Deeply engaging, this book's long section on labor exhibits excellent scholarship, displaying all the qualities we've come to expect from this author. Domhoff reorganizes and extends his earlier analysis by incorporating more recent empirical findings, new archival data, and more. The story comes to life in the historical narrative of labor's rise and decline, which offers a richness of detail and analytical coherence that makes the account both engaging and accessible to a wide readership. This book can be used in advanced undergraduate or entry-level graduate courses in political sociology (and related sociology courses on social problems and economics) and courses in other disciplines that deal centrally with politics, inequality, and American society, particularly in political science, public policy, and American culture.

Howard Kimeldorf, Professor Emeritus of Sociology, University of Michigan

This book offers an analysis of U.S. politics and social/economic policy from the Progressive Era into the early twenty-first century, based on extensive archival and secondary sources. The book analyzes three of the more important realms of federal policy: regulation of labor unions, social benefits, and foreign relations, focusing especially on trade. It sharply contrasts an analysis of the power elite to Marxist and institutional theories, and then throughout the book specifies how the power elite analysis yields better explanations for historical change and for the particularities of U.S. political economy than previous explanations. The book dramatically advances our understanding of the role of race, racism, and racial conflict in the making of policy in the United States, offers an historical explanation for the emergence of a divided power elite made up of corporate moderates and ultraconservatives, and identifies the mechanisms through which the elite shaped public policy. It also traces the making of labor policy, explaining why labor militancy had a limited effect due to the enduring divisions of craft and industrial workers and their unions, racism, and the usually united corporate interests. Taken together, these chapters offer the most sophisticated and accurate history of labor in the United States yet written.

Richard Lachmann, Professor of Sociology, State University of New York at Albany

The Corporate Rich and the Power Elite in the Twentieth Century

The Corporate Rich and the Power Elite in the Twentieth Century demonstrates exactly how the corporate rich developed and implemented the policies and created the government structures that allowed them to dominate the United States. The book is framed within three historical developments that have made this domination possible: the rise and fall of the union movement, the initiation and subsequent limitation of government social-benefit programs, and the postwar expansion of international trade.

The book's deep exploration into the various methods the corporate rich used to centralize power corrects major empirical misunderstandings concerning all three issue-areas. Further, it explains why the three ascendant theories of power in the early twenty-first century—interest-group pluralism, organizational state theory, and historical institutionalism—cannot account for the complexity of events that established the power elite's supremacy and led to labor's fall. More generally, and convincingly, the analysis reveals how a corporate-financed policy-planning network, consisting of foundations, think tanks, and policy-discussion groups, gradually developed in the twentieth century and played a pivotal role in all three issue-areas. Filled with new archival findings and commanding detail, this book offers readers a remarkable look into the nature of power in America during the twentieth century, and provides a starting point for future in-depth analyses of corporate power in the current century.

G. William Domhoff is the author or co-author of 16 books on the American power structure, four of which appeared on a list of the top-50 best-sellers in sociology from the 1950s through the early 1990s, including his now-classic, *Who Rules America?* He is a Distinguished Professor Emeritus in Sociology and remains active as a Research Professor at the University of California, Santa Cruz. *Who Rules America?* was published in a revised and updated version in 2014 and has been in print and used in many classrooms for 52 years.

The Corporate Rich and the Power Elite in the Twentieth Century

How They Won, Why Liberals and Labor Lost

G. William Domhoff

Routledge
Taylor & Francis Group
NEW YORK AND LONDON

First published 2020
by Routledge
52 Vanderbilt Avenue, New York, NY 10017

and by Routledge
2 Park Square, Milton Park, Abingdon, Oxon, OX14 4RN

Routledge is an imprint of the Taylor & Francis Group, an informa business

© 2020 Taylor & Francis

The right of G. William Domhoff to be identified as author of this work has been asserted by him in accordance with sections 77 and 78 of the Copyright, Designs and Patents Act 1988.

All rights reserved. No part of this book may be reprinted or reproduced or utilised in any form or by any electronic, mechanical, or other means, now known or hereafter invented, including photocopying and recording, or in any information storage or retrieval system, without permission in writing from the publishers.

Cover image: Benton, Thomas Hart (1889–1975). America Today; a) Instruments of Power; b) City Activities with Dance Hall; c) City Activities with Subway; d) Deep South; e) Midwest; f) Changing West; g) Coal; h) Steel; i) City Building; j) Outreaching Hands. Panel a) Instruments of Power. 1930–31. Egg tempera with oil glazing over Permalba on a gesso ground on linen mounted to wood panels with a honeycomb interior, 92 x 160 in. (233.7 x 406.4 cm). The Metropolitan Museum of Art, Gift of AXA Equitable, 2012 (2012.478a-j).

Photo Credit: Image copyright © The Metropolitan Museum of Art. Image Source: Art Resource.

Trademark notice: Product or corporate names may be trademarks or registered trademarks, and are used only for identification and explanation without intent to infringe.

Library of Congress Cataloging-in-Publication Data
A catalog record for this title has been requested

ISBN: 978-0-367-25202-1 (hbk)
ISBN: 978-0-367-25389-9 (pbk)
ISBN: 978-0-429-28752-7 (ebk)

Typeset in Bembo
by codeMantra
Printed by CPI Group (UK) Ltd, Croydon CR0 4YY

Contents

Preface, Acknowledgments, and Stylistic Notes	ix
List of Acronyms	xiii
Introduction	1

PART 1
The Rise and Fall of Labor Unions · 41

1 The Uphill Battle for Unionism from the 1820s to 1932	43
2 The Origins of the National Labor Relations Act of 1935	91
3 Stronger Unions, a Weaker National Labor Relations Act, 1936–1960	137
4 Union Victories, Corporate Pushback in the 1960s	165
5 The Corporate Moderates Reorganize to Defeat Unions, 1969–1985	191

PART 2
How the Corporate Moderates Created Social Insurance Programs, and Later Tried to Undermine Them · 227

6 The Origins of the Social Security Act	229
7 Revising and Augmenting Social Security, 1937–1973	292
8 Social Disruption, New Social Benefits, and then Cutbacks, 1967–1999	317
9 The Circuitous Path to the Affordable Care Act, 1974–2010	342

viii   Contents

PART 3
The Rise of an International Economic
System, 1939–2000   371

10 The Council on Foreign Relations and World Trade   373

11 The Grand Area and the Origins of the International
    Monetary Fund   397

12 The Grand Area Strategy and the Vietnam War   429

13 Rebuilding Europe in the Face of Ultraconservative
    Resistance, 1945–1967   446

14 From Turmoil to the World Trade Organization, 1968–2000   469

PART 4
Conclusions   497

15 The Shortcomings of Alternative Theories   499

    Archival Sources Consulted   521
    Index   523

Preface, Acknowledgments, and Stylistic Notes

This book draws on, updates, and chronologically extends the work I have done in a wide range of archival sources over the past 30 years, including a few archives that had never been utilized before for research in political sociology (see Archival Sources Consulted following Chapter 15). I have written previously on unions, based on archival sources, in *The Power Elite and The State* (1990, Chapter 4), *Class and Power in The New Deal* (co-authored with sociologist Michael J. Webber) (2011, Chapter 3), and for the postwar era in parts of various chapters in *The Myth of Liberal Ascendancy* (2013b). Here the story is told in a chronological fashion, as augmented by new sources and more detailed reading in the voluminous earlier sources.

Similarly, I have written on the Social Security Act in different eras in *State Autonomy or Class Dominance?* (1996, Chapter 3), *Class and Power in the New Deal* (2011, Chapter 4), and parts of chapters in *The Myth of Liberal Ascendancy* (2013). The account here is now more seamless because it is presented in a chronological order and has more depth. Finally, I have written scattered pieces on international trade in *The Power Elite and the State* (1990, Chapters 5 and 6), parts of *The Myth of Liberal Ascendancy* (2013), and in the journal *Class, Race and Corporate Power* (2014). Building on an amended version of these past writings, my analysis of trade policy is now extended to the final 30 years of the twentieth century.

The book also makes use of the even larger corpus of original archival research produced by experts on labor relations, by social scientists and historians on government social insurance and benefits, and by historians and sociologists on the creation of a new international economic trading system in the decades after World War II. These various archive-based sources are supplemented by a handful of interviews I carried out with policy experts employed by nonprofit organizations financed and directed by the owners and managers of large corporations. The insights and methods of many other sociologists, historians, and political scientists are incorporated as well.

In the case of labor relations, I draw in particular on three books on the history of the National Labor Relations Board by James A. Gross (1974; 1981; 1995), work on the United Automobile Workers union (UAW) by historian Kevin Boyle (1995; 1998; 2013), new ideas developed by sociologist Howard Kimeldorf (1988; 1999; 2013) on the basis of his own historical research, a comparative history of labor relations in the United States, the United Kingdom, and France in the nineteenth century by sociologist Kim Voss (1993), a study of the origins of the Business Roundtable by law professor Marc Linder (1999), work on unions from the 1950s through 1970s by sociologist Jill Quadagno (1994), a history of the role of corporate leaders in the creation of the National Labor Board in 1933 by historian Kim McQuaid (1976; 1979), and a study of the involvement of John D. Rockefeller, Jr. in labor relations from 1914 into the 1930s by historian Howard Gitelman (1984; 1988).

For the chapters on the origins of government social insurance programs, the book relies heavily on original research by political scientist Michael K. Brown (1999) and sociologists Linda Bergthold (1990; 1995), Donald Fisher (1993), Jill Quadagno (1994; 2005), and Paul Starr (2011; 2017). My analysis of the expansion of international trade relations in the postwar era is based on archival work by historians Allen Matusow (1998), Laurence Shoup (1974; 1975; 1977), and Charlie Whitham (2016), as well as archival work by sociologist Nitsan Chorev (2007), and quantitative analyses using statistical methods linked to network analysis by sociologists Michael Dreiling (2011), and Dreiling and Derek Darves (2016), to understand the major trade expansions of the 1990s.

Based on the work of this wide range of scholars, the book presents a new empirical synthesis that can be read as a series of informative case studies on landmark legislative acts that have not been fully explored in the past. The empirical shortcomings of similar past efforts along these lines are pointed out as the analyses unfold. The new findings and synthesis also can be deployed to assess the usefulness of the theoretical perspectives that had gained ascendancy in the social sciences by the end of the twentieth century. These theories are presented and discussed in the final chapter.

I am deeply grateful to sociologist Richard Lachmann, whose work has an impressive historical scope that includes Europe as well as the United States, for his careful reading of the whole manuscript. Several of his many useful suggestions sent me back to basic sources to learn more about labor issues in the 1830s and 1920s, and as a result I have placed some issues in a larger context. Similarly, I am very grateful to sociologist Howard Kimeldorf, whose knowledge of labor history in the United States is in my judgment unsurpassed, for reading the five labor chapters. He, too, caused me to read more and to think more carefully about several issues. The result is a more balanced and nuanced account on several key issues.

On the topic of healthcare policy in the 1970s and 1980s, I am grateful to sociologist Linda Bergthold for the perspective she provided me through her answers to my many questions to her via email, which supplemented her original research on which I relied a great deal. Similarly, I thank healthcare expert John McDonough for answering my equally numerous questions concerning the origins of the healthcare act in Massachusetts that presaged the Affordable Care Act, as well as on the Affordable Care Act itself, especially since he played an important role in both of those legislative victories. Sociologist Larry King of the University of Massachusetts, Amherst, also provided several helpful suggestions that improved the chapter relating to the Affordable Care Act. I also benefited from theoretical comments and suggestions from sociologist Tom Morrione of Colby College concerning my discussions of both gift-giving and religion in a section on my general theoretical perspective in the Introduction. Finally, I thank political scientist Seth McKee of Texas Tech University, an expert on issues relating to Congress and elections, especially in the case of the South, for his frank comments and very useful suggestions and bibliographical updates in relation to the sections on Congress in the Introduction. However, all five of these generous experts should be considered entirely blameless for the angles I have taken on several issues related to their specialties.

I have had the benefit of careful editorial readings of the Introduction and last chapter, which cover much new ground for me, by social psychologist Richard L. Zweigenhaft. Happily, he is used to taming and focusing drafts of my work due to our decades of collaboration on research relating to diversity at the highest levels of American society, some of which is cited in this book. And once again, I want to thank my great editor, Dean Birkenkamp, for taking a chance with another of my books, even though this one is longer than he expected, and far longer than most of the many excellent books that he has brought to the light of day.

Stylistically, I have tried to keep the welter of names of people in the text to a minimum, especially those from the distant past. I followed the rule of thumb that people should only be named if they appear more than once or are so well known their names are recognizable to just about everyone. I adopted this approach because I often feel overwhelmed by names in reading otherwise interesting historical accounts. But I know that some readers familiar with the literature would prefer to know the names of the persons I am talking about, and I apologize to them in advance.

Similarly, I have tried to keep the abbreviations and acronyms to a minimum, but the ones that remain are generally used repeatedly, and I occasionally revert to the full name of an agency or organization as a kind of reminder. I signal this repetition by writing when I first use an acronym that it will "usually" be used. In addition to the occasional in-text reminders, there is also a list of abbreviations following these initial comments, which can be referred to if readers lose track of an acronym's meaning.

Although I end these prefatory notes with a feeling of closure, I suspect that I am likely to return to some of these issues in the future. Newly available archives are increasingly compelling and fascinating to me on issues through which I lived and thought I understood at the time. But for now, it will be good to be back in the twenty-first century after spending so much time thinking about the past during the last three years.

List of Acronyms

AAA	Agricultural Adjustment Act/Agricultural Adjustment Administration
AALL	American Association for Labor Legislation
AARP	American Association of Retired Persons
ACA	Affordable Care Act
ACPTN	Advisory Council on Trade Policy and Negotiations
ACW	Amalgamated Clothing Workers
AFL	American Federation of Labor
AHA	American Hospital Association
AHIP	American Health Insurance Plans
AMA	American Medical Association
BAC	Business Advisory Council
CDC	Community Development Corporation
CEA	Council of Economic Advisors
CED	Committee for Economic Development
CES	Committee on Economic Security
CFR	Council on Foreign Relations
CIO	Congress of Industrial Organizations
CUAIR	Construction Users Anti-Inflation Roundtable
ECAT	Emergency Committee for American Trade
EITC	Earned Income Tax Credit
GATT	General Agreement on Trade and Tariffs
HMO	Health Maintenance Organization
IMF	International Monetary Fund
IRC	Industrial Relations Counselors, Inc.
LLRC	Labor Law Reform Group
NAACP	Nation Association for the Advancement of Colored People
NAFTA	North American Free Trade Agreement
NAM	National Association of Manufacturers
NCF	National Civic Federation
NFIB	National Federation of Independent Business
NICB	National Industrial Conference Board

NLB	National Labor Board
NLRB	National Labor Relations Board
NPA	National Planning Association
NRA	National Recovery Administration
NSC	National Security Council
NWLB	National War Labor Board
PCEEO	President's Committee on Equal Employment Opportunity
SEIU	Service Employees International Union
SSRC	Social Science Research Council
STR	Special Trade Representative
TCF	Twentieth Century Fund
UAW	United Automobile Workers
WBGH	Washington Business Group on Health
WTO	World Trade Organization

Introduction

This book demonstrates exactly how the corporate rich (the owners and managers of large incorporated properties) developed the policies and created the governmental structures that allowed them to dominate the United States in the twentieth century. By "dominate" I mean that the corporate rich were able to establish the organizational structures, rules, and customs through which most people carried out their everyday lives, due to their control of many millions of jobs and their success in convincing government officials to adopt their top policy priorities.

Domination by the corporate rich, in other words, was the institutionalized outcome of their great economic and political power. Even when there were loud vocal complaints from highly visible individuals or groups, and a considerable degree of organized protest and resistance, the routinized ways of acting in the United States mostly followed from the rules and regulations needed by the big banks and corporations to continue to make profits. Domination also allowed the corporate rich to maintain a distinctively luxurious lifestyle, which further imbued them with feelings of superiority, and reinforced their implicit belief that they were entitled to dominate.

The main focus of the book is on three policy issues that made overall domination possible: successfully resisting unions, initiating and then limiting government social programs, and creating a postwar international trading and investment system.

The Corporate Community

Although corporations were in constant competition with each other throughout the twentieth century, and frequently at risk of being taken over by investment bankers, rival corporations, or equity funds, they also shared the same goals and values, especially and most obviously the profit motive. All of them were eager to control relevant labor markets, minimize government regulations, and avoid taxation to the greatest extent possible. Large corporations and financial institutions also had several other common bonds, including shared ownership, the use of the same legal, accounting, advertising, and public relations firms, and longstanding patterns of supply and purchase. They also were pulled together through belonging to one or more business associations that looked out for their general interests.

The fact that the corporate rich were opposed in varying degrees by the labor movement, liberals, leftists, and strong environmentalists reinforced their sense of being a small, beleaguered group. Although the corporate rich overestimated the coordination among these oppositional groups, most of them were in fact members of a loosely knit liberal–labor alliance that began to form in the late 1920s and became more solidified by the mid-1930s as one part of the New Deal. This alliance was able to challenge the corporate rich on a wide range of issues for the remainder of the twentieth century, including the three issues focused on in this book. However, the large divisions that developed within the liberal–labor alliance in the late 1960s over several issues, starting with the civil rights movement, led to its decline in the 1970s and near-collapse by the 1980s.

At the outset of the twentieth century, the wealthy industrialists and several other business sectors were concerned with the need for new ways to regulate the ruthless competition among them, as well as the need for protection against populist farmers, middle-class reformers, and socialists. In particular, government antitrust legislation led more industrialists to take advantage of the rights and privileges that legislatures and courts were granting to the legal device called a "corporation" (Parker-Gwin and Roy 1996; Roy 1997).

This combination of economic, sociological, and legal factors led to the development of a *corporate community* by 1900. It was at this point that the wealthy became *the corporate rich*, with their fortunes in all business sectors (later including "agribusiness") protected by their incorporated fortresses, which successfully pushed for further legal protections and legal rights in ensuing decades. These corporations also shared common (overlapping) members on their boards of directors.

The use of shared directors began among wealthy Boston merchants and mill owners in the New England textile industry in the late eighteenth and early nineteenth centuries, who more importantly shared ownership in many Massachusetts companies. By the 1840s they had reached out regionally to play a large role in financing the nation's early railroads (Dalzell 1987). To take another example, by 1816 the ten largest banks and ten largest insurance companies in New York were tightly interlocked, which reflected shared ownership as well as shared interests (Bunting 1983). National interlock networks connecting railroad, coal, and telegraph companies existed by 1886; they were further integrated through shared connections to the banks on Wall Street that provided them with the capital to expand. Then a national corporate network emerged between 1897 and 1905, which included industrial corporations and other incorporated sectors of the economy for the first time (e.g., Carosso 1970; Roy 1983). This network persisted throughout the twentieth century (Davis, Yoo, and Baker 2002; Mizruchi 1982).

However, too much can be made too quickly about the possible implications of nationwide interlocks among corporations after the 1890s for a variety of reasons (e.g., Davis, Yoo, and Baker 2002; Mills 1956, pp. 123–124, 402 note 12; Mintz and Schwartz 1983; Zweigenhaft and Domhoff 1982, pp. 18–19, 39–43). Attempts in the 1970s and 1980s to show that interlocks between companies had economic or political consequences did not meet with any success (e.g., Gogel and Koenig 1981; Koenig and Gogel 1981; Palmer 1983). Mixed results in subsequent studies, based on resource dependency theory (Pfeffer 1972), led to the strong conclusion, in a retrospective overview of the entire literature, that "Resource dependency theory seemed of little use to explain corporate interlocks" (Fennema and Heemskerk 2017, p. 17). Membership on two or more corporate boards is therefore best viewed simply as (1) evidence for social cohesion, (2) an opportunity to develop a business outlook that extends beyond one company, and (3) a starting point for discovering the involvement of corporate leaders in a wide range of nonprofit organizations, including those involved in policy-making (Davis, Yoo, and Baker 2002; Domhoff 1974, Chapter 3; Domhoff 1975; Eitzen, Jung, and Purdy 1982; Salzman and Domhoff 1983; Useem 1979; Useem 1984).

Despite their shared interests, common opponents, and interlock structure, the leaders in the corporate community were not united on all issues. Based on divisions that arose on a wide range of policy issues, it was discovered decades ago that the corporate community included both moderately conservative and ultraconservative factions among its owners and managers (McLellan and Woodhouse 1960; Mills 1948, pp. 25–27, 240–250; Weinstein 1968; Woodhouse and McLellan 1966). No one factor has been found through systematic studies to be the sole basis for the division into corporate moderates and ultraconservatives. There may have been a tendency for the moderate conservatives to be executives from the very largest and most internationally oriented of corporations, but there were numerous exceptions to that generalization. Nor were there significant differences based on business sector or geographical location (e.g., Domhoff 1990, pp. 35–37; Domhoff 2014, pp. 17–18, 75–76).

There is a need for more research on the reasons for this division while resisting any attempts to prematurely reduce it to differences in economic interests without also considering ethnic, religious, and psychosocial factors as well. Whatever the admixture of factors that may account for the differences between moderate conservatives and ultraconservatives within the corporate community, however, these differences existed throughout the twentieth century, and they are readily apparent in all three policy domains discussed in this book.

Plantation Owners and Southern Democrats

For all the emphasis on the corporate community in this book, Southern plantation owners and their satellite business associates in the South, and in major trade and financial centers, such as New York, played a pivotal role in deciding the outcome of many policy battles. Although plantation owners were junior partners in relation to the burgeoning corporate community after their defeat in the Civil War, they nonetheless exercised total domination in the former slave states. Their terrorist-based imposition of a caste status on African Americans through racial stigmatization at birth, disenfranchisement, neighborhood and school segregation, and the prohibition of black-white marriages was nearly complete as the twentieth century began (Berreman 1960; Berreman 1981, pp. 265–266, 273–277; Davis, Gardner, and Gardner 1941; Dollard and Leftwich 1957; Myrdal 1944, Chapter 31). They also disenfranchised, but did not entirely segregate, many low-income whites through a variety of means (e.g., Key 1949; Kousser 1974). The plantation owners and their allies were then able to project their unity, wealth, and power to the national level through their predominant role in the Democratic Party.

The breadth of the potential power base for the plantation owners is first of all evidenced by the fact that there were 17 slave states and territories before the Civil War, all of which had established legalized segregation in all walks of life by the early twentieth century. (West Virginia became a separate slave state during the Civil War and Oklahoma was a slave-and-segregation territory before it became a state in 1907.) School segregation was not declared unconstitutional until 1954, and for the most part it continued by means of private and suburban schools for well-off whites throughout the century. (In that same year, 27 states still banned racial intermarriage, with all of them in the South, Great Plains, or Rocky Mountains, with the exception of Indiana, which has been heavily shaped by its early links to the South.)

The Civil Rights Act of 1964 and the Voting Rights Act of 1965 outlawed the other forms of segregation, and the Supreme Court declared laws against marriage between Caucasians and African Americans unconstitutional in 1967, at which point it overturned the remaining 17 antimarriage state laws, all of which were in the former slave states. In the case of housing, there was legalized housing segregation throughout the United States until 1968 due to laws and rulings at the federal, state, and local levels, which in turn meant that most public schools remained segregated in a caste-like fashion (Rothstein 2017, for the highly detailed evidence for these conclusions on residential and school segregation). Experts on neighborhood segregation call it the American version of apartheid, and note that it is the most important basis for continuing racial stratification (Massey 2016; Massey and Denton 1993).

By the late 1960s, and despite the legal changes at the federal level, the informal norms and customs that shaped the South in general, and the rest of the country as far as housing, school segregation, and racial intermarriage were concerned, were firmly in place. People of African heritage remain unique in that they are the only Americans who have faced the combined effects of race, slavery, and segregation (Pettigrew 1988, pp. 24–26). Any changes therefore turned out to be very slow and small (Pettigrew 2008). At the same time, the gradual transition of a majority of white Democrats in the South into the Republican Party was underway, which made increases in integration in the South even more difficult (McKee 2019, Chapter 4).

The transition of white Southerners from the Democrats to the Republicans was a cautious one at the state and local levels due to a traditional party identity in part based on the resentment of "Yankees," but also due to the realization that the South would lose power in Congress if established Southern Democrats gave up their seniority and committee chairships. Even though more and more white Southerners voted for Republicans at the presidential level, and drifted away from any identification with the Democratic Party, it did not make sense for Southern Democrats to change parties before they were certain that there would be a Republican majority in the House and Senate. For the most part, Southern whites voted Republican at the presidential level in 1968 and thereafter, and Democratic at the state and local level, which created a "one-and-a-half" party system while excluding and isolating black voters to the extent that few African Americans held office at any level of government well into the 1980s (Black and Black 2002; Davidson and Grofman 1994a; Davidson and Grofman 1994b).

Corporate Dominance Through Four Networks

The corporate community and its plantation counterparts, sometimes in complete agreement, but sometimes in conflict with each other, dominated the United States in the twentieth century through four network-based processes: the special-interest process, the policy-planning process, the opinion-shaping process, and the candidate-selection process. Taken together, these four processes, which provided dense links between the corporate community and the American government at all levels, can be understood as the "party" of the corporate rich, defined as the means by which they tried to influence communal action in a planned manner (Weber 1998).

The special-interest process was focused on the specific and short-run policy concerns of wealthy families, individual corporations, and the many different business sectors within the corporate community. For example, limiting the taxes paid by the corporate rich to the greatest extent possible

6 Introduction

is the province of the "wealth defense industry" within the special-interest process, a small army of accountants, tax lawyers, investment advisers, and lobbyists (Winters 2011). More generally, the special-interest process operated primarily through lobbyists, company lawyers, and trade associations, with a focus on congressional committees, departments of the executive branch, and regulatory agencies. Many lobbyists were former elected or appointed officials who were capitalizing on their experience in government and their connections within it. This process has been examined in thousands of scholarly case studies. These studies almost always show that one or another business group usually won, sometimes in battles with other business groups.

In the face of corporate-wide issues, however, such as conflicts with employees over unions, the problems generated by the Great Depression, and the possibility of increased international trade, the corporate rich gradually developed a set of policy-discussion groups and think tanks. These separate nonprofit organizations then evolved into a more general policy-planning network that was further cemented by common funding sources and overlapping boards of trustees. The policy-planning process based in this network was the main way in which corporate leaders attempted to reach policy consensus among themselves and impress their views upon government.

The *opinion-shaping process* attempted to influence public opinion and keep some issues off the public agenda. It usually took its direction from the major organizations within the policy-planning network. In addition to the large public relations firms and many small organizations within it, the opinion-shaping network included a wide variety of patriotic, anti-tax, and other single-issue organizations funded by corporate foundations, family foundations, and individual members of the dominant class. However, many excellent studies of public opinion provide no evidence that the corporate rich were able to shape long-term public opinion in general despite their efforts to do so (e.g., Page 2008; Page, Bartels, and Seawright 2013; Page and Hennessy 2010; Page and Jacobs 2009; Page and Shapiro 1992). At best, then, the opinion-shaping process was able to aid in complex legislative battles or in times of crisis only if the leaders and organizations in it were able to create doubt and hesitation, or introduce plausible alternatives or reasons for delay (e.g., Domhoff 2014, Chapter 5; Michaels 2008; Oreskes and Conway 2010; Potter 2010). The corporate-dominance theory put forth in this book therefore is not based on concepts such as false consciousness, ideological hegemony, elite manipulation, or manufactured consent via the media.

However, this does not mean that public opinion, which tended to favor generous social-insurance programs and a less aggressive foreign policy than government leaders in the White House and Congress (e.g., Moore 2007; Page 2008; Page and Jacobs 2009), had any impact. In fact, there is good evidence that majority public opinion had little or no impact. This conclusion is based on studies of the results from 1,779 survey questions asked between 1981 and 2002 by many different survey organizations, which were compared with Congressional voting outcomes (Gilens 2012, pp. 57, 60, and Chapter 2 more generally, for data and methods). On the other hand, the same studies show that 43 interest groups and a small sample of people worth $10 million dollars or more had significant impacts on legislative outcomes (Gilens 2012, Chapter 5; Page and Gilens 2018, pp. 66–69 for a brief summary).

The researchers therefore conclude that their findings are consistent with a theory of "biased pluralism" (in which "corporations, business associations, and professional groups predominate"), and with a theory of corporate domination such as the one presented in this book (Gilens and Page 2014, pp. 564–565, 573–574). Even so, it was also the case that some "average citizens fairly often get what they want" because they "fairly often agree with the policies that are also favored (and won) by their affluent fellow citizens who *do* have a lot of clout" (Page and Gilens 2018, p. 69, their italics). This book explains these various new findings on the minor role of public opinion on the basis of the strong influence of the corporate rich and the Southern rich in Congress through two voting coalitions that are discussed later in this chapter.

Fourth and finally, there was a candidate-selection process, which focused on the election of politicians that were sympathetic to the agenda put forth by the corporate rich through the special-interest and policy-planning processes. Indeed, success in this process was one of several reasons why elected officials could ignore public opinion because it produced a majority of office holders that were impervious to national public opinion. It operated through large campaign donations and hired political consultants. Northern industrialists and bankers from Anglo-Saxon Protestant backgrounds primarily supported the Republican Party. On the other hand, the Democrats were favored by the Southern rich and by urban land, real estate, and department store owners throughout the country. The urban land and real estate interests worked together as growth coalitions to turn cities into "growth machines," because their primary goal was to find ways to make money by intensifying land use and thereby increase land values (Domhoff 1986; Logan and Molotch 2007; Molotch 1976; Molotch 1998). Moreover, the urban rich more often came from ethnic and religious backgrounds that differed from those of the white Protestants from the United Kingdom and Northern Europe, who discriminated again them in high-status law firms, banking firms, and social clubs (e.g., Baltzell 1964; Domhoff 1990, Chapter 9; Webber 2000; Zweigenhaft and Domhoff 1982).

For the purposes of this book, the policy-planning network is the most important of the four processes, but it could *not* have had the successes it did without sufficient victories in the candidate-selection process, along with occasional help in conflicts over complex legislative issues from leaders in the opinion-shaping process through the dissemination of messages that generated doubt, spread confusion, or provided reasons to delay (e.g., Michaels 2008; Oreskes and Conway 2010).

The organizations within the policy-planning network, and in particular the policy-discussion groups, gradually developed five specific functions within the corporate community and three roles in relation to the small "attentive public," that is those who paid attention to legislative issues and government appointments and communicated with others about their opinions through conversations and various forms of media (Nisbet and Kotcher 2009):

1. They provided a setting in which corporate leaders could familiarize themselves with general policy issues by listening to and questioning the experts from think tanks and university research institutes.
2. They provided a forum in which conflicts among corporate leaders could be discussed and a compromise reached, usually by including experts within the discussion groups that had conservative and centrist policy perspectives, along with an occasional liberal on some issues.
3. They provided an informal training ground in which corporate leaders could decide which of their peers might be best suited for government service, either as high-level appointees in the White House or in departments of the executive branch.
4. They provided an informal recruiting ground for determining which policy experts might be suitable for government service, either as staff aides to the corporate leaders who accepted government positions or as high-level appointees in their own right.
5. The major conclusions reached in the policy-discussion groups frequently resulted in a set of policy prescriptions, including plans for new governmental committees and agencies. These policy recommendations were conveyed to appointed and elected officials through a variety of avenues, including testimony before Congressional committees, service on departmental advisory committees, membership on special presidential commissions, and, not least, appointments to high-level positions in departments of the executive branch. Due to these multiple channels, the policy recommendations were often adopted by the federal government almost as they were written, or in a partially modified form. The frequent implementation of a wide range of policy proposals, as documented in this book, adds up to "state-building" by the corporate rich, which contradicts the widely held idea that government officials build state structures in the United States and thereby give themselves a considerable degree of autonomy.

In addition, the policy groups had three useful roles in relation to the attentive public, most of whom, but not all, were highly educated and often members of one or another profession:

1. These groups legitimated their members to the attentive public as fair-minded, serious and expert persons capable of government service. This image was created because members of the policy-discussion groups were portrayed as giving of their own time to take part in highly selective organizations that were both nonpartisan and nonprofit in nature.
2. They conveyed the concerns, goals, and expectations of the corporate community to those young policy specialists and professors who wanted to further their careers by receiving foundation grants, invitations to work at think tanks, and invitations to take part in policy-discussion groups.
3. Through such avenues as books, journals, policy statements, press releases, and speakers, these groups tried to influence the climate of opinion on important policy issues in Washington and among the attentive public, sometimes directly, sometimes through special single-issue committees, and sometimes through the use of organizations in the opinion-shaping network.

In an important social-psychological sense, this bird's-eye sociological view of the policy-planning process makes the interactions within it sound far too straightforward, reasonable, and rational, which ignores the human tendencies toward self-serving ambition, combativeness, compartmentalized thinking, and group-think. Without question, the thousands of people that participated in one or another aspect of this policy-planning process *experienced* their involvement as a chaotic and rancorous competition over ideas, status, and prestigious appointments. In other words, corporate leaders and experts also suffer from the all-too-human pettiness, self-importance, and interpersonal competitiveness that lead to an egosystem within any group or institution (Crocker and Canevello 2015). This is also the way in which the process and its participants were observed and written about by journalists. It all became just another human-interest story.

To be sure there are no misunderstandings, the emphasis in this book is on the fact that potential leaders were *informally* socialized, educated, selected, and vetted within this network by its members in general as they cycled in and out of various roles within it, as well as in and out of government positions. There were also many instances in which participants "deselected" themselves because they did not want to take part in this competition, or else they found the level of discourse to be banal and conventional, as revealed over the decades by resignations from policy-discussion organizations by highly visible professors and other expert advisers.

However, this book is not concerned with the subjective or interpersonal levels of human experience. Instead, it focuses on the sociological level, on the *results* ("output") of the interactions within the corporate community and the policy-planning network in terms of the leaders that emerged and the collective statements that were written. These leaders and collective statements often left many members of the corporate rich grumbling and unhappy, and only partly in agreement. But in terms of the limits of human rationality, these group-based outcomes were the best the corporate rich could do at that moment given the circumstances, the information available, and time constraints.

The Power Elite

The corporate rich maintained their domination through a leadership group called "the power elite." This power elite is defined as those people who served as directors or trustees in profit and nonprofit institutions controlled by the corporate rich through stock ownership, financial support, involvement on governing boards, or some combination of these factors. This definition differs somewhat from the original definition provided by sociologist C. Wright Mills (1956, pp. 3–4, 18–20). It agrees with his definition in stating that the power elite are those individuals who have a superior amount of power due to the institutional hierarchies they command, but it differs in a theoretically important way by restricting the term to persons who are in command positions in institutional hierarchies controlled by the corporate rich.

More specifically, this revised conception of the power elite makes it possible to integrate class and organizational insights in order to create a more complete theory of power in America, which makes it a more resilient theory than the class-based Marxist theory and a more encompassing theory than the perspectives discussed in Chapter 15. Empirically, it leads from the corporate community to the foundations, think tanks, and policy-discussion groups that made up the policy-planning network, as well as to the major organizations in the opinion-shaping network (Domhoff 2014, Chapters 4 and 5). These were in fact the institutions that were involved in the key decisions. The military, contrary to Mills (1956, p. 6 and Chapters 8–9), was not central to any of the key decisions discussed in this book, or in any other policy arena in the twentieth century that has been studied (Domhoff 1967, pp. 115–127; Domhoff 1996, Chapter 6; Huntington 1961; Janowitz 1960). Nor were those Mills defined as the "political directorate" (the top appointed officials in executive departments of the federal government) an independent group. As shown in numerous past studies, they were members of the corporate community and the policy-planning network (e.g., Burch 1980; Burch 1981; Domhoff 1998, pp. 247–256; Mintz 1975; Salzman and Domhoff 1980).

Although the power elite were a leadership group, the phrase is always used with a plural verb to emphasize that the power elite were also a collection of individuals who had some internal policy disagreements as well as ambitions for the same government appointments. They sometimes had bitter personal rivalries that received detailed media attention and often overshadowed the general policy consensus. In other words, the power elite were not a monolithic leadership group. In that regard, the book adheres to Mills' (1959, p. 6) view that the sociological imagination stands at the intersection of personal biography and the class and institutional structures that history hands down to each new generation. To reiterate in order to avoid possible misunderstandings, a set of for-profit and nonprofit organizations provided the institutional basis for the exercise of power on behalf of the owners of all large income-producing properties.

In the early decades of the twentieth century, there were relatively few members of the Southern rich who were part of the power elite. Those who were, tended to serve on the boards of directors of Northern banks and corporations with economic interests in the South. In addition, some of the richest of the Southerner planters and bankers participated in a few of the organizations in the policy-planning network. For the most part, however, the policy interactions between the corporate rich and the plantation owners took place through a few formal business associations that focused on specific business sectors, such as agriculture or banking. The corporate rich and the plantation owners in the past also interacted indirectly through elected Congressional members and their staffs, which meant Northern Republicans and Southern Democrats until very late in the twentieth century.

Challengers and Supporters of the Power Elite

As briefly noted earlier, unions, grassroots environmentalists, social-justice groups, consumer groups, and political liberals in general were the most frequent challengers to the efforts that were initiated through all four of the networks that connect the corporate rich to the government. They lobbied on specific issues that arose within the special-interest process, created temporary coalitions to oppose new policies generated in the policy-planning process, and, most of all, supported liberal and pro-union candidates within the Democratic Party, both in primaries and general elections. More generally, these groups were the mainstays of the liberal-labor alliance that came into existence in the context of the early New Deal. As also mentioned earlier, this alliance figured prominently on all three of the major policy issues that are analyzed in this book.

However, the liberal-labor alliance was severely handicapped from the outset by the fact that a single-member-district plurality electoral system left them with little choice but to work within the Democratic Party. The alternative would have been to take the big risk of allowing ultraconservative Republicans to win even more elections (e.g., Lipset 1963, pp. 295–311, for a sweeping cross-national and historical synthesis; Rosenstone, Behr, and Lazarus 1996, for an updated focus on the American case). By depriving the Democrats of a significant percentage of their voters, an independent third party on the left would be ignoring the short-run daily needs of low-income Americans and people of all colors, who would suffer a setback under Republicans, as everyday working people well knew. Research comparing income growth during Democratic and Republican administrations between 1948 and 2014 has demonstrated this point in a systematic fashion (Bartels 2016, pp. 69–73). The result was a less-than-ideal political alliance with Southern Democrats.

On the other end of the political spectrum, the Republicans had potential allies on many issues of concern to them when they could convince these would-be allies to eschew the rightist third parties that sometimes appeared. These potential allies were the result of a combination of sociological and psychological factors that predispose some individuals in all social classes to varying degrees of social or economic conservatism. These factors include a preference for hierarchy over group decision-making, strong religious or nationalist beliefs, anti-immigrant and anti-government sentiments, a belief in white superiority, and/or an authoritarian personality (e.g., Domhoff 2013a; Pettigrew 2017; Tomkins 1964). These extremely conservative individuals created a variety of conservative organizations, which often received financial support from wealthy conservatives through personal donations and foundation grants. As a result, the disparate conservative groups and the corporate community joined together in the political arena as a corporate-conservative alliance.

The Power Elite, the Liberal-Labor Alliance, and Congress

Although there is good direct evidence that the corporate community and the policy-planning network had a strong relationship with the White House and other departments and agencies of the executive branch, these links were not sufficient for corporate domination. It was also essential for the power elite to be able to reach and influence Congress as well. The legislative branch was and is a strong and independent part of the federal government, and potentially an arena of contention on every major issue that comes before it, in part because of the potential role of majority public opinion.

In the case of Congress, the four networks that linked the corporate rich and the power elite to government were adapted to deal with the emergence of two enduring voting coalitions, the conservative coalition and the spending coalition. These two voting coalitions primarily

Introduction 13

reflected general corporate dominance from the late 1930s onward, but within a context of some important policy differences within the corporate community, along with the importance of the liberal-labor alliance to the spending coalition. (Before the New Deal, corporate and plantation dominance of Congress was so obvious that it has not been questioned.) However, there were also some very important issues, such as the National Labor Relations Act of 1935, on which unusual voting coalitions emerged, and still others on which the liberal-labor alliance was able to achieve at least partial success.

The conservative coalition, which is called a cross-party coalition in some sources, consisted at its core of a majority of Southern Democrats voting with a majority of Republicans. It most often formed on three general issues of great concern to employers North and South, which in essence defined the substance of their conflict with the liberal-labor alliance at the national policy level: legislation relating to labor unions, overly generous social benefits, and government regulation of business (see Clausen 1973; Mayhew 1966, for systematic studies pointing to the concerns shared by the conservative coalition). This coalition formed on anywhere from 14 to 40 percent of the contested votes in different sessions of Congress between 1939 and 1980, and it rarely lost, except for the 89th Congress (1965–1966) (Shelley 1983, pp. 34, 39). Since 1939, it has never lost on any legislation having to do with unions (e.g., Brady and Bullock 1980; Katznelson, Geiger, and Kryder 1993).

The spending coalition, on the other hand, consisted of a majority of Southern and non-Southern Democrats voting together to provide subsidies, tax breaks, and other government benefits to their most important supporters. A majority of the non-Southern Democrats supported agricultural subsidies and price supports, which greatly benefited plantation owners, ranchers, and agribusiness interests in the South, Midwest, and California. The Southerners in turn were willing to support government spending programs for roads, urban redevelopment, hospital construction, public housing, school lunches, and even public assistance, which were the main concerns of the urban real estate interests (i.e., the growth coalitions mentioned briefly earlier in the chapter). These growth coalitions financed the political machines and remained in place even though the political machines gradually disappeared or were transformed after the mid-1970s—except in Chicago and a few other cities (Domhoff 2005b; Logan and Molotch 2007; Molotch 1999). This mutual back-scratching bargain, which had its origins in the decades after the Civil War, provided the Democrats with their major policy basis (once again, see Clausen 1973; Mayhew 1966, for indications based on systematic studies that this second coalition existed).

Most, if not all, of these spending programs were opposed in principle by the majority of Northern Republicans and their ultraconservative

14 Introduction

supporters in the corporate community, although not always by corporate moderates until they hardened their views on social insurance in the 1980s.

The Conservative Coalition

Theoretically speaking, the conservative coalition is best defined as "an informal, bipartisan bloc of conservatives whose leaders occasionally engage in joint discussions of strategy and lining up votes" (Shelley 1983, p. 15). Its existence is most clearly demonstrated by rigorous, computationally intensive simulation studies of the persistence of voting patterns that are extremely unlikely to be random (Jenkins and Monroe 2014), and by longitudinal studies based on time-series analysis (Shelley 1983).

However, the existence of the conservative coalition was also attested to in interviews with two of its leaders in the House from the late 1930s to mid-1960s, after their retirements. According to Howard Smith of Virginia, a leader of the Southern Democrats:

"Our group—we called it our 'group' for want of a better term—was fighting appropriations. We did not meet publicly. The meetings were not formal. Our group met in one building and the conservative Republicans in another, on different issues" (Manley 1973, p. 231). Smith's counterpart on the Republican side, Joseph W. Martin of Massachusetts, who first won election to the House in 1938, independently corroborated this account, noting that he would seek out Smith or Representative Eugene Cox of Georgia, asking them if they could "get me some votes" on one or another issue (Manley 1973, p. 232).

Operationally, the Democratic component of the conservative coalition is initially defined in terms of the Democrat members of Congress from 13 of the 17 Southern states that were slave states or territories until the Civil War, and had legally institutionalized segregation until the Brown v Board of Education of Topeka decision by the Supreme Court in 1954 and the passage of the civil rights laws of 1964 and 1965: Alabama, Arkansas, Florida, Georgia, Kentucky, Louisiana, Mississippi, North Carolina, Oklahoma, South Carolina, Tennessee, Texas, and Virginia. This starting point tends to err on the side of caution in that it does not include the four former slave-and-caste states that slowly differentiated themselves from other former slave-and-caste states and territories in varying ways for somewhat different reasons (Delaware, Maryland, Missouri, and West Virginia).

However, this potential problem of erring on the side of caution is in effect remedied by expanding the operational definition of the conservative coalition to include those Democratic members of the House or Senate who agreed with the positions taken by its core Republican and Democratic supporters on 50 percent or more of the votes on which the coalition formed in any given session of Congress (Shelley 1983, p. 150). This expanded and more realistic definition encompasses the conservative Democrats from outside the 13 Southern states. (Recall that the conceptual definition of the conservative coalition is "an informal, bipartisan bloc of conservatives whose leaders occasionally engage in joint discussions of strategy and lining up votes," so this expanded operational definition is consistent with the conceptual definition (Shelley 1983, p. 15).) These additional conservative Democrats were often from districts in the former slave-and-caste states of Missouri and West Virginia, but also in rural districts in states bordering on the South and in rural districts in upstate New York and the West.

Based on this operational definition, which encompasses the full range of conservative Democrats, the conservative coalition included a majority of the House members in all but four sessions between 1939 and 1980: 1960, 1965, 1966, and 1975 (Shelley 1983, pp. 151–152, Table 8.5). It also had a majority in the Senate except for 1939–1941, 1960–1961, 1963–1967, 1973–1976, and 1978 (Shelley 1983, pp. 153–154, Table 8.6). As a glance at these numbers reveals, the House was the stronghold of the conservative coalition, which was sufficient for blocking legislation. Although a majority in the Senate was obviously necessary as well for passing legislation, the conservative coalition in the Senate was always large enough to sustain a filibuster until 1975, when the Senate changed its rules to say that a super-majority of 60 votes could end a filibuster. (At that point, ironically, it in effect became necessary to have a super-majority of 60 votes to pass any controversial legislation in the Senate).

Moreover, the scattered sessions in which the conservative coalition did not have a majority in the House were usually followed by its large comebacks that broke any momentum the liberal-labor alliance might have been developing. For example, after falling to 45 percent of all House members in 1959, it was back to 56 percent in 1961. Similarly, in 1965 the conservative coalition was down to 46 percent of all House members, but it was at 60 percent in 1967 (Shelley 1983, pp. 151–152, Table 8.5).

The overall results of these quantitative analyses provide impressive evidence that the conservative coalition seldom lost, except in a handful of instances during a few sessions of Congress. However, this big-picture view needs to be made more specific by discussing the conservative coalition's role on the major issues that are examined in this book. This makes it possible to provide a nuanced look at its power, as well as the limits on its power. In fact, some of its losses are more interesting for theoretical purposes than its many successes.

The longitudinal academic database containing information on the conservative coalition ends in 1980. However, the findings on the conservative coalition compiled each year by the *Congressional Quarterly*, based on the Democratic side of the coalition on only 13 Southern states, are useful through 1994 because the conservative coalition remained essential for several important conservative victories between 1981 and that year (e.g., CQ 1987; CQ 1996). It usually appeared ten or more times in each legislative session during that later time period, and it won 87 percent or more of the time in 13 of those 14 years in the Senate, and 80 percent or more in nine of the 14 years in the House, as shown in *Vital Statistics On Congress* (Ornstein, Mann, Malbin, Rugg, and Wakeman 2014, Table 8.5).

However, the conservative's need for Southern Democrats declined greatly after the 1994 elections, in good part because the Republicans rather suddenly became a majority in the 11 Deep-South states between 1992 and 1994. They did so through a bargain with African American Democrats in the South, which gave African American political figures 17 new seats that they never would have received from white Southern Democrats (Berman 2015, pp. 187–206; Zweigenhaft and Domhoff 2018, pp. 212–216). In exchange, the Republicans were able to carve out many new districts for themselves, partly by redrawing them in such a way that white Democratic incumbents had as few of their former white voters in the new district as possible, and partly by taking away the loyal black Democratic voters the white Democratic incumbents had depended upon to provide the winning margin (McKee 2010, for innovative work that provides the complete picture). As a result, the Southern Republicans in the House gained nine seats in 1992, 16 in 1994, and seven in 1996, for a total of 32 new Southern Republicans in the space of just three elections (McKee 2010, p. 72). (In addition, five white Southern Democrats in the House and one in the Senate switched to the Republican side after the 1994 elections.)

Due to the changes in the size and composition of the Democratic and Southern delegations to Congress, the concept of a conservative coalition was rendered meaningless. In any case, it did not appear at all in 1999, and the *Congressional Quarterly* stopped compiling the data. The conservative coalition is now ancient history, but it was essential to the corporate community and the power elite in dealing with the liberal-labor alliance in a generally successful manner between 1939 and 1994.

The Spending Coalition

The concept of a spending coalition emerged from my analyses of several specific pieces of legislation from the vantage points of the corporate community, Southern plantation owners, and the growth coalitions. These analyses were augmented by studies of more general issue clusters by political scientists (e.g., the findings in Clausen 1973; Mayhew 1966; Sinclair 1982, provided good starting points). As noted a few paragraphs ago, the primary concern of the spending coalition was to provide subsidies and tax breaks to its most important supporters, such as agricultural subsidies and price supports for plantation owners, ranchers, and agribusiness interests, along with redevelopment grants, urban renewal subsidies, and roads for the urban real estate interests at the heart of local and (increasingly) regional growth coalitions, which usually dominate city politics on all of the issues of concern to it (Domhoff 2005b; Gendron and Domhoff 2009, for a discussion of the exceptions to this generalization).

The concept of a spending coalition has considerable overlap with political scientist Aage Clausen's (1973) agricultural, social welfare, and government management dimensions, but in each case those three general issue-areas contain specific issues that do not quite belong and are successfully opposed by the conservative coalition. Similarly, the concerns of the spending coalition overlap with aspects of political scientist Byron Shafer's (2016, pp. 10–11, 38–39) economic welfare dimension, but that dimension does not put enough stress on the subsidies and tax breaks that go to wealthy agricultural and urban real estate interests, and can give the impression that the primary focus of economic spending is on lower-income citizens. In a word, the concept of a spending coalition is both a little wider and a little more selective than other ways of slicing the databases built from the votes of the individual legislators. On the other hand, due to this book's focus on the conflicts between the power elite and the liberal-labor alliance, it does not try to encompass all the legislative issues that might be relevant to a more general theory of Congressional voting behavior (e.g., Grossman 2014, whose "networks of governance" rarely touch on any of the policy issues discussed in this book, or assign much importance to corporations).

The core of the spending coalition included the approximately 90-to-100 Democrats from the 13 former slave-and-caste states and the roughly 50-to-60 Democrats that were members of urban political machines outside the South, which are called "patronage-based organizations" in some accounts, and contrasted with the liberals from "reform clubs" (e.g., Shafer 2016, p. 34). The Southern Democrats and the machine Democrats controlled the House and Senate for most of the years between 1932 and 1975, after which urban Democrats that were not part of classical machines came to the fore until the Republican congressional victories in 1994 (Domhoff 2005b; Logan and Molotch 2007).

Even without the political machines, however, the growth coalitions maintained their local involvement with urban Democrats through campaign finance while at the same time entering into the special-interest process at the national level through the National Association of Real Estate Boards, the National Association of Building Owners and Managers, the Mortgage Bankers Association of America, and the U.S. Building & Loan League (Farkas 1971; Tolchin and Tolchin 1971). They also had a strong influence on urban Democrats through an urban policy-planning network, financed by the same large foundations that were important funders of the policy-planning organizations focused on national-level issues. This urban

18 Introduction

dimension of the policy-planning network is described in somewhat more detail in Chapter 1 (Brownlow 1958, Chapters 22–24; Domhoff 1978, pp. 160–171, for a detailed historical account; Roberts 1994, for an in-depth look at its funding sources).

The Southern and urban Democrats used their seniority and choice of committee chairships to control Congress through stacking the committees of most concern to them, such as the Agriculture, Ways and Means, and Rules committees in the House and the Finance Committee in the Senate. The only exceptions to complete Democratic control of Congress before 1994 were Republican control of the House in 1947–1948 and 1953–1954, and Republican control of the Senate from 1954 to 1956 and from 1981 to 1986.

The spending coalition in the House was managed for most of the years between 1939 and 1989 by Southern Democrats from a few districts in Texas and southern Oklahoma, in conjunction with Democrats from the Boston area. The three leaders of this "Austin-Boston Alliance" (the Speaker of the House, the House majority leader, and the majority whip) shared a strong interest in bringing government spending projects to their districts, both of which had a low percentage of black constituents compared to most Southern states and the big Northern cities that were the basis of the urban political machines. They also shared a moderate or centrist stance compared to their more conservative colleagues in the case of the Southerners and their more liberal colleagues in the case of the Bostonians. The one exception to the Austin-Boston leadership regime was a moderate Southern Democrat from New Orleans, who was the majority whip from 1962 through 1970, and then the majority leader during 1971 and most of 1972, when he died in a plane crash (Champagne, Harris, Riddlesperger, and Nelson 2009).

Although the Northern and Southern Democrats were on opposite sides when the Southerners joined the conservative coalition, these disagreements were not as divisive as they might seem to be. The machine Democrats always backed their Southern counterparts on the all-important issues of party leadership and on the retention of the seniority system, which made it possible for the Southerners to use Congressional committees to delay or modify legislation they did not support. Then, too, the machine Democrats' voting records were not always as impressive as they seemed to be on labor, civil rights, and social welfare. They often helped the Southerners water down such legislation within committees. "By voting right," concluded a reporter who covered Congress for the *Wall Street Journal* in the 1960s, "they satisfied liberal opinion at home; by doing nothing effective, they satisfied their Southern allies in the House" (Miller 1970, p. 71).

This reporter's observations are supported by a systematic quantitative study based on all committee roll call votes from 1970 to 1980. The conservative coalition formed on 908 of the 4,219 substantive committee votes, about the same as on the floor, and it was successful 8 percent more of the time than on floor votes. Southern committee chairs sided with the conservative coalition within the committee 66.9 percent of the time, as might be expected. But Northern chairs also did so on 32.6 percent of the roll call votes, which led to success for the conservatives on 66.7 percent of those votes within committees (Unekis 1993, pp. 96–97).

From the 1960s onward, the urban Democrats and Southern Democrats shared another common objective, even though it could not be discussed publicly: limiting the power of African American voters. As the number of African Americans in many Northern cities steadily grew from the mid-1930s to majorities or near majorities by the 1960s, their potential voting strength became even more of a threat to the white urban Democrats than African American voters in the South were to the white Southern Democrats after the passage of the Voting Rights Act of 1965. In fact, African Americans gradually displaced many of the machine Democrats in the North over the 30-year period from 1970 to 2000.

Although the Democratic spending coalition seldom broke apart, Southern support for it always was conditional, based on the acceptance of three provisos: the spending programs could not contain any attacks on segregation, they had to be locally controlled so the Southerners could limit benefits to African Americans to means-tested programs, and they had to differentially benefit Southern states, even on such matters as hospital spending and urban renewal funds (Brown 1999, pp. 182–200). In other words, the spending coalition was premised on excluding African Americans from the jobs provided by its projects and many of its other policy benefits. (This is one of the reasons why the civil rights movement in the North took to the streets and blocked construction sites in the early 1960s, as discussed in Chapter 4: to force government agencies staffed by New Deal sympathizers to change their traditional rules and open up patronage networks related to jobs, housing, and education (Quadagno 1994).)

The core of the spending coalition was augmented by two important elements. First, it had the strong support of the building-trades unions in the American Federation of Labor (AFL). They aided the political machines' slates by helping to bring blue-collar voters to the polls, and later in the century began to make campaign contributions as well. When necessary, they served as political bulldozers against environmentalists and other liberals who opposed one or another specific growth project advocated by the local growth coalitions. They did so in the name of "jobs," which put liberals on the defensive because they did favor more jobs as a rule, albeit through major spending programs at the federal level (Molotch 1998; Molotch 1999). Put another way, local construction unions were the allies of the growth coalitions in terms of bringing new projects to a city or region, even though they also did battle with urban corporate interests over wages and working conditions.

20 Introduction

Despite the criticisms of liberals by building-trades unions in some cities on some issues, the approximately 90–100 liberal Democrats elected to Congress during the New Deal and thereafter (i.e., those non-Southern Democrats who were not beholden to machine bosses) were important supporters of the spending coalition because of their general belief that government, and the federal government in particular, should expand social spending that would benefit middle- and low-income people. Indeed, their votes were crucial on some issues during the postwar era. For the most part, however, they received little or nothing in return on the other issues of importance to them, including unions and civil rights. Instead, they had to settle for incremental improvements on economic and welfare issues crucial to the lives of average Americans, which they were often able to win when they could attract the support of machine and Southern Democrats, and even corporate moderates on a few issues between 1945 and 1975.

These liberal-labor victories included increases in the minimum wage, old-age pensions, unemployment benefits, and welfare payments, along with the expansion of the availability of food stamps and rent subsidies, and the addition of disability insurance to the Social Security Act. Since the ultraconservatives in the corporate community and in Congress opposed liberals on these issues, these liberal-labor successes can be counted as defeats for the ultraconservatives.

The Pivotal Role of Southern Democrats

Based on this analysis of the two main Congressional voting coalitions, the Southern Democrats were clearly the pivotal voting group in Congress because all but a very few of them shared three general views: (1) they supported racial segregation; (2) they were opponents of organized labor, not only to insure their domination of the plantation owners' traditional workforce, but to attract companies in the North that were in heavily unionized states; and (3) they knew that the South needed subsidies for the plantation owners as well as welfare-type supports for their subjugated workforce.

If the Southern Democrats sided with the Republicans on an issue, which meant that the representatives of major employers in the South and North were united, then the conservative coalition triumphed on a great majority of its appearances in most sessions of Congress. However, even though the Southern Democrats were essential to the conservative coalition, the degree to which it was a success depended on the number of Republicans in the House or the Senate. For that reason, the conservative coalition could only be successful if Republicans could defeat large numbers of moderate and liberal Democrats outside the South (e.g., Shafer 2016, pp. 36–38). In fact, the correlation between the size of the Republican delegation and success for the conservative coalition was .59 (Shelley 1983, p. 145). Although the size of the Republican delegation was critical, the Southern Democrats maintained a leadership role through the many committees they chaired due to the overall Democratic majority in most sessions of Congress, which gave them their choice of chairships due to the Democrats' adherence to the seniority system (e.g., Irish 1942).

The conservative coalition mostly played a defensive role between 1939 and 1977, eliminating New Deal agencies and spending programs, or else cutting back or blocking new liberal-labor proposals. However, in 1946–1947 and 1953–54, when Republicans temporarily controlled both houses of Congress, and after 1977, it showed it could play an initiatory role as well, passing or reshaping legislation that was useful to it.

Most strikingly, there are only two instances when the conservative coalition did not stay together on a labor issue critical to either Northern or Southern employers. The Southern Democrats abandoned the corporate community in 1935 by supporting the passage of the National Labor Relations Act, as explained in Chapter 2. Conversely, Republicans left the Southern plantation owners and their business allies high and dry when they withdrew their support for the Southern Democrats' filibuster of the Civil Rights Act of 1964 (e.g., Klinkner and Smith 2002; Whalen and Whalen 1985).

Based on this analysis, the fact that Democrats formally controlled Congress during most of the years between 1939 and 1994 is in fair measure irrelevant in terms of understanding the corporate community's domination of crucial government policies. Instead, the essential point is that a conservative majority had predominant power in Congress on issues related to corporate power throughout most of these years, including on union issues in the two most liberal sessions of Congress in American history, 1965–1966 and 1975–1976, as shown in Chapters 4 and 5.

Still, it is important to reiterate that the ultraconservatives within the corporate community, who are discussed in many social-science accounts as if they represented the entire business community, lost on some of their issues due to the existence of the spending coalition (Domhoff 2013b, pp. 80, 116–121, 135–138). In fact, in a detailed study of 107 successful pieces of legislation between 1953 and 1984, the ultraconservatives lost on 52.3 percent of them, a finding based on the use of the policy stances taken by the Chamber of Commerce as the index of the policy preferences of the ultraconservatives in the power elite (Smith 2000). The ultraconservatives often lost to the spending coalition on issues concerning subsidies for housing or urban real estate interests, which usually enjoyed the support of corporate moderates as well. The ultraconservatives also lost to agribusiness interests on votes for the agricultural subsidies that were vital to plantation owners and other large agribusiness interests. They lost to the spending coalition and the corporate moderates four times—in 1958,

22 Introduction

1963, 1965, and 1972—on programs that provided federal aid to public schools in depressed areas and to universities to support graduate students and basic research in science and engineering. They were defeated on government regulations mandating equal pay for women in 1963 and outlawing age discrimination in the workplace in 1967. Then, too, and as already noted in discussing the success of liberals within Congress, the ultraconservatives were unsuccessful in their opposition to some forms of income support for low-income workers and retirees.

Moreover, in spite of intense opposition by ultraconservatives in the corporate community and the conservative coalition in Congress, the liberal–labor alliance was largely responsible for putting Medicare on the legislative agenda, and the civil rights movement created the disruption that led to the Civil Rights Act of 1964 and the Voting Rights Act of 1965. These instances are exceptions to the generalizations presented in this discussion of the power elite and Congress, but they are important ones that are discussed in more detail later in the book.

A General Theory of Social Power

It is not entirely necessary to present a more general theoretical framework to encompass the historically circumscribed and policy-oriented focus of this book, which can stand or fall on its own merits. Nevertheless, it is useful to present a larger theoretical context in order to highlight the book's contrast with most other theoretical perspectives. This alternative framework begins at an abstract level with the idea that power, defined as the ability to achieve desired social outcomes, has both collective and distributive dimensions (Mann 1986; Parsons 1960; Wrong 1995).

"Collective power," the capacity of a group, class, or nation to be effective and productive, concerns the degree to which a collectivity has the technological resources, organizational forms, and social morale to achieve its general goals. "Distributive power" is the ability of a group, class, or nation to be successful in conflicts with other groups, classes, or nations on issues of concern to it (Mann 1986, pp. 6–7). Both collective and distributive power arise from the same basis: organizations. Organizations are at bottom sets of rules and roles that human beings develop so they can accomplish a particular purpose; they provide ways in which people do something together in a routinized fashion.

Once an organization is established, a permanent division of labor gradually emerges as it grows in size because of the advantages large-scale organizations provide in efficiency, ease of training new personnel, and greater overall effectiveness, all of which increase collective power. However, the division of labor also leads to a hierarchical distribution of power within the organization itself: "Those who occupy supervisory and coordinating positions have an immense organizational superiority over the others" (Mann 1986, p. 7). This suggests that those who lead organizations can turn them into power bases.

Reinforcing this sociological possibility, systematic studies of the social psychology of power in controlled laboratory settings indicate that participants in small-group experiments, after being randomly assigned to power roles without their realizing it, soon fail to understand the viewpoints and arguments of those randomly assigned to have less power. They come to believe they have more control over events than they in fact do and are more likely to condemn cheating, while cheating more often themselves (e.g., Fast, Gruenfeld, Sivanathan, and Galinsky 2009; Galinsky, Magee, Inesi, and Gruenfeld 2006; Lammers, Stapel, and Galinsky 2010; Piff 2014). They also tend to distance themselves from others, to think more abstractly, and to objectify others as instruments for personal gain, whereas those who lack power in experimental situations become more deferential, inhibit the expression of their actual attitudes, and suffer from impairments in their thinking abilities, even though they were as capable as other participants before the studies began (Keltner, Gruenfeld, Galinsky, and Kraus 2010; Kraus, Piff, Mendoza-Denton, Rheinschmidt, and Keltner 2012; Miyamoto and Ji 2011; Smith 2006; Smith, Jostmann, Galinsky, and Dijk 2008). These studies reveal that attitudes of superiority and inferiority can develop very quickly, and then be exploited by the powerful.

In addition, observational field studies and questionnaires concerning how power is in essence given to some people and not others, such as in student dormitories, sororities, and fraternities, suggest that members of new groups tend to see people who appear outgoing, and as having everyone's interests at heart, as natural leaders. They tell social psychologists within the first week or two the group is together that such people are informal leaders, and they continue to report the same opinions after they have come to know everyone better (Keltner, Gruenfeld, Galinsky, and Kraus 2010). But, as the experimental studies summarized in the previous paragraph show, being treated as the leader soon leads people to distort the situation, objectify others, and show tendencies toward what (in settings in which there is more at stake) might be called "corruption."

These studies suggest there is a "paradox to power;" it is more or less naturally given ("afforded") to some individuals at the interpersonal level in order to benefit the group as a whole, but that affordance is soon abused by the leaders as they become more self-important and self-absorbed. Thus, just as distributive power arises more or less naturally out of collective power, so too small-group studies suggest that informal leaders are chosen by the group, but soon come to dominate the group. These generalizations seem to be applicable to the leaders of any large-scale organization, such as religious leaders who take advantage of their congregation, or elected officials who ignore the preferences of those who voted for them, as well as to leaders of large corporations.

24   Introduction

Since human beings have a vast array of purposes, they have formed an appropriately large number of organizations. But only four of these organizations weigh heavily in terms of generating societal power: ideology/religious organizations, economic organizations, military organizations, and political organizations, which (from their first letters) become the basis for the IEMP model of social power creatively constructed by sociologist Michael Mann (1986) after immersing himself in a wide-ranging study of Western history These four organizational bases are conceptualized as overlapping and intersecting sociospatial networks that have widely varying extensions in physical space at different times in Western history.

Ideology organizations, the most prominent of which throughout human history have been religious organizations, are concerned with meaning, ethical norms, and ritual practices, but such an abstract statement sounds too benign in that it belies the depths of human anxiety, fear, and irrationality that lie within religion's purview. Religious organizations gain loyalty and financial support (through "sacrifices" and "tithing") by providing answers to such universal concerns as the origins of humanity, the purpose of life, the reasons for guilt, and the meaning of death. Psychologically, tithing may be the deepest form of the important social rite of gift exchanges; tithing is a gift to the gods in exchange for emotional calmness, and the temple becomes a storehouse of wealth and a base for power (Halls 2000; Mauss 1924/1969). Of almost equal importance, religions develop "rites of passage," all of which involve rituals of separation, periods of uncertainty and transition, and rituals of reincorporation into the society. They provide help in coping with the varying mixtures of anxiety, anger, guilt, and exhilaration that inevitably accompany momentous events, such as birth, puberty, marriage, and death (Van Gennep 1909/1960). Religious organizations also provide "community" and an opportunity to share collective joy and gratitude with those of a kindred spirit (Durkheim 1912/1965).

The economic network consists of a set of organizations concerned with satisfying material needs through the "extraction, transformation, distribution and consumption of the objects of nature" (Mann 1986, p. 24). The economic network gives rise to "classes," which are defined as positions in a social structure that are shaped by their relationship to, and power over, the different parts of the economic process. These economic classes, in turn, have the potential to create relatively cohesive social classes—"large group[s] of families approximately equal in rank and differentiated from other families with regard to characteristics such as occupation, prestige, or wealth" (Gilbert 2018, p. 262). As stressed by theorists of different persuasions, the members of a social class see each other as equals, socialize together, and freely intermarry.

Numerous studies, including those of the social organizations created by the wives and daughters of male corporation owners, demonstrate that an upper social class, based in the economic ownership class, does exist in the United States; it is in effect the social manifestation of the corporate community (Baltzell 1958; Domhoff 1970, Chapters 1–4; Kendall 2002; Ostrander 1984). The social cohesion generated by interactions within the social institutions of the upper class then plays a role in making policy cohesion possible within the policy-planning network (Domhoff 1974, Chapter 3; Domhoff 2005a). On the other hand, non-owning economic classes are less likely to develop a strong sense of social-class identity. In the United States, non-owners tend to self-identify and involve themselves in social groups in terms of high-status professional credentials, white-collar and blue-collar occupational roles, ethnic organizations, and religious organizations.

According to the four-network theory, the most powerful economic class, the owners of the key economic organizations, is called a "dominant" or "ruling" class if—and only if—it has been successful in organizing its members for collective action and subordinating the leaders in the other three networks. Thus, it is not inevitable that owners will become a dominant class. Geographically extensive classes arose very slowly in Western history because they were dependent upon advances in infrastructure. For the first 2,500 years of Western civilization, for example, economic networks were extremely localized, especially in comparison to the military and political networks discussed shortly.

Economic classes are also social relationships between groups of people, who often have different interests in terms of how the economic system is organized and how its output is distributed. The economic network may therefore generate class conflicts, which are disagreements over such matters as wage rates, working conditions, unionization, profit margins, and, on rare occasions, the fact of private ownership itself. Class conflicts can manifest themselves in ways that range from workplace protests and strikes to industry-wide boycotts, collective bargaining, and on up to nationwide political actions. However, class conflict is not inevitable, because both owners and workers, the usual rival classes in recent history, have to have the means to organize themselves over an extended area of social space for conflict to occur. For much of Western history, there have been relatively organized dominant classes, but class conflict has been important only in certain periods of it, such as in ancient Greece, early Rome, and the present era. This is because members of the non-owning economic class usually find it very difficult to organize themselves into a coherent oppositional force. Most of the time they are "organizationally outflanked" because they are "embedded within collective and distributive power organizations controlled by others" (Mann 1986, p. 7). Viewed from an individualistic perspective that starts with the competitiveness among individuals within any group or class, the American corporate rich are slightly less disorganized than those who would like to challenge

26   Introduction

them. Once again, that is, this book recognizes there are individualistic and rancorous tendencies within the people in all economic classes.

The third major organized power network, the military network, is rooted in organized physical violence. It is based on the ability to generate direct and immediate coercion that leads to death, captivity, imprisonment, or enslavement. Military networks had a greater range throughout most of Western history than either economic or political networks. Historically, many armies, based in societies on the fringes of recently established civilizations, were able to create "empires of domination" by taking over the newly arisen civilizations, which were based almost entirely on the intertwining of economic, religious, and political networks, the last of which very likely emerged from the religious network (Mann 1986, Chapter 3; Mann 2016; Yoffee 2005).

In recent centuries, military power is most often one aspect of the political network discussed in the next two paragraphs, but there are at least four reasons for keeping military and political power analytically distinct. First, and as noted in the previous paragraph, there were long periods of early history in which conquests were undertaken by armies that were not controlled by governments. Second, most historical states did not control all the military forces within the territory they attempted to regulate. Third, the frequent emergence of guerrilla armies and terrorist organizations shows that organized violence can still arise separately from government. Fourth, even in modern-day nation-states, the military is often set apart from other government institutions, which facilitates the in-group morale, sense of separateness, and independent hierarchical structure that make it possible for ambitious military leaders to overthrow governmental leaders, especially in times when governmental leaders appear to be weak in the face of economic problems or threats from other countries.

Turning to the fourth and final power network, the political network regulates activities within the geographical area for which it is responsible, including the movement of people, economic goods, and weapons in and out of its territory. This network, which is usually called the "state" or the "government," is separate from the other networks first of all because the people in a large social group need the regulatory and judicial services the political network provides. Groups of people may be in general cooperative, as studies in both developmental and social psychology show, but there are always disagreements that flair up between individuals or families, and there are inevitably a few people who dispute every issue or ignore laws and customs, thereby creating problems for everyone.

For example, in the case of the highly complex economic networks of the modern era, these are extremely dependent upon the political network because competing businesses have failed in their repeated attempts to regulate themselves due to the fact that some of them try to improve their market share or profits by reducing wages, adulterating products, colluding with other companies, telling half-truths, or even organizing shake-down gangs to extort other businesses. Thus, it is very difficult if not impossible for an economic network, with its dependency on at least reasonably fair and open markets, to survive without some degree of market regulation. Political networks also enforce property and contract rights, and in even more recent times they have taken on the added duties of creating money, regulating banks, and influencing interest rates.

The necessary services provided by the political network make it potentially independent from the other networks, including the economic network, and it gains further potential autonomy due to the fact that it interacts with other states, especially through warfare (e.g., Mann 1977; Mann 1984; Mann 1988; Skocpol 1979). Modern-day leaders in the economic network therefore greatly fear government independence, and constantly rail against it. At the same time, they know they need government's help in structuring the economy, as dramatically shown in the banking crises of the 1980s and 1990s that soon faded from memory and were repeated in 2008.

Once the four networks are solidly established historically, interorganizational alliances among two or more of them often generate a more general power structure that has the potential to greatly increase collective power, as well as to provide even more distributive power to people on the top. But the process of creating an overall power structure is fraught with tensions and dangers for the society as a whole because the mobilization of greater collective power depends on the resolution of prior questions about distributive power arrangements within and between the four power networks. Who has power over whom has to be settled within organizations, classes, and nation-states before collective power can be exercised in any useful way. Otherwise, relentless infighting among rival organizational leaders greatly weakens a society. It can lead to the collapse of dominant economic classes, armies, or governments, as hundreds of historical examples over many centuries amply confirm (e.g., Lachmann 2000; Lachmann 2010; Mann 1986; Mann 1993).

Struggles for power among the four networks to the side for the time being, it is important to stress that the emphasis on the relative independence of the four networks of power in this theory generates a dynamic and open-ended view of the future. The organizations in these networks interact and come into conflict in constantly changing ways due to newly created organizational forms, newly invented technologies, new methods of communication, military innovations, and new spiritual movements. Thus, there is an emergent and constantly changing quality to social organization that makes the present very different from the past, which suggests that it is illusory to think that the future can be predicted.

As a consequence of the many different possible outcomes of the interactions among organizational power bases, comparative studies are of

28   Introduction

limited value, even among modern-day Western European and North American countries. The primary focus therefore has to be on "historical, not comparative, sociology" (Mann 1986, p. 503). Every country is distinctive enough that detailed historical analyses are necessary. This generalization includes the United States, and provides the theoretical rationale for the predominantly historical approach that is used in this book. However, there are a few comparisons with Canada and countries in Western Europe that illuminate some of the unique features of the United States, including one that is presented in the next subsection.

Corporate-Dominance Theory and Marxism

Because the concept of "class" is so strongly identified with Marxism in the social sciences, it may be useful to contrast the general starting point for this book with Marxism to anticipate possible misunderstandings. As is well known, Marxism begins at a very abstract level with a theory of history in which there is an inevitable and growing clash between owners (e.g., feudal lords, capitalists) and non-owners (e.g., slaves, peasants, workers). For a variety of reasons, Marxists claim that capitalism inevitably leads to more intense economic crises, heightened class struggle, the inevitable collapse of capitalism due to its internal contradictions, the eventual triumph of the property-less proletariat (workers), and the replacement of capitalism with a non-market planned economy called socialism. By contrast, proponents of the four-network theory argue that it is only barely possible to discern any patterns in history and do not forecast any inevitable outcomes (e.g., Lachmann 2015; Mann 1986, Chapter 16; Mann 2013, Chapters 12–13; Mann 2016).

The labor theory of value, the idea that commodities have value only in so far as human labor power has been used to produce them, is a central feature of the historical process according to Marxism. Although the extraction of the surplus value created by non-owners is transparent in slave and feudal societies, where it is often violent and brutal, in capitalist societies the expropriation of profit in private ownership, market-based societies is said to be disguised by the operation of markets. In other words, the idea of a fair day's pay for a fair day's work masks the power that capitalists exercise in markets. This expropriation behind the backs of workers is further veiled by parliamentary democracy. In this view, any semblance of democracy is a sham, not a hard-won and often-lost achievement: "Democracy in the parliamentary shell hides its absence in the state bureaucratic kernel; parliamentary freedom is regarded as the political counterpart of the freedom in the marketplace, and the hierarchical bureaucracy as the counterpart of the capitalist division of labor in the factory" (O'Connor 1984, p. 188).

Moreover, the dominant variant within Marxism in the 1970s, structural Marxism, turned out to be very wrong in its claims and predictions due to factors that had not been anticipated. As a leading structural Marxist of that era later wrote about in his highly regarded book: "The fact remains that *Fiscal Crisis* [*of the State*] failed to anticipate the rise of neo-liberalism and globalization and the reestablishment of U.S. political hegemony after the fall of the Soviet empire" (O'Connor 2002, p. xviii). Similarly, one of the sociologists who was a prominent participant in this theory group later concluded: "One of the tacit assumptions in much Marxist work of the early 1970s was the conviction that the statist turn in capitalism could not be dramatically reversed," which meant that "no one seriously envisioned the wholesale dismantling of the welfare state, the deregulation of markets, the partial reversal of statist capitalism as a way of coping with the crisis tendencies of the period" (Wright 2004, p. 252).

Thus, the only conceptual agreement with Marxism in this book is that class conflict in the economic sense is a useful conceptual building block for an understanding of the American power structure. However, that agreement is due to the absence of four power bases that already existed in most European countries before the rise of capitalism: feudalism (a rival ownership class, with which the rising capitalists had to contend), a strong centralized state, a large standing army, and an established church. These power bases, which existed before capitalism, were able to shape capitalism's development within the context of those countries, and to force a sharing of power with unions that successful American corporate leaders never had to face (e.g., Hamilton 1991; Mann 1993; Mann 2004; Voss 1993).

In addition, this book disagrees with Marxian analyses of the United States in relation to the policy domains that are discussed in it. In particular, they tend to overestimate the potential for unity and militancy in the working class from the late 1820s, when the first small city-based working-class political parties and unions briefly appeared, into the 1930s and beyond. Nor do they give sufficient weight to the electoral rules that lead inexorably to a two-party system, especially in a presidential system. Marxists also tend to overstate the degree to which corporate leaders feared leftists in the 1930s. In the case of the National Labor Relations Act, for example, this book argues that it is incorrect to claim that corporate leaders instituted reforms out of a fear of working-class militancy (e.g., Davis 1986; Goldfield 1989), or in cooperation with AFL leaders who purportedly shared their fears (e.g., Aronowitz 1973; Aronowitz 2003).

Nor is it likely that the decline in union strength throughout most of the postwar era was due to the pro-labor response by the Democratic Party during the Great Depression, which was said by one Marxian sociologist to be co-optive (Eidlin 2016; Eidlin 2018), and thereby able to draw working-class voters away from nascent left-wing third parties that they might otherwise have joined at this possible formative moment for a stronger working-class identity. Marxists also tend to underestimate the

30 Introduction

flexibility of the corporate moderates; for example, the archival record does not support the assertion that no corporate moderates supported the Social Security Act (e.g., Lichtenstein 2002, p. 105).

Although I have used the phrase "class dominance" or "corporate dominance" in one or another of my past books, depending upon the main focus of the book, I use the phrases "corporate dominance" and "corporate domination" in this book for two reasons. First, it does not put forth the full case that the corporate rich are a dominant social class, in part for reasons of space, in part because it is not necessary for a study of specific government policies. Second, the use of the concept of corporate dominance may help to remind readers that this book draws upon concepts adapted from several different theories and is not a version of Marxism.

Neoliberalism

Nor does this book make any use of the concept of "neoliberalism." The cutbacks in government social-insurance benefits and business regulation encompassed by this term, which are usually characterized as developing in the 1970s or 1980s, were in fact the essence of an ultraconservative policy perspective that goes back to the division between corporate moderates and ultraconservatives, which was clearly discernible in the first ten years of the twentieth century (Lo 2018, pp. 199–200; Weinstein 1968). Neoliberalism is therefore neither a new set of policies nor dependent upon the ideas of ultraconservative economists of the 1940s and 1950s.

In addition, theorists who invoke a relatively recent rise in "neoliberalism" are in effect implying a degree of moderate unity in the corporate community as a whole that never existed. They thereby overlook the differences between corporate moderates and ultraconservatives during the first six decades of the twentieth century, as well as the changes the corporate moderates made in their policy positions in the late 1960s and early 1970s, based on their own needs and reasoning. Neoliberal theorists are therefore unable to understand the growing attack on unions in the late 1960s, the attempt to limit the expansion of social-insurance programs after 1980, or the accelerating development of the international economy beginning in the 1970s.

The term "neoliberalism" also inevitably leads to confusion with twentieth-century American political liberalism, which is in no way similar to "neoliberalism" (Block and Somers 2014, for a critique of the concept of neoliberalism that makes this point, among several others; Lachmann 2015, for a wider-ranging critique of neoliberalism). The people who eventually called themselves "liberals" differentiated their views from classical nineteenth-century liberalism during the first three decades of the twentieth century because its sole focus remained on property rights, the proper functioning of markets, and the minimal involvement of government in civil society and markets as the key to liberty. For modern liberals, however, the increasing exclusion of African Americans in the 17 slave-and-caste states, along with the refusal by classical liberals to extend the right of association to unions, violated the basic tenets of liberalism relating to individual rights.

In other words, the twentieth-century liberals believed that liberalism could accommodate greater inclusion without any basic challenge to property rights or markets (e.g., Starr 2007, Chapters 4–6). To deal with these new societal issues in the context of United States history, the Americans who labeled themselves as liberals by the late 1920s concluded that the scope of the federal government would have to be extended on some issues if individual liberty was going to be accorded to everyone. Due to their knowledge of American history and their lived experience, they knew from the early twentieth century onward that only the federal government could (1) insure basic individual freedoms and the right to vote to everyone in slave-and-caste states and (2) make it possible for unions to develop in the states that were completely dominated by anti-union property owners. Based on this analysis, there is nothing "neoliberal" about modern-day liberalism.

But in one frequently cited Marxian-oriented version of the rise of neoliberalism, three longstanding prominent liberals, Paul Krugman, George Soros, and Joseph Stiglitz, are called "earlier enthusiasts" of neoliberalism who have "now turned critical, even to the point of suggesting some sort of return to a modified Keynesianism..." (Harvey 2005, p. 186). More generally, as frankly stated by American historian Sean Wilentz (2018, p. 31), who follows politics closely as a political liberal, the once-academic concept of neoliberalism "has morphed into a sweeping pejorative against liberals, progressives, and European social democrats not of the hard left," and is being invoked at "both ends of the political spectrum..." The implicit premise of these condescending critiques by leftist critics of liberals—that a majority of voters in the United States would respond to a strong liberal-leftist platform, or to a new left-oriented third party—seems to be more an expression of longstanding political hopes by leftists, who generally scorn liberals, than an empirically based theoretical analysis. By contrast, this book has no implicit political agenda or any prescriptions about what people of one or another political persuasion should do.

Instead, this book takes a stance similar to that in a comment by Mills (1957/1968, p. 249). This comment appears in a reply to criticisms by theorists of all stripes that his book on *The Power Elite* (1956) was "too pessimistic" or "too negative." In response, Mills said he had "never been able to make up my mind whether something is so or not in terms of whether or not it leads to good cheer;" rather his view was that: "First you try to get it straight, to make an adequate statement." Then, "If it's gloomy, too bad; if it's cheerful, well fine" (Mills 1957/1968, p. 249). The goal of the book is to get it as straight as possible based upon available archival sources.

References

Aronowitz, Stanley. 1973. *False promises: The shaping of American working class consciousness.* New York: McGraw-Hill.

———. 2003. *How class works: Power and social movement.* New Haven: Yale University Press.

Baltzell, E. Digby. 1958. *Philadelphia gentlemen: The making of a national upper class.* New York: Free Press.

———. 1964. *The Protestant establishment: Aristocracy and caste in America.* New York: Random House.

Bartels, Larry M. 2016. *Unequal democracy: The political economy of the new Guilded Age.* Princeton: Princeton University Press.

Berman, Ari. 2015. *Give us the ballot: The modern struggle for voting rights in America.* New York: Farrar, Straus and Giroux.

Berreman, Gerald. 1960. "Caste in India and the United States." *American Journal of Sociology* 66:120–127.

———. 1981. *Caste and other inequities.* New Delhi: Manohar Book Services.

Black, Earl and Merle Black. 2002. *The rise of Southern Republicanism.* Cambridge: Harvard University Press.

Block, Fred and Margaret Somers. 2014. *The power of market fundamentalism: Karl Polanyi's critique.* Cambridge: Harvard University Press.

Brady, David and Charles Bullock. 1980. "Is there a conservative coalition in the House?" *Journal of Politics* 42:549–559.

Brown, Michael K. 1999. *Race, money and the American welfare state.* Ithaca: Cornell University Press.

Brownlow, Louis. 1958. *A passion for anonymity: The autobiography of Louis Brownlow,* Vol. 2. Chicago: University of Chicago Press.

Bunting, David. 1983. "Origins of the American corporate network." *Social Science History* 7:129–142.

Burch, Philip 1980. *Elites in American history: The New Deal to the Carter administration,* Vol. 3. New York: Holmes & Meier.

———. 1981. *Elites in American history: The Civil War to the New Deal,* Vol. 2. New York: Holmes & Meier.

Carosso, Vincent. 1970. *Investment banking in America.* Cambridge: Harvard University Press.

Champagne, Anthony, Douglas Harris, James Riddlesperger, and Garrison Nelson. 2009. *The Austin/Boston connection: Five decades of House Democratic leadership, 1937–1989.* College Station: Texas A&M Press.

Clausen, Aage R. 1973. *How Congressmen decide: A policy focus.* New York: St. Martin's Press.

CQ. 1987. *Power in Congress: Who has it, how they got it, how they use it.* Washington: Congressional Quarterly.

———. 1996. "Will the rise of 'blue dogs' revive the partisan right?" *Congressional Quarterly,* December 21, pp. 3436–3438.

Crocker, Jennifer and Amy Canevello. 2015. "Relationships and the self: Egosystem and ecosystem." Pp. 93–116 in *APA handbook of personality and social psychology: Interpersonal relations,* vol. 3, edited by M. Mikulincer, P. R. Shaver, J. A. Simpson, and J. F. Dovidio. Washington: American Psychological Association.

Dalzell, Robert F. 1987. *Enterprising elite: The Boston Associates and the world they made.* Cambridge: Harvard University Press.

Davidson, Chandler and Bernard Grofman. 1994a. *Quiet revolution in the South: The impact of the Voting Rights Act, 1965–1990.* Princeton: Princeton University Press.

———. 1994b. "The Voting Rights Act and the second Reconstruction." Pp. 378–387 in *Quiet revolution in the South: The impact of the Voting Rights Act, 1965–1990,* edited by C. Davidson and B. Grofman. Princeton: Princeton University Press.

Davis, Allison, Burleigh Gardner, and Mary Gardner. 1941. *Deep South: A social anthropological study of caste and class.* Chicago: University of Chicago Press.

Davis, Gerald F., Mina Yoo, and Wayne Baker. 2002. "The small world of the American corporate elite, 1982–2001." *Strategic Organization* 1:301–326.

Davis, Mike. 1986. *Prisoners of the American dream: Politics and economy in the history of the US working class.* London: Verso Press.

Dollard, John and Adrian Leftwich. 1957. *Caste and class in a southern town.* New York: Doubleday.

Domhoff, G. W. 1967. *Who rules America?* Englewood Cliffs, NJ: Prentice Hall.

———. 1970. *The higher circles.* New York: Random House.

———. 1974. *The Bohemian Grove and other retreats: A study in ruling-class cohesiveness.* New York: Harper & Row.

———. 1975. "Social clubs, policy-planning groups, and corporations: A network study of ruling-class cohesiveness." *The Insurgent Sociologist* 5:173–184.

———. 1978. *Who really rules? New Haven and community power re-examined.* New Brunswick: Transaction Books.

———. 1986. "The growth machine and the power elite: A challenge to pluralists and Marxists alike." Pp. 53–75 in *Community power: Directions for future research,* edited by R. Waste. Newbury Park, CA: Sage Publications.

———. 1990. *The power elite and the state: How policy is made in America.* Hawthorne, NY: Aldine de Gruyter.

———. 1996. *State autonomy or class dominance? Case studies on policy making in America.* Hawthorne, NY: Aldine de Gruyter.

———. 1998. *Who rules America? Power and politics in the year 2000.* Mountain View, CA: Mayfield Publishing Company.

———. 2005a. "Social cohesion & the Bohemian Grove: The Power Elite at Summer Camp." WhoRulesAmerica.net: http://whorulesamerica.net/power/bohemian_grove.html.

———. 2005b. "The political economy of urban power structures." WhoRulesAmerica.net: https://sociology.ucsc.edu/whorulesamerica/power/local.html#economy.

———. 2013a. "The left and the right in thinking, personality, and politics." WhoRulesAmerica.net: https://www2.ucsc.edu/whorulesamerica/change/left_and_right.html.

———. 2013b. *The myth of liberal ascendancy: Corporate dominance from the Great Depression to the Great Recession.* Boulder: Paradigm Publishers.

———. 2014. *Who rules America? The triumph of the corporate rich.* New York: McGraw-Hill.

Durkheim, Emile. 1912/1965. *The elementary forms of religious life: A study in religious sociology.* New York: Free Press.

34　Introduction

Eidlin, Barry. 2016. "Why is there no labor party in the United States? Political articulation and the Canadian Comparison, 1932 to 1948." *American Sociological Review* 81:488–516.

———. 2018. *Labor and the Class Idea in the United States and Canada.* New York: Cambridge University Press.

Eitzen, D. Stanley, Maureen A. Jung, and Dean A. Purdy. 1982. "Organizational linkages among the inner group of the capitalist class." *Sociological Focus* 15:179–189.

Farkas, Suzanne. 1971. *Urban lobbying: Mayors in the federal arena.* New York: New York University Press.

Fast, Nathaniel, Deborah Gruenfeld, Nio Sivanathan, and Adam Galinsky. 2009. "Illusory control: A generative force behind power's far-reaching effects." *Psychological Science* 20:502–508.

Fennema, Meindert and Eelke M. Heemskerk. 2017 "When theory meets methods: The naissance of computer assisted corporate interlock research." *Global Networks.* Global Networks Partnership and John Wiley & Sons.

Galinsky, Adam, Joe Magee, M. Ena Inesi, and Deborah Gruenfeld. 2006. "Power and perspectives not taken." *Psychological Science* 17:1068–1074.

Gendron, R. and G. W. Domhoff. 2009. *The leftmost city: Power and progressive politics in Santa Cruz.* New York: Routledge.

Gilbert, Dennis. 2018. *The American class structure in an age of growing inequality.* Los Angeles: Sage.

Gilens, Martin. 2012. *Affluence and influence: Economic inequality and political power in America.* Princeton: Princeton University Press.

Gilens, Martin and Benjamin Page. 2014. "Testing theories of American politics: Elites, interest groups, and average citizens." *Perspectives on Politics* 12:564–581.

Gogel, Robert and Thomas Koenig. 1981. "Commercial Banks, interlocking directorates and economic power: An analysis of the primary metals industry." *Social Problems* 29:117–128.

Goldfield, Michael. 1989. "Worker insurgency, radical organization, and New Deal labor legislation." *American Political Science Review* 83:1257–1282.

Grossman, Matt. 2014. *Artists of the possible: Governing networks and American policy change since 1945.* New York: Oxford University Press.

Halls, W. D. 2000. *Gift: The form and reason for exchange in archaic societies.* New York: Norton.

Hamilton, Richard 1991. *The bourgeois epoch: Marx and Engels on Britain, France, and Germany.* Chapel Hill: University of North Carolina Press.

Harvey, David. 2005. *A brief history of neoliberalism.* New York: Oxford University Press.

Huntington, Samuel. 1961. *The common defense.* New York: Columbia University Press.

Irish, Marion. 1942. "The Southern one-party system and national politics." *Journal of Politics* 4:80–94.

Janowitz, Morris. 1960. *The professional soldier.* New York: The Free Press.

Jenkins, Jeffery and Nathan Monroe. 2014. "Negative agenda control and the conservative coalition in the U.S. House." *Journal of Politics* 76:1116–1127.

Katznelson, Ira, Kim Geiger, and Daniel Kryder. 1993. "Limiting liberalism: The Southern veto in Congress 1933–1950." *Political Science Quarterly* 108:283–306.

Keltner, Dacher, Deborah Gruenfeld, Adam Galinsky, and Michael Kraus. 2010. "Paradoxes of power: Dynamics of the acquisition, experience, and social regulation of social power." Pp. 177–208 in *The social psychology of power*, edited by N. Guinote and T. Vescio. New York: Guilford Press.

Kendall, Diana. 2002. *The power of good deeds: Privileged women and the social reproduction of class*. Lanham, MD: Rowman & Littlefield.

Key, V. O. 1949. *Southern politics in state and nation*. New York: Random House.

Klinkner, Philip and Rogers Smith. 2002. *The unsteady march: The rise and decline of racial equality in America*. Chicago: University of Chicago Press.

Koenig, Thomas and Robert Gogel. 1981. "Interlocking corporate directorships as a social network." *The American Journal of Economics and Sociology* 40:37–50.

Kousser, J. Morgan. 1974. *The shaping of Southern politics: Suffrage restriction and the establishment of the one-party South, 1880–1910*. New Haven: Yale University Press.

Kraus, Michael, Paul Piff, Rodolfo Mendoza-Denton, Michelle Rheinschmidt, and Dacher Keltner. 2012. "Social class, solipsism, and contextualism: How the rich are different from the poor." *Psychological Review* 119:546–572.

Lachmann, Richard. 2000. *Capitalists in spite of themselves: Elite conflict and economic transformation in early modern Europe*. New York: Oxford University Press.

———. 2010. *States and power*. Malden, MA: Polity Press.

———. 2015. "Neoliberalism, the origins of the global crisis, and the future of states." Pp. 463–484 in *The sociology of development handbook*, edited by G. Hooks, S. Makaryan, and P. Almeida. Berkeley: University of California Press.

Lammers, Joris, Diederik Stapel, and Adam Galinsky. 2010. "Power increases hypocrisy: Moralizing in reasoning, immorality in behavior." *Psychological Science* 21:737–744.

Lichtenstein, Nelson. 2002. *State of the Union: A century of American labor*. Princeton: Princeton University Press.

Lipset, Seymour. 1963. *The first new nation: The United States in historical and comparative perspective*. New York: Basic Books.

Lo, Clarence Y.H. 2018. "'Fairness' in Presidential economic policy: Disagreements among upper class elites." Pp. 182–204 in *Studying the power elite: Fifty years of who rules America?* edited by G. Domhoff. New York: Routledge.

Logan, John and Harvey Molotch. 2007. *Urban fortunes: The political economy of place*. Berkeley: University of California Press.

Manley, John F. 1973. "The conservative coalition in congress." *American Behavioral Scientist* 17:223–247.

Mann, Michael. 1977. "States ancient and modern." *Archives of European Sociology* 18:226–298.

———. 1984. "The autonomous power of the state: Its origins, mechanisms, and results." *Archives of European Sociology* 25:185–213.

———. 1986. *The sources of social power: A history of power from the beginning to A.D. 1760*, Vol. 1. New York: Cambridge University Press.

———. 1988. *States, war and capitalism: Studies in political sociology*. Cambridge: Blackwell Publishers.

———. 1993. *The sources of social power: The rise of classes and nation-states, 1760–1914*, Vol. 2. New York: Cambridge University Press.

———. 2004. *Fascists*. New York: Cambridge University Press.

———. 2013. *The sources of social power: Globalizations, 1945–2011*, Vol. 4. New York: Cambridge University Press.

———. 2016. "Have human societies evolved? Evidence from history and prehistory." *Theory and Society* 45:203–237.

Massey, Douglas. 2016. "Residential segregation is the linchpin of racial stratification." *City & Community* 15:4–7.

Massey, Douglas and Nancy Denton. 1993. *American apartheid: Segregation and the making of the underclass*. Cambridge: Harvard University Press.

Mauss, Marcel. 1924/1969. *The gift: Forms and functions of exchange in archaic societies*. London: Cohen & West.

Mayhew, David 1966. *Party loyalty among congressmen: The difference between Democrats and Republicans, 1947–1962*. Cambridge: Harvard University Press.

McKee, Seth C. 2010. *Republican ascendency in southern U.S. House elections*. Boulder: Westview Press.

———. 2019. *The dynamics of Southern politics: Causes and consequences*. Thousand Oaks: CQ Press.

McLellan, David and Charles Woodhouse. 1960. "The business elite and foreign policy." *Western Political Quarterly* 13:172–190.

Michaels, David. 2008. *Doubt is their product: How industry's assault on science threatens your health*. New York: Oxford University Press.

Miller, Norman. 1970. "The machine Democrats." *Washington Monthly*, pp. 70–73.

Mills, C. Wright. 1948. *The new men of power: America's labor leaders*. New York: Harcourt, Brace, and Company.

———. 1956. *The power elite*. New York: Oxford University Press.

———. 1957/1968. "Comment on Criticism in Dissent Magazine." Pp. 229–250 in *C. Wright Mills and The Power Elite*, edited by G. W. Domhoff and H. Ballard. Boston: Beacon Press.

———. 1959. *The sociological imagination*. New York: Oxford University Press.

Mintz, Beth. 1975. "The president's cabinet, 1897–1972: A contribution to the power structure debate." *Insurgent Sociologist* 5:131–148.

Mintz, Beth and Michael Schwartz. 1983. "Financial interest groups and interlocking directorates." *Social Science History* 7:183–204.

Miyamoto, Yuri and Li-Jun Ji. 2011. "Power fosters context-independent, analytic cognition." *Personality and Social Psychology Bulletin* 37:1449–1458.

Mizruchi, Mark. 1982. *The American corporate network, 1904–1974*. Beverly Hills: Sage Publications.

Molotch, Harvey. 1976. "The city as a growth machine." *American Journal of Sociology* 82:309–330.

———. 1998. "Urban America: Crushed in the growth machine." Pp. 53–71 in *Social policy and the conservative agenda*, edited by C. Lo and M. Schwartz. Malden, MA: Blackwell.

———. 1999. "Growth machine links: Up, down, and across." Pp. 247–265 in *The urban growth machine: Critical perspectives, two decades later*, edited by A. Jonas and D. Wilson. Albany: State University of New York Press.

Moore, Gwen. 2007. "From Vietnam to Iraq: American elites' views on the use of military force." *Comparative Sociology* 6:215–231.

Myrdal, Gunnar. 1944. *An American dilemma: The Negro problem and modern democracy*, Vol. 1. New York: Harper and Brothers.

Nisbet, Matthew and John Kotcher. 2009. "A two-step flow of influence? Opinion-leader campaigns on climate change." *Science Communication* 30:328–354.

O'Connor, James. 1984. *Accumulation Crisis*. New York: Blackwell.

———. 2002. "New introduction to the transaction edition of The Fiscal Crisis of the State." Pp. i-xx in *The fiscal crisis of the state*, edited by J. O'Connor. New Brunswick: Transaction Books.

Oreskes, N. and E. Conway. 2010. *Merchants of doubt: How a handful of scientists obscured the truth on issues from tobacco smoke to global warming*. New York Bloomsbury Press.

Ornstein, Norman J., Thomas E. Mann, Michael J. Malbin, Andrew Rugg, and Raffaela Wakeman. 2014. *Vital statistics on Congress*. Washington: The Brookings Institution.

Ostrander, Susan A. 1984. *Women of the upper class*. Philadelphia: Temple University Press.

Page, Benjamin. 2008. *The foreign policy disconnect: What Americans want from our leaders but don't get*. Chicago: University of Chicago Press.

Page, Benjamin, Larry Bartels, and Jason Seawright. 2013. "Democracy and the policy preferences of wealthy Americans." *Perspectives on Politics* 13:51–73.

Page, Benjamin and Martin Gilens. 2018. *Democracy in America?* Chicago: University of Chicago Press.

Page, Benjamin and Cari Hennessy. 2010. "What affluent Americans want from politics." in *Meetings of the American Political Science Association*. Washington.

Page, Benjamin and Lawrence Jacobs. 2009. *Class war? What Americans really think about economic inequality*. Chicago: University of Chicago Press.

Page, Benjamin and Robert Y. Shapiro. 1992. *The rational public: Fifty years of trends in Americans' policy preferences*. Chicago: University of Chicago Press.

Palmer, Donald. 1983. "Interpreting corporate interlocks from broken ties." *Social Science History* 7:217–231.

Parker-Gwin, Rachel and William G. Roy. 1996. "Corporate law and the organization of property in the United States: The origin and institutionalization of New Jersey corporation law, 1888–1903." *Politics & Society*, June, pp. 111–136.

Parsons, Talcott. 1960. "The distribution of power in American society." Pp. 199–225 in *Structure and process in modern society*, edited by T. Parsons. New York: Free Press.

Pettigrew, Thomas. 1988. "Integration and pluralism." Pp. 19–30 in *Modern racism: Profiles in controversy*, edited by P. A. Katz and D. A. Taylor. New York: Plenum.

———. 2008. "Still a long way to go: American Black-White relations today." Pp. 45–61 in *Commemorating Brown: The social psychology of racism and discrimination*, edited by G. Adams, M. Biernat, N. Branscombe, C. Crandall, and L. Wrightsman. Washington: American Psychological Association.

———. 2017. "Social psychological perspectives on Trump supporters." *Journal of Social and Political Psychology* 5:107–116.

Pfeffer, J. 1972. "Size and composition of corporate boards of directors: The organization and its environment." *Administrative Science Quarterly* 17: 218–228.

38   Introduction

Piff, Paul. 2014. "Wealth and the inflated self: Class, entitlement, and narcissism." *Personality and Social Psychology Bulletin* 40:34–43.

Potter, Wendell. 2010. *Deadly spin: An insurance company insider speaks out on how corporate PR is killing health care and deceiving Americans.* New York: Bloomsbury Press.

Quadagno, Jill. 1994. *The color of welfare: How racism undermined the war on poverty.* New York: Oxford University Press.

Roberts, Alasdair. 1994. "Demonstrating neutrality: The Rockefeller philanthropies and the evolution of public administration, 1927–1936." *Public Administration Review*, pp. 221–228.

Rosenstone, Steven J., Roy L. Behr, and Edward H. Lazarus. 1996. *Third parties in America: Citizen response to major party failure.* Princeton: Princeton University Press.

Rothstein, Richard. 2017. *The color of law: A forgotten history of how our government segregated America.* New York: Liveright.

Roy, William G. 1983. "Interlocking directorates and the corporate revolution." *Social Science History* 7:143–164.

———. 1997. *Socializing capital: The rise of the large industrial corporation in America.* Princeton: Princeton University Press.

Salzman, Harold and G. William Domhoff. 1980. "The corporate community and government: Do they interlock?" Pp. 227–254 in *Power structure research*, edited by G. W. Domhoff. Beverly Hills: Sage.

———. 1983. "Nonprofit organizations and the corporate community." *Social Science History* 7:205–216.

Shafer, Byron 2016. *The American political pattern: Stability and change, 1932–2016.* Lawrence University Press of Kansas.

Shelley, Mack. 1983. *The permanent majority: The conservative coalition in the United States Congress.* Tuscaloosa.: University of Alabama Press.

Sinclair, Barbara. 1982. *Congressional realignment, 1925–1978.* Austin: University of Texas Press.

Skocpol, Theda. 1979. *States and social revolutions: A comparative analysis of France, Russia, and China.* New York: Cambridge University Press.

Smith, Mark A. 2000. *American business and political power.* Chicago: University of Chicago Press.

Smith, Pamela. 2006. "You focus on the forest when you're in charge of the trees: Power priming and abstract information processing." *Journal of Personality and Social Psychology* 90:578–596.

Smith, Pamela, Nils Jostmann, Adam Galinsky, and Wilco Dijk. 2008. "Lacking power impairs executive functions." *Psychological Science* 19:441–447.

Starr, Paul. 2007. *Freedom's power: The true force of liberalism.* New York: Basic Books.

Tolchin, Martin and Susan Tolchin. 1971. *To the victor ... Political patronage from the clubhouse to the White House.* New York: Random House.

Tomkins, Silvan. 1964. "Left and right: A basic dimension of personality and ideology." Pp. 388–411 in *The study of lives*, edited by R. W. White. New York: Atherton Press.

Unekis, Joseph. 1993. "Blocking the liberal agenda in house committees: The role of the conservative coalition." *Congress & the Presidency* 20:93–99.

Useem, Michael. 1979. "The social organization of the American business elite and the participation of corporate directors in the governance of American institutions." *American Sociological Review* 44:553–571.

———. 1984. *The inner circle: Large corporations and the rise of business political activity in the U.S. and U.K.* New York: Oxford University Press.

Van Gennep, Arnold. 1909/1960. *The rites of passage.* Chicago: University of Chicago Press.

Voss, Kim. 1993. *The making of American exceptionalism: The Knights of Labor and class formation in the nineteenth century.* Ithaca: Cornell University Press.

Webber, Michael J. 2000. *New Deal fat cats: Business, labor, and campaign finance in the 1936 presidential election.* New York: Fordham University Press.

Weber, Max. 1998. "Class, status, and party." Pp. 43–56 in *Social class and stratification: Classic statements and theoretical debates,* edited by R. F. Levine. Lanham, MD: Rowman & Littlefield.

Weinstein, James. 1968. *The corporate ideal in the liberal state.* Boston: Beacon Press.

Whalen, Charles and Barbara Whalen. 1985. *The longest debate: A legislative history of the 1964 Civil Rights Act.* Washington: Seven Locks Press.

Wilentz, Sean. 2018. "The High Table Liberal." *The New York Review* February 8:31–33.

Winters, Jeffry. 2011. *Oligarchy.* New York: Cambridge University Press.

Woodhouse, Charles and McLellan. 1966. "American business leaders and foreign policy: A study in perspectives." *The American Journal of Economics and Sociology* 25:267–280.

Wright, Erik Olin. 2004. "Introductory comments to 'Alternative perspectives in Marxist theory of accumulation and crisis'." Pp. 251–254 in *Enriching the sociological imagination: How radical sociology changed the discipline,* edited by R. F. Levine. Boulder: Paradigm Publishers.

Wrong, Dennis. 1995. *Power: Its forms, bases, and uses.* New Brunswick: Transaction Publishers.

Yoffee, Norman. 2005. *Myths of the archaic state: Evolution of the earliest cities, states, and civilizations.* New York: Cambridge University Press.

Zweigenhaft, Richard L. and G. William Domhoff. 1982. *Jews in the Protestant establishment.* New York: Praeger.

———. 2018. *Diversity in the power elite: Ironies and unfulfilled promises.* Lanham, MD: Rowman & Littlefield

Part I

The Rise and Fall of Labor Unions

Part 1 pivots on the origins of the National Labor Relations Act in 1935 and its gradual dismantling between 1938 and 1985. The act represents both a major turning point in American labor history and a major theoretical challenge to a corporate-dominance theory. It promised to put the power of government behind the right of workers to organize unions and bargain collectively with their employers about wages, hours, and working conditions. Whatever its shortcomings and long-term failures, it changed the American power structure for nearly 45 years between the mid-1930s and the late 1970s. In telling this story, these chapters show that corporate moderates had a larger role in creating the National Labor Relations Act than is usually understood, even though they fiercely opposed its final form and led the charge against it from the day it became law. These chapters also show the crucial role of the Southern rich in allowing the act to pass, and then making its gradual dismantlement possible by turning against it completely in 1938.

The first chapter briefly overviews the first appearance of unionism and workers' political parties in the late 1820s and early 1830s, which then fell into abeyance for a variety of reasons. It then turns to the pitched battles between corporations and union organizers from the late 1870s until the late 1890s. It includes a comparison with the more successful unionization efforts beginning in several European countries in the 1880s, which helps to explain why unions had relatively little success in the United States, except for their important role from the mid-1930s to the late 1970s.

Following a detailed chapter on the clashes and precedents that informed specific aspects of the National Labor Relations Act, along with explaining why it passed and the successes of the union movement in the first three years after it passed, later chapters describe the step-by-step dismantling of the act. This dismantlement was temporarily halted by the need for national unity during both World War II and the Korean War. The way in which the increasing white resistance to the civil rights movement in the 1960s contributed to the downfall of the unions is also analyzed. The series of defeats for private-sector unions after the 1970s, which

42 The Rise and Fall of Labor Unions

was partly compensated by the growth of public-sector unions, along with a brief analysis of a failed legislative initiative in 2009, provide the conclusion to Part 1.

Some degree of quantitative structure and precision is given by making use of the concept of "union density" as a rough index of liberal-labor power, as measured by the percentage of nonagricultural employees that are members of a union in any given year. Union density is by no means a perfect measure of liberal-labor power because it in part reflects changes in the rate of unemployment. However, no indicators in the social sciences are fully accurate in terms of the concept they are measuring, including in economics (Diener, Lucas, Schimmack, and Helliwell 2009, Chapter 3; Domhoff 2014, pp. 4–8, 193–197; Lazarsfeld 1966; Morgenstern 1963). To provide an indication of its variation, and hence of its possible usefulness, union density was only 1.6 percent when any semblance of a sound estimate could be made in 1880. After gradual growth in the remainder of the nineteenth century, followed by a significant increase over a five-year period to 17.4 percent in 1921, due to World War I, there was a decline to a low point of 11.0 percent in 1933. Union density surged in the late 1930s and reached high points at the end of World War II (34.2 percent in 1945) and the Korean War (33.5 percent). Thereafter it gradually declined to 14.0 percent in 1995, when this invaluable time series ends (Freeman 1998, Table 8A.2). These large variations suggest there was a rise and fall in union power at various times over the span of the 115 years, which is useful in verifying the events that were turning points in union history.

References

Diener, Ed., Richard Lucas, Ulrich Schimmack, and John Helliwell. 2009. *Well-being for public policy.* New York: Oxford University Press.

Domhoff, G. W. 2014. *Who rules America? The triumph of the corporate rich.* New York: McGraw-Hill.

Freeman, Richard B. 1998. "Spurts in union growth: Defining moments and social processes." Pp. 265–296 in *The defining moment: The Great Depression and the American economy in the twentieth century,* edited by M. Bordo, C. Goldin, and E. White. Chicago: University of Chicago Press.

Lazarsfeld, Paul. 1966. "Concept formation and measurement." Pp. 144–202 in *Concepts, theory, and explanation in the behavioral sciences,* edited by G. DiRenzo. New York: Random House.

Morgenstern, Oskar. 1963. *On the accuracy of economic observations* Princeton: Princeton University Press.

Chapter 1

The Uphill Battle for Unionism from the 1820s to 1932

Labor organizations in the early years of the United States were largely mutual aid societies or craft guilds that restricted entry into a craft and enforced workplace standards, as was also the case in Western Europe. This form of worker organization did not generate major opposition because craft workers were relatively few in number and very narrow in their aims, and most of the companies that employed them were small. But the reorganization of the workplace by business owners, in response to new opportunities and increased competition in the growing national economy, widened the gap between employers and skilled workers. By the 1820s, skilled workers were engaging in increasing numbers of protests and strikes over wage cuts, longer workdays, or layoffs, which were threats to both their economic well-being and social standing.

As the first halting steps beyond separate craft guilds began to occur, employers reacted strongly by charging that strikes and related activities were an attack on their own rights as individuals, as well as being subversive and in violation of the workers' obligations to society (Voss 1993, pp. 30–31). In sharp contrast to the story told by the "free-market" advocates of that era, whose emphasis was already on the way in which market demand was the best regulator of wages and prices, the union activists asserted that they were being dispossessed of rights that their forbears already had earned for skilled workers as patriots and soldiers in the founding of the United States.

Skilled workers knew that the participation of the "middling" classes of yeoman farmers and artisans had been essential to the members of the upper-middle and upper classes that had opted for a Revolutionary War, and that in return they had insisted upon special conventions, based on duly elected representatives, to meet and develop each state's constitution. Not only had they helped to win the war, but also they feared the potentially onerous property laws and taxation policies that might be written into the state constitutions by those who were known at the time as their "betters." They were thereby the source of the new idea that "the people" were the basis for legitimate power in the new United States (Palmer 1959; Piven 2006, Chapter 3).

In the end, these middling-level insurgents of the Revolutionary War era only won the right to both a constitutional convention of elected delegates and a vote on subsequent ratification in Massachusetts in 1780. But in 1789 the authors of the new federal constitution did not try to promulgate their new federal constitution, primarily designed to more fully protect private property and compromise some of their basic disagreements, without asking for the consent of the governed. In the process they were forced to add the Bill of Rights to ensure the constitution's acceptance, and an increasingly high percentage of adult white males won the right to vote between 1790 and 1850, which was often extended to new immigrants as the areas to the west of the original states competed for settlers (e.g., Keyssar 2009, Chapter 2; Starr 2007, pp. 90–92). Based on this cultural and political heritage, the skilled workers of the 1820s and 1830s felt every right to cast any attempts by employers to cut wages or increase the length of the workday as a threat to the new Republic itself. They in effect claimed that the early market fundamentalists were trying to strip them of their rights and independence as free white male citizens. The defense of labor was thereby equated with the defense of American republican government (e.g., Lambert 2005, for a fine account of how the early craft unionists viewed the world; Voss 1993, pp. 26–29, for a succinct overview).

Building on their nascent unions and their republican beliefs, the strikes of the 1820s were accompanied by brief flurries of independent political action in 1829 and 1830 by skilled workers and their higher-status sympathizers in numerous cities in 16 states, led by Philadelphia and New York, the two largest manufacturing centers at the time (Laurie 1989, p. 74). However, the political organizations did not last for more than a year due to a lack of success for most of their candidates and the adoption of key parts of their platforms by Jacksonian Democrats in the early 1930s. Both skilled and unskilled workers, and perhaps especially the recent immigrants among them, who were openly reviled by the new conservative party of Whigs, found it difficult to support pro-worker third parties that might lead to the defeat of the Jacksonian Democrats that were sympathetic to them.

Politics aside, union activity reached new heights between 1833 and 1837, with unions appearing in most sectors of the urban economy, and with the creation of the equivalent of citywide labor councils "in more than a dozen urban centers, ranging from Philadelphia and Boston to Cincinnati and Newark" (Voss 1993, p. 30). In addition, union leaders from several cities met yearly under the name General Trades' Union, although there was little coordination beyond the city level. However, all of this organizational growth was "destroyed in the nation's first industrial depression that began in 1837 and lasted for seven painful years," including most local unions, and in any case there had remained "an enormous boundary between skilled and unskilled workers" (Voss 1993, p. 33, 35).

Nonetheless, many skilled workers had won the 10-hour day by 1840, and in the 1840s there was agitation for the 10-hour day for factory workers, which met with limited success until the 1860s.

With few exceptions, such as the longshoremen's union organized in Boston in 1847, any post-1837 efforts at unionization were not successful until skilled workers were able to take advantage of a short-lived Civil War boom to revive past craft unions and start some new ones as well. In their first 15 years, some of the activists built a national labor organization that promised to have some staying power. This national labor organization, the Noble and Holy Order of the Knights of Labor (usually shortened to the Knights of Labor), was founded in 1869 as a secret society by a handful of Philadelphia garment cutters, after they gave up on their own craft union because they did not think it had any chance to succeed. Their credo emphasized citizenship rights, action in support of general social progress, cooperative forms of organization for the society as a whole, and, significantly, the inclusion of workers of all crafts and races in one union for the first time (Voss 1993, pp. 73–82). They also started reading rooms, held parades, and supported local labor parties.

Based on their understanding of the importance of organizational survival, the older and more seasoned leaders were ambivalent about strikes due to their past experience. They worried that disruptive actions alienated both employers and the general public, and made unions vulnerable to collapse. They therefore tended to focus on education, persuasion, and legislative changes. Although they emphasized their openness to unskilled as well as skilled workers, to women as well as men, and to African Americans as well as whites, they were in fact mostly white male craft workers when the union grew to a few thousand members nationwide in 1877.

In 1877 a major political bargain between Northern and Southern political leaders, memorialized in history books as the Compromise of 1877, handed the disputed 1876 presidential election to the Republicans. The Republicans agreed in return to help subsidize the reconstruction of the Southern infrastructure and to remove the remaining troops from the South, which gave the former slaveholders an opening to regain their ascendancy by any means necessary. Four months after the bargain, and just weeks after the last remaining federal troops were removed from the former Confederate states, labor relations in the North suddenly took a violent turn. This violence turned out to be the start of a new era that lasted for decades and reshaped the nature of the American union movement. It began when the Baltimore and Ohio Railroad announced in mid-July that it would impose an immediate 10 percent pay cut, the third for that year. In the face of an ongoing depression that had lingered since 1873, other railroads had already made draconian wage cuts without major protest. But the announcement by the Baltimore and Ohio led to a spontaneous

46 The Rise and Fall of Labor Unions

strike in the company's rail yards in Martinsburg, West Virginia, which did not end quickly.

City officials called out the local militia, but its members were reluctant to use force against workers who were part of their own community. The governor asked for federal troops, leading to a clash in which workers stopped trains and destroyed railroad property. The strike rapidly spread to other nearby cities. The violence was especially extensive in Pittsburgh, already a growing industrial center based in the iron and steel industry. When militia brought in from Philadelphia fired at the demonstrators, killing several people, the angry mob burned down 39 buildings and destroyed 104 locomotives and 1,245 freight and passenger cars. The strike became national in scope, drawing in nearly 100,000 workers, and at one point had stopped half the nation's rail freight from moving (Bruce 1959; Foner 1977). In all, governors in seven different states had to call out their militia, which is a clear demonstration of how important it is for business owners to ensure that there are government officials who are supportive of their property rights (*pace* Lindblom 1977; Lindblom 1978, who ignores class conflict and violence in claiming that elected officials must perforce cater to business, lest they lose the next election because people suffering from unemployment or inflation will vote them out of office).

Traveling from city to city via trains, government troops finally quelled the uprising after two weeks of effort. In the process, over 100 people were killed and many more were imprisoned (Stowell 1999, for a thorough account). Based on the traditional, more tolerant responses to strikes, the extent of the violence came as a shock to both workers and employers. Up until that time, Americans generally had viewed strikes as a legitimate form of action because employees had an independent stature that reflected both their valued work skills and their belief in republican values (Lambert 2005). Courts had sometimes condemned strikes as conspiracies or restraints of trade, but fines were usually small and there were no imprisonments. In addition, the Massachusetts Supreme Court had rejected the conspiracy and restraint of trade charges in a case that came before it in 1854 (Dubofsky and Dulles 2004, pp. 59–61). The only previous known deaths from strike activity—two in number—had occurred in New York City in 1850 when police shot into a crowd to break up a strike by tailors, who were protesting wage cuts (Lambert 2005, p. 22).

Since 1877, though, the United States has had "the bloodiest and most violent labor history of any industrial nation in the world," with the exception of Russia (Mann 1993, p. 644). The strongly held American belief in the right of business owners to have complete control over their property, along with business dominance of both political parties, provided the starting point that led to an ideological appeal to classical liberalism and then to moral justifications. Moreover, the history of violence in dealing with Native Americans and slaves, not to mention the horrendous casualty

The Uphill Battle for Unionism 47

rate in the Civil War, made the pitched labor battles seem as normal and expectable to most Americans as they were to Russians, with their totally different history. Between 1877 and 1900, American presidents sent the U.S. Army into 11 strikes, governors mobilized the National Guard in somewhere between 118 and 160 labor disputes, and mayors called out the police on numerous occasions to restore order (Archer 2007, p. 120; Cooper 1980, pp. 13–16; Lambert 2005, p. 44).

In the aftermath of the summer of violence in 1877, a few railroad corporations began to consider the use of employee benefits, such as accident insurance and old-age pensions, to mollify workers, which is a topic that will be discussed in more detail in Part 2. Generally speaking, though, very little changed in terms of employer/employee relations. Instead, corporate leaders put their efforts into creating stronger military forces to control workers when necessary, starting with reorganized militias and fortified local armories. In addition, militia units were often directly funded and supplied by corporate leaders. For example, the founder of International Harvester equipped an Illinois National Guard regiment, and a group of Chicago businessmen funded five cavalry companies (Smith 2003). The regular army also developed close ties to the industrial companies in urban areas. Three business leaders in Chicago, to provide another example, donated the money for a military base just 20 miles north of their city (Archer 2007, pp. 121–122; Cooper 1980, pp. 85–86). Thus, it can be seen that the close relationship between the corporate community and the military in the United States developed very early, with the corporate leaders in charge from the beginning. Contrary to all subsequent claims of a separate "military-industrial" complex (e.g., Hooks 1991), the corporate community as a whole was a military-industrial complex from the late 1870s until at least the end of the twentieth century (e.g., Domhoff 1996, Chapter 6; Pilisuk and Hayden 1965).

The use of private security forces in labor disputes also grew. Business leaders paid for and directed the activities of deputy sheriffs and deputy marshals, regularly employed Pinkerton Detective Agency strikebreakers (the company had 30,000 regular and reserve agents in 1890), and attempted to establish and control their own police forces (Norwood 2002; Smith 2003). In fact, at this point the private Pinkerton forces that owed their livelihood to the corporate community had more armed employees than the United States military (Mann 1993, p. 646).

The violence of 1877 also led to a change of strategy by many local affiliates of the aforementioned Knights of Labor, which decided that the strikes had failed because they lacked the proper leadership and organization. Reflecting the changing circumstances as businesses grew in size and power, the Knights decided to drop their semi-secret ways and take a more active role in creating the kind of organizations they thought would be able to counter employers and even challenge the new industrial

48   The Rise and Fall of Labor Unions

companies. They also emphasized again that their doors were open to membership for both skilled and unskilled workers as well as women and people of all racial and ethnic backgrounds. With the economy improving at the same time, the Knights claimed to have 50,000 members in 1883, a claim that may be reflected in the gradual growth of union density from 1.6 percent in 1880 to 2.8 percent in 1883 (Freeman 1998, Table 8A.2).

It was at this point that the Knights seemed to be on the verge of major success due to highly publicized strikes by railroad shop men in 1883 and 1884 against one of the most notorious Robber Barons of the day, a railroad magnate. The successes only involved the restoration of wage cuts, but local activists saw them as evidence for the potential power of unions and their strike weapon, and more workers began to join: "In its wake, thousands of workers—particularly semiskilled and unskilled workers— joined the Order. By the summer of 1885, membership had doubled and a local assembly [the Knights' term for a local chapter] had been established in nearly every city and mid-sized town in the country" (Voss 1993, pp. 75–76).

Buoyed by their new hopes, many assemblies decided to join a general strike to force employers to grant the eight-hour day. The Federation of Organized Trades and Labor Unions, a loose-knit national labor organization to which some of the Knights also belonged, first advocated this action. The strike was set for May 1, 1886. The leaders of the Knights opposed the idea, fearful that such a strike could not be won, but sociologist Kim Voss (1993, p. 77) concludes that large numbers of workers were taken with the idea that they could establish the eight-hour day on their own initiative, a step toward imposing their own work rules (cf. Lambert 2005, p. 56). The seeming caution of the labor leaders, which then and thereafter received heavy criticism from the strongest activists, was based on a fear of losing everything if the organization was destroyed, as the Knights soon were (Dubofsky 2000). In other words, any claims about labor bosses who "sell out" to the corporate leaders is a vast overstatement, if not totally inaccurate. Such criticisms are due to a failure to understand that defeated unions disappear, or have to make unsavory deals with employers, or organized crime syndicates, to save the remnants.

As workers across the country prepared for the upcoming general strike, another Knights-affiliated union went on strike against another of the Robber Barons' railroads, this time in the Southwest. The union demanded a daily wage of $1.50 for unskilled workers and the reinstatement of a worker who had been fired for attending a union meeting. Workers across the country became members of the Knights out of sympathy for this strike, but the owner held firm this time. As the strike against the railroad in the Southwest dragged on, the May 1 strike for the eight-hour day began with over 1,500 work stoppages throughout the country, involving

The Uphill Battle for Unionism 49

several hundred thousand people. It looked for a moment as if this relatively spontaneous action might succeed.

But the tide turned against the mass action just two days later when police in Chicago fired into a crowd of 30,000 pro-strike demonstrators and killed two people, with several more wounded. At that point anarchists came into the picture by calling for a massive protest rally the next day, which attracted 50,000 people to Haymarket Square. After two hours of speeches and many reminders that the event was to be nonviolent, and with the demonstrators starting to disperse, a major disaster suddenly erupted. A bomb was thrown at the police when they suddenly started to break up the gathering, killing one policeman and wounding 70 others. The police then began shooting, which killed one worker and wounded many more (Lambert 2005; Voss 1993).

The big industrialists and their allies in city governments across the country used what was quickly labeled as the Haymarket Riot as a pretext for a major counterattack by federal troops and private business armies. They now defined all union leaders as communists, socialists, and, especially, anarchists. The result of the corporate and government repression was a complete defeat for the Knights of Labor on both the eight-hour day and the railroad strike. Moreover, the organization gradually collapsed over the next few years, losing 90 percent of its membership in four years (e.g., Lambert 2005, p. 57). This sudden rise and more rapid fall in the strength of the union movement is reflected in the rise of union density from 4.1 percent in 1885 to 10.0 percent in 1986, followed by a decline to 5.5 percent in 1889 (Freeman 1998, Table 8A.2).

As for the May Day demand for an eight-hour day, it was totally ignored. President Franklin D. Roosevelt, an advocate of the eight-hour day, did not achieve this goal until the Fair Labor Standards Act passed in 1938, with the help of the liberal-labor alliance that gradually developed in the early years of his administration. However, some unions won the eight-hour day here and there along the way, such as coal miners in 1890 and printers and typographers in 1905. Still other workers were granted the eight-hour day during World War I.

Several different factors seem to have contributed to the decline of the Knights, including tensions between craft and unskilled workers. Voss (1993, pp. 186–204) uses cross-national comparisons with the United Kingdom and France, and a close look at the rise and decline of Knight assemblies in New Jersey, to argue that the most important factor was the unusual strength and cohesion of American employer associations. These associations could display brutal determination in combating the growth of labor unions because they dominated local governments and political parties. At this point Voss (1993, pp. 238–239) draws an important contrast between the United States, the United Kingdom, and France when she shows that the British and French governments in effect forced employers

50   The Rise and Fall of Labor Unions

to compromise with workers. For a combination of reasons, including the continuing power of land-based aristocrats and the greater strength of these two national governments, the business owners did not dominate in either of these countries (cf. Guttsman 1969; Hamilton 1991; Mann 1993). This is in fact a major difference from the United States that is sometimes not fully appreciated for its importance.

The repression of 1886 led to a rapid decline for the Knights of Labor, but the events of that year also gave rise to a very different kind of union movement, the American Federation of Labor (AFL), which took several lessons away from the failures of the Knights. These lessons eventually made it possible for the AFL to force moderates in the corporate community to consider the possibility of collective bargaining as an acceptable compromise in the face of ongoing labor strife, which ranged from slowdowns to strikes to sabotage and the destruction of equipment. But a possible compromise was still more than a decade in the future.

The new federation was founded in early December 1886, a few months after the general strikes during the spring and summer had ended in defeat. Convinced that the organizational structure of previous unions was too diffuse and fragmented to withstand the violence that companies could bring to bear against workers, its leaders organized as a federation of narrow, self-interested craft unions, which included iron molders, miners, typographers, tailors, bakers, furniture workers, metal workers, carpenters, and cigar makers. It was the separate unions, not the AFL itself, that conducted the main activities of organized labor (such as recruitment, bargaining, and calling strikes), and the federation itself was always dependent upon its constituent organizations for finances. By 1892, the AFL included 40 unions, most of them with a few thousand members. The carpenters (57,000), typographers (28,000), cigar makers (27,000), iron and steel workers (24,000), and iron molders (23,000) were the five largest (Foner 1955, p. 171).

Craft unions, with exclusive membership jurisdictions and high membership dues, were able to grow stronger than the Knights' assemblies because they used new organizational measures to survive the combined onslaught of employers and government authorities when they called strikes. In order to secure the long-term loyalty of their members, they first provided sickness, unemployment, and strike benefits in addition to the burial insurance that had been a staple of craft guilds since the colonial era. Second, craft unions became more centralized, such that authority for strike action had to come from the national-level leadership. This organizational form reduced the potentially fatal consequences for a nationwide organization if there were independent strike initiatives by local affiliates. AFL leaders also tried to mitigate the influence of local anarchists and other types of activists who were not always part of the unions themselves, although in later decades leftist political activists often joined fledgling unions in an attempt to become part of the leadership or advocate more militant tactics. At the same time, as later events showed, a centralized form of organization can provide a potential base for dictatorial leaders (Shefter 1994, p. 153). In other words, an organization is a double-edged sword, but in a large-scale society any form of organization, for all its potential defects, is usually better in terms of confronting well-organized power rivals than no organization at all.

Despite their considerable autonomy and independence, however, the national-level craft leaders ceded some authority to speak for them on general policy issues to the leader of the federation, who was voted into office for two-year terms by delegates from each union at national meetings. Samuel Gompers, the federation's founding president, originally a leader of the cigar makers' union, served as the AFL's president for all but two years from 1886 until his death in 1924. He was the face of the AFL and its main spokesperson for nearly 40 years.

With their organizational strategy in place, the craft unions then girded for the focused strike actions and boycotts they selectively employed. The preamble to their original constitution described these activities as a "struggle" that was going on "between the oppressors and the oppressed of all countries, a struggle between the capitalist and the laborer, which grows in intensity from year to year, and will work disastrous results to the toiling millions if they are not combined for mutual protection and benefit" (e.g., AFL 1901). This ringing general analysis was used against the AFL ever after by editorial writers and conservatives of all stripes. At the same time, though, the federation also adopted a more pragmatic and less politically threatening strategy toward employers and the government. It emphasized higher wages, shorter working hours, and better working conditions, not general class conflict. This narrow agenda of "pure and simple unionism" was supposed to be accomplished through direct actions against employers, so it is not as if the AFL members were afraid of confrontation or unaware of the violence with which most employers would react.

As part of this confrontational but narrowly focused approach, the AFL tried to avoid involvement in broad-based political organizations, especially at the national level, although they generally sided with Democrats in national elections after 1900. They feared that political activity might divide their unions in a context in which the nation's electoral rules and the history of the two dominant political parties made it highly unlikely that workers could form their own political party. Believing that the political activism of the Knights of Labor, and especially the frequent disagreements between craft unions and various groups of socialists within the organization, had contributed to its downfall, the AFL tried to keep anarchists and Marxists at a distance, and treated any claims they made with suspicion (Shefter 1994, p. 156).

In reality, however, the AFL did involve itself in politics in many instances, especially at the state and local levels, and it was in constant dialogue and disagreement with various leftist groups and parties over the next three decades. At one point in the early twentieth century, about one-third of the AFL affiliates were controlled by socialists (Weinstein 1968, p. 5).

The Important Issue of "Replacement Costs"

In addition to their tight organizational structures, narrow agendas, and attempts to avoid involvement with political parties and leftists, the unions within the AFL that had any degree of success had one other factor that weighed in their favor. Workers in some occupations succeed because the "replacement costs" for bringing in strikebreakers and replacement workers are very high for their employers, for different reasons in different industries (Kimeldorf 2013, for these original and invaluable insights). In some cases, replacement costs are high due to the employees' possession of rare skills, as in the case of the printers, who successfully organized in that era, and of professional sports players in the late twentieth century (who had some of the strongest unions in the country, which is why they made big money, not just because they were sterling athletes). Replacement costs also can be high for companies that have fast turnaround times, such as shipping and railroads in the late nineteenth and early twentieth centuries, or UPS in the modern era, which is one big reason why UPS drivers were able to maintain a strong union and keep their wages high. Then, too, in the late nineteenth and early twentieth centuries it was often impossible to recruit strikebreakers and replacement workers due to the geographic isolation of the workplace (e.g., mining, logging, and other extractive industries). For example, immigrant replacement workers from urban areas might be injured or killed by strikers if they took temporary jobs in coalmines in unfamiliar hill country settled several generations earlier by people of a different ethnicity or color.

When replacement costs are high, the use of militant strikes and violence can play a role in organizing a union, but primarily as a means of keeping replacement workers from entering job sites, not as a general strategy. Most of this violence is between strikers and replacement workers (called "scabs" by union organizers and members), or between police and strikers, with destruction of equipment and other forms of sabotage relatively rare, even though it was sometimes threatened. However, some skilled workers, such as construction workers of various kinds, were able to do costly damage if they decided to sabotage equipment or destroy what they had partially built. In the railroad industry, as seen graphically in the deadly violence and destruction in the spontaneous strikes in 1877, the companies were vulnerable to highly expensive repairs to locomotives and other valuable equipment.

Employer Resistance Continues

In the face of well-organized craft unions and potentially high replacement costs if workers went on strike, the employers nonetheless continued to resist the union pay scales, elaborate work rules, and apprenticeship limits that skilled craft workers wanted to institutionalize. This point is important to underline because it shows that the employers' primary concern was full control of the workplace and the greatest possible profits, not a fear of socialist ideas. In addition, the employers increasingly sought to speed up the labor process with new forms of work organization (e.g., Zieger and Gall 2002, pp. 27–28). They also employed growing numbers of unskilled immigrant laborers at lower wages in an attempt to rid themselves of skilled workers by taking advantage of the new machines and forms of work organization, such as assembly lines, that were becoming available.

To counter this business counterattack, the craft unions within the AFL opposed the continuing influx of unskilled industrial workers into the country. They saw the introduction of more workers and mass-production technologies as detrimental for their wages and social status. Instead of trying to fight industrialists by joining with the growing number of unskilled workers, as many assemblies of the Knights of Labor had attempted to do, they decided that their best hope was in limiting the number of available workers in order to keep their wages and replacement costs as high as possible. That is, they knew that the control of labor markets was the key power issue for both them and their employers.

The fact that the newly arriving immigrants were largely from Eastern and Southern Europe, and often from Catholic and Jewish religious backgrounds as well, only heightened the resolve of these white male craftsmen, who were overwhelmingly Protestants of British and Northern European heritage. Over time, as political scientist Gwendolyn Mink (1986, p. 17) convincingly argued, "ethnic differences and skill differences converged within an expanding labor market to precipitate organizational and nativist anxieties among skilled unionizing workers of older immigrant stock." As the craft unions' objections to immigrant industrial workers mounted, "ethnic exclusion solidified craft-based exclusion, stripping union economic action of its class-based potential" (Mink 1986, p. 72). The result was a political division in the working class, with immigrant industrial workers tending to support the pro-immigrant Republicans from 1896 to the late 1920s, or the Socialist Party during the Progressive Era. Members of the AFL were more likely to vote Democratic because urban political machines were more tolerant of unions, perhaps due to the high costs of hiring skilled replacement workers in the building trades (e.g., carpenters, bricklayers, plasterers, and painters) (Kimeldorf 2013; Mink 1986, p. 155). Indeed, throughout the twentieth century, and as mentioned in the Introduction, building-trades unions usually supported the local land owners, developers, and related real estate interests because the growth of a city means more construction and thus more work for all types of building-trades workers (Logan and Molotch 2007; Molotch 1979; Molotch 1999).

For all the AFL's careful planning and hopes, pure and simple trade unionism for skilled workers organized into craft unions did not enjoy much success within big industrial companies in its first decade. The problems are seen in the sudden collapse of the Amalgamated Association of Iron, Steel and Tin Workers, which provided the AFL with 10 percent of its members and had a contract with the steel companies owned by one of the richest and most powerful men of his era, Andrew Carnegie. When the union refused to accept the introduction of highly profitable new technology and changes in wage rates in 1892, Carnegie and his executives in effect forced a strike by cutting wages by nearly 18 percent at the Carnegie Steel Works in Homestead, Pennsylvania. The ensuing confrontation led to the deaths of ten workers and three of the 300 armed Pinkerton Detective Agency guards that had been brought in to attack the strikers (Bernstein 1969, pp. 432–434; Scheinberg 1986, pp. 7–9).

Eight thousand members of the Pennsylvania National Guard then occupied Homestead; the nationwide union was but a shell thereafter (e.g., Dubofsky and Dulles 2004, pp. 153–170). Similarly, when an estimated 150,000 workers in the railroad industry went on strike in 1893–1894 to protest wage cuts in the midst of a severe depression, roughly 32,000 state troopers were called out in 20 of the 27 states affected, along with nearly 16,000 federal soldiers out of an available regular force of 20,000 (e.g., Cooper 1980, pp. 144–164; Lambert 2005, pp. 58–63). In battles with large corporations, as discussed in more detail shortly, there is a second ingredient that is necessary for unions to succeed. When push comes to shove, government has to side with the unions, as already substantiated in the comparative analysis by Voss (1993).

In the aftermath of these dramatic defeats, however, the AFL did make some headway outside the manufacturing sector, where disruptive efforts could succeed because the replacement costs for bringing in strikebreakers for some kinds of jobs were prohibitive. As briefly noted earlier, the newspaper industry had to accede to the unionization demands of printers and typographers because of the unique skills these workers possessed, including most of all their literacy. Similarly, the building-trades unions grew from 67,000 in 1897 to 391,600 in 1904 because these skilled construction workers could capitalize on their disruptive capacities due to the decentralized nature of the construction industry and also their connections to the urban political machines (Brody 1980, p. 24; Zieger and Gall 2002, p. 22).

It was in this context of high replacement costs, business pushback, and frequent violent interventions by Pinkertons and the U.S. military that

The Uphill Battle for Unionism 55

an "Era of Good Feelings" began in the late 1890s, which encouraged some AFL leaders to accept overtures from a group of corporate moderates within the emerging corporate community.

Corporate Moderates and Ultraconservatives

The appearance of a reasonably cohesive group of corporate moderates just as the twentieth century began was due to two loosely related developments in the last three decades of the nineteenth century, a 30-year span that included major technological and transportation advances as well as the rise of a factory system that transformed the economic landscape. First, there were the several intensely violent conflicts between workers and employers, which were discussed earlier in the chapter. Second, as mentioned in the Introduction, there was a gradual adoption of the corporate form of ownership by business owners, which was originally intended to raise more capital, limit liability for owners, and allow businesses to continue after the death of their founding owners (Roy 1997).

This corporatization process began with textile companies and railroads in the early nineteenth century, then spread to coal and telegraphs companies after mid-century (Roy 1983). These companies also became increasingly connected by interlocking directors, which in that era usually reflected common ownership or shared economic interests (Bunting 1983). At the same time, commercial and investment banks on Wall Street took an integrative role in these developments through their ability to raise capital in the United Kingdom, France, and Germany (Carosso 1970). Bankers also contributed to the general leadership of the nascent corporate community and provided large campaign donations to candidates in both political parties (e.g., Alexander 1992; Overacker 1932). For example, investment banker August Belmont, an immigrant from France, who worked closely with Parisian financial interests, became a major donor to the Democratic Party and had business relationships with plantation owners and shipping companies in the South, as did his son, August Belmont II, a generation later (Katz 1968; Overacker 1932).

Until the late 1880s and early 1890s, however, industrial companies were not part of this gradual corporatization. Instead, they were organized as partnerships among a few men or families. They tended to stand apart from the financial institutions and the stock market (Roy 1983). Detailed historical and sociological studies of their shift to the corporate form reveal no economic efficiencies that might explain the relatively sudden incorporation of industrial companies. Instead, and contrary to those social scientists who think primarily in terms of organizational efficiency and rationality, it is more likely that industrial companies adopted the corporate form of organization for a combination of economic, legal, and sociological reasons. The most important of these reasons were a need to

(1) regulate the competition among industrial companies that was driving down profits, which of course contradicted their own rhetorical emphasis on competition and free markets, and (2) gain better legal protection against the middle-class reformers, populist farmers, and socialists who had mounted an unrelenting critique of "the trusts," meaning agreements among industrialists to fix prices, divide up markets, and/or share profits (Roy 1997).

Then, too, there were further pressures on industrialists due to a new depression in the early 1890s, which led to another round of wage cuts and then strikes by angry workers. Furthermore, the Sherman Anti-Trust Act of 1890 had outlawed the industrialists' resort to trust arrangements to manage the vicious price competition among them, which was bringing them to potential collective ruin. This combination of events set the stage for industrialists to take advantage of the increasing number of rights and privileges that legislatures and courts were gradually granting to the legal entity called a "corporation" (Parker-Gwin and Roy 1996).

It was at this point that a more integrated set of financial, rail, coal, and industrial companies began to develop. Between 1897 and 1904 alone, $6 billion worth of corporations were organized, six times the worth of all incorporations in the previous 18 years, leading to a situation in which the top 4 percent of companies produced 57 percent of the industrial output: "By any standard of measurement," concludes historian James Weinstein (1968, p. 63), "large corporations had come to dominate the American economy by 1904" (cf. Bunting 1987; Mizruchi 1982; Mizruchi and Bunting 1981; Roy 1997). The result was the emergence of a corporate community that fits the criteria outlined in the Introduction. More generally, at this point the corporate community was not only held together by overlapping ownership patterns, common financial backers, and interlocking boards of directors, but by a shared concern to limit the power of employees and a common desire to keep the role of government at a necessary minimum (Weinstein 1968).

It was the combination of a more integrated corporate community, continuing labor strife, and the return of prosperity after three years of depression that led to the emergence of the Era of Good Feelings. As a result, moderate conservatives in some of the new corporations began to differentiate themselves from their ultraconservative colleagues. They did so by indicating to union leaders that they might be willing to make bargains with them as a possible way to reduce industrial conflict. Moreover, companies were urged by some of the expert advisers of the day to organize themselves into employer associations. These associations purportedly would make it possible for companies to enter into the multi-employer collective bargaining agreements that were thought to be essential if unions were going to be useful in helping to stabilize a highly competitive industry (Swenson 2002). Then, too, some smaller businesses, especially in bituminous (soft) coal mining, thought that unions that could insist on a minimum wage might be one way to limit the wage competition that plagued their industries (Gordon 1994; Ramirez 1978).

On the other side of this class divide, several AFL leaders decided that unions could not defeat the burgeoning industrial corporations through strikes and spontaneous work stoppages. In addition, they long ago had abandoned any hope that elected officials or judges might aid them. They saw political entanglements as divisive and were convinced that the new corporate titans dominated government at all levels. They therefore decided it might make sense to react positively to the overtures from corporate moderates. Then, too, a few trade union leaders were among the voices encouraging employers to form their own organizations, on the grounds that such organizations would make cooperation and multi-employer bargaining between corporations and labor all the easier (Brody 1980, pp. 23–24). In other words, most labor leaders were far from being labor bosses who had sold out.

The United Mine Workers (UMW), a union that later played a lead role in the union upsurge during the New Deal, was one of the first to take advantage of this new opportunity. The union was formed in 1890 when two rival unions agreed to set aside their differences. In the process, they enacted a constitutional ban on racial, ethnic, and religious discrimination in order to provide a basis for solidarity. The founders also realized they had to ignore craft divisions among them if they were to have any chance to succeed after years of failure. Nevertheless, the union did not have much if any success until it was able to win recognition, wage increases, and an eight-hour day in 1898 in five Midwestern states in which soft coal was mined. It then won a strike for anthracite (hard) coal miners in eastern Pennsylvania in 1902, and by the end of World War I it was one of the largest unions in the country, assuming a leadership role that lasted into the 1940s (Laslett 1996; Phelan 1996).

Part of the UMW's early success was based on the importance of coal as an essential fuel of that era, but demand for coal fluctuated widely from summer to winter, and from recessions to booms, leaving miners unemployed for months at a time. It was also easy for would-be coal operators to open a small company, thereby creating cutthroat competition that often led to downward wage spirals as coal region fought coal region. As a result, coal operators and coal miners both needed greater stability via cooperation and wage floors, and both sides therefore took advantage of the new era.

The most visible new organization to develop in this changed atmosphere was the National Civic Federation (hereafter usually called the NCF). Formed in 1900 and composed of leaders from both big corporations and major trade unions, it also included well-known leaders from the worlds of finance, academia, and government. Building on this cross-section of

58 The Rise and Fall of Labor Unions

leaders, it was the first national-level policy-discussion group formed by the newly emerging corporate community. It therefore has been studied extensively from several different angles (e.g., Cyphers 2002; Green 1956; Jensen 1956; Weinstein 1968). The explicit goal of the NCF was to develop means to harmonize capital-labor relations, and its chosen instrument for this task was the trade union agreement (now called collective bargaining). The hope for the NCF rested on the fact that some of its corporate leaders stated publicly that the right kind of trade unions could play a constructive part in reducing labor strife and in helping American business to sell its products overseas, which is one of the clear early signs that Wall Street and the corporate moderates already had worldwide ambitions. (The fact that they were thwarted in these ambitions by ultraconservatives for many decades is discussed in Part 3 as part of the analysis of the creation of an international economy after World War II.)

In particular, the first president of the NCF, Senator Mark Hanna of Ohio, a mining magnate and Republican kingmaker, who had a major role in the election of Republican President William McKinley in 1896 and 1900, was respected by labor leaders for the fair-minded way he had dealt with striking miners on some of his properties. Hanna also worked to convince his colleagues that the improved productivity and efficiency that would follow from good labor relations would make it possible for American products to compete more effectively in overseas markets. The finished goods, he argued, would be of both a higher quality and a lower price as a result of more cooperation. In exchange, labor would be able to benefit through employment security and the higher wages that would come with increased productivity and sales (Weinstein 1968, Chapter 1). In terms of one strand of present-day theorizing, Hanna and the NCF were trying to create a cross-class coalition, or alliance, that would be beneficial for both parties (Swenson 2002, pp. 143–144).

The charismatic and widely respected leader of the UMW, John Mitchell, along with Gompers, the president of the AFL, were among the labor leaders who responded positively. Mitchell's faith in trade union agreements was strengthened by the fact that leaders in the NCF helped to settle the 1902 strike in the hard-coal region of Pennsylvania in a way that was satisfactory to the miners (Laslett 1996, pp. 41, 68). At that point Mitchell became a heroic figure to most coal miners, and many members of the working class more generally, and employers respected him because they could trust him to carry out bargaining agreements (Phelan 1996, p. 72).

Nor did the NCF hesitate to seek the advice of experts, including some who were considered reformers, which is another reason for thinking that the corporate moderates were somewhat different from the ultraconservatives. The most famous of these reform-oriented experts was an atypical economist, John R. Commons, who had been part of many reform efforts in the previous decade. Commons became a researcher and strike mediator for the NCF while managing its New York office from 1902 to 1904. He adopted the NCF emphasis on collective bargaining and argued for the concept ever afterwards. When he left for a position at the University of Wisconsin, half of his salary was paid by moderate conservatives in the NCF who admired his efforts. Commons later claimed that his years with the NCF were among the "five big years" of his life (Commons 1934, p. 133). It is worth noting here that Commons figures prominently in Part 2 because of his work over a 30-year period on several of the government social-insurance programs that became part of the safety net. His former students played a prominent role in creating and administering the Social Security Act of 1935, and a few testified in favor of the final version of the National Labor Relations Act in that same year.

The National Civic Federation also revealed its differences with the ultraconservatives in the corporate community through its role in creating the Federal Trade Commission in 1913 to deal with several different problems of concern to it, such as cutthroat competition in numerous business sectors, variations in business regulation from state to state, and the criticism from populists, reformers, organized labor, and socialists over the lack of adequate federal government supervision of corporations. After losing in Congress in 1908 to ultraconservative and middle-sized business associations on an earlier regulatory bill, the NCF formed a private committee in 1912 that included corporate members and economists, and enjoyed the full-time assistance of the legal counsel of the Iron and Steel Institute (Weinstein 1968, p. 87). The draft bill created by the new working group was sent to President Woodrow Wilson, the Commissioner of Corporations, and a senator who was also a member of NCF.

Although Congress and the executive branch received other suggestions on how to regulate corporations, the NCF version "was almost a model for the final legislation," except that there were no federal licensing provisions for interstate businesses and two fewer commissioners than the NCF recommended (Weinstein 1968, p. 89). In this early successful effort at state-building by the corporate rich and the power elite through the nascent policy-planning network, NCF members were clearly reacting to outside pressures, and readily said so at the time. The important issue from their point of view was that the reforms did not interfere with the growth and profitability of large corporations.

At first glance, the NCF focus on collective bargaining may seem to reflect the corporate moderates' acceptance of an equal relation between capital and labor in a pluralistic American context. But from a corporate-dominance perspective, collective bargaining is not about pluralism or values or decency, none of which had been in evidence in the years following 1877. Instead, the process of collective bargaining is the outcome of a power struggle that reflects the underlying balance of power in favor of the corporations. From the corporate point of view, a focus on collective

60 The Rise and Fall of Labor Unions

bargaining involved a narrowing of demands by AFL unions to a manageable level. It held out the potential for satisfying most craft-union members at the expense of the unskilled workers and socialists in the workforce, meaning that it decreased the possibility of constant disruption and even of a challenge to the economic system itself.

However farfetched it seems in hindsight, the possibility of such a challenge appeared to have at least some validity in the early twentieth century due to the volatility of capitalism, the seeming plausibility of at least some aspects of Marx's theory of inevitable collapse, and the strong socialist sentiments of a small but growing minority of workers and intellectuals. From the corporate moderates' point of view, which did not have the benefit of twentieth-century history as a guide, it is understandable that they preferred unions for skilled workers to periodic disruption by frustrated workers or constant political challenges from socialists, who actually won an increasing number of city and state legislative elections in the first 10 to 15 years after they founded a new political party in 1901 (e.g., Weinstein 1967).

From the labor standpoint, collective bargaining over wages, hours, and working conditions seemed to be the best that it could do at that juncture. Despite the growing agitation by socialists, most skilled workers apparently did not think it was worth the costs in time, and the sacrifice of their everyday lives with family and friends, to organize a political challenge to capitalism, or even attempt to organize unions that included both skilled and unskilled workers, as the Knights of Labor tried to do between 1869 and 1886. They therefore decided to fight for what their power to disrupt in some contexts forced the corporate leaders to concede in principle. This strategic decision to work toward unions based on bargaining for better wages, hours, and working conditions was embraced by the committed socialists who predominated in one-third of the unions, including the Brewery Workers Union and the International Association of Machinists (Laslett 1970). More generally, both the leftist and apolitical unions, which often fought each other very vigorously, "relied on labor solidarity, mass mobilization, and unrestricted direct action to find their way across what was still a largely uncharted organizational landscape" (Kimeldorf 1999, p. 149).

Thus, the process and content of collective bargaining is actually a complicated power relationship that embodies the strengths and weaknesses of both sides. Its existence reveals the power of organized labor, but the narrowness of the unions and the substance of what is bargained about reflect the power of corporations. Collective bargaining is "both a result of labor's power as well as a vehicle to control workers' struggles and channel them in a path compatible with capitalist development" (Ramirez 1978, p. 215). Drawing on Kimeldorf's (2013) formulation concerning the importance of replacement costs in union success, this point can be generalized to say that unionization is only possible without government support when workers can exercise a disruptive potential that threatens profits. That is, the unions that were organized in the late ninetieth and early twentieth centuries had a high disruptive capacity that was rooted in the difficulty (and thus high costs) of finding adequate replacement workers in a timely fashion in the face of strikes.

However, it is important to add that the unionization and collective bargaining that sometimes developed in industries in which workers had disruptive potential was not quite a standoff in which both sides had the same amount of power. They were close to equal when it comes to collective bargaining once the ability of workers to organize and disrupt had been demonstrated. But it is also the case that it is very difficult to sustain most unions if governments use their legal or coercive powers to support employers in their refusal to recognize unions. Thus, political power has to be added to the collective bargaining equation. It serves as the tipping point if collective bargaining fails and one or both sides resort to organized violence. In this context, the matter of who controls key government offices, starting with the presidency, once again can be seen as a crucial factor in class conflicts.

To avert potential misunderstandings on this issue, it needs to be repeated that the unionism the NCF leaders were willing to support was a narrow one, focused almost exclusively on skilled or craft workers, to the exclusion of the unskilled industrial workers in mass-production industries. Furthermore, the corporate leaders in the NCF objected to any "coercion" of non-union workers by union members and to any laws that might "force" employers to negotiate. Everything was to be strictly voluntary, although government could be called in to mediate when both sides agreed to arbitration. Indeed, there was precedent for such voluntary arbitration in federal legislation passed in 1898, which allowed for mediation between interstate railroads and those unionized employees that worked on the trains themselves (e.g., engineers, brakemen, conductors).

Within this limited perspective, the NCF and other corporate moderates seemed to be having at least some success in their first two years. Leaders in the new employers' associations not only signed agreements with their workers, but spoke favorably of the NCF and its work. None was in a major mass-production industry, however, and the new era did not last very long. As the unions' membership grew and they began making more demands, the employers' unwillingness to concede any control of their workforce to unions resurfaced accordingly. In other words, class conflict once again emerged, which soon led to organized opposition to unions within the very same employer associations that had been created to encourage trade agreements. This sequence of events reveals the difficulties of maintaining cross-class coalitions, which were to break down more often than not in future decades as well. Either the workers try to

62 The Rise and Fall of Labor Unions

impose conditions that employers find unreasonable, or else some employers, known as "chiselers" in that era, try to gain market share or earn higher profits by undercutting the terms of the agreement.

This usual sequence of events was most dramatically illustrated when the National Metal Trades Association, which included a wide range of manufacturers that made use of metal in their production processes, broke its agreement with the International Association of Machinists only 13 months after signing it in May 1900. The turnabout occurred when the machinists tried to place limits on the number of apprentices in a shop and resisted piece rates and doubling up on machines (Swenson 2002, pp. 49–52). The angry employers announced in a Declaration of Principles "we will not admit of any interference with the management of our business" (Brody 1980, p. 25). The failure of the attempt to employ collective bargaining to resolves disputes is also exemplified by the refusal of steel unions even to consider the terms offered in 1901 by J. P. Morgan, the most powerful financier of the day, who was open to dealing with the established unions in subsidiaries of his newly organized behemoth, U.S. Steel. Instead, the union actually "called a general strike against the corporation to force immediate agreements on its entire tin plate, sheet steel, and steel hoop operations, thus breaking current agreements in some of them" (Swenson 2002, p. 51).

Despite this abrupt rebuff by the union, Morgan, whose name is best known today by its enshrinement in the JPMorgan Chase bank, extended an olive branch to the union, perhaps because he wanted to avoid public controversy about the new company as well as possible government investigations of it. He therefore "assured the union leaders that he wished to maintain friendly relations with labor" (Garraty 1960, p. 13). In reply, the union leaders upped the ante by breaking existing contracts and trying to extend the strike to skilled workers in all the subsidiaries of the new company, most of which had never been unionized. In the process, the steel union leaders deeply angered Gompers of the AFL, who had good information on Morgan's intentions via intermediaries, and was highly critical of the union's leadership in a federation newsletter (Gompers 1901, p. 428).

Even so, Morgan met with the union leaders again, offering to sign contracts in factories in which the skilled workers already had been unionized, but not in factories that did not have established locals of the union (Neill 1913, p. 506). However, his offer was rejected, and he then gave an order to break the strike. Despite the earlier provocation, Morgan allowed the declining union to persist until 1909 in spite of its resistance to new technologies and the continuing insistence by the staunchly anti-union presidents of the many U.S. Steel subsidiaries that it should be crushed immediately (Garraty 1960, p. 26).

Thus, what happened between Morgan and the steel unions is an example of the mutual suspicions and recriminations that ended the Era of Good

Feeling. More ominously, and unlike at U.S. Steel, at least 198 people were killed and 1,966 were injured between 1902 and 1904 in the many labor disputes that soon followed in a variety of industries (Archer 2007, p. 121). Nevertheless, union membership grew an average of 2 percent a year from 1904 to 1915 despite the renewed warfare (Nelson 1997, pp. 92–93; Zieger and Gall 2002, pp. 18–19).

The anti-union sentiments of individual employers and the employer associations were reinforced and given added clout when an industry-wide employers' association, the National Association of Manufacturers (NAM), moved into their ranks. This move by the NAM was not without irony and conflict. It was founded in 1896 to encourage the marketing of American products overseas, and its first president was also an early member of the NCF, so there were good reasons to avoid any discussion of management-labor issues within the organization. However, when anti-union employers took over the association in late 1902 in a three-way race for the presidency, it quickly turned into the largest and most visible opponent of trade unions in the United States. It also took part in the defeat of the NCF's 1908 regulatory bill. The NAM soon came to be seen as the core organization for the ultraconservatives in the corporate community, a role it played for the rest of the century, but always buttressed by the organizations established by specific industries, such as the Iron and Steel Institute and the American Automobile Manufacturers Association.

The rise of the anti-union movement caused the NCF to draw back from its collective-bargaining emphasis, but it continued to endorse collective bargaining as a principle even though it no longer pushed for it. It thereby kept the concept of trade union agreements alive, which later became one basis for the plans that corporate moderates put forth during the New Deal to cope with the increase in demands for union recognition, as shown later in this chapter (Piven and Cloward 1977, p. 110). From the corporate moderates' point of view, collective bargaining still held out the potential for satisfying the demands of the relatively small number of Protestant craft workers, while at the same time allowing corporations to oppose unions for the large number of "ethnic" unskilled workers.

At the same time, though, the NCF had redirected its attention to trying to persuade all corporations to adopt various social-benefit programs, ranging from on-site technical education courses to recreational facilities, as a way to deal with worker discontent (Cyphers 2002). "After 1905," says Weinstein (1968, p. 18), "welfare work increasingly was seen as a substitute for the recognition of unions." These widespread efforts were successful in many large corporations and were an important forerunner of the welfare-capitalism strategy to combat unions emphasized during the 1920s and discussed in several chapters in Part 2. In fact, the Welfare Department within the NCF played a large role in disseminating this perspective (Cyphers 2002). In the terminology employed in one current of

64 The Rise and Fall of Labor Unions

present-day theorizing, these large-scale employers, many of them using advanced production technologies, were paying "efficiency wages" in an effort to increase profits through enhanced productivity and at the same time protect themselves against disruption, sabotage, and the destruction of equipment.

Mitchell of the UMW and NCF was a major casualty of the renewed class warfare. In 1904, fearing that his union could not survive a strike, he argued within the union for acceptance of a 12-percent wage reduction that was demanded by the coal companies. The miners backed his argument for rejecting a strike call by giving him 60 percent of the vote over the objections by most other leaders within the union, and most vehemently by the socialists within the union (Phelan 1996, pp. 94–95). When the coal operators decided to keep the wage reductions in place in 1906, and indicated that they would try to drive hard bargains in the next round of contract negotiations, the miners decided to strike, despite Mitchell's warnings and objections. Mitchell then won assent to negotiate separate contract settlements, beginning with the more sympathetic companies, in hopes of quick settlements, but the result was a near-disaster for the union (Phelan 1996, pp. 96–97).

As his popularity declined even further, Mitchell resigned from the presidency of the UMW in 1908; a few months thereafter he took a paid position within the NCF after recovering from severe alcoholism that developed while he felt pulled in both directions. He still thought that trade agreements were the one best hope, but he was soon marginalized and ineffective in the NCF, and resigned his position in 1911 (Phelan 1996, pp. 98, 103). He became an implacable foe of both the socialists and the hierarchical union leadership that replaced him.

Despite the NCF's greater emphasis on welfare issues after 1905, and the intransigent conflicts between corporations and unions that have persisted ever since, the existence of both the NCF and the NAM signified a larger point that was presaged in the Introduction and that takes on greater significance in the analyses in the rest of the book. Without a doubt, the presence of these two somewhat different corporate organizations, the NCF and the NAM, demonstrates (some might say "personifies") the solidification of two somewhat different tendencies (some might say "factions") in the corporate community—the moderate conservatives and the ultraconservatives. The moderate conservatives were somewhat more open to conciliation and compromise, and they were certainly more willing to listen to the ideas of independent experts, and even to those experts that were critical of corporations, or of capitalism itself.

The ultraconservatives, on the other hand, were standpatters who wanted to stick with what they believed were tried and true principles, which added up to a hard-shelled, nineteenth-century version of classical liberalism. They had no use for any experts who might argue with them.

They were only interested in experts who might come up with new ways to carry out the strategies they wanted to pursue. Some of them therefore looked upon corporate moderates with great suspicion, and as potential deserters and turncoats. In their later incarnations, they opposed the efforts by corporate moderates to expand overseas trade and investment from the 1920s into the 1970s, as demonstrated in Chapter 14 (e.g., McLellan and Woodhouse 1960; Woodhouse and McLellan 1966).

More generally, ultraconservatives advocated market fundamentalism in opposition to the corporate moderates many decades before the presumed rise of neoliberalism. By the 1920s the ultraconservatives began to make more nationalistic and nativist appeals for a "white Protestant nation" whenever they found themselves losing an argument (e.g., Lichtman 2008). In the 1960s and 1970s this appeal was broadened to include previously excluded Catholics through calls for a "white Christian nation." Then the exclusionary and openly anti-democratic nature of American ultraconservatism was augmented by the ideas put forth by the libertarian economist James B. Buchanan at the University of Virginia, which first emerged in the immediate aftermath of the Supreme Court's unanimous Brown v Board of Education of Topeka decision in 1954 (MacLean 2017). This new libertarian strand, which did not have any impact until the 1970s, when its ideas were widely disseminated by a new generation of anti-government billionaires, focused on the many ways in which economic arguments concerning property rights, efficiency, and markets could be used to widen the appeal of school vouchers, eliminate Social Security pensions, and limit voting (MacLean 2017, for archival evidence concerning these efforts, which is based on Buchanan's correspondence and other documents that MacLean brought to light; Mayer 2017, for a detailed account of how billionaire ultraconservatives used nonprofit organizations and advocacy groups to advocate these ideas).

Those social scientists that are skeptical about the importance of the differences between moderate conservatives and ultraconservatives within the corporate community say they add up to a distinction without a difference. They are especially unmoved because there is no one economic factor that has been shown to cause the differences, such as smaller versus bigger businesses, or labor-intensive versus capital-intensive businesses, as already noted in the introductory chapter. As this book shows, however, taking intra-class differences as well as class conflict seriously provides a much better understanding of how some power struggles are resolved, just as the occasional appearances of cross-class alliances help to explain puzzling legislative outcomes. In the case of the National Labor Relations Act, for example, a cross-class alliance between the corporate community and conservatives within the AFL played a role in undermining that legislation in the late 1930s (Gross 1981). Moreover, the longstanding intra-class differences between moderate conservatives and ultraconservatives

66 The Rise and Fall of Labor Unions

demonstrate that neoliberalism did not develop in the 1960s or 1970s, and thereby directs attention to the need for a better explanation for the more conservative policies advocated by the power elite after the 1968 elections.

Another Round of Violence Triggers New Initiatives

In spite of the efforts by the NCF and other corporate moderates to deal with labor conflict after 1904 through welfare and education programs instead of collective bargaining, there was another wave of industrial violence in 1911. Dynamite attacks at many construction sites across the country, and on the *Los Angeles Times'* entire building, by what turned out to be apolitical but militant members of the bridge and structural ironworkers' union, were of particular surprise and concern. In reaction, President William Howard Taft sponsored legislation to create a Commission on Industrial Relations to examine the causes of industrial unrest and labor sabotage, which resulted in further legitimation for the collective-bargaining agreements sought by the AFL.

Although the NCF had by then abandoned its organizational emphasis on collective bargaining, several of its individual members nonetheless played the major role in the commission's deliberations. The nine-member commission, which was appointed by President Woodrow Wilson in 1913, consisted of three corporate leaders, all members of the NCF; three labor leaders, also members of the NCF; and three public members, two of whom, Commons and a well-known socialite and reformer of the era, Mrs. Borden Harriman, were members of the NCF. The only non-NCF member was the chair, Frank P. Walsh, an attorney, reformer, and advocate for the poor. Walsh was more than a match for the other eight members, leading the commission into investigations and arguments, both of which angered the non-labor members (Adams 1966; Weinstein 1968, Chapter 7).

The commissioners could not come to general agreement after hearing hundreds of hours of testimony and debating numerous legislative proposals. However, it is important to note, in the light of the eventual passage of the National Labor Relations Act in the mid-1930s, that the weight of the members' several separate reports in 1915 favored greater use of collective bargaining. As Commons noted in a report that also was signed by Mrs. Harriman and the business members, but not the labor members, the important issue was "whether the labor movement should be directed towards politics or toward collective bargaining" (Weinstein 1968, p. 202). Commons went so far as to recommend new legislation empowering government advisory boards to mediate capital-labor relations and channel protest into collective bargaining. His report clearly foreshadowed the kinds of solutions that eventually were tried during the early New Deal.

World War I Provides Unions with a New Opportunity

As the Commission on Industrial Relations was winding down, the sudden and unexpected outbreak of World War I in Europe in July 1914, gradually led to an economic boom that changed the power balance between business and organized labor as unemployment fell from 7.9 percent in 1914 to 5.1 in 1916 and 1.4 in 1918 (Rockoff 2004, p. 6). At the same time, the supplies of new labor from Europe virtually dried up, and the federal government expanded its role in the economy. Many AFL unions took advantage of the situation, especially after the United States entered the war in early 1917, by calling strikes to gain union recognition. In exchange for a no-strike pledge, President Wilson promised to support the right of unions to exist and to bargain collectively.

One of the fledgling unions that benefited greatly from the war, the Amalgamated Clothing Workers (ACW), was second only to the United Mine Workers in its importance during the New Deal. The new union had been organized in the fall of 1914 amidst the frustrations and failures of the small rival clothing-workers unions, which had been engaged in unending internecine battles. In particular, the new union broke away from the AFL's United Garment Workers, which was dominated by native-born tailors who were wary of the many new immigrants in the needle trades, from predominantly Italian and Jewish backgrounds. The ACW defection was completely unacceptable to Gompers, and he did everything he could to defeat it. Moreover, the ACW's socialist founders, based in New York, readily abandoned the distinctions among types of workers that were drawn by the craft unions. By that point, they simply wanted to organize as many tailors of varying skill levels, ethnicities, and sewing traditions as possible in as many states as possible.

The founding members then recruited a highly successful garment worker and union organizer from Chicago, Sidney Hillman, who had won acclaim by leading the effort to unionize the large wholesale and retail menswear firm, Hart, Schaffner & Marx, in the face of hesitations by the leadership of the United Garment Workers. In the process Hillman also had gained the admiration and support of the progressive reformers of that era, many of whom were well-to-do women who were part of the settlement house movement and supporters of the Woman's Trade Union League (Davis 1967; Domhoff 1970, pp. 44–54, on upper-class women and labor reform; Fraser 1991, pp. 81, 100; Kessler-Harris 1982).

Hillman and the new ACW quickly won a series of major strikes in four large cities, including Boston and Baltimore. By late 1914 the union had established the eight-hour day and better working conditions through its contracts, and in the process shown that it was willing to work with union-friendly businesses in a constructive way (Fraser 1991, pp. 95–96).

68 The Rise and Fall of Labor Unions

However, the union made no further progress and its foothold remained tenuous until the federal government began to contract for military clothing in 1916 and 1917 in the context of increasing labor shortages, especially in the case of skilled tailors. In terms of replacement-cost theory, the ACW had two factors working in its favor: the need for skilled workers and the need for timely deliveries of military clothing. As employers tried to return to long hours and dangerous working conditions to fulfill wartime orders and make windfall profits, Hillman used his connections with elite women, some of them socialists, to meet with the progressive Democrats appointed to positions in the War Department.

The resulting Board of Control and Labor Standards for Army Clothing eliminated child labor in the industry, created safer working conditions, and enforced a policy of union recognition in exchange for a no-strike pledge. This accord and the intervention by appointees in the War Department made it possible for the ACW to organize Rochester, an important site for garment manufacturing. By the end of the war, most army clothing was made by firms that had been unionized by the ACW; between 1916 and 1920, its membership burgeoned from 48,000 to as many as 170,000 members (Fraser 1991, p. 115; Wolman 1924, p. 51). At that point the ACW was the fourth-largest industrial union after the miners, the machinists, and railroad workers (Fraser 1991, p. 115).

General labor unrest and ongoing criticisms of the war by some members of the Socialist Party continued throughout 1917. In response, President Wilson created a National War Labor Board in April 1918, to mediate conflicts and ensure a smooth flow of war materiel. Composed of corporate and trade union leaders, it was co-chaired by former President Taft and Frank P. Walsh, the intrepid investigator who had served as chair of the recently disbanded Commission on Industrial Relations. AFL membership increased from two million in 1916 to 3.2 million in 1919, mostly in unions that had existed since 1897, with the ten largest national unions accounting for nearly half the increase (union density rose from 9.5 percent in 1912 to 17.4 percent in 1921) (Dubofsky and Dulles 2004, p. 191; Freeman 1998, pp. 291–293). The war labor board supported the eight-hour day and the right to organize unions and bargain collectively, with President Wilson using the powers of his office to ensure compliance. While all this was going on, anti-war dissenters from radical unions and the Socialist Party were put in jail.

Leaders within the AFL were hopeful that this renewed harmony and success would continue after the war, but such was not to be the case. Within a few months after the war ended in early November 1918, nearly four million workers (21 percent of the workforce) took disruptive action in the face of employer reluctance to recognize or bargain with unions. There were major strikes in the nation's coalfields and among longshoremen in New York City and police officers in Boston, as well as a general strike in Seattle. The ACW was challenged by a four-month lockout by anti-union employers in New York, but ended up with contracts with roughly 85 percent of the garment manufacturers in the city. The largest strike took place in the steel industry, in an attempt to gain the right to bargain. Led by U.S. Steel, the biggest and most powerful manufacturing company in the country at the time, the employers launched a strong counterattack, branding the strike leaders as foreign radical agitators, this time trying to link them to Bolshevism, not anarchism. Corporations also hired numerous replacement workers, including 30,000 African Americans completely excluded from unions. Anti-union forces attacked picket lines with impunity and broke up union meetings. With President Wilson appearing to favor steel executives, the defeat of the steel strike in December 1919 sealed the fate of collective bargaining in the ensuing decade (Zieger and Gall 2002, pp. 39–41).

Moreover, the courts, including the Supreme Court, were more sympathetic to the labor injunctions that employers increasingly filed to halt strikes and boycotts even before they had begun. Courts also ruled that it was legal for employers to demand that potential workers sign a contract stipulating that they would not join a union as a condition of their employment (Bernstein 1960, pp. 194–196, 218–219). At that point there was no reasonable legal avenue to organizing a new union, which was of concern to moderates and centrists in terms of what angry workers might do in the future if they became desperate.

In the face of court injunctions and all-out employer opposition led by the NAM, unions lost strike after strike during the 1920s. Many of the wartime advances by organized labor were reversed. Over the course of these lean years for organized labor, union membership declined from five million in 1919 to just under three million in 1933 (Bernstein 1960, p. 84). The United Mine Workers fell from 500,000 in 1919 to under 80,000 members in the early 1930s. The garment unions were also devastated—the ACW declined from 170,000 in 1920 to 60,000 in 1933 (with only 7,000 of those members paying dues), and the International Ladies' Garment Workers Union went from 120,000 in 1920 to around 40,000 in 1933.

The biggest unions were now in construction, transportation, entertainment, and printing, all of which still had the advantages of high replacement costs (Zieger and Gall 2002, pp. 69–70). There were virtually no union members in mass-production industries. Even so, total union membership never dipped below 1917 levels, no major unions disappeared, and there were some gains for the building trades, railroad brotherhoods, and the Teamsters (Nelson 1997, pp. 98–99). But union density dropped from the new high point of 17.4 percent of the nonagricultural labor force in 1921 to 11.0 percent in 1933 (Freeman 1998, pp. 291–292, Table 8A.2).

Despite the corporate successes, there remained a few corporate moderates who wanted to control labor by giving workers some representation. They sought to avoid the kind of violent confrontations that the leaders of the NAM and other ultraconservatives were willing to undertake when necessary. These efforts toward conciliation were led by the richest man of that era, John D. Rockefeller, Jr., who had no direct involvement in the management of any corporation. His new plans later had a large impact on New Deal labor policy, but things did not turn out as he and his extensive network of advisers intended them.

The Rockefeller Factor

Although the name Rockefeller is now synonymous with wealth, foundation giving, and power, the full scope of Rockefeller wealth and the massive role of the family's corporations, bank, foundations, advisory groups, and charities in the years between 1915 and 1985 is not fully appreciated today because the family is no longer involved in any large corporations and includes many liberal and/or environmentally concerned members. In fact, leaders in the current generation of the family have taken a major role in fighting the biggest of the former Rockefeller oil companies, Standard Oil of New Jersey (now named Exxon) because the company well understood the dangers of carbon-based fuels by the 1980s, but nonetheless gave large amounts of money to a network of climate-denial organizations (e.g., Oreskes and Conway 2010; Union of Concerned Scientists 2007).

Then, too, social scientists of all theoretical persuasions usually shy away from any suggestion that the Rockefellers were a powerhouse in their day because of the exaggerated claims that were made about the alleged hidden power of the five grandsons of John D. Rockefeller, Sr. from the 1950s to the 1980s. Such unfounded claims about the Rockefeller family in general continued into the early twenty-first century, at a time when there were no Rockefellers in positions of any importance in the corporate community. The most visible member of the family, John D. Rockefeller, IV, was the longtime Democratic senator from West Virginia, with a liberal voting record overall. (He retired from the Senate in 2015.)

The story of Rockefeller involvement in labor legislation is not well known despite some revealing archival work on the topic in the late twentieth century, and is therefore met with skepticism or denial. The story therefore has to be unfolded carefully if the conventional wisdom in the social sciences is ever to be questioned by future generations of social scientists.

In the early 1920s, the descendants of John D. Rockefeller, Sr., who were led by his son, John D. Rockefeller, Jr., were worth an estimated $2.5 billion. As a first approximation of Rockefeller power in that era, that figure happens to be 2.5 times higher than their nearest rivals, the Fords,

The Uphill Battle for Unionism 71

Mellons, and du Ponts (Lundberg 1937, pp. 26–27). Not only was the Rockefeller family far and away the richest family of that era, but also John D. Rockefeller, Sr., may have been the richest man in American history if the size of fortunes is calculated as a percentage of the Gross National Product for any given era; by this index, the Rockefeller fortune surpassed the wealth of even a Bill Gates of Microsoft (Klepper and Gunther 1996). Although Rockefeller, Sr. lived to 1937, when he was 97 years old, most of his fortune was inherited or controlled, as already noted, by Rockefeller, Jr. He and his numerous personal employees managed most of the rest of the family's wealth for his sisters and their families. (From this point on, John D. Rockefeller, Jr., will be called simply "John D. Rockefeller" or "Rockefeller," and his father will be referred to as "John D. Rockefeller, Sr.," on the few occasions that his name appears.)

The Rockefeller fortune was based primarily in five of the oil companies created in 1911 out of the original Standard Oil, after it was broken up by antitrust action. In the 1920s and 1930s, the Rockefellers held the largest blocks of stock in these companies and had considerable influence on their management. Four of the five companies were in the top 11 corporations in terms of their assets in 1933. Standard Oil of New Jersey, the fourth largest, was by far the most important and politically involved of these companies. Rockefeller had his offices in its headquarters building, which was located near Wall Street in New York. He was close to the senior management throughout the 1920s and 1930s, especially the president during these years, Walter C. Teagle.

Teagle, a grandson of one of John D. Rockefeller, Sr.'s, original partners, worked as an executive for various Standard Oil companies for 15 years before heading Standard Oil of New Jersey from late 1917 until his retirement in 1937. By the 1930s he was a director of White Motors in Cleveland and Coca Cola in Atlanta due to personal friendships with their CEOs. He served on the Petroleum War Service Board in World War I and chaired a Share-the-Work campaign for Hoover in 1932, making dozens of speeches across the country (Wall and Gibb 1974, Chapter 15). If the close and mutually respectful relationship between Teagle and Rockefeller can be kept in mind, and if Teagle's independent judgment is appreciated, then the idea of "Rockefeller" power in labor relations can be considered with a more open mind, especially after other dramatis personae are added to the picture.

Despite the huge amount of wealth the Rockefellers retained in the Standard Oil companies, they had diversified their holdings. Most importantly, by the early 1930s they controlled the largest bank in the country, Chase National Bank, chaired by Rockefeller's brother-in-law, Winthrop Aldrich, who took the lead on Wall Street in calling for the separation of commercial and investment banking in early 1933. (Chase National Bank was memorialized as part of a merger that created JPMorgan Chase in

72　The Rise and Fall of Labor Unions

2000, which also owes its gargantuan size to the assimilation of several other large banks in New York City between 1982 and the late 1990s.)

In addition, the Rockefeller family owned a major coal company, Consolidation Coal, and several minor railroads. The family also diversified into real estate in the early 1930s by building Rockefeller Center in New York City with the help of a large loan from Metropolitan Life Insurance, a company with which Rockefeller enjoyed a close relationship, including the placement of one of his several policy-oriented personal employees on its board of directors. The largest development of its kind up until that time, Rockefeller Center opened in the early 1930s and lost money for many years thereafter (Fitch 1993; Okrent 2003). By the 1970s, however, it was at the center of the Rockefeller fortune, with any involvement in the oil companies long in the past. Similarly, involvement in Chase Manhattan Bank, as it was renamed in 1955, ended in the early 1980s with the retirement of David Rockefeller (Rockefeller's fifth and youngest son) after being either its president or chair since 1960.

Most fatefully in terms of the development of American labor relations, the Rockefellers owned Colorado Fuel & Iron, a relatively small mining company, with Rockefeller serving as a member of its board of directors, along with two or three of his personal employees. The company and Rockefeller became infamous because they played the central role in a prolonged and deadly labor dispute in 1913–1914. The dispute came to be known as the Ludlow Massacre after 20 people died in a confrontation between the Colorado National Guard and striking miners. The total included ten women and two children, who burned to death after machine gun fire ignited the makeshift tent city in which they were living after being evicted from company housing. More generally, at least 66 people died in the open warfare between labor and mine operators in Colorado between May and September of 1914; the violence only ended when President Wilson sent Federal troops to the area (Zieger and Gall 2002, p. 23). Rockefeller's reaction to this disaster reshaped corporate-moderate policy thinking about labor relations over the next 15 years, and, unlikely as it may sound in the twenty-first century, had a direct impact on labor policy in the early New Deal.

In addition to his corporate involvement and great personal wealth, Rockefeller also controlled three foundations: the General Education Fund, the Rockefeller Foundation, and the Laura Spelman Rockefeller Memorial Fund. Although he did not take a direct role in all of the foundations, he had an executive committee, made up of his main employees from each of them, which met with him to determine whether he should give his own money directly to a project or if the project should be assigned to one of the foundations. In addition, he chaired the board of the Rockefeller Foundation, which had its offices in the Standard Oil of New Jersey Building from its founding in 1913 until 1933. Rockefeller and his

The Uphill Battle for Unionism 73

foundations supported a wide array of think tanks and policy-discussion organizations within the larger context of massive financial donations for medical research, education, national parks, museums, and ecumenical Protestant organizations (Schenkel 1995). It needs to be stressed, however, for a sense of proportion, that he spent far more money on organizations that had nothing to do with policy than he did on think tanks and policy-discussion groups, including one of his favorite personal projects, the restoration of Colonial Williamsburg.

The general importance of the three Rockefeller foundations can be seen through figures on assets and donations in 1933–1934. At a time when a mere 20 foundations held 88 percent of the assets held by all foundations, the assets of the three Rockefeller foundations (which were the largest, second-largest, and seventh-largest on the list) were more than the combined assets of the other 17 foundations (Lundberg 1937; TCF 1935). As another indication of how concentrated foundation giving was at the outset of the New Deal, three Rockefeller-related and four Carnegie-related foundations accounted for well over half of the donations in 1934. To provide one stark contrast, the most liberal and socially oriented foundation of the 1930s, the Russell Sage Foundation, was the thirteenth-largest donor in 1934, with just over $267,000 in donations. By comparison, the Rockefeller Foundation alone gave $11.8 million, 44 times as much. As for most of the other foundations in the top 20, they gave donations to local charities, educational institutions, libraries, and museums, and were not concerned with public policy.

The Rockefeller network's specific philanthropic involvement in the policy-planning network was widespread. The Rockefeller Foundation alone supported the founding of the Institute of Government Research in 1916 and gave it money for specific projects in the 1920s (Saunders 1966, pp. 14–16, 25, 49). Two of Rockefeller's personal employees sat on its board of directors as well. Between 1924 and 1927, the Laura Spelman Rockefeller Memorial Fund became an ambitious fund for the advancement of the social sciences (Harr and Johnson 1988, pp. 187–192). The Memorial, as it was known at the time, supported basic research in the social sciences at levels that had never been heard of before, creating what sources usually call a golden age of the social sciences (Bulmer and Bulmer 1981; Harr and Johnson 1988, pp. 187–192; Lagemann 1989, pp. 69–70).

As one part of its overall effort, the Memorial spearheaded the development of a new coordinating and grant-giving organization for social science research, the Social Science Research Council (SSRC), established in 1923. Over 90 percent of the SSRC's funding in its first ten years came from the Memorial and other Rockefeller foundations, a pattern of support that continued into the 1940s. The SSRC quickly became an important source of policy expertise through committees set up to discuss policies related to agriculture, unemployment insurance, and industrial relations.

The advisers who served on the agricultural committee, under the direction of the president of the Memorial, had the major role in the creation of the Agricultural Adjustment Act. Their plan was eagerly embraced in 1932–1933 by corporate leaders, plantation owners, and the American Farm Bureau Federation (hereafter usually Farm Bureau) (Domhoff and Webber 2011, Chapter 3).

The Memorial also gave the National Bureau of Economic Research between 14 percent and 16 percent of its income from 1923 to 1928, and Rockefeller philanthropies in general gave the organization over 60 percent of its income in 1932 and 1933 (Bulmer and Bulmer 1981, p. 393). Overall, the Rockefeller Foundation and the Memorial were the National Bureau of Economic Research's largest single contributors in its first 30 years (Alchon 1985, pp. 117, 157, 165, 217–232; Fosdick 1952, p. 213).

The Rockefeller family and foundations also had a part in creating an urban-oriented policy-planning network in the Progressive Era through both general financial support and the founding of an array of organizations encompassing every aspect of city government and public administration, as spelled out in considerable detail in one history of public administration (Roberts 1994). In conjunction with a political scientist at the University of Chicago, the Spelman Fund (a $10 million spin-off from the Laura Spelman Rockefeller Memorial Fund when it was folded into the Rockefeller Foundation in 1928–1929) helped create the Public Administration Clearing House in 1930–1931, which served as a new coordinating organization for the nascent urban policy-planning network. Shortly after the clearinghouse was established, virtually every municipal, public administration, and social-welfare organization in the country moved its headquarters to a building not far from the University of Chicago, in which the clearinghouse also had its headquarters. These agencies then developed in their scope and importance with the help of Rockefeller philanthropies, especially the new Spelman Fund (Brownlow 1958, Chapters 22–24; Domhoff 1978, pp. 160–171; Karl 1974; Roberts 1994). They had a highly influential role in convincing the newly elected President Roosevelt in 1933 that local private and public relief agencies could not deal with the growing unemployment and unrest (Brown 1940, p. 135).

The growing foundational support for these and other nonprofit organizations by the Rockefeller family and other members of the corporate rich helped to create an enduring institutional basis for the policy-planning network, which meant that the power elite had been broadened beyond the leaders in the corporations, financial institutions, corporate law firms, and trade associations within the corporate community. By this point the power elite began to include the top leaders in foundations, think tanks, and policy-discussion groups. Moreover, this wider institutional base continued to grow during and after World War II.

The Rockefeller Labor-Relations Network

For all that Rockefeller and his many personal employees and foundations did to aid in the general development of the policy-planning network at all levels, their most direct contribution to the New Deal was the creation of a group of experts and policies in reaction to the violent labor conflicts in not one, but two, Rockefeller companies between 1913 and 1916. As explained a few paragraphs ago, Rockefeller's personal concern with new policies for dealing with labor strife began unexpectedly when Colorado Fuel and Iron became involved in its murderous labor battle with striking miners in 1913. As the tensions and violence escalated, Rockefeller resisted appeals to intervene because he firmly believed the company's managers were upholding an inviolate principle he shared with his father: employees should have the right to resist joining a union when they are allegedly being pressured by supposed outside agitators that want to exploit both the men and the companies. In essence, Rockefeller believed that union leaders ran a protection racket. All of this and more has been documented through work in the Rockefeller Archives by historian Howard M. Gitelman (1984; 1988, Chapter 1).

After first denying any direct involvement in the events leading to the Ludlow Massacre, Rockefeller then endured grueling appearances before the presidential Commission on Industrial Relations, which was discussed briefly in the previous subsection. Its chair then released many damaging and incriminating documents about Rockefeller's involvement in key decisions leading to the confrontation (e.g., Weinstein 1968, pp. 191–198). The most detailed historical account of Ludlow and its aftermath, based on documents at the Rockefeller Archives, proved that Rockefeller had no information on the actual working conditions at the company and had no interest in examining independent reports that were offered to him (Gitelman 1988).

In fact, his first step in the midst of the crisis was to hire a famous public relations expert of that era, who worked for Rockefeller from then until his death many years later. His next step, well after the massacre occurred, was to hire a Canadian labor-relations expert, MacKenzie King, who had worked for 12 years in his country's Ministry of Labour. After several long discussions between King and Rockefeller, which led to a deep personal relationship that lasted until the end of their lives, King then served as one of Rockefeller's closest advisers until he became Prime Minister of Canada, after leading the Liberal Party to victory in 1921.

Rockefeller's original idea was to hire King to direct a new Department of Industrial Relations within the Rockefeller Foundation, an idea that was immediately criticized by reformers and journalists as a blatant misuse of nontaxable family money to further the interests of the corporate community. The proposal was quickly abandoned and Rockefeller hired

King out of his own pocket, a practice he continued in his future efforts to manage class conflict.

Once King's employment status was settled, he proceeded to acquaint Rockefeller with the basic tenets of welfare capitalism and convince him to foster "employee representation plans," whereby workers within a plant could elect their own representatives to talk with management periodically on company time about their grievances. This plan was based on the theory that there is a potential "harmony of interests" between the social classes if employers and workers begin to think of each other as human beings working together on a common endeavor that has mutual, although admittedly differential, rewards. The stress was on "human relations" in industry. According to most analysts, employee representation plans, called "company unions" by their critics, were designed as a way to avoid industry-wide labor unions, although Rockefeller and virtually everyone who ever worked for him always insisted otherwise (Gilson 1940, for an informative exception).

King and Rockefeller were not the first to propose employee representation plans as a way to deal with labor conflict in the United States. In a discussion of several similar efforts in small American companies, well before King came on the scene, historian Daniel Nelson (1982) concluded that the origins of the idea go back at least to 1905 when the liberal Filene family, owners of William Filene & Sons, a major department store in Boston, offered their employees a way to discuss management–employee relationships in the store, even though there was no apparent labor conflict with their primarily female workforce. However, King and Rockefeller were the first to develop a systematic plan, publicize it widely, and install it in major corporations. When workers at Colorado Fuel and Iron voted for the plan and it seemed to work, Rockefeller received considerable praise in the media as a statesman and reformer. He then urged its adoption at the other companies in which he had major stock interests. (Shortly thereafter, Colorado Fuel and Iron endured the first of four strikes by the United Mine Workers over a period of 15 years before it was unionized in 1933.)

However, the plan did not come soon enough at Standard Oil of New Jersey's main plant in Bayonne, New Jersey. Major violence ripped through the company in July 1915, in a strike over wage levels, after the company refused any arbitration and blamed the strike on outside agitators. Several days of fighting led to the death of six workers and a score of injuries, many at the hands of a private detective agency the company hired to protect the refineries (Gibb and Knowlton 1956, Chapter 6; Gitelman 1988, p. 159). Once the men agreed to return to work, they received a pay increase and shorter hours, as they had demanded. Just over a year later another strike in Bayonne resulted in the deaths of three people and 30 serious injuries during a week of fires and rioting (Gibb and Knowlton 1956, p. 152). Rockefeller then asked the company's board of directors to consider the adoption of his new approach to labor relations, which was a more difficult request for him to make than it might seem for the son of the founder, and a major stockholder in his own right. Revealing once again the divisions among owners about how to deal with workers, the board had rejected his efforts to change labor policy a few years earlier, leading him to resign from the board (Gitelman 1988, p. 217). But this time the board agreed.

To implement the program, Rockefeller brought in Clarence J. Hicks, a former YMCA employee turned industrial adviser at, first, International Harvester, chaired by another one of Rockefeller's brothers-in-law, Cyrus McCormick, Jr., and then Colorado Fuel and Iron. Hicks became the vice president of industrial relations at Standard Oil of New Jersey in 1917, where he served until his retirement in 1933. He reported directly to Teagle, the president of Standard Oil of New Jersey, which put him at the center of the Rockefeller industrial relations network. More generally, the core of the Rockefeller labor-relations network was Teagle, Rockefeller, and Hicks, but others will be added as the story unfolds.

The Special Conference Committee

After pushing for the installation of employee representation plans at several other companies in which he had an ownership interest, in 1919 Rockefeller used Standard Oil of New Jersey as a launching pad for creating what came to be called the Special Conference Committee. It was an informal and off-the-record meeting group for the presidents of the largest corporations of that era and their industrial relations vice presidents. (Since the 1970s the top executive in a company has been called the chief executive officer—CEO—so I will henceforth use that term to avoid any confusion.) Hicks of Standard Oil of New Jersey was the chair from its inception. Its purpose was to keep these key executives in touch with each other on major labor relations and social-insurance issues, and to push the idea of Rockefeller's Employee Representation Plan whenever possible. In addition to Standard Oil of New Jersey, the group included ten of the largest corporations in the country and one bank: U.S. Steel, General Motors, General Electric, AT&T, DuPont, Bethlehem Steel, International Harvester, U.S. Rubber, Goodyear, Westinghouse, and Irving Trust (e.g., Gordon 1994, pp. 152–155; Scheinberg 1986, pp. 152–158). Eight of the ten original companies in the Special Conference Committee had adopted employee representation plans by 1925 (Sass 1997, p. 45). However, they did so with varying degrees of enthusiasm and diligence.

The vice presidents for industrial relations met with each other several times a year and the presidents joined them for one meeting a year. Between meetings they were kept informed of ongoing developments in the field of labor relations by an executive secretary, Edward S. Cowdrick, a former journalist from Colorado. He was hired by Rockefeller as a personal public relations employee after he wrote a favorable magazine article in 1915 on company representation plans (Gitelman 1988, p. 185). He served as the committee's secretary from 1922 until his death in 1951. In addition to his efforts for the Special Conference Committee, Cowdrick worked on several projects with industrial relations experts who were part of the Rockefeller circle. He was deeply involved in battles over labor legislation during the New Deal, but he was for the most part a minor figure who did both internal organizational maintenance and kept in touch with a wide range of journalists and industrial relations experts.

Although the Special Conference Committee was unknown at the time, its correspondence and other records were later subpoenaed and published in the Congressional Record by a Senate committee investigating corporate violence against union organizers in the late 1930s. We therefore know with certainty that it is not the figment of someone's imagination, which matters because of its role in shaping labor legislation in the early New Deal (Auerbach 1966; Senate 1939). The Special Conference Committee is also of interest later in the chapter because it provides evidence that the proneness of the corporate community to violence post-1877 continued into at least the 1930s. It turned out that several of the companies in it were stockpiling dynamite and other weapons in the mid-1930s. And all but one or two of the corporations included in the Social Conference Committee were part of the failed attempt, coordinated by Cowdrick, to defeat the National Labor Relations Act in 1935.

Industrial Relations Counselors, Inc.

In 1921, at the urging of King and one of Rockefeller's most trusted personal employees, lawyer Raymond Fosdick, Rockefeller formed an industrial consulting group, Industrial Relations Counselors, Inc. (The organization was usually called the IRC at the time and will be so named in the remainder of the book.) Its purpose was to generalize the results of the experiences within the Rockefeller-influenced companies and develop a program of research on industrial relations. The new consulting firm, the first of its kind according to labor historian Irving Bernstein (1960, pp. 168–169), began as a subgroup of Fosdick's law firm, which was on a retainer to Rockefeller. In 1926 it became an independent entity with a little over 20 employees, financed almost entirely by Rockefeller's personal fortune at the cost of about $1.4 million a year in 2018 dollars, which is not much money for the expertise it generated (Gitelman 1988, pp. 33ff on the IRC).

The group was soon doing highly detailed studies of labor relations in Rockefeller-related companies, providing reports (available through the Rockefeller Archives) that clearly stated any faults its investigators found. The reports included suggestions to improve working conditions and labor relations. It strongly advocated employee representation plans and identified those foremen and executives that treated workers harshly (see Kaufman 2009, for a detailed analysis of IRC reports on companies and for its general impact on how managers treated employees in the workplace). As shown in two chapters in Part 2, relying heavily on the IRC's confidential newsletter to major corporate clients, it had an even larger and more lasting impact on the Social Security Act than it did on the National Labor Relations Act.

The trustees for the IRC at the time of its formal incorporation in 1926—two corporate leaders, two Rockefeller employees, and the president of Dartmouth College—provide a good sense of how well the Rockefeller group was integrated into the corporate community, the nascent policy-planning network, and the two political parties. One of the most noted corporate executives of the era, Owen D. Young, was the chair of General Electric and a Democrat; he sat on the boards of General Motors, Radio Corporation of America, the National Broadcasting Company, and the National Bureau of Economic Research. One of Rockefeller's brothers-in-law, Cyrus McCormick, Jr., who was a director of National City Bank of New York and a trustee of Princeton University, in addition to being the chair of International Harvester, was also on the IRC board. Like Young, he was a Democrat and in addition had been a strong backer of Woodrow Wilson's presidential candidacy in 1912.

The two Rockefeller employees on the IRC board, Arthur Woods, a Republican and friend of Herbert Hoover, and Raymond Fosdick, a Democrat and acquaintance of Franklin D. Roosevelt, served as directors of corporations, foundations, and think tanks for Rockefeller. Woods was a vice president at Colorado Fuel and Iron, a director of Bankers Trust and Consolidation Coal, and a trustee of the General Education Board, the Rockefeller Foundation, and the Laura Spelman Rockefeller Memorial Fund. Fosdick, one of Rockefeller's lawyers since 1912, sat on the boards of Consolidation Coal, Davis Coal, and Western Maryland Railroad, and was a trustee of the Institute of Public Administration, the Rockefeller Foundation, the General Education Board, the Laura Spelman Rockefeller Memorial Fund, and the Rockefeller Institute for Medical Research. He served as the president of the Rockefeller Foundation from 1936 to 1948 (Fosdick 1952).) As one of Rockefeller's two or three closest advisers on labor relations, along with Teagle and Hicks, Fosdick was part of the Rockefeller labor-relations network during the New Deal. As for the fifth and final IRC trustee, Ernest Hopkins, the president of Dartmouth College, he also served as a trustee for the Laura Spelman Rockefeller Memorial Fund at the time.

Over and beyond the applied work by the IRC employees, Rockefeller and his aides started industrial relations institutes at major universities in order to develop the expertise needed to bring about harmonious labor relations. The first grant supported a new Department of Industrial Relations within the Wharton School of Business at the University of Pennsylvania, chaired by Joseph Willits. Willits then became involved in the work of the Social Science Research Council shortly thereafter. In 1939 he was appointed director of the Rockefeller Foundation's Division of Social Sciences (Fisher 1993, pp. 54–55, 121, 183). Their second initiative involved the formation of an Industrial Relations Section in the Department of Economics at Princeton, starting with direct overtures from Rockefeller and Fosdick. (Fosdick was a graduate of Princeton; John D. Rockefeller 3rd was a student there at the time). This project was developed under the guidance of Hicks from his post at Standard Oil of New Jersey. Industrial relations institutes were also created at several other universities, including MIT, the University of Michigan, and Stanford, and in the late 1930s another one was developed at the California Institute of Technology (Gitelman 1984, p. 24).

More generally, the Rockefeller foundations began to fund studies relating to human relations in industry. For example, they took an interest in the work of an Australian immigrant, Elton Mayo, whose grandiose claims about the importance of psychology in work relations greatly intrigued Hicks and his colleagues. They soon began to fund his research and then helped him to obtain a position at the new Harvard Business School. He is best known for his "Hawthorne Studies" at General Electric, which were in fact very poorly done and inaccurate, but which nonetheless gave a major boost to human relations studies before the inadequacy of the research and his inflated credentials were fully understood (Hoopes 2003, Chapter 5; Jacoby 1997, pp. 221–228).

The creation of employee representation plans and support for the new academic field of industrial relations made Rockefeller a leading figure among the moderate conservatives within the corporate community, which led ultraconservative corporate leaders to criticize him openly for his efforts. However, his policies were hardly a success. Less than 4 percent of manufacturing companies with 10 to 250 employees had employee representation plans in 1929, and only 8.7 percent of the companies with over 250 employees had plans (Gitelman 1984, p. 38). At that point, the Rockefeller industrial relations network had a core of five to ten members, along with many ties to corporate vice presidents that dealt with labor issues, and some potential outposts in the academic community, but the IRC was not a center of power.

Moreover, the policy prescriptions advocated by the Rockefeller labor-relations network were a step backward from the positions taken by the National Civic Federation at the beginning of the twentieth century because of their insistence that conflict could be eliminated through good human relations practices. Few members of the NCF in its heyday had gone so far as to think that government should enforce any worker rights to collective bargaining, but some of them understood that conflict between owners and employees might be inevitable, and that collective bargaining was the best practical way of regulating that conflict. The Rockefeller group's unwillingness to accept this lesson led to a major defeat for it on labor legislation during the New Deal, but only after it had laid the groundwork for the National Labor Board (hereafter usually NLB) in 1933, which eventually led to the National Labor Relations Act of 1935 and the creation of the more powerful National Labor Relations Board, a perfect example of the law of unintended consequences.

Two Legislative Precedents Set the Stage for Later Union Success

Even though the courts were thwarting union organizing at every turn, the NAM was physically attacking unions when need be, and the Rockefeller labor-relations network was trying to woo workers away from unions through employee representation plans, there were nonetheless two legislative enactments in the 12 years of Republican rule from 1921 to 1932 that carved out a legal path for the establishment of collective bargaining under the aegis of a government regulating board. This path was very different from what most Democrats had advocated up to that point.

The Railway Labor Act of 1926, which proved to be an important precedent for the National Labor Relations Act nine years later, reflected the leverage that skilled workers could generate when their replacement costs were high and they had the potential to disrupt an industry crucial to the functioning of the entire economy. Setting the stage for this 1926 legislative victory, skilled railroad workers had gained strength during World War I because the railroad owners were forced to accept collective bargaining and government regulation in the face of worker unrest at a time of international crisis. They also insisted upon an eight-hour day at the same wages they had received previously for a ten-hour day. Furthermore, the federal government had to take over the railroads in 1917 because their owners could not make deliveries in a timely and efficient way, thereby hampering the war effort. As a result of this series of events, skilled railroad workers had the opportunity to organize and win a greater role in railroad labor relations.

Railroads had been returned to private ownership after the war, but both owners and workers were forced to accept a Railroad Labor Board as part of the Transportation Act of 1920, which gave the new board the power to issue non-binding proposals to resolve labor disputes (Nelson 1997, pp. 99–100). However, the immediate result of this new law was several years of renewed conflict that led to a stalemate due to a combination of the skills of many rail workers, the need for timely delivery of industrial goods and passengers, and the vulnerability of expensive engines and train

82 The Rise and Fall of Labor Unions

cars to possible sabotage. Faced with a standoff due to the government's involvement, the corporate executives in the Association of Railway Executives and the leaders of four railroad craft unions finally agreed in 1926 to accept legislation creating a government mediation board. The railroad owners could console themselves with the knowledge that the law did not prohibit them from attempting to force their unskilled workers into employee representation plans, and the skilled workers were not inclined to support unionization efforts by unskilled workers (O'Brien 1998, pp. 98–100). But the new legislation passed against the wishes of the ultraconservative NAM, which opposed it on principle because it contained "the first explicit congressional endorsement of the right of collective bargaining" (Zieger 1986, p. 34).

Most important in terms of future legislation, the Railway Labor Act of 1926 created a new procedure for dealing with contract disputes. It established a U.S. Mediation Board with five members appointed by the president and approved by the Senate (Bernstein 1960, p. 218; O'Brien 1998, p. 254 note 78). As part of its duties, the board had the obligation to "protect the procedural rights of all workers," which was one major reason why all craft unions could support it (O'Brien 1998, p. 119). If the permanent board could not settle a contract dispute, the president had the discretion to appoint a temporary emergency board to examine the case. Neither companies nor unions could make any changes while the emergency board was deliberating, which created a powerful incentive for both sides to accept the decisions of the U.S. Mediation Board. In fact, the mediation board was by and large reasonably successful at a time when few major disputes occurred.

Although the overall legislation failed in many respects, including on its procedures to settle workplace grievances, the U.S. Mediation Board proved to be the germ of an agency with government enforcement powers that would be acceptable to the Supreme Court. Two earlier Supreme Court decisions had affirmed that workers had individual rights in relation to their jobs, including the right to designate a union as their representatives (O'Brien 1998, pp. 39–41, 57, 97, 157). At the same time, the Supreme Court decisions had made clear that the unions themselves did not have any legal standing. They were simply the temporary "agents" of the individual workers, which linked this individual right to the established tradition of agency law (O'Brien 1998, pp. 5–6, 16–17, 157–158, 172).

Progressive Republicans in both the Senate and House saw the distinction between individual rights for workers and the lack of any permanent legal standing for unions as a crucial one in terms of their principled support for individual rights, including the right to enter into contracts. They contrasted this approach with their distaste for the legalization of any organization (in this case unions) that would impinge upon the individual rights of others (in this case business owners). Based on this distinction,

The Uphill Battle for Unionism 83

they believed they could create a foundation for a "responsible unionism" that would differ from the "statism" and "collectivism" they saw as underlying the attempts by union-friendly Democrats sympathetic to the AFL (O'Brien 1998, pp. 16–17). Further, this distinction would make it possible to create state agencies, such as the U.S. Board of Mediation and the later National Labor Relations Board, which could "represent the public good" in adjudicating between the rights of individual workers and individual employers (O'Brien 1998, pp. 17, 146).

With this set of understandings in hand, one of the leading Progressive Republicans in the Senate, George Norris of Nebraska, enlisted the help in late May 1928, of three well-known professors of constitutional law from prestigious law schools. All three were conversant with the relevant legal precedents and sympathetic to the Progressive Republican's approach concerning labor issues. (One of them, Felix Frankfurter of Harvard, was a friend and adviser of future president Franklin D. Roosevelt, who used Frankfurter as an informal adviser during the first five years of his presidency and nominated him for the Supreme Court in 1938.) The three law professors were joined by an expert legislative draftsman, who had developed a special expertise on labor injunctions, after receiving his training in economics at the University of Wisconsin from John R. Commons.

The four experts built on past Supreme Court decisions and accepted regulatory principles, including those included in the Railway Labor Act of 1926. They devised a series of necessary procedural steps that would hem in the issuance of labor injunctions and greatly reduce their use. They found indirect ways to eliminate contracts that forced new employees to forego union membership as a condition of employment, and made it illegal to sue unions for the unlawful acts of individual members, except when there was clear proof that unions had taken part in or authorized the actions (Bernstein 1960, pp. 397–400; O'Brien 1998, pp. 154–158).

It seemed unlikely that the legislation could have been passed at the time it was written, or as long as ultraconservative Republicans controlled Congress. In any event, its sponsors were delayed for nearly two years before they could introduce it into the Senate because the AFL was resistant to the idea that its unions would have no legal standing, despite the defeats AFL unions had suffered throughout the postwar 1920s. Its leaders instead lobbied their allies in the Democratic Party, including the party's 1928 presidential candidate, to call for the recognition of unions and a ban on injunctions. After that effort failed, they took another year before they suggested their own set of amendments to the proposed legislation. The original drafters rejected these suggestions as being unhelpful and very likely unconstitutional (Bernstein 1960, p. 403). When the labor leaders finally agreed to support the bill, Senator Norris introduced it for the first time in the spring of 1930, with the full support of a coalition of

84 The Rise and Fall of Labor Unions

Progressive Republicans and liberal Democrats. It died in a Senate Committee shortly thereafter (Bernstein 1960, pp. 409–410).

By the time the bill was reintroduced and passed nearly two years later—in January 1932—after making slight alterations in it, and with the additional sponsorship of Fiorello LaGuardia, a progressive member of the House from New York City, two things had changed. First, the Supreme Court had ruled in May 1930, that the railroad owners had violated the rights of their unskilled workers to select their own representatives through their behind-the-scenes efforts to promote their employee representation plans as legitimate worker representation; this ruling amounted to another court vindication of the Progressive Republican arguments and a repudiation of company unions (Bernstein 1960, pp. 405–406).

Second, the stock market crash in late September 1929, and the sudden rise in the unemployment rate thereafter, led to a Democratic takeover of the House and a reduction of the Republican majority in the Senate to one seat, which could be overcome on labor legislation by the presence of seven Progressive Republicans and a Farmer-Labor senator from Minnesota. This time the coalition of Progressive Republicans and liberal Democrats won with great ease in both the House and the Senate, with all Democrats in support in the Senate (Bernstein 1960, p. 413). The act clearly posed no threat to plantation owners and Southern Democrats, and it did not contain an agency, such as the U.S. Mediation Board in the case of railroads, that could mandate employers to enter into collective bargaining.

Even with the Railway Labor Act and the Norris-LaGuardia Act on the law books, it did not seem likely that the weakened union movement would have any power to influence the New Deal that arrived a year after the Norris-LaGuardia Act was enacted. However, the AFL did have institutional legitimacy and a heritage of over 45 years of labor organizing. Workers had the right to vote and the potential to disrupt production and destroy plants and equipment. The dynamiting of the *Los Angeles Times'* building and several construction sites in 1911, the deadly strikes at Standard Oil of New Jersey in 1915 and 1916, the work stoppages by railroad workers and other workers during World War I, and the massive U.S. Steel strike in 1919 were only the most recent reminders of these disruptive capabilities.

There also was one new factor. The ongoing depression and the near-collapse of many unions led to pivotal changes in several AFL policy positions at its convention three months before the 1932 presidential election. The craft unions abandoned their opposition to national-level labor standards, unemployment insurance, and old-age pensions, although they continued to be hostile to minimum-wage legislation. In all, though, the changes meant that organized labor could become part of a new liberal-labor alliance after Roosevelt, the Democratic challenger to the incumbent

Republican, won the presidential election and included liberals in his governing coalition. As the unemployment rate rose to nearly 25 percent, and the lines of hungry people waiting for bread and soup grew ever longer, the AFL was in a position in which it might be able to influence the federal government to pass labor laws favorable to workers. With these new possibilities in mind, the next chapter presents a detailed account of how labor conflict and the legacies of past labor legislation led to the National Labor Relations Act, but there were many strike actions and several unexpected twists before the act was passed.

References

Adams, Graham. 1966. *The age of industrial violence, 1910–1915*. New York: Columbia University Press.

AFL. 1901. *Proceedings of the Federation*. New York: American Federation of Labor.

Alchon, Guy. 1985. *The invisible hand of planning: Capitalism, social science, and the state in the 1920s*. Princeton: Princeton University Press.

Alexander, Herbert E. 1992. *Financing politics: Money, elections, and political reform*. Washington: CQ Press.

Archer, Robin. 2007. *Why is there no Labor Party in the United States?* Princeton: Princeton University Press.

Auerbach, Jerold S. 1966. *Labor and liberty: The LaFollette Committee and the New Deal*. Indianapolis: Bobbs Merrill.

Bernstein, Irving. 1960. *The lean years: A history of the American worker, 1920–1933*. Boston: Houghton Mifflin.

———. 1969. *Turbulent years: A history of the American worker, 1933–1941*. Boston: Houghton Mifflin.

Brody, David. 1980. *Workers in industrial America: Essays on the twentieth century struggle*. New York: Oxford University Press.

Brown, Josephine. 1940. *Public relief, 1929–1939*. New York: Henry Holt & Company.

Brownlow, Louis. 1958. *A passion for anonymity: The autobiography of Louis Brownlow*, Vol. 2. Chicago: University of Chicago Press.

Bruce, Robert. 1959. *1877: Year of violence*. Indianapolis: Bobbs-Merrill.

Bulmer, Martin and Joan Bulmer. 1981. "Philanthropy and social science in the 1920s: Beardsley Ruml and the Laura Spelman Rockefeller Memorial, 1922–29." *Minerva* 19:347–407.

Bunting, David. 1983. "Origins of the American corporate network." *Social Science History* 7:129–142.

———. 1987. *The rise of large American corporations, 1889–1919*. New York: Garland.

Carosso, Vincent. 1970. *Investment banking in America*. Cambridge: Harvard University Press.

Commons, John. 1934. *Myself*. New York: Macmillan.

Cooper, Jerry M. 1980. *The army and civil disorder: Federal military intervention in labor disputes, 1877–1900*. Westport, CT: Greenwood Press.

Cyphers, Christopher. 2002. *The National Civic Federation and the making of a new liberalism, 1900–1915*. New York: Praeger.

86 The Rise and Fall of Labor Unions

Davis, Allen. 1967. *Spearheads for reform.* New York: Oxford University Press.

Domhoff, G. W. 1970. *The higher circles.* New York: Random House.

———. 1978. *Who really rules? New Haven and community power re-examined.* New Brunswick: Transaction Books.

———. 1996. *State autonomy or class dominance? Case studies on policy making in America.* Hawthorne, NY: Aldine de Gruyter.

Domhoff, G. W. and M. Webber. 2011. *Class and power in the New Deal: Corporate moderates, Southern Democrats, and the liberal-labor coalition.* Palo Alto: Stanford University Press.

Dubofsky, Melvyn. 2000. *Hard work: The making of labor history.* Chicago: University of Illinois Press.

Dubofsky, Melvyn and Foster Rhea Dulles. 2004. *Labor in America.* Seventh edition. Wheeling, IL: Harlan Davidson.

Fisher, Donald. 1993. *Fundamental development of the social sciences: Rockefeller philanthropy and the United States Social Science Research Council.* Ann Arbor: University of Michigan Press.

Fitch, Robert. 1993. *The assassination of New York.* New York: Verso.

Foner, Philip. 1955. *The history of the labor movement in the United States: From the founding of the American Federation of Labor to the emergence of American imperialism,* Vol. II. New York: International Publishers.

———. 1977. *The great labor uprising of 1877.* New York: Pathfinder Press.

Fosdick, Raymond. 1952. *The Story of the Rockefeller Foundation.* New York: Harper & Brothers.

Fraser, Steven. 1991. *Labor will rule: Sidney Hillman and the rise of American labor.* New York: Free Press.

Freeman, Richard B. 1998. "Spurts in union growth: Defining moments and social processes." Pp. 265–296 in *The defining moment: The Great Depression and the American economy in the twentieth century,* edited by M. Bordo, C. Goldin, and E. White. Chicago: University of Chicago Press.

Garraty, John. 1960. "The United States Steel Corporation versus labor: The early years." *Labor History* 1:3–38.

Gibb, George and Evelyn Knowlton. 1956. *The resurgent years, 1911–1927: History of the Standard Oil Company (New Jersey),* Vol. 2. New York: Harper & Brothers.

Gilson, Mary. 1940. *What's past is prologue: Reflections on my industrial experience.* New York: Harper.

Gitelman, Howard M. 1984. "Being of two minds: American employers confront the labor problem, 1915–1919." *Labor History* 25:189–216.

———. 1988. *Legacy of the Ludlow Massacre.* Philadelphia: University of Pennsylvania Press.

Gompers, Samuel. 1901. "The steel strike. Mr. Shaffer, his accusations, their refutation." *The American Federationist*:415–431.

Gordon, Colin. 1994. *New Deals: Business, labor, and politics in America,1920–1935.* New York: Cambridge University Press.

Green, Marguerite. 1956. *The National Civic Federation and the American Federation of Labor, 1900–1925.* Washington: Catholic University of America Press.

Gross, James A. 1981. *The reshaping of the National Labor Relations Board.* Albany: State University of New York Press.

The Uphill Battle for Unionism 87

Guttsman, W. L. 1969. *The English ruling class*. London: Weidenfeld & Nicholson.

Hamilton, Richard 1991. *The bourgeois epoch: Marx and Engels on Britain, France, and Germany*. Chapel Hill: University of North Carolina Press.

Harr, John and Peter Johnson. 1988. *The Rockefeller century*. New York: Charles Scribner's Sons.

Hooks, Gregory. 1991. *Forging the military-industrial complex: World War II's battle of the Potomac*. Urbana: University of Illinois Press.

Hoopes, James. 2003. *False prophets: The gurus who created modern management and why their ideas are bad for business today*. New York: Perseus Book Group.

Jacoby, Sanford. 1997. *Modern manors: Welfare capitalism since the New Deal*. Princeton: Princeton University Press.

Jensen, Gordon. 1956. "The National Civic Federation: American business in the age of social change and social reform, 1900–1910." Ph.D. dissertation Thesis, History, Princeton University, Princeton, NJ.

Karl, Barry. 1974. *Charles E. Merriam and the study of politics*. Chicago: University of Chicago Press.

Katz, Irving. 1968. *August Belmont: A political biography*. New York: Columbia University Press.

Kaufman, Bruce. 2009. *Hired hands or human resources: Case studies of HRM practices and programs in early American industry*. Ithaca: Cornell University Press.

Kessler-Harris, Alice. 1982. *Out to work: A history of wage-earning women in the United States*. New York: Oxford University Press.

Keyssar, Alexander. 2009. *The right to vote: The contested history of democracy in the United States*. New York: Basic Books.

Kimeldorf, Howard. 1999. *Battling for American labor: Wobblies, craft workers, and the making of the union movement*. Berkeley: University of California Press.

———. 2013. "Worker replacement costs and unionization: Origins of the U.S. labor movement." *American Sociological Review* 78:1033–1062.

Klepper, Michael and Robert Gunther. 1996. *The Wealthy 100: From Benjamin Franklin to Bill Gates—A ranking of the richest Americans, past and present*. New York: Carol Publication Group.

Lagemann, Ellen. 1989. *The politics of knowledge: The Carnegie Corporation, philanthropy, and public policy*. Middletown, CT: Wesleyan University Press.

Lambert, Josiah. 2005. *If the workers took a notion: The right to strike and American political development*. Ithaca: Cornell University Press.

Laslett, John. 1970. *Labor and the left: A study of socialist and radical influences in the American labor movement, 1881–1924*. New York: Basic Books.

———. 1996. "Introduction: 'A model of solidarity?' Interpreting the UMWA's first hundred years, 1890–1990." Pp. 1–25 in *The United Mine Workers of America: A model of industrial solidarity?* edited by J. Laslett. State College, PA: Pennsvylania State University Press.

Laurie, Bruce. 1989. *Artisans into workers: Labor in nineteenth-century America*. New York: Hill and Wang.

Lichtman, Allan 2008. *White Protestant nation: The rise of the American conservative movement*. New York: Atlantic Monthly Press.

Lindblom, Charles. 1977. *Politics and markets: The world's political economic systems*. New York: Basic Books.

88　The Rise and Fall of Labor Unions

Lindblom, Charles. 1978. "Why Government must cater to business." *Business and Society Review* 27:4–6.

Logan, John and Harvey Molotch. 2007. *Urban fortunes: The political economy of place*. Berkeley: University of California Press.

Lundberg, F. 1937. *America's 60 families*. New York: Vanguard.

MacLean, Nancy. 2017. *Democracy in chains: The deep history of the radical right's stealthy plan for America*. New York: Viking.

Mann, Michael. 1993. *The sources of social power: The rise of classes and nation-states, 1760–1914*, Vol. 2. New York: Cambridge University Press.

Mayer, Jane. 2017. *Dark money: The hidden history of the billionaires behind the rise of the radical right*. New York: Penguin Random House.

McLellan, David and Charles Woodhouse. 1960. "The business elite and foreign policy." *Western Political Quarterly* 13:172–190.

Mink, Gwendolyn. 1986. *Old labor and new immigrants in American political development, 1870–1925*. Ithaca: Cornell University Press.

Mizruchi, Mark. 1982. *The American corporate network, 1904–1974*. Beverly Hills: Sage Publications.

Mizruchi, Mark and David Bunting. 1981. "Influence in corporate networks: An examination of four measures." *Administrative Science Quarterly* 26:475–489.

Molotch, Harvey. 1979. "Capital and neighborhood in the United States: Some conceptual links." *Urban Affairs Quarterly* 14:289–312.

———. 1999. "Growth machine links: Up, down, and across." Pp. 247–265 in *The urban growth machine: Critical perspectives, two decades later*, edited by A. Jonas and D. Wilson. Albany: State University of New York Press.

Neill, Charles. 1913. *Report on the conditions of employment in the iron and steel industry in the United States, vol. III: Working conditions and the relations of employers and employees*. Washington: U.S. Government Printing Office.

Nelson, Daniel. 1982. "The company union movement, 1900–1937: A reexamination." *Business History Review* 56.

———. 1997. *Shifting fortunes: The rise and decline of American labor from the 1820s to the present*. Chicago: Ivan R. Dee.

Norwood, Stephen H. 2002. *Strikebreaking and intimidation: Mercenaries and masculinity in Twentieth-Century America*. Chapel Hill: University of North Carolina Press.

O'Brien, Ruth. 1998. *Worker's paradox: The Republican origins of New Deal labor policy, 1886–1935*. Chapel Hill: University of North Carolina Press.

Okrent, Daniel. 2003. *Great fortune: The epic of Rockefeller Center*. New York: Viking.

Oreskes, N. and E. Conway. 2010. *Merchants of doubt: How a handful of scientists obscured the truth on issues from tobacco smoke to global warming*. New York Bloomsbury Press.

Overacker, Louise. 1932. *Money in elections*. New York: Macmillan.

Palmer, Robert R. 1959. *The age of the democratic revolution: A political history of Europe and America, 1760–1800*. Princeton: Princeton University Press.

Parker-Gwin, Rachel and William G. Roy. 1996. "Corporate law and the organization of property in the United States: The origin and institutionalization of New Jersey corporation law, 1888–1903." *Politics & Society*, June:111–136.

Phelan, Craig. 1996. "John Mitchell and the politics of the trade agreement, 1898–1917." Pp. 72–103 in *The United Mine Workers of America: A model of industrial solidarity?* edited by J. Laslett. State College: Pennsylvania State University Press.

Pilisuk, Marc and Thomas Hayden. 1965. "Is there a military-industrial complex which prevents peace?" *Journal of Social Issues* 21:67–117.

Piven, Frances. 2006. *Challenging authority: How ordinary people change America.* Lanham, MD: Rowman & Littlefield.

Piven, Frances and Richard Cloward. 1977. *Poor people's movements: Why they succeed, how they fail.* New York: Random House.

Ramirez, Bruno. 1978. *When workers fight.* Westport, CT: Greenwood Press.

Roberts, Alasdair. 1994. "Demonstrating neutrality: The Rockefeller philanthropies and the evolution of public administration, 1927–1936." *Public Administration Review* 54:221–228.

Rockoff, Hugh. 2004. *Until it's over, over there: The U.S. economy in World War I.* Cambridge: National Bureau of Economic Research.

Roy, William G. 1983. "Interlocking directorates and the corporate revolution." *Social Science History* 7:143–164.

———. 1997. *Socializing capital: The rise of the large industrial corporation in America.* Princeton: Princeton University Press.

Sass, Steven A. 1997. *The promise of private pensions: The first hundred years.* Cambridge: Harvard University Press.

Saunders, Charles B. 1966. *The Brookings Institution: A fifty-year history.* Washington: The Brookings Institution.

Scheinberg, Stephen. 1986. *Employers and reformers: The development of corporation labor policy, 1900–1940.* New York: Taylor and Francis.

Schenkel, Albert. 1995. *The rich man and the kingdom: John D. Rockefeller, Jr., and the Protestant establishment.* Minneapolis: Fortress Press.

Senate, U.S. 1939. *Violations of free speech and rights of labor, Part 45: The Special Conference Committee.* Washington: U.S. Government Printing Office.

Shefter, Martin. 1994. *Political parties and the state: The American historical experience.* Princeton: Princeton University Press.

Smith, Robert M. 2003. *From blackjacks to briefcases: A history of commercialized strikebreaking and unionbusting in the United States.* Athens: Ohio University Press.

Starr, Paul. 2007. *Freedom's power: The true force of liberalism.* New York: Basic Books.

Stowell, David. 1999. *Streets, railroads and the Great Strike of 1877.* Chicago: University of Chicago Press.

Swenson, Peter. 2002. *Capitalists against markets: The making of labor markets and welfare states in the United States and Sweden.* New York: Oxford University Press.

TCF. 1935. *American foundations and their fields, 1934.* New York: Twentieth Century Fund.

Union of Concerned Scientists. 2007. "Smoke, mirrors, & hot air." Cambridge: Union of Concerned Scientists.

Voss, Kim. 1993. *The making of American exceptionalism: The Knights of Labor and class formation in the nineteenth century.* Ithaca: Cornell University Press.

Wall, Bennett and George Gibb. 1974. *Teagle of Jersey Standard.* New Orleans: Tulane University Press.

Weinstein, James. 1967. *The decline of socialism in America, 1912–1925.* New York: Monthly Review Press.

———. 1968. *The corporate ideal in the liberal state.* Boston: Beacon Press.

Wolman, Leo. 1924. *The growth of American trade unions, 1880–1923*. http://www.nber.org/books/wolm24-1. Cambridge: National Bureau of Economic Research.

Woodhouse, Charles and McLellan. 1966. "American business leaders and foreign policy: A study in perspectives." *The American Journal of Economics and Sociology* 25:267–280.

Zieger, Robert. 1986. *American workers, American unions, 1920–1985*. Baltimore: Johns Hopkins University Press.

Zieger, Robert and Gilbert Gall. 2002. *American workers, American unions: Third edition*. Baltimore: Johns Hopkins University Press.

Chapter 2

The Origins of the National Labor Relations Act of 1935

After the passage of several pieces of enduring emergency legislation in the spring of 1933 to save the banks, the plantation owners in the South, and the corn-hog farmers in the Midwest, Roosevelt was inclined to end the special session of Congress he had called to deal with the dire emergencies the country was experiencing. He thought that the new legislation, which at least temporarily solved the problems facing finance and agriculture, dealt with the most pressing problems facing the nation, and he did not want to push his luck any further. However, he had been alerted through memos from members of his small expert advisory committee (the Brain Trust) that corporate leaders were working on a plan for industrial reorganization. Their plan would free corporations from the constraints of the antitrust laws, thereby making more cooperation among them possible (e.g., price setting and limits on production). In addition, he also had received memos and personal White House visits from representatives of the NAM and the U.S. Chamber of Commerce, which urged the corporate plans upon him. But Roosevelt was not convinced that any of these plans had jelled sufficiently or were politically feasible (Himmelberg 1976/1993, Chapter 10).

Then the political equation suddenly changed on April 6, 1933, when the Senate unexpectedly approved a liberal bill concerning wages and hours, which would cut the workweek to 30 hours for the same daily wage. It meant a significant pay increase despite a likely decrease in productive output. Sponsored by one of the few Southern liberals in the Senate, Hugo Black, later to be appointed to the Supreme Court by Roosevelt, the bill was based on the argument, heartily supported by organized labor, that the measure would spread work and increase purchasing power at the same time. Neither Roosevelt nor any business group liked the idea for a variety of reasons. Leaders of the NAM, along with several corporate moderates, including Teagle of Standard Oil, testified against it, which reminds us that Teagle was an important figure on policy issues of major concern to the entire corporate community. Secretary of Labor Frances Perkins found the legislation unacceptable for her own reasons: in particular, it did not include a minimum-wage provision.

92 The Rise and Fall of Labor Unions

Faced with so much disagreement, but deciding that the time might be right, Roosevelt then insisted on an industrial reorganization plan that was acceptable to both organized business and organized labor, which is nothing to be sneezed at because it would at least put the unions' desires on the agenda. The search for an alternative began on April 11 when Roosevelt told the head of his three-person Brain Trust to ask the Democratic senator from New York Senator Robert F. Wagner of New York, who had served as a justice on the New York Supreme Court from 1919 to 1926, and was an urban liberal with good relations with the AFL, to bring together a drafting group. The resulting legislation, the National Industrial Recovery Act, passed in June 1933. It had some surprising outcomes, but acceptable labor legislation turned out to be two years away.

The composition of Wagner's committee provides testimony to the increasing role of think tanks and policy-discussion groups in shaping government. In addition to a prominent banker from Rochester, who had once served in the House as a liberal Democrat, it included as members one of the leaders of the NAM, who was also the CEO of Remington Rand, the presidents of The Brookings Institution and the National Industrial Conference Board, and one of the founders of the National Bureau of Economic Research. The group also included a Progressive Republican senator from Wisconsin and a Progressive Republican member of the House from Pennsylvania, as well as John L. Lewis, the president of the United Mine Workers, and an economist who was an adviser to Lewis' union.

Based on a two-year suspension of the antitrust laws, a plan for a National Recovery Administration emerged from this committee and other discussions within the Roosevelt Administration. It would bring together business owners in each sector of the economy, usually through their trade associations, to create codes of fair competition. The codes would set minimum wages, minimum prices, and production levels in a very wide range of business sectors. The business owners were supposed to be joined in this effort by representatives of workers and consumers, although in practice labor was only represented by even one person in fewer than 10 percent of the cases, usually in various garment trades (Hawley 1966, pp. 56–57; McQuaid 1979). In theory, these separate and self-policed "code authorities" would eliminate cutthroat competition, reemploy workers, and increase purchasing power, thereby restarting the economy.

Although the National Industrial Recovery Act was a hasty response to Black's 30-hour bill, corporate leaders had been discussing its basic ideas for over a decade. According to every historian who has studied the matter, the fingerprints of various corporate leaders and policy experts can be found on every part of it (e.g., Hawley 1966; Himmelberg 1976/1993; Schlesinger 1958; Vittoz 1987). The main ideas for it were developed in the aftermath of the seeming success of the business-government partnership during the limited industrial mobilization for World War I. Then, too, the idea of instituting peacetime equivalents of the National War Labor Board was widely discussed by businessmen through their trade associations over the next 12 years. Roosevelt, as president of the American Construction Council from 1922 to 1928, was one of those "encouraging industrial self-government as an alternative to government regulation," so the idea was not foreign to the new president (Schlesinger 1957, pp. 374–375).

Roosevelt not only was familiar with the basic plan and the corporate support for it. He knew he was trying to bring about recovery within the constraints that were likely to be set by the Supreme Court if the executive branch tried to regulate the economy. Roosevelt and his advisers feared that the extremely conservative court, with a majority of former corporate lawyers, most of whom were market fundamentalists, would find legislation regulating wages to be unconstitutional. It was likely to do so on the grounds that regulating wages was an infringement on the right of individuals to freely negotiate contracts, as it had done just ten years earlier. Roosevelt therefore decided that the only way to obtain the minimum wage and maximum hour laws he wanted was through agreements hammered out by business and labor leaders in each industry. Unfortunately for the liberals and labor, the White House had to find ways to induce those agreements by giving business something it wanted even more, the ability to set minimum prices and restrict output without fear of antitrust prosecution (Schlesinger 1958, p. 101).

Given the nearly unanimous scholarly opinion that the corporate community had the major impact on the shaping of the National Industrial Recovery Act, the most interesting question in terms of an eventual understanding of the origins and passage of the National Labor Relations Act in 1935 is how the 1933 legislation came to include the idea that labor should have the right to bargain collectively through representatives of its own choosing. The clause that eventually gave support to this right began as a one-sentence declaration that came to be known as "section 7(a)." It simply said "employees shall have the right to organize and bargain collectively through representatives of their own choosing." However, it is important to emphasize that the NCF first articulated these principles 33 years earlier and that organized labor had insisted upon them in exchange for its participation in the National War Labor Board 16 years earlier (Conner 1983, Chapter 11). Although the NCF itself had outlived its usefulness by World War I, and during the 1920 was primarily a soap box for one of its original organizers, its early work had an impact on aspects of New Deal labor legislation.

Moreover, the Railway Labor Act of 1926 and Norris-LaGuardia Act of 1932 included the idea of collective bargaining. It therefore seems plausible that Wagner, the two Progressive Republicans, and Lewis were able to include section 7(a) despite the likely objections from the NAM leader and the presidents of The Brookings Institution and the National Industrial Conference Board. There is also some evidence that at least a handful of business executives and economists from the policy-planning network supported the idea, apparently because they believed unions could play a positive role in stabilizing such highly competitive and wage-cutting industries as coal mining and garment making (e.g., Gordon 1994, Chapter 3; Vittoz 1987, Chapters 2 and 3). However, as subsequent resistance to union involvement in the code authorities demonstrates, most of the corporate leaders who at first seemed willing to accept some degree of union involvement became highly opposed to unions.

Ultimately, the act included section 7(a) because labor leaders and liberals demanded it (e.g., Bernstein 1950, pp. 37–38; Schlesinger 1958, p. 99). At a final meeting with Roosevelt, the two most important liberals in Washington, Senator Wagner and Secretary of Labor Frances Perkins, were adamant in their insistence that it be included, which reveals their sympathy for unions. Wagner, as the most respected and visible spokesperson for urban liberals in Congress, told Roosevelt that there would be no law without the clause. Perkins, who had supported unions for decades, even though she found them narrow and shortsighted, made an appointment for her and AFL president, Green, to see Roosevelt. Roosevelt decided the conflict by agreeing that the clause would remain in the legislation (Cohen 2009, p. 240). This series of events demonstrates that the nascent liberal-labor alliance had the power to put its clause in the bill for two reasons. First, organized labor, small though it was in numbers at the time, nonetheless had the potential to initiate disruptive actions through strikes, boycotts, and property destruction in key business sectors at a vulnerable moment for the economy. Second, Roosevelt's decision showed that he considered the liberals who backed unions as one part of the New Deal coalition.

However, the fact that Roosevelt considered liberals to be part of his coalition does not mean that he was personally in favor of unions, or of union militancy. In his view, the federal government should defend workers and guarantee their rights, but it should do so through satisfying both business and labor, not through encouraging the independence of unions (Daniel 1981, pp. 167–170). Historians of the New Deal in general agree. For example, Arthur S. Schlesinger, Jr. (1958, p. 402) concludes that Roosevelt was "reared in the somewhat paternalistic traditions of prewar progressivism and of the social work ethos." In other words, Roosevelt believed that creating wages and hours legislation, pensions, and unemployment benefits was better than recognizing collective bargaining rights, so he was not in complete agreement with the liberal Democrats and the Progressive Republicans on matters such as an independent labor-relations board and the use of majority rule. His doubts proved to be a source of hesitation and delay even in the days before the National Labor Relations Act was passed in mid-1935. Moreover, Roosevelt did not think that the weakened union movement was likely to become larger or more activist in the foreseeable future (Daniel 1981, pp. 167–170).

The apparent weakness of unions to one side, there was apprehension on the part of Southern Democrats and plantation owners about the possible inclusion of agriculture as an "industry." At this point they did not want to provide any encouragement whatsoever toward unionization on the part of their completely subjugated, and overwhelmingly African American, workforce. Their concern mattered greatly because Southern Democrats still held 35 percent of the seats in both the House and the Senate. Moreover, due to the seniority system, Southern Democrats chaired nine of the 14 most important committees in the Senate and 12 of 17 in the House (Texas alone had nine chairs of permanent committees). For Roosevelt's part, he owed the Southerners for his nomination at the presidential convention in 1932, was personally acquainted with many of them going back several decades, and per force had to rely on them, as the top leaders in both the Senate and House, to manage New Deal legislation on the floor of Congress (*pace* Shafer 2016, pp. 7–8, who says that by 1934 the Northern Democrats did not need the Southern Democrats because they were such a large majority, and that Roosevelt had only "minimal reason to worry" about them). In addition, Southern Democrats were adept at utilizing various parliamentary devices, especially the filibuster, to obstruct legislation they deemed inimical to white Southern interests (e.g., Potter 1972).

In response to Southern concerns, Wagner insisted that agriculture was excluded from the purview of the legislation (Farhang and Katznelson 2005, p. 12). There was also implicit agreement that any issues having to do with agriculture and its labor force came under the jurisdiction of the Agricultural Adjustment Administration, which was known to be safely in the hands of conservative Democrats. Thus, this potentially divisive issue did not cause any further problems within the Democratic Party during the legislative process. From this point forward on the uncertain path to the NLRA, the concerns of Southern Democrats were always paramount. More generally, Wagner's willingness to exclude agricultural workers from the benefits of a pro-union provision, along with Roosevelt's acceptance of this decision, once again shows just how important the plantation owners and Southern Democrats were at the time.

With the Southern Democrats fully accommodated due to Wagner's interventions, the AFL was able to propose an important, and controversial, amendment to the National Industrial Recovery Act of 1933 once it reached Congress. It insisted that language from the Norris-LaGuardia Act be added to the simple declaration of the right to collective bargaining in section 7(a). The additional clause stated that employees "shall be free from the interference, restraint, or coercion of employers of labor or their agents..." (Bernstein 1969, p. 31). Moreover, the AFL wanted a seemingly small change in a clause stating that "no employee and no one seeking employment shall be required as a condition of employment to join any organization or to refrain from joining a labor organization of his own choosing." In a phrase aimed directly at the Rockefeller industrial relations network, the AFL further requested that the word "organization" be replaced by "company union," which raised the corporate moderates' hackles immediately (Bernstein 1969, p. 31). But the AFL's amendments made it into the bill passed by the House despite the NAM's desire to eliminate section 7(a) entirely. However, at this juncture the NAM did not have the support of the Chamber of Commerce on this issue because it had made a private agreement with the AFL that it would accept the collective-bargaining provision in exchange for labor's support for the price-setting provisions (Bernstein 1950, p. 35).

The ultraconservatives represented by the NAM carried their fight against section 7(a), and especially the amendments to it, to the floor of the Senate. By this time they had the support of the Chamber of Commerce again, which felt that the AFL amendments went too far. And yet, their united effort to soften section 7(a) was soundly defeated, 46 to 31, by the overwhelming Democratic majority. This vote clearly showed the potential power of the liberal-labor alliance within Congress when the Southern Democrats did not oppose it.

Once the National Industrial Recovery Act passed, the moderate conservatives and ultraconservatives reacted very differently to the success of the liberal-labor alliance in carving out a small space for union initiatives within the framework of the NRA. The corporate moderates believed they could live with collective bargaining if they had to, an attitude reinforced by the way in which the Railway Labor Act of 1926 had led to a moderate railroad unionism focused on a relatively few skilled jobs. They also had confidence that employee representation plans, as honed by the efforts of the IRC, could keep out independent unions. Most of all, corporate moderates believed they had won the day against unionism. Thus, historian Robert Himmelberg (1976/1993, p. 107) concludes that "few" corporate reformers felt modification of the new language in section 7(a) was an "absolute condition" for their support of the whole bill. In effect, they shared Roosevelt's sense that unions were not strong enough to play a significant role.

On the other hand, the National Association of Manufacturers and other ultraconservatives opposed section 7(a) to the bitter end. Moreover, NAM's general counsel believed Wagner had betrayed business on the issue when he agreed to the AFL amendments in the course of his own testimony before the House committee. Thus began an increasingly acrimonious relationship between the NAM and Wagner. But for the time being, the ultraconservatives, recognizing that there were no penalties for violating section 7(a), decided to stonewall the pro-union provisions by claiming that the law did not outlaw company unions or designate trade unions as the sole bargaining agents within a plant. Everything now depended on who administered the NRA and how the vague guidelines were interpreted.

Based on the direct and overwhelming corporate involvement in the creation of this legislation, and the fact that the inclusion of section 7(a) had some business support and no enforcement mechanism, most social scientists and historians apparently accept Himmelberg's (1976/1993, Chapter 10) conclusion to his highly detailed analysis of the origins of the National Industrial Recovery Act: the legislation marked a victory for business revisionists, the group of business leaders called corporate moderates in this book. So far, then, my account hews closely to the mainstream views on labor legislation, except for the addition of the Rockefeller industrial relations network as a key factor.

Any qualms about the administration of the act seemed to disappear for the ultraconservatives when someone they trusted, whose name and story need not sidetrack us here, was appointed as the National Recovery Administration's director (Domhoff 1996, pp. 67, 105–107, for background on this colorful pro-business, but chaotic and haphazard administrator). To the great satisfaction of ultraconservatives, he immediately made an interpretation of the collective-bargaining section that discouraged unionization. He also accepted many other suggestions made to him by corporate leaders, including various mechanisms for setting industry-wide prices. Further, he ended any lingering concerns on the part of Southern Democrats by ruling that the Agricultural Adjustment Administration would deal with any issues concerning agricultural labor, a ruling that was backed up with a series of executive orders by Roosevelt (Farhang and Katznelson 2005, p. 12).

To provide him and the many business leaders in the National Recovery Administration (hereafter usually called the NRA) with advice, the NRA director set up an Industrial Advisory Board. He drew its members from a unique governmental advisory agency formed in the early spring of 1933 by Roosevelt's Southern-born Secretary of Commerce, Daniel Roper, a former lobbyist for corporations, with extensive contacts throughout the corporate world. The new advisory committee, originally called the Business Advisory and Planning Council of the Department of Commerce, soon shortened its name to the Business Advisory Council (hereafter usually BAC).

Although the BAC was a government advisory group, the corporate community itself selected its members. Through consultation with the leading policy groups and trade associations, the corporate leaders who set it up made a deliberate attempt to enlist highly visible and respected members of the corporate community (McQuaid 1976; McQuaid 1982). The BAC thereby became a policy-discussion group within the policy-planning network, as well as a quasi-government committee. Moreover, it was at the center of the policy-planning network and the corporate community for the next 35 years. Then its leading members in the late 1960s and early 1970s played a central role in creating the Business Roundtable in 1972, so there was an unbroken continuity between the largest corporations and the central organization in the policy-planning network from the 1930s to the end of the century (e.g., Burris 1992; Burris 2008; Dreiling and Darves 2016; Moore, Sobieraj, Whitt, Mayorova, and Beaulieu 2002; Salzman and Domhoff 1983).

The BAC had 41 members at its outset in 1933–1934, representing a cross-section of business and financial executives. Several members of the Special Conference Committee were in this group, as well as officers of other large banks, retail firms, policy groups, and trade associations. Eighteen of the 60 largest banks, railroads, utilities, and manufacturing corporations of the day were linked to the BAC through the multiple corporate directorships held by some BAC members. There were also numerous regional and local businessmen from across the country.

Gerard Swope, the president of General Electric, and a friend of the New Deal, was named chair of the BAC. Teagle was selected as chair of its Industrial Relations Committee, which demonstrates the central role of the Rockefeller labor-relations network in the corporate community once again. One of Teagle's first decisions was to appoint all the vice presidents that were members of the Special Conference Committee to the BAC's Industrial Relations Committee. He thereby made that private group into a governmental body, which is a small, temporary instance of state-building by the corporate community. Rockefeller's personal employee, Edward S. Cowdrick, the aforementioned secretary of the Special Conference Committee, was made secretary of the new BAC committee.

Reflecting the seamless overlap of the corporate community and government in the early New Deal, Cowdrick wrote as follows to an AT&T executive. The memo deserves to be quoted because it reveals one of the ways the corporate leaders explained their involvement in government advisory groups. The members were told to think of themselves as attending as individuals, not as representatives of their companies or as members of the Special Conference Committee. It also tells them to avoid any mention of the Special Conference Committee, even though the government advisory meetings were part of Special Conference Committee meetings:

> Each member is invited as an individual, not as a representative of his company, and the name of the Special Conference Committee will not be used. The work of the new committee will supplement and broaden—not supplant—that of the Special Conference Committee. Probably special meetings will not be needed since the necessary guidelines for the Industrial Relations Committee's work can be given at our regular sessions.
>
> (Senate 1939, p. 16800)

Not surprisingly, perhaps, the first task of the new Industrial Relations Committee was to prepare a report on employee representation and collective bargaining, which favored employee representation plans and criticized unions (Scheinberg 1986, p. 163). However, it did not really take a report from the new BAC to prod the corporate community, including those in the NAM, into defensive action by quickly installing employee representation plans (Jacoby 1997, pp. 157–159).

As if to signal that it meant to continue the central role it had taken since the early years of the twentieth century in resisting unions, U.S. Steel hired the longtime director of the IRC, Arthur H. Young, as its vice president in charge of industrial relations. Young, who had worked for both International Harvester and Colorado Fuel and Iron before joining the IRC, received a personal letter of congratulations from John D. Rockefeller, which thanked him for his years of service and told him that "I shall follow with interest your course in this new position" (Rockefeller 1934). At the least, this letter shows that Rockefeller was paying attention, or having someone pay attention for him. Young soon announced a new employee representation plan and assured everyone that the plan would generate "sound and harmonious relationships between men and management," which he likened to the "sound and harmonious relationship between a man and his wife" (Bernstein 1969, p. 455). Within a year, at least 93 steel companies had employee representation plans that covered over 90 percent of the workers in the industry.

At the BAC's first general meeting in Washington on June 26, 1933, ten days after the NRA itself was created, the NRA director asked Teagle to chair the NRA's Industrial Advisory Board, which drew the majority of its members from the BAC as well (McQuaid 1979, p. 685–686). Teagle brought Hicks, his recently retired industrial relations vice president at Standard Oil of New Jersey, to join him in Washington as his personal assistant. (At this point Hicks was paid about $107,000 a year as a personal consultant to Rockefeller, in addition to his $178,000 a year pension from Standard Oil of New Jersey—both of those figures are in terms of 2018 dollars). Shortly thereafter, when Teagle spent much of the summer of 1933 in Washington helping to set up the administrative apparatus for the National Recovery Administration, he brought Hicks with him to help keep him abreast of what was unfolding.

In short, the overlap between the corporate community, the Rockefeller labor-relations network, and the NRA was very extensive. This seems to be even more the case when it is added that other top businesspeople came to Washington to serve the NRA as "presidential industrial advisers" on temporary loan from their corporations. In other words, the corporate community was subsidizing, staffing, and building a new state agency. Moreover, contrary to some social scientists, this process was unfolding at the very time that the corporate community supposedly had lost power and legitimacy (e.g., Hacker and Pierson 2004; Hacker and Pierson 2010).

But the many efforts to prevent worker unrest and labor organizing did not work out as expected. The inclusion of section 7(a) in the enabling legislation for the NRA turned out not to be benign after all. Instead, it inspired a huge organizing drive. "Those provisions," conclude two protest-disruption theorists, Frances Fox Piven and Richard Cloward (1977, p. 110), "were to have an unprecedented impact on the unorganized working people of the country, not so much for what they gave, as for what they promised." Or as sociologist Rhonda F. Levine explains (1988, p. 82): "Ironically, contrary to its design, the National Industrial Recovery Act and the NRA's implementation of the act actually worked to disorganize the capitalist class and to organize the working class." The idea of collective bargaining seemed to have arrived due to the support and legitimation it received from the legislative and executive branches of the federal government.

Labor's organizing efforts met with success in some industries, especially those in which the companies were small or the workers were organized into one industry-wide union in narrowly defined and circumscribed business sectors. This success was greatest for the United Mine Workers, who were able to thwart attempts by mine operators to bring in replacement labor. However, the mineworkers did not succeed in unionizing the "captive" coal mines that were owned by large corporations that had their major operations in other business sectors, which in particular meant U.S. Steel (Johnson 1970). This basic fact, which meant the union was always vulnerable to a counterattack, was perhaps the major reason why Lewis, the leader of the coal miners, eventually widened his horizons to create successful unions in major manufacturing industries such as steel (Johnson 1970; Swenson 2002, pp. 146–160).

Similarly, the Amalgamated Clothing Workers (ACW) grew rapidly by organizing the men who worked for the many small clothing companies in New York and other Eastern cities; the International Ladies Garment Workers did the same for women (Swenson 2002, pp. 146–160) Once again, as in the case of the United Mine Workers, the garment workers' unions had a self-interested reason to try to build a larger union movement when the opportunity arose. They were vulnerable to attack by the large Southern textile mills that supplied the cloth to garment shops. "Hillman's nightmare," as his biographer put it, was that the garment manufacturers would flee to the South; he feared that the textile mills "menaced the ACW directly," so his attempt to unionize them three years later, against great odds, was at least in part "a desperate act of self-defense" (Fraser 1991, p. 386).

Worker Disruption and a New Labor Board

The unexpected labor strife in Northern industrial cities six weeks after passage of the NRA was so great that major business figures felt it necessary to contemplate a compromise with organized labor. The BAC members on the Industrial Advisory Board of the NRA therefore hosted a private meeting with the Labor Advisory Board of the NRA on August 3, 1933, which included Lewis of the mine workers, Hillman of the garment workers, and Green of the AFL as key participants. BAC minutes reveal that Teagle opened the meeting by suggesting a "truce" (this war-derived metaphor suggests that Teagle perhaps believed that there was a class-based war going on) until the NRA could establish the numerous codes that would set price, hours, and wages in a wide variety of industries. According to notes from the meeting, he emphasized that he had no complaint with labor's efforts. "It was only natural," he said, "for labor to try to use this opportunity to organize and for employers to resist," a statement that also suggests that Teagle thought in terms of a class-conflict theory (McQuaid 1979, p. 688). As Teagle further stated, some degree of harmony was needed so that the recovery process could begin. He therefore proposed that the two boards create an agency to arbitrate the problems that were being caused by differing interpretations of section 7(a).

The labor leaders were skeptical about Teagle's proposed truce because he also was asking that organizing drives and strikes be halted. Hillman countered that he might agree to forego strikes if the right to continue organizing was stated clearly by the Industrial Advisory Board, but Teagle did not like this suggestion. Swope of General Electric, searching for compromise, then suggested that a small subcommittee of four people, including himself, meet for a short time to see if it could work out a common declaration on labor policy.

The subcommittee came back to the full meeting with a proposal for "a bipartisan arbitration board composed equally of Industrial Advisory Board and Labor Advisory Board members, which would be headed by an impartial 'public' chairman" (McQuaid 1979, p. 680). The similarity of the proposed board to the earlier National War Labor Board was not lost on any of the participants; several of them had been involved in management-labor cooperation during World War I. The problem of union organizing was left unmentioned, but to reassure the labor leaders, Swope suggested Senator Wagner as the public member and chair. While there was general acceptance of Wagner, Hillman remained doubtful about the overall plan. He repeated his opinion that the "right to organize on the part of labor" should be announced as an overall board policy. In response, Green, who was far more cautious than Hillman or Lewis, responded that Hillman's view was as "extreme" as Teagle's proposal to halt all organizing drives for the duration. Green, like Swope, wanted to maintain a "cooperative spirit" by leaving the issue of organizing rights for the future (McQuaid 1979, pp. 689–690).

After further discussion, the two groups reached general agreement on the subcommittee proposal and they formally approved it the following

102 The Rise and Fall of Labor Unions

day. President Roosevelt accepted the agreement immediately and the next day announced the formation of a National Labor Board (NLB) to arbitrate strikes and seek voluntary consent to section 7(a). Corporate moderates therefore had forged a compromise with labor leaders in the way that fit with their general approach to most problems, along with the earlier efforts of the National Civic Federation on labor issues. In the process they developed a new government structure (another example of state-building by the corporate rich) and thereby gave renewed legitimacy to collective bargaining and government mediation of labor disputes.

In all, the written record provides practically a minute-by-minute account of how the corporate community, drawing on ideas and experts from its policy-planning network, worked with organized labor to create a new government agency. And it did so with little or no involvement of the White House, although it is likely that Roosevelt was aware of this activity and tacitly approved of it. The creation of the labor board is also a classic example of how new government legislation, in this case the National Industrial Recovery Act, can lead to outcomes that no group anticipated or desired. It is also a demonstration of the importance of the policy-planning network and the executive branch of the federal government in shaping—and even inadvertently supporting—working-class organization.

The new NLB, renamed the National Labor Relations Board (NLRB), was strengthened in 1934, despite opposition by corporate leaders, and then further strengthened by the passage of the National Labor Relations Act in 1935 in the face of complete resistance by a united corporate community; it consisted of men that had been present for the meeting during which it was proposed. The labor representatives on the new NLB in 1933 were Lewis, Green, and Leo Wolman, the latter of whom worked as an adviser to Hillman and as a professor of economics at Columbia University. The three business members were Teagle, Swope, and Louis Kirstein, a vice president of William Filene & Sons, the Boston department store. Like Teagle and Swope, Kirstein was a member of the NRA's Industrial Advisory Board and had been present at the August 3 meeting with the labor leaders. The Filene family for whom Kirstein worked had been proponents of liberal business policies for several decades, as seen by their role in creating the Twentieth Century Fund, and one of its members was on the BAC.

From the tenor of the August 3 meeting of corporate and labor leaders, and a look at the composition of the new labor board, it appeared that moderate conservatives within the corporate community were prepared to adopt a more cooperative stance toward organized labor. It seemed that they might be willing to accept the collective-bargaining solution that had been urged by the National Civic Federation and the Commission on Industrial Relations in the Progressive Era, then implemented for the duration of World War I, then reluctantly accepted by railroad executives in 1926, then supported by the Norris-LaGuardia Act, and then legislated by Congress as part of the NRA deal. The presence of Swope and Teagle seemed to signal that two of the most respected and powerful corporate leaders in the country were now in favor of a more cooperative approach to labor strife.

The new board registered considerable success in its first few weeks by establishing regular procedures and settling several strikes. On August 11, just six days after the board was created, it announced a five-step procedure that was successful in ending a strike at 45 hosiery mills in Reading, Pennsylvania. Drafted by Swope, and soon to be known as the "Reading Formula," the procedure was as follows, with the provision for secret elections conducted by the NLB as the most crucial aspect:

1. the strike would end immediately;
2. the employers would reinstate strikers without discrimination;
3. the NLB would supervise a secret election by workers to determine whether or not they wished to have a union as their representative;
4. the employer would agree to bargain collectively if the workers voted for a union;
5. all differences not resolved by negotiation would be submitted to an arbitration board or the NLB itself for decision (Gross 1974, pp. 20–21; Loth 1958, pp. 228–229).

Most of the successes under the Reading Formula were with small businesses in minor and fragmented industries, which were not able for different reasons to overcome the problem of replacement costs, especially coal mining, clothing, and building construction. These three business sectors accounted for fully half of all union members in 1934, when union density had crept up to 11.5 percent, about what it had been in 1904 and 1918 (Freeman 1998, p. 292, Table 8A.2). It also seemed possible that at least some of the employers in those industries had reason to hope that bargains with unions might help put an end to destructive competition through cuts in wages and prices (Swenson 2002, p. 144). Despite its auspicious start, however, the NLB's authority and prestige were diminished in late 1933 by the lack of a legal underpinning and enforcement powers to overcome opposition by the large industrial employers and strong trade associations, which refused to accept the board's decisions.

In October, for example, several companies declined to appear at board hearings, and on November 1 the NAM launched a vigorous public attack on the legitimacy of the board itself. The NAM claimed that its procedures were unfair and objected in particular to Swope's idea of representation elections, 75 percent of which were won by trade unions from August through December of 1933. NAM even objected to the corporate members of the board, claiming that "the representatives of the manufacturers are usually chosen from among those who are known from their expression of views to have a strong leaning towards labor" (Gross 1974, p. 44). In two major cases in December 1933, Weirton Steel and Budd Manufacturing openly defied the NLB and brought the agency to a dead halt (Bernstein 1969, p. 177).

Workers in large-scale industries were therefore defeated in the first surge of unionizing efforts, but it was not simply because the companies they were up against were large, well organized, and treated gingerly by Roosevelt and his advisers. Union organizers also were handicapped by the fact that they were under the jurisdiction of numerous craft unions. In keeping with the principles that had led to the original success of the AFL, they had little interest in organizing the growing number of industrial workers. The organizational structure that had made the union movement successful in some business sectors was now hampering its future growth.

By December 1933, Wagner had decided that the basic principles established by section 7(a) and the Reading Formula, along with various board rulings concerning procedures for implementing them, had to be written into law outside the structure of the NRA (Bernstein 1950, p. 62). To that end, he held a meeting in early January with labor leaders and a lawyer from the Department of Labor to decide what topics would be covered. This meeting began a process that led to an eventual defeat for the corporate moderates, so it is important to note that the following account of it makes use of new archival findings that were not available until 2011, and were either not generally known or not taken seriously by most social scientists and historians as of 2019.

Although no employer representatives were present at that first meeting to plan for new labor legislation, it did not take long for Hicks of Standard Oil of New Jersey and the Special Conference Committee to write Wagner on January 16, saying that he liked section 7(a) as written because in many cases workers did need unions. However, he did not like the possibility that section 7(a) would be modified at labor's request so that employee representation plans would be forbidden because they were allegedly company dominated: "I have noticed, however, that the A.F. of L is recommending a change in this Section which would forbid employers to cultivate friendly relations with their own employees. Such a change would in my opinion, work a great injustice to both employers and employees" (Hicks 1934a).

Hicks went on to explain that it would not be fair to allow union leaders to "have a free hand to secure members on a voluntary basis" while at the same time saying that "such men as Mr. Teagle, Mr. Swope, and Mr. Kirstein should be forbidden to encourage and cultivate cooperative relations with their own employees..." Wagner replied with a cordial thank-you letter two weeks later, but a prohibition against employee representation plans sponsored by a company nonetheless appeared in the first draft of the legislation in early February. At that point the corporate representatives on the NLB began planning a dinner meeting with Wagner for February 13, during which they hoped to convince him to adopt their plan for organizing the board for its current work, with Hicks playing an administrative role. But no changes were made on the basis of the dinner meeting.

As these maneuverings signal, the strong opposition from steel, autos, and the NAM soon led to differences of opinion within the board itself, which had been enlarged from seven to 11 members so there would always be three business people able to come to Washington at relatively short notice to deal with new cases needing immediate attention. One of those new members was BAC member Pierre S. du Pont, chair of DuPont Corporation, and a member of the then closely knit du Pont family of Wilmington, Delaware, the third-richest family of the era (Lundberg 1937, pp. 26–27). Since Pierre du Pont was the family's leader at the time and a key figure in a split in the NLB that was about to emerge, a few details on him and his family may be relevant.

The family's main corporate base was in the DuPont Corporation, which had grown very large during World War I through munitions orders from the government. It was the tenth-largest American corporation in 1933, when it earned $26 million despite the depression; by 1936, its profits were over $90 million, which is roughly the equivalent of $1.6 billion in 2018 (Zilg 1974, p. 345). Although not in favor of employee representation plans, it was a member of the Special Conference Committee. In addition, the du Pont family owned about 25 percent of the stock in General Motors, the third-largest corporation in 1933, and about 20 percent of the stock in United States Rubber, both of which were also in the Special Conference Committee. It also owned the National Bank of Detroit and the Wilmington Trust Company, and had at least partial ownership in Continental American Life Insurance, North American Aviation, and Remington Arms Company.

Although highly conservative and anti-government, the du Ponts became Democrats in the 1920s to push for repeal of prohibition, which they favored for reasons that are still disputed—maybe to make federal income taxes less necessary through the collection of taxes on alcoholic beverages, or to keep the role of the federal government in American life to a minimum, or to make sure that respect for government was not lost through the flagrant disregard for the law (Okrent 2010; Webber 2000, Chapter 2). They also were drawn to the Democrats because one of their top employees, John J. Raskob, who served as vice president for finance for both General Motors and the DuPont Corporation, backed fellow Catholic Al Smith for president in 1928, and then took over as the head of the Democratic National Committee.

Raskob and the du Ponts were opposed to Roosevelt at the Democratic National Convention in 1932, but they were pleased with the repeal of prohibition and other early New Deal measures. Then tensions gradually developed over tax and labor policies, with a special focus on the majority rule decision by the NLB. The du Ponts and their allies soon led a successful effort by ultraconservatives to install new leadership at the top of the NAM in 1934, at a point when its financial situation was very grim due to the loss of small-business members hit hard by the depression (Burch 1973). After the takeover, the du Ponts then increased the NAM's advertising and public relations budget from $36,500 in 1933 to $467,759 by 1936 (Lichtman 2008, pp. 62–63).

In May 1934, Pierre du Pont stopped making regular donations to the Democratic National Committee to help pay off its campaign debts, and then joined with Raskob in August of that year to form the American Liberty League, an ultraconservative political action group funded by a handful of multimillionaire ultraconservatives. The league immediately began media attacks on the New Deal based on traditional ultraconservative, market-fundamentalist principles. In 1935, it published and disseminated more than 135 different pamphlets to members, newspapers, and universities. It also supported numerous radio broadcasts and recruited college students and conservative professors in an effort to publicize its cause. In addition, it supported legal challenges to the constitutionality of most New Deal legislation through a lawyer's committee headed by the general counsel of U.S. Steel (Lichtman 2008, pp. 70–71). Needless to say perhaps, it hoped to defeat Roosevelt in the 1936 elections by publicizing criticisms of him, starting with those by highly visible Democratic leaders from the past who had become disenchanted with the New Deal (Webber 2000; Wolfskill 1962).

Pierre du Pont, made his first public dissent as a member of the NLB on March 1, 1934, when the majority on the board ruled that the union or employee representation plan chosen by a majority of the employees voting in a representation election had to be recognized as the sole bargaining agent for all the employees in the plant, factory, or office. This decision, if enforced, would have cut the ground from under one of the major tactics of anti-union employers, who insisted, based on a doctrine called "proportional representation," that they had the right and duty to bargain with their company unions and individual employees as well as trade unions. Although the industrialists' claim was based on lofty arguments about the rights of numerical minorities and individuals, it was believed by most observers at the time to be a divide-and-conquer strategy that would allow them to avoid serious negotiations with unions.

For many years thereafter, Pierre du Pont was portrayed as the villain, in contrast to Teagle and Swope. For example, the former general counsel employed by the NLB, Columbia Law School professor Milton Handler, remembered du Pont as a person who tended to vote automatically for the business side in a dispute. He added that this was unlike Teagle and Swope, whom he recalled as "very, very fair-minded men and they called the shots as they saw them" (Gross 1974, p. 44). Another member of the board's staff said:

> My experience with Pierre du Pont [was] that when he spent a little time in Washington subject to discussions with us, he would be well educated to the purpose of the act and interested in carrying out its functions . . . and then he'd go back to Wilmington for two weeks . . . (listening . . . to the people in his own organization who must have told him what a horrible thing the whole 7(a) idea was) . . . and by the time he came back again, we'd have to go through the whole process all over again.
>
> (Gross 1974, pp. 44–45)

However, there is evidence that both Teagle and Swope opposed the decision as well. When the board majority attempted to use their decision in one case to "establish majority rules as a principle, Teagle called it 'an attempt to interpret the law—something which I believe should only be done on the basis of actual court decisions'" (Tomlins 1985, p. 114). Even more surprising, my findings in the General Electric Archives show that Swope also opposed majority rule. As he wrote in a letter to du Pont on February 26, he was on the panel that heard the Denver Tramways case in December, during which "the officers of the Amalgamated had at no time asked for Tramways to deal exclusively with them as representing all employees, and the contract recites that they were dealing on behalf of the members of the union who were employees of the Tramways" (Swope 1934b). Swope therefore was "heartily in agreement" with du Pont's view that the decision should say that "the Amalgamated shall represent the 353 employees who voted for them, and the representatives for whom 325 employees voted shall represent them, and the Tramways is to deal individually with the 36 employees who cast no ballot, until such time as part or all of them choose some method of collective bargaining" (Swope 1934b). He added that he had told Wagner that this was his conclusion.

March 1 was also the day that Wagner introduced his labor disputes bill into the Senate. Building on the precedent of the NLB, it called for a tripartite board of business leaders, union leaders, and individuals representing the public interest. Although several judicial functions were now included in the board's mandate, its primary focus would continue to be mediation (Gross 1974, p. 65). Every one of its specific provisions was meant to deal with roadblocks to collective bargaining that the NLB had faced in its ten months of existence (Gross 1974, p. 67). Surprisingly, both the supporters and critics of the proposed legislation were opposed to a tripartite structure and an emphasis on mediation: "The one point on which both the opponents and supporters of the labor disputes bill agreed, however, was that the experience of the NLB had proved that its partisan representation approach had failed to bring about union recognition and collective bargaining and that what was needed was an independent, neutral, quasi-judicial agency free from the necessity of compromise" (Gross 1974, pp. 65–66). Secretary of Labor Perkins favored this change, as did the general counsel of the NLB. Thus, those who wanted to allow labor unions to develop were being moved toward the model of the U.S. Mediation Board established by the Railway Labor Act of 1926 (O'Brien 1998, Chapter 8).

As far as the bill's specific provisions were concerned, the corporate moderate Swope did not like them any better than the ultraconservatives did, revealing that the differences between the liberal-labor alliance and the corporate community in general were beginning to emerge more clearly. Swope immediately wrote to one of his vice presidents at the company's plant in Schenectady on March 2 asking him what he thought:

> I suppose you saw in the paper this morning about the bill of Senator Wagner for the strengthening of the NLB and also combat the company union. Senator Wagner's statement to me was that it would not affect our so-called company unions, but the way I read this bill, I am not so sure of this. What do you think?
>
> (Swope 1934a)

The vice president quickly wrote back on March 5 saying he read the proposed legislation in the same way: "The provisions are far reaching and my feeling is like yours that they do touch the General Electric Company's various Employees Representation Plans as they operate today" (Peck 1934). By March 12 Swope had sent a rush telegram to Wagner in Washington outlining his objections to the bill and suggesting ways to change it. He first of all wanted to make sure that employee representation plans could survive by adding language that would specify that employees could be paid for the time they spent meeting with managers and that a manager would have the right to discuss "matters relating to his business" (Swope 1934c). He also thought that the act in general was unfair because it "imposes no obligations whatever on employees." Further, he did not think the board should be permitted to make decisions "without legal evidence and to proceed in disregard of ordinary rules of evidence" (Swope 1934c). In short, the corporate moderate Swope had as many reservations about the direction Wagner was heading as the ultraconservative du Pont.

While the du Ponts and NAM made plans to block any labor legislation that would strengthen section 7(a), Teagle, Kirstein, Swope, and Hicks lobbied Wagner for modifications in the draft legislation that would make it more palatable to them in case it did pass. They did so through a memorandum of suggested changes, many of them similar to Swope's comments via telegram. Teagle and Kirstein handed the memorandum to Wagner when the three of them had dinner in Washington on March 14 (Teagle 1934b). As Teagle summarized the results of the meeting in a letter to Swope the next day, "Generally speaking, the Senator expressed himself as feeling that most of the points we had made were sound and that the draft of the Bill should be modified accordingly" (Teagle 1934a).

One of the suggestions eventually accepted by Wagner, small though it may be, concerned a change in the title for his "Labor Disputes Bill." Teagle felt that the word "disputes" contained what today would be called a self-fulfilling prophecy. As the memorandum dryly noted, "some of the provisions of the law, unintentionally of course, seem to have been framed expressly to invite such industrial disagreement." Teagle's memorandum then went on to suggest that henceforth the term "labor relations" be used: "I am sure that you, as the sponsor of this measure, had quite the opposite field in mind and I, therefore, take the liberty of suggesting that the title be made "Labor Relations Act" (Teagle 1934b). (When a new board was constituted by a presidential executive order three months later, it was called the National Labor Relations Board, and the law that Roosevelt eventually signed in July 1935, was called the National Labor Relations Act.)

The memorandum made several other suggestions that were standard items in the employers' argument by then. For example, coercion by labor organizers as well as coercion by employers should be banned and efforts should be made to solve problems through cooperative means. But the sticking point in the memorandum at the dinner discussion concerned a section of the draft legislation that banned employee representation plans that had been founded and financed by companies. Teagle and Kirstein argued that the issue was domination, not origins, but Wagner held firm, at least for the time being:

> The principal point, on which the Senator seemed to be still in doubt, was as to our suggestion that on Page 5 "Section 5 (3)" [which in effect outlawed all employee representation plans] should be struck out. We had quite a debate about this, and I am sorry to say that I am doubtful whether the arguments we advanced were in themselves sufficient to convince the Senator as to the desirability of the elimination of this paragraph.
>
> (Teagle 1934a)

As the tensions increased over labor issues, Fosdick wrote an extremely revealing letter to Rockefeller on March 22, 1934, warning him that he and the IRC had to keep a very low profile because there were likely to be strong clashes with labor. Fosdick began by stressing the importance of the

IRC, but then said he had "to introduce a caveat which is not in any sense inconsistent with the enthusiasm which I have just expressed" (Fosdick 1934). He then noted, "One of my responsibilities in the 21 years I have been associated with you has been to point out possible dangers ahead in connection with your multifarious interests." By this he meant that Rockefeller and the IRC might be drawn into the class conflict between corporations and unions, which he deftly reframed and softened as "a head-on collision between the labor union and the company union." Due to these conflicts, he was "not entirely convinced that the detached attitude which we have thus far held can be maintained."

Fosdick then brought Hicks' opinion into the picture by saying that "Mr. Hicks with entire frankness has pointed out to me that the very nature of the work of Industrial Relations Counselors implies a sympathy toward the company union which as an organization we do not have toward the labor union." He then delivered the clear warning: "If this is true—and I fear it may be—it is possible that the charge might be made that you were financing an organization to fight union labor, and you might thereby be maneuvered into an uncomfortable public position." He then qualified this warning by reminding Rockefeller that "I am not saying you would be dragged in" (underlining original). Indeed, he thought it likely that "Industrial Relations Counselors might—and indeed probably can—steer clear of this fighting issue in the future as we have in the past." Fosdick then closed by saying, "I feel I have a duty, however, just to mention the possibility of unpleasantness—and with this mention I again subscribe to my belief in the value of the organization" (Fosdick 1934).

Although Hicks and Fosdick in effect suggested that the IRC lie low on union issues, Hicks and Teagle continued their individual efforts to influence the legislation. On March 26, four days after Fosdick's letter to Rockefeller, Hicks wrote another long letter to Wagner on the issue of employee representation plans, agreeing that employers initiated "practically all" of them, but denying that the employers "have in any sense dominated employees." He pointed to the higher wages paid by Standard Oil of New Jersey as evidence for this point, along with the company's willingness to accept outside arbitration when workers and management disagreed. Then he reminded Wagner that Teagle, Swope, and Kirstein felt strongly about this matter:

> Mr. Teagle tells me that he and Mr. Swope and Mr. Kirstein are agreed in feeling that these provisions would be disastrous to the plans now in operation in the companies which they represent. I know that you believe in the sincerity of these men and I hope that you will see to it that these particular provisions, which they and many others deplore, are stricken from the bill.
>
> (Hicks 1934b)

Based on this lobbying, the provisions banning all employee representation plans were removed from the draft legislation in late March. This series of events suggests that Teagle and Swope still had some leverage with Wagner, especially when it is added that amendments to the Railway Labor Act in 1934 had banned company unions.

But Teagle and Swope did not have the clout to bring about all the changes they wanted. For example, they wanted the bill to ban coercion by union organizers as well as by corporations, but that ban was rejected by the liberal-labor alliance. Most of all, in my view, they wanted to eliminate the provision for "majority rule," which required that all members of a factory or company be included in the union that received the largest number of votes. The corporate moderates insisted upon proportional representation, as explained several paragraphs ago, which meant that there might be several separate unions in the same factory, each representing different workers (Gross 1974, pp. 57–58, 89–103, 136–139).

Liberals and most union leaders agreed with the many independent observers that perceived proportional representation as a divide-and-conquer strategy on the part of the corporate community, although craft unions had their own reservations about majority rule, as discussed in detail later in the chapter. Proportional representation, as envisioned by corporate leaders, would allow Employee Representation Plans to coexist with unions, or make it possible to deal with craft unions separately from unions for unskilled workers if the corporate moderates' Employee Representation Plans lost out entirely.

At that point the conflicts over the composition of the board, its mandate, and majority rule versus proportional representation were in effect postponed. New circumstances led Roosevelt to make a decision that derailed the proposed legislation. At the moment when Wagner was dropping the elimination of Employee Representation Plans, standing firm against banning coercion by labor leaders, and insisting on majority rule, Roosevelt intervened in a conflict between the NLB and the automobile industry over unionization, which put an end to the corporate moderates' concerns for the time being. As part of Roosevelt's decision to move jurisdiction over automobile companies to a separate labor board, he rejected the principle of majority rule. It seemed to be a clear concession to the du Ponts and General Motors, and it was a great disappointment to liberals and union leaders. Roosevelt's decision meant that company unions could flourish alongside trade unions, thereby undercutting serious negotiations by employers with independent unionists (Gross 1974, pp. 61–62). If there had been any hope of restraining anti-union employers, this decision by Roosevelt seemed to kill it, at least for the time being.

Still, although it was clear by this point that Roosevelt was not supporting Wagner's proposal, there may have been more than meets the eye to Roosevelt's decision than pressure from the du Ponts and the automobile industry. First, he needed the automobile industry to lead the way to recovery; the industry had accounted for one-fourth of the increase in national payroll between January and February, 1934 and was in general, along with large steel and rubber corporations, leading the economic rebound (e.g., Levine 1988, pp. 104–106). Second, he was well aware that the AFL union could not win a strike against the powerful and well-organized automobile executives, who were widely known for their willingness to use violent methods if necessary. It may even be that some union leaders conveyed their desire to avoid a showdown to the president (Fine 1969, pp. 220–222).

Whatever Roosevelt's reasons for his decision, the moderate conservatives Teagle and Kirstein were privately pleased with it. They believed the NLB now would fall by the wayside. They were abandoning a government agency they had played a major role in creating. In effect, they were admitting that they had made a mistake in suggesting the labor board, and were glad to see that it was being undone. As Teagle wrote to Kirstein in a private note in April 1934:

> Just between you and me and the lamp-post it strikes me that the President's decision in the automobile controversy has put the Labor Board out of the running. I am sure that neither you nor I will shed any tears if such is the case.
>
> (McQuaid 1982, p. 46)

Any remaining hope for Wagner's revised legislation collapsed at this point. Roosevelt saw to it that the new draft was given to another Democratic senator, David I. Walsh of Massachusetts, whose Committee on Education and Labor proceeded to suggest legislation that was even more sympathetic to employer concerns. However, the committee's revised legislation did not include any mention of excluding agricultural and domestic labor, a glaring omission in the eyes of the wary Southern Democrats. That problem was remedied by five of the Democrats on the committee (Farhang and Katznelson 2005, p. 13). Once the exclusion of agricultural and domestic labor was in the bill, there was no further mention of the issue by either supporters or opponents of the bill. Industrial workers were the focus of the floor debate and the amendments that were offered. Despite the many amendments that were added, the NAM, Chamber of Commerce, Special Conference Committee, and industrial trade associations worked to make sure that even this tepid legislation did not pass. As part of their effort, they brought in large numbers of employees from several different companies with employee representation plans to testify to their satisfaction with the plans, which Cowdrick thought to be the most influential statements heard by the Senate (Senate 1939, p. 16807).

Corporate executives who supported employee representation plans were especially vigorous in their criticism. Arthur H. Young, identified earlier as the former director of the IRC as well as the vice president for industrial relations at U.S. Steel, criticized the bill as "in its entirety both vicious and undesirable because of its fundamental philosophy as to the certain and complete clash of interest as between employer and employee" (Stark 1934, p. 1).

The refusal by the corporate moderates to accept majority rule in March 1934, when they still had control of the overall legislative and administrative situation, encapsulates the complex change in class forces that had occurred over the previous four to six years. At the surface level, the corporate moderates had an obvious concern to protect the employee representation plans they had established in their various companies. At a deeper level, they were committed to proportional representation because it allowed them to deal with craft workers separately from industrial workers, thus helping to maintain the segmentation of the working class. Proportional representation had been the basis for the agreement between big business and organized labor during World War I, because it allowed the craft-oriented AFL to look out for its workers while leaving industrial workers to the tender mercies of their anti-union employers. In suggesting a similar board in 1933, the business leaders were assuming that AFL leaders once again would accept the same sort of cross-class bargain (McQuaid 1979; McQuaid 1982).

But AFL leaders were no longer willing to accept this bargain, as they once did as members of the temporary War Labor Board during World War I. They now realized they could not defeat most corporations without stronger government backing. In particular, and as noted earlier in this chapter, Lewis and Hillman wanted to organize industrial unions outside their own industries. Lewis was determined to organize the steel workers because the steel companies would not allow him to organize the coal miners in the many mines they owned. These "captive mines" left the United Mine Workers completely vulnerable to the employers, who had almost destroyed the union in the 1920s, so Lewis was determined that such a near-catastrophe would not happen again (Dubofsky and Van Tine 1977; Johnson 1970).

Hillman had his own similar strategic reasons to support industrial unions. He needed to organize textile workers to protect his clothing workers union. As the textile companies accelerated their move to the South to undercut the unionization of some of their northern mills, cut labor costs, and be closer to the source of their cotton, Hillman feared that the garment companies would soon follow suit and thereby destroy the ACW. In terms of replacement-cost theory, Lewis and Hillman's change in their stance toward proportional representation reflected their realization that their unions were not strong enough to raise replacement costs high enough to deal with large, anti-union industries.

114 The Rise and Fall of Labor Unions

If it were only a matter of Lewis and Hillman in coal and garments, perhaps the corporate moderates might have conceded the point on majority rule, although the du Ponts, the steel industry, the textile industry, and Northern ultraconservatives would have objected mightily, and the Southern Democrats might have filibustered. However, there was an even more serious issue facing the entire corporate community: the growing unity and militancy among white craft and industrial workers, especially in steel, rubber, autos, and other heavy industries.

The idea of collective bargaining was acceptable to the corporate moderates if it was voluntary and involved craft workers, but not if it was mandatory and contained the potential for uniting all workers. True enough, there is a small amount of evidence that some business leaders, usually in highly competitive sectors containing many small companies, could see the benefits of unions in helping to limit competition among businesses by enforcing a minimum wage scale. However, even the historian who presses this point the furthest concludes that in the final analysis almost all business owners rejected unions as a threat to the right to manage their enterprises exactly as they pleased (Gordon 1994, p. 238). At the most general level, then, the problem boiled down to the fact that virtually no corporate leaders, whether moderates, ultraconservatives, or those with small businesses in highly competitive sectors, wanted the government to have the power to aid in the creation of a fully organized working class (e.g., Skocpol 1980, p. 181).

The rejection of majority rule by the corporate moderates meant that the president and Congress, not corporate executives, would decide labor policy in the near term. They would do so in the context of labor militancy on the one side and a corporate willingness to use physical attacks to resist unionization on the other, as exposed in great detail by Senate hearings in late 1936 and early 1937 (Auerbach 1966). Roosevelt, as a member of the labor board for naval shipyards in World War I, and a participant in a few discussions at the National Civic Federation in the 1920s, was most closely identified with those corporate leaders who favored a conciliatory, although partial and paternalistic, approach toward workers. He also slowly came to agree with the growing number of labor-relations experts from several different schools of thought, including Commons and several of his former students, who had concluded stronger unions were necessary to limit corporate power, based on their experience during the previous two years (Manza 1995, pp. 147–149, 156–173, for detailed evidence on this point).

As Roosevelt's decision to give the automobile industry its own labor board clearly showed, however, he was willing at the least to make temporizing decisions that reflected the complex balance of issues and political alliances at any given moment. Francis Biddle (1962, p. 220), a corporate lawyer who served as chair of a temporary National Labor Relations

Board established by executive order in 1934, reflecting many years later on Roosevelt's approach to labor conflict, admiringly concluded that he had "a strong sense of the incidence of power..."

Although Roosevelt, most corporate leaders, and top AFL craft-union leaders surely understood this shifting power equation, they probably did not fully grasp the growing militancy of a significant number of industrial workers or the increasing acceptance of trade unionism by Congressional liberals and labor-relations experts, which of course fed on each other. The corporate policy-planning network had helped to legitimate an idea—collective bargaining—and create a government agency—the National Labor Board—that were fast taking on lives of their own, although it might be more accurate to say that these ideas had gained new supporters in the face of corporate resistance to a governmental role in shaping the economy, and through the realization by some members of the liberal-labor alliance that they needed a new approach to the problem they faced. Put another way, the moderate conservatives had lost control of the concept of collective bargaining to liberals and industrial unionists. In 1935, Senator Wagner, Lewis, Hillman, the lawyers for the NLB (most of them law school professors or corporate lawyers), and prominent labor-relations experts came to the center of the stage to fight for an improved version of the labor board that corporate moderates in the Rockefeller labor-relations network had created and then abandoned.

Roosevelt's decision to establish an automobile labor board, in conjunction with the watering down and forthcoming defeat of the 1934 version of Wagner's bill, was deeply disheartening to militant unionists, many of whom felt they had been betrayed by the Democrats. It thereby gave activists inspired by Marxism their opening. The result was a series of violent strikes that broke out in April and May in San Francisco (where Communists joined with syndicalists and independent radicals to lead the way), Toledo (where small Marxist groups sparked the confrontation), and Minneapolis (where Marxist-Leninists who followed Leon Trotsky had the lead role) (see Brecher 1997, for a detailed discussion of these strikes, which includes a full accounting of leftist leadership and police violence). Importantly, the fact that the corporate community and the Senate rejected the first version of Wagner's bill at a time of high militancy undercuts claims that the corporate leaders were afraid of a working-class uprising by this point.

For all the tensions and calls for repressive force by the ultraconservatives, Roosevelt was able to deal with all three of these serious upheavals when they reached the boiling point that summer by sending special mediators to bring the adversaries to the bargaining table. Temporary arrangements acceptable to both sides were hammered out after several deaths, scores of injuries, and hundreds of arrests (Bernstein 1969, Chapter 6). Despite all this violence and the militancy of the striking workers, Roosevelt might have put aside labor legislation entirely. But he faced a problem that could not be easily handled, the threat of an industry-wide steel strike in mid-June, which might slow economic recovery as well as lead to more violence. The strike was first proposed by a small group of leftist labor leaders, who had taken over several moribund locals of the Amalgamated Association of Iron, Steel, and Tin Workers. It was then agreed to by the union as a whole in mid-April as a last resort if the steel companies would not bargain with it. As the steel companies prepared for physical conflict by stocking munitions, putting up barbed wire fences, and hiring extra employees, the top AFL leadership was able to head off the strike, which the union almost surely would have lost, by convincing Roosevelt to set up an impartial committee to mediate the dispute (Bernstein 1950, pp. 76–77). Once again, leftist activists, including Communists, had forced an issue that Roosevelt did not want to face and that most labor leaders thought would be too risky in terms of organizational survival.

Still, the near-collision in steel was enough to convince Roosevelt that he needed a temporary labor board to handle unexpected disputes. A temporary board also might buy him the time he needed to see if the National Recovery Administration would be able to bring back economic prosperity. The result was a Public Resolution, created by Roosevelt on the basis of suggestions from lawyers in the Department of Labor, which Congress immediately adopted in late June. It gave the president the power to appoint a National Labor Relations Board that would have what corporate leaders felt confident were very limited powers. Young of U.S. Steel and the IRC, who had made the spirited attack on Wagner's proposed legislation two months before, wrote a private memo expressing his pleasure with the outcome, suggesting that victory could be declared:

> I view the passage of the joint resolution with equanimity. It means that temporary measures that cannot last more than a year will be substituted for the permanent legislation proposed....I do not believe there will ever be given as good a chance for the passage of the Wagner Act as exists now, and the trade is a mighty good compromise. I have read carefully the joint resolution, and my personal opinion is that it is not going to bother us very much.
>
> (Bernstein 1950, p. 81, ellipsis in the original)

However, Young may have misunderstood Roosevelt's perspective on labor issues. As Roosevelt wrote to one of his most trusted advisers, Harvard Law School Professor Felix Frankfurter, in August 1934, his long-term goal was to salvage the National Industrial Recovery Act's provisions for "(1) minimum wage, (2) maximum hours, (3) collective bargaining, and (4) child labor," which would require legislation that could pass muster with a Supreme Court dominated by eight former corporate lawyers (four ultraconservatives, two moderate conservatives who provided the swing votes, and two liberals); Frankfurter then passed this information along to Justice Louis Brandeis, one of the two liberals, in a handwritten note (Davis 1986, p. 517).

Moreover, the new temporary board proved to be more important than Young expected. Although it lacked the authority to enforce its own decisions, as well as any specific provisions that would have led to strong opposition by the corporate community, Roosevelt had decided to make it possible for the board to move in the more legalistic direction advocated by the friendly critics of Wagner's recent failed legislative effort. He instituted "an impartial board of three full-time paid neutrals" that would focus on administration (Gross 1974, p. 77). In the context of the U.S. Mediation Board created by the Railway Labor Act of 1926, this decision may have involved an acknowledgment that the Progressive Republicans, who were his ardent supporters on most domestic issues, had created some important precedents that might prove useful.

The new board's chair was Lloyd K. Garrison, a corporate lawyer who started his career in the early 1920s with one of the most prestigious firms in New York, and was the dean of the law school at the University of Wisconsin at the time of his appointment. After meeting with the other two appointees (a former Commissioner of Labor for the state of Massachusetts, and an economics professor who was a well-known labor mediator and the current president of the American Economic Association), Garrison announced the board would forego any form of mediation and take a legalistic direction, with a focus on making binding decisions (Gross 1974, p. 77). With the aid of a staff of young lawyers, some of whom were law school professors, others fresh out of law school, the board began to create the case law on labor issues that eventually provided part of the basis for a stronger version of the National Labor Relations Act in 1935.

Among other things, Garrison was a strong opponent of proportional representation. A year later he wrote that "I have never yet seen a case in which these arguments were advanced by a bona fide minority group generally concerned with negotiating a collective agreement applying to all" (Bernstein 1950, p. 103n). In instituting majority rule, the board argued that it had adopted "traditional *political* forms of representation," which it thought would give the concept a public legitimacy it had previously lacked within the context of labor relations (Tomlins 1985, p. 135, my italics). But majority rule also had been instituted in the Railway Labor Act of 1926, and by 1935 Wagner had concluded it was absolutely necessary if his legislation was going to have any impact (O'Brien 1998, pp. 173, 175–176, 181–184). When Garrison resigned after several months to return to the University of Wisconsin, he was replaced by Francis Biddle, whose corporate law firm boasted the Pennsylvania Railroad as its most prominent client among several blue-chip corporations; he proved to be even more liberal and persistent on unions issues than Garrison (Bernstein 1969, pp. 318–319; Biddle 1962).

The temporary National Labor Relations Board resolved very few labor disputes, and no employer complied with its directives (O'Brien 1998, p. 190). But Garrison, Biddle, and other union-friendly corporate lawyers with a sound understanding of corporate law, were aiding the stymied efforts of the liberal-labor alliance. They were explaining—and helping Wagner craft—a strategy and set of provisions that might make it possible to control corporate power within the context of (1) long-established property laws, (2) a powerful corporate community, (3) a very conservative Supreme Court, and (4) the precedents set by the Progressive Republicans through the Railway Labor Act and the Norris-LaGuardia Act. They were far from doing the bidding of the corporate owners and managers, who wanted plant-level employee representation plans or at best a few small craft unions. They were in essence far-seeing corporate moderates who also might well qualify as liberals on this particular issue.

Shortly after the new board was formed and Garrison was appointed chair, Industrial Relations Counselors, Inc. (IRC) began printing a periodic brief Memorandum to Clients. As an inadvertent by-product of its efforts, it created a behind-the-scenes paper trail that provides a new window into the mindset of the corporate moderates, which has been used only twice in the past, and for slightly different reasons than in this and subsequent chapters (Kaufman 2003, with my thanks for making these newsletters available to me; Scheinberg 1986). The purpose of the occasional memorandums was to update a wide range of industrial relations executives on unfolding events in Washington relating to labor relations, unemployment insurance, and old-age pensions. Most of these executives were members of the Special Conference Committee or worked for the many companies related to Rockefeller interests.

These memorandums provide revealing insights into the perspectives of corporate moderates during these years, and new specific evidence that might make it possible for social scientists and historians to rethink their past conclusions on business involvement in labor legislation. Generally speaking, the memorandums are very circumspect in discussing labor issues, but at the least they prove that IRC employees were able to keep a close eye on the personnel, inner workings, and decisions of the new labor board. As demonstrated in Chapter 6, the memorandums are much more revealing of insider information on the Social Security Act, which the IRC openly supported and on which it could provide considerable detail because its employees were involved in writing it.

The first memorandum, dated July 10, 1934, provided a two-page overview of the powers of the new labor board and the backgrounds of its three appointees. Somewhat ominously, the opening paragraph noted that the president's executive order "gave it more authority than was contemplated" in the resolution passed by Congress, then went on to characterize the three board members for its clients (Industrial Relations Counselors 1934, p. 1). An accurate account of Garrison's impressive career is provided, followed by the reassuring information: "Apparently he has a pleasant personality and has favorably impressed the business men with whom he has been in contact." It further stated: "He is said to have 'advanced ideas on economics,' but not to be radical on labor questions." Similar positive comments are provided on the other two board members, who were judged to be open to established employee representation plans (Industrial Relations Counselors 1934, pp. 3–4).

Meanwhile, the "temper of the American Federation of Labor from 1933 to 1935 was one of discord, dissension, division, and disunion," and its Executive Council's minutes added up to a "military chronicle of a hundred wars within the labor movement" (Bernstein 1969, pp. 352, 354). Most of these internal arguments involved the fact that a strong majority of the leaders of the many different craft unions continued to reject the idea of organizing workers into industrial unions, despite the ongoing failure of craft forms of organizing and the presence of an activist ferment within many factories that might be capitalized upon. Bluntly stated, the craft-based organizational structure "reflected the industrial world of a half-century earlier: small shops, a simple technology, and the highly skilled workman;" by the 1930s much of American industry consisted of "great corporations, large plants, a complex technology, division of labor, and dilution of skills" (Bernstein 1969, p. 353).

For example, the head of the machinists' union was adamantly opposed to industrial unions in the automobile industry, even though virtually no machinists in it belonged to a union. If machinists in heavy industry were somehow organized into a temporary industrial union, he insisted they would have to be reassigned to his craft union at some point (Bernstein 1969, pp. 353–354, 359–365). But labor organizing went nowhere from 1934 until after the passage of the National Labor Relations Act in the summer of 1935, which again suggests that the corporate community and the New Dealers were not as afraid of labor militancy as some sociologists and historians have claimed.

Disruption or no disruption, Wagner was determined to develop legislation that would give workers the right to unionize and bargain collectively. His revised draft of the National Labor Relations Act, introduced in February of 1935, benefited greatly from the experience of the temporary board appointed by Roosevelt in the summer of 1934. It also more fully embraced the strategy advocated by Progressive Republicans in that it created a government-appointed three-person board that would make rulings on disputes over collective bargaining. The new version also may have had more legitimacy with political leaders due to the numerous speeches by Biddle, the labor board's chair, to business groups and middle-class voluntary associations across the country. He extolled the proposed legislation's sensible approach, which was based on long experience, the widely accepted principle of majority rule, and many legal precedents (Biddle 1962). Moderate and liberal lawmakers also may have been impressed, as noted earlier, by the large number of labor-relations experts from diverse schools of thought who now thought stronger unions were needed for the New Deal to succeed (Manza 1995, pp. 156–174).

With Biddle and other board members overseeing their efforts, the key provisions in the act came from the board's legal staff, led by former Harvard Law School professor Calvert Magruder (Gross 1974). Wagner's only staff member at the time, Leon Keyserling, a 24-year-old Columbia law school graduate, then put these ideas into traditional legislative language (Casebeer 1987). Keyserling is often given a little too much credit for some of the specific aspects of the act, as revealed by the archival and interview work on the origins of the NLRA by labor-relations scholar James A. Gross (1974), but he did fully understand that the Norris-LaGuardia Act provided the legal precedents that the Supreme Court would be most likely to accept (O'Brien 1998, pp. 190–191). However, there was one aspect of the 1934 version that remained unchanged. Agricultural and domestic labor was excluded with the same language that the Committee on Education and Labor introduced in 1934. And once again, there were no questions raised about this exclusion in the floor debates (Farhang and Katznelson 2005, p. 13).

The new version of Wagner's legislation, which is often called the "Wagner Act" out of respect for his reasonableness, tenacity, courage, and grasp of the relevant law statutes through his years as a justice on the New York Supreme Court in the first half of the 1920s, in effect established the National Labor Relations Board as a permanent mini- Supreme Court of labor law, which would focus on the enforcement of rights, not on mediation. Its members would be from backgrounds similar to those of the previous board's members, and this time the board would have the right to enforce its decisions. It would also determine the appropriate remedies for workers who had been fired for union activities. Moreover, the new legislation gave companies the right to appeal the board's decisions in courts of law, another necessity if the legislation were to have any chance of surviving, but which also later proved to be one key factor in its eventual undoing. The proposed legislation drew upon precedents set by earlier quasi-judicial government regulatory agencies, such as the Federal Trade Commission and the U.S Mediation Board, which had been upheld by federal courts (e.g., Bernstein 1969, pp. 323–324).

In addition, the legislation called for majority rule and gave the board the right to exercise its discretion on several issues. According to political scientist Ruth O'Brien (1998, p. 17), in a convincing analysis of the legal origins of the National Labor Relations Act, "The National Labor

Origins of National Labor Relations Act 121

Relations Board gave state managers, not organized labor or the business community, the discretion to safeguard the public interest" in a way that was fully acceptable to Progressive Republicans and very likely to a majority on the Supreme Court as well. In the process of making her argument, O'Brien (1998, pp. 5, 174) invokes sociologist Max Weber's conclusion that "legal formalism" makes it possible for the legal system to "operate like a technically rational machine," which "guarantees to individuals and groups within the system a relative maximum of freedom, and greatly increases for them the possibility of predicting the legal consequences of their actions."

However, despite the craft-union leaders' seeming acceptance of the Progressive Republicans' rationale, they became more uneasy about majority rule and two other issues (discussed shortly) within the context of an impartial board. It was one thing for them to support majority rule when a tripartite board ensured that the voice of the longstanding craft unions and their entrenched leaders would be heard, but quite another when an impartial board would be making decisions at a time when there was growing worker sentiment for industrial unions.

In addition to majority rule, craft leaders were upset by a provision that would allow the board to determine whether the workers' votes to accept or reject union representation would take place within a company as a whole, or each one of its factories, or within factory departments. This issue was discussed in terms of the "size of the bargaining unit," which could even include a whole industry. Employers as well as unions saw the size of the bargaining unit as a crucial battleground as they jockeyed for advantage. Craft unions naturally favored small, craft-dominated voting units, while proponents of industrial unions strongly preferred company-wide, or even industry-wide, voting units, and corporations favored voting units that would allow their employee representation plans to survive. The new legislation therefore gave the power to decide this issue to the board because it was more likely to be impartial (Millis and Brown 1950, p. 138, and more generally 138–146 for a full account). Then, too, the leaders of craft unions were uncertain as to how the board might view agreements that had been reached earlier between craft unions and companies, which were discussed in terms of "existing contracts."

To deal with these concerns, the AFL offered several amendments, each of which would "safeguard the freedom of the established national unions to formulate their own organizing strategy," and more generally "ensure that they received recognition as autonomous institutions with established rights" (Tomlins 1985, p. 139). But Wagner and the lawyers who worked closely with him would not accept any of the proposed amendments due to a fear that they would make it even more difficult to gain court approval in the face of the lawsuits corporations surely were going to file. Despite the rejection of their amendments, however, the craft-union leaders accepted these defeats. Empowering a permanent National Labor Relations Board as an independent administrative agency with enforcement powers still "seemed a necessary price to pay to overcome employer intransigence" (Tomlins 1985, p. 141). Once again, the overriding issue was the need to find a way to control corporate power that would be approved by a majority on a conservative Supreme Court, in spite of the many past legal precedents that the most conservative justices might invoke in order to protect corporations.

In the case of majority rule, its acceptance was somewhat more palatable for the craft unions because they would not be prohibited from continuing their longstanding exclusion of African American workers (e.g., Foner 1974, Chapter 15, for the AFL's continuing race-based exclusion of African Americans during the New Deal; Lieberson 1980, Chapter 10, for evidence of exclusion early in the century; Linder 1999, Chapter 9, for the history of exclusion). Nor was it just the craft unions several of the nascent industrial unions were still excluding African Americans at the time (e.g., Stepan-Norris and Zeitlin 2003, p. 243; Weiss 1983, pp. 163–166). The National Association for the Advancement of Colored People (hereafter NAACP) and the Urban League put forth a variety of amendments that would have prevented exclusion, such as labeling discrimination as an unfair labor practice, or stating that black workers hired as replacement workers during strikes would be protected, or even resorting to proportional representation if necessary. All of them were defeated with little or no Congressional discussion (Frymer 2008, p. 29). As early as the 1934 version of the legislation, Wagner had wanted to include a clause making closed shops legal only if they did not practice racial exclusion, but the AFL strongly opposed it, and he dropped the idea (Weiss 1983, p. 164).

Significantly, Teagle, Swope, and other corporate leaders made very little effort to influence the legislation this time around, probably because they knew that they could not have any general impact. In February 1935, Teagle sent Wagner a copy of a new booklet that Standard Oil of New Jersey had created to extol the virtues of its employee representation plan and employee benefits. Wagner replied that the booklet was "quite helpful," adding "the need for social legislation would be much less pressing than it is" if "conditions everywhere were such as described in your booklet" (Wagner 1935b). On a more important theoretical note, Swope made a successful effort to amend a section of the bill pertaining to employee representation plans by sending Wagner a letter containing language suggested by Teagle. Creating an employee representation plan would not be prohibited, but dominating or interfering in one would be illegal. In addition, language was once again added to make it possible to pay workers for the time they spent in meetings with management as officers of an employee representation plan (Swope 1935). While this language did not stop the subsequent union onslaught, it did turn out to help Rockefeller oil companies and a few other companies to retain their employee representation plans for several more years, as discussed later in the chapter.

The IRC Memorandum to Clients, No. 8, dated March 1, reported on the new version of the legislation in a descriptive and neutral tone. It included a comparison of the 1934 and 1935 drafts provided by an unnamed "client company." It noted at the outset that the legislation "creates a National Labor Relations Board with authority superior to any existing labor board or agency and with powers of enforcement far exceeding those of the present National Labor Relations Board" (Industrial Relations Counselors 1935a, p. 1).

The memorandum also contained an attachment with a list of questions and answers, beginning with the status of employee representation plans, which once again was provided by the unnamed client company. The first question asked whether an employee representation plan can still "continue to function if the bill were passed," and the answer was "yes," but only as long as "it is not dominated by the management and involves no practices ruled illegal by the bill" (Industrial Relations Counselors 1935a, attachment, p. 1). The illegal practices were then listed, including financial support beyond paying workers their wages while meeting with management. The memorandum's assured tone in claiming employee representation plans remained legal fits with the language that Wagner added to the bill at Teagle and Swope's request.

The second question in the memorandum concerned majority rule, and noted that: "The Board shall decide whether...the unit appropriate for the purposes of collective bargaining shall be the employer unit, craft unit, plant unit, or other unit" (Industrial Relations Counselors 1935a, attachment, p. 1, ellipsis in the original). (It is the phrase "other unit" that made industry-wide bargaining a possibility.)

Nor did the IRC and its corporate allies sit by while Congress was debating the final legislation. Its Memorandum to Clients for March 27, No. 9, reported that "spokesmen for employee representation plans in a number of steel plants testified before the committee March 26, asserting that many thousands of employees were satisfied with employee representation plans as a method of collective bargaining." But it also said on the basis of "advice received from Washington this morning" that the new bill was likely to pass. Again documenting IRC's concern for the preservation of employee representation plans as their only remaining possibility, the memorandum added that "it is hoped that certain amendments which have already been considered by the Senate Committee on Education and Labor will be adopted; these amendments are designed principally to ensure recognition of employee representation" (Industrial Relations Counselors 1935b, p. 8).

Although the hoped-for amendments were adopted, Cowdrick and the Special Conference Committee nonetheless coordinated an all-out battle

124   The Rise and Fall of Labor Unions

against the act, a fact revealed in documents subpoenaed by a Senate investigating committee (Auerbach 1966; Senate 1939, pp. 16806–16809). No business sector or visible corporate leaders supported it. Most of the favorable testimony came from Garrison, Biddle, and others who had worked for earlier incarnations of the labor board. The act also had public support from prominent labor-relations experts, as expressed in testimony before Congress (Manza 1995, Chapter 3).

On May 14, Roosevelt refused Wagner's request to make the act "must" legislation, but the Senate nonetheless passed the bill two days later by a strong 63-12 vote. The Senate's approval, which included virtually all of the Southern Democrats, made the final outcome a foregone conclusion because the Democrats also had an overwhelming majority in the House. On May 20 the lawyers at the temporary National Labor Relations Board wrote to Wagner saying they thought it was imperative that the bill go to the White House "this week" because of "the imminence of a decision in the Schechter case, which will in all probability be adverse to the government" (Levy 1935). In other words, the lawyers at the temporary National Labor Relations Board expected the NRA to be declared unconstitutional, which would eliminate the foundation for labor relations in section 7(a).

Nevertheless, Roosevelt still tried to make changes in the legislation from behind the scenes. In a meeting at the White House on May 24, which included the secretary of labor, the executive director of the NRA oversight board, an assistant attorney general, and labor leaders Green and Hillman, Roosevelt asked Wagner to consider changes in some of the act's main provisions, one of which would have allowed unions to determine the unit for collective bargaining (O'Brien 1998, pp. 198, 274, note 113). When the Supreme Court decision was announced three days later, Roosevelt decided that the new National Labor Relations Act was essential as it stood and put an end to his call for further negotiations (O'Brien 1998, p. 198).

The certain passage of the National Labor Relations Act once Roosevelt expressed his support for it was the final straw for most corporate leaders, who had become increasingly uncomfortable with the direction the New Deal was taking. They had expressed their dissatisfaction in early May by replacing a corporate moderate as the president of the Chamber of Commerce with an ultraconservative, who made fiery speeches about the perfidy of the New Dealers. From that point forward most corporate leaders were in all-out revolt against New Deal policies, with the important exception of the Social Security Act, as explained in two chapters in Part 2. Young of IRC and U.S. Steel was so incensed by the act that he delivered a rant to the audience at a banquet on May 24, at which he received a gold medal from the American Management Association for "his outstanding and creative work in the field of industrial relations." Young told those assembled that he would "prefer to go to jail or receive a conviction as a felon and yet be true to the principles of peaceful cooperation in industry," than to accept any provision of the National Labor Relations Act. He further asserted that the act was being "imposed on us by demagogues" (NYT 1935).

The Supreme Court decision on May 27 created a potential stumbling block that had to be removed before the vote on the new act took place. The justices had declared that the act enabling the National Recovery Administration was both an impermissible delegation of congressional power to the president and an overreach on the power that Congress had to regulate commerce, *unless* a direct impact on interstate commerce could be demonstrated. Concerned by the substance of the court's ruling, Wagner asked that the House delay its vote so he could change the preamble to the labor act in light of the court's argument. The new preamble omitted any appeal to the general welfare clause of the constitution. It focused on the fact that the failure of employers to recognize and bargain with unions was a major cause of strikes, which stopped the production of goods intended for interstate commerce, and therefore had a very direct effect on the flow of goods beyond single states (Bernstein 1950, pp. 120–122; Cortner 1964, pp. 82–83). The revised bill passed the House by a voice vote and then was supported once again in the Senate.

Two days before Roosevelt signed the new legislation on July 5, IRC's Memorandum No. 13 provided a summary of the bill, along with a criticism of it for its efforts to upend employee representation plans:

> Many provisions of this act are clearly intended to prevent not only coercion but also any active interest on the part of the employer in the matter of collective bargaining so far as it concerns employees. It may fairly be stated that the act encourages the organization of outside unions and discourages employee representation plans.
> (Industrial Relations Counselors 1935c, p. 1)

The memorandum further claimed that union organizers were using the act to argue that employee representation plans had been "outlawed," but the memorandum then reminded readers that:

> The bill states otherwise, and employers and employees should bear in mind that employee representation plans are specifically named in the act as a recognized form of "labor organization for dealing with employers concerning grievances, labor disputes, wages, rates of pay, hours of employment, or conditions of work," and employers and employees should be prepared to maintain before the Labor Board and in the courts their right to continue friendly relations.
> (Industrial Relations Counselors 1935c, pp. 1–2)

126 The Rise and Fall of Labor Unions

The memorandum then urged employers to "study carefully the list of five specified unfair labor practices and under advice of counsel instruct all connected with management to refrain from any statements or actions which could be construed as coming within that list" (Industrial Relations Counselors 1935c, p. 2). It next presented six steps that needed to be taken to assure that an employee representation plan could not be banned because it was deemed to be employer-controlled. They included employee-controlled elections, separate meetings of employee representatives in addition to their meetings with management, statements by employee representatives to fellow employees assuring them that the organizations were independent of management, and the withdrawal of any company subsidies to the organizations.

Clearly, the IRC was not prepared to give up on its employee representation plans. In fact, the memorandum argued, "genuine employee representation plans should be strengthened rather than weakened by this legislation" (Industrial Relations Counselors 1935c, p. 2). But in spite of all the hope and effort on the part of IRC and the members of the Special Conference Committee, the union movement overwhelmed most employee representation plans in 1937, quickly winning the support of most of the two million members enrolled in these plans. However, Standard Oil of New Jersey and several other Standard Oil companies were among the relative handful of companies that were able to maintain their employee representation plans. As late as 1962, when the Industrial Relations Section at Princeton last supported a study, there were still 1,400 "single-company" unions, as employee representation plans were called at that point.

Most of them were descendants of earlier employee representation plans, representing 400,000 workers. (To put these numbers in perspective, there were about 16.0 million members in independent unions at that time.) Single-company unions were "the dominant form of labor organization in the chemical industry and close to being so in the telephone and petroleum industries," which means that the employee representation plans at companies such as DuPont, AT&T, and Standard Oil of New Jersey were able to hold on by offering higher salaries and better employee benefits than in most industries (Shostak 1962/1973, p. 1). So Rockefeller's efforts had not been totally in vain (Jacoby 1997, Chapter 5, for a general account of company unions after the New Deal).

Meeting shortly after Roosevelt signed the act, members of the Special Conference Committee reaffirmed their decision, already made two months earlier, to challenge its constitutionality. They asserted that it "is generally agreed among industrialists and their legal advisers that the Wagner Act is unconstitutional as applied to manufacturing industry" (Senate 1939, p. 16809). They also stressed that the behavior of corporations should look good in the eyes of the general public. Executives should make themselves more accessible to newspaper reporters. "Industrial relations" and "public relations" were declared to be interdependent, which shows once again that a concern with public image arose within the corporate community well before the television era, the Internet era, or the social-media era (Senate 1939, p. 16850).

The major question that must be answered by any theory attempting to demonstrate corporate dominance is how an act so vehemently opposed by organized business groups could pass so easily despite their very large lobbying effort. For some social scientists, the passage of the act shows that corporate leaders had lost whatever power they once had in Washington. For others, the increased unity and militancy of the working class forced a worried corporate community and a timid New Deal to accede to labor demands. For still others, it was a joint effort by corporate moderates and AFL leaders to limit the rise of leftist leadership in the labor movement.

But any emphasis on fear-driven concessions or a general loss of power by the corporate community is first of all contradicted by the way in which the same Senate and House that passed the National Labor Relations Act treated other liberal legislation, namely, public utility regulation and changes in the Federal Reserve System. To begin with, the bankers who controlled many of the utility companies through holding companies were successful in removing the most stringent forms of utilities regulation (e.g., Parrish 1970). One historian concludes that the House was rebuking Roosevelt through this vote because a majority of its members were "annoyed at what they considered Roosevelt's undue hostility to free enterprise" (Patterson 1967, p. 56). Then, too, the proposed reforms in the Federal Reserve Act were changed so that New York bankers retained some of their traditional power through the Open Market Committee, and the act ended up acceptable to the American Banking Association (Schlesinger 1960, pp. 300–301). Most of all, the severe limits that Southern Democrats and their allies were able to place on labor legislation is demonstrated by the fate of the Fair Labor Standards Act of 1938 in the even more liberal Congress that was elected in 1936.

The New Deal's Last Gasp

The Fair Labor Standards Act of 1938 set federal standards for maximum hours and a minimum wage, and abolished child labor as well. It was resisted for over a year when it was first introduced in May 1937, in the context of ongoing battles over union organizing drives and the aftermath of Roosevelt's attempt to add more justices to the Supreme Court in the hopes of making it more liberal.

Southern Democrats, emboldened by their successes in 1937 and early 1938 in defeating the anti-lynching bill, the Court-packing plan, executive reorganization, and regional planning authorities ("the seven little

TVA's"), and deeply upset by the sit-downs in the North and by attempts by the Congress of Industrial Organizations (CIO) to organize integrated textile unions in the South, led the vigorous opposition to the law. Southern business leaders therefore opposed the Fair Labor Standards Act, this time led by the lumber interests, which spent $200,000 annually lobbying against it. Most Northern industrialists also opposed the act, although a few of them actually supported it in the hope that it would protect them from cheap labor competition from the South. However, the corporate moderates had no stake in this legislation, and there were too few ultra-conservative Republicans in the Congress at the time to matter, so the real battles were between Southern conservatives and the liberal-labor alliance.

As a result of Southern power, the wage floor was very low, 25 cents per hour, with yearly increases of 5 cents per year to a limit of 40 cents (Wright 1986, p. 219). Almost 20 percent of Southern industrial workers earned below the new minimum as compared to fewer than 3 percent in the rest of the country, and the new law affected 44 percent of Southern textile workers but only 6 percent in the North. Organized labor not only supported the act on principle, but also out of fear that the low Southern wage rates might begin to undermine their relatively successful efforts to raise wages in the North (e.g., Biles 1994, p. 100; Kennedy 1999, pp. 344–346). The final legislation was riddled with exemptions and exclusions, particularly for agricultural workers and women workers; 22.8 percent of male workers, including many nonwhite workers, were excluded, along with 42.2 percent of the female workforce (e.g., Biles 1994, p. 100; Mettler 2002, p. 248).

Moreover, Congress kept the power to adjust minimum wages for itself rather than giving it to the secretary of labor, as the draft legislation proposed. This power made it possible for the conservative coalition to allow the minimum wage to decline in real dollars for years at a time from 1939 onward, with the exception of the 1960s. Even with its limitations, however, the Fair Labor Standards Act was a major accomplishment for the Roosevelt Administration and the liberal-labor alliance (Leuchtenburg 1963 pp. 261–263; Smith 2007, pp. 408–409). But its limitations were a harbinger of the harsh treatment that labor legislation would receive in the future.

Why, Then, did Congress Pass the National Labor Relations Act?

Based on the way in which conservative Democrats in Congress limited other reforms between 1935 and 1938, it seems likely that the National Labor Relations Act was a unique piece of legislation even for a liberal Congress, which means it is not possible to explain its passage with generalities such as a general "loss of business power." Nor does it seem likely that the labor militancy of the spring and summer of 1933 and 1934 can

Origins of National Labor Relations Act   129

provide an explanation because the 1934 version of the National Labor Relations Act was defeated in the midst of that militancy. Moreover, there was relatively little militancy in the following year, when the new—and stronger—version did pass.

It is much more likely that liberals and labor leaders were able to pass this legislation for very different reasons than are usually put forth. First and foremost, the liberal-labor alliance was able to convince most moderate and conservative Democrats in Congress to vote for the act willingly by excluding agricultural and domestic labor from its purview. This purposeful exclusion meant that the great bulk of the Southern workforce would not be covered, making it possible for Southern Democrats to support the legislation (cf., Farhang and Katznelson 2005). The exclusion of farm labor also made it easier for the Progressive Republicans of the Midwest and West (who were often critical of corporations and always supportive of agriculture) to vote for the act. Translated into class terms, the exclusion of agricultural and domestic workers meant that the plantation owners and related agribusinesses did not have any direct stake in opposing the act. In other words, the corporate leaders did not lose power in general, despite the calamity of the depression. Instead, they lost on this issue because their key allies, the plantation owners and Southern Democrats, did not stick with them.

Wagner understood the necessity of this exclusion. As far back as the debate over the National Industrial Recovery Act, he had insisted that the act did not cover agricultural labor, and he had seen the 1934 version of his anti-lynching bill die without even making it out of committee. That is, he fully realized that Southern Democrats still controlled the Democratic Party and Congress despite the large majority of Democrats from the North and West. He knew that Southern Democrats would not be reluctant to use the filibuster in the Senate if all else failed, as they did against later versions of the anti-lynching bill. When the leader of the Socialist Party, Norman Thomas, wrote to Wagner to complain about the exclusion of farm labor, Wagner replied as follows on April 2, 1935, a month before the bill was voted on in the Senate:

> I am very regretful of this, because I should like to see agricultural workers given the protection of my bill, and would welcome any activity that might include them. They have been excluded only because I thought it would be better to pass the bill for the benefit of industrial workers than not to pass it at all, and that inclusion of agricultural workers would lessen the likelihood of passage so much as not to be desirable.
>
> (Wagner 1935a)

The importance of satisfying Southern Democrats is also seen in an interview many years later with Keyserling, the Columbia Law School graduate and Wagner employee who helped craft the National Labor Relations Act to meet likely objections by members of the Supreme Court. As he told the interviewer, Secretary of Agriculture Henry Wallace did not want to include farm labor because "[h]e was entirely beholden to the chairmen of the agricultural committees in the Senate and House, who were all big Southern landowners like Senator Smith and Congressman Bankhead" (Casebeer 1987, p. 334). Moreover, Keyserling knew whereof he spoke from his lived experienced. His father was one of the major cotton growers in South Carolina, the state in which he grew up.

The National Labor Relations Act also passed handily because it was ultimately acceptable to the centrists and liberals who controlled the executive branch on this issue, meaning Roosevelt, Perkins, and the corporate lawyers and law professors who worked for the temporary National Labor Relations Board. Although Roosevelt and Perkins originally had little use for unions, and preferred governmental paternalism through legislation protective of workers, they believed through long experience that unions were a safe and sensible method for dealing with workers. And from the point of view of moderate and liberal corporate lawyers, the act had a very respectable regulatory pedigree that had worked well for the corporate community in the past, including the Interstate Commerce Commission, the Federal Trade Commission, the Securities and Exchange Commission, and the Railroad Labor Board, all of which had been accepted by the Supreme Court. From an historical perspective, the New Deal's collective-bargaining legislation "gathered up the historical threads and wove them into law" (Bernstein 1950, p. 18).

Third, the legislation passed because of the newly developed electoral cohesion between the native-born craft workers and predominantly immigrant and African American industrial workers in the Northern working class, who began to vote together for Democrats in the early 1930s, helping to overcome to some extent the divisions that had existed since at least the 1880s (e.g., Mink 1986; Stepan-Norris and Zeitlin 2003). Many of them also worked together in an effort to create industrial unions in heavy industry, and almost all of them supported union leaders and liberal elected officials in their efforts on behalf of the National Labor Relations Act. As already shown, some of the most important craft-union leaders in the AFL had reservations about the act because they knew it would put them at the mercy of labor-board decisions on voting procedures and on the determination of the size of bargaining units. However, they backed passage of the act even though none of their suggested amendments to the proposed legislation was incorporated, and they were at least somewhat assuaged by the fact that their exclusion of black workers in construction and other trades would not be challenged (Frymer 2008, pp. 25–29; Tomlins 1985, pp. 139–140).

Finally, the National Labor Relations Act passed because Roosevelt had entered into a political alliance on this issue with leaders of the industrial segment of the working class, which had gained his attention through the disruptions its activists and leaders had been able to generate. That is, the key labor leaders on this issue were Hillman and Lewis, precisely the people that would create the new movement for industrial unions after the passage of the act. Furthermore, a range of labor-relations experts had reassured Roosevelt that experience had shown that stronger unions provided the best hope for limiting corporate power, although he did try to make changes in the days before he finally gave his assent.

Roosevelt faced a choice between trade unions regulated by the government and the continuing use of force to repress militant labor activists in the face of provocations and violent physical attacks by private police squads employed by members of the corporate community. As far and away the most important leader of the new liberal-labor alliance, as well as the most cautious and enigmatic, Roosevelt chose unions over periodic violence and property destruction of the kind that had first broken out in 1877. But he only did so after the liberal-labor alliance proved that it could produce a voting majority in Congress that included the Southern Democrats, and after his own attempt at last-minute amendments had failed.

In summary, then, the National Labor Relations Act passed for a confluence of reasons, starting with the fact that the Great Depression led to both social upheaval and a united working class, which in turn led corporate moderates to suggest a new government institution that soon took on a life of its own—in the sense that liberals, a handful of corporate lawyers serving in government, labor leaders, and labor-relations experts refashioned it to their own liking within the context of past Supreme Court decisions and the Norris-LaGuardia Act. The union leaders who spoke for the working class found allies in the liberal Democrats they had helped to elect to Congress and in the pragmatic patrician liberal they helped elect to the presidency. It was possible for the liberals and Roosevelt to work with labor on this issue because the plantation owners and large-scale farmers outside the South had been satisfied by the removal of their workforce from the purview of the legislation. Although the election of moderate-to-liberal Northern Democrats to Congress and the militancy of a united working class were necessary conditions, as rightly mentioned by most of the scholars who have studied this legislation, it was in fact the Southern Democrats that had the final say-so on this critical piece of legislation.

As shown in the next chapter, this analysis is supported by the events that followed during the three years after the act passed, all of which had to do with race relations in both the North and the South, and the desire on the part of plantation owners for complete control of labor markets in the Southern states. The wealthy Southerners turned against the act in 1937 when the new CIO unexpectedly tried to organize integrated industrial unions in the South. Their sudden and very adamant change of heart meant that the entire ownership class became united against the National Labor Relations Act.

At the same time, the AFL and CIO entered into an intra-class war, which included both the skilled/unskilled divide and a racial dimension. Thus, the working class became more divided at the same time that owners and managers North and South were becoming more united. When the Republicans gained enough seats in the House and Senate in 1938 to forge an effective conservative voting coalition with the Southern Democrats, which could stop any legislation that employers North and South did not want, the handwriting was on the wall for the development of a strong union movement in the United States. In fact, as explained in the next chapter, the outbreak of World War II and then of the Korean War were the main factors that made it possible for unions to solidify their gains by 1954, and then fend off the corporate community and the power elite for the next two decades.

References

Auerbach, Jerold S. 1966. *Labor and liberty: The LaFollette Committee and the New Deal.* Indianapolis: Bobbs Merrill.

Bernstein, Irving. 1950. *New Deal collective bargaining policy.* Berkeley: University of California Press.

———. 1969. *Turbulent years: A history of the American worker, 1933–1941.* Boston: Houghton Mifflin.

Biddle, Francis. 1962. *In brief authority.* New York: Doubleday.

Biles, Roger. 1994. *The South and the New Deal.* Lexington: University Press of Kentucky.

Brecher, Jeremy. 1997. *Strike!* Cambridge: South End Press.

Burch, Philip. 1973. "The NAM as an interest group." *Politics & Society* 4:100–105.

Burris, Val. 1992. "Elite policy-planning networks in the United States." *Research in Politics & Society* 4:111–134.

———. 2008. "The interlock structure of the policy-planning network and the right turn in U.S. state policy." *Research in Political Sociology* 17:3–42.

Casebeer, Kenneth. 1987. "Holder of the pen: An interview with Leon Keyserling on drafting the Wagner Act." *University of Miami Law Review* 42:285–363.

Cohen, Adam. 2009. *Nothing to fear: FDR's inner circle and the hundred days that created modern America.* New York: Penguin.

Conner, Valerie. 1983. *The National War Labor Board.* Chapel Hill: University of North Carolina Press.

Cortner, Richard. 1964. *The Wagner Act cases.* Knoxville: University of Tennessee Press.

Daniel, Cletus. 1981. *Bitter harvest.* Ithaca: Cornell University Press.

Davis, Kenneth. 1986. *FDR: The New Deal Years, 1933–1937* New York: Random House.

Domhoff, G. W. 1996. *State autonomy or class dominance? Case studies on policy making in America.* Hawthorne, NY: Aldine de Gruyter.

Dreiling, Michael and Derek Darves. 2016. *Agents of neoliberal globalization: Corporate networks, state structures and trade policy.* New York: Cambridge University Press.

Dubofsky, Melvyn and Warren R. Van Tine. 1977. *John L. Lewis: A biography.* New York: Quadrangle Books.

Farhang, Sean and Ira Katznelson. 2005. "The Southern imposition: Congress and labor in the New Deal and Fair Deal." *Studies in American Political Development* 19:1–30.

Fine, Sidney. 1969. "Sit-down: The General Motors strike of 1936–1937." Ann Arbor: University of Michigan Press.

Foner, Philip. 1974. *Organized labor and the black worker, 1619–1973.* New York: Praeger.

Fosdick, Raymond. 1934. "Letter to John D. Rockefeller, March 22." In *Rockefeller Family Archives, Record Group 2 (OMR), Economic Reform Interests, Box 16, Folder 127.* Sleepy Hollow, NY: Rockefeller Archive Center.

Fraser, Steven. 1991. *Labor will rule: Sidney Hillman and the rise of American labor.* New York: Free Press.

Freeman, Richard B. 1998. "Spurts in union growth: Defining moments and social processes." Pp. 265–296 in *The defining moment: The Great Depression and the American economy in the twentieth century,* edited by M. Bordo, C. Goldin, and E. White. Chicago: University of Chicago Press.

Frymer, Paul. 2008. *Black and blue: African Americans, the labor movement, and the decline of the Democratic Party.* Princeton: Princeton University Press.

Gordon, Colin. 1994. *New deals: Business, labor, and politics in America, 1920–1935.* New York: Cambridge University Press.

Gross, James A. 1974. *The making of the National Labor Relations Board.* Albany: State University of New York Press.

Hacker, Jacob and Paul Pierson. 2004. "Varieties of capitalist interests and capitalist power: A response to Swenson." *Studies in American Political Development* 18:186–195.

———. 2010. *Winner-take-all politics: How Washington made the rich richer—and turned its back on the middle class.* New York: Simon & Schustser.

Hawley, Ellis. 1966. *The New Deal and the problem of monopoly.* Princeton: Princeton University Press.

Hicks, Clarence. 1934a. "Letter to Senator Robert F. Wagner, January 16." in *Wagner Papers, General Correspondence.* Washington: George Washington University.

———. 1934b. "Letter to Senator Robert F. Wagner, March 26." in *Wagner Papers, General Correspondence.* Washington: Georgetown University.

Himmelberg, Robert. 1976/1993. *The origins of the National Recovery Administration.* New York: Fordham University Press.

Industrial Relations Counselors, Inc. 1934. "Memorandum to Clients No. 1." New York: IRC.

———. 1935a. "Memorandum to Clients, No. 8." New York: IRC.

———. 1935b. "Memorandum to Clients, No. 9." New York: IRC.

———. 1935c. "Memorandum to Clients, No. 13." New York: IRC.

Jacoby, Sanford. 1997. *Modern manors: Welfare capitalism since the New Deal*. Princeton: Princeton University Press.

Johnson, James P. 1970. "Reorganizing the United Mine Workers of America in Pennsylvania during the New Deal." *Pennsylvania History: A Journal of Mid-Atlantic Studies* 37.

Kaufman, Bruce. 2003. "Industrial Relations Counselors, Inc.: Its history and significance." Pp. 31–112 in *Industrial relations to human resources and beyond: The evolving process of employee relations management*, edited by B. Kaufman, R. Beaumont, and R. Helfgott. Armonk, NY: M.E. Sharpe.

Kennedy, David. 1999. *Freedom from fear: The American people in depression and war, 1929–1945*. New York: Oxford University Press.

Leuchtenburg, William 1963. *Franklin D. Roosevelt and the New Deal, 1932–1940*. New York: Harper & Row.

Levine, Rhonda F. 1988. *Class struggle and the New Deal*. Lawrence: University of Kansas Press.

Levy, Philip. 1935. "Letter to Senator Robert F. Wagner, May 20." in *Keyserling Papers, Labor Series, Box 1, Folder 10*. Washington: Georgetown University Library.

Lichtman, Allan 2008. *White Protestant nation: The rise of the American conservative movement* New York: Atlantic Monthly Press.

Lieberson, Stanley. 1980. *A piece of the pie: Blacks and white immigrants since 1880*. Berkeley University of California Press.

Linder, Marc. 1999. *Wars of attrition: Vietnam, the Business Roundtable, and the decline of construction unions*. Iowa City: Fanpihua Press.

Loth, David. 1958. *Swope of G. E. The story of Gerard Swope and General Electric in American business*. New York: Simon and Schuster.

Lundberg, F. 1937. *America's 60 families*. New York: Vanguard.

Manza, Jeff. 1995. "Policy experts and political change during the New Deal." Ph.D. dissertation Thesis, Sociology, University of California, Berkeley.

McQuaid, Kim. 1976. "The Business Advisory Council in the Department of Commerce, 1933–1961." *Research in Economic History* 1:171–197.

———. 1979. "The frustration of corporate revival in the early New Deal." *Historian* 41:682–704.

———. 1982. *Big business and presidential power from FDR to Reagan*. New York: Morrow.

Mettler, Suzanne. 2002. "Social citizens of separate sovereignties: Governance in the New Deal welfare state." Pp. 231–271 in *The New Deal and the triumph of liberalism*, edited by S. Milkis and J. Mileur. Amherst: University of Massachusetts Press.

Millis, Harry and Emily Brown. 1950. *From the Wagner Act to Taft-Hartley: A study of national labor policy and labor relations*. Chicago: University of Chicago Press.

Mink, Gwendolyn. 1986. *Old labor and new immigrants in American political development, 1870–1925*. Ithaca: Cornell University Press.

Moore, Gwen, Sarah Sobieraj, J. Allen Whitt, Olga Mayorova, and Daniel Beaulieu. 2002. "Elite interlocks in three U.S. sectors: Nonprofit, corporate, and government." *Social Science Quarterly* 83:726–744.

NYT. 1935. "Rather go to jail than accept Wagner Bill, says U.S. Steel executive, getting medal." P. 1 in *The New York Times*, May 25.

O'Brien, Ruth. 1998. *Worker's paradox: The Republican origins of New Deal labor policy, 1886–1935.* Chapel Hill: University of North Carolina Press.

Okrent, Daniel. 2010. *Last call: The rise and fall of Prohibition.* New York: Scribner.

Parrish, Michael E. 1970. *Securities regulation and the New Deal.* New Haven: Yale University Press.

Patterson, James T. 1967. *Congressional conservatism and the New Deal: The growth of the conservative coalition in Congress, 1933–1939.* Lexington: University of Kentucky Press.

Peck, Darius 1934. "Letter to Gerard Swope, March 5." in *General Electric Archive, Downs Collection, 898.15.1, Series 5, Box A-19a.* Schnectady: Schenectady Museum Archive.

Piven, Frances and Richard Cloward. 1977. *Poor people's movements: Why they succeed, how they fail.* New York: Random House.

Potter, David. 1972. *The South and the concurrent majority.* Baton Rouge: Louisiana State University Press.

Rockefeller, John D. 1934. "Letter to Arthur Young, February 10." In *Rockefeller Family Archives, Record Group 2F, Box 16, Folder 127.* Sleepy Hollow, NY: Rockefeller Archive Center.

Salzman, Harold and G. William Domhoff. 1983. "Nonprofit organizations and the corporate community." *Social Science History* 7:205–216.

Scheinberg, Stephen. 1986. *Employers and reformers: The development of corporation labor policy, 1900–1940.* New York: Taylor and Francis.

Schlesinger, Arthur. 1957. *The decline of the old order.* Boston: Houghton Mifflin.

———. 1958. *The coming of the New Deal.* Boston: Houghton Mifflin.

———. 1960. *The politics of upheaval.* Boston: Houghton Mifflin.

Senate, U.S. 1939. *Violations of free speech and rights of labor, Part 45: The Special Conference Committee.* Washington: U.S. Government Printing Office.

Shafer, Byron 2016. *The American political pattern: Stability and change, 1932–2016.* Lawrence: University Press of Kansas.

Shostak, Arthur. 1962/1973. *America's forgotten labor organization: A survey of the role of the single-firm independent union in American industry.* Westport, CT: Greenwood Press.

Skocpol, Theda. 1980. "Political responses to capitalist crisis: Neo-Marxist theories of the state and the case of the New Deal." *Politics & Society* 10:155–202.

Smith, Jean. 2007. *FDR.* New York: Random House.

Stark, Louis. 1934. "Steel men assail 'vicious' labor bill." P. 1 in *The New York Times,* April 5.

Stepan-Norris, Judith and Maurice Zeitlin. 2003. *Left out: Reds and America's industrial unions.* New York: Cambridge University Press.

Swenson, Peter. 2002. *Capitalists against markets: The making of labor markets and welfare states in the United States and Sweden.* New York: Oxford University Press.

Swope, Gerard. 1934a. "Letter to Darius Peck, March 2." in *General Electric Archives, Downs Collection, 898.15.1, Series 5, Box A-19a.* Schenectady: Schenectady Museum Archive.

———. 1934b. "Letter to Pierre du Pont, February 26." in *General Electric Archives, Downs Collection, 898.15.1, Series 5, Box A-19a.* Schenectady: Schenectady Museum Archive.

136   The Rise and Fall of Labor Unions

———. 1934c. "Telegram to Senator Robert F. Wagner, March 12." in *General Electric Archives, Downs Collection, 898.15.1, Series 5, Box A-19a*. Schenectady: Schenectady Museum Archive.

———. 1935. "Letter to Senator Robert F. Wagner, March 28." in *Wagner Papers, General Correspondence*. Washington: Georgetown University.

Teagle, Walter. 1934a. "Letter to Gerard Swope, March 15." in *General Electric Archives, Downs Collection, 898.15.1, Series 5, Box A-19a*. Schenectady Schenectady Museum Archive.

———. 1934b. "Memorandum to Senator Robert F. Wagner, March 14." in *General Electric Archives, Downs Collection, 898.15.1, Series 5, Box A-19a*. Schenectady: Schenectady Museum Archive.

Tomlins, Christopher. 1985. *The state and the unions: Labor relations, law and the organized labor movement in America, 1880–1960*. New York: Cambridge University Press.

Vittoz, Stanley. 1987. *New Deal labor policy and the American Iindustrial economy*. Chapel Hill: University of North Carolina Press.

Wagner, Robert F. 1935a. "Letter to Norman Thomas, April 2." in *Wagner Papers, General Correspondence*. Washington: George Washington University.

———. 1935b. "Letter to Walter Teagle, February 23." In *Wagner Papers, General Correspondence*. Washington: Georgetown University.

Webber, Michael J. 2000. *New Deal fat cats: Business, labor, and campaign finance in the 1936 presidential election*. New York: Fordham University Press.

Weiss, Nancy. 1983. *Farewell to the party of Lincoln: Black politics in the age of FDR*. Princeton: Princeton University Press.

Wolfskill, George. 1962. *The Revolt of the Conservatives*. Boston: Houghton Mifflin.

Wright, Gavin. 1986. *Old South, new South*. New York: Basic Books.

Zilg, Gerald. 1974. *DuPont: Behind the nylon curtain*. Englewood Cliffs, NJ Prentice Hall.

Chapter 3

Stronger Unions, a Weaker National Labor Relations Act, 1936–1960

Although the corporate community suffered a major defeat when the National Labor Relations Act passed, its leaders and trade associations nonetheless continued to resist unionization through a multi-pronged attack. With the Industrial Relations Counselors, Inc. (IRC) frequently reminding its clients that employee representation plans were legal if the employer did not control them, industrial relations executives restructured their plans with the hope they would find favor with their employees. Top corporate chieftains made preparations to challenge the constitutionality of the act in the Supreme Court, with a long list of corporate lawyers employed by the American Liberty League taking the lead by means of a lengthy brief they already had prepared (Shamir 1995, pp. 85–92, for the most complete list of corporate lawyers and Wall Street law firms that filed cases against the National Labor Relations Act or supported the American Liberty League). Further, they obtained injunctions to prohibit the National Labor Relations Board (hereafter usually the NLRB) from carrying out the duties assigned to it by the legislation until the Supreme Court ruled on the constitutionality of the act.

Finally, many corporations prepared for violent confrontations with labor organizers by stockpiling guns and dynamite, hiring labor spies and infiltrating union groups, organizing squads of men to attack pro-union activists, and in a few cases making contact with right-wing vigilante groups. These efforts were uncovered in Senate hearings in early 1937, which embarrassed the corporate community and put many corporations on the defensive (Auerbach 1966). Among the corporations preparing to use violence against their employees were General Motors and Goodyear Tire and Rubber, both members of the Special Conference Committee, and in good part controlled by the du Pont family (Scheinberg 1986, Chapter 7).

Labor leaders were of course elated by the passage of the National Labor Relations Act, and many workers at the plant level were inspired to make new demands, with the number of strikes increasing significantly in 1936. Although spontaneous sit-downs by workers in the rubber industry in the

138 The Rise and Fall of Labor Unions

face of wage cuts in early 1936 led to an increase in the membership of the United Rubber Workers, top-level American Federation of Labor (AFL) leaders made no immediate attempt to take advantage of the new labor act through the encouragement of massive organizing drives. Three important issues delayed organizing efforts until early 1937, which gave the corporate community ample time to put all its defenses in place.

First, there was the ongoing disagreement over the form the new unions would take, craft or industrial, which heated up within weeks after the National Labor Relations Act passed. This issue was not "resolved" until November 1936, when several unions, including one or two craft unions, defied the AFL leadership majority by forming a new Committee of Industrial Organizations (CIO) to create industrial unions. (It later changed its name to the Congress of Industrial Organizations when it broke with the AFL.) The word "resolved" is in quotes because this division in fact never healed, and thereby permanently crippled the efforts toward a union movement, as hindsight clearly tells us. In the short run, however, the outcome discussed in the following few paragraphs did allow union organizers to take advantage of the moment and create a power base that carried into the 1970s.

Lewis and Hillman, as the main leaders in favor of a new CIO, argued that large corporations could only be organized if workers with varying levels and types of skills were part of one industrial union. In doing so they pointed to the failure of most union drives in heavy industry in 1933 and 1934 and the success of their own unionization efforts. They also claimed that workers in industries such as steel, rubber, and automobiles wanted to be in one industrial union (Bernstein 1969, Chapters 8 and 9). For the leaders of traditional craft unions, ranging from carpenters to railroad engineers to photoengravers, the battle boiled down to a power struggle. The powerful craft-union leaders perceived Lewis as too ambitious for power, claiming he had been working to gain control of the AFL since 1931 (Tomlins 1985, p. 142). In their view, the argument over craft vs. industrial unions was a secondary matter. But they perhaps felt vulnerable in the face of the potential influx of previously non-unionized workers, who were more likely to be relatively unskilled immigrants from eastern and southern Europe, or African Americans (e.g., Stepan-Norris and Zeitlin 2003).

One of the most perceptive labor-relations experts of that era, William Leiserson, who had been a major figure on the original National Labor Board in 1933–1934, and was in close contact with other experts on labor relations, thought that it was in fact a power struggle. "The issue of craft versus industrial organization is quite a side issue now [and] could be easily settled by a fair compromise on the basis of the San Francisco resolution of the A.F. of L.," he wrote in a letter to a fellow labor-relations expert who was working for the New Deal. "The real issue now is a struggle for power as to who shall control the A.F. of L" (Tomlins 1985, p. 142). In the end, the basis for the strong disagreements within the AFL may have involved a complex entanglement of reasons, which may not be fully understood as yet, if it ever will be, but the sociological fact that there was a serous division is the important point in understanding the events that followed.

Even if there had been agreement within the AFL, which would have made it possible to issue charters for both craft and industrial unions, there was another difficulty that caused delay: the need for experienced organizers, who were woefully few within the AFL. Lewis decided to solve this problem in good part by reaching out to his perennial enemies in the Communist and Socialist parties, which had opposed him on many occasions in the 1920s, leading him on one occasion to have the Communist members of his union roughed up and expelled. These overtures to his former opponents, which were formally denied at the time, began with an interview Lewis gave to the Communist Party's *Daily Worker* in December 1935. They were made possible by the fact that the American Communists had quietly signaled a change in strategy by closing down their rival unions and allowing their organizers to work with the most militant local trade unionists. This change of line was formally announced in February 1936, after Moscow gave its reluctant approval. Months of negotiations with Lewis and his lieutenants then ensued, finally ending with an agreement in mid-1936. It led to the hiring of many dozens of Communist labor organizers, who were highly experienced due to their past organizing efforts. Because the Communists had to gain approval from Moscow for this new alliance, the detailed reports in the Soviet archives, opened in the early 1990s, make it possible to see the arrangement in fascinating detail from the Communist perspective (Haynes, Klehr, and Anderson 1998, pp. 53–70).

Third, Lewis and Hillman knew that they could not successfully organize large corporations run by ultraconservatives unless Roosevelt won reelection in 1936 and non–Southern Democrats retained enough seats in Congress to fend off a potential pro-employer alliance between Southern Democrats and Northern Republicans. Labor leaders also wanted to elect sympathetic governors and local officials in key industrial states such as Pennsylvania, the heart of the steel industry, and Michigan, the center of the automobile industry.

The unions were particularly concerned about a possible Republican victory because of the highly visible but ultimately futile efforts of the American Liberty League. The du Pont family and their close allies, the Pew family, which owned Sun Oil, gave nearly one million dollars to the Republicans ($18.2 million in 2018 dollars) and one-third of the Republican National Finance Committee was identified with the Liberty League (Wolfskill 1962, pp. 205–206). The du Ponts also gave another $350,000 ($6.4 million in 2018 dollars) and the Pews provided an additional $20,000 ($380,800 in 2018) to the Liberty League and other extreme right-wing groups (e.g., Webber 2000, p. 27). This money was used to supplement the Republican campaign in a variety of ways. (The Koch brothers' huge donations to Republicans in the 1980s and thereafter, along with their network of nonprofit support groups, are therefore nothing new. However, they have provided even more massive funding, to the tune of hundreds of millions instead of mere tens of millions, along with some new (libertarian) ideas on how to undermine government (MacLean 2017; Mayer 2017).)

To help win Democratic victories against the combined Republican and Liberty League efforts, labor played a major role in a presidential campaign for the first time in American history as foot soldiers for candidates and as financial contributors to campaigns. Between 1906 and 1935, the AFL had given a meager $95,000 to national political campaigns, but in 1936 organized labor contributed $803,800 to the Democratic Party and political organizations aligned closely with it, which represented 16 percent of the $5.1 million spent by the Democrats (Overacker 1937, p. 46; Webber 2000, page 116, Table 7.2). A little over three-fourths of that money came from just three unions—the United Mine Workers, the International Ladies Garment Workers Union, and the Amalgamated Clothing Workers of America. What makes these donations all the more interesting in terms of how shared enemies bring previous foes together is that Lewis had voted for President Hoover in 1932 and the leaders of the other two unions, David Dubinksy and Sidney Hillman, had voted for the Socialist Party candidate.

Contrary to any claims that Roosevelt had major backing in the corporate community, he did not have significant support in any business sector except one, the alcoholic beverages industry, which paid "its debt of gratitude to the Democratic Party" for Roosevelt's successful efforts to end prohibition by providing 5.7 percent of the party's donations of $1,000 or more (Overacker 1937, p. 487). There was no support from an alleged "capital-intensive international segment of the capitalist class," as one economic reductionist in political science insisted without looking at the systematic donation records (Ferguson 1995; Webber 2000, Chapter 4, for the full range of systematic evidence against the reductionist claims). Nor did Roosevelt receive disproportionate support from purported "proto-Keynesians" in mass-consumption industries (e.g., department stores, chain stores, manufacturers of household electrical equipment), as one historian partial to economic reductionism believes to be the case (Fraser 1989; Fraser 1991; Webber 2000, Chapter 3, for a full empirical refutation of these claims).

Instead, two different studies, using campaign contributions as an indicator of political preferences, in an election in which virtually no business executives gave to both parties, found that Roosevelt had support from only 17–20 percent of the corporate executives who gave $100 or more to either party. The first study was based on 270 corporate directors who held four or more directorships in the 250 largest banks and corporations of that era (Allen 1991). The second and more wide-ranging study used a large random sample of 960 executives and directors listed in *Poor's Register of Corporations Executives, and Directors* (Webber 2000, p. 13).

Four factors, all of which are consistent with findings by scholars who study voting patterns, were the best predictors of business support for Roosevelt: region (Southerners in most business sectors gave more to Democrats than Republicans); religion (Catholics and Jews in the capital-intensive and mass-consumption sectors were much more likely to give to Democrats than Protestants were); the size of the business (smaller businesses tended to support Roosevelt); and as already mentioned, involvement in the manufacture or sale of alcoholic beverages. Nor did Roosevelt lose any of his 1932 business backers, except the du Pont family and their key employees and close associates (Webber 2000, for detailed evidence for all the assertions in this paragraph).

Due to the strong corporate support for the Republican challenger, Roosevelt was outspent $8.8 million to $5.1 million, and most major newspapers endorsed his opponent. But he won 62.5 percent of the two-party vote, documenting once again that those with the biggest war chest do not always win and that the influence of the mass media can be greatly overstated. The ultraconservatives' appeal to traditional values, their claims that the constitution was being shredded, and their insistence that the New Deal was socialism in liberal clothing, themes that have been used by Republicans ever since, fell on deaf ears at that time. Organized labor's efforts seemed to make the difference in Ohio, Illinois, Indiana, and Pennsylvania, including "crucial local elections in the steel and coal towns of Pennsylvania and Ohio" (Dubofsky 2000, p. 157). The Democrats increased their already overwhelming margins in both the Senate and House, and also elected New Deal Democrats to the governorships in Pennsylvania and Michigan, precisely the states that the unions' leaders knew would be crucial to the success of organizing efforts.

With New Deal Democrats in key positions of power at the federal level and in Michigan, the newly hired organizers employed by the CIO targeted an automobile assembly plant in Flint, Michigan, in early January 1937, for a sit-down strike that would serve as an ideal starting point and a signal of what was to come. The automobile factory in Flint was chosen because it belonged to General Motors and was a critical link in the company's network of factories. Success would bring much of General Motors' production to a halt. Moreover, a victory over the third-largest corporation in the country was likely to bring hope to industrial workers everywhere because its profits had rebounded in 1935 and 1936, leading to $10 million in salaries and bonuses for 350 officers and directors in 1936, while its workers averaged $900 a year, well below the $1,600 that was considered to be the minimum necessary for a family of four (Zilg 1974, p. 330). Led in good part by Communist and Socialist factions in the fledgling United Auto Workers, the sit-downers held the factory for six weeks despite attacks by police, legal threats from local authorities, and demands by the owners that the liberal governor put an end to this illegal takeover of private property (Fine 1969).

All in all, this was the heroic effort it is usually said to be. However, it is too easily overlooked that stopping production long enough for it to hurt a large corporation is based on the premise that the government's legal authority and military force will not be used to remove the strikers from what is after all private property that the government is committed to protecting. In terms of a full power analysis from a corporate-dominance perspective, the essential point is that neither the governor of Michigan nor the president of the United States would accede to the corporation's demand that they enforce the owners' property rights. They thereby forced the leaders of General Motors to negotiate with the union and to suffer a major defeat at the hands of the CIO.

While the Flint drama was unfolding, the chair of U.S. Steel decided for several reasons that it was time to make a deal with the unions, starting with the fact that New Deal Democrats controlled Pennsylvania, where the company had many of its mills (Bernstein 1969, pp. 466–473; Gordon 1994, p. 229). Furthermore, the CIO's Steel Workers Organizing Committee was winning over many members of the company's employee representation plan. In effect, union organizers were building an industrial union at U.S. Steel, and elsewhere, through the employee representation plans, which of course has to be seen as ironic (Jacoby 1997, pp. 158–159; Zieger 1995, pp. 54–59).

As a result, the steel company's chair began secret meetings with Lewis that led to a signed agreement shortly after the United Auto Workers' victory over General Motors. The agreement saved Lewis from expending resources on what could have been a very long and tough battle, kept the many Communist organizers from rising to important positions in what was basically a top-down union, and provided a visible symbolic victory because U.S. Steel was still the largest industrial company in the United States. Change came easily and more completely at General Electric, where Gerard Swope and Owen Young, a director of Industrial Relations Counselors since the 1920s, were still in charge. When the workers voted to unionize, Young and Swope recognized the union immediately and began bargaining. The fact that the union was the largest of the Communist-dominated unions in the CIO made the bargaining all the more notable, but the fact that the leaders were Communists made no difference in terms of the company's willingness to deal with the union. As a result of these and other victories, the percentage of the nonagricultural workforce in unions rose from 11.5 percent in 1934 to 21.8 in 1937 and 26.6 percent in 1938 (Freeman 1998, p. 292, Table 8A.2).

By 1937 the IRC was keeping its distance from labor conflicts. As Rockefeller said in a letter to King, the creator of his employee representation plan, in late April 1937, just a few days after the Supreme Court ruled that the National Labor Relations Act was constitutional, he thought that employee representation plans "were generally doomed." Rockefeller went on to note that "the Harvester Company, the Goodyear Company, and now the subway company in New York City, have given up their industrial relations plans, which have worked successfully for many years, and are carrying on collective bargaining with the union, while the Steel Company has recognized the unions, which I assume is tantamount to the same thing." Although he did not look forward to unions "in our own companies," he did not think it "either wise or possible to withstand the pressures from outside for union recognition even though the employees themselves may prefer the present plan" (Rockefeller 1937).

However, several problems soon arose that slowed the CIO's progress. First, the ultraconservatives in the somewhat smaller steel companies were able to defeat unionization efforts in the second half of 1937, with the help of the state police in Ohio, Indiana, and Illinois, whose governors were not as sympathetic to unions as their counterparts in Michigan and Pennsylvania. The corporations also had the unanticipated necessity of having to lay off thousands of workers due to the sudden economic downturn triggered by Roosevelt's misguided decision to balance the budget. Second, a similar organizing drive in the textile industry, which was spread out over several states, was stalled later in the year for a similar combination of reasons, along with the earlier mentioned fact that many textile companies were by then located in the South. Nor did it help morale, or strengthen the resolve of those elected Democrats who supported unions, that by this point public opinion polls, which were just coming into their own on a sound social-science basis, suggested that a majority of the population was opposed to unions. As early as February 1937, for example, two-thirds of the respondents to a Gallup poll "believed that GM was right not to negotiate with the sit-downers and strong majorities sympathized with the employers" (Kennedy 1999, p. 316).

Perhaps even worse from the point of view of further union success, Southern Democrats became adamantly opposed to the NLRB because of the sit-down strikes in the North and the attempt to organize integrated unions in the South, as noted at the end of the previous chapter. The fact that the CIO organizing drives were interracial in both the North and South only added fuel to the fire. Led by Senator James Byrnes of South Carolina, one of Roosevelt's closest allies in previous years, the Southern Democrats began a series of actions within Congress that created problems for the CIO and the National Labor Relations Board. They ranged from passage of a "sense of the Senate" resolution that sit-downs were illegal to attacks on the labor board's budget (Gross 1981; Patterson 1967, pp. 135–137). The Southerners also were acting upon their growing animosity toward Roosevelt's unexpected court-packing scheme, introduced as a complete surprise on February 5, 1937. The plan stirred their fears of an eventual court attack on the Jim Crow system. More generally, the effort to hamstring the National Labor Relations Board helped to create a new conservative coalition that came to dominate Congress on labor issues in 1939 (Patterson 1967).

To make matters even more difficult for pro-union forces, the AFL became extremely bitter toward the NLRB because of its belief that the board's decisions favored the CIO. As the AFL craft leaders had feared might happen before passage of the act, the board was using its power to create large bargaining units that included workers in a wide range of occupations. AFL leaders felt from early 1937 on that the NLRB was aiding the CIO, but the decision that "could not be forgiven" occurred in June 1938, when the board ruled that the entire West Coast would be the bargaining unit for longshoremen and warehousemen, thereby eliminating the AFL in the four ports where it had small locals (Gross 1981, p. 56). Then the board voided an AFL contract because it was allegedly a sweetheart deal between the company and the AFL that was meant to keep out the CIO. AFL officials also were upset by the ruling in the Mobile Dry Dock Company case in Alabama; it allowed for plant-wide elections in which the 500 "white, highly skilled mechanics" would be outnumbered by the 1,000 African American laborers (Gross 1981, pp. 59, 85). The AFL retaliated by claiming that Communists dominated both the labor board and the CIO, which escalated their grievances with the CIO into a public political battle.

The result of Southern and AFL disenchantment with the National Labor Relations Board was a new alignment of class forces. The Southerners were once again in an alliance with a united Northern business community that had planned for amendments to the National Labor Relations Act from the day of its passage. The working class, on the other hand, was now split. Moreover, and far more surprising for scholars who focus solely on class conflict, the most conservative segments of the ownership and working classes entered into an alliance after decades of unrelenting hostility. Beginning in July 1938, leaders of the NAM began meeting in private with AFL lawyers to decide upon those amendments to the National Labor Relations Act that would best serve their common interest in thwarting the CIO (Gross 1981, pp. 67ff.). Rather clearly, this series of events is an ideal example of why both class conflicts and intra-class conflicts have to be taken seriously to have a more accurate understanding of why the American corporate rich have triumphed.

Adding further complexity to the picture, and despite its complaints about the labor board, the AFL was growing by the late 1930s in regulated industries, such as railroads and trucking, in which both owners and workers could benefit from the higher prices made possible by government oversight (Nelson 2001). Construction unions also grew in late 1939 and 1940 when the economy slowly began to revive, due in part to the rise in defense spending. In addition, the AFL made gains in service industries. By 1941 the AFL had almost twice as many members as the CIO, a fact that was masked at the time by the CIO's inflated membership claims (Bernstein 1969, p. 774). Furthermore, the 106 AFL affiliates were in a far wider range of business sectors than the 41 CIO unions, which were concentrated in mining and manufacturing, with its mining, automobile, steel, electrical, clothing, and textile unions accounting for 71 percent of its membership. But these figures were not the basis for the perceptual reality, so discourse on the strength of the CIO, encouraged by both writers that were enthusiastic about industrial unions and those who despised them, claimed that the CIO was far larger and more powerful than the AFL. And that "social fact" shaped thinking and actions at the time.

At this point the Roosevelt "Recession" of 1937–1938 entered into the equation once again, this time via the electoral system. This unexpected recession was induced by both budget cutbacks to reassure business and a concern with "excessive reserves" on the part of the Federal Reserve Board (don't ask, but it's the money that banks hold beyond what is required, and it had happened inadvertently); the net result was a 13-month economic decline, the third-worst depression of the twentieth century, exceeded only by the depressions of 1920 and 1929 (Jaremski and Mathy 2017; Waiwood 2013). As shown in detail in a study that examined the national elections throughout the 1930s, as well as making state-by-state comparisons in 1938, the rise in unemployment to a nationwide average of 20 percent was the main factor in the large gains for the Republicans in both the Senate and the House, which thereby changed the balance of power in Congress (Achen and Bartels 2016, Chapter 7). The result was a nearly unbeatable conservative coalition, at least on union-related issues, which could weaken the NLRB and slow any further union gains. Soon thereafter, the union movement received another hammer blow. The Supreme Court ruled in February 1939 that sit-down strikes were illegal, thereby depriving union organizers of a potent tactic that makes it impossible to bring in replacement workers (Gross 1981, pp. 26, 83–84).

Buoyed by the 1938 election results and the Supreme Court decision in early 1939 banning sit-downs, the political leadership that was needed to stop the drive for industrial unions was provided by a Southern Democrat in the House, Howard Smith, who also was the chair of a local bank in his hometown of Alexandria, Virginia. The new Southern Democrat/ NAM/AFL coalition greatly weakened the NLRB in late 1939 and early 1940 through damaging revelations in House committee hearings, which undermined the board's credibility and caused Roosevelt to make changes in its personnel (Gross 1981, p. 2). Moreover, it was the bill fashioned by this coalition that was the basis for the TaftHartley Act, a fact the AFL later tried to deny or ignore. As Gross (1981, p. 3) summarizes his discoveries:

146 The Rise and Fall of Labor Unions

The Hartley Bill was written in Smith's office using Smith's 1940 bill as a model, and the TaftHartley Act of 1947 contained most of the more severe provisions of the Hartley Bill. The AFL-business-conservative southern Democrat alliance during the first half of the twelve years between the Wagner and TaftHartley Acts has had a lasting effect on labor history and on labor law.

Overall union density, which had risen another percentage point to 27.6 percent by 1939, had declined to 25.0 percent by 1942. This decline suggests that the union movement—and most likely the CIO in particular—had been stalled. Moreover, the union movement might have experienced further decline if it had not been for the very large change in power relations due to World War II (e.g., Freeman 1998, pp. 269, 292, Table 8A.2).

World War II Leads to Union Growth

Based on the setbacks the CIO suffered in Little Steel and textiles in the latter half of 1937, and in Congress from July 1938, to 1940, the union movement was stalemated at best and most likely on the defensive by 1940. However, organizers were able to overcome the weaknesses of the union movement at that moment due to a very rapid increase in the defense build-up. This dramatic industrial conversion of unprecedented speed and proportions put everyone to work, including previously excluded women and African Americans. The tight labor markets that resulted made it possible for the unions to renew their upsurge. This turn of events caused Roosevelt to create a National War Labor Board (NWLB) in January 1942, which was similar to the one that had been created in the context of labor agitation during World War I. Although the National Labor Relations Board had its hands full during the war, conducting thousands of representation elections and making several thousand rulings on complaints concerning unfair labor practices, the NLWB took the lead role. It was in charge of ensuring that the industrial conversion for war production was not slowed by strikes and other labor disputes (Gross 1981, pp. 243–244).

The NWLB consisted of four employers, four union leaders, and four representatives of the general public. The retired president of Standard Oil of New York, Walter Teagle, who had a central role in both instituting and doing battle against the National Labor Relations Board, was the most visible corporate member. He was joined on the business side by a San Francisco shipping magnet, the owner of *The Washington Post*, and one of the more liberal members of the IRC network, who was employed as the director of industrial and public relations at Goodyear. Their counterparts on the labor side included the presidents of the CIO and the International Brotherhood of Railway Clerks, the secretary-treasurer of the AFL, and the secretary-treasurer of Lewis's United Mine Workers.

The most prominent public member was the president of the University of North Carolina, who served as chair. He was joined in the public group by a corporate lawyer who earlier had served under Perkins in the Department of Labor, a New York lawyer with experience as a labor mediator, and a University of Pennsylvania economist who was close to Hillman. Its executive director and chief counsel was Lloyd K. Garrison, the former chair of Roosevelt's 1934 temporary National Labor Relations Board. In early 1944 he became a member of the board itself and served as its chair during its final year of existence.

Although the corporate executives on the NWLB initially resisted rulings that would aid unions, the public and labor representatives gradually convinced them to accept a "maintenance of membership" provision through which newly employed workers would automatically be part of already existing unions in exchange for a no-strike pledge by union leaders. This agreement provided organizers with the opportunity to boost union membership from 9 million in 1941 to 15 million in 1945, an increase that would not have occurred outside the context of a two-front war against two highly militarized countries (Gross 1981, Chapter 13; Schatz 2013). By the end of 1945, union density for nonagricultural wage and salary workers was at 34.2 percent, the highest point it ever reached, because corporations could not employ their usual instruments of intimidation and repression (Freeman 1998, p. 292, Table 8A.2). At this point unions provided a large and solid base for the liberal-labor alliance, a base that endured for the next 30–35 years.

The NWLB also accepted the essence of the union agenda in terms of improving working conditions and social benefits for union members. It mandated seniority, grievance systems, vacation pay, night-shift supplements, sick leave, and paid mealtimes as standard working-class "entitlements" (Lichtenstein 2002, pp. 101–102). These decisions, along with decisions concerning the tax-free status of social benefits, which are discussed later in the chapter, set important precedents that union negotiators fought for and often won in postwar collective-bargaining sessions (Schatz 2013, for evidence and a convincing critique of the NWLB's leftist historian critics). In fact, some of the precedents set by the NWLB may have saved the unions from a rapid decline in the aftermath of crippling postwar alterations in the National Labor Relations Act, as explained later in the chapter.

The Corporate Community and Wartime Mobilization

But it was not only the unions that benefited from the needs of the federal government during World War II. The corporate community, with the Business Advisory Council playing a central role in placing corporate executives in key positions, increased its direct involvement within the government as the leaders of the industrial conversion to a war-based economy (Domhoff 1996, Chapter 6; Holl 2005; Waddell 2001). In leading this effort, corporate executives defeated the liberal-labor alliance on virtually every administrative and legislative issue that arose, even when Roosevelt made the final decision.

Moreover, members of the BAC, with a major assist from the secretary of commerce, an extremely wealthy Texan, created a new policy-discussion group in 1942 that went on to formulate the economic policies that prevailed in the early postwar era. This organization, the Committee for Economic Development (CED), provides an ideal window into the mindset of the corporate moderates during and after World War II. Its published policy statements, along with letters and memos in its archives, reveal how corporate moderates dealt with ultraconservatives, the liberal-labor alliance, and government officials in the years of its strongest influence, from the late 1940s to the early 1970s.

The CED's primary focus at its outset was an effort to create moderately conservative policies that would help to guard against the return of depression-era economic conditions after World War II ended. It enjoyed several successes during and after the war on issues having to do with social-insurance benefits and foreign economic policy, which will be discussed at appropriate places in chapters in Parts 2 and 3. Most importantly, it created a business-friendly version of Keynesian economics, which soon won the day and was later chronicled as a "fiscal revolution in America" (Stein 1969/1996). These policy preferences came to be known as "business" or "commercial" Keynesianism (Collins 1981).

The CED's version of Keynesianism is best understood by contrasting it with the liberal Keynesianism that already had been crafted by American economists working closely with the liberal-labor alliance. The liberal Keynesians advocated the management of future economic downturns through tax cuts for middle-income and lower-income workers, the provision of government jobs, and increases in government spending. On the other hand, they wanted to head off periods of inflation by raising taxes on the well-to-do and cutting government expenditures, which would decrease buying power and at the same time provide enough of a government surplus to pay down the federal debt.

CED trustees opposed these liberal-labor policy preferences without at the same time embracing the ultraconservatives' economic orthodoxy about balancing the budget each year. In the interest of limiting the expenditures called for by liberal Keynesians as much as possible, the CED suggested its own formula for a "stabilizing budget policy." It prescribed setting tax rates at a level that would balance the budget over a period of several years while providing for a high level of employment. This "stabilizing budget policy" purportedly would be accomplished by allowing tax receipts to be lower in times of economic recession, thereby leading to automatic deficit spending by the federal government (CED 1944; CED

1947b). Contrary to the version of Keynesianism advocated by the liberal-labor alliance, there was no suggestion that the government should make investments in the economy, hire unemployed workers, or increase spending (CED 1947b).

Moreover, long before the market fundamentalists among economists had attained any visibility or legitimacy, the CED emphasized the use of monetary policy (i.e., changes in the size and rate of growth in the money supply) to stimulate the economy when necessary, or to reduce demand if inflation increased. It claimed monetary policy was a better alternative because the Federal Reserve Board and its Open Market Committee could move more quickly than Congress. It therefore could have a more immediate impact by simply buying or selling government securities on the open market, increasing or decreasing the banks' reserve requirements, changing the rate at which banks could borrow from each other overnight (the "federal funds rate"), or changing the rate at which banks could obtain short-term loans from a Federal Reserve Bank ("the discount rate") (CED 1948).

Perhaps best of all from the CED's point of view, a mix of fiscal and monetary policies did not necessitate any expansion of the traditional functions of government, a view most fully articulated in a speech by a leading trustee, which the CED published (Thomson 1954). Then, too, a commercial Keynesian that emphasized the use of monetary policy would be useful in power struggles with the liberal-labor alliance because it could induce recessions by raising interest rates, which in effect made unemployment for workers, not higher taxes for the corporate rich, the way in which inflation would be controlled. The differences between liberal and commercial Keynesianism may at first seem small, and they are often glossed over or ignored in accounts of postwar America that talk in terms of a "Keynesian consensus." This is perhaps especially the case for the social scientists who have written about "Keynesianism" since the 1970s as if the commercial Keynesianism practiced by the Kennedy, Johnson, and early Nixon administrations were the same as the liberal and left-liberal Keynesianism proposed by the economists who were part of the liberal-labor alliance.

In fact, in terms of class and power, and in terms of who would benefit the most from a growing economy, the differences between liberal and commercial Keynesian were very large. They were the form that class conflict took in arguments over taxes and budgets in Congress, and over interest rates on the Federal Reserve Board in the postwar era. The mainstream concept of a "Keynesian consensus" therefore obscures far more than it illuminates (Stein 1969/1996, a longtime economist for the CED, and the main source for this view). The corporate moderates were well armed for this class-based conflict over wages, taxes, and interest rates, and their use of commercial Keynesianism played a significant role in their success over the next 25 years in a wide range of policy domains.

The Conservative Coalition Also Gains Strength

Due to Republican successes in the 1942 and 1944 Congressional elections, the conservative coalition also became stronger as the number of liberal Northern Democrats declined (Whitham 2016, Chapter 4). In 1943, it won on all of the 18 occasions it formed in the House, and it won 15 of 17 times in 1944 (88.2 percent) (Shelley 1983, p. 34, Table 2.3). In addition, and despite the efforts by Roosevelt and the NWLB to dampen class conflict in order to successfully prosecute a two-front war against powerful nation-state enemies, the conservative coalition continued to search for ways to hamper union organizing.

It found the opening it was looking for when Lewis, who had refused to sign the no-strike pledge, ordered the mineworkers to strike for a $2-a-day wage increase in early June 1943. In response, Congress immediately passed the War Labor Disputes Act, which gave the president the power to take over industries essential to prosecuting the war when they were threatened by strikes. It also prohibited unions from using membership dues for campaign donations to political candidates. Roosevelt vetoed the bill, but the conservative coalition and its moderate allies on this issue easily overturned the veto. And despite his veto, Roosevelt used the act a year later when 10,000 unionized transit workers went on a six-day strike to protest a ruling by the Fair Employment Practices Commission that the city's transit authority had to employ African Americans as trolley and rapid transit operators. In addition, the president sent 8,000 U.S. army troops to operate the system, and announced that any workers who did not return to work would be subject to the draft (Klinkner and Smith 2002, p. 191). This openly race-based attempt at exclusion by Northern white workers was one of many indications during the war years that the caste-based divide within the working class would become a major problem for unions in the postwar era, and thereby undercut the gains the unions made during the war.

Union Setbacks in the Early Postwar Era

Despite the clear signs of serious divisions among workers along racial lines before and during World War II, the growth in union membership during the war nevertheless caused union leaders to develop the same optimism about their likely postwar successes that their predecessors harbored during and after World War I. At the same time, the AFL muted its antagonism toward the CIO in the postwar years because it had gained in strength and members. Moreover, the AFL and CIO started to work together in the months after the end of the war as workers lost ground due to a strong one-two punch. First, there was an abrupt end to overtime pay due to the end of defense production. Second, there was a rise in inflation because the ultraconservatives inside and outside Congress insisted upon the immediate end of price controls, even though the economy was not producing enough consumer goods to be ready for that step. The ensuing strike actions by several major unions failed in the face of united opposition by the reinvigorated corporate leaders. Instead, the strikes created a backlash that gave the conservative coalition the opportunity in early 1946 to legislate many of the restrictions that the Southern Democrats and the NAM had decided upon in 1939. Only a veto by Truman, upheld by liberals and moderates in the House, kept those restrictions from becoming law at that early postwar juncture.

Then, in the election a few months later, at a time when 65 percent of those polled in a nationwide survey thought "well" of the Chamber of Commerce, but only 50 percent and 26 percent thought the same about the AFL and CIO, respectively, the Republicans won big (Collins 1981, pp. 92–93). They gained control of Congress for the first time in 18 years, with 246 seats in the House and 51 in the Senate; only 75 of 318 candidates endorsed by organized labor's political action arm were elected. These results were a clear sign that a majority of the electorate, which consisted of only 38 percent of those eligible to vote in that election, was not sympathetic to organized labor, including some liberals who thought the labor leaders had acted in an irresponsible fashion (e.g., Griffith 1988, p. 145).

From this point forward, the story is one of legislative defeats for the liberal-labor alliance on union issues. Each setback took its small toll on union strength, as best indicated once again by the gradual decline of union density from its wartime high in 1945. This decline was in part due to the inability of unions to expand into other sectors of the economy, but also because they could not stop the gradual movement of factories to the low-wage, non-union South, which became the original "off-shore" platform for both large and small corporations. The first in this unending and unbroken string of reversals (in Congress and in the courts) was the passage of the Taft-Hartley Act in 1947, despite another Truman veto (Gable 1953). This act crippled unions in numerous ways.

A Major Setback for Organized Labor

The Labor-Management Act of 1947, best known as the Taft-Hartley Act because of its primary sponsors, Robert Taft (R, OH) in the Senate and Fred Hartley (R, NJ) in the House, severely hampered organized labor's ability to establish new unions in non-unionized economic sectors, especially in the least unionized parts of the country. Building on the anti-union amendments developed by the Southern Democrats, the NAM, and the AFL in 1939, the Taft-Hartley Act put its greatest emphasis on adding new rights for corporate executives in relation to labor, which in effect gave management more latitude to pressure workers. For one thing, the Taft-Hartley amendments included new language that downgraded the importance of collective bargaining in the name of free speech for both

152 The Rise and Fall of Labor Unions

employers and workers. In practice, this meant employers could refuse to bargain and more readily propagandize workers through pamphlets, flyers, and speeches at meetings workers had to attend. Veiled threats to move the plants elsewhere were often made and companies did increase their efforts to move factories to the South whenever possible. In addition, the softening of provisions against unfair management practices aided in the defense and extension of company unions (Jacoby 1997, pp. 183–191, 200–203).

The act also added a list of unfair labor practices that hampered union organizing by outlawing tactics that were used in the 1930s to win union recognition, such as mass picketing and secondary boycotts. Unauthorized ("wildcat") strikes by the rank and file on the shop floor were prohibited, which took power from those on the bottom of the union and at the same time forced the labor leaders to police their dissident members or else be in violation of the law (e.g., Gross 1995, Chapter 1). Drawing on the precedents in the War Labor Disputes Act of 1943, another statute in the Taft-Hartley Act gave the president the power to represent the general public's interest through the declaration of an emergency, which would delay a strike with a 60-day cooling-off period. Still another statute limited the power of labor-board appointees by giving their top staff member, the general counsel, more discretion as to what cases to investigate and bring before the board.

The law included a direct attack on the several CIO unions that were led by members of the Communist Party by making it necessary for union leaders to sign an affidavit stating they were not Communists (Gross 1981 Chapter 13; Gross 1995, Chapter 1). Not least, and a mistake by the ultraconservatives in retrospect, it also decreed that employer contributions to a union health fund were illegal. This seemingly minor amendment abolished a union-controlled benefits fund that the United Mine Workers had won for its members in a 1946 strike. It therefore became necessary for unions to share responsibility for benefit funds with management, which created an opening for unions in terms of negotiating over social benefits, as explained shortly (Brown 1999, p. 158).

In addition, the act legitimated laws already passed in 11 states that allowed employees to decline to pay dues to an established union if they so desired. In effect, these "right-to-work" laws, as the ultraconservatives successfully named them, based on their usual market fundamentalism, hold out the temptation to workers of being "free riders." In other words, they could benefit from any union successes, but would not have to help pay for the efforts to win them (Dempsey 1961, pp. 25–27). There followed decades of legislative conflict over "Section 14b," the clause that allows states to have right-to-work laws (Gall 1988). With the ultraconservatives constantly on the attack, unions had to put a very large amount of their resources into trying to fend off new right-to-work laws (Dixon 2007; Dixon 2010). There were 19 right-to-work states in 1965, with a majority in the South. By the end of 2000, there were 21 right-to-work states—11 in the South, five in the Great Plains, four in the Rocky Mountain region, and one in the Southwest (Arizona).

Ultraconservatives in the corporate community fervently supported the Taft-Harley Act in a highly public way (Gable 1953; Gross 1995). But the act also had the quiet support of the Committee for Economic Development, which was not moderate when it came to unions. (However, its trustees were willing to work with unions on other issues when necessary, as shown in relevant chapters in Parts 2 and 3.) Up until 1947, the CED had steered clear of any labor issues as it worked closely with liberals and union leaders in a mostly vain attempt to smooth the transition to a peacetime economy in the face of ultraconservative intransigence once World War II ended (Domhoff 2013, Chapter 3).

CED's (1947a) statement on collective bargaining, *Collective Bargaining: How to Make it More Effective*, supported most of the key provisions of the Taft-Hartley Act. For example, it suggested more leeway for employers to tell their side of the story to their employees, called for limits on the power of appointed board members by giving more decision-making latitude to the board's general counsel, and supported the ban on both secondary boycotts and jurisdictional strikes. It agreed with other business groups that foremen and other supervisors should be defined as management and excluded from union bargaining units. It also argued for strengthening an already existing government mediation agency by turning it into an independent Federation Mediation Service; this widely shared business recommendation was included in the final legislation as the Federal Mediation and Conciliation Service (Schriftgiesser 1967, pp. 161–162).

The CED report relating to the Taft-Hartley Act was not needed because ultraconservatives in the NAM had formulated the key ideas, so its report is therefore useful primarily as an indication of how corporate moderates continued to view unions in the postwar era. By the mid-1950s, CED statements on unions became more direct and critical. In the 1960s, the CED came to the forefront of a more confrontational corporate effort to limit the power of unions. For now, the important point is that all members of the corporate community remained as opposed to unions as they were at the time the National Labor Relations Act was enacted.

Union Tensions with Communists Over a Third Party in 1948

Highly motivated by the desire to undo key aspects of the Taft-Hartley Act, members of the AFL and CIO worked together even more closely than in the early postwar period to help restore strong Democratic majorities to both houses of Congress in 1948. They also worked very hard for the reelection of Truman so that any legislative rollbacks on Taft-Hartley would not be defeated by a Republican presidential veto (pollsters had concluded that the Republican candidate was favored to win the election). However, the liberal-labor alliance faced what it perceived as a major peril. A widely known and admired farm owner and hybrid seed developer from Iowa, Henry A. Wallace, who had been Roosevelt's Secretary of Agriculture from 1933 to 1940, and his vice president from 1941 to 1944, decided to run for president as the leader of a new left-wing third party—the Progressive Party.

Although this third-party effort ultimately had no impact on the electoral outcome at either the presidential or congressional levels, it did have a big impact on the union movement because of the possibility that Wallace might win enough votes to give the Republicans a plurality victory, and cost the Democrats some House seats as well. Moreover, union leaders felt certain, based on their own informants, that the Communist Party and the CIO unions it controlled were the backbone of the new party. Communists denied these claims at the time, and there were many non-Communist liberals in the party, including Wallace, but in fact the AFL and CIO leaders were absolutely correct, as historical archives fully demonstrate (Devine 2003). Worse, the decision to back Wallace was made late in the pre-election planning by the left wing of the Communist Party in October 1947, as the best way to fulfill Moscow's very recent and unexpected directive that everything should be done to stop a massive American foreign-aid plan for Europe, a plan that is discussed in Chapter 13 (Devine 2003; Stepan-Norris and Zeitlin 2003, pp. 289–295; Weinstein 1975, pp. 104–111; Weinstein 2003, pp. 256–259).

Since the several Communist-dominated unions were in the CIO, the CIO's top leaders therefore expelled the Communist unions because they believed Communists had put the entire union movement at risk by backing a third party. Their decision to expel the Communists deprived the CIO of activists and organizers that were useful to the union movement when they were not following Soviet foreign policy directives. But to allow Communists to continue to control some affiliates of the CIO, even though they had shown they were willing to put the union movement at risk in the pursuit of their own goals, would have been far worse as far as the top union leaders were concerned. In terms of the fortunes of militant leftists, the Communists' risky venture into a third party may have hastened the demise of the "combative, class-conscious industrial union movement" they had hoped to build within the larger context of the CIO (Stepan-Norris and Zeitlin 2003, p. 296).

The Conservative Coalition Successfully Defends Taft-Hartley

Despite the initial threat posed to the liberal-labor alliance and the Democratic Party by the Progressive Party challenge, the Democrats nonetheless returned Truman to the White House and reclaimed majorities in both houses of Congress, in part due to the all-out efforts of organized labor. Having defeated both the leftist third-partyists and the Republicans, labor leaders believed they also could reverse some of the changes brought about by the Taft-Hartley Act. However, the union movement was blocked in this effort. As always since at least the mid-1930s, the power of the Southern Democrats was the determining factor. A united working class could do nothing against the Southern Democrats, who of course had the support of most Republicans as well.

As one labor historian explained: "Despite labor's electoral and financial contributions and the Democrats' successes in 1948, the Eighty-first Congress failed to move energetically on Taft-Hartley" (Zieger 1986, p. 119). President Truman supported the revisions called for by the liberal-labor alliance, but the fact remained that "Southern Democrats, almost uniformly hostile to the labor movement, dominated key congressional committees" (Zieger 1986, p. 119). Most of the Democratic senators and congressmen outside the South announced they would vote for the labor agenda, but the liberal-labor alliance could not overcome the power of the conservative coalition.

As suggested earlier in the chapter, several provisions in the Taft-Hartley Act very likely have played a significant role in the gradual decline of the union movement. However, it is difficult to pinpoint any one act or ruling, or any one piece of the Taft-Hartley Act, as "the" turning point in undermining the union movement. To begin with, unions already had lost their most potent prewar organizing tactic, the sit-down strike, due to the 1939 Supreme Court decision alluded to earlier in the chapter. The Supreme Court issued another damaging decision in 1951 when it ruled that it was illegal for a union to close down an entire construction site over an argument with a single contractor or subcontractor; this issue is discussed in later conflicts using the phrase "common-situs picketing" (Gross 1995, pp. 83–84, 341).

When union leaders signed on with liberals in supporting the National Labor Relations Act in 1935, they were well aware of the risk they were taking by giving up traditional organizing tactics in exchange for promises of government protection through the NLRB and the courts. They took that risk in part because they were having little or no success except for a few business sectors in which employers could not afford to bring in replacement workers. Furthermore, the usefulness of the original act for union organizers was not automatic. Its value depended on the protection and possible extension of the several specific statutory guarantees that were included in it. But the Taft-Hartley Act and many later decisions by both Congress and the NLRB narrowed or withdrew those guarantees in what turned into class warfare at the legislative and regulatory levels.

However, the Taft-Hartley Act did result in one unanticipated consequence for the corporate community. It reinforced union leaders' resolve to bargain for health and pension benefits as the only way to overcome the challenges to the long-term viability of unions. The possibility for such negotiations was created by two separate government decisions during World War II, which once again demonstrate the positive impact of the war for unions. First, and as already mentioned earlier in the chapter, the Internal Revenue Service ruled that corporations could count health and pension benefits as expenses for tax purposes. Then, as also noted earlier, the National War Labor Board ruled that wage controls did not apply to increases in fringe benefits.

Union leaders did not seize upon these possibilities immediately because they still had hopes for victory in the political arena. But after a postwar drive to unionize the South failed badly, thereby making it impossible to unseat Southern Democrats or force compromises from them, labor leaders fully realized that any improvements in worker security would have to come through collective bargaining for social benefits, not government programs. They thus had to take a different direction from the one taken by social democrats and union activists in most European countries, which again shows the limits of cross-national comparisons and the importance of taking the history of every country seriously.

In a word, it was the Taft-Hartley Act's challenge to the very existence of unions that changed the terms of the power equation. As political scientist Michael K. Brown (1999, p. 154) concludes, "unions found that collectively bargained social rights provided an escape hatch from the threat to their security posed by Taft-Hartley; fringe benefits obtained on union terms provided the 'virtual equivalent' of a closed shop." In 1948 the National Labor Relations Board, with all of its members appointed by a Democratic president, backed the earlier wartime rulings by the National War Relations Board concerning social benefits by deciding that bargaining over health and welfare funds was legal. Then that ruling was supported by the majority on the Supreme Court, which by that time consisted entirely of Roosevelt and Truman appointees. The wartime rulings, along with the decisions by the NLRB and the Supreme Court, therefore "opened the door to bargaining over social rights and left legislative derailment as the only way to shut down unionized welfare capitalism." After a Truman-appointed strike settlement board ruled in 1949 that the steel industry had to accept the United Steelworkers' demand for pensions and social insurance "in the absence of adequate Government programs," the die was cast, to the outrage of steel executives and other industrialists (Brown 1999, pp. 154, 159, for the information and quotes in this paragraph).

Although the established unions were able to withstand the worst of the Taft-Hartley setbacks, thanks to rulings by Democratic Party appointees, and even gain a more solid base within major industries by winning good benefit packages, the union movement as a whole lost its momentum. It could not organize the unorganized in the face of the strategic weapons it had lost due to the courts and Congress. Its members enjoyed another 25 to 30 years of good wages and improved benefits in several mass-production industries, including steel and autos, but it was not very successful in the strongly anti-union industries in staunchly anti-union states. The percentage of wage and salary workers in unions declined from its high point of 34.2 in 1945 to 30.5 percent in 1950. It then received a temporary boost due to new wartime controls and restrictions necessitated by the outbreak of the Korean War, which brought the unions close to their 1945 density peak by 1954 (33.5 percent). However, that second war-induced peak was followed by a gradual decline in the late 1950s and 1960s, from which the union movement never recovered (Freeman 1998, p. 291, Table 8A.2, for union-density figures; Goldfield 1987, for a detailed account of the general decline).

The Eisenhower Years: Further Setbacks for the Unions

Once a truce to end the fighting in Korea was finally signed in mid-1953, the corporate community built on the Taft-Hartley Act to make further progress during the Eisenhower years in limiting the regulatory and legal support for unions. It did so first and foremost through the deployment of corporate-oriented practitioners of labor law, who often had experience as aides for Republicans on Congressional labor committees, or as former staff members for the National Labor Relations Board. To start with, Eisenhower made conservative appointments to the NLRB, which soon began to issue rulings that strongly favored corporations. For example, the new board majority rapidly expanded the rights of employers to resist unions through speeches and pamphlets, which bordered on threats of job loss. These rulings went well beyond what the Taft-Hartley Act had mandated as "free speech." Then it further restricted union organizers' ability to use some of their most potent economic weapons, such as boycotts of companies and picketing of delivery sites. In addition, Eisenhower appointees to the board exempted even more of the medium-sized and strictly local firms from its purview than was called for in the Taft-Hartley Act, and made it easier for employers to fire union activists (Gross 1995, pp. 102–103).

The board majority replaced longtime staff members in regional offices with conservatives, and, by December 1954, it had reversed most of the precedents developed by Democratic boards between 1937 and 1952. At the same time the new NLRB majority ignored the dubious practices used by an increasing number of firms to defeat unionization drives and devise new ways to bring about the decertification of already established unions. Their methods included the use of psychological tests to screen out potential employees with leadership abilities, and the creation of seemingly neutral discussion groups to identify employees who might be sympathetic to unions (Smith 2003, Chapter 4). Those scholars who think that there was ever a "limited, uneasy partnership," based on the usefulness of unions (Bell 1960, p. 216), or a "capital-labor accord" between corporate moderates and labor (e.g., Mizruchi 2013, pp. 86–100, 108–110) are misguided (e.g., Boyle 2013, for a critique of such claims; Gross 1995, for evidence that that there was no truce, partnership, accord, or pact).

Buoyed by their success within the NLRB, the ultraconservatives turned their attention to corrupt leadership and criminal behavior in several unions through hearings in the Senate, chaired by the senior Democratic senator from Arkansas. Although the main fireworks came a few years later, the hearings began in 1955 and provided material for headlines and television clips based on testimony, wiretaps, and subpoenaed documents, with the International Brotherhood of Teamsters, the International Longshoremen's Association, and the United Mine Workers as the major targets. The legislation that emerged from these hearings, the Labor-Management Reporting and Disclosure Act of 1959, had a complex history, starting with rival bills created by the labor committees in the House and Senate in 1958. However, the final act was based for the most part on a version written by corporate lawyers serving on the Chamber of Commerce's Labor Relations Committee, and it dealt further setbacks to unions (Gross 1995, p. 140). The Chamber's draft was introduced on the floor of the House through a rarely used parliamentary procedure by a Democrat from Georgia, Phil Landrum, and a Republican from Michigan, Robert Griffin, which led to the legislation being called the Landrum–Griffin Act in most historical accounts.

The Landrum–Griffin Act was aimed first and foremost at boss control and racketeering in the labor movement, requiring unions to hold secret elections that could be reviewed for fairness by the Department of Labor. It gave more rights and protections to union members, required unions to file financial reports with the government, and in other ways limited the power that leaders had over their members. However, in addition to these democratizing reforms, the Chamber's lawyers also used the legislation as an opportunity to hamper union organizing by making it illegal for a unionized business to agree to demands by union organizers that it cease doing business with non-union companies that unions were trying to organize. It also strengthened the laws against secondary boycotts through the closing of small loopholes. Laws that restricted picketing were made even more constraining by prohibiting roving pickets from being present when the delivery trucks of anti-union companies arrived at their destinations (Gross 1995, p. 139).

Unions were clearly on the defensive in the face of the revelations during the Congressional hearings, but leaders within the AFL-CIO were confident they could limit the damage. Their confidence was heightened because they had contributed campaign workers and money to the Democratic Party's success in the 1958 midterm elections, which gave the party margins of 64-36 in the Senate and 283-153 in the House, in the context of the kind of sluggish economy that is one of the primary factors, along with strong party identification, that shapes voting in the United States (Achen and Bartels 2016). They further believed they might be able to remove some of the more onerous provisions of the Taft-Hartley Act as a trade-off for accepting the new restrictions on their management of the unions' financial resources. In making their calculations, however, organized labor ignored the fact that the conservative coalition still had the potential to win 59 percent of the votes in the House and 52 percent in the Senate, with potential defined, as stated in the Introduction, as *all* those Democrats who voted with a majority of Southern Democrats and a majority of Republicans 50 percent or more of the time (Shelley 1983, pp. 151, Table 8.2, and 154, Table 8.6).

The chair of the Senate Labor Committee, John F. Kennedy of Massachusetts, who already had his eye on the 1960 presidential race, tried to convince his union allies that changes in the Taft-Hartley Act should not be included in the new legislation, but the labor leaders rejected his arguments. With Kennedy's acquiescence, the Senate passed the union's version of the bill in April 1959 (Gross 1995, p. 141). But the Senate version was not able to survive in the House, in which the conservative coalition had the support of 95 Democrats, including all 92 Southerners, and 136 of 153 Republicans. The result was a surprising victory for the Landrum-Griffin version of the act.

Before joining with Republicans in voting for the revised legislation, however, the Southern Democrats insisted upon the elimination of several clauses they feared might provide openings for civil rights efforts in the South. In addition, the Republicans promised to continue to join the Southern Democrats in blocking civil rights legislation in the future, casting aside any pretense that it was any longer the "Party of Lincoln" when it came to civil rights. All the while, the NAM and Chamber of Commerce reminded Southern Democrats that passage of the act was essential to keep unions out of their region and thereby maintain its attractiveness to industry (McAdams 1964, p. 212). The final version of the act that emerged from the compromises within the conference committee was not as restrictive for unions as the House bill fashioned by Landrum and Griffin had been. But the outcome was primarily a defeat for unions nonetheless because it strengthened the regulation of internal union affairs by government officials far more than AFL-CIO leaders desired and added the restraints on secondary boycotts and roving pickets discussed earlier in this subsection. However, the long-term impact of the further restraints on boycotting and picketing was obscured by the fact that the new legislation had no immediate negative effects for the large established unions that practiced some semblance of internal democracy. Instead, its impact was more serious for the long run because it made organizing new unions much more difficult, especially in smaller industries, and particularly in the South.

At the same time, there were a few small favors for construction unions on picketing issues in the final bill, suggesting that at least some moderate Republicans in the Northeast still hoped to win support from them. In addition, the bill also required anti-union consulting firms to "file an 'Agreements and Activities Report' within thirty days after agreeing to persuade their client's employees to reject unionization" (Smith 2003, p. 102). This seemingly minor provision quickly led to the near disappearance of union busting for the next 15 years. The most important of these firms, Labor Relations Associates, which figured prominently in the Senate hearings, was a thinly disguised arm of Sears, Roebuck. Founded by the director of the company's employee relations department in 1939, with the ostensible goal of providing advice to any company that needed its services, it primarily funneled Sears, Roebuck money to the Teamsters in exchange for the Teamsters' help in decertifying other unions. Fully exposed during the Senate hearings, it went out of business in 1962 (Smith 2003, pp. 98–102).

Problems Within the Union Movement

Despite the setbacks for organized labor at the hands of the Taft-Hartley Act, the Supreme Court, and the Eisenhower Administration, by the late 1950s the major unions were well entrenched in the large industrial companies that stood at the heart of the corporate community. Nor had the Landrum-Griffin Act directly damaged the large industrial unions, and they no longer had to deal with the direct threats posed by the anti-union "consulting" firms. Indeed, the 1950s were sometimes claimed to be the heyday of a "hidden affair between big labor and big business," as one journalist called it (Nossiter 1959), and later as the beginnings of a truce between the corporate community and unions, as mentioned earlier in the chapter. The unions' strong position seemed to be indicated by the fact that the union–density percentage had hovered around 32 since its Korean War high point of 33.5 in 1954, although it did drop to 30.4 percent in 1960. In addition, a merger between the AFL and CIO in 1956 held out the hope that the union movement might develop greater political clout now that it spoke with one voice.

However, the unions in fact faced several major difficulties. To begin with, less than a majority of union members were registered to vote (Boyle 1995, Chapter 5). Further, the number of workers in unions had stagnated at about 16 million between 1954 and 1960. Most of all, perhaps, unions faced serious internal problems because of the unwillingness of white workers to support the integration of African Americans into craft unions, especially in the construction industry (Frymer 2008, pp. 54–65). In 1959 the NAACP passed a resolution warning labor leaders that it might ask the National Labor Relations Board to decertify the many unions that were discriminating against black workers at the local level in both the North and the South. When black trade unionists brought several resolutions concerning discrimination to the floor of the annual AFL-CIO convention in that same year, the only support for the defeated measures came from the liberal UAW delegates, despite the racial discrimination practiced by a large percentage of their union's rank and file (Boyle 1995, Chapter 5; Frymer 2008, Chapter 3; Quadagno 1994, p. 62; Roof 2011, p. 120).

Up to that point, the racial animus harbored by many white union members had not had much if any impact on the growth and solidarity of the union movement overall, although integrated unions had lower wage differentials among members and more avenues for input by rank-and-file members (Stepan-Norris and Zeitlin 2003). However, caste-based racial exclusion in housing, schools, marriage, and jobs came to matter in a major way in the face of the civil rights movement and the uprisings and rioting in many cities across the country between 1964 and 1968, leading to defeats for both the Democratic Party and the union movement.

References

Achen, Christopher and Larry M. Bartels. 2016. *Democracy for realists: Why elections do not produce responsive governments.* Princeton: Princeton University Press.

Allen, Michael P. 1991. "Capitalist response to state intervention: Theories of the state and political finance in the New Deal." *American Sociological Review* 56:679–689.

Auerbach, Jerold S. 1966. *Labor and liberty: The LaFollette Committee and the New Deal.* Indianapolis: Bobbs Merrill.

Bell, Daniel. 1960. "The subversion of collective bargaining." *Commentary* 29:185–197.

Bernstein, Irving. 1969. *Turbulent years: A history of the American worker, 1933–1941.* Boston: Houghton Mifflin.

Boyle, Kevin. 1995. *The UAW and the heyday of American liberalism, 1945–1968.* Ithaca: Cornell University Press.

Boyle, Kevin G. 2013. "The Treaty of Detroit and the postwar labor accord." Pp. 324–326 in *The Oxford encyclopedia of American business, labor, and economic history,* vol. 2, edited by M. Dubofsky. New York: Oxford University Press.

Brown, Michael K. 1999. *Race, money and the American welfare state.* Ithaca: Cornell University Press.

CED. 1944. *A postwar federal tax plan for high employment.* New York: Committee for Economic Development.

———. 1947a. *Collective bargaining: How to make it more effective.* New York: Committee for Economic Development.

―――. 1947b. *Taxes and the budget: A program for prosperity in a free economy* New York: Committee for Economic Development.

―――. 1948. *Monetary and fiscal policy for greater economic stability.* New York: Committee for Economic Development.

Collins, Robert M. 1981. *The business response to Keynes, 1929–1964.* New York: Columbia University Press.

Dempsey, Joseph R. 1961. *The operation of right-to-work laws: A comparison between what the state legislatures say about the meaning of the laws and how state court judges have applied these laws.* Milwaukee: Marquette University Press.

Devine, Thomas. 2003. "The Communists, Henry Wallace, and the Progressive Party of 1948." *Continuity: A Journal of History* 26:33–69.

Dixon, Marc. 2007. "Limiting Labor: Business political mobilization and union setback in the states." *Journal of Policy History* 19:313–344.

―――. 2010. "Union threat, countermovement organization, and labor policy in the states 1944–1960." *Social Problems* 57:157–174.

Domhoff, G. W. 1996. *State autonomy or class dominance? Case studies on policy making in America.* Hawthorne, NY: Aldine de Gruyter.

―――. 2013. *The myth of liberal ascendancy: Corporate dominance from the Great Depression to the Great Recession.* Boulder: Paradigm Publishers.

Dubofsky, Melvyn. 2000. *Hard work: The making of labor history.* Chicago: University of Illinois Press.

Ferguson, Thomas. 1995. *Golden rule: The investment theory of party competition and the logic of money-driven political systems.* Chicago: University of Chicago Press.

Fine, Sidney. 1969. "Sit-down: The General Motors strike of 1936–1937." University of Michigan Press, Ann Arbor.

Fraser, Steven. 1989. "The 'labor question'." Pp. 55–84 in *The rise and fall of the New Deal order, 1930–1980,* edited by S. Fraser and G. Gerstle. Princeton: Princeton University Press.

―――. 1991. *Labor will rule: Sidney Hillman and the rise of American labor.* New York: Free Press.

Freeman, Richard B. 1998. "Spurts in union growth: Defining moments and social processes." Pp. 265–296 in *The defining moment: The Great Depression and the American economy in the twentieth century,* edited by M. Bordo, C. Goldin, and E. White. Chicago: University of Chicago Press.

Frymer, Paul. 2008. *Black and blue: African Americans, the labor movement, and the decline of the Democratic Party.* Princeton: Princeton University Press.

Gable, Richard. 1953. "NAM: Influential lobby or kiss of death?" *Journal of Politics* 15:254–273.

Gall, Gilbert. 1988. *The politics of right to work: The labor federations as special interests, 1943–1979.* New York: Greenwood Press.

Goldfield, Michael. 1987. *The decline of organized labor in the United States.* Chicago: University of Chicago Press.

Gordon, Colin. 1994. *New deals: Business, labor, and politics in America, 1920–1935.* New York: Cambridge University Press.

Griffith, Barbara. 1988. *The crisis of American labor: Operation Dixie and the defeat of the CIO.* Philadelphia: Temple University Press.

Gross, James A. 1981. *The reshaping of the National Labor Relations Board.* Albany: State University of New York Press.

———. 1995. *Broken promise: The subversion of U.S. labor relations policy.* Philadelphia: Temple University Press.

Haynes, John, Harvey Klehr, and K. M. Anderson. 1998. *The Soviet world of American Communism.* New Haven: Yale University Press.

Holl, Richard. 2005. *From the boardroom to the war room: America's corporate liberals and FDR's preparedness program.* Rochester: University of Rochester Press.

Jacoby, Sanford. 1997. *Modern manors: Welfare capitalism since the New Deal.* Princeton: Princeton University Press.

Jaremski, Matthew and Gabriel Mathy. 2017. *How was the Quantitative Easing Program of the 1930s Unwound?* NBER Working Paper No. 23788. http://www.nber.org/papers/w23788. Cambridge: National Bureau of Economic Research.

Kennedy, David. 1999. *Freedom from fear: The American people in depression and war, 1929–1945.* New York: Oxford University Press.

Klinkner, Philip and Rogers Smith. 2002. *The unsteady march: The rise and decline of racial equality in America.* Chicago: University of Chicago Press.

Lichtenstein, Nelson. 2002. *State of the union: A century of American labor.* Princeton: Princeton University Press.

MacLean, Nancy. 2017. *Democracy in chains: The deep history of the radical right's stealthy plan for America.* New York: Viking.

Mayer, Jane. 2017. *Dark money: The hidden history of the billionaires behind the rise of the radical right.* New York: Penguin Random House.

McAdams, Alan. 1964. *Power and politics in labor legislation.* New York: Columbia University Press.

Mizruchi, Mark. 2013. *The fracturing of the American corporate elite.* Cambridge: Harvard University Press.

Nelson, Daniel. 2001. "The other New Deal and labor: The regulatory state and the unions, 1933–1940." *Journal of Policy History* 13:367–390.

Nossiter, Bernard. 1959. "The hidden affair between big business and big labor." *Harper's Magazine*, July, pp. 32–39.

Overacker, Louise. 1937. "Campaign funds in the presidential election of 1936." *American Political Science Review* 31:473–498.

Patterson, James T. 1967. *Congressional conservatism and the New Deal: The growth of the conservative coalition in Congress, 1933–1939.* Lexington: University of Kentucky Press.

Quadagno, Jill. 1994. *The color of welfare: How racism undermined the war on poverty.* New York: Oxford University Press.

Rockefeller, John D. 1937. "Letter to Mackenzie King, April 30." In *Rockefeller Family Archives, Record Group III, 2H, Box 72, Folder 557.* Sleepy Hollow, NY: Rockefeller Archive Center.

Roof, Tracy. 2011. *American labor, Congress, and the welfare state, 1935–2010.* Baltimore: Johns Hopkins University Press.

Schatz, Ronald. 2013. "National War Labor Board, World War II." Pp. 14–16 in *The Oxford encyclopedia of American business, labor, and economic history*, vol. 2, edited by M. Dubofsky. New York: Oxford University Press.

Scheinberg, Stephen. 1986. *Employers and reformers: The development of corporation labor policy, 1900–1940.* New York: Taylor and Francis.

Schriftgiesser, Karl. 1967. *Business and public policy.* Englewood Cliffs, NJ: Prentice Hall.

Shamir, Ronen. 1995. *Managing legal uncertainty: Elite lawyers in the New Deal*. Durham, NC: Duke University Press.

Shelley, Mack. 1983. *The permanent majority: The conservative coalition in the United States Congress*. Tuscaloosa.: University of Alabama Press.

Smith, Robert M. 2003. *From blackjacks to briefcases: A history of commercialized strikebreaking and unionbusting in the United States*. Athens: Ohio University Press.

Stein, Herbert. 1969/1996. *The fiscal revolution in America: Policy in pursuit of reality*. Washington: The AEI Press.

Stepan-Norris, Judith and Maurice Zeitlin. 2003. *Left out: Reds and America's industrial unions*. New York: Cambridge University Press.

Thomson, J. Cameron. 1954. *Balance and flexibility in fiscal and monetary policy*. New York: Committee for Economic Development.

Tomlins, Christopher. 1985. *The state and the unions: Labor relations, law and the organized labor movement in America, 1880–1960*. New York: Cambridge University Press.

Waddell, Brian. 2001. *The war against the New Deal: World War II and American democracy*. DeKalb: Northern Illinois University Press.

Waiwood, Patricia. 2013. "Recession of 1937–1938." *Federal Reserve History* https://www.federalreservehistory.org/essays/recession_of_1937_38.

Webber, Michael J. 2000. *New Deal fat cats: Business, labor, and campaign finance in the 1936 presidential election*. New York: Fordham University Press.

Weinstein, James. 1975. *Ambiguous legacy: The left in American Politics*. New York: Franklin Watts.

———. 2003. *The Long Detour*. Boulder: Westview.

Whitham, Charlie. 2016. *Post-war business planners in the United States, 1939–1948*. New York: Bloomsbury Publishing.

Wolfskill, George. 1962. "The revolt of the conservatives." Boston: Houghton Mifflin.

Zieger, Robert. 1986. *American workers, American unions, 1920–1985*. Baltimore: Johns Hopkins University Press.

———. 1995. *The CIO, 1935–1955* Chapel Hill: University of North Carolina Press.

Zilg, Gerald. 1974. *DuPont: Behind the nylon curtain*. Englewood Cliffs, NJ Prentice Hall.

Chapter 4

Union Victories, Corporate Pushback in the 1960s

For all the problems the union movement faced by the end of the Eisenhower Administration, its immediate future looked rosy with the election of a former senator seen as friendly to organized labor, Democrat John F. Kennedy, as president. Although most of Kennedy's high-level appointments to his cabinet and other important positions were moderate political leaders or members of the corporate community and the policy-planning network, this was not true for his appointments to the National Labor Relations Board. Taking advantage of an unexpected opportunity to make two appointments in his first month in office, Kennedy quietly liberalized the NLRB.

His first appointment, Frank McCulloch, came from a liberal family that had been strongly supportive of integration since the early twentieth century. McCulloch graduated from Williams College in 1926, earned a law degree from Harvard, and then worked for a law firm in Chicago for five years in the mid-1930s. Leaving his legal career behind, he took a position as the industrial relations secretary for the Council of Social Action, in Chicago, a church-based organization. From 1949 until his appointment as chair of the NLRB, he worked as an aide and liaison to unions for a liberal Democratic Senator from Illinois.

Kennedy's second appointment was a longtime NLRB employee, Gerald Brown, a regional director working out of San Francisco at the time of his appointment. Brown had a BA in history from West Texas State and an MA in economics from the University of Texas in Austin. McCulloch and Brown joined with a holdover Eisenhower appointee, John Fanning, a Democrat with a law degree from Catholic University, to give the board a liberal majority throughout the 1960s, to the growing frustration of both corporate moderates and ultraconservatives in the corporate community. Fanning's first job after he received his law degree was in the Department of Labor, followed by a high-level position in the Department of Defense in which he was in charge of industrial relations and had dealings with many craft unions working on the construction of military installations. He was appointed to the board in 1957 at the urging of Eisenhower's secretary of labor, a former defense department executive and industrial relations manager at Bloomingdale's (Gross 1995, pp. 147–152).

Kennedy's labor advisers and friendly Democrats in the House attempted to aid the NLRB in its work by formulating a reorganization plan. It would allow the board's regional offices to make final reviews on issues of fact, rather than allowing appeals to the board itself. Their aim was to decrease the large backlog of undecided cases, which grew from 410 in 1958 to 1,151 in 1961, due in good part to the increasing number of requests by corporations for board-level reviews. But the NAM and Chamber of Commerce objected vigorously, claiming that any delegation of authority would deny the right of review by "presidentially appointed board members," which they preferred because they thought that board members "were more vulnerable to political and public pressure than trial examiners obscured from public view" (Gross 1995, pp. 157–159). The conservative coalition then blocked the reorganization plan by a 231-179 vote in the House in July 1961. This outcome served notice that the NLRB was under close scrutiny by the corporate community as well as by Congressional conservatives. It was also another defeat on labor issues for the liberal–labor alliance.

The new Democratic majority on the labor board moved quickly to regulate collective bargaining more fully than in the past in order to force resistant corporations to take the process seriously. It began by restricting what employers could say to their employees about joining a union, ruling out any claims that they would go out of business, relocate, or shut down for some period of time. It also ruled that unions had greater latitude in picketing businesses and in passing out information about a company's anti-union tactics than the Republican-dominated board had allowed. In addition, it made penalties for violations of labor laws somewhat stiffer, although it was hampered in this regard by the refusal of many courts to enforce such orders and by the conservative coalition's ability to block new labor legislation. The new board majority further aided unions by defining the size of bargaining units in ways that gave labor organizers an advantage.

These and other decisions elicited immediate protests from the corporate community, but the NLRB majority dismissed these outcries as the usual overstatements by ultraconservatives. They did so based on the false assumption, widely shared at the time in liberal and academic circles, that the biggest and most reasonable corporations had come to accept collective bargaining as a stabilizing influence, especially when they could raise prices after a contract settlement to levels that more than compensated for the higher wages and benefits they had to pay.

As this belief started to harden into conventional wisdom, rulings by the National Labor Relations Board in 1963 and 1964 took the reality and depth of class conflict to a new level because they represented a distinctly greater threat to the corporate community. These rulings provided new openings for organized labor to take part in management decisions, including such volatile issues as the removal of some in-plant functions to other companies ("outsourcing"), the closure of whole factories, and the movement of factories to new locations. In the eyes of all members of the corporate community, the labor board's decisions on these issues were a challenge to their "right to manage," a phrase that had been invoked since the 1940s to indicate that a sacrosanct line had been crossed (Harris 1982).

The first round in this protracted conflict, which the corporate community did not win until 1971, involved a seemingly minor matter. Fibreboard, the 364th-largest publicly held company in the country at the time, outsourced maintenance work previously carried out by the company's own employees. By farming this work out to a low-wage, non-union company, Fibreboard lowered its labor costs and undercut its unionized workforce at the same time. To make matters more complicated, the Republican majority on the NLRB originally decided the case in favor of the corporation in early 1961, before Kennedy made his appointments to the board. But the local union protested that the company's decision should have been subject to collective bargaining because it involved changes in the work process and the layoff of workers. The AFL-CIO therefore lodged a strong protest.

Shortly thereafter, with the two Kennedy appointees now on the board, the holdover general counsel to the board decided that the case needed a new hearing. One board member was unable to participate, and another volunteered not to participate so that the case could be reconsidered in a timely fashion, which resulted in a 2-1 decision in favor of the union. Fibreboard, with the encouragement of the corporate community in general, made an immediate appeal to the courts.

Corporate leaders were not only upset by a highly unusual board action that put the right to manage at stake. They also worried that the decision would "hamper economic expansion by prohibiting the movement of capital to lower-wage areas; prohibiting employers from obtaining the lowest cost of production; preventing the discontinuance of unprofitable lines or products; inhibiting automation, mergers, and consolidations..." (Gross 1995, p. 173). In other words, they were concerned about the rising competition with foreign corporations and their ability to modernize their factories and eliminate workers by means of new machinery and production processes. As demonstrated in detail in Part 3 the corporate moderates had purposely created this competition as the price they had to pay to create a world market for their own investments and products, and to ensure that the Soviet Union and China were not successful in their efforts to extend communism into other countries. As the most detailed original research on the NLRB and the impact of its decisions concluded, "[e]mployers were particularly interested in becoming more

168 The Rise and Fall of Labor Unions

efficient through technological change, ending inflationary contract settlements with unions, and in other ways seeking to overcome the labor cost advantage enjoyed by foreign competitors" (Gross 1995, p. 190).

Moreover, the Fiberboard decision on outsourcing was not an isolated example of a controversial ruling on a topic of major concern to the corporate community. The board also generated corporate opposition through a ruling on a decision by the ultraconservative owner of a textile company in 1956 to close his plant in Darlington, South Carolina, for the sole reason that its local workers had voted for a union. Although the Eisenhower-era NLRB had opened its investigation of the shutdown soon after it occurred, a series of delays and legal challenges kept the case from reaching the board until the 1960s. Joined by one Republican holdover, the three Democrats voted that it was an unfair labor practice to shut down a plant in order to eliminate a union. The board held the company liable for back pay and ordered it to offer jobs to its former employees in its other mills in the South. The result was another court appeal.

By then the CED had also made its displeasure with recent events known through a statement that was highly critical of unions and suggested remedies to rein them in. The chair of the subcommittee was the chair of one of the major industrial corporations of the day, American Can Company, and the committee members included the CEOs of Alcoa, American Electric Power, Corning Glass, and U.S. Steel, among others (CED 1964). It asserted that unions are a primary cause of inflation because they are often able to win settlements that go beyond productivity gains. It endorsed right-to-work laws, greater restraints on secondary boycotts, and the removal of any constraints on individual employers or groups of employers to use lockouts in the face of labor disputes. It urged that courts should be authorized to issue restraining orders or injunctions against unions for strikes that violated a labor agreement (CED 1964, pp. 17–18).

The Rise of Public-Employee Unions

As if all this were not enough for the corporate community to worry about, public-employee unions suddenly became another potential problem for it. Public-employee unions not only could bring in many new members and win new benefits for public employees, but they could add muscle to what was in fact a sagging union movement in the private sector.

Although the origins of the American Federation of Teachers, the International Firefighters Association, and the National Federation of Federal Employers go back to World War I, few public-employee unions managed to gain a toehold in cities and states until the 1950s, usually by signing up white-collar workers in municipal governments. A bill introduced into both the House and Senate in the late 1950s to give federal employees the right to organize offered new hope, but it did not cause a stir until it was introduced once again at the outset of the Kennedy years. Suddenly, the bill was not only seen as threatening by most members of the conservative coalition, but by government executives as well. Several Kennedy aides, fearful that Congress "might enact a bill that gave workers too many rights and unions too much power," suggested that the president issue an executive order "intended to placate his labor allies while ensuring that the advent of collective bargaining in the federal service would alter labor relations as little as possible" (McCartin 2011, pp. 35–36). Organized labor, on the other hand, greeted the proposed legislation with enthusiasm, hoping to organize workers at the federal level, and then turn to state and municipal employees in the parts of the country in which union organizing in the private sector had failed.

Lawyers for the Department of Defense wrote the first draft of the preemptive executive order, based on the claim that unionized employees might impede defense production. The drafters emphasized that 92 work stoppages between 1956 and 1961 by skilled craftsmen at the National Aeronautic and Space Administration were the primary basis for their concern. After learning of this effort, Secretary of Labor Arthur Goldberg, a lifelong labor lawyer within the union movement, who had been serving as the general counsel for the United Steel Workers at the time of his appointment, took control of the process. He then created a task force that included representatives from several departments and agencies, including the Department of Defense, the Bureau of the Budget, and the Civil Services Commission, all three of which wanted the most narrow order possible in order to limit union powers.

The executive order finally issued in 1962 was narrow in scope. It emphasized that federal employees need not join a union, ruled out strikes, included few of the procedures the AFL–CIO requested, and was soon made even more restrictive through interpretations by the Civil Service Commission. But union leaders praised it in public because it gave them the right to organize federal workers. As the labor organizers had anticipated, there was a rapid rise in membership for most public-employee unions, including at the state and local levels, with 23 states passing laws permitting public-sector bargaining by 1970. For the most part, they were states in which liberal unions had used a variety of activist tactics and the Democrats had a legislative majority (Miller and Canak 1995a). The growth in public-employee unions was "the biggest breakthrough for labor since the New Deal" (McCartin 2011, p. 43). By 1973, the 3.1 million members of public-sector unions constituted 15.3 percent of the 18.1 million workers in unions (Hirsch and Macpherson 2018, for the membership figures from which this percentage was derived).

The corporate community's reactions to this new organizing drive broke along moderate/ultraconservative lines. The NAM and Chamber of Commerce insisted that public-employee unions should be restricted to

170   The Rise and Fall of Labor Unions

the right to meet and confer, but with no right to collective bargaining. The corporate moderates proceeded more cautiously by using their positions as foundation trustees to suggest background studies. To begin with, the Carnegie Corporation provided money in 1966 for a joint study by two associations of governmental executives, the National Government Center and the Council of State Governments, which were part of the urban policy-planning network.

Shortly thereafter, in 1967, the Ford Foundation provided The Brookings Institution with funds for a parallel study. Formally published in 1971, but widely circulated before that date, the Ford/Brookings report suggested that public officials stress the right not to join a union in talking with their employees, and offered specific ways to discourage unionization efforts. In effect, sociologists Berkeley Miller and William Canak (1995b, pp. 28–29) conclude, the report suggested ways in which public officials could "avoid unionization by contracting out public services to private employees, leaving them entirely to free enterprise, or by skillfully resisting union organizing drives." The corporate moderates thus wanted to use contracting out in government agencies in the same way they wanted to use outsourcing in their corporations—to lower labor costs and weaken unions. By 1970, the Ford Foundation had given $445,000 to a consortium of urban policy-planning groups to establish a new Labor-Management Relations Service to train government administrators to deal with unions. The Ford Foundation also helped create the National Public Employers Association, a national-level labor relations association for public officials at all levels of government. Its Business Research Advisory Committee included representatives from Eastern Airlines, Ford Motor, General Electric, and Republic Steel (Miller and Canak 1995b, pp. 28–29).

The Corporate Community and the Unions React to the Civil Rights Movement

The one bright spot for the corporate community as a whole in the first half of the 1960s, not just the corporate moderates, concerned their positive response to the demands of the Civil Rights Movement, and in particular the Civil Rights Act of 1964, which ended up strengthening their hand against organized labor. At the same time, the response by most unions, and especially the construction unions, hurt and divided the union movement due to their general resistance to the full integration of black workers into their unions.

The difference in the corporate and union reactions appeared immediately after President Kennedy took legal action against segregation in the workplace two months after his inauguration. His executive order banned discrimination in hiring decisions on the basis of race, religion, or national origins by federal agencies or by companies that had federal contracts. In addition, borrowing a phrase that was first used in the National Labor Relations Act, the order called for "affirmative action" in future hiring. Significantly, the order applied to unions that controlled apprenticeship programs as well as to corporations. To oversee the executive order, the president created the President's Committee on Equal Employment Opportunity (PCEEO), which had the power to ask for a company's employment statistics, to publicize the names of companies that discriminated, and to suspend government contracts (Delton 2009, p. 177; Golland 2011, Chapter 2).

Although usually opposed to government regulations on principle, corporate leaders did not respond negatively to Kennedy's order, and several of them agreed to serve on PCEEO (including the CED trustees who ran American Electric Power, Federated Department Stores, and General Electric). They were joined by several highly visible figures in a range of civic and cultural organizations. Specific corporate leaders aside, the idea of fair and open employment fit with the corporate community's emphasis on the individual freedom of each worker. In addition, the industrial relations departments that corporations created after World War I were well enough staffed to take on the responsibility for issues of integration and compliance, albeit with some additional training. Moreover, a fully integrated work force did not conflict with an anti–union bias: "Racial integration did not require that businesses give up their fundamentally conservative goals" (Delton 2009, p. 279).

Shortly after the PCEEO was in operation, its director told the Air Force that a new billion-dollar contract for Lockheed to manufacture massive cargo planes in the company's plant just outside Atlanta would not be certified. The company was not in compliance with the new rules. At the same time, the NAACP Legal Defense Fund filed a lawsuit against Lockheed to test the strength of the new executive order. Although corporate leaders often react negatively to rulings that might hamper their operations, the decisions by the leaders of this California-based company set an important precedent. They agreed to what in the heat of the moment was called a "plan for progress." After negotiations involving the highest levels of Lockheed and several other companies, the companies pledged to change their hiring and promotion practices (Feild 1967, pp. 27–28). Several other defense companies soon signed on to similar plans, although there is reason to doubt their effectiveness in the first years (Golland 2011, Chapter 2).

NAM, which first put itself on record in support of equal employment for African Americans and women at its annual meeting in 1940, gradually realized the possibilities for industry contained within the plans for progress. Although its legal department sent a 26-page statement to the White House in an effort to ensure that companies would not be subject to any arbitrary government sanctions, it quietly supported the integration effort after the White House oversight committee clarified the details of the executive order and tightened up the procedures and guidelines (Delton 2009, p. 182).

In June 1963, leaders in the corporate community, led by those who served on the White House oversight committee, organized and financed a new quasi-independent advisory council, which they named Plans for Progress. Initially, it consisted of 19 executives from defense companies. Demonstrating once again how often committees of the corporate rich and the power elite become part of the government, they insisted that their private Plans for Progress committee remain a part of the White House committee in charge of overseeing the executive order, which kept them in formal contact with the president on employment issues. NAM supported Plans for Progress, touting it as a way to "maintain the credibility of voluntarism and to increase businesses' leadership role in equal employment opportunity" (Delton 2009, p. 182). NAM also saw Plans for Progress as protection against criticisms and possible boycotts.

On the other hand, with a few exceptions, most craft unions reacted very negatively to the executive order because it banned discrimination by their apprenticeship programs as well as discrimination by employers. On the other hand, most industrial unions signed a voluntary pledge to end discrimination, which they called Union Programs for Fair Practices to distinguish it from Plans for Progress. However, most of the craft unions refused to sign such a pledge. Even after they eventually did so, they continued to exclude African Americans from apprenticeship programs, or refused to take them into their unions if they gained accreditation through government programs.

Most unions saw Kennedy's executive order as the beginning of an attack on what they had slowly achieved, a job niche that paid well and that could be passed on to their children or the children of their friends and neighbors. In sociologist Jill Quadagno's (1994, p. 65) telling phrase, they felt they had "property rights" in their jobs that were more basic than the right to equal access. In terms of their moral justification, the construction unions resisted on the basis of a gradualist version of liberalism that had been articulated by the liberal-labor alliance in the postwar era, which made it more difficult for civil rights advocates to counter their arguments against any form of affirmative action (Sugrue 2001).

The general union resistance to integration soon led African Americans to initiate protests and temporary shut-downs at construction sites in the North, especially in Philadelphia, where months of serious confrontation developed just as strife-ridden efforts to bring about integration in Birmingham were unfolding in April 1963. Although some of these demonstrations were called in support of the nonviolent protesters in Birmingham, the Northern activists were also reacting to two years of adamant resistance to their efforts at local job integration by white craft workers, and they expressed little respect for a nonviolent approach. When

Kennedy sent his secretary of labor and members of his White House staff to survey the situation in several different cities, their reports revealed an increasing potential for violence.

This alarming conclusion led Kennedy to make a major civil rights speech on June 11. Eleven days later, he issued a second executive order related to civil rights, this one explicitly banning discrimination on all construction sites that involved a federal contract. The day after the executive order was announced, Walter Reuther, the liberal and assertive president of the United Auto Workers, joined Martin Luther King, Jr. in leading a "Walk for Freedom" in Detroit. Ominously, few of the 125,000 to 200,000 marchers were white (Sugrue 2008, p. 298). Shortly thereafter, the importance of the new executive order, and any possible confrontations over it, were overshadowed by Kennedy's announcement that his administration had begun the process of drafting new civil rights legislation that would deal with all forms of discrimination.

Several top industrial union leaders then stated their willingness to change their policies, but the most that the construction unions would do was to express support for training programs (Quadagno 1994, pp. 64–74). This resistance, bolstered by the claim that their individual rights were being violated, widened the longstanding racial split in the union movement, and set the stage for union defeats at the hands of their own white members at the voting booth in 1966 and 1968.

The Supreme Court Makes Labor Law

In theory, it would have been easy enough for the federal government to use a variety of its economic powers to force companies to comply with the decisions by the National Labor Relations Board that had angered the entire corporate community. For example, it could have excluded companies that violated the law from bidding on government contracts, which involve far more than defense spending, including purchases of everything from trucks and automobiles for government departments and agencies to uniforms, linens, food and much else by the Department of Defense. But the conservative coalition could block legislation to implement such penalties when it came to labor issues. Moreover, President Kennedy, and the vice president who replaced him after he was assassinated in late 1963, Lyndon B. Johnson, were reluctant to issue executive orders on what had become a highly contentious issue for the corporate community. In this context of stalemate, the Supreme Court in effect made labor law in the 1960s, and it did so to the detriment of unions. This step in the decline of unions was a subtle one, and did not have immediate impacts on existing unions, so it is often overlooked. But it was crucial to events that unfolded during the presidency of Richard M. Nixon in relation to the destruction of the union movement.

174 The Rise and Fall of Labor Unions

The court setbacks for unions seem all the more surprising because the "Warren Court," overseen by a moderate Republican chief justice from California, Earl Warren, was an anathema for Northern ultraconservatives and Southern Democrats. They believed it was a hotbed of liberals and radicals because it had allegedly destroyed the country's foundations through its unanimous ruling against school segregation in 1954. Moreover, the court had further inflamed ultraconservatives North and South with its "one man, one vote" reapportionment rulings between 1962 and 1964, which outlawed the thinly populated rural House districts that greatly favored the conservative coalition. It also outraged ultraconservatives between 1962 and 1966 by outlawing mandatory school prayer, extending the right to privacy into the bedroom, and giving new rights and protections to those arrested for alleged criminal acts. The court seemed to be remaking America in many ways.

However, for all the court's liberalism on the rights of individuals, its decisions on labor issues tilted in the direction of the corporate community by making decisions that set the stage for corporate success in the 1970s in the ongoing counterattack on unions. To begin with, the court first upheld the Fibreboard decision on extremely narrow grounds. The top leaders' "freedom to manage the business" had not been abridged because "no capital investment was involved" and the company "merely replaced existing employees with those of an independent contractor to do the same work under similar conditions of employment" (Gross 1995, p. 192). So the decision was not the sweeping vindication the board needed, leaving the more general decision for perhaps another day. But even this narrow victory turned out to be a temporary and hollow one for the NLRB and organized labor. Justice Potter Stewart wrote a damaging separate concurring decision, which was joined by two other justices. It included the vague but clearly pro-management assertion that employers were not obligated to bargain over decisions that were "at the core of entrepreneurial control" or were "fundamental to the basic direction of the corporate enterprise" (Gross 1995, p. 193). Those two phrases became the basis for many future anti-union court decisions at all levels of the court system.

As disheartening as the Fibreboard decision was for the liberal-labor alliance, the decision concerning Deering Milliken's shutdown in Darlington was an even greater setback. It gave employers the right to go out of business for any reason whatsoever, "even if vindictiveness toward the union was the reason for the liquidation" (Gross 1995, p. 193). It then sent the case back to the labor board for further consideration. The court also overturned two NLRB rulings that were based on the idea that employer lockouts created too great an imbalance of power over unions. The court held that power imbalances were not the issue. So henceforth employers had the right to lock out workers whenever they wished to do so, including during contract negotiations.

Summing up the arguments that were waged all the way to the Supreme Court, the corporate community had gained two new weapons that could do considerable damage. They could use lockouts with impunity, and they could close down factories if worse came to worse. However, a united corporate community was not fully satisfied with the outsourcing decision in the Fibreboard case, and it still thought that the NLRB was too powerful in general.

Corporate Moderates Mobilize to Change Labor Laws

Despite their general success in the Supreme Court, the corporate moderates decided to organize a new attempt to bring about changes in labor law through the legislative process. The outcome of this attempt was not what they originally hoped for, but their major efforts between 1965 and 1970 did set the stage for victory by another route in the 1970s. It is important to describe this all-out effort so readers can decide for themselves if those social scientists and historians that claim business was not well organized until the early 1970s are correct (e.g., Hacker and Pierson 2010; Phillips-Fein 2009; Vogel 1989).

The corporate community began its new initiative in 1965 through the "No-Name Committee," a small group of management lawyers and industrial relations vice presidents from a dozen major companies, including AT&T, B.F. Goodrich Ford, General Dynamics, General Electric, Macy's, Sears, Roebuck, and U.S. Steel (Gross 1995). The organizational chores within the new committee, which eventually changed its name to the Labor Law Reform Group (LLRG), fell to Douglas H. Soutar, a lawyer employed as an industrial relations manager by American Smelting and Refining. In the course of carrying out his role within the LLRG, Soutar also inadvertently secured himself a place in the history of labor-management conflict because he was a detailed note-taker and careful record keeper, including for his innumerable telephone conversations. After his retirement, he donated his files to the Industrial and Labor Relations Library at Cornell. His detailed files made it possible for James A. Gross (1995, pp. 200–205, 234–237) to tell the full story of the origins of the corporate community's new offensive in detail for the first time.

With the LLRG providing the general framework, the corporate leaders hired three pro-management lawyers to draft new legislation for eventual introduction into Congress. One worked as a legislative counselor to General Motors, Chrysler, and General Electric, a second represented Chrysler and General Motors after working on both the Taft-Hartley and Landrum-Griffin acts, and the third was an influential management attorney in Washington. Two had served on the National Labor Relations Board at one time or another. In all, these lawyers were a small subsection of the general category of corporate lawyers who became the most prestigious figures in the law profession in the late nineteenth century as they rose to prominence and influence as part of the ascendancy of corporations. Corporate lawyers became hired guns for corporations and important go-betweens with government (Domhoff 2014, pp. 29–31, for a summary of several studies; Nelson 1988, for a detailed study of four corporate law firms, and especially pp. 232, 264, 269). Many of them are even more specialized as Wall Street lawyers, who work closely with commercial and investment bankers, and they often are appointed to cabinet-level positions in Washington (Smigel 1964).

The work of the corporate lawyers hired by the LLRG was checked over by a "Blue Ribbon Committee," which consisted of corporate lawyers specializing in labor issues at 100 large corporations. The drafting work was also coordinated with the Labor Policy Association (a meeting ground for hundreds of corporations with labor-law units) through its president, who was a former lobbyist for several corporations (Gross 1995, p. 202–203). Clearly, this was an extensive effort involving a large number of corporations, not the work of a few ultraconservatives or maverick isolates.

With the work of the three draftsmen under way, aided by financial support from the NAM and the Chamber of Commerce, the LLRG laid plans for "phase two," a large public education project aimed at the country's "thought leaders." It would also include a widespread media campaign directed by a major public relations firm. There was a third phase as well, an attempt to gain the help of a Southern Democrat in the Senate, who would hold hearings on the National Labor Relations Act. Lawyers involved with the LLRG would use the hearings to criticize the NLRA and lay the groundwork for the changes suggested by the drafting committee and the Blue Ribbon Committee (Gross 1995, pp. 205–207). However, it was early 1968 before phases two and three could be put into action.

By late 1967 the Labor Law Reform Group had a final draft of its proposed changes in the National Labor Relations Act. First and foremost, the draft put more emphasis on the right of employees to join or not join a union, and on the right of management to talk with employees about this decision. The plans to shape public opinion and influence Congress were also in place, but at the same time members of the LLRG were well aware "there was no chance of changing the law unless Republicans triumphed in the 1968 presidential and congressional elections" (Gross 1995, p. 205). The public education phase of the campaign was carried out by Hill and Knowlton, the world's largest public relations firm, which handled publicity and lobbying for numerous industries (Gross 1995, pp. 207–208).

The LLRG's main legal counsel (i.e., top lobbyist) for the Congressional phase of the campaign was a Washington lawyer who had worked on the Landrum-Griffin Act with other corporate lawyers, first as the general counsel to the House labor committee, then as a White House liaison to Congress. With Soutar of American Smelting and Refining playing a coordinating role, the LLRG then directed its efforts through a senior senator from North Carolina, a strong supporter of the textile industry. He created a select subcommittee of the Senate Judiciary Committee, appointed himself chair, and then added a large majority of anti-union senators to the committee. Seventy percent of the testimony came from corporate lawyers working with the LLRG, although none of them mentioned this fact.

Despite all this preparation, the hearings had little or no impact for a variety of unexpected reasons. They were completely obscured by anti-war demonstrations, the scramble for the Democratic presidential nomination after Johnson announced he would not run again, and the assassinations of Martin Luther King, Jr., and Senator Robert F. Kennedy of New York. Although the Republicans gained five seats in the Senate in 1968, and five in the House as well, the labor committees in both houses still had too many non-Southern Democrats to make significant changes in labor laws possible. The overall campaign therefore ended in failure, but it once again revealed just how coordinated 100 or more corporations were for lobbying Congress and connecting with opinion-shaping organizations. It also showed their determination to prevail one way or another on this issue, and prepared them to work closely with the newly elected Republican president, Richard M. Nixon. However, more context is needed from the Kennedy-Johnson years before turning to the constraints and options that faced the Nixon Administration.

Conflicts Over Wage-Price Guidelines

As the NLRB was delivering its pro-union rulings in the early 1960s and the LLRG was beginning to develop its plan, the corporate community was dealing with another challenge, in this instance from the White House. It involved the imposition of wage-price guidelines by the federal government to control inflation. Although their possible usefulness had been mentioned in an earlier CED report (1958) on inflation, which caused tensions within the organization, any wage-price committee or agency remained unacceptable to most corporate moderates, as well as all ultraconservatives. The corporate community viewed any form of government mediation or intervention of this nature as a challenge to their power to determine prices and wages. As it turned out, unions had their own reasons for disliking wage-price guidelines, but from the outset corporate leaders feared the possibility of an eventual government-labor alliance on wage-price issues. The almost immediate and complete failure of this initiative is therefore an important dimension of the escalating struggle between corporations and unions because it eliminated one of the

178 The Rise and Fall of Labor Unions

options, short of wartime wage and price controls, for limiting the inflation that developed shortly thereafter due to the Vietnam War.

Fully aware of the possible minefield that lay before it, the Kennedy Administration had introduced voluntary wage-price guidelines into the policy mix soon after it took office. It did so gingerly by first appealing to the need to preserve foreign markets in the face of a potential wage-price spiral that might jeopardize the international competitiveness of American corporations: "We cannot afford unsound wage and price movements which push up costs, weaken our international competitive position, restrict job opportunities, and jeopardize the health of our domestic economy," Kennedy wrote in a special message to Congress two weeks after the inauguration (Barber 1975, p. 141). Since the issue of foreign trade during the Kennedy Administration will be dealt with in detail in Chapter 13, the important contextual point for now is that the corporate moderates were eagerly advocating the Trade Expansion Act of 1962 at this point, and Kennedy was fully supportive of their efforts. In effect, he was trying to take advantage of the corporate moderates' desire for trade expansion to make a pitch for their support for wage-price guidelines.

As a first step, Kennedy appointed an Advisory Committee on Labor-Management Policy, consisting of top business leaders and major union presidents, which was charged with the responsibility of recommending measures to meet the goal of wage-price stability. However, the committee could not achieve consensus, and the corporate members strongly rejected any semblance of government guidelines or hearings in relation to price increases. While the labor-management advisory committee floundered, the administration carried out discrete efforts behind the scenes (largely through members of the Council of Economic Advisors and its staff) to limit the size of any wage increase resulting from the 1962 contract negotiations between the United Steel Workers and the steel industry. As part of this effort, Secretary of Labor Goldberg put his credibility on the line with organized labor by urging the steelworkers to keep their wage demands within the bounds set by productivity gains. Kennedy then talked personally with the president of the steelworkers, leading to the latter's reluctant acceptance of the Kennedy-Goldberg pleas to maintain political solidarity with the pro-labor president. The White House also thought it had reached an understanding with U.S. Steel, the industry's price leader, that it would not raise prices. In fact, Kennedy and Goldberg had met with the president of the steelworkers and Roger Blough, the chair of U.S. Steel since 1955, as a final step in the lengthy negotiations leading to an agreement (Barber 1975, pp. 167–168). Blough, who figures prominently in the corporate community's anti-union efforts over the next ten years, was a former Wall Street lawyer representing the J. P. Morgan financial interests, which at the time still had a close involvement in U.S. Steel.

Two weeks after the settlement was announced, Blough asked for a White House appointment on only a few hours' notice. He then told

Union Victories, Corporate Pushback   179

Kennedy that U.S. Steel had decided to raise its prices by $6 a ton. Kennedy was taken by surprise, but he knew he was not the first president to have problems with the steel industry. Truman faced three similar confrontations between 1946 and 1952, ordering the combatants to the White House to resume negotiations in 1946 and temporarily taking over the industry in 1952, only to have the Supreme Court rule that his action was illegal. Similarly, the Eisenhower Administration was drawn into an intermediary role in a steel strike in 1956. It kept its involvement secret, set the terms for the settlement of a 116-day strike, and specifically prohibited an increase in steel prices (Gordon 1975, pp. 128–129). A study prepared by two economists for the Joint Economic Committee in 1959 concluded that increases in steel prices in the 1950s "had contributed greatly" to inflation (Barber 1975, p. 155).

With the prestige of the presidency and the concept of wage-price guidelines at stake, as well as his own image in the eyes of the union movement, Kennedy immediately took several highly publicized actions to force Blough to rescind the price increase. In doing so, he was not only taking on the steel industry, but one of the most powerful members of the corporate community as well, because Blough was the chair of the Business Council (a new name the Business Advisory Council had adopted in 1962 after a dispute with the White House) and a trustee of the CED (Domhoff 2013, p. 103 for the details of this dispute and its aftermath). Blough also had served on the CED subcommittee that issued a strong anti-union report in 1964. (Even before signing the CED report, he had made his anti-union views clear in the late 1950s in a series of three lectures at Columbia University in which he concluded that unions "adopt objectives that largely contradict the competitive principle itself," with the result that "wages and costs have spiraled so far out of line that enough profits cannot be accumulated to buy the needed new tools" (*Time* 1958).) Due to his central role in the policy-planning network, he had an increasingly large role in most of the key events between 1963 and 1973, including the steps that led to the formation of the Business Roundtable in 1972.

Kennedy's strong reactions to what he saw as a double-cross by Blough included the exercise of powers he would not consider using in order to help unions: threats of antitrust actions, other types of government investigations, and the transfer of government steel purchases to companies that did not raise their prices. The battle was over in 72 hours when U.S. Steel announced that it would rescind its price increases. For Blough and other corporate leaders, it was a worrisome reminder of the potential power of the government to dictate to the corporate community, at least in the short run (Schlesinger 1965, pp. 636–639). This incident was highly publicized at the time and is still used by some scholars as strong evidence that corporations have little power when it comes to governmental policy.

Although the Kennedy Administration soon claimed that the outcome of its first serious attempt at institutionalizing restraint by both corporations and unions was on balance a successful one, even though there were subsequent piecemeal price hikes by most steel companies, it was hesitant thereafter to become actively involved in contract negotiations. In the aftermath, one of Kennedy's Council of Economic Advisors (CEA) appointees did a careful study of the experience of several European governments with wage-price policies. He concluded that they did not do any better in holding down wages and prices, even though those governments had more power over these issues than did the American government (Barber 1975, p. 175).

Moreover, the episode reinforced organized labor's wariness of guidelines as more likely to restrain wages than prices, partly because wages are more easily monitored than prices, but also because of the corporate community's general clout. In addition, agreeing to wage-price guidelines would imply that organized labor tacitly accepted the current distribution of income between wages and profits as being fair, but that seemed morally wrong to many union activists, liberals, and leftists, especially at a time when profits were soaring (Dark 2001, pp. 64–66).

The same story repeated itself for President Johnson two weeks after he assumed office. Reuther, one of the labor leaders Johnson worked very hard to cultivate, told members of the CEA that the UAW intended to demand large wage increases in the light of record profits at General Motors and other automobile companies during the previous year. Since the industry was making great gains in productivity as well as profits, Reuther in effect challenged the administration to "enforce the price guideposts in the automobile industry," which would mean wage increases without price increases (Cochrane 1975, pp. 199–200). Not only were automobile company profits high, but Reuther also worried that he would look weak to the rank and file by accepting only moderate wage gains while the Teamsters and the construction unions were winning large increases. The competitive antagonisms within the union movement thereby caused problems for unions in general. When the CEA checked with its main contact at General Motors, it learned that GM would insist on a price increase if it had to raise wages by a significant amount.

In response to the likelihood that other union and corporate leaders were thinking much the same way, Johnson approved plans for a more elaborate system of gathering information and influencing contract negotiations in 1964 than Kennedy had been willing to consider. However, the AFL-CIO made its opposition to these efforts clear in May of 1964 with a long statement saying that guidelines were unnecessary because "inflation is not today's threat. Today's threat is idle men, idle plants, and idle machines." This public announcement bothered the chair of the CEA, who wrote to Johnson that this opposition was "pretty serious business so soon after you have told them you regard the guideposts as 'sensible and fair' and 'in the public interest'" (Dark 2001, p. 65, also for the statements by the AFL-CIO and the CEA chair). Meanwhile the secretary of commerce, the former CEO of a large pharmaceutical company and a member of the Business Council, did not make any effort to enforce the guidelines (McQuaid 1982, p. 239).

Still, the steelworkers did limit themselves to a 3.2 percent increase during contract discussions in 1965, to the great relief of Johnson and his CEA chair (Matusow 1984, pp. 156–158), However, the steel companies ignored the implicit bargain once again by making small price increases on different products over a period of several months. Shortly thereafter, the wage-price guidelines were a dead letter as far as labor, corporations, and Johnson were concerned. The CEA chair summarized the government's dilemma when he remarked that "[s]omewhere, sometime, we have to find a way to convince the unions they cannot continually push wage costs up and to convince business that profit margins cannot continually rise" (Cochrane 1975, p. 262). The failure of wage-price guidelines reverberated far beyond management-labor issues by the end of 1965. The CEA had underestimated just how close the economy was to full employment, and the Pentagon had seriously underestimated the amount it would be spending on the Vietnam War.

The Rise of Inflation and New Complications

Johnson and the corporate moderates headed into 1965 with a firm resolve to keep taxes low and stay within the budget. But that year turned out to be the beginning of a rapid increase in social-services spending at a rate of 8 percent a year, and by 1966 increased war spending and rising medical costs were overheating the economy as well. The result was tight labor markets, increasing conflicts between the corporate community and unions, and inflation. The inflation created dilemmas for both the White House and the corporate community concerning (1) government involvement in wage-price issues, (2) the need for higher taxes, and (3) the power of unions. Inflation was also impacting the corporate community's plans for expanding international trade, an issue that will be discussed in Chapter 14.

For Johnson, wage-price guidelines were essentially out of the question by mid-1966, just at the time that inflation really took off, because of his failed efforts to make them work in the first two years of his presidency. By late 1966 tax increases therefore seemed to be the only remedy for dealing with inflation in a situation in which government spending could not be cut. Tax increases for high-income earners and profitable corporations, which were the remedy recommended by liberal-labor Keynesian economists, were the most pressing need. Johnson completely understood this basic point, but political considerations once again made him hesitate. Asking for a tax increase would be to admit that the Vietnam War was expensive and going badly. It would also incur the wrath of the corporate rich and the large number of Americans in general with strong anti-tax sentiments, and thereby put the large contingent of new Democratic members of Congress at risk in 1966 in their traditionally Republican districts and states. Equally problematic, the conservative coalition, with Southern Democrats still serving as the chairs of key Congressional committees, and in particular the House Ways and Means Committee, made it clear that the price for such a tax increase was cutbacks in social spending. But the reductions in social spending sought by ultraconservatives risked more conflict among black activists, organized labor, and city officials.

Instead of calling for wartime wage-price controls and a tax increase, as Democratic presidents did during World War II and the Korean War, but which Johnson wanted to avoid, to downplay the extent of the war, he instead asked the corporate community to show voluntary restraint in investing overseas. In theory, lower overseas investments might help tame inflation by reducing the growing balance of payments problem. But voluntary restraint is a chimera, whether on the part of business or labor, and it was bound to fail. In my view, then, the root cause of the domestic inflation was the failure to fully mobilize on a war footing for the battle in Vietnam in which Johnson and the corporate community had decided to engage, as will be discussed in Chapter 12. And the main reason for the failure to mobilize on the home front was the increasingly militant opposition to a war that made no sense to a growing percentage of the population.

As might be expected, the Business Council would not support a temporary suspension of the investment tax credit, but Johnson was nonetheless able to convince Congress to take this small step. Then the CED rejected this legislative action in the context of a policy statement on *The Dollar and the World Monetary System* (1966b). Instead, the CED called for cuts in both domestic spending and overseas development assistance (Schriftgiesser 1967, p. 129). In other words, in late 1966 corporate moderates were still more concerned with defending the dollar through budget cuts than they were with the growing tensions in the inner cities and the South.

The Committee for Economic Development, once again demonstrating that its moderation and foresight had their limits, also wanted to reduce the corporate tax burden by adopting a value-added tax, which would provide more revenue for the government and "a better balance in federal taxes on business," to quote the title of its new tax proposal (CED 1966a). In the process, the corporate income tax would be dropped from 48 to 38 percent, which was the rate that prevailed before the Korean War. According to corporate leaders, the 48-percent corporate tax rate deterred necessary corporate investment and reduced their ability to create more jobs. With Johnson delaying a request for a general tax increase throughout 1966, an inflation rate that had been a mere 1.3 percent from 1961 to 1965 increased to 2.9 percent in 1966 and 3 percent in 1967 (Collins 2000, p. 75).

Union Victories, Corporate Pushback 183

While 3 percent inflation may seem minor by later standards, it was upsetting to the corporate community. Republicans decried it as a sign of worse things to come because they realized they had a good chance of bouncing back in the 1966 elections by running a scare campaign. In fact, white centrist and moderate voters did cut deeply into the Democratic Congressional majorities in those elections. Their votes may have been cast partly in reaction to an unpopular war and rising inflation, but most of all they were an expression of their increasing frustration with the demands of the civil rights movement, as documented in the concluding subsection of this chapter. The Republicans gained 47 seats in the House, including two more in the lower South, which restored the strength of the conservative coalition. The Republicans' success ensured that the conservative coalition could make good on its threats to extract cuts in domestic social spending in exchange for any tax increases, which no doubt would fall differentially on middle-income voters.

The ultraconservatives also added three new seats in the Senate. Their gains included a seat in Illinois that had been held for 18 years by a liberal Democratic incumbent, who received less than half of the UAW vote, a strong indication of just how disaffected white workers were becoming. But the impact of racial divisions was seen most dramatically in California, where UAW members who had voted two-thirds for Johnson in 1964, cast half their votes for the successful Republican challenger for governor, Ronald Reagan. The future president hammered on issues relating to white resistance to the pace of the civil rights movement, especially in the case of recent state legislation that enabled the integration of neighborhoods. This legislation was then rejected by 65.4 percent of the voters in a statewide initiative put on the ballot by ultraconservatives in 1964 (Boyle 1995, p. 222).

Due to these increasing conservative pressures, the options for dealing with the wage-price spiral were narrowing. By a process of elimination, the only acceptable remedy for inflation was higher interest rates, which had been the CED's preferred option since the late 1940s. This option reduces inflation by reducing consumer demand and throwing people out of work. It has the added advantage of weakening unions, but domestic turmoil had made it impossible to take this step in 1967 or 1968. In other words, the issue was power, not the correctness of one or another economic theory. The concerns of the corporate moderates had changed from a need to insure consumer demand, due to a lingering fear of what happened in the 1930s, and to a need to control inflation and labor unions. Put another way, the moderate conservatives in the corporate community changed their economic policies for political reasons. They wanted to defeat unions as the alleged source of cost-push inflation, to eliminate any government inclination to develop wage-price controls, and to make sure inflation was controlled only by using higher Fed interest rates, not by

Summary: The Beginning of the End for Union Power

As demonstrated in the next chapter, serious union decline began in the late 1960s for two separate reasons. First, corporate resistance to unions stiffened as manufacturing companies faced stronger competition from abroad, along with a need to continue to automate their production processes. Corporate leaders were not willing to have their "right to manage" challenged under any circumstances, but they thought the issue was especially critical in the new competitive environment they had created for themselves through their strong lobbying for tariff reductions. (As already noted, this issue is discussed in detail in chapters in Part 3.)

Second, the growing divisions between liberals and labor over how to react to the civil rights movement's demands for integration of neighborhoods, schools, and workplaces made the unions vulnerable to a renewed corporate attack. As the disruption generated by activists in the black community (and then the anti-war movement) continued to escalate after 1965, it soon became apparent that the liberal trade unions could not organize a large voting coalition in favor of the government programs they favored. Even in the case of the UAW, its leaders' hopes for an enlarged welfare state on the basis of a black-white worker's coalition in both the North and the South, with the segregationist Southern Democrats finally displaced, were "little more than ashes" by 1968 (Boyle 1998, Chapter 8). More exactly, the UAW simply did not have the ability "to maintain a cross-class, biracial coalition committed to continued reform" (Boyle 1998, p. 230). Instead, it lost the support of its major allies and the confidence of many of its white members: "For very different reasons, African-Americans, white workers, liberals, and the New Left all came to see the UAW, as they saw the Johnson Administration, as a prop for the status quo," historian Kevin Boyle (1998, p. 230) concludes in a concise summary of his masterful full-length study of the UAW between 1945 and 1968, published three years earlier (Boyle 1995). Far from any notion that labor had sold out, lacked militancy, or betrayed its promise, its story was one "of struggles fought—and lost" (Boyle 1998, p. 230). More generally, there was an unraveling of the liberal-labor alliance, just a little over 30 years after it first came together (Boyle 1995, Chapters 9–10; Matusow 1984).

To make matters worse, longstanding tensions increased between Reuther, who was the de facto leader of the liberal unions, and the president of the AFL-CIO, George Meany, a former plumber with a classic craft-union mentality and little interest in helping African American workers, if any. Meany's support for the Vietnam War and foot-dragging on integration exacerbated the tensions. Reuther withheld UAW dues to the AFL-CIO to express his displeasure with Meany's leadership, which led Meany to suspend the UAW from the AFL-CIO. Reuther then formed a new Alliance for Labor Action in July 1968, which was joined by "the most unlikely of partners," the Teamsters, noted for corruption and political conservatism. The failure of the Alliance for Labor Action reflected the UAW's isolation, and that of the liberal unions in general, from the rest of the labor movement at that point (Boyle 1995, pp. 246–247).

However, that fact provided no comfort for the corporate community. It was far more concerned that the most powerful of the private-sector unions, liberal or not liberal, could still use slowdowns, work stoppages, and strikes to win wage increases, cost-of-living clauses, and better benefits in a context of tight labor markets and domestic turmoil. As noted a moment ago, these tactics were being used at the same time as corporations were facing more foreign competition in American markets and trying to sell more goods overseas. As a consequence, reducing union power became the primary concern for both moderates and ultraconservatives in the corporate community by 1968, whether the immediate issue was inflation, wage rates, profit margins, or foreign trade.

This renewed emphasis on defeating unions occurred just as Richard M. Nixon prepared to assume the presidency, thanks to a narrow victory over Hubert Humphrey in the popular vote by a 43.4 to 42.7 percent margin, which led to a 301 to 191 victory in the Electoral College. Nixon's triumph was in part made possible by the defection of white Democrats to the third-party candidacy of Alabama's segregationist governor, George Wallace, who won five Southern states and 13.5 percent of the nationwide popular vote. His strong support in 1968 in two highly populated Midwestern industrial states, Ohio (where he had 11.8 percent of the vote) and Illinois (where he had 8.5 percent), may have contributed to Nixon's narrow victory in them. All that said, Nixon's victory owed even more to the white Democrats who cast their votes for him instead of Humphrey.

The sea change in white voting patterns due to racial issues actually first manifested itself in early 1964, when Governor Wallace of Alabama won 30 percent of the white Democratic vote in primaries in Indiana, with his strongest support in a heavily black area in the northern part of the state and a fundamentalist Christian area in central Indiana, where few African Americans resided (Rogin 1969). He also won 33 percent of the Democratic vote in Wisconsin, and 47 percent in the former slave-and-caste state of Maryland (Carleson 1981, pp. 31–37; Rogin 1969). In Maryland, he won 16 of 23 counties, many of which were on the state's eastern plantation shores, along with the state capitol and the white "ethnic" neighborhoods of Baltimore (Carter 2000, p. 215).

The large and rapid changes in voting preferences by white union members has been pieced together from Gallup polls since the late 1930s and

186 The Rise and Fall of Labor Unions

from more detailed studies by the American National Elections Studies at the University of Michigan since 1952. They first of all indicate that between 72 and 80 percent of union members had voted for the Democratic presidential candidate between 1936 and 1948 (Frymer 2008, p. 4, Figure 1.1). Despite the white workers' increasing concern with the demands of the civil rights movement, as evidenced by the George Wallace vote in three Democratic Party primaries in 1964, the percentage of white union members voting for Johnson in the national elections rose to a record 84 percent (Frymer 2008, p. 3). This was at least in part due to ultraconservative Republican presidential candidate Barry Goldwater's strong anti-union record, his talk of privatizing Social Security, and his musings about perhaps dropping nuclear bombs on Vietnam if necessary. But Johnson's record-setting Democratic percentage in 1964 fell to 40 percent in 1968, a shocking turn of events, and the Democratic percentage of the union vote sank to a new low of 36 percent in 1972 (Frymer 2008, p. 3).

The reasons for this very large change can be seen in Boyle's (1995) study of the UAW, which drew in part on surveys of its members commissioned by the union's research department. The passage of the Civil Rights Act in 1964 already had led to a considerable increase in integration in automobile factories in 1965 and 1966. For example, the percentage of African Americans in the UAW's unskilled membership ranks rose from 12 percent to almost 20 percent between 1960 and 1967 (Boyle 1995, p. 213). By 1965, one-third of white UAW members said the civil rights movement was moving too fast, and by 1967 one-half of the union's white members "opposed further integration" (Boyle 1995, p. 220). In 1968 the Democratic presidential candidate's support in one blue-collar county near Detroit fell by 19 percentage points from 1964, and by 22 percentage points in a county near Flint, the city in which the UAW had proven its mettle; Wallace won 14.2 percent of the vote near Detroit and 15.4 percent near Flint (Boyle 1995, pl. 255–256). Even though the Democrats ended up winning Michigan because of the three-way split in the vote, the fact remains that "[h]alf of the voters in United Auto Worker areas [i.e., city neighborhoods or nearby suburban communities] had cast their ballots for conservative candidates, a profound change for a union whose members had been among the Democrats' most loyal supporters," and they continued to "move away from the Democratic party" over the next two decades (Boyle 1995, p. 256).

At the same time as many Northern white union members were moving toward the Republicans, so too were Southern whites. In 1964, the five Deep-South states with the highest percentage of African Americans (Alabama, Georgia, Louisiana, Mississippi, and South Carolina) cast the majority of their votes for Goldwater. They knew that his strong advocacy of "states' rights" meant that he would do nothing to change race-based caste relations in the South. In 1968, the white majority in eight of the 17 former slave-and-caste states voted for Nixon and another five states voted for George Wallace on his third-party ticket. As a result, the Democratic Party only won Texas in the South, along with three small, former slave-and-caste states, Delaware, Maryland, and West Virginia.

Although it is true that the Vietnam War was extremely divisive, and resulted in undying enmity between some groups, it is unlikely that very many defections to Nixon or Wallace by previous Democratic supporters can be attributed to opposition to the war or the anti-war movement. Instead, polls suggested that even though a majority of blue-collar and white-collar employees disliked the anti-war movement, they were opposed to the war as well (Boyle 1995, pp. 220–223; Hamilton 1972, Chapter 4; Hamilton 1975, Chapter 5; Mueller 1973; Mueller 1984). It therefore seems more plausible that the defections were due to the white resistance to the liberal Northern Democrats' support for integration, which many white Democrats perceived as a challenge to white dominance and the property rights they had in their jobs.

Based on these changes in white voting patterns in the second half of the 1960s, it is the Democrats' loss of many of its white voters, in conjunction with the harder line being taken by the corporate moderates, that prepared the way for a right turn. The allegedly improved organization and outreach of the ultraconservatives does not explain the right turn in the United States on labor or any other issues (*pace* Hacker and Pierson 2010; Mizruchi 2013; Phillips-Fein 2009). A fractured liberal-labor alliance was defeated by an enlarged corporate-conservative alliance because many white Americans at all class levels resented and resisted the demands by the civil rights movement, and soon thereafter by feminists and the LGBT movement (e.g., Hardisty 1999). Thus, in the same time period between 1965 and 2000 in which individual rights and freedoms expanded for people of color, women, and people with alternative sexual orientations, corporate domination also unexpectedly increased. Individual freedom turned out to be one thing, and collective power turned out to be quite another in a society riven by racial exclusion, religion, and ethnicity.

As a result of white voting shifts based on one of more of these new challenges to the status quo, the overwhelmingly anti-union Republican Party, dominated by conservatives and ultraconservatives in both the North and the South, now was in charge of the White House. Republicans therefore had the power to shape the NLRB and the Supreme Court. In addition, they could count on the rejuvenated conservative coalition, which had expanded its potential strength to 60 percent of the vote in the House and 52 percent in the Senate, thanks to the outcome of the 1968 elections (Shelley 1983, pp. 151, Table 8.5 and 154, Table 8.6).

I realize all this may sound a little unusual coming from a corporate-dominance theorist, but it's a multivariate world. People have racial, ethnic, and religious identities as well as class identities. Based on the United

States' history of slavery and continuing waves of immigration from many different countries, factors such as race, religion, and ethnicity came to be more important than class in shaping voting behavior from the mid-1960s to the end of the century (Manza and Brooks 1997; Manza and Brooks 1999; Zweigenhaft and Domhoff 2018, pp. 201–216). The explanation for the right turn is therefore not to be found in the idea that the corporate community or its ultraconservative wing somehow pulled its act together and asserted itself.

This corporate-assertiveness theory is the great conceit of the conventional academic wisdom of the twenty-first century. It comes close to explaining away the white defections from the liberal-labor alliance and the complicity of white trade unionists, however accidental or shortsighted, in the decline in industrial unions over the next 15 years. Contrary to this conventional academic wisdom, white resentments and resistance to integration, gender equality, and tolerance for all sexual orientations were the final, and critical, ingredients in the equation that changed the power structure between the 1968 and 1976 elections. A significant segment of everyday white voters made it possible for the corporate moderates to begin the right turn they had wanted to make by 1968 for their own reasons. The corporate moderates' reasons are explored in detail in the next chapter.

References

Barber, William. 1975. "The Kennedy years: Purposeful pedagogy." Pp. 135–192 in *Exhortation and control: The search for a wage-price policy 1945–1971*, edited by C. Goodwin. Washington: The Brookings Institution.

Boyle, Kevin. 1995. *The UAW and the heyday of American liberalism, 1945–1968*. Ithaca: Cornell University Press.

———. 1998. "Little more than ashes: The UAW and American reform in the 1960s." Pp. 217–238 in *Organized labor and American politics 1894–1994: The labor-liberal alliance*, edited by K. Boyle. Albany: State University of New York Press.

Carleson, Jody. 1981. *George C. Wallace and the politics of powerlessness: The Wallace campaigns for the presidency, 1964–1976*. New Brunswick, NJ: Transaction Books.

Carter, Dan 2000. *The politics of rage: George Wallace, the origins of the new conservatism, and the transformation of American politics*. Baton Rouge: Louisiana State University Press.

CED. 1958. *Defense against inflation: Policies for price stability in a growing economy*. New York: Committee for Economic Development.

———. 1964. *Union powers and union functions: Toward a better balance*. New York: Committee for Economic Development.

———. 1966a. *A better balance in federal taxes on business*, New York: Committee for Economic Development.

———. 1966b. *The dollar and the world monetary system*. New York: Committee for Economic Development.

Cochrane, James. 1975. "The Johnson Administration: Moral suasion goes to war." Pp. 193–293 in *Exhortation and control: The search for a wage-price policy 1945–1971*, edited by C. Goodwin. Washington: The Brookings Institution.

Collins, Robert M. 2000. *More: The politics of economic growth in postwar America.* New York: Oxford University Press.

Dark, Taylor. 2001. *The unions and the Democrats: An enduring alliance.* Ithaca: Cornell University Press.

Delton, Jennifer. 2009. *Racial integration in corporate America, 1940–1990.* New York: Cambridge University Press.

Domhoff, G. W. 2013. *The myth of liberal ascendancy: Corporate dominance from the Great Depression to the Great Recession.* Boulder: Paradigm Publishers.

———. 2014. *Who rules America? The triumph of the corporate rich.* New York: McGraw-Hill.

Feild, John. 1967. "Oral history interview, January 16." in *John G. Feild personal papers.* Boston: John F. Kennedy Presidential Library and Museum.

Frymer, Paul. 2008. *Black and blue: African Americans, the labor movement, and the decline of the Democratic Party.* Princeton: Princeton University Press.

Golland, David. 2011. *Constructing affirmative action: The struggle for equal employment opportunity.* Lexington: University Press of Kentucky.

Gordon, R. Scott. 1975. "The Eisenhower Administration: The doctrine of shared responsibility." Pp. 95–134 in *Exhortation and control: The search for a wage-price policy 1945–1971*, edited by C. Goodwin. Washington: The Brookings Institution.

Gross, James A. 1995. *Broken promise: The subversion of U.S. labor relations policy.* Philadelphia: Temple University Press.

Hacker, Jacob and Paul Pierson. 2010. *Winner-take-all politics: How Washington made the rich richer—and turned its back on the middle class.* New York: Simon & Schustser.

Hamilton, Richard 1972. *Class and politics in the United States.* New York: Wiley.

———. 1975. *Restraining myths: Critical studies of U.S. social structure and politics.* New York: Sage Publications.

Hardisty, Jean. 1999. *Mobilizing resentment: Conservative resurgence from the John Birch Society to the Promise Keepers.* Boston: Beacon Press.

Harris, Howell. 1982. *The right to manage: Industrial relations policies of American Business in the 1940s.* Madison: University of Wisconsin Press.

Hirsch, Barry and David Macpherson. 2018. "Union membership and coverage database from the CPS." http://www.unionstats.com.

Manza, Jeff and Clem Brooks. 1997. "The religious factor in U.S. presidential elections, 1960–1992." *American Journal of Sociology* 103:38–81.

———. 1999. *Social cleavages and political change: Voter alignments and U.S. party coalitions.* New York: Oxford University Press.

Matusow, Allen. 1984. *The unraveling of America: A history of liberalism in the 1960s.* New York: Harper & Row.

McCartin, Joseph. 2011. *Collision course: Ronald Reagan, the air traffic controllers, and the strike that changed America.* New York: Oxford University Press.

McQuaid, Kim. 1982. *Big business and presidential power from FDR to Reagan.* New York: Morrow.

Miller, Berkeley and William Canak. 1995a. "Laws as a cause and consequence of public employee unionism." *Industrial Relations Research Association Series* 13:346–357.

———. 1995b. "There should be no blanket guarantee: Employers' reactions to public employee unionism, 1965–1975." *Journal of Collective Negotiations in the Public Sector* 24:17–35.

Mizruchi, Mark. 2013. *The fracturing of the American corporate elite.* Cambridge: Harvard University Press.

Mueller, John E. 1973. *War, presidents, and public opinion.* New York: Wiley.

———. 1984. "Reflections on the Vietnam antiwar movement and on the curious calm at the war's end." Pp. 151–157 in *Vietnam as history: Ten years after the Paris Peace Accords,* edited by P. Braestrup. Washington: University Press of America.

Nelson, Robert L. 1988. *Partners with power: The social transformation of the large law firm.* Berkeley: University of California Press.

Phillips-Fein, Kim. 2009. *Invisible hands: The making of the conservative movement from the New Deal to Reagan.* New York: W.W. Norton & Company.

Quadagno, Jill. 1994. *The color of welfare: How racism undermined the war on poverty.* New York: Oxford University Press.

Rogin, Michael. 1969. "Politics, emotion, and the Wallace vote." *British Journal of Sociology* 20:27–45.

Schlesinger, Arthur 1965. *A thousand days: John F. Kennedy in the White House.* Boston: Houghton Mifflin.

Schriftgiesser, Karl. 1967. *Business and public policy.* Englewood Cliffs, NJ: Prentice Hall.

Shelley, Mack. 1983. *The permanent majority: The conservative coalition in the United States Congress.* Tuscaloosa: University of Alabama Press.

Smigel, Erwin. 1964. *The Wall Street lawyer: Professional organization man?* New York: Free Press.

Sugrue, Thomas. 2001. "Breaking through: The troubled origins of affirmative action in the workplace." Pp. 31–52 in *Color lines: Affirmative action, immigration, and civil rights options for America,* edited by J. Skrentny. Chicago: University of Chicago Press.

———. 2008. *Sweet land of liberty: The forgotten struggle for civil rights in the North.* New York: Random House.

Time. 1958. "Business: Roger Blough." June 8, *Time Magazine.* http://content. time.com/time/magazine/article/0,9171,892625,00.html.

Vogel, David. 1989. *Fluctuating fortunes: The political power of business in America.* New York: Basic Books.

Zweigenhaft, Richard L. and G. William Domhoff. 2018. *Diversity in the power elite: Ironies and unfulfilled promises.* Lanham, MD: Rowman & Littlefield.

Chapter 5

The Corporate Moderates Reorganize to Defeat Unions, 1969–1985

Despite the best efforts of the Labor Law Study Group and the Committee for Economic Development between the mid-1960s and 1969, the corporate community had been unable to subdue the private-sector unions, which were now bolstered in terms of overall union numbers by the gradual growth of public-sector unions, which had 4.0 million members by 1970 (Miller and Canak 1995, p. 17, Table 1). At first the Nixon Administration, heavily influenced by its corporate backers and numerous appointments from within their ranks, tried to win this battle through continuing the fight against inflation with the usual Committee for Economic Development (CED) approach via commercial Keynesianism—higher interest rates and budget balancing.

But inflation rose from 4.4 percent in January 1969, to 6.2 percent one year later, and was only back down to 4.4 percent in July 1971. During the same 31-month period, unemployment grew from 3.4 percent to 6.0 percent. Very quickly, leaders within the corporate community complained that not enough was being done in a timely fashion. This was especially the view of executives who managed companies rushing to complete new factories. Wages and fringe benefits for workers in plant construction increased by 10 percent between June 1968 and June 1969. Wage increases in plant construction also contributed to a rise in housing prices due to the fact that the unionized workers that built residential housing insisted on the same wage and benefit scales established in industrial construction.

Although the corporate chieftains publicly blamed the resulting wage increases on unions, they had contributed to the problem, and many of them understood that fact. In their search for higher profits and greater market share in a booming economy, they encouraged contractors to take on extra workers, and to pay overtime wages if necessary, in order to finish new projects on time. They thereby tightened labor markets over and beyond what a strong economy was already causing, which made it possible for unionized construction and industrial workers to keep up with the inflationary spiral for a short time. In some cases, workers apparently were able to win settlements that improved their wages, temporarily pushing their gains above increases in the Consumer Price Index (Edsall 1984, p. 157). However, these gains were usually short-lived, especially if the actual number of hours they were able to work each year are added into the equation (Linder 1999, p. 196).

Paralleling the administration's efforts to reduce inflation through higher interest rates and a tighter budget, several corporate leaders, heeding calls from leaders within the construction industry, created a new organization in May 1969, at a regularly scheduled meeting of the Business Council in Hot Springs, Virginia. Its initial goal was to enforce self-restraint and provide aid to construction companies in trying to put an end to cost-of-living adjustments and lucrative union contracts (Linder 1999, pp. 187–188, 190, for the evidence that the corporate leaders were responding to entreaties and criticisms from within the construction industry). Called the Construction Users Anti-Inflation Roundtable (CUAIR), its founding members included the CEOs of General Electric, Standard Oil of New Jersey, Union Carbide, Kennecott, General Motors, and AT&T, all of whom were also trustees of the CED as well as being members of the Business Council.

Planning for the new group had been going on for several months, but it was slowed by the usual problems of creating any new organization, along with the need to convince the leader they had agreed upon, Roger Blough, recently retired from his 14 years as the CEO of U.S. Steel, that he should take the position. Blough finally agreed to become the CUAIR chair, but only on the condition that the CEOs on the coordinating committee would personally attend the group's biweekly meetings, which they by and large did for a four-year period. (As discussed in the next subsection of the chapter, CUAIR was merged with the LLRG to form the Business Roundtable in late 1972 (Linder 1999, pp. 190, 197).)

According to one of the labor-relations lawyers who worked with Blough closely during these years, CUAIR was informally called "Roger's Roundtable" because he was self-effacing and widely respected for his leadership throughout his long legal and business careers, and as a member of many key policy-planning organizations (Soutar 1996). But it was also the case that the steel industry was under especially strong pressure to hold down construction costs due to the increasing international competition from foreign mills, which were more productive than the American plants and had lower labor costs (Swenson 2002, pp. 308–310). In fact, Blough (1968/1972) had already called for import quotas because the steel industry was losing a big part of the American market and could no longer pass along rising production costs to its corporate customers.

As part of its effort to help construction companies resist demands by unions, CUAIR also quietly encouraged them to become "double-breasted," a euphemism for adding a new unit to the company that could bid on non-union contracts. Backed by the big industrial corporations, the Associated General Contractors of America also developed a strike insurance fund to provide money to companies that resisted union demands for wage increases that exceeded the inflation rate. In addition, CUAIR urged the formation of several dozen local construction user groups, called "local Roundtables," with the goal of organizing smaller companies and influencing city and county governments. For example, the chair of Inland Steel was chair of the Chicago Construction Users and the chair of New York Telephone was the chair of the local council in New York City (Linder 1999, pp. 212–213). To aid in the development of these local Roundtables, CUAIR hired the former president of the National Constructors Association, an organization of the large construction companies that built plant and equipment for corporations. He had a large network of friends and acquaintances in the construction industry (Linder 1999, pp. 10–11, 156). This outreach strategy was later put to nationwide use by CUAIR's successor, the Business Roundtable, at the state level in the 1980s on health-insurance issues, and then in the 1990s to lobby Congress for trade legislation, as shown in Chapters 10 and 15.

By mid-July 1969, Blough and his CEO advisers had decided that their specific goals were to (1) refrain from scheduling overtime despite their desire to expand their companies, and (2) support contractors who resisted settling strikes by acquiescing to demands for large wage hikes. In terms of increasing the pool of skilled labor, which would require help from the federal government, they wanted to include more members of the minority groups that the white construction unions had almost entirely excluded, which for the most part in that era meant African Americans. This was a possibility that had been raised several times by corporate labor advisers in the months before CUAIR was established (Linder 1999, pp. 192, 250–251).

Blough met with several top officials in the Nixon Administration during the summer months of 1969 to discuss CUAIR's concerns and policy goals. They included the secretary of labor, the chair of the Council of Economic Advisors, and a counselor to the president, Arthur Burns, an economist with many connections to the corporate community through his longtime leadership within the National Bureau of Economic Research. Blough also met with the postmaster general, himself the owner of a large construction company in Alabama. The new Postmaster General also was one of the leaders in the National Constructors Association that had been urging the large international corporations to find new ways to help contractors limit the power of construction unions (Linder 1999, pp. 190, 192). By mid-August, information on CUAIR was widely available to members of the corporate community and leaders in the union movement through reports in newsletters for the construction industry (e.g., the *Construction Labor Report* on August 6) as well as in *The Wall Street Journal* (August 14) and *The New York Times* (August 21) (Linder 1999, pp. 194–195).

194 The Rise and Fall of Labor Unions

Several of the Nixon appointees that Blough met with told him it would be difficult for them to confront the construction unions because they had given the administration considerable support during and after the elections. However, these appointees did relay Blough's concerns to the president. On September 4, Nixon issued a statement decrying the shortage of skilled labor in the industry, and then established a six-person Cabinet Committee on Construction. The new committee consisted of the secretaries of commerce, labor, transportation, and housing and urban development, along with the postmaster general and the chair of the CEA (Linder 1999, p. 234). Nixon also told several departments to work with the Department of Labor on expanding programs to train more skilled construction workers. Employers in general were not satisfied with these small steps and lobbied for more, but the new cabinet committee did become a formal communication link for them. For example, Blough spoke at its meetings in late October and December 1992.

In response to CUAIR's desire for further actions, and with the advice of the Secretary of Labor, George Shultz, who was the former dean of the University of Chicago School of Business, as well as a frequent adviser to the CED in the 1960s, Nixon established a Construction Industry Collective Bargaining Commission two weeks later. It was charged with mediating disputes and finding new ways to moderate wage increases (Marchi 1975, pp. 310–311). The members included employers, union officials, and public members. However, CUAIR decided not to express public support for the commission, reasoning that management would be outvoted 8-4 on the 12-person committee (Linder 1999, pp. 236–237).

In the short run, though, inflation continued to rise. In late April 1970, Nixon's main economic adviser, Burns, by this time the chair of the Federal Reserve Board, gave a speech in which he said that the demand-driven inflation of the late 1960s had been replaced by a wage-push inflation that was due to the wage-price spiral. Therefore, he added, "making monetary and fiscal policies still more restrictive not only would be ineffective but would invite recession" (Marchi 1975, p. 316). He instead advocated short-term controls and even a reconsideration of an incomes policy, an idea corporate leaders did not like any better then than they had earlier.

In June of 1970, Blough and three CUAIR staff members met with the Cabinet Committee on Construction to advocate stronger measures. They first of all wanted several steps taken to limit the power of union-controlled hiring halls in supplying workers to construction companies. They argued that union control of hiring halls made it possible for union leaders to create labor shortages even when there was evidence of high unemployment (Linder 1999, pp. 198–199, 236). CUAIR also wanted the committee to recommend suspension of a 1931 law that put a floor under construction wages. Fashioned in that bygone era by Republicans James Davis, a senator from Pennsylvania, and Robert Bacon, a representative from New York, the law has been known ever since simply as "Davis-Bacon." Originally intended to keep contractors from making the lowest bids on a contract on the basis of extremely low wages for workers they brought in from low-income regions of the country, Davis-Bacon required federal contractors to pay the local "prevailing wage" to construction workers. In practice, though, the prevailing wage soon came to be set by government officials through informal negotiations with construction unions, which meant that the wage usually did not decline and often increased.

However, Secretary of Labor Schultz opposed bypassing union hiring halls as unlikely to work, and also opposed the suspension of Davis-Bacon. Instead, with the help of one of his assistant secretaries, a former vice president of labor relations at Standard Oil of New Jersey, he continued to reshape apprenticeship programs by taking the power to select new apprentices away from construction unions. Based on predictions of an imminent labor shortage that never materialized, he also increased the size of apprenticeship programs. This series of actions increased the supply of construction workers, brought about some integration in the building trades, and at the same time began to erode the power of unions (Quadagno 1994, pp. 79–84).

Following Schultz's advice, Nixon delayed on the suspension of Davis-Bacon, and took no action related to the union domination of hiring halls. By this point, though, the leading corporate moderates, such as those in the Business Council and the CED, had heard enough about patience and long-term policy. Contrary to any claim that the Business Council was "aloof from political engagement" at this time (e.g., Phillips-Fein 2009, p. 166), the corporate leaders used a regular meeting of the Business Council with White House and cabinet officials as the occasion to send the White House a "message of censure" in October 1970. The Business Council leaders charged that the federal government had failed "to check excessive wage and price increases" (Marchi 1975, p. 326). As acknowledged at the time by one of the members of Nixon's CEA, who previously had been employed as an economist by the CED for 23 years, the views presented by the Business Council leaders in this and subsequent meetings had an impact: "Their views become a part of our information in policy making. It's a fact that the growing feeling in the Business Council of the need to do something on the inflation front was a definite contribution to the decision we took" (Fowlkes 1971, p. 2307).

In effect, the corporate executives now wanted to rely on two confrontational options for dealing with inflation, which could be used separately or together. One would hold the line on wage increases, thereby forcing blue-collar and white-collar employees to absorb the costs of inflation through cuts in their real wages. This course was justifiable in employers' minds because they thought that workers, and construction workers in

196 The Rise and Fall of Labor Unions

particular, had been making excessive wage demands. The other option would increase unemployment by using high interest rates set by the Federal Reserve Board to reduce consumer demand, housing construction, and business investments, despite the warnings by Burns as to the likelihood that this course of action might fail.

Faced with these pressures and criticisms, Nixon nonetheless tried to maintain a gradualist policy for dealing with inflation to avoid alienating the union leaders that supported his Vietnam policies. But with the inflation rate averaging 18 percent for the first year on new government construction contracts, he asked the members of his Construction Industry Collective Bargaining Commission in mid-January 1971 to come up with a plan within 30 days for dealing with inflation. When the business executives and labor leaders on the commission could not agree to a plan, Nixon turned to the remedy favored by CUAIR, a suspension of the Davis-Bacon Act in February 1971. The suspension ended a month later with the trade unions agreeing to a new Construction Industry Stabilization Committee, "whose task it was to abate wage increases to something like the rate that had prevailed from 1961 to 1968" (Marchi 1975, p. 332). All settlements would have to be approved first by craft-level dispute boards and then by the new industry stabilization committee.

Nixon was still not prepared to institute a wage-price freeze or make the transition to a government board that would recommend caps on wage and price increases. There were strong divisions within his administration over taking those steps. But the Business Council decided that it did not want to wait any longer for action. In a meeting at the White House with Nixon in May 1971, the president of a major corporation of that era, Cummins Engine, "espoused the immediate adoption of temporary wage and price controls." Then the Business Council as a whole took "the unprecedented step of taking a straw vote on the issue, subsequently conveying to the president an expression of discontent at the administration's failure to secure smaller wage and price increases" (Marchi 1975, p. 340). Strikes in several different industries in the summer of 1971, which resulted in major wage hikes, including a 30 percent wage increase over a three-year period for the United Steel Workers, finally forced Nixon's hand (Matusow 1998, p. 110).

To deal with these problems, and help ensure his reelection, Nixon instituted a temporary wage-price freeze in August 1971. There was no freeze on dividends or profits rates, which in itself was a commentary on the administration's solicitude toward the corporate rich. Imminent pay raises for 1.3 million employees were frozen, even though they had been agreed to earlier in negotiations between union leaders and management. Most interest groups and the general public, including the corporate community, responded to the freeze with strong approval, but unions reacted negatively because they thought it was aimed at them. As historian Allen

Matusow (1998, p. 157) explained: "Everyone knew the real purposes of the freeze. It was to halt the excessive wage settlements driving up cost-push inflation." In a famous phrase of the time, Nixon had "zapped labor."

At the end of the 90-day wage-price freeze, Nixon established separate pay and price boards, which were fashioned in part to satisfy organized labor. Their charge was to establish guidelines and limit the size of any increases that went beyond them. The pay board, with five labor representatives, five business representatives, and five public representatives, voted ten to five against retroactive pay increases for the 1.3 million employees whose raises had been frozen (Matusow 1998, p. 162). Its later decisions may have restrained wage increases somewhat, but several of its early settlements were very permissive. The price board, with seven public members, did not even do that well. However, it turned out that inflation was declining for normal economic reasons, and unions were being somewhat more cautious in what they demanded.

At the same time that Nixon originally instituted the wage-price freeze, he also announced that the United States would no longer exchange American gold for the massive amount of American dollars held by other nations. This decision signaled the end of an agreement signed by the United States and 43 other nations in 1944. (The origins and purposes of this agreement are discussed in detail in Chapter 11.) Taken together, the two policies were meant to give corporations and the Nixon Administration more flexibility in dealing with inflation and unions at home, while at the same time improving the competitiveness of American corporations abroad. The policies succeeded on both counts (Matusow 1998, Chapter 5).

The American government's refusal to provide gold when presented with dollars left its stunned allies with no good alternatives. They had to capitulate to this raw exercise of American power. In the end, they were forced to put the value of their currencies at the mercy of market forces. Not insignificantly, the cumulative impact of this unilateral change, along with shocks to the world economy by sudden oil increases in 1973 and 1979 by the major oil-producing countries of that era, increased the volatility in currency values around the world. The Nixon Administration's policy thereby contributed to the destabilization of the economies in many countries, and to the return of old-fashioned ultraconservative austerity economics (renamed "neoliberalism") in the United Kingdom, not to mention the rise of authoritarian regimes in other countries (e.g., Fourcade-Gourinchas and Babb 2002; Krippner 2011; Mann 2013, Chapter 6). (The international aspects of the decision to take the dollar off the gold standard are discussed further in Chapter 14.)

Within the United States, inflation dipped as low as 2.7 percent 11 months after Nixon announced the new policies. It stood at a tolerable 3.4 percent when he was reelected in a landslide vote in 1972. But another round of inflation began in early 1973 that led to major changes

198 The Rise and Fall of Labor Unions

in economic policy. According to the moderate Keynesian economists that advised the CED, this time it was a cost-push inflation, generated by a series of external, supply-side economic shocks that were caused by worldwide agricultural shortages, shortages in some natural resources, and most of all, an Arab oil embargo in October 1973. Inflation exploded to 8.7 percent by the end of the year and to 12.3 percent by the end of 1973. At the same time, unemployment rose from 4.9 percent in January 1973, to as high as 9.0 percent in May 1975.

This completely new set of circumstances was explained in a detailed fashion to CED trustees at a special CED conference in May 1975, by one of their longtime Keynesian economic advisers, Charles Schultze (CED 1975). Schultze had first consulted for the CED in the late 1950s, before he spent several years as an assistant director of the Bureau of the Budget during the Kennedy Administration and as its director in the Johnson Administration from 1965 to 1968. He then became a frequent adviser to CED subcommittees and a member of its Research and Advisory Board. Based at The Brookings Institution, he served as the chair of the Council of Economic Advisors during the Carter Administration, two years after his mid-1970s talk to CED.

According to Schultze's moderate Keynesian analysis, the sudden downturn in the economy was caused by a sharp decline in consumer demand, which was primarily due to the costs of paying for the rising prices that were the results of the three unexpected supply-side shocks. To begin with, farm prices rose sharply due to poor harvests around the world; this problem was exacerbated in the United States by the sale of grain and soybean reserves to the Soviet Union in 1972 and 1973 for strategic reasons, which strained American reserves. The increases in farm prices took $7.0 billion (in 2018 dollars) out of consumers' pockets. Then the costs of non-petroleum raw materials went up as well, which cost consumers another several billion dollars (CED 1975).

The third and biggest shock came from the six-month Arab oil embargo in late 1973, in response to the perceived American support for Israel when it was suddenly attacked by Egypt and Syria. The embargo quadrupled the price of oil and sent $36.6 billion of consumer purchasing power to oil-producing countries (again in 2018 prices), only $5.1 billion of which came back to commercial and investment banks in the United States for loans and investments. The resulting inflationary spiral pushed individuals and corporations into higher tax brackets, removing another $55–60 billion from consumption and investment. Then, due to the overall major decline in demand caused by the cumulative effects of these events, employers began to lay off workers, which of course increased the unemployment rate and further depressed demand (CED 1975).

This analysis is supported by later studies of this time period (Blinder 1979; Blinder and Rudd 2008, pp. 6–7, 15–16). In addition, the effect of lifting the temporary Nixon price controls, which lasted in a gradually weakened form from late 1971 into 1973, also played a role. Although Schulze's years of work for the CED gave him considerable credibility with its trustees, they rejected his recommendation to hold interest rates down and at the same time lower taxes on low-income workers, perhaps through a temporary suspension of their Social Security taxes. The corporate moderates had already decided they were going in another direction: higher interest rates, which also might resolve their conflict with unions by causing unemployment to rise.

However, the corporate moderates' desires for higher interest rates to undercut unions, as reflected in a CED report on *Fighting Inflation and Promoting Growth* (1976), could not be fully realized until late in the Carter Administration. In 1979, business economist Paul Volcker, the president of the Federal Reserve Bank of New York, who had been employed off and on since 1957 by the Chase Manhattan Bank when he was not in government, was appointed as chair of the Federal Reserve Board. (Before becoming president of the Federal Reserve Bank of New York, he served as the under secretary of treasury for international monetary affairs in the Nixon Administration, as discussed in Chapter 14.) As chair of the Federal Reserve Board, a position he occupied from 1979 to 1987, Volcker immediately announced his focus would be on tightening the money supply, which had been expanding for a variety of reasons, such as the greater liquidity of mutual funds and the increasing use of credit cards. Although reigning in the money supply has the same effect as the indirect actions that raise interest rates, Volcker argued that it was better to tighten the money supply because the average person understood that inflation involved too much money at a time when there were not enough goods to buy.

Volcker's policy focus was seen by some outside observers at the time as evidence that he had become an advocate of monetary theory, which he neither confirmed nor denied. But to economists that had experience in relation to the Federal Reserve Board and its policies, his concentration on the money supply seemed to be a clever political maneuver. For example, one of the members of Carter's CEA, Lyle Gramley, believed from the outset, due to his previous experience working for the Fed, that Volcker's policies were politically motivated. He based his opinion on research by economists showing that manipulating the federal funds rate could control the growth in the money stock with considerable precision. He then noted that Volcker "was well aware of this, and ninety-eight percent of the reason for going in this direction [i.e., attempts at direct control of the money supply] was a cover." "He felt," Gramley continued, "and perhaps quite justifiably, that the central bank could not take responsibility for setting interest rates when interest rates might have to go as high as they did, in order to stop inflation" (Biven 2002, p. 315, ftn 18).

Carter's CEA chair, Charles Schultze, initially opposed Volcker's plan because controlling the money supply is not easy to do, and can lead to volatility in interest rates. But he soon realized that the new policy was ideal from a political point of view because people would be less likely to blame either Carter or the Fed for the decline in the economy. In the early 1980s, for example, Schultze told two economists, who were interviewing him for a book on the continuity of policy advice by the CEA over the decades, that he was "morally certain" that Volcker had political motives for donning the monetary mantle (Hargrove and Morley 1984, pp. 486). In the late 1980s, Schultze told a conference on the Carter Administration that "no democratically elected president can or would" take the overt steps that were needed to stop inflation by increasing unemployment from 6 to 10 percent (Biven 2002, p. 244). In other words, it took a relatively independent central bank to halt the inflationary spiral in a way that was acceptable to the corporate community, that is, without using the liberal Keynesian prescription of large increases in high-end taxes, an incomes policy, and/or government controls on wages and prices.

In 1991, long after any of this mattered to anyone but academicians, Schulze provided his fellow economist, Carl Biven, who was writing a book on the Carter Administration, with an even more frank and complete analysis: "Either consciously or unconsciously," he began, "Volcker was absolutely dead right on the politics of it" (Biven 2002, p. 242). That is, "[i]n order to do what had to be done to stop and reverse inflation, the Fed had to jack interest rates up to unprecedented heights." However, if the Fed had used its usual methods, setting a federal funds target every month, "then, in the eyes of the public, the Fed would have been driving those rates up," which might have angered political activists. Thus, "the genius of what Volcker did, during the period when you had to get the public used to this, was to adopt a system which came to the same thing, but in which he said we are not raising interest rates, we are just setting a non-inflationary path for the money supply, and the markets are raising the interest rates." It was this stratagem, Schultze concluded that "enabled the Fed to do politically, during that transition period, what it couldn't have done in a more direct way" (Biven 2002, p. 242).

Although it is likely that Gramley and Schultze are right in their political analysis, it was not simply a matter of Volcker resorting to political chicanery. At the urging of leaders in the conservative coalition, in 1975 Congress had passed a Concurrent Resolution that required the Federal Reserve to "report to Congress its objectives for annual growth of the money supply," and conservatives later formalized this directive as one of their amendments to the Humphrey-Hawkins Act, which passed one year before Volcker swung into action (Biven 2002, p. 242). Just as Volcker provided Carter and the Fed with political cover, so, too, conservatives in Congress, whether inadvertently or not, had provided legislative legitimacy for the action Volcker took, as he very likely knew.

However, over and beyond the political dimension of a focus on the money supply, the decision was also based on an intuitive sociological assumption about the potential for social unrest. After years of domestic tranquility, the corporate community and the Carter Administration implicitly understood that high unemployment would not lead to social disruption. There would be complaints and rallies, but there would be no major strikes, widespread sit-ins, physical destruction of private property, violent confrontations with Special Weapons and Tactics (SWAT) teams and riot police, or votes for liberal Democrats. In short, there were no longer any social risks to inducing high employment.

With Volcker in effect raising interest rates, the corporate community now tried to build political support in Washington for sustaining the new policies for as long as they were needed. This concern was fully revealed in the private discussions that corporate executives and conservative economists held at CED headquarters in preparing a new report, *Fighting Inflation and Rebuilding a Sound Economy* (CED 1980a). (Most discussions at the CED were taped and then transcribed for use in future discussions and policy statements, so there may be a treasure trove awaiting text-mining data scientists.) At one early meeting, an outspoken conservative economist, Martin Feldstein, a professor of economics at Harvard, and the president of the National Bureau of Economic Research, who later served as the chair of Reagan's Council of Economic Advisors, suggested that high interest rates and the resulting high employment were the only way to control inflation.

An economist employed fulltime at the CED, Frank Schiff, a moderate Keynesian, then asked: "Are you saying that the answer is a period of high and protracted employment?" Feldstein replied: "It may be." Schiff then asked: "That is the only answer?" Feldstein then replied in a way that suggested the CED had to make sure it did not become part of the problem: "It may be. Certainly, if the CED says the opposite, that makes it harder." Feldstein then suggested that CED had to back Volcker in staying the course with high interest rates until the inflationary spiral was broken (CED 1980b, p. 82, for this dialogue).

At this point, the chair of this CED subcommittee, Reuben Mettler, who was the CEO of TRW, the 68th largest corporation in 1980, spoke for the first time. He did so in the name of the corporate community, making it clear that he and his fellow CEOs favored high interest rates to cut demand, although he used a more neutral term, "demand management:" "I think there is widespread support for persistent, steady demand management in the business community. There is strong support there" (CED 1980b, p. 82). In addition to being a CEO and a trustee of the CED,

Mettler was an active member of the National Alliance of Businessmen and a member of other policy-discussion groups, including the one to be discussed in the next subsection, the Business Roundtable.

Based on this and subsequent discussions, Mettler later commented that the final draft was "quite different than the one you saw earlier," with a stronger emphasis "on demand restraint and on not relaxing at the first sign of some recovery" (CED 1980b, pp. 4–5, 9–10). The published report called for reductions in government regulations, the use of cost-benefit analysis for deciding whether or not to issue new regulations, the use of market pricing to control energy use, a series of tax credits for corporations designed to improve productivity and investment, and most of all, steady restraint in fiscal and monetary policies in order to reduce the inflation rate.

The CED leaders who crafted the report realized these policies might well lead to another recession, but they argued that inflation was a greater danger in the long run than a short-term recession. The blunt comments by Feldstein in his exchange with Schiff, which suggested that the Fed would have to persist with high interest rates, even though many people would lose their jobs, were stated in a more indirect way in the report:

> A major risk is that recession will lead to an abandonment of the battle against inflation. This could happen if observed reductions in the inflation rate, combined with growing concern over the social and economic effects of the recession, should lead to relaxation of the degree of demand restraint needed to overcome inflation in the long run. Such a policy would be very shortsighted.
>
> (CED 1980a, p. 4)

Once the report was available, it became the basis for a major lobbying campaign aimed at members of Congress. For the most part, though, the lobbying effort took the form of meeting informally with elected officials and giving them or their staff copies of the report.

Back to 1972: Enter the Business Roundtable

In 1972, encouraged by their success in combating the construction unions and in shaping the National Labor Relations Board between 1969 and 1971, corporate leaders made the Labor Law Study Group and the Construction Users Anti-Inflation Roundtable into the two main committees in a new, stronger, and more publicly visible organization, the Business Roundtable. This new organization combined policy-formation, lobbying, advocacy, and public relations in a way that previous policy-discussion organizations had not done before. It was incorporated in October, announced in mid-November, and began putting together an administrative structure in early 1973, just as Nixon's second term began. The full story is presented by Gross (1995, pp. 234–235) in his account based on a detailed look at the Business Roundtable's archival papers. However, despite his factual account, as supplemented by work in the Business Roundtables' organizational files (Linder 1999, Chapter 7), many accounts of the origins of the Business Roundtable remain inadequate, at least in part because of the mistaken belief that the ultraconservatives had the major role in the right turn during the 1970s (e.g., Hacker and Pierson 2010; Harvey 2005; Phillips-Fein 2009).

The Business Roundtable's Labor Law Reform Committee continued to be chaired by Soutar, carrying on the effort initiated in 1965 to bring about changes in labor law and influence appointments to the National Labor Relations Board. The Construction Committee, chaired by an industrial relations lawyer at General Electric, continued the lobbying and legal work started by the Construction Users Anti-Inflation Roundtable. In fact, this GE lawyer had urged the formation of the Business Roundtable because he objected to the fact that "the proposals issue by the NAM and Chamber of Commerce were worked out by their staffs and thus did not necessarily represent the views of CEOs or business in general" (Linder 1999, p. 207).

Several months later, the Business Roundtable added a fledgling group of 40 chief executives leaders and their Washington representatives, who were working on ways to influence Congress and sway the electorate. It became the Business Roundtable's Public Information Committee, which tried to shape the climate of opinion concerning corporations (but without any luck). It worked for months on thinly disguised advocacy pieces that appeared in 1975 in the *Reader's Digest*. This committee soon faded in importance.

One of the main mistakes made in several accounts of the Business Roundtable is that it was formed to fight new regulatory rules concerning workplace safety and the environment (e.g., Hacker and Pierson 2010; Mizruchi 2013). However, its early 1973 statement of purpose, "The Business Roundtable: The Purpose and Challenge," suggests otherwise. It begins by claiming that inflation had been the most "persistent" and "pervasive" of all the problems that faced the United States in the previous decade, and predicts that it was "likely to be the dominant economic challenge of the Seventies." It blames the inflation on "the cost of labor," which means that "runaway unit labor costs will make economic stability impossible." Labor's pressure for higher wages therefore results "in a never ending circle [that] is the most difficult economic issue of our time" (Business Roundtable 1973, pp. 1–2).

This assertion is softened a few paragraphs later with the qualification that the government's fiscal and monetary policies share "some of the blame" because they, too, create inflation, and it is noted that food prices were "advancing rapidly." Still, the primary problem is the cost of labor because "a limited recovery from low profit margins" would necessitate that increased labor costs "would have to be quickly transmitted to the public through higher price costs" (Business Roundtable 1973, pp. 2–3). Once again, that is, the power of organized labor is said to be at the heart of the inflation problem, and government was at fault for aiding unions. Government "interference" in capital-labor relations, couched in terms of various kinds of interference in the market, including labor markets, was the primary object of the Business Roundtable's lobbying over the next eight years.

The manifesto contained many suggestions. For example, Business Roundtable leaders wanted to repeal the prevailing wage provision in Davis-Bacon and block future increases in minimum wages, which were carryovers from an earlier suggestion by its predecessor, the Construction Users Anti-Inflation Roundtable. It claimed that restrictive work practices were cutting into the rate of growth in productivity. The Roundtable founders were especially annoyed by what they believed to be a rise in the use of food stamps by strikers, although the numbers were miniscule at best. The House of Representatives had rejected attempts to ban the practice in both 1971 and 1972, but the Business Roundtable nonetheless claimed that this alleged practice violated the intent of the law for the relatively few families of strikers that actually qualified for support. While noting that it could not put a dollar figure on the amount of support food stamps provided to strikers, the manifesto cited case studies by industrial relations experts at the Wharton School in claiming that the amounts were substantial enough to add to inflation (Thieblot and Cowin 1972).

Working within the new political climate of the early 1970s, the resistance organized by the Construction Users Anti-Inflation Roundtable, and later by the Business Roundtable, put the building-trades unions on the defensive. They urged and aided the Department of Labor's initiatives to weaken unions through the restructuring of apprenticeship programs and the integration of construction sites financed by federal contracts. As a result, an estimated 40 percent of new construction jobs were non-union by 1975 (Levitan and Cooper 1984, p. 120).

Although strong unions were still winning good contracts in the first half of the 1970s, overall membership hit a stasis at between 18 and 19 million from 1968 to 1973, and union density declined from 26.9 to 24.6 percent (Freeman 1998, pp. 292–293, Table 8A.2). The fall-off would have been even greater if not for the continuing growth of the public-sector unions, which had gained over 1 million members since 1970 and reached a union density of 38.0 percent by 1974 (Miller and Canak 1995, p. 19, Table 1).

The anti-labor manifesto to one side for the moment, the Business Roundtable is also of interest because by 1976 it was at the center of the policy-planning network (e.g., Burris 1992; Burris 2008; Dreiling and

Darves 2016). It also began to take positions on a wider range of issues, including health insurance, as shown in two chapters in Part 2, and by the 1980s at the latest it was leading the way on the internationalization of the American economy, as shown in Part 3 (Dreiling 2001). In addition to moving to the center of the network, archival and interview evidence reveals that by 1975–1976 its leaders had made their former main policy-discussion organization, the Committee for Economic Development, into a more narrowly focused subsidiary of the Business Roundtable (Domhoff 2013, Chapters 9–10). Henceforth the CED was used primarily to generate research and reports, while continuing to carry out what one of its employees, Frank Schiff, called "non-lobbying lobbying" in my two-day interview with him, a form of lobbying that kept the CED within the rules for nonprofit groups (Domhoff 2013, p. 233; Schiff 1990).

The most powerful and active of the corporate moderates, the CEOs of very large corporations, pushed the CED to the sidelines primarily because they became increasingly unhappy with its mild, and occasionally somewhat liberal, policy statements about inflation in the late 1960s and early 1970s, as revealed by their numerous and often strongly worded dissents at the end of these statements (Domhoff 2013, pp. 167–168, 173–174, 196–197, 208–211). In addition, they also were upset by a tentative 1975 proposal by two of the more liberal trustees and the organization's hired president to study the possibilities of more government planning to stabilize the economy. The planning proposal was quickly withdrawn in the face of strong objections without any further mention, and the CED president, a former Federal Reserve economist, decided to retire early at age 63 after a 20-year tenure (Domhoff 2013, pp. 198–201).

In effect, the creation of the Business Roundtable in the early 1970s by the most powerful CEOs in the CED marginalized the two or three liberal CED trustees that owned consulting and real estate businesses, along with a liberal vice president from a large financial institution, retired CEOs that had outsized roles in the discussions of several policy statements, and the more liberal-leaning economists among the economists employed by the CED. These changes demonstrate that organizations in the policy-planning network can wax and wane in their importance, and be shifted to secondary roles as well (Domhoff 2013, Chapters 10–11).

The Myth of the Powell Memo

This account of the efforts by the Labor Law Reform Group, the Construction Users Anti-Inflation Roundtable, and the Business Roundtable in shaping the right turn that began in the late 1960s can be usefully compared with studies that attribute the origins of the right turn to a memo that a corporate lawyer in Richmond, Lewis Powell, wrote for the Chamber of Commerce in late August 1971, at the request of a Chamber leader

206 The Rise and Fall of Labor Unions

who wanted it to take a more active role (e.g., Hacker and Pierson 2010, pp. 117–119; Phillips-Fein 2009, pp. 156–165). According to one widely read perspective on neoliberalism, it is "hard to tell" just how "directly influential this appeal to engage in class war was," but "we do know" that the Chamber of Commerce "subsequently expanded its base" and that the Business Roundtable "was founded in 1972, and thereafter became the centrepiece of collective pro-business action" (Harvey 2005, p. 43).

But these claims are about a memo that appeared long after corporate moderates initiated the right turn in 1968 and 1969. Nor is there any causal connection between the 1971 memo and the establishment of the Business Roundtable, as already documented with archival information in this chapter. These assertions are furthermore irrelevant because the Chamber of Commerce always had held to the free-market principles espoused in the memo, and always had been vigilant and active. Moreover, there is no evidence that the influence of the Chamber of Commerce had spread beyond its longstanding ties with the right wing of the Republican Party and the conservative coalition in Congress at that point. Although "the document broke little new ground" conceptually, because "business leaders had been voicing many of the same concerns for years," there is evidence that the Chamber beefed up its own structure and lobbying activities in 1974 and 1975 in reaction to this memo (Waterhouse 2014, p. 59, for the quotations, and pp. 58–63 for the origins and impact of the memo within the Chamber itself, including the fact that it took a few years before this 1971 memo was implemented).

In addition, it would be several more years, well after the right turn was in full swing, before the various ultraconservative think tanks mentioned in these Powell-based accounts began to have any influence in the policy arena, primarily in Republican administrations beginning with the Reagan Administration. In fact, as political scientist Joseph Peschek (1987, pp. 170–177) demonstrated, The Brookings Institution was headed in a more conservative direction by 1975. Even in the Reagan Administration from 1981 to 1988, the top appointments and the major policy initiatives came from the moderate-conservative groups within the policy-planning network, not the ultraconservative ones, which had to settle for secondary positions and for relentless attacks on specific agencies (Domhoff 1983, pp. 139–141, for what was then new evidence on these points, as well as many citations to other empirical studies of the issue).

By focusing on the Powell memo, the social scientists that make use of it overlook or downplay the role of the corporate moderates in initiating the right turn, as well as the importance of the white voters who switched from the Democrats to the Republicans in making it possible for this agenda to be implemented. They thereby miss all the complexity of the corporate community, and they relieve white workers of any responsibility for the demise of the private-sector unions. In dismissing the importance of the white resistance to the black demands of the 1960s, one pair of analysts

Corporate Moderates Reorganize   207

who make use of the Powell memo claim that "[t]his near-universal narrative is colorful, easy to tell, and superficially appealing," and then add that it "misses the real story" (Hacker and Pierson 2010, pp. 95–96). That "real story" is based on the continuing high levels of government activism and social spending from 1964 to 1977: "nothing unraveled" as far as "spending, taxation, regulation, and all the other things that government does…" (Hacker and Pierson 2010, p. 96). (The continuing high level of spending and alleged activism, which started to suffer cutbacks by 1974–1975, is explained in Chapter 8.)

Reshaping the National Labor Relations Board

While the conflicts over inflation and wages were unfolding between 1969 and 1973, the corporate community's Labor Law Reform Group (known as the Labor Law Reform Committee after 1972) was working patiently behind the scenes in the early months of the Nixon Administration to change the composition of the National Labor Relations Board in ways that would have long-term impacts on a wide range of management-union issues (Gross 1995, Chapter 12). Its members understood that the changes had to be gradual because of Nixon's desire to maintain labor leaders' support for the Vietnam War while at the same time controlling civil disturbances and gaining as much blue-collar electoral support as possible. They also realized that pro-labor Democrats still controlled the labor committees in both Houses and could block anti-labor appointees. Despite these obstacles, the direction of the NLRB was quietly changed in dramatic ways by late 1971.

With Soutar of the LLRG designated by his corporate superiors to work with the Nixon Administration on all labor-related appointments, including to the NLRB, the secretary of labor rejected the LLRG's initial suggestion for a new chair of the labor board. Instead, he asked for a Republican who was not from either wing of the party. The result was the appointment of a corporate lawyer, Edward Miller, a partner in a large Chicago firm, and a member of the Blue Ribbon Committee that helped guide the work of the LLRG. Miller said little about his views before or after his appointment in 1970, but he did indicate he believed that protecting the freedom of employees to join or not join a union was more important than the encouragement of collective bargaining. Meany formally opposed Miller's appointment, but not so vigorously that Democrats on the Senate labor committee voted against him. Nor was there any opposition to Nixon's second appointment, Ralph Kennedy, a longtime staff member of the NLRB, who had become a regional director during the Eisenhower Administration (Gross 1995, pp. 220–221).

Joining with a Republican holdover on the board, Miller and Kennedy diluted or reversed many of the decisions made by the board during the Kennedy-Johnson years. They began by ruling that the board was limited in the penalties it could impose on companies that violated the law, and then gradually allowed more anti-union statements by employers in the name of free speech (Windham 2017, p. 63). However, their most important decision came in 1971, when the majority ruled that there was no duty for corporations to bargain on decisions that involved basic managerial issues (Gross 1995, p. 226).

The new case that provided the occasion for this reversal concerned General Motors' right to sell a truck dealership to an independent company that would be doing business in space it leased from General Motors. In other words, the independent company, which would be doing business inside the General Motors truck dealership, was not really independent at all. But a piece of paper said it was independent, so the majority ruled that General Motors only had to bargain about the "effects" of the sale, not about the sale itself. It drew this fine distinction because the sale "was financial and entrepreneurial in nature" (Gross 1995, p. 193).

The difference may seem small, but it had major consequences because it rendered unions powerless in such carefully constructed pseudo-entrepreneurial circumstances. The Democratic majority had ruled in the Fibreboard case in 1962 that there was a duty to bargain about the decision itself, which meant that it had to happen *before* the decision was made. Although the Supreme Court supported the NLRB's Fibreboard decision on narrow grounds in its 1964 opinion, the Republican majority on the labor board now focused upon the comment in Justice Potter Stewart's concurring decision about management control over decisions that were entrepreneurial or fundamental to the direction of the company (Gross 1995, p. 226).

This change opened the way for outsourcing and plant removal without any notice or consultation with unions, which led to declining wages and benefits for lower-income workers. According to one study of the issue, the outsourcing of low-wage and middle-income jobs may account for as much as 20 percent of the increase in income inequality between 1989 and 2014 (Cobb and Lin 2017). In the specific cases of janitors and security guards, their income fell by between 4 and 7 percent for janitors and between 8 and 24 percent for security guards when comparing companies that did and did not outsource these jobs (Dube and Kaplan 2010)

This fateful NLRB decision, in combination with other decisions by corporations and government agencies, thereby facilitated the unimpeded movement of production to low-wage American states and Third-World countries at the same time as communication and transportation costs were declining. These costs declined even more dramatically in the late 1970s and early 1980s due to the development of international standards for shipping containers, which made it possible to mechanize on-loading from freight trucks and to use double-stacking of the containers in giant cargo ships. In other words, the outflow of jobs, which is now often viewed as one inevitable part of "globalization," did not just naturally somehow happen due to the "efficiency" of the market and technological changes, but due to a power struggle that the corporations won and the unions lost in the United States.

In other countries, such as Canada, unions were not decimated because the government was stronger and enforced labor laws (Warner 2013). In addition, profits from economic growth due to worldwide trade were more widely shared in many countries through higher wages for the remaining workers, better government job-training programs for those who lost jobs, and higher government taxes on profits, which were used to strengthen social benefits for all citizens. In the United States, however, the corporate rich and their corporations reaped virtually all of the benefits of outsourcing and off-shoring. In subsequent years, social scientists and historians sometimes used general concepts that are a basic part of economics, economic sociology, and traditional organizational sociology to explain the results of the internationalization of the economy as largely economic and inevitable, which for the most part leaves power and class conflict out of the picture.

From 1971 on, then, once the NLRB had made its union-killing decisions, the battle between the corporate community and organized labor was fully joined on new terms at all levels. The new anti-union offensive also included the return of consulting firms that advised corporations on how to keep out or disestablish unions. By the late 1970s there were dozens of such firms, with one of the largest, West Coast Industrial Relations Associates, claiming to have as many as 1,500 clients a year (Smith 2003, pp. 102–104). Anti-union consultants often encouraged corporations to fire workers who tried to create unions, even though such an action was illegal. They calculated that it was worth paying the relatively small fines and back wages when the case was finally decided, if unions could be defeated in the meantime. They also attempted to decertify unions that already had been established. In addition, the ongoing movement of unionized factories out of Northern states to the South and lower-wage foreign destinations made workers more hesitant to ask for large wage increases. This wide-ranging corporate attack, from the NLRB to the factory gates, and the consequent loss of union power, is one of the major reasons for the decline in income for average workers in the 1970s and thereafter (Bluestone and Harrison 1982; Volscho and Kelly 2012; Western and Rosenfeld 2011).

Union Hopes Rise Post-Nixon

For all the problems unions encountered in the early 1970s in the face of the new corporate pushback, few people were thinking that they were down for the count. In fact, hope sprang anew when the Democrats won a large majority in the 1974 Congressional elections in the aftermath of

Nixon's resignation in early August of that election year. Most crucially, Democrats from outside the South had an even larger delegation in the House (211) than they had enjoyed in 1965 (194), and their representation in the Senate was up to 49, just three fewer than it was in 1965. Neither of those numbers added up to enough to beat the conservative coalition in the House or the Senate. As for the new Republican president, Gerald Ford, he was an anti-union ultraconservative with a veto power that would be difficult to override.

Liberals in Congress understood these realities, and decided to wait until after the 1976 elections to push for their full agenda, when they thought their majority would grow larger, and that there might be a Democrat in the White House as well. Democrats therefore spent much of their time preparing for future battles by making procedural reforms that might make new legislation possible in spite of the conservative coalition. These proposals had been prepared for House members by the staff of the Democratic Study Group, a liberal caucus created in 1959, which had experienced a gradual growth in its size and analytical capabilities (Roof 2011, pp. 136–139, 144).

When these proposals were taken to the Democratic members of the House, they first agreed that the party's newly established Steering and Policy Committee, not the party members on the Ways and Means Committee, would make future committee assignments. They also agreed that committee chairs would be selected by a majority vote within the Democratic caucus, not by their years of seniority. Under the new rules, members of the Democratic group as a whole could call for a vote if they wanted to challenge the automatic ascension of a senior member to the chair or replace an aging chair.

Once its new rules were in place, the House Democrats caused a major stir by displacing three longtime committee chairs from the South. One used his position as head of the Agricultural Committee to keep subsidy payments flowing into Southern agribusiness, as it was by then called; another used his top post on the Armed Services Committee to deliver defense contracts to companies in the South and keep military bases open; and the third, a populist from Texas, used his position on the Banking and Currency Committee to make investigations of big New York banks and fling jeremiads at the Federal Reserve System.

These changes may have moved at least some Southern Democrats closer to the center, and perhaps contributed to the fraying bonds between the Southern rich and the Democratic Party (e.g., McKee 2010, pp. 148–154, for a concise account of the larger context within which the liberal challenges became possible). Nevertheless, they had little apparent impact in terms of the renewed attack on organized labor that was underway. For that matter, the liberal reforms within the Democratic Party did not have any effect on the other two major policy domains discussed in this book either, as shown in later chapters. According to one historical account, the changes ended up strengthening the role of conservatives in Congress over the next 20 years (Zelizer 2007).

On the other hand, liberals in the Senate were able to make a procedural change that unexpectedly had a major unintended impact by making it easier for a determined minority of 41 Senators (historically, the conservative coalition, and after 1994, the Republican Party) to block legislation through a filibuster. The tradition of blocking legislation through a filibuster went back to the 1830s, when one or a handful of senators could block legislation indefinitely as long as they had the energy to keep talking on the Senate floor. Between 1917 and 1949, and then again after 1959, the Senate made it somewhat easier to end a filibuster through a two-thirds vote by the senators present and voting. As part of the mid-1970s reforms, liberal senators proposed that the threshold for cutting off debate should be lowered to three-fifths of those present and voting. However, the conservative coalition would only agree to lower the barrier to three-fifths of the Senate as a whole. The result was that it became necessary to have a super-majority of 60 votes to pass any legislation that was slightly controversial, in part because the liberals also agreed to a compromise that made it unnecessary to sustain a prolonged debate on the Senate floor for days or weeks at a time. Obstruction therefore became easier and more frequent on many issues, so there were no major gains by the liberal-labor alliance (Binder and Smith 1997, pp. 181–182; Roof 2011, p. 130).

Despite the liberal Democrats' doubts about the political wisdom of attempting substantive legislation on any major issue until after the 1976 elections, organized labor insisted that it could win on a bill that would allow common-situs picketing in the construction industry, which had remained a high-level priority for union leaders since the Supreme Court banned such activity as an illegal secondary boycott in 1951. The minutes from Business Roundtable meetings reveal that its leaders were extremely concerned about the possibility this new legislation might pass, and it did everything it could through its Construction Committee to alter its contents or derail the bill entirely (Linder 1999, Chapter 4).

The new legislation nonetheless included compromises that were negotiated by Ford's secretary of labor, a Harvard professor and prominent labor mediator. The two sides agreed on a 10-day notice of union intentions to picket and a 30-day limit on how long the picketing could last. After the bill passed in the House and the liberal-labor alliance overcame a Senate filibuster with a cloture vote, Ford broke his promise to sign the compromise bill due to enormous lobbying pressure from a united corporate community, including the Business Roundtable and the construction industry's trade association. The secretary of labor, who had worked for several years to craft a management-labor accord in construction that could tame inflation, resigned shortly after the veto (Greene 1995, pp. 96–98).

The defeat did not augur well for unions, but it did not involve the loss of an existing right.

More generally, the liberal–labor alliance had to endure 66 Ford vetoes over a period of 29 months, 54 of which were upheld by core members of the conservative coalition, including his veto of the common-situs picketing bill.

An Unexpected Defeat for Labor in the Carter Years

Democrats regained the White House in 1976 with the election of a moderate Southern Democrat, Jimmy Carter, but the House and Senate hardly changed in their overall composition. Still, the threat of a veto no longer made new legislation all but impossible. In addition, Carter and all of his main White House advisers supported the unions' agenda for changes in labor law, and thought these changes should be brought forward in one package to maximize their chances for success. However, union legislative strategists once again insisted that common-situs picketing could pass easily on its own because virtually the same Congress had supported it so strongly in 1975. After making the bill slightly stronger than the one Ford vetoed, union leaders put most of their efforts into persuading the necessary 60 senators to support the bill, assuming it would face its greatest opposition in the Senate.

Well aware that the labor leaders were focusing their initial efforts on the Senate, a united corporate community, this time calling its lobby the National Action Committee on Secondary Boycotts, lobbied the conservative majority in the House relentlessly in order to stop the bill even before it reached the Senate. The corporate lobbyists framed the issue as one in which union bosses were trying to gain even higher wages for overpaid construction workers, and then targeted undecided or hesitant representatives, especially those who had been elected for the first time in 1974 or 1976. As the vote neared, the liberal–labor alliance fell back to a more moderate bill similar to the one vetoed by Ford. But this retreat and a few other compromises could not save the bill from a 217-205 defeat, which meant that 92 percent of the conservative coalition's potential supporters had opposed the bill (Shelley 1983, p. 141, Table 8.1). Despite a large contingent of Northern Democrats in the House and a Democrat in the White House, labor had lost for a second time on common-situs picketing (Eccles 1977; Levitan and Cooper 1984, pp. 121–122).

1977: The Labor Law Reform Act

With virtually all members of the corporate community breaking labor laws with impunity throughout the first seven years of the 1970s, and using a variety of tactics to delay votes on union recognition, organized labor wanted several procedural changes in the laws that ensured and protected workers' rights. In particular, it wanted to (1) expand the size of the National Labor Relations Board from five to seven members to deal with a backlog that had by then grown from 1,151 in 1961 to 19,000 cases; (2) introduce procedures that would lead to certification votes only a few weeks after labor organizers filed petitions asking for them; (3) provide stronger penalties against companies that fired activist employees; (4) increase the back payments owed to workers fired for union activities; and (5) prohibit companies that violated the law from bidding on government contracts.

The final bill had President Carter's endorsement after the White House held lengthy negotiations with the Business Roundtable, the Chamber of Commerce, and the NAM, which led Carter's chief domestic policy adviser to assure the president that corporate concerns were "vastly muted" and that their reaction likely would be "less vociferous" (Windham 2017, p. 78). The White House also had long negotiations with union leaders, who dropped three important policy objectives, and in the process became convinced through their own discussions with corporate leaders that some corporations might support the bill or not raise major objections (Windham 2017, p. 78).

The White House and union optimism was due to the fact that the new legislation would not require that state-level right-to-work laws be overridden. Nor would it include the proposal that cards signed by 50 percent or more of a company's employees would be sufficient for a union to be recognized, which unions had said was necessary because employers were delaying recognition elections even longer than they had in the past. So, too, the White House had insisted that unions drop their demand that new owners of a business should not have the right to repudiate an existing union contract (Fink 1998, p. 245; Windham 2017, p. 77).

For the purposes of this campaign, the corporate community created the National Action Committee on Labor Law Reform, with a vice president for industrial relations from Bethlehem Steel directing the lobbying team. The Council on a Union-Free Environment, founded in 1977 by the NAM in anticipation of the effort by unions to reform labor legislation, aided the effort. Although the bill covered only 20 percent of American businesses, the corporate campaign stressed the alleged dangers of the legislation for small businesses (Akard 1992, p. 605). Due to this emphasis on the plight of small business, social scientists later paid a great deal of attention to the efforts of the National Federation of Independent Business (hereafter usually NFIB), the organization that they mistakenly saw as the representative of the smallest of small businesses (e.g., Hacker and Pierson 2010, p. 119; Vogel 1989, p. 199).

Since many social scientists and historians take the role of the NFIB at face value, this organization is worthy of a closer look. It is also given a

214   The Rise and Fall of Labor Unions

prominent role as the alleged representative of small business on health-insurance initiatives in 1993–1994 and 2009–2010, as discussed in Chapter 9. In contrast to its image, the NFIB is best understood as an ultra-conservative political lobby, a spin-off from the Chamber of Commerce. In fact, it began as a small business itself, incorporated in 1943 in Northern California by a former Chamber of Commerce employee, who became a political entrepreneur in order to make profits on membership fees while lobbying for ultraconservative policy preferences (Zeigler 1961, pp. 31–32).

Unlike the standard-issue voluntary associations, including business associations, which figure strongly in mainstream accounts of the American power structure (and which the NFIB is apparently assumed to be), the NFIB did not have general meetings or votes for officers, and membership turnover was very large each year (White 1983). It was financially based on annual memberships, sold to small businesses by several hundred traveling sales representatives, working strictly on commission. In short, the NFIB was a front group for the ultraconservatives in the corporate community, and an arm of the ultraconservatives in Congress as well. At best, only a small percentage of the NFIB's paid-up members had enough employees to be subject to the proposed reforms in the Labor Law Reform Act, which made its involvement on the alleged behalf of small business all the more irrelevant.

The business owners that joined the NFIB received membership stickers for their store windows, a newsletter with suggestions for small businesses, and periodic surveys on a wide range of issues. Called "mandates" to give the surveys more apparent heft, the surveys are now known to have been slanted to evoke conservative responses. The results were compiled at state and national headquarters and mailed to state and national legislators as "mandates" from small-business owners. Comparisons of the results of these surveys, which typically are returned by only about 20 percent of the members, with the results from national surveys suggest that the ultraconservative claims made on the basis of the mandates are not representative of small-business owners, who mostly shared the attitudes of their ethnic group and/or local community (Hamilton 1975, Chapters 2 and 7).

The organization switched to a nonprofit status in the late 1970s, shortly after the Labor Law Reform Act played out, but not before the founder and outgoing president was given a golden handshake of $800,000, which is a little over $2 million in 2018 dollars (White 1983). At that point, another former Chamber of Commerce employee became its president. Despite its transition to a nonprofit status, and the placement of its headquarters in Nashville, it continued to be financially based on the sale of membership stickers by traveling salesmen.

Returning to the Labor Law Reform Act of 1978, there was one moment of drama shortly before Congress took up the legislation. It was due to differences within the Business Roundtable on whether or not to join the coalition. Several companies that were said to have good relationships with their unions, along with some companies that had small or harmless unions, did not want to become involved. In the end, the Roundtable's policy committee voted 19-11 to enter the fray on the anti-reform side, but the fact that there had been an argument and that the vote was made public gave the Business Roundtable some legitimacy with corporate critics. The split vote nurtured the liberal-labor hope that at least some corporate leaders still might be as flexible on at least some labor issues as they were on civil rights and diversity issues. It also caused some ultraconservative staffers and lobbyists to criticize the corporate moderates in off-the-record interviews. The chair of NL Industries (formerly National Lead Company) defended the Business Roundtable with the comment that "the organization tries to deal rather pragmatically with what is possible;" he viewed any danger of alienating the Chamber and NAM as "an acceptable loss" in pursuing Business Roundtable goals (Green and Buchsbaum 1980, p. 103).

The campaign by the National Action Committee on Labor Law Reform was large and extensive, and it included the usual very expensive effort to influence public opinion. Business-oriented journalists also claimed that organized labor's resistance to the Carter Administration's inflation guidelines might make some members of Congress less favorable toward the legislation. But in spite of all these efforts by the corporate community, and the predictions of possible defeat for the bill by the business punditry, it passed the House by a large margin, 257-163, in early October. Nor did the efforts of organized business or any alleged Senatorial hostility toward labor for opposing inflation guidelines keep the Senate's Human Resources Committee from approving the bill by a 13-2 vote in late January 1978. However, the bill was then delayed for four months while the Senate debated the Panama Canal treaty, which was higher on Carter's list of priorities than labor-law reform. Even with this extra time for the National Action Committee for Labor Law Reform to lobby Senators and influence public opinion, it could not keep 58 senators from going on record to end a filibuster that was undertaken by the hard core of the conservative coalition (Roof 2011, pp. 157–162).

Despite its ability to achieve strong majorities in both the House and the Senate, the liberal-labor alliance could not overcome the resistance sustained by most Republicans and virtually all Southern Democrats, along with Democratic senators from the right-to-work states of Nebraska and Nevada. The senatorial opponents were bolstered in their efforts by the full support of corporate lawyers employed by the Business Roundtable, who provided 65 time-consuming amendments and an Employee Bill of Rights that were introduced to prolong the debate.

Along the way, organized labor offered further compromises, exempting even more businesses, but the hard-core conservatives' resistance still could not be broken. The bill was recommitted to the Senate Committee

216 The Rise and Fall of Labor Unions

on Human Resources for further review in late June, never to emerge again. The corporate community won, but it did so because the hard core of the conservative coalition in the Senate stayed together. As political scientists Taylor Dark (2001, pp. 111–113) and Tracy Roof (2011 p. 161) rightly stress, this fact is often overlooked by those who say that organized labor lost all of its political power in the 1970s. In fact, the liberal-labor alliance won 58 percent of the vote in the House and 59 percent in the Senate, which would be more than enough in a Congress in which the majority rules. Based on the way in which the American system of power works, however, it had lost on another union-oriented initiative, which marked 42 years of legislative defeats since the National Labor Relations Act based in 1935.

All that said, it is not certain, or even likely, that the enactment of the Labor Law Reform Act would have helped organized labor in its attempt to reverse the decline in private-sector union density. This is because the bill "still would have had to undergo the same judicial and agency review that so effectively gutted the legislative intent of the NLRA" in general (Fink 1998, p. 241). Nor was it clear that union organizers could overcome employer resistance at the company gates. The ongoing, and perhaps widening, racial divisions among workers, along with the continuing movement of factories to the South and overseas, not to mention the strong-arm tactics of the anti-union industrial relations firms, might have been too much to overcome. By 1980, union density was down to 22.2 percent, a decline of 4 percentage points since 1970, even though the number of members in public-employee unions had risen from 4.0 to 5.7 million in the same time period (Freeman 1998, pp. 292–293, Table 8A.2; Miller and Canak 1995, p. 19, Table 1).

The Reagan Administration Finishes Off Industrial Unions

Unions were just one of several items on President Ronald Reagan's cutback agenda when he took office in 1981, but they were high on that agenda. He received an unexpected, and even unwanted, opportunity to zap labor at the outset of his presidency. PATCO (the air traffic controllers' union), which had supported him for the presidency after years of relative failure under Democratic presidents, threatened to violate federal law by going on strike. Although Reagan initially tried to arrange a very generous settlement with the union, its adamant and frustrated leaders demanded even more. The president then felt he had no other recourse but to fire them, and the legend of his determination to set an example by breaking the union began to develop (McCartin 2011).

Whatever his original intentions, Reagan's eventual decision was dramatic and decisive, sending shock waves through both the corporate community, which knew an opportunity when it saw one, and the union movement, which recognized a disaster in the making when the president disbanded one of its unions. For starters, there was an immediate decline in actions by public-sector unions, although they were able to hold on in most areas of the country (McCartin 2011, pp. 338–350). The corporations swung into action. Taking advantage of a 1938 Supreme Court ruling declaring that companies had the right to hire "permanent replacements" for workers who went on strike for "economic reasons," they were emboldened to make even more use of union-busting consulting firms that offered replacement workers. The consulting firms also became more confrontational in dealing with strikers, using video cameras and other high-tech devices as part of their intimidating surveillance efforts. One firm had its own heavily armored SWAT team (Goldfield 1987, pp. 189–195; Smith 2003, pp. 119, 121–123).

At the same time, the unions were being shredded by the recession generated by the Fed through high interest rates. This corporate-backed attempt to control inflation through high interest rates hurt workers because it made domestic manufacturing goods too expensive to compete against imports from Western Europe and Japan, thereby encouraging industrial firms to move their production overseas and then import the finished product back into the United States. High interest rates also caused problems for the housing industry, which led to higher unemployment for the construction unions as well.

The Reagan Administration insisted the high rates were necessary in order to break the back of inflation, but a study by researchers at the Urban Institute concluded that one-third to one-half of the decline was due to unexpected decreases in world prices for food and oil. There also was a decrease in the price of imports to the United States due to the high value of the dollar, which was caused in good part by the high interest rates (Stone and Sawhill 1984, p. 2). The rest of the decline could be attributed to the high unemployment rates and the demand compression induced by the high interest rates.

Despite the economic costs of Reagan's policies for both workers and some business sectors, most corporate leaders found the recession of 1981–1982 to be worthwhile because of its numbing impact on workers, according to a survey in the spring of 1982. In the face of the large number of small-business bankruptcies and the high unemployment rate, "a majority of the 800 executives at large and medium-sized companies" said that the recession was good for the country; they believed this because of its sobering effect on the liberal-labor alliance in general and on workers seeking wage increases in particular (Vogel 1989, p. 256). They also believed that the humbling of unions would mean that automatic cost-of-living adjustments would no longer feed into core inflation when commodity prices rose very suddenly due to food shortages or oil embargoes. On this

218   The Rise and Fall of Labor Unions

score they proved to be very right. Later research showed increases in commodity prices impacted core inflation in the 1960s and 1970s, but not afterwards (Krugman 2011; Krugman 2012, pp. 154–155).

While high unemployment rates and direct corporate attacks were decimating unions, Reagan applied the final blow by appointing a series of ultraconservatives to the National Labor Relations Board. The appointment process was drawn out and contentious in each case because some Reagan advisers did not consider the low-key ultraconservatives suggested by Soutar on behalf of the Business Roundtable to be conservative enough. After tumultuous confirmation hearings along with subsequent exchanges of personal insults among the ultraconservative appointees, the board made extremely conservative decisions even while experiencing turnover and tension. In the process, it reversed even more of the pro-labor decisions by the Democratic majority during the Kennedy, Johnson, and Carter administrations (Gross 1995, pp. 246–265). The only solace for organized labor was that up to that point it had fended off repeated efforts by the conservative coalition to eliminate the Davis-Bacon Act and restrict union involvement in politics (Roof 2011, pp. 190–191).

Coda: One Last Try (and Defeat) in 2009

Although this analysis of the defeat of organized labor ends with the systematic archival data and historical studies that carry the story to 1985, it is possible to extend the account into the early twenty-first century through a brief discussion of a defeat for unions in 2009. Before that moment, of course, there was no chance for labor to win any legislative changes during the second Reagan Administration or the subsequent administrations of George H. W. Bush, Bill Clinton, and George W. Bush between 1989 and early 2009. Using the time series that stretches back to the early 1880s and ends in 1995, union density declined from 20.7 percent in 1982 to 14.0 percent in 1995, which fully reflects the defeat of private-sector unions, and of industrial unions in particular, during those years (Freeman 1998, p. 293, Table 8A.2).

Switching to the official statistics provided by the government's Bureau of Labor Statistics, whose estimates are generally about a percentage point or two higher than those provided by Freeman (1998), it is possible to parcel out the relative contributions of private-sector and public-sector unions in 1970 and thereafter, which shows that public-sector unions gradually rose to a position of ascendancy. In 1970, the members of public-sector unions were 17.3 percent of the 18.1 million overall union members. By 2000 they were 48.6 percent of 16.3 million union members and in 2009 they became a small majority of a shrinking union membership (51.5 percent of 15.3 million union members (Hirsch and Macpherson 2018, for the membership figures from which these percentages were derived). As for the private sector, which is what counts the most for corporations, union density stood at 7.2 percent in 2009, about one-fifth of what it had been in 1945, and less than half of what it was as recently as 1985 (BLS 2018).

Despite these general declines and the parlous state of the private-sector unions, which had all but disappeared from industrial corporations, there was a new glimmer of hope with the election of Barack Obama to the presidency in 2008, along with a Democratic congress. Labor had one main legislative goal in return for the money and campaign workers it put into the field for Democratic candidates, including Obama. It needed a way to have newly organized unions certified even if employers tried to use their very successful strategy of delaying elections for as long as possible, while at the same time threatening and supposedly reeducating their workforces. Labor leaders therefore advocated their Employee Free Choice Act, which would instruct corporations to recognize and bargain with unions if a majority of their employees signed a card expressing their desire to be represented by a union (Greenhouse 2008).

As a senator, President Obama had voted for a similar (unsuccessful) proposal in 2007, and he expressed his support for the Employee Free Choice Act during his 2008 presidential campaign. Early in 2009, however, he told journalists that the pressing priorities created by the financial implosion of 2008, and the need for government health insurance, would be at the top of his agenda. The card-check legislation would have to wait. Moreover, some of his largest financial donors let it be known they hoped that the legislation would not be considered. For example, three Chicago billionaires who had backed his campaign, all of them with interests in hotels that unions were trying to organize, let it be known to him that they opposed the bill (Lippert and Rosenkrantz 2009).

In anticipation of a Congressional vote on the bill in 2009, the corporate community launched a multimillion-dollar media campaign through new lobbying coalitions, with names such as Workplace Fairness Institute and the Coalition for a Democratic Workplace, which claimed that the legislation would take away workers' right to vote for or against unionization in a secret ballot. From the union point of view, this claim was especially galling and hypocritical because it was the corporations that did everything they could to block such elections. The NAM president, a former Republican governor of Michigan, warned that the unionization of Wal-Mart's 1.4 million workers alone would add $500 million a year in union dues, part of which would be used to support pro-labor Democratic candidates (Greenhouse 2009). "We like driving the car," the CEO of Wal-Mart told stock market analysts in October, 2008, "and we're not going to give the steering wheel to anybody but us" (Kaplan 2009, p. 10).

While all this was going on, the 41 Republican senators remaining in the Senate after the large Democratic gains in 2008 announced they would not support new labor legislation. Three Democrats, all from

220 The Rise and Fall of Labor Unions

right-to-work states, said they would not support it either. Since only 41 votes were needed to sustain a filibuster, the bill never came up for a vote.

Conclusion

The union movement in the United States rose and fell for a complex combination of reasons that are relatively unique to the United States, if not completely unique. First, and this is common to many if not all industrialized democracies, there is the fact that a small percentage of unionized workers can persist because of the problems some owners face in dealing with the issue of replacement costs, whether due to the necessity of highly skilled workers, timeliness in delivery or shipment, or the inaccessibility of the work site for many potential replacement workers (Kimeldorf 2013). Short of highly authoritarian training and work structures, and/or the use of physical violence condoned or carried out by government agencies, the business sectors with high replacement costs may provide a small irreducible union base.

Second, in the United States there was a united corporate opposition to unions and the liberal–labor alliance from 1934 onward, which was joined in 1937–1938 by plantation owners in the South. The resources available to the corporate community meant that even established unions were always on the defensive, which in turn meant that resources that might be put into expanding the union movement had to be used to defend the few gains that had been made. However, this constant pressure was not enough to halt the rise of the unions and their persistence as a major power base into the late 1970s in some industrial sectors, and even into the early 1980s in a few instances.

There were two key variables in terms of the rise and fall of unions: the stance of the Southern rich, rooted in agricultural exports of extremely valuable cash crops, and the voting decisions of middle-income whites outside the South, blue collar and white collar, union and non-union. As demonstrated in Chapter 2, it was the liberal-labor alliance's accommodation of the Southern Democrats in 1935 that made the passage of the National Labor Relations Act possible, but it was the Southern Democrat's growing opposition to sit-down strikes and interracial organization in 1937–1938 that turned their most important benefactors, the Southern rich, into its unrelenting opponents, and thereby united the full power elite against the act.

But even that united opposition was not enough to defeat the union movement once World War II intervened and the unions and their members could provide a strong base for the Northern Democrats in Congress and for Democratic presidents. As a result, the highly organized corporate challenges to the union in the 1950s and 1960s had to settle for limiting the spread of unions outside of their base in the Northeast, Midwest, and

Corporate Moderates Reorganize 221

some parts of the West Coast. In doing so they used a variety of means, including state-level right-to-work laws, decisions by the National Labor Relations Board during the Eisenhower Administration, and decisions by the Supreme Court in the 1950s and 1960s on common-situs picketing and plant closings, all of which hampered union organizing.

Thus, it was not until a large minority of middle-income whites switched their votes to the Republicans (and the openly racist Southerner, George Wallace), starting in 1964 in the South, and in 1966 and 1968 outside the South, that the corporate community and the conservative coalition could make any major advances despite their ongoing efforts. (At the same time, an increasing number of white professionals began voting for the Democrats, which staved off the full impact of the switch by the white working class for many years (Manza and Brooks 1999).)

As was the case at the end of the 1960s, when unions began to suffer political and organizing defeats, so too for the 1970s and 1980s. It was not that union leaders sold out or made mistakes, or that activists did not try hard enough or were not militant enough. Instead, it was once again a matter of battles fought and lost, as labor historian Kevin Boyle (1995; 1998; 2013) concluded in the case of the largest, most powerful, and most liberal industrial union of the 1950s and 1960s, the United Automobile Workers.

Even with all that, it is not as if there had been "majority rules" via Congress on union issues. As seen most clearly in the case of the Labor Law Reform Act of 1977, the defeats were at the hands of a determined minority that had clear strategic advantages, including the filibuster for many decades. Despite the Democratic reforms of the Senate in the mid-1970s, it still would have taken 60 senators to pass the relatively mild pro-union legislation in 1977, which failed in the face of opposition from 42 senators, almost all of them from right-to-work states.

While all this was going on, the Supreme Court made several decisions that gradually took away many of the statutory guarantees of protection against employers that had been granted to workers by the National Labor Relations Act, in exchange for labor peace. Decisions made by the NLRB during the Nixon, Ford, and Reagan administrations created a long list of prohibitions on actions by unions and their organizers. By 1985, a law that was originally meant to facilitate unionization and collective bargaining, as a moderate and nonviolent way to handle class conflict, had been turned into an employer-protection, anti-union law. That is a strong and counterintuitive conclusion, but sociologist Holly McCammon (1990; 1994; McCammon and Kane 1997) has provided the evidence that makes her conclusion one that is hard to deny.

In 1932, when there were few or no public-sector workers in unions, union density stood at its lowest level since 1918, 11.0 percent. In 2009, when the card-check act advocated by unions was not even voted on because 44 senators had stated they would not support it, union density in the private sector was only 7.9 percent. Union density therefore can be seen as an excellent indicator of the lack of union power, and of working people's power more generally, in the United States.

References

Akard, Patrick. 1992. "Corporate mobilization and political power: The transformation of U.S. economic policy in the 1970s." *American Sociological Review* 57:597–615.

Binder, Sarah and Steven Smith. 1997. *Politics or principle? Fiibustering in the United States Senate.* Washington: The Brookings Institution.

Biven, W. Carl. 2002. *Jimmy Carter's economy: Policy in an age of limits.* Chapel Hill: University of North Carolina Press.

Blinder, Alan. 1979. *Economic policy and the great stagflation.* New York: Academic Press.

Blinder, Alan and Jeremy Rudd. 2008. *The supply-shock explanation of the great stagflation revisited.* Cambridge: National Bureau of Economic Research.

Blough, Roger. 1968/1972. "The case for limiting steel imports (*Los Angeles Times*, September 20, 1968)." Pp. 427–431 in *Issues in business and society*, edited by G. Steiner. New York: Random House.

BLS. 2018. *Union Membership (Annual) News Release: Union members – 2009 (USDL-10–0069).* Bureau of Labor Statistics. Washington: Department of Labor.

Bluestone, Barry and Bennett Harrison. 1982. *The deindustrialization of America: Plant closings, community abandonment, and the dismantling of basic industry.* New York: Basic Books.

Boyle, Kevin. 1995. *The UAW and the heyday of American liberalism, 1945–1968.* Ithaca: Cornell University Press.

———. 1998. "Little more than ashes: The UAW and American reform in the 1960s." Pp. 217–238 in *Organized labor and American politics 1894–1994: The labor-liberal alliance*, edited by K. Boyle. Albany: State University of New York Press.

———. 2013. "The Treaty of Detroit and the postwar labor accord." Pp. 324–326 in *The Oxford encyclopedia of American business, labor, and economic history*, vol. 2, edited by M. Dubofsky. New York: Oxford University Press.

Burris, Val. 1992. "Elite policy-planning networks in the United States." *Research in Politics and Society* 4:111–134.

———. 2008. "The interlock structure of the policy-planning network and the right turn in U.S. state policy." *Research in Political Sociology* 17:3–42.

Business Roundtable. 1973. "The Business Roundtable: The purpose and the challenge." in *Business Roundtable*. Washington: Files of the Laborers' International Union of North America.

CED. 1975. *Progress toward recovery of the economy: CED Symposium.* New York: Committee for Economic Development.

———. 1976. *Fighting inflation and promoting growth* New York: Committee for Economic Development.

———. 1980a. *Fighting inflation and rebuilding a sound economy.* New York: Committee for Economic Development.

———. 1980b. "Transcript/subcommittee on inflation." in *Committee for Economic Development Archives, Transcript Library.* Washington: Committee for Economic Development.

Cobb, J. Adam and Ken-Hou Lin. 2017. "Growing apart: The changing firm-size wage effect and its inequality consequences." *Organization Science* 28:429–446.

Dark, Taylor. 2001. *The unions and the Democrats: An enduring alliance.* Ithaca: Cornell University Press.

Domhoff, G. W. 1983. *Who rules America now? A view for the '80s.* New York: Simon and Schuster.

———. 2013. *The myth of liberal ascendancy: Corporate dominance from the Great Depression to the Great Recession.* Boulder: Paradigm Publishers.

Dreiling, Michael. 2001. *Solidarity and contention: The politics of class and sustainability in the NAFTA conflict.* New York: Garland Press.

Dreiling, Michael and Derek Darves. 2016. *Agents of neoliberal globalization: Corporate networks, state structures and trade policy.* New York: Cambridge University Press.

Dube, Arindrajit and Ethan Kaplan. 2010. "Does outsourcing reduce wages in the low-wage service occupations? Evidence from janitors and guards." *Industrial and Labor Relations Review* 63:287–306.

Eccles, Mary. 1977. "House rejects labor-backed picketing bill." *Congressional Quarterly*, March 26, pp. 521–524.

Edsall, Thomas B. 1984. *The new politics of inequality.* New York: W. W. Norton.

Fink, Gary. 1998. "Labor law reform and the end of the postwar era." Pp. 239–257 in *Organized labor and American politics 1894–1994: The labor-liberal alliance*, edited by K. Boyle. Albany: State University of New York Press.

Fourcade-Gourinchas, Marion and Sarah Babb. 2002. "The rebirth of the liberal creed: Paths to neoliberalism in four countries." *American Journal of Sociology* 108:533–579.

Fowlkes, Frank. 1971. "Business Council shuns lobbying but influences federal policy." *National Journal*, November 20:2302, 2307.

Freeman, Richard B. 1998. "Spurts in union growth: Defining moments and social processes." Pp. 265–296 in *The defining moment: The Great Depression and the American economy in the twentieth century*, edited by M. Bordo, C. Goldin, and E. White. Chicago: University of Chicago Press.

Goldfield, Michael. 1987. *The decline of organized labor in the United States.* Chicago: University of Chicago Press.

Green, Mark and Andrew Buchsbaum. 1980. *The corporate lobbies: Political profiles of the Business Roundtable & the Chamber of Commerce.* Washington: Public Citizen.

Greene, John. 1995. *The presidency of Gerald R. Ford.* Lawrence: University Press of Kansas.

Greenhouse, Steven. 2008. "Unions look for new life in world of Obama." *The New York Times*, December 28, p. A1.

———. 2009. "Bill easing unionization under heavy attack." *The New York Times*, January 9, p. A14.

Gross, James A. 1995. *Broken promise: The subversion of U.S. labor relations policy.* Philadelphia: Temple University Press.

Hacker, Jacob and Paul Pierson. 2010. *Winner-take-all politics: How Washington made the rich richer—and turned its back on the middle class.* New York: Simon & Schuster.

Hamilton, Richard 1975. *Restraining myths: Critical studies of U.S. social structure and politics.* New York: Sage Publications.

Hargrove, Erwin and Samuel Morley. 1984. *The president and the Council of Economic Advisers: Interviews with CEA chairmen.* Boulder: Westview.

Harvey, David. 2005. *A brief history of neoliberalism.* New York: Oxford University Press.

Hirsch, Barry and David Macpherson. 2018. "Union membership and coverage database from the CPS." http://www.unionstats.com.

Kaplan, Esther. 2009. "Can American labor revive the American dream?" *The Nation,* January 26, pp. 10–14.

Kimeldorf, Howard. 2013. "Worker replacement costs and unionization: Origins of the U.S. labor movement." *American Sociological Review* 78:1033–1062.

Krippner, Greta. 2011. *Capitalizing on crisis: The political origins of the rise of finance.* Cambridge: Harvard University Press.

Krugman, Paul. 2011. "The Un-COLA era." in *The New York Times,* February 1. http://krugman.blogs.nytimes.com/2011/02/01/the-un-cola-era.

———. 2012. *End this depression now!* New York: W. W. Norton.

Levitan, Sar and Martha Cooper. 1984. *Business lobbies: The public good & the bottom line.* Baltimore: Johns Hopkins University Press.

Linder, Marc. 1999. *Wars of attrition: Vietnam, the Business Roundtable, and the decline of construction unions.* Iowa City: Fanpihua Press.

Lippert, John and Holly Rosenkrantz. 2009. "Billionaire donors split with Obama on law that may hurt hotels." in *Bloomberg.com,* May 7. http://www.bloomberg.com/apps/news?sid=a6A3G.MZZqIw&pid=newsarchive.

Mann, Michael. 2013. *The sources of social power: Globalizations, 1945–2011,* Vol. 4. New York: Cambridge University Press.

Manza, Jeff and Clem Brooks. 1999. *Social cleavages and political change: Voter alignments and U.S. party coalitions.* New York: Oxford University Press.

Marchi, Neil. 1975. "The first Nixon Administration: Prelude to controls." Pp. 295–352 in *Exhortation and control: The search for a wage-price policy 1945–1971,* edited by C. Goodwin. Washington: The Brookings Institution.

Matusow, Allen. 1998. *Nixon's economy.* Lawrence: University Press of Kansas.

McCammon, Holly J. 1990. "Legal limits on labor militancy: U.S. labor law and the right to strike since the New Deal." *Social Problems* 37:206–229.

———. 1994. "Disorganizing and reorganizing conflict: Outcomes of the state's legal regulation of the strike since the Wagner Act." *Social Forces* 72:1011–1049.

McCammon, Holly J. and Melinda D. Kane. 1997. "Shaping judicial law in the post-World War II period: When is labor's legal mobilization successful?" *Sociological Inquiry* 67:275–298.

McCartin, Joseph. 2011. *Collision course: Ronald Reagan, the air traffic controllers, and the strike that changed America.* New York: Oxford University Press.

McKee, Seth C. 2010. *Republican ascendency in Southern U.S. House elections.* Boulder: Westview Press.

Miller, Berkeley and William Canak. 1995. "There should be no blanket guarantee: Employers' reactions to public employee unionism, 1965–1975." *Journal of Collective Negotiations in the Public Sector* 24:17–35.

Mizruchi, Mark. 2013. *The fracturing of the American corporate elite*. Cambridge: Harvard University Press.

Peschek, Joseph. 1987. *Policy-planning organizations: Elite agendas and America's rightward turn*. Philadelphia: Temple University Press.

Phillips-Fein, Kim. 2009. *Invisible hands: The making of the conservative movement from the New Deal to Reagan* New York W.W. Norton.

Quadagno, Jill. 1994. *The color of welfare: How racism undermined the war on poverty*. New York: Oxford University Press.

Roof, Tracy. 2011. *American labor, Congress, and the welfare state, 1935–2010*. Baltimore: Johns Hopkins University Press.

Schiff, Frank. 1990. "Personal Interview with G. William Domhoff, August 9." Berkeley Springs, WV.

Shelley, Mack. 1983. *The permanent majority: The conservative coalition in the United States Congress*. Tuscaloosa: University of Alabama Press.

Smith, Robert M. 2003. *From blackjacks to briefcases: A history of commercialized strikebreaking and unionbusting in the United States*. Athens: Ohio University Press.

Soutar, Douglas. 1996. "Telephone interview with G. William Domhoff."

Stone, Charles and Isabell Sawhill. 1984. *Economic policy in the Reagan years*. Washington: Urban Institute Press.

Swenson, Peter. 2002. *Capitalists against markets: The making of labor markets and welfare states in the United States and Sweden*. New York: Oxford University Press.

Thieblot, Armand and Ronald Cowin. 1972. *Welfare and strikers: The use of public funds to support strikers*. Philadelphia: Industrial Research Unit, Wharton School of Finance and Commerce, University of Pennsylvania.

Vogel, David. 1989. *Fluctuating fortunes: The political power of business in America*. New York: Basic Books.

Volscho, Thomas and Nathan Kelly. 2012. "The rise of the super-rich: Power resources, taxes, financial markets, and the dynamics of the top 1 percent, 1949 to 2008." *American Sociological Review* 77:679–699.

Warner, Kris. 2013. "The decline of unionization in the United States: Some lessons from Canada." *Labor Studies Journal* 38:110–138.

Waterhouse, Benjamin. 2014. *Lobbying America: The politics of business from Nixon to NAFTA*. Princeton: Princeton University Press.

Western, Bruce and Jake Rosenfeld. 2011. "Unions, norms, and the rise in U.S. wage inequality." *American Sociological Review* 76:513–537.

White, Donald. 1983. "Golden handshake: Small business big bonanza." P. 23 in *San Francisco Chronicle*. San Francisco.

Windham, Lane 2017. *Knocking on labor's door: Union organizing in the 1970s and the roots of a new economic divide*. Chapel Hill: University of North Carolina Press.

Zeigler, Harmon. 1961. *The politics of small business*. Washington: Public Affairs Press.

Zelizer, Julian. 2007. "Seizing power: Conservatives and Congress since the 1970s." Pp. 105–134 in *The transformation of American politics: Activist government and the rise of conservatism*, edited by P. Pierson and T. Skocpol. Princeton: Princeton University Press.

Part 2

How the Corporate Moderates Created Social Insurance Programs, and Later Tried to Undermine Them

The origins and fate of the Social Security Act of 1935 and related national-level social-insurance programs is a very different story than what happened in the case of unions. By and large, government social-benefit programs were not seen as a mortal threat by corporate moderates, although they resisted them or tried to cut back on them if they (1) impinged upon wage levels in low-wage industries; (2) became large enough to threaten corporate control of labor markets; or (3) began to be expensive enough to cut into profits in a serious way. As a result of the corporate moderates' relative moderation on social-insurance programs, they were sometimes amenable to social programs when there was social upheaval or working-class pressures. At that point, they either created social-benefit programs within their policy-planning network or shaped those put forward by the liberal-labor alliance to their liking.

The corporate moderates were even more amenable to a social-welfare program if it had major benefits for them, as turned out to be the case with the provisions of the Social Security Act of 1935, which was the first large-scale social-benefits program ever created by the federal government. As will be shown in great detail, some of the same companies that led the fight against the liberal-labor version of the National Labor Relations Act of 1935, such as Standard Oil of New Jersey and General Electric, were strong supporters of the Social Security Act. In addition, experts employed by Industrial Relations Counselors, Inc. had a major role in shaping two of the legislation's most important provisions, old-age pensions and unemployment insurance.

Most Americans, as well as many social scientists and historians, assume that big business has always been opposed to Social Security. They make that assumption for several reasons, starting with the fact that the most outspoken business leaders of the 1930s, the leaders of the NAM and the Chamber of Commerce, railed against it when it was considered by Congress, and tried to undermine it ever after. Moreover, as one part of the general right turn by corporate moderates, they joined the effort to cut back on these programs in the late 1970s, although they only partially succeeded in terms of programs concerning old-age pensions.

The original Social Security Act is also interesting for what it did not include, government spending for health (medical) insurance. A legislative drafting committee actually spent a large amount of time trying to craft a satisfactory program, but the resistance on the part of the American Medical Association, backed by ultraconservatives, was so intense that the attempt was abandoned (e.g., Starr 2017, pp. 267–269; Witte 1963, pp. 174–186). However, the eventual provisions for health insurance (in the form of Medicare and Medicaid in 1965, and the Affordable Care Act in 2010) were included under the umbrella of the Social Security Act.

The fact that many Americans now have government-supported health insurance owes much to the efforts of the liberal-labor alliance, but the story is more complicated than that because at a certain point in the late 1940s and early 1950s many hospitals started to need government subsidies to survive. Then government medical insurance became a financial cornucopia for private insurance companies, pharmaceutical companies, medical technology companies, and doctors, which dramatically changed the nature of healthcare in the United States. The history of Medicare and Medicaid is recounted as part of Chapter 7, and the story of the Affordable Care Act, which was supported by corporate moderates, is discussed in the final subsection in Chapter 9.

There is also a political angle to the twenty-first century's conventional wisdom about all forms of social insurance. This conventional wisdom, inside and outside of academia, says that corporate leaders were always against all forms of social insurance. Conversely, the liberal-labor alliance was their champion. Since most moderate conservatives within the corporate community became outspoken critics of the Social Security Act beginning in the 1980s, and wanted to cut back on government pensions, they were perfectly willing to blame liberals for the existence of these programs, and in any case may not know that corporate moderates provided the guidelines for the Social Security Act in the 1930s. Members of the liberal-labor alliance, on the other hand, were happy to accept credit for the creation of the programs they now defended so vigorously. In doing so they either do not know or ignore the fact that the liberals of the 1930s thought the old-age pensions and unemployment insurance provisions of the Social Security Act of 1935 were too centrist. Nor do they remember that the liberal-labor alliance was disappointed by the final versions of both the Medicare Act of 1965 and the Affordable Care Act of 2010.

References

Starr, Paul. 2017. *The social transformation of American medicine: The rise of a sovereign profession and the making of a vast industry.* New York Basic Books.

Witte, Edwin E. 1963. *The development of the Social Security Act.* Madison: University of Wisconsin Press.

Chapter 6

The Origins of the Social Security Act

The primary focus of this chapter is on the origins of the two largest and most theoretically contentious programs contained within the overall Social Security Act of 1935—old-age insurance (which is what is now meant by Social Security, or pensions, in everyday parlance) and unemployment insurance (which is usually called unemployment benefits). But it is also essential to emphasize that the other provisions in the overall Social Security Act were then and remained extremely important in many people's lives. However, those provisions were not as controversial, at least in the 1930s, and in the decades since the 1960s they have not been the focus of strong theoretical disagreements about the origins of the Social Security Act among social scientists and historians.

For example, there was a provision called old-age assistance, which provided means-tested benefits for the elderly, that is, payments to low-income elderly people who had not worked long enough for enough money to be part of the original insurance program. Although old-age assistance remained crucial for many elderly people, it is only of interest from an academic perspective because the proponents of old-age insurance always saw it as a potential threat to their own program. That is, they knew from the start that ultraconservatives would insist that old-age assistance is all that is necessary. From the somewhat different perspectives of corporate moderates and members of the liberal-labor alliance, an ultraconservative victory on this issue would have been highly undesirable because it would have stigmatized funds for the elderly as "welfare," which might have led to a reluctance to raise benefits to keep pace with inflation (Altman 2005).

Then, too, there is a title in the Social Security Act, advocated by liberal women activists of the 1930s, whose efforts actually started in the Progressive Era. It provided benefits for unmarried mothers, which was not controversial at the time because the single mothers were most often white widows, and there were relatively small numbers of them. But as the program grew and was reshaped after World War II, it was soon stigmatized as "welfare" for allegedly undeserving women (Gordon 1994b; Mink

1995; Poole 2006, Chapter 5). Although the amounts of money involved were small in terms of the overall federal budget, and the individual payments were meager, the program was constantly attacked by ultraconservatives as a generous handout to allegedly lazy people of color, even though a majority of the recipients were white. The ultraconservatives' distaste for the program also became one part of their successful effort to win over just enough white middle-income workers to put Republicans in the White House for most of the years between 1968 and 2008.

After 40 years of effort, the ultraconservatives succeeded in drastically cutting back on the provisions for single mothers in 1996. They then renamed the original provision for it in the Social Security Act as "The Personal Responsibility and Work Opportunity Act" in order to reinforce the idea that those on welfare had supposedly lost moral fiber and needed to look harder for work opportunities. This "reform" was the outcome of President Bill Clinton's 1992 campaign promise to "end welfare as we know it." His attempt to salvage the welfare program with some middle-of-the road changes (harsh enough in themselves) were made more stringent by the Republicans' insistence that his provisions for child care and health insurance for those on welfare had to be eliminated (Quadagno and Rohlinger 2009). The act put time limits on the number of years a person could receive welfare, added a work component, and reduced assistance for immigrants, due to the strong Republican belief that many immigrants come to the United States with the hope of receiving welfare assistance.

Old-Age Pensions and Unemployment Insurance

According to some historians and political scientists, there are many precedents for old-age pensions that can be found in the nineteenth century, especially old-age pensions for former union soldiers in the Civil War. In their telling, these programs provided paths, precedents, and social learning that guided the government officials that created the Social Security Act (e.g., Skocpol 1992, Chapter 2). As for unemployment insurance, it first gained attention in the first decade of the twentieth century and received extended discussion in the 1920s, in part based on the experience of European countries with various forms of social insurance.

In the case of disability benefits and pensions for the civil war veterans, they were used by nineteenth-century Republicans, almost totally beholden to northern manufacturers and bankers, to win votes in key Northern states after the Civil War. At the same time, these pensions were also useful because they were a benign way to spend some of the surplus government funds that eventuated from the high tariffs the Republicans had enacted to protect American industries. These benefits were later extended to widows and children of the veterans, and in general allegedly became so corrupt that they soured people on government pensions for all elderly citizens (Skocpol 1992, Chapter 2). As a result, this tainted program may have become a negative example, which delayed consideration of old-age insurance for everyone. But there were only 424,000 people receiving such pensions by 1915, so it seems more likely that their impact would be minimal (Domhoff 1996, pp. 234–236, for a detailed critique, which concludes that Civil War pensions are irrelevant to the origins of the Social Security Act).

From the perspective of a corporate-dominance theory, the first faint glimmer of the principles embodied in the old-age provisions of the Social Security Act arose in the 1870s when a few corporate leaders thought about providing company pensions, not government pensions, for their elderly workers. From that time until the Great Depression, members of the corporate community always saw pensions as having two main purposes, which varied in their importance from era to era, depending on circumstances. First, old-age pensions were most often seen as a way to replace superannuated workers with more productive younger workers. This point is demonstrated by a program put in place in 1875 by American Express, whose employees had to move heavy freight on and off railroad cars, as well as transport securities and currency.

Second, the spontaneous strike and large-scale property destruction by railroad workers in 1877, as discussed in Chapter 1, led some railroad owners to think of old-age pensions for loyal employees as a potential way to quell labor disruption, at the least by creating new openings for restive and/or unemployed younger workers. However, in terms of dealing with labor unrest, it is also the case that both railroad owners and other corporate leaders regarded death benefits, accident insurance, and unemployment compensation as potentially more important than old-age pensions (e.g., Graebner 1980; Sass 1997).

Either way, by 1900 the Pennsylvania Railroad, the third-largest railroad in the country at the time, had a full-fledged pension plan for all employees at age 70, and a few other railroads had smaller programs. Similarly, and as part of its efforts to avoid worker protests and maintain union-free factories, in 1910 U.S. Steel instituted accident and death benefits for all workers, and old-age pensions for workers over age 60 (Garraty 1960, pp. 31–32). For now, though, it is the railroad pensions that are worth keeping in mind because militant railroad workers in the late 1920s and early 1930s created the pressures that set in motion the series of events that led to the Social Security Act.

In the case of unemployment insurance, the first push, primarily on a state-by-state basis, was based on what were considered to be sound business principles that would appeal to corporate moderates. The initial plan came from a small group of experts, many of them university professors, who formed the American Association for Labor Legislation (AALL) in 1906 to promote "uniform progressive state and local labor laws and,

232 Social Insurance Created and Undermined

where possible, national labor legislation" (Eakins 1966, p. 59). Due to the fact that several of its founders were included in the National Civic Federation (NCF), the policy-discussion group discussed in Chapter 1, the experts in the AALL came to believe that some corporate moderates might be sympathetic to unemployment insurance, as well as some of the other labor reform laws that progressives in economics, political science, and sociology had been working on since the 1880s (with little success, be it noted) (Slaughter and Silva 1980). In other words, this is another example of the way in which corporate moderates and policy experts have discussed issues and worked together in the policy-planning network since the early twentieth century.

The founders of the AALL began their efforts by doing careful research, writing model legislation, and encouraging discussion of labor issues in the journal they created, the *American Labor Legislation Review*. They thereby served as a clearinghouse that answered questions from all levels of government across the country. They also did educational outreach work with professionals, government officials, and party leaders through speeches, conferences, books, press releases, and legislative testimony. It was a small expert group that in no way reached out to the general public.

The AALL had several overlaps in leadership and financing with the NCF, but it also included reformers and even a few socialists who were not invited to take part in NCF deliberations. In addition, progressive women reformers from the settlement house movement, the National Consumers' League, and the Women's Trade Union League served on its advisory board. The AALL was financed by a small number of wealthy individuals, including some of the political economists and women activists themselves, who came from the upper and upper-middle classes (Domhoff 1970, pp. 172–173). In other words, some of the members and supporters of the AALL were more than moderate conservatives, but it is once again notable that moderate conservatives were willing to discuss programs with them.

The key figure in the AALL, economist John R. Commons, briefly introduced in Chapter 1, was not from a wealthy background. Instead, he came from humble circumstances and involved himself in a variety of reform efforts in the 1890s while teaching at various colleges. However, recall from Chapter 1 that in 1902 he took a job running the New York office of the NCF, and also did research and involved himself in mediating labor disputes. Based on his experience dealing with business leaders in the NCF, he became convinced that the secret to reform was appealing to the profit motive.

Although he was by then a professor at the University of Wisconsin, Commons served as the secretary of the New York-based AALL from 1907 to 1909. He was succeeded as secretary by one of his Wisconsin students, John B. Andrews, who directed the organization and most of its activities from that point until his death in 1943, when the organization became inactive, and disbanded soon thereafter. Many of Commons' other students, it should be noted here, worked on projects for the AALL over the next several decades, and eventually for the government committees that formulated the Social Security Act. In doing so, they followed Commons' lead by building their reform measures on business principles. They also gradually decided to concentrate on the state level because of the many defeats the AALL suffered at the federal level between 1906 and 1925 (Moss 1996). By the late 1920s, the AALL was focused even more on the state level because of its fear that the Supreme Court, based on several of its earlier rulings, would rule federal labor legislation unconstitutional. This is important to mention because it later brought the AALL into arguments with those corporate moderates who eventually had the biggest impact on shaping the Social Security Act in the 1930s. That is, on this issue the corporate moderates of the 1930s were willing to go further than the AALL stalwarts.

The AALL also had the support of one of the most brilliant and persuasive minds of the early twentieth century, Louis Brandeis, a corporate lawyer turned reformer. In addition, Brandeis was appointed to the Supreme Court in 1916 and became a powerful behind-the-scenes player in Washington. Born into wealth in 1856 and a graduate of Harvard Law School, Brandeis worked as a conventional corporate lawyer from 1879 until the late 1890s. At that point he became a critic of the "curse of bigness" and signed on as the legal counsel for the National Consumers' League, where his sisters-in-law, Josephine and Pauline Goldmark, were top leaders (Baltzell 1964, pp. 188–192; Gordon 1994b, pp. 83–84). He also joined the AALL's Advisory Council, and in 1911 wrote draft legislation for unemployment insurance that contained an incentive feature meant to induce employers to minimize unemployment. The proposed bill lowered the required premiums for businesses if they had low layoff records.

During its nearly 40 years of existence the AALL worked on a wide variety of labor legislation that ranged from old-age pensions to unemployment insurance to accident insurance, with varying degrees of success. It had a strong impact on the health of workers through the legislation it helped write to combat industrial diseases, while failing on unemployment insurance (Domhoff 1970, pp. 174–175; Pierce 1953, pp. 27–34). However, there is one labor issue it did not include on its agenda, support for unions, which is a major reason why it could attract the financial support and participation of some corporate moderates as well as include reformers and socialists in its discussions. It is also noteworthy that the AALL's legislative approach did not attract much support from the American Federation of Labor (AFL) until the New Deal because of the AFL's general wariness toward government, which its leaders assumed to be controlled by corporate interests (Skocpol 1992, pp. 208–209). As this wariness demonstrates, there was no liberal-labor alliance in the United States until the 1930s, which is later than the one that formed in the United Kingdom, as well as being later than the labor-leftist coalitions that formed in several European countries (Ahmed 2013; Mann 1993; Starr 2007).

The AALL also had one state-level plan, health insurance, that went nowhere after drawing some interest (Moss 1996, Chapter 8, for a detailed history of this failed effort; Starr 2017, pp. 243–257 for a more wide-ranging and contextualized account). Initially, it even received some short-lived positive reactions from one of the executives in the insurance industry that was sympathetic to the general concerns of the organization, but he quickly became its most vociferous critic because he perceived it as a threat to the insurance industry (Moss 1996, pp. 139, 147–148). Gompers of the AFL was its fierce opponent as well, as were the well-organized physicians, working through the American Medical Association (AMA), who zealously defended their autonomy (Moss 1996; Starr 2017, pp. 248, 252–253). The AMA soundly defeated the AALL whenever it tried to move beyond workmen's compensation and industrial health and safety regulations.

Although the AALL had only marginal success in most of its campaigns, and none at all with health insurance, it did achieve great success on its first, and most important, insurance issue, workmen's compensation. In fact, this initiative became the first step in an unlikely and indirect route to the Social Security Act. Workmen's compensation may seem far from old-age pensions, but it was conflict over workman's compensation that started the giant insurance companies of that era thinking about old-age insurance. This was because workmen's compensation, not old-age pensions or unemployment insurance, was the big issue of the early twentieth century, due to the fact that industrial accidents were a major personal tragedy for tens of thousands of workers and a costly and disruptive problem for American industry. The result was worker discontent and numerous individual liability lawsuits in which juries found against the companies and awarded expensive settlements to injured workers. As corporations lost more and more lawsuits, they became open to new alternatives (e.g., Castrovinci 1976; Fishback and Kantor 2000; Weinstein 1968, Chapter 2).

In an effort to provide accident insurance for workers in a way that would be acceptable to employers, the AALL developed a plan that was structured to induce companies to reduce their rate of accidents in exchange for lower insurance payments. It began in 1906 by sending its model legislation to business executives, labor leaders, academic experts, and government officials, and by discussing it with NCF leaders. Just a year later, the members of the NCF decided to support the AALL initiative as a way to reduce uncertainty and expenses. Some corporate chieftains also argued that workmen's compensation might help reduce support for unions as well, since the high accident rate was such a contentious issue

(Weinstein 1968, Chapter 2). In short, the experts built on business principles, and the corporate moderates were receptive, which was the winning combination on most social-insurance issues, including health insurance, in the twentieth century.

By 1910, even most members of the ultraconservative National Association of Manufacturers also favored workmen's compensation as a legal right. However, the ultraconservatives still differed from the corporate moderates because they were not willing to pay taxes for a plan administered by state governments. They therefore urged private insurance companies to develop commercial plans, which led to a trip to England by insurance company experts and NAM representatives to study European precedents (Klein 2003; Sass 1997). The result was a rival proposal for legally enforceable mandates that would stipulate that companies had to provide their employees with private accident compensation insurance. This approach also came to be preferred by many members of the NCF, because it embodied their own inclination toward as little government involvement in their affairs as possible. As this example suggests, the corporate moderates sometimes accept the ultraconservative alternative when they think it will work. More generally, the back-and-forth arguments between the moderate conservatives and ultraconservatives on this issue provide another specific instance in which they were able to compromise their differences—and for the most part win out, as demonstrated in the next few paragraphs.

The original reaction by Samuel Gompers and other AFL leaders to the AALL's model legislation had been to oppose any form of social insurance that involved government due to their belief that the domination of government by corporations would lead to unsatisfactory programs. Instead, labor leaders preferred to continue to take their chances in individual court cases. By 1908, however, they had been persuaded by their corporate counterparts in the NCF to support insurance on this specific issue. But they reacted negatively to the NAM push for the involvement of private insurance companies, as did many reformers and all members of the rising and highly visible Socialist Party of the pre-World War I era. The result was two rival camps that were pushing for two different approaches to government-mandated accident insurance programs. The AALL, NCF, and NAM were on one side, and organized labor, liberal reformers, and the Socialist Party were on the other. This line-up suggests that the argument over workmen's compensation was edging toward being a class conflict.

When the AALL/NCF/NAM campaign for legislation began in 1910 and 1911, the battles primarily centered on the disagreement over government versus commercial insurance, although there were also arguments concerning compensation rates, breadth of coverage, and other particularistic but vital issues that are not relevant here. In the end, corporate executives usually held firm for private insurance and conceded higher payout rates in exchange, which were generally above 50 percent of a week's pay. It was a compromise that organized labor and their liberal and Socialist Party allies only reluctantly accepted. By 1920, only six states, all in the South, lacked workmen's compensation laws (Fishback and Kantor 2000; Weinstein 1968). Workmen's compensation therefore can be seen as a success story for the corporate-financed policy-planning network.

Over and beyond the immediate beneficial impacts of this legislation for the many thousands of workers injured each year, the battle over accident insurance had two long-lasting effects that influenced debates about social insurance during the New Deal. First, success on workmen's compensation reinforced AALL members in their belief that the use of sound business principles and the right incentives might convince corporations to drop their opposition to unemployment compensation. As a result, the AALL tried to kindle interest in Brandeis's company-specific unemployment insurance plan, which was structured to encourage companies to minimize layoffs for their workers through better anticipation of market fluctuations and more careful planning of production schedules. (Under this plan, recall, lower layoff rates would lead to lower payments into the unemployment insurance fund.) And once again, legislation would be passed by individual states.

Later experience proved once again what had been demonstrated many times before: there is no chance that individual companies can have any effect on a major systemic problem such as unemployment. For that reason, the AALL emphasis on company layoff rates, individual company accounts, and state-level legislation became flashpoints of conflict when other experts within the policy-planning network came to believe that a federal system with uniform tax rates was necessary. What therefore needs to be underscored and remembered is that the long policy battle on unemployment insurance that is discussed later in this chapter is between two rival business-oriented plans. At bottom it is another round in the ongoing argument about how much government involvement could be forced upon the well-organized ultraconservatives in the corporate community and the Southern Democrats (who were, to repeat, the representatives of the plantation/agribusiness owners in that era and into at least the 1970s as well).

As to the second, and even more important, long-lasting effect of the conflict over workmen's compensation, it provided the starting point for the old-age insurance provisions of the Social Security Act. It convinced private insurance companies that they might be able to underwrite other forms of group social insurance, starting with group life insurance programs for corporations, and maybe old-age pensions as well. Two of the three largest insurance companies, Equitable Life and Metropolitan Life, which shared many directors in common with major banks and corporations, began making the analyses necessary to offer such packages to corporations as a way to make profits and at the same time head off any push for government insurance programs. Both companies also came to believe they could do a better job with private pensions than individual corporations, but only if contributions were made by both the companies and their employees (Klein 2003; Sass 1997). (Plans that mandate contributions by both the company and its employees are called "contributory" plans.)

The gradual move toward actuarial soundness for private old-age pensions received a boost in 1918 from the president of the Carnegie Foundation for the Advancement of Teaching, another early arm of the policy-planning network, which was initially established to provide pensions for professors. It was one of five foundations created by Andrew Carnegie, one of the richest of the steel barons of that era, who was mentioned briefly in Chapter 1 for his attacks on unions at Homestead, PA, in 1892. The largest of Carnegie's foundations, which shared directors with other Carnegie foundations, and was second only to the Rockefeller Foundation in its importance, was given the name "Carnegie Corporation." It has had an impact in a wide range of policy areas, but with a major emphasis on foreign policy and the shaping of the educational system (e.g., Darknell 1975; Darknell 1980; Lagemann 1989; Weischadle 1980). All five of the Carnegie-endowed foundations were among the 20 largest foundations in 1934 (TCF 1935, p. 15).

The pension plan for retired professors established by the Carnegie Foundation for the Advancement of Teaching was put on a solid actuarial footing by creating the Teachers Insurance and Annuity Association, a life insurance company, which then fashioned the first fully insured pension system (it is now part of a giant company called TIAA-CREF) (Sass 1997, p. 65). It was at this point that the experience of the private insurance companies and the Carnegie Foundation for the Advancement of Teaching also began to have an influence on pension programs for government officials. This point is best demonstrated by the pension program designed for federal civil service employees in 1920 by a fledgling think tank of that day, the Institute of Government Relations, which was one of three policy-oriented institutes that were merged to create The Brookings Institution in 1927 (Graebner 1980, pp. 77, 87; Saunders 1966, p. 25). In other words, by 1920 large corporations and organizations in the policy-planning network were shaping government insurance programs based on their own principles and experience. Thus, whatever small influence that lingered from pensions for the Union Army veterans and their survivors, or from a few other small government pension plans of the past, had been swept aside by this point (Domhoff 1996, pp. 234–236).

Although group insurance plans engaged the interest of corporate moderates during the 1920s, it is important to avoid any misunderstandings by stressing that group insurance plans provided coverage for only a tiny

238 Social Insurance Created and Undermined

percentage of the elderly at the time. Most people bought old-age insurance from actuarially unsound plans sponsored by fraternal organizations, ethnic lodges, or trade unions, but by the end of the 1920s almost all of those plans had failed. As a consequence of these failures, there was a gradual movement toward support for state-level government pensions by organizations such as the Fraternal Order of Eagles and some local and state union federations, using plans drawn up for them by the AALL. A more liberal reform-oriented group, the American Association for Old Age Security, joined these efforts in the mid-1920s. It advocated comprehensive social insurance at the state level paid for by general taxes, and thereby directly challenged the AALL approach (Loetta 1975). The incipient battle between the two reformist groups to one side for the moment, as many as 25 states passed legislation allowing for old-age pensions in the late 1920s and early 1930s, usually without any state funding and at the option of individual counties. As a result, few people received a state pension and the benefits were meager if they did so.

As for any plans for unemployment insurance, which continued to be based on the AALL's emphasis on encouraging employers to prevent unemployment with an incentive-based insurance plan, they went nowhere in the 1920s (Nelson 1969, Chapter 6). Most unions ignored plans for government unemployment insurance and tended to favor the company-oriented incentive plans offered by the AALL and corporate moderates. One of the few exceptions involved the pragmatic leftists in the clothing industry, the Amalgamated Clothing Workers, the same union that had played a large role in the origins of the National Labor Relations Act through its president, Sidney Hillman. As in the case of the garment workers' ability to win strikes, they had enough solidarity to push for programs to which companies and workers both contributed (Nelson 1969, Chapter 6). And, as discussed shortly, an expert employed by the Amalgamated Clothing Workers to help with this plan was soon hired away by John D. Rockefeller, Jr., to work on corporate social insurance plans.

Despite the various grassroots efforts overviewed in the previous two paragraphs, the major developments in the mid-1920s, the ones that impacted the Social Security Act, were being made by large individual corporations that had insurance plans of their own. In addition, the insurance companies already had made their group programs sounder and less expensive by having both employers and employees contribute. By 1923, for example, Metropolitan Life was confident that it had a group pension plan that was better than anything any one corporation could offer on an equally sound basis. One of its main spokespersons therefore eagerly presented the new plan to the corporate executives that his company invited to a special conference.

However, even though this executive presented evidence that most corporate plans were unsound, the biggest corporations of the era were not

The Origins of the Social Security Act   239

prepared to abandon their own plans. They liked to run their own show, and some of them still believed their pension plans were helpful in controlling their workforces and limiting strikes. (As a result, corporate plans sometimes had clauses saying a pension could be lost if the individual participated in a strike.) The corporate leaders present at the conference also liked the fact that they did not legally have to pay benefits if they decided not to do so.

When an executive from Otis Elevator frankly told the Metropolitan Life speaker that the circumstances of each corporation varied too greatly to go along with what the insurance companies had to offer, the insurance representative argued back. His reply led to a sharp rebuke by none other than the top industrial relations executive at Standard Oil of New Jersey, Clarence Hicks, who figures as prominently in this chapter as he did in the account of the National Labor Relations Act in Chapter 2. Hicks put an end to the discussion with these frank words:

> It is impossible and impracticable. For 20 years the [Standard Oil] company has been experimenting on plans. I do not know why it becomes suitable at this time to stop experimenting. If we had done this a week ago, we would not have had the benefit of what we did today.
> (Sass 1997, p. 72)

After Hicks concluded his remarks, the executive from Otis Elevator made a motion to end the meeting and offer Metropolitan Life a "hearty thanks," which led to immediate adjournment (Sass 1997, p. 72). So it is not like these corporate executives were far seeing and immediately sensible in any big-picture sense. They wanted to hold on to their baronial power as long as their corporate fiefdoms made that possible. In this case, it took the crisis of the Great Depression to expand their horizons, as will soon become apparent. Moreover, they only begrudgingly learned that their individual company plans did not help with control of the workforce, and were not even actuarially sound, so Hicks and his likeminded counterparts are more accurately called blinkered and shortsighted on this issue. Soon after the Metropolitan Life conference, for example, a meat packing company went bankrupt, sold its assets, and left its 400 retirees with 14 months of benefits (Sass 1997, p. 57). So it was not long before the Metropolitan Life plan became more attractive to smaller companies, if not yet to large ones, especially when it packaged group old-age pensions with life, health, or disability insurance.

Industrial Relations Counselors, Inc.

It was at about this time that another organization entered the picture, one that was destined to have far more impact on the Social Security

240 Social Insurance Created and Undermined

Act than anyone ever would have imagined at the time. Moreover, it is an organization—Industrial Relations Counselors, Inc. (IRC)—that is already familiar to readers due to its attempts to combat unions and diminish labor-management conflict through Employee Representation Plans, but also due to its vigorous campaign to scuttle the National Labor Relations Act. Failure though it was in relation to the National Labor Relations Act, its parallel work on company-level old-age pension and unemployment compensation plans provided the basis for the Social Security Act.

The IRC's major role in relation to the Social Security Act was made possible by its employment of two very well trained independent experts on these issues, Murray Latimer and Bryce Stewart, who avoided any involvement in union-related issues and ended up at the center of the legislative drafting for the Social Security Act, beginning in 1934. Latimer, a 25-year-old instructor in finance at the Harvard Business School at the time he was hired in 1926, was born and educated in Clinton, Mississippi, where his father owned an automobile dealership. (Latimer received an MBA from the Harvard Business School in 1923 before joining its faculty.) During his years at the IRC, Latimer helped to establish new pension plans at Standard Oil of New Jersey as well as three other Rockefeller oil companies and an independent steel company, American Rolling Mill.

Latimer's book for IRC on *Industrial Pension Systems in the United States and Canada* (1932) was well known and respected at the time, and is still frequently cited in historical accounts (Klein 2003; Orloff 1993; Sass 1997). Latimer also did a study of union pension plans for the AFL in 1928–1929, shortly before the stock market crash, concluding that "the experiments are far from having reached a sound basis and that unless drastic financial reorganization is made they are almost certain to end in failure in the relatively near future" (Klein 2003, pp. 56–57).

Stewart, 44 years old when he joined the IRC staff in 1927, was a Canadian with many years of experience working with employment and labor issues. A graduate of Queens University in Kingston, Ontario, he earned a Ph.D. at Columbia University and worked as a researcher, chief statistician, and editor for the Canadian Department of Labor, and then as an organizer and director of the Employment Service of Canada (Kelly 1987). Most interesting of all in terms of my emphasis on the relative openness of moderate conservatives in the corporate community on unemployment and pension issues, Stewart is the person I was referring to earlier as an employee of the Amalgamated Clothing Workers in Chicago. He came back to the United States in 1922 to develop and administer an employment exchange for the union, which was later supplemented by an unemployment insurance fund.

Created at Hillman's request, the Amalgamated's employment exchange and its insurance fund were jointly financed by labor and management, but controlled by the union. Stewart (1925) wrote an article for the

International Labor Review about this "American experiment." After leaving the union to join the IRC staff, he became its director of research in 1930. He held that position until his retirement in 1952, except for a return to Canada as deputy minister of labor during World War II. Like Latimer, he was well known in the early 1930s for his publications on social insurance (Stewart 1928; Stewart 1930).

Latimer and Stewart are not mystery people who are unknown to the social scientists that have examined the origins of the Social Security Act, but their personal employment by Rockefeller at the IRC is not considered very relevant. For example, one pair of political scientists claims that information on the connections between corporate moderates and policy experts ignores the differences between corporate executives and policy experts, and also overlooks the "multiple affiliations" and "complex career histories" of the independent policy experts; they say that my kind of research "implies that all policy designers with past or present ties to corporate-funded research groups accurately reflect the sentiments of big business, ignoring the multiple affiliations and complex career histories of many of these experts, as well as the overwhelming number of New Deal figures, especially in top positions, who had no such ties" (Hacker and Pierson 2002, p. 308). Besides, they continue, to the degree that the corporate moderates had any involvement in the Social Security Act, their stance was a "strategic accommodation, driven by fear of less attractive alternatives," by which they mean "the Townsend movement," a legislative pressure group formed in the summer of 1934; it will be discussed later in the chapter (Hacker and Pierson 2002, pp. 298, 307–308). For now, perhaps readers can keep this critique in mind as they assess the persuasiveness of the evidence for the importance of Latimer, Stewart, and the IRC.

Returning to the specifics on Latimer and Stewart, and their network of committee and individual affiliations, they were often joined in their efforts by economist J. Douglas Brown, the director of the Rockefeller-financed Industrial Relations Section of the Department of Economics at Princeton. Since he, too, figures in the origins of the Social Security Act, a few words about him are in order. The son of an industrial executive in Somerville, New Jersey, Brown received his B.A. and Ph.D. at Princeton and taught for a year in the industrial relations program at the Wharton School at the University of Pennsylvania. He then returned to Princeton as a professor. Brown also worked closely with Hicks, the industrial relations executive at Standard Oil of New Jersey, and later helped him write his autobiography (Hicks 1941, pp. 163–167). In addition, Brown hosted an annual industrial relations conference at Princeton in conjunction with Hicks and the IRC staff. Still another of his assignments was to talk with corporate executives around the country and make periodic reports to Hicks and John D. Rockefeller, III, who was overseeing the IRC for his father at the time. For example, Hicks wrote the following letter to

242 Social Insurance Created and Undermined

Rockefeller to alert him to a forthcoming report from Brown, who was also going to tell Hicks about the work agenda for the Industrial Relations Section at Princeton during the next year:

> During this past summer Mr. J. Douglas Brown, who has charge of the Industrial Relations Section at Princeton, has been making a trip as far west as California, interviewing representatives of a large number of corporations and getting in personal touch with the industrial relations situation in various sections of the country. Tomorrow, Friday, he is coming to take luncheon with me to review his trip and to discuss the work of the Industrial Relations Section for the coming year.
>
> (Hicks 1930)

A pamphlet written for the American Management Association in 1928 by Edward S. Cowdrick, the former journalist personally employed by Rockefeller, as discussed in Chapter 1, best exemplifies the pre-depression thinking about company pensions within the Rockefeller-financed industrial relations network. Furthermore, the pamphlet reflects the thinking of other corporate moderates as well, as shown shortly. According to Cowdrick's detailed analysis, which contains discussions of the moral, economic, and technical issues involved in industrial pensions, a pension is part of a good personnel program. Especially in the case of corporations that have been around for many years, a pension is "a means, at once humane and approved by public opinion, of purging its active payroll of men who, by reason of age or disability, have become liabilities rather than assets" (Cowdrick 1928, p. 10). Pensions also provide the "opportunity to promote their younger subordinates." Cowdrick concluded with the prediction that industrial pensions will be "increasingly valuable to employers" (Cowdrick 1928, pp. 11, 21).

Cowdrick's summary aside, and returning to the IRC, it undertook its first consulting for a government agency in 1928 when Frances Perkins, recently appointed by Governor Franklin D. Roosevelt as New York's industrial commissioner, established an Advisory Committee on Employment Problems "to effect some improvement in the State Employment Service" (Perkins 1930). Very striking in terms of my emphasis on the importance of the corporate-funded network of foundations, think tanks, and policy-discussion groups, the legislation enabling the demonstration project called for private funding from foundations. Perkins therefore wrote to the director of the Spelman Fund, which was by then a relatively small policy-oriented foundation because most of the Laura Spelman Rockefeller Memorial Fund, as briefly mentioned in Chapter 1, had been folded into the Rockefeller Foundation as its Social Sciences Division. She asked him "if the Spelman Fund of New York would grant an annual appropriation of $25,000 for a period of three to five years," which

The Origins of the Social Security Act 243

was one-third of the estimated annual expenses (Perkins 1930). Her letter indicated that another foundation was also willing to help out, so all this adds up to the fact that the policy-planning network was going to finance this government project.

At about the same time, Perkins appointed the director of the IRC, Arthur H. Young, as the chair of her advisory committee. (Readers may recall from Chapter 2 that Young went to work as an industrial relations vice president at U.S. Steel in 1934 and later famously said that he would rather go to jail than support the National Labor Relations Act.). His report to Perkins recommended that demonstration projects be developed to test the effectiveness of public employment centers. The recommendation led to a demonstration project in Rochester in 1931, based on a grant of $75,000 over a three-year period by another one of the Rockefeller philanthropies. Stewart was put in charge of the project as chair of the Committee on Demonstration, through which he came to know Perkins. The Rochester project also brought Stewart into contact with a transplanted Southerner, Marion Folsom, the assistant treasurer of Eastman Kodak, who had taken a leadership role since the early 1920s in experimenting with forms of unemployment insurance, with the approval and support of the company president. (Since Folsom becomes involved in the effort to pass the Social Security Act, it should be added that he was born and raised in southeastern Georgia, where his father was a merchant and a trustee of Southern Georgia College, then educated at the University of Georgia and the Harvard Business School, and then hired by the treasury department at Eastman Kodak in 1915. After serving as a captain in World War I, he returned to Eastman Kodak and was soon promoted to assistant treasurer (Jacoby 1993; Jacoby 1997, pp. 206–220).)

At the same time, Stewart also worked for a three-person federal government study group on unemployment in 1931, which included Senator Robert Wagner of New York, the leader of the urban liberals in the Senate, who was discussed in Chapter 2 as the main advocate for the National Labor Relations Act (Huthmacher 1968, p. 83). Clearly, then, the IRC and the Spelman Fund had developed close connections, well before there was any thought of the 1932 presidential elections, or that Perkins would become President Franklin D. Roosevelt's secretary of labor, with other corporate moderates and with the two liberals—Senator Wagner and future Secretary of Labor Perkins—that would play a lead role in shaping the New Deal on social insurance issues.

Although corporate moderates and IRC employees had a strong interest in old-age pensions and unemployment compensation plans, they had no desire at this point to move toward government old-age pensions, a point demonstrated in a report by the National Industrial Conference Board in 1931. Based on work by IRC employees and a survey of a large number of industrial executives, *Elements of Industrial Pension Plans* concluded that

244 Social Insurance Created and Undermined

pension plans were becoming more important in the minds of industrialists and urged that the plans be made actuarially sound, in part through having employees contribute to them. No longer was there any mention of the usefulness of these plans in controlling employees. Now the emphasis was on staving off government programs by demonstrating that industry can "take care of its worn-out workers through pension plans resting on voluntary initiative and cooperation" (NICB 1931,p. vi). Showing even more clearly how much the corporate leaders wanted to avoid government pensions, the report stated:

> In proportion as such plans are established and become successful there is thus effected a reduction in the number of dependent aged that must be taken care of by society or the state. The extension throughout the field of industry of pension plans adequate in their provisions, equitably administered, and soundly financed, will do much toward removing any real need or excuse for resort to the dubious expedient of state pensions.
>
> (NICB 1931. p. vi)

At the same time that the insurance companies and IRC were shoring up company pension plans, IRC employees also became involved in the growing problem of unemployment. Although most members of the Rockefeller group had accepted the cautious and optimistic approach to dealing with the depression that Hoover insisted upon, they nonetheless began to take new initiatives. Very quickly, the Rockefeller Foundation, which was chaired by Rockefeller, came to the fore as the center of the Rockefeller network's efforts to help combat the social impacts of the deep depression. Its first step in this new direction was the creation of an Economic Stabilization Program in early 1930, a framework that was used to fund a variety of initiatives over the next three years. The second step was to tell the Social Science Research Council (hereafter SSRC) that there would be no further grants for general academic research. Times were tough and money was tight, so from then on only socially useful applied research would be supported. Henceforth the SSRC consisted of policy-oriented committees made up primarily of experts and business executives (Fisher 1993). It was to become even more of a think tank within the policy-planning network than it had been before. (In the postwar era, as already stressed in Chapter 1, it was relegated to the role of funding and organizing conferences for social scientists, and was no longer a part of the policy-planning network.)

Shortly thereafter, in February 1930, the SSRC created a Committee on Unemployment. Arthur Woods, the personal Rockefeller employee mentioned in Chapter 1, who was also a friend of President Hoover, chaired the new committee. His vice chair was another person introduced in Chapter 1, Joseph Willits, from the Wharton School and the SRCC

(Fisher 1993, p. 122). Stewart of IRC was a member, as were two other men who figure later in the creation of the Social Security Act: William Leiserson, a Wisconsin-trained economist and well-known labor mediator (who worked for the original National Labor Board); and corporate moderate Morris Leeds, the president of Leeds & Northrup (a manufacturer of precision instruments in Philadelphia). Leeds was a director of the AALL and a member of the SSRC's Committee on Industry and Trade.

By October 1930, Hoover was less certain that prosperity was just around the corner, so he appointed a President's Emergency Committee on Employment, drawing heavily on the think tanks in the policy-planning network, including The Brookings Institution, the National Bureau of Economic Research, and the SSRC. In spite of his concerns, Hoover was at the same time fearful that such a committee might contribute to an atmosphere of pessimism and a renewed call for greater involvement by the federal government in creating employment. He therefore stressed the temporary nature of the committee and limited its options to voluntary efforts at the state and local level. He chose his friend Woods as the chair, who then dovetailed the work of the emergency committee with that of the SSRC committee he also chaired (Fisher 1993, p. 122). Thus, the SSCR committee became a government committee—in other words, a temporary agency of the White House. In addition to Woods, there were ten other business leaders on the 33-person presidential committee, along with eight experts from the policy-planning network, including Willits, Stewart, Brown, and the director of the Spelman Fund from the network of Rockefeller-supported experts. Further blurring the line between the policy-planning network and the government, the Rockefeller Foundation gave the presidential committee $50,000 in 1930 and $75,000 in 1931 to help with its work. The Spelman Fund provided an additional $25,000 in 1931.

The committee's experts drafted a proposed message to Congress for Hoover, which presaged much of what the New Deal would eventually do. It called for "a public works program, including slum clearance, low-cost housing, and rural electrification" (Schlesinger 1957, p. 170). They recommended speeding up a large program of highway construction and advocated a national employment service, but there was no mention of unemployment insurance. These suggestions were resisted by Hoover, however. When Woods asked Hoover to start an emergency program in the near-starvation conditions of Appalachia, he was sent to the Red Cross, which refused to help because the problem was not due to a natural disaster, such as a flood or drought. At that point the Rockefeller philanthropies provided money to charitable and community groups for the Appalachian relief effort (Bernstein 1960, p. 301).

Woods later removed most hints of the considerable tensions between Hoover and the presidential committee from the historical account of the committee's efforts, leading to a long delay in the appearance of the book written about it. As one of Woods' aides later wrote to a key Rockefeller lawyer: "Colonel Woods was somewhat doubtful as to the wisdom of publishing the report in exactly the form as first prepared by Mr. Hayes, since it went into considerable detail as to certain differences of view which arose between the Committee and President Hoover" (Eden 1936). (Wood's decision, unfortunately, denied future researchers the opportunity to learn more about corporate-moderate thinking in the face of the Great Depression.) Willits of Wharton and the SSRC was assigned the task of making the manuscript revisions. These conflicts highlight the difference between anti-government market fundamentalists and the more pragmatic approach of the moderate conservatives within the corporate community.

Despite the obvious failure of the emergency employment committee, it had longer-term research consequences, although they were not at first apparent. It did so through a supplemental Advisory Committee on Unemployment Statistics chaired by Willits, with Stewart as its technical adviser. The committee sent out questionnaires to businesses and government agencies all over the country; its main finding was the inadequacy of unemployment figures and the impossibility of determining the number of people needing direct relief (Hayes 1936, p. 29). This finding supported later SSRC efforts to develop better data-gathering capabilities under governmental auspices.

The work by Hoover's emergency committee also led to research collaboration between the IRC and the Economic Stabilization Research Institute at the University of Minnesota on a pilot program on the usefulness of employment centers. The Rockefeller Foundation's Economic Stabilization Program awarded the institute a two-year grant for $150,000 to carry out the research, which was supplemented by smaller grants from the Carnegie Corporation and the Spelman Fund. One of the outcomes of this collaboration was a book presenting a plan for unemployment insurance, written by Stewart in conjunction with three University of Minnesota employees. The first of these three co-authors, economist Alvin Hansen, who later had a staff role in the creation of the Social Security Act, the International Monetary Fund, and much else, was soon to be appointed a professor at Harvard, where he became persuaded of the correctness of Keynesian theory in 1937. The second, Merrill Murray, trained in economics at Wisconsin and, previously employed by the Wisconsin Industrial Commission, was in charge of the actual field study and took part in an unsuccessful campaign to pass an unemployment insurance bill in the state. Four years later he joined with Stewart in writing a draft of the unemployment insurance provisions of the Social Security Act. The third co-author, Russell Stevenson, the dean of the School of Business Administration at the University of Minnesota, had no further role in the events recounted in this chapter.

The Origins of the Social Security Act 247

Although this multi-authored book is only of historical interest now, its preface has a noteworthy comment that highlights the way in which research carried out in the policy-planning network helps to bring about a new consensus. Hansen, Murray, and Stevenson report that they had come to doubt the usefulness of the AALL plan to create incentives that presumably would induce businessmen to reduce unemployment. Now they favored a national-level rather than a state-level plan, crediting Stewart for their change of view: "Many of the modifications in the original plan are the result of the research and thought brought to bear upon the subject by Bryce M. Stewart of the Industrial Relations Counselors, Inc., and his staff" (Hansen, Murray, Stevenson, and Stewart 1934, p. v). The experts should be given full credit on this idea, as critics of corporate-dominance theory emphasize, even while remembering the source of their financial sustenance.

The Rockefeller Foundation's Economic Stabilization Program made a series of grants to the IRC throughout 1931, drawing what had been a business-oriented consulting group further into the governmental arena. The first grant, for $30,000, provided at Woods' request, paid for a study of unemployment insurance plans in the United Kingdom. The second, for $16,000, supported a study of the administration of employment offices, supplemented a year later with $7,500 to support the IRC's role in the demonstration projects on employment offices in Rochester and Minneapolis. Another $16,000 made possible a study of employment offices in Europe. Finally, the IRC received $10,000 to help it set up the New York State Employment Service, which brought it into collaboration with Perkins once again. In short, the IRC was on its way to developing unique expertise on the administration of employment offices and on unemployment insurance, based on the provision of $1.3 million in Rockefeller Foundation grants in terms of 2018 dollars.

Even with this increased support from the Rockefeller Foundation, the great bulk of IRC's funding continued to come directly from Rockefeller himself, who was still kept informed of its activities by John D. Rockefeller III, Hicks, and Fosdick, his trusted personal lawyer. It is thus significant that Fosdick wrote to Rockefeller as follows in 1933 in regard to the IRC's work on social insurance:

> As to the value of the work of this organization I cannot speak too highly. In reviewing the current year's work, I would mention the completion of our series of reports on Unemployment Insurance, which are everywhere acclaimed as authoritative and timely, and the publication of the report on Industrial Pension Systems.
>
> (Fosdick 1933)

Fosdick also noted that the quality and visibility of the work of the IRC "has led to engagement of our staff by the Wisconsin Industrial Commission and the Minnesota Employment Stabilization Research Institute to

248   Social Insurance Created and Undermined

assist in shaping and administering legislation." But he does not neglect what IRC was doing to stabilize pension funds in several different companies, by switching over to contributory plans. Several of these companies were oil and pipeline companies owned by Rockefeller:

> There is much concern over the problem of funding of pensions plans just now, and in the last two years we have directly aided the New York Transit Co., National Transit Co., Buckeye, Northern, Indiana, Cumberland, Eureka, Southern and South West Pennsylvania Pipe Line Companies, Standard Oil Company of Ohio, Solar Refining Co., Ohio Oil Co. and other clients in revising and refunding their plans on a sound basis, in nearly all cases securing adoption of a plan providing for assumption of part cost by the employees, and other desirable and conservative provisions that have aggregated several millions of dollars in savings to those companies as well as affording greater security to the employees. This work has required intimate consideration of the financial status of the companies and on several occasions has permitted us to make suggestions of general management and economic value which I believe Mr. Debevoise [Rockefeller's lawyer for business matters and a close friend] or Mr. Cutler [a personal Rockefeller employee who was a director of Metropolitan Life] could attest.
>
> (Fosdick 1933)

Fosdick's mention of concern about pensions reflected a new reality that now faced corporations: by 1932 the ongoing depression was starting to take its toll on even the best of the company plans. More workers were reaching retirement age and retirees were living longer at a time when corporate profits had been flat or declining for three straight years. In addition, low interest rates meant that the investments by corporate pension funds were not generating the cash flow that was needed to pay current monthly obligations. As economic historian Steven Sass (1997, p. 88) concludes: "The Great Depression of the 1930s sent a massive shock wave through the nation's fragile private pension system." This was especially the case for the railroads, which had an older workforce than many other industries as well as unsound pension plans. Even the switch to contributory plans over the previous three years had not been enough to save the railroad pension plans. But it was not just corporate plans that were in trouble: the handful of small pension plans controlled by the AFL and other unions also began to suffer, as Latimer had predicted they would even before the depression began.

As the depression deepened and Roosevelt took office in March 1933, the Rockefeller Foundation created a Special Trustee Committee to administer emergency funds of up to $1 million in an expeditious manner (to keep things in perspective, that is $18.7 million in 2018 dollars). The committee consisted of Rockefeller, Fosdick, and Walter Stewart, an investment banker (no relation to Bryce Stewart), who served as a trustee of the Rockefeller Foundation. In addition, Woods and other advisers were sometimes present for the committee's deliberations. The largest of ten projects for that year was $100,000 for work by the SSRC's Committee on Governmental Statistics and Information Services, which followed up on concerns expressed by Willits, Stewart, and others about the dismal state of government statistics. This project, the largest undertaken by the SSRC to that date, led to the creation of a new Central Statistics Board for the federal government, the first small exercise in state-building on social insurance at the national level by the corporate rich, the power elite, and their policy-planning network (Fisher 1993, pp. 128–129). Then, too, the foundation gave $5,000 to the SSRC's Committee on Unemployment for a study of unemployment reserves by Bryce Stewart.

The IRC Joins the New Deal

Members of the IRC contributed their first direct official service to the New Deal in 1933 when Stewart became chair of a committee to advise Secretary of Labor Perkins on selecting the members for her Advisory Committee to the Department of Labor. He also served as a member of the Advisory Council of the United States Employment Service and chaired its Committee on Research (Stewart 1933). At the same time, Latimer provided the Department of Commerce with estimates on the amount of pension income that was being paid out in the country. He became a member of the Advisory Committee of the Department of Labor, where he spent part of his summer months assisting "in the revision of the employment and payroll indexes and in making studies which would lead ultimately to the revision of the price indexes" (Latimer 1933).

As this mundane statistical work was grinding along, a grassroots effort by the railroad workers in craft unions, which had been building since 1929, began to pick up momentum. It did so in good part because the railroads owners announced they would be making 10 percent cuts in both salaries and pensions. In a context in which at least 84 percent of railroad workers had been covered by pension plans since the early 1920s, and with young workers backing the retirement plans for older workers so they could move into the senior jobs, the rank and file organized on their own because of the lack of interest in government pensions on the part of their union leaders (Klein 2003; Latimer and Hawkins 1938; Sass 1997). In 1931 and 1932, the railroad workers' independent actions—organized as the Railways Employees National Pension Association, which was outside the confines of their union leadership—generated major support among workers in the face of the impending pension crisis in the railroad industry.

250 Social Insurance Created and Undermined

At the least, it was enough to convince Senator Henry D. Hatfield, a one-term Republican Senator from West Virginia, to introduce legislation in 1932 that ended up having a big impact on corporate thinking about government pensions.

Hatfield, a physician who was a staunch supporter of unions and a former governor of his home state, had a special sympathy for railroad workers. He had worked for 18 years as a surgeon for the Norfolk and Western Railroad. Significantly, the legislation he introduced, written for the most part by the Railways Employees National Pension Association, called for contributions by workers and employers as well as an option for early retirement and generous benefits. This legislation grabbed the attention of the railroad union leaders. "As pension agitation mounted, labor leaders began to recognize that their indifference to the pension issue was alienating them from the rank and file, and in the same year they succeeded in inducing Senator Wagner to introduce an alternative proposal" (Quadagno 1988, p. 73). The liberal Hatfield version and the more cautious Wagner version were eventually reconciled, so Congress passed the Wagner-Hatfield bill in 1933, despite strong opposition from railroad executives, (see also Graebner 1980, pp. 171–176; Huthmacher 1968, p. 177).

Although the federal coordinator of transportation advised Roosevelt to sign the legislation because "it is in line with sound social policy," he added that he would have preferred to wait in order to improve it (Latham 1959, p. 160). One of the problems he worried about was the actuarial soundness of the plan. This concern caused him to bring Stewart, Latimer, and Brown to Washington in late 1933 as members of an Employment Advisory Council that would design the new social-insurance system for railroad workers. At this point the empirical and theoretical problems seem to mount even higher for social scientists and historians who deny the importance of the corporate moderates and their policy-planning network in the creation of the Social Security Act:

> The group of us that went down [to Washington] on that centered very much on Industrial Relations Counselors, in New York... So Latimer and I began working on the old-age protection of railroad workers. We put Hawkins [a student of Brown] to work on the dismissal compensation. Bryce Stewart worked on the unemployment insurance.
>
> (Brown 1965, p. 6)

Latimer, Stewart, and Brown lacked the information needed for the actuarial studies on which to base a sound program, and they did not have an army of clerks at their disposal to develop the information. They therefore applied for a $300,000 grant ($5.5 million in 2018) from the recently established Civilian Works Administration, and then hired laidoff railroad clerks that had dealt with the relevant employment records for their respective companies. As a result, 1,500 people ended up collecting records on 400,000 employees and 110,000 pensioners. The threesome also hired a staff of 500 in New York to analyze the data (Brown 1965, pp. 8–9; Latimer and Hawkins 1938, p. 111). The result was a new set of records within the space of a few months, which proves how rapidly government capacity can be created when there is the desire to create it. This may seem to be a small point, but some political scientists say that it is a big problem when a state lacks "capacity," and that the American state lacked capacity at the outset of the New Deal (e.g., Finegold and Skocpol 1995; Skocpol and Amenta 1985; Skocpol and Finegold 1982; Skocpol and Ikenberry 1983). But if capacity can be created very rapidly, as was also the case in the industrial conversion to fight World War II, based on the extant resources and expertise in the corporate community and the policy-planning network, then the possibility arises that the corporate community—and the plantation owners in the South, who will come into the Social Security picture very shortly—wanted to limit the capacity of the American government as much as they could.

Latimer, Stewart, and Brown then crafted a plan that was satisfactory to all concerned, even though the benefit levels were lower than those originally proposed. Everyone supported it because the study discovered that the original actuarial assumptions were unsound (Latimer and Hawkins 1938, pp. 123–127). Employers were pleased because they were relieved of the cost of private pensions and their tax rates were lower. Railroad workers accepted the plan because the pensions were satisfactory—in fact, much higher than those later established for the Social Security Act—and there were disability and survivor benefits as well (Latimer and Hawkins 1938, p. 274). In the end the Railroad Retirement Act was a victory for all those who were willing to allow the government to play a role in providing social insurance. Because of this work, Latimer was appointed chair of the three-person Railroad Retirement Board in the summer of 1934.

Strikingly, the railroad workers' success did not lead to similar efforts by other workers, which Quadagno (1988, p. 74) attributes to the division of American workers along craft lines. This lack of involvement by other unions supports my contention, fully demonstrated later in this chapter, that pressures from organized labor in general had very little to do with the development of the Social Security Act over the next two years.

However, the lessons from this successful effort were not lost on Latimer, Stewart, and Brown. They slowly began to realize the possibilities for using the group insurance policies developed by the private insurance companies, with whom they were always in close contact, as a model for government insurance plans. It dawned on them that they could package old-age pensions and unemployment compensation in a way that would be compatible with the major concerns of corporate leaders. They also figured out

252 Social Insurance Created and Undermined

that such plans would be far less expensive for corporations than having their own programs, some of which were on increasingly shaky ground in any case. From this point forward they worked to convince corporate executives, fellow experts, liberal reformers, and social workers of the soundness of their ideas. Their efforts are a textbook example of how experts function in the United States, which contradicts any theoretical emphasis on independent experts as well as anything could, while at the same time showing there is originality and complexity built into their role, as always has been understood by class-dominance theorists.

The large amount of time being spent in government service by IRC employees led to another series of grants from the Rockefeller Foundation to the IRC beginning in January 1934. The first grant request, entitled "Grant from Rockefeller Foundation to Cover Expense of Cooperation with Government Agencies," captures much of the argument for the growing importance of the IRC in the policymaking process. The grant request, written by Young, also relates to the issue of state-building because these privately employed experts were creating new agencies. It begins by noting "increasing inroads have been made on our time by such agencies as the New York State Advisory Council on Employment Problems, the Labor Statistics Committee of the American Statistical Association and the Social Science Research Council" (Young 1933, p. 1).

The proposal then outlines the many governmental and SSRC tasks undertaken by Stewart and Latimer, including work on the railroad retirement program, and in addition reports that another employee had been serving full time as the assistant director of the United States Employment Service for the previous six months. Young then listed his own government involvements "as a member of the Federal Advisory Council of the United States Employment Service, as a member of the Executive Committee, and chair of the Committee on Veterans' Placement Service and, since June as a special representative of the United States Department of Labor, actively assisting the Director of the United States Employment Service in the organization and administration of the National Reemployment Service" (Young 1933, p. 2).

All of this service, the grant proposal continues, was voluntary, and it had been costing IRC money in both salary expenses and lost opportunities to do paid consulting work for businesses. The proposal concludes with a request for "an emergency appropriation of twenty-five thousand dollars," which was granted by the foundation shortly thereafter (Young 1933, p. 3). Similar supplemental grants were approved for $10,000 in June 1935 and $6,000 in February 1936. Even when Latimer began to be paid by the government, he stayed on the IRC payroll and turned over his government salary to the organization (Latimer 1934).

This series of grants has large theoretical implications. In effect, the Rockefeller Foundation became part of the government by paying the

The Origins of the Social Security Act 253

salaries of men who were de facto state employees. The foundation thereby provided the capacity to build new processes and agencies into the government through the expertise of a private consulting firm, Industrial Relations Counselors, Inc. Thus, government officials did not build the government's new capacity, and those who administered it were not independent of the corporate community and its closely affiliated policy-planning network. In fact, this is the best example of state-building by the corporate rich, the power elite, and their policy-planning network presented up to this point in the book.

By November 1933, the experts in the policy-planning network, who had been working on social insurance for nearly four years by this point, felt confident enough with what they had accomplished to bring it to the attention of experts just outside their circles. They did so through a small conference in Washington under the auspices of the SSRC. Meredith Givens, an economist trained by Commons at the University of Wisconsin, who had been a member of the research staff at the National Bureau of Economic Research since 1928, made the arrangements. Givens also became the executive secretary to the SSRC's Committee on Industry and Trade in 1929 and was the main force behind the successful effort to create the aforementioned Central Statistics Board within the government. In addition, he served as a staff member for the SSRC's Committee on Unemployment Insurance, often working with Stewart. His example, like those of Alvin Hansen and Merrill Murray in the case of the IRC/University of Minnesota collaboration, suggests that the line between the John R. Commons and IRC camps was not a hard and fast one.

Twenty-two people attended this conference, representing a wide range of social service organizations as well as government agencies related to social insurance and social provisioning. Fourteen of the 22 had served on an SSRC committee or were connected to the policy-planning network in some other way. Several were affiliated with the urban policy-planning network briefly overviewed in Chapter 1 (Roberts 1994). The most prominent representative of the social service organizations was Edith Abbott, one of the most famous women reformers of the Progressive Era, and since 1921 the dean of the School of Social Service Administration at the University of Chicago. The social-welfare representatives also included the director of the Public Administration Clearing House and leaders from the Institute of Public Administration and the American Association of Social Workers.

Perhaps the most important government official present was Harry Hopkins, the head of the Federal Emergency Relief Administration (Cohen 2009, Chapters 8 and 9). Arthur Altmeyer, Perkins's main assistant on social-insurance issues, was second only to Hopkins. Altmeyer, who was yet another former Commons student, had been the executive secretary of the Wisconsin Industrial Commission for many years before joining

254 Social Insurance Created and Undermined

the New Deal. Also present were John Dickinson, the Assistant Secretary of Commerce, who helped draft the National Industrial Recovery Act just a few months before; Morris Leeds, the aforementioned president of Leeds and Northrup; Isador Lubin, a former Brookings Institution employee who had been appointed by Perkins as the commissioner of labor statistics; and Mary Anderson, the director of the Women's Bureau in the Department of Labor, which had jurisdiction over the "mother's pensions" that would become known as "welfare payments" when they were enfolded into the new Social Security Act. (Anderson, who grew up in the working class, became involved in social reform through the outreach efforts during the Progressive Era of Jane Addams and Hull House (Anderson and Winslow 1951, p. 32).) There were also several experts present that worked closely with government agencies, starting with Brown, the director of the Industrial Relations Section at Princeton, who had worked on the railroad retirement plan. Frank Bane, head of the American Public Welfare Association, who had played a key role in a November, 1932 conference in Chicago that established the principles for the new federal relief program, attended as an adviser to Hopkins (Brown 1940; Domhoff 1996, pp. 147–148, Table 5.3, for the full list of attendees and their affiliations).

The starting point for the discussions at the SSRC conference was a document prepared by Stewart, which listed the nature of the studies needed to understand several problems that had to be resolved to design a comprehensive social-insurance program. It set the stage by noting that his earlier work, focused strictly on issues of unemployment and relief, had soon led him to the realization that these issues were linked to many other questions. For example, they related to the ability to return to the work force due to old age or physical or mental disabilities, as well as to the relation of government unemployment insurance to recently established government employment centers meant to aid job seekers, and to programs for vocational training. He added that it also would be necessary to explore the need for minimum wages to guard against any tendency by employers to reduce wage rates to help pay their unemployment insurance taxes.

In the case of old-age pensions, the draft plan embodied three principles that the corporate moderates insisted upon, based on several years of experience with private pension plans, especially in conjunction with the efforts of the major life insurance companies. First, the level of benefits must be tied to salary level, thus preserving and reinforcing the values established in the labor market. Second, unlike the case in many countries, there would be no government contributions from general tax revenues, if at all possible. Instead, there would be a separate tax for old-age pensions, which would help to limit the size of benefits. Third, there had to be both employer and employee contributions to the system, which would limit the tax payments by the corporations.

The Origins of the Social Security Act   255

Although the attendees were unanimous in encouraging the SSRC to move forward in refining its proposal, the liberals and reformers of that era, many of them social workers, did not give their approval without expressing their disagreements with what they called "the insurance crowd," which meant experts such as Latimer and Stewart. This difference flared up most prominently over the issue of funding old-age pensions when Abbott stated her preference for "one welfare statute," which would be paid for out of general tax revenues and "available to all without stigmatizing qualifications" (see Gordon 1994b, p. 261 for Abbott's general views; see Witte 1963, pp. 15–16, for the fact of disagreement). Moreover, liberals and social workers did not like the idea of employee contributions to unemployment compensation because they agreed with labor leaders that unemployment was a failure of the economic system that should be paid for by its primary beneficiaries, the owners, perhaps with the help of general tax contributions. These differences of opinion suggest that Stewart and other insurance-oriented experts in the policy-planning network were not liberals in the eyes of the liberals of that era.

The same group of people then met for a second SSRC conference in early April 1934, to consider a second version of Stewart's proposal, this one co-authored with Givens. However, they did so under very different circumstances because Senator Wagner had introduced a new state-oriented unemployment insurance bill on February 5. He did so on behalf of the AALL reformers, who were being provided with ideas, advice and encouragement from behind the scenes by Supreme Court Justice Louis Brandeis. Brandeis conveyed his policy ideas through a number of different people, the most important of whom was his daughter, Elizabeth Brandeis, who had been a professor of economics at the University of Wisconsin since the late 1920s after studying with Commons. He also conferred with his daughter's husband, Paul Raushenbush, also an economist at Wisconsin. Raushenbush was in charge of administering the state's unemployment insurance law passed in 1932, which included the AALL's incentive policy. Both Elizabeth Brandeis and Paul Raushenbush were leaders in the AALL and championed its basic principles.

Louis Brandeis also had an extensive network of legal and political contacts, especially among lawyers who had clerked for him or former Justice Oliver Wendell Holmes (e.g., Carter 1934, pp. 315–316). His most important confidant was Felix Frankfurter, a professor at Harvard Law School and an informal adviser to Roosevelt since working with him during World War I. Frankfurter was renowned for sending his students to both corporate law firms and the New Deal (Irons 1982). One of those students, Thomas Corcoran, worked very closely with Roosevelt and served as a direct communication link between Brandeis and Roosevelt. In short, the AALL was not simply a group of academic experts by the time of the New Deal, but a part of the prestigious Brandeis/Frankfurter network, which

256 Social Insurance Created and Undermined

was rooted in the stature and resources of the Supreme Court, Harvard Law School, the University of Wisconsin, and the state government in Wisconsin. It also had financial help from a small handful of well-to-do donors and corporate moderates.

In addition to the incentive provisions, the legislation introduced by Wagner included a new feature suggested by Brandeis that would apply strong pressure on states to create unemployment insurance plans. Called the "tax offset plan," it imposed a federal tax on employers to pay for federal unemployment insurance, but it would not be collected if they paid an equivalent tax to their state government. This was of course an incentive for state-oriented employers and elected officials to urge passage of an unemployment insurance plan in their home states (Nelson 1969, p. 199).

Reformers to the left of the AALL, such as those involved in the American Association for Old Age Security, which had just changed its name to the American Association for Social Security, vowed to defeat the AALL/ Wagner bill because it was so cautious. They also feared it would undercut their efforts toward more liberal programs in several states, which they thought had a good chance of legislative success. At the same time, most business groups were equally opposed to the AALL/Wagner bill for their own reasons. Nonetheless, Perkins urged Roosevelt to push for this legislation and held a conference on February 14–15 to drum up support for it. However, Roosevelt soon made it clear in the midst of all the strong disagreement that he wanted a contributory unemployment compensation plan as part of a larger social-insurance plan that included old-age pensions, but the origins of his preferences are not certain (Nelson 1969).

Within this context, Roosevelt invited Gerard Swope, the president of General Electric, to the White House on March 8. (Swope, who was introduced in Chapter 2 as a key figure in the process leading to the NLRA, was in Washington for a meeting of the Business Advisory Council). Roosevelt and Swope then had a long discussion on social insurance that may have had considerable impact on Roosevelt. During their discussion Swope argued that it was feasible to have government social insurance for everyone. It would begin at birth with a government life insurance policy, and would require small payments from the parents until their children were grown. At age 20 both the individual and the employer would contribute (Loth 1958, p. 234). Swope also outlined plans for unemployment and old-age insurance, which had proven to be workable through the experience of private corporate plans, and he stressed the need for employee contributions. Although Swope thought that one-third of the cost from employees and two-thirds from employers would be sufficient, Roosevelt thought that the split should be fifty-fifty.

According to Swope in extensive interviews with his biographer, Roosevelt expressed enthusiasm for these ideas and asked for a detailed memo outlining a plan, which Swope sent him two weeks later (Loth 1958,

The Origins of the Social Security Act   257

p. 235). His plans later were seen as too ambitious by Roosevelt's other advisers, but at the least the visit from Swope may have led Roosevelt to anticipate support for a comprehensive social-insurance program from the corporate moderates on the Business Advisory Council (BAC). If so, this fits with political scientist Peter Swenson's (2002, Chapters 9–10) expectations theory of why the Roosevelt Administration moved ahead with social-insurance legislation despite the possible opposition of ultraconservatives in the corporate community. According to this view, political leaders often put forth plans that they have reason to believe will be accepted by groups that are initially hesitant or skeptical.

In the context of the legislative disagreements swirling around in Congress on social insurance, the second meeting of the informal SSRC-sponsored group took place in early April. It gave its general approval to the evolving plan that had emerged from the IRC/Rockefeller Foundation/SSRC efforts over the past several years. Stewart and Givens then revised their report to take into account concerns expressed at the meeting. They also emphasized their support for the kind of unified plan that Roosevelt was now talking about. As they explained in a report to the SSRC, which has some elements of the proverbial smoking gun: "In a draft report, revised following the April conference, the unified character of the task of planned protection was developed, and the several phases of relief and social insurance were considered in terms of (a) the problems of planning, administration, and coordination, (b) the present state of knowledge in each field, and (c) further work specifically required for the proper integration of each major segment into a unified program" (Stewart and Givens 1934b, p. 1).

Stewart and Givens sent Perkins and Hopkins copies of their conference report in an effort to reinforce the idea that general, not piecemeal, legislation was necessary. From their point of view, their efforts were successful in influencing the creation of the Cabinet-level Committee on Economic Security, as explained in the same SSRC report of November 16 that was just quoted. I find the following paragraph to be strong evidence that the experts within the policy-planning network were working closely with Perkins and Hopkins to shape the government's agenda:

> At the request of officials of the Department of Labor [I read that as Altmeyer and Perkins] and the Federal Emergency Relief Administration [I read that as Bane and Hopkins], these materials were made informally available in the formulation of plans for a government inquiry. A draft plan for such an inquiry, developed upon the basis of the exploratory study, was placed in the hands of a Cabinet committee, and *these plans have eventuated in the establishment* by Executive Order, June 29, 1934, of the Committee on Economic Security. Thus *the original project became merged in a major planning venture at the Administration.*
> (Stewart and Givens 1934b, p. 1, my italics)

258 Social Insurance Created and Undermined

Perhaps it could be argued that Stewart was overstating his and IRC's role when he reports to his sponsor, the SSRC, that plans on which he worked "have eventuated in the establishment" of the Committee on Economic Security and that "the original project became merged in a major planning venture at the Administration." However, it is unlikely that he was making sure he received future grants, and he never tried to take any credit in public for any aspect of the Social Security Act. It therefore seems plausible to take this report at face value.

Once the Roosevelt initiative was announced, Stewart and Givens anticipated (on the basis of the liberal social workers' dissents at the two SSRC conferences, and the strength of conservatives in Congress) that there might be aspects of the final legislation that would not be acceptable to corporate moderates. They therefore revised their earlier proposal for immediate research funds from the SSRC to make it a call for a large SSRC study that would begin *after* the shape of the final legislation became clear. They argued it was not likely that any new legislation would be thoroughly satisfactory, which meant that future SSRC studies would be important in influencing inevitable revisions in the program (Stewart and Givens 1934a, p. 1). Thus, members of the policy-planning network were already preparing for likely amendments—and for shaping the administration of the Social Security Act—well before the plan was finalized and sent to Congress in early 1935 (cf. Fisher 1993). In this regard, the experts deserve great credit for the far-sightedness they are paid to develop.

As this brief history demonstrates, experts from the policy-planning network, and especially those in and around the IRC and SSRC, were actively involved in developing plans for social insurance right up until the moment the governmental process began. Latimer and Stewart had been employees of the IRC since 1926, and it was still funded primarily by Rockefeller at the time, although consulting fees and foundation grants were providing more of its revenue. Arthur Young went back a few years before that. Brown and Willits worked in university industrial relations units funded primarily by Rockefeller monies, and the National Bureau of Economic Research and the SSRC received a majority of their funding from Rockefeller foundations.

However, it remains to be determined whether or not the same people and organizations were involved in the drafting process inside the government and if so, if they had any impact.

The Drafting Process

Roosevelt announced the plan for a comprehensive study of a program for economic security on June 8, 1934. A cabinet-level committee, the Committee on Economic Security (CES), chaired by Perkins and including Hopkins, who always was in attendance at its meetings, would conduct

The Origins of the Social Security Act 259

the study. The committee also included the secretary of agriculture, who sometimes sent his very liberal Assistant Secretary of Agriculture, Rexford Tugwell, to represent him. The others on the committee included the secretary of treasury, who often sent one of his economic advisers, and the attorney general, who always sent an assistant that was instructed to vote with Perkins. A "Technical Board," a group of 20 government-employed experts that was drawn from several different agencies, assisted the CES. (However, many of these experts had been employees of foundations, think tanks, and universities until shortly before the process leading to the Social Security Act began).

The CES also had the input of an Advisory Council on Economic Security, which was made up of 23 private citizens, including many prominent corporate moderates, labor leaders, and social-welfare advocates. The members of the advisory council were supposed to have a minimal role and serve in part as window dressing, but they nonetheless inserted themselves into the process with considerable vigor, to the growing dismay of Roosevelt and Perkins. The business representatives included four corporate moderates that have been mentioned earlier in this chapter as being heavily involved in social-insurance issues: Swope of General Electric, Teagle of Standard Oil of New Jersey, Leeds of Leeds & Northrup, and Folsom of Eastman Kodak (who was by then its treasurer). The advisory council also included a corporate moderate not yet mentioned, Sam A. Lewisohn, the scion of a mining and investment banking fortune, and the vice president of his family's Miami Copper Company.

In addition, there were five labor leaders, including the head of the AFL, but they attended few meetings and generally did not have any impact. However, they had an influence on the financing of unemployment insurance, as shown shortly. There were also several public members, who came from advocacy organizations and voluntary associations that stretched back to the Progressive Era. The public members also included representatives from the social service organizations housed at the Public Administration Clearing House (Chambers 1952, pp. 255–256; Roberts 1994; Witte 1963, pp. 49–53). In today's terms, the representatives from the social services organizations could be thought of as the sensible and acceptable liberals on the advisory council.

In addition, the National Grange (a farm organization), and the Fraternal Order of Eagles, which had advocated for old-age pensions since the 1920s with an AALL model bill, were represented. These two representatives wanted some form of social insurance, but were cautious and centrist.

Significantly, the most visible reformers on the general issue of social insurance, who had worked at the grassroots for well over a decade and written several influential books, were not included in the formal process. They most prominently included Abraham Epstein, the leader of the American Association for Social Security, and Isaac Rubinow, who had

260 Social Insurance Created and Undermined

both a Ph.D. in economics and an M.D. degree, and made his living as an actuary. Like the acceptable liberals and the social workers, they advocated protection for everyone without qualification and wanted to finance the program out of general taxes. But they were far less willing to compromise than were the social workers, who were part of the New Deal coalition through their many connections to Eleanor Roosevelt, Perkins, Anderson of the Women's Bureau, and several other government appointees.

Rubinow, Epstein, and their colleagues and followers had made it clear that they would disagree with several of the basic premises of the corporate moderate/IRC approach, which would therefore slow down the drafting process. In addition, it was feared that their involvement would serve as a red flag and rallying point for ultraconservative opponents in the corporate community and Congress. Their agitation, writing, and lobbying may have helped to create a more favorable climate for doing something about old-age pensions, and it was their phrase—"social security"—that came to designate what variously had been called "economic security," "social insurance," or "industrial pensions" up until that time (Klein 2003, pp. 78–80). Although they were briefly consulted when the process was well under way, they had no direct involvement in formulating the act, which led to many personal tensions among the supporters of Social Security.

On the basis of a strong recommendation from Altmeyer, Perkins offered the important position of staff director to Edwin Witte. Witte had studied with Commons at the University of Wisconsin and then was appointed as the executive secretary of the Wisconsin Industrial Commission in 1917. In 1922 he became the chief of the Legislative Reference Library, a service for the state's legislators who needed help in writing their bills. He became a professor of economics at the University of Wisconsin in 1933, shortly before he was hired to direct the social security drafting process. He did collaborative work with Commons and wrote reports on labor law for him, but he respectfully disagreed with Commons and the AALL that incentives to encourage employers to reduce unemployment would have any impact (Nelson 1969). Once again, not all AALL members were of exactly the same mind.

Unknown to anyone at the time, Witte maintained a diary of the unfolding events to help him keep things straight in a complex situation. The diary became the basis for a memorandum he wrote in 1936 at the request of the SSRC's Committee on Public Administration, which used it as part of its efforts to help shape the administration of the Social Security Act (Witte 1963, p. xi). Later the SSRC asked Witte if it could have his permission to publish his memorandum as a book, which appeared in 1963 and became the basis for just about every analysis of the origins of the Social Security Act since that time. It remains a valuable book, and it contains many statements supporting the idea that IRC experts had a key role, but it is too brief and incomplete to tell the whole story in detail.

The Origins of the Social Security Act   261

This background material on Witte and his book provides a good context for assessing the importance of the policy-planning network in general, and the IRC in particular, for the act itself. The first interesting fact is that Altmeyer, Givens, and Stewart developed the structure and process for the research program, and much of its agenda, based on the report written after the second SSRC conference (Schlabach 1969, p. 99). This conclusion, based on interviews and a statement in the CES files written for Roosevelt by Altmeyer, Givens, and Stewart, is consistent with Stewart and Givens' (1934b) statement in their SSRC report that their proposals were made informally available to government officials. In addition, and a clincher to my way of thinking, Witte (1963, pp. 15–16) notes that he made "some little use" of the research suggestions in this report "in outlining the fields to be covered by various members of the staff." Moreover, Stewart was put in charge of unemployment studies and Givens oversaw the study of employment opportunities (Witte 1963, pp. 13–14, 31). All in all, this is impressive evidence that the policy-planning network, and the IRC employees, were an integral part of the governmental process.

To our unexpected good fortune, it is at this point that IRC experts began to send industrial relations executives inside information on the drafting process, as already mentioned in Chapter 2. They did so through the periodic IRC memorandums for members of the Special Conference Committee and the IRC's smaller clients. In other words, and to repeat a point made in Chapter 2, the IRC memorandums were prepared for a rich and powerful group of people: Rockefeller, his personal employees, the top executives at the oil, mining, and railroad companies in which he had a strong ownership position, and the presidents and industrial relations vice presidents at several of the largest industrial corporations in the country.

The first of the memos, for July 10, 1934, provided a thorough overview of how the drafting process would be carried out by the CES, concluding that: "It is patent that the Administration is determined to develop a program of social welfare to be presented at the next session of Congress, and that broad departures in the field of industrial relations may be anticipated" (Industrial Relations Counselors 1934a, p. 2). Two paragraphs later it reminded its readers "to prepare for the advent of various forms of social insurance." There is no question, then, that we are being treated to insider information. Three pages later in that first memorandum, the IRC staff began an analysis of the various alternatives for unemployment insurance by noting the role of two key outposts of the corporate community: "The United States Chamber of Commerce has suggested to the code authorities [i.e., the National Recovery Administration] that they should consider the development of industrial plans of unemployment insurance, and the Industrial Relations Committee of the Business Advisory Council [i.e., the Special Conference Committee, in its formal governmental role] has also been giving the subject much attention" (Industrial Relations

262 Social Insurance Created and Undermined

Counselors 1934a, page 5). In other words, the IRC was in touch with the industrial relations vice presidents on this issue. The analysis in the memorandum outlines the advantages of a plan such as Stewart would be proposing to the CES. It is noteworthy that the Annual Report for the Special Conference Committee for 1934 also stated that "there probably will be need for funds built up and administered under the direction of public authorities" (Gordon 1994a, p. 256).

To do the necessary detailed work on the many possible provisions within the proposal that might eventuate, the cabinet-level Committee on Economic Security, with considerable help from Witte, hired a large research staff made up of experts brought in from the IRC, SSRC, other think tanks, and universities. It was the staff's job to draft the proposals to be discussed by the appropriate committees of the Technical Board and the Advisory Council on Economic Security before they were passed up the hierarchy to the CES (and Roosevelt from behind the scenes through his interactions with Perkins and Hopkins). Finally, there was an executive director, Witte, to lead the staff and serve as secretary to the CES.

Although most of the proposals eventually went forward, there were two that did not. The first, which stated that it might be feasible to include agricultural workers in the old-age and unemployment programs, received virtually no attention (Alston and Ferrie 1999). As in the case of including agricultural workers within the purview of the National Labor Relations Act, as discussed in Chapter 2, it was considered a non-starter for old-age pensions as well because of the adamant objections that would be made by Southern Democrats.

Similarly, the fraught issue of health insurance, which had been so strongly opposed by the American Medical Association and some insurance companies when it was proposed by the AALL during the Progressive Era, once again went nowhere due to the AMA's strong objections (Starr 2017, pp. 267–269). However, at first there seemed to be some faint hope for at least studying health insurance, so Witte had enlisted the services of the prestigious and highly visible Milbank Memorial Fund, a nonprofit organization lavishly funded by the extremely wealthy Milbank family (Borden's Milk, Wall Street investments). One of the family's members was a name partner in the Wall Street firm, Milbank, Tweed, Hope & Webb, which had strong business connections with John D. Rockefeller. The fund's goal since its establishment in 1905, under a slightly different name, had been to improve health for individuals and groups by applying the findings from established scientific research, and to that end it published a well-known journal, the *Milbank Quarterly* (Fox 2006, for a history).

Two of the Milbank Memorial Fund's high-level physician employees were "loaned to the committee" by the third-generation member of the Milbank family who was its president, with the intention that they would draft the necessary legislation (Witte 1963, p. 31). But the physicians and ultraconservatives who strongly opposed any form of federal health insurance immediately made their displeasure with this arrangement known by calling for a boycott of Borden's milk products. The Milbank family was on the defensive, but in any case there were so many other dangers to including such a volatile proposal that it did not survive the drafting process, and was never presented to Congress (Fox 2006, pp. 14–17 for how the Milbanks backed away from their foundation's involvement and fired their longtime chief executive for causing them embarrassment; Witte 1963, pp. 30–31, 173–189). The bigger problem was that the AMA remained far too formidable a foe for the Roosevelt Administration to tackle.

Nor was the process easy in the case of old-age pensions and unemployment insurance, but they did survive. To anticipate what might be expected by this point, the corporate moderates and IRC experts had extensive day-to-day involvement in the development of both of these plans.

Old-Age Insurance (Pensions)

Describing his search for a staff to study old-age pensions and draft a proposal, Witte (1963, p. 29) reported that "[i]t was agreed by everyone consulted that the best person in the field was Murray Latimer, who was unavailable because he was chair of the Railroad Retirement Board." That is a strong endorsement of an IRC employee, and it shows once again that he and the organization were well known at the time. In any case, Latimer was able to take a role in the process by serving as chair of the Technical Board's Committee on Old Age Security, an important policy role in itself. He also was given the opportunity to recommend a leader for the pension research staff, and then worked closely with the staff in drafting the legislation. His suggestion for staff leader was his friend and co-worker J. Douglas Brown, one of his collaborators on the railroad retirement study, whom he also knew through the IRC and annual conferences at Princeton on social insurance (Witte 1963, p. 3). When Brown decided that he could only give part of each week to the work at hand, Professor Barbara Nachtrieb Armstrong, a professor in the law school at the University of California, Berkeley, was placed in charge of the old-age study (Armstrong 1965, p. 36). Latimer and Brown worked very closely with her, along with Otto Richter, an actuary on loan from AT&T.

Armstrong is an intriguing and interesting figure who by all accounts was an inspirational professor and an outstanding researcher (Armstrong 1965; Graebner 1980; Traynor, Kragen, Kay, Riesenfeld, Kagel, Dinkelspiel, and Gehrels 1977). She also figures importantly in current theoretical disagreements because she is one of the few examples of an independent expert who was important in the drafting of the Social Security Act. She had "multiple affiliations" and a "complex career history" as well (Hacker 2002, p. 102). She is worthy of further discussion to determine if her involvement contradicts an emphasis on the policy-planning network.

Armstrong earned her law degree in 1915 at the University of California, Berkeley, and went to work for California's Commission on Social Insurance. She wrote a report on sickness as a cause of poverty in California, which earned her a Ph.D. at Berkeley in 1921. Armed with both an L.L.B. and a Ph.D., she then taught both law and economics at UC Berkeley for the next several years before becoming the first woman to be appointed a professor of law at a major university in the United States. During the 1920s she immersed herself in the study of European social-insurance systems and produced one of the most respected books in the field at the time, *Insuring the Essentials* (1932), with the help of an SSRC grant. In addition to all else, she is indeed an example of an independent expert.

Armstrong (1965, p. 38) reports in an oral history that she knew no one in Washington when she was asked to join the research staff, and never learned who suggested her inclusion. She says she had received positive letters about her book from Roosevelt intimates Swope and Frankfurter, and speculates that Swope may have been responsible for her selection (Armstrong 1965, p. 30). However, since she also knew many of the experts in the field and was highly respected for her book, it may be that one of the other experts recommended her. Originally hired to work on the unemployment compensation program, she was switched to old-age insurance when she arrived because Latimer and Brown did not have the time to take on the task. The last-minute nature of the reassignment to old-age pensions may be telling in itself. She was an afterthought on that key issue.

However, like Latimer and Brown, she favored a nationwide contributory system administered by the federal government, which may be a key factor in why they were glad to have her as their leader. Further, Armstrong soon clashed with Witte because she had little use for his ideas about social insurance, derived in good part from the AALL/Wisconsin tradition, calling them "absurd" (Altmeyer 1968, pp. 5–6; Armstrong 1965. p. 42). Nor did she have much respect for Perkins, who never bothered to meet with her, which Armstrong attributed to Perkins's preference for the AALL/Wisconsin approach (Armstrong 1965, p. 31). In turn, Perkins was highly critical of Armstrong; she characterized Armstrong as an "arrogant academic" (Downey 2009, p. 234). Her former colleagues and law school students, on the other hand, characterized her as bursting with energy, enthusiasm, frankness, and insight, and as not afraid to challenge the accepted wisdom of her era (Traynor, Kragen, Kay, Riesenfeld, Kagel, Dinkelspiel, and Gehrel 1977).

In contrast to her views of Witte and Perkins, Armstrong had the highest regard and affection for Brown and Stewart, whom she describes as kind and gentle people. She told the interviewer for the oral history project that she felt sorry for Stewart because he was not as tough as she was. "He suffered awfully at their hands," she continued, meaning Perkins, Altmeyer, and Witte (Armstrong 1965, p. 36). After playing a central role in the drafting process, she returned to California, never returning to Washington to testify before Congress, in part because of time pressures, in part because she feared she might be too acerbic as a witness before congressional committees (Graebner 1980, p. 187).

Armstrong went on to gain renown in family law and as an administrator of rent control in San Francisco during World War II, all the while teaching at the UC Berkeley law school, raising her daughter, and enjoying life with her businessman husband, an importer. As impressive and admirable as she was, this brief overview of her policy preferences and personal priorities suggests that it is not correct to claim that the one person involved in the policy-formation process who was not part of the IRC/Rockefeller or the AALL/Wisconsin network casts doubt on the role of the policy-planning network. This is especially the case when it is added that her role was fully noted in my earlier account of the origins of old-age pensions in the Social Security Act, which is where the critics originally learned about her involvement (Domhoff 1996, pp. 151–153; Hacker and Pierson 2002).

The plan prepared by Armstrong and her colleagues, which contained all the provisions the IRC had come to advocate, sailed through the Technical Board's Committee on Old Age Pensions. However, its two main features, its national scope and the inclusion of employee contributions, were worrisome to Perkins and the other members of the CES for a combination of political and legal reasons. Nevertheless, the original plan prevailed on both issues when the CES finally voted. Thus, the process produced a clear policy victory for the approach first developed by the insurance companies and the experts at IRC. But their plan did contain one funding issue that emerged later and caused last-minute problems. To keep taxes on both employers and employees as low as possible, they said there would be a need for a government contribution from general tax revenues beginning in 1965 (30 years in the future!) and lasting for another 15 years, unless payroll taxes were increased (Witte 1963, pp. 147–149). When Roosevelt grasped the details of this funding plan several months later, just before the proposal was about to be sent to Congress, he insisted that payroll taxes should be set at a higher rate to maintain his rhetorical fiction that the funding came from "contributions," not taxes. The result would be a very large reserve fund, which neither the corporate moderates nor the liberals wanted. This result led to amendments after the plan passed, which are discussed in the next chapter, but for now this series of events is a reminder of the very complex relationship between policy proposals and political considerations (e.g., Jacobs and Shapiro 2000, for a detailed analysis and good examples).

266 Social Insurance Created and Undermined

Of more immediate concern, the plan may have faced a different kind of challenge. There may have been some inclination on the part of Roosevelt, Perkins, and Witte to exclude old-age insurance from the final package sent to Congress because they feared that opposition to it might interfere with the passage of the program that mattered the most to them, unemployment insurance. Perkins and Witte always denied there was any such move afoot, but Armstrong, Brown, and Latimer were convinced otherwise. They quickly spoke off the record to reporters to that effect after they were jolted to attention by an ambiguous comment by Roosevelt in a speech to a national conference on economic security in Washington in November 1934. "I do not know," Roosevelt intoned, "whether this is the time for any federal legislation on old age security" (Davies 1999, p. 60). The immediate uproar in the newspapers led to assurances by all concerned that old-age pensions would be included in the legislative proposal (Armstrong 1965, pp. 88–89; Brown 1965, p. 13; Schlabach 1969, p. iii, based on his interview with Latimer).

Shortly after the public phase of this dust-up ended, the corporate moderates came into the picture in a supporting role through their membership on the Advisory Council on Economic Security. According to Armstrong (1965, pp. 82–83) and Brown (1972, p. 21), the corporate moderates were crucial in convincing Roosevelt and Perkins to retain the old-age provisions in the legislation. As Brown recalled it:

> The likelihood of gaining the support of the Cabinet Committee for our proposals was still in doubt. At this critical time, December 1934, help came from an unexpected source, the industrial executives on the committee's Advisory Council. Fortunately included in the Council were Walter C. Teagle of the Standard Oil Company of New Jersey, Gerard Swope of General Electric, and Marion Folsom of Eastman Kodak, and others well acquainted with industrial pension plans. Their practical understanding of the need for contributory old-age annuities on a broad, national basis carried great weight with those in authority. They enthusiastically approved our program. Just as the newspaper writers had carried us through the November crisis, the support of progressive industrial executives in December ensured that a national system of contributory old-age insurance would be recommended to the President and Congress.
>
> (Brown 1972, p. 21)

Brown also summarized what he called the "American philosophy of social insurance" in his retrospective book. Echoing Cowdrick in his 1928 pamphlet for the American Management Association, Brown's (1972, pp. 90–91) emphasis was on "the need for a perpetual corporation to assure a flow of effective and well-motivated personnel for the year-by-year operation of the company." More specifically, "retirement programs with

The Origins of the Social Security Act 267

adequate pensions became necessary to prevent an excessive aging of staff or the loss of morale which the discard of the old without compensation would involve;" thus, old-age insurance was simply "a charge on current production to be passed on to the consumer" (Brown 1972. pp. 90). This is exactly the conclusion most corporate moderates and a few ultraconservatives had reached by the late 1920s. It was an industrial relations plan, not a social-welfare plan, contrary to what some social scientists claim (e.g., Orloff 1993; Orloff and Parker 1990). However, as mentioned earlier, it did take the "massive shock wave" of the Great Depression (Sass 1997, p. 88), along with the grassroots efforts of the Railways Employees National Pension Association, and careful actuarial work by Latimer, Stewart, Brown, and other experts, to convince the corporate moderates that they would have to realize their purposes through a narrowly circumscribed government program.

This sequence of events demonstrates a clear, but not-yet-complete, victory for the corporate moderates and their employees at the IRC. Their success built on private insurance company plans going back 20 years by that point, and on the experience of a few big companies in the 1920s, as refined by the IRC staff.

Drafting Plans for Unemployment Insurance

Turning to unemployment compensation, the other major title of the Social Security Act of theoretical interest, the story begins as another apparent triumph for the corporate moderates and experts in the policy-planning network. Not only was Stewart put in charge of the staff study, he installed one of his co-authors from the Minnesota study, Merrill Murray, as his principal assistant, and then insisted on using employees of IRC to make the study. As Witte (1963, p. 29) explained, Stewart would only take the position if he could also stay with IRC in New York and use his own staff as well:

> It developed that he did not feel that he could leave his position and would consider only an arrangement under which his work for the committee could largely be done in New York, and under which he could use his own staff to assist him. Such an arrangement was objected to by some members of the technical board, but was finally made. Almost the entire research staff of the Industrial Relations Counselors, Inc., was placed on the payroll of the Committee on Economic Security, so that the arrangement in effect amounted to employing the Industrial Relations Counselors, Inc., to make this study.

Witte then explained a little further in a footnote:

> Dr. Stewart himself was never on the payroll of the Committee on Economic Security, pursuant to his express request. Instead, his staff

was put on the payroll, with the understanding that both he and the staff would work simultaneously for the committee and the Industrial Relations Counselors, Inc.

(Witte 1963, p. 29, ftn. 24)

This seems to be a strong set of demands for a government free of corporate dominance to accept, and suggests that the government lacked policy-planning capacity on insurance issues at that time. To retain the services of the expert it needed, the CES had to hire staff members from a private firm that everyone in Washington knew to be closely affiliated with Rockefeller and Standard Oil of New Jersey, and it had to allow them to stay in New York as well. On top of that, Stewart and his staff were also consulting at the same time for Teagle, who was chair of the Business Advisory Council's newly formed Committee on Unemployment Insurance in addition to being on the president's Advisory Council on Economic Security. It therefore seems very likely that Teagle, Stewart, and the IRC were the main links in a network that included key corporate moderates and government officials on the issue of unemployment compensation. The substance of the IRC memorandums cited in the remainder of this chapter also supports this inference.

It would thus appear the story of unemployment insurance should have a similar ending to the one on old-age insurance, but it doesn't. Stewart did recommend that unemployment compensation should be a national system, not a state-by-state one. He and his colleagues wanted to ensure there would be adequate and uniform standards of taxation and benefits, and that employees should contribute to the fund as well as employers. But these recommendations generated enormous conflict, causing the CES to change its recommendation several times.

In the end, Stewart and the corporate moderates lost because the CES finally decided on the federal-state system favored by the AALL and Southern Democrats (i.e., the plan favored by plantation owners, who did not want to pay into Social Security or have their field hands collect pensions of any kind, private or public). The CES also eliminated contributions to unemployment insurance by employees and the government. Nor were there any minimum standards that states had to meet, to the chagrin of both Stewart and members of the AALL. In terms of the theoretical issues addressed in this book, the interesting question is why the corporate moderates lost on unemployment insurance.

The answer to the question posed at the end of the previous paragraph can be found in the details of arguments within the overall CES, along with political considerations that had to be taken seriously. Stewart's report first went to the Technical Board's Committee on Unemployment Insurance. The committee was chaired by Murray, the economist who had worked with Stewart on the Minnesota project, and served as his

The Origins of the Social Security Act 269

principal assistant in writing the report for the CES. The Executive Secretary of the Business Advisory Council, Edward Jensen, also served on this committee, along with another one of Stewart's former co-authors, economist Alvin Hansen. In addition, the committee also included William Leiserson, the economist who was also a member of an SSRC Committee on Unemployment; Thomas Eliot, a lawyer from a longstanding upper-class family, who worked for Perkins at the Department of Labor; and economist Jacob Viner from the University of Chicago, who was an adviser to the Department of the Treasury. (Viner later played a major role in the creation of the International Monetary Fund through his work for a corporate policy-discussion group and the Department of the Treasury, as shown in Chapters 11 and 12.)

Perhaps it will come as no surprise that the committee was unanimous in its general support for Stewart's proposal, but differed on a few details (Witte 1963, pp. 112–113). The committee's recommendations then went to the executive committee of the Technical Board, where Altmeyer of Wisconsin presided. The executive committee made a very general statement of endorsement, but expressed concern about the idea of any "public contribution," meaning funds from general taxes, and about the constitutionality of a national-level system. Because of this hesitation, Perkins and other members of the CES asked for more definite recommendations before they reached any conclusions. A month of discussions then followed, which included experts who had not been consulted before on this specific issue, including Barbara Armstrong and J. Douglas Brown, who weighed in on Stewart's side.

As disagreement and acrimony increased, the germ of a compromise was finally proposed. It would allow the federal government to collect taxes from employers and employees, but then return the money to the individual states "subject to the state's compliance with standards to be prescribed by the federal government" (Witte 1963, pp. 115–116). (It became known as the "subsidy" plan, even though there were no subsidies involved, but it was sometimes called the "federal" plan as well.) Stewart, Armstrong, and Brown saw it as an acceptable fallback position because it gave some assurance of federal standards, that is, it helped insure that firms in low-wage states would not be able to undercut large national firms by paying less than their share into the fund for unemployment insurance.

Industrial Relations Counselors Memorandum to Clients, No. 4, for October 31, provided readers with an overview of most of these issues, but first it urged its clients to keep the memorandum confidential because of IRC's direct involvement and its concern with "possible embarrassment":

> We have refrained from comment until we could have the advantage of the discussion in meetings held during the past week. Because this organization has worked with various committees and interests, much

270 Social Insurance Created and Undermined

of our information is confidential. Therefore, to avoid any possible embarrassment, we request that the following discussion be limited to confidential circulation among the executives of our client companies. (Industrial Relations Counselors 1934b, p. 1)

In addition to discussing the conflicts over unemployment insurance, the memorandum notes that there were rumors that old-age insurance might be delayed because "the administration is trying to improve business psychology," that is, postpone any program that business thought to be an impediment to recovery. But the memorandum is certain that unemployment insurance would be enacted in the next Congress: "At this stage the outstanding feature of the development is that some kind of legislation on unemployment insurance seems fairly certain to be enacted in the next Congress" (Industrial Relations Counselors 1934b, p. 2).

The first-round success enjoyed by Stewart's plan did not last long because the unemployment insurance committee of the Technical Board reversed its earlier decision when it met again in early November. Now it unanimously supported the cooperative federal-state system favored by Roosevelt, Perkins, Witte, and the AALL. This plan differed from the federal approach in that states would collect the money and set their own tax levels and benefit payments. The Technical Board apparently was influenced by questions of constitutionality and political viability (Schlabach 1969, p. 118).

When the proposal went to the CES for a second look, the members met with Altmeyer, Hansen, Stewart, and Viner to hear a debate on the issues before making a decision. The CES members then concluded that a fully national system was out of the question, but the issue of the federal plan favored by Stewart versus the cooperative federal-state plan favored by many AALL members was left somewhat open. Nonetheless, Perkins immediately told Roosevelt the sentiment was primarily in favor of the federal-state system. Roosevelt liked that recommendation and supported it in a speech on November 14, the same speech mentioned earlier in which he gave at least some listeners the impression that the old-age insurance plan might not be included in the legislative package (Witte 1963, pp. 118–119). Put another way, it may be that Roosevelt was using this speech to try to shape the legislation before it was sent to Congress.

It would seem to be the end of the matter once the president had spoken. But Stewart and his colleagues would not accept the decision. The next day Stewart discussed the issue with a group of experts that he personally invited to an informal discussion. They voted 14 to 3 in favor of a national plan over a statefederal one (Witte 1963, p. 121). Stewart also contacted the business members on the Advisory Council on Economic Security. Three of the five (Teagle, Swope, and Leeds) were also members of the Business Advisory Council's unemployment insurance committee for which Stewart and the IRC were serving as consultants. Stewart and

The Origins of the Social Security Act 271

Armstrong also lobbied the chair of the Advisory Council on Economic Security, who was also the president of the University of North Carolina, at a dinner party arranged by a mutual friend (Burns 1966, p. 44).

There then followed a battle within the Advisory Council on Economic Security, much to the displeasure of Roosevelt, Perkins, and Witte. The full council heard directly from Stewart, Armstrong, and Murray. Then it created a committee on unemployment insurance to draft its own proposal, with the help of Stewart and Murray. But the committee's efforts failed because the same divisions appeared within the Advisory Council when it discussed the committee report (Witte 1963, pp. 56–57). Finally, on December 9, the Advisory Council on Economic Security voted nine to seven in favor of the nationally oriented federal plan over the AALL's federal-state plan. Three liberals and the president of the AFL joined with the five business executives in supporting the federal plan. Voting in opposition to a federal plan were the representative from the Fraternal Order of Eagles, the president of the Wisconsin Federation of Labor, and the five people from charity and social work backgrounds that were not supporters of the "insurance crowd" (i.e., IRC, Stewart, and Latimer). That is, one of the corporate moderates' major problems had surfaced once again: they were not able to gain the full support of the social workers and liberals they first tried to persuade at the SSRC conference in November, 1933.

However, the corporate moderates were not deeply concerned, as Folsom explained in a long letter to Frank W. Lovejoy, the president of Eastman Kodak, after discussing the outcome of the vote:

> The Committee was almost evenly divided as to the Wagner-Lewis type [i.e., the AALL type in my terms] and the subsidy [federal] type of bill. The employers all favored the subsidy type because under that plan it would be possible to set up inter-state industry funds, in which Mr. Teagle, Mr. Lewisohn, and Mr. Swope are very much interested. The subsidy plan received a majority vote but it seems that the Cabinet Committee and the Technical Board favor the Wagner-Lewis bill. We have it protected, I think, so that under either plan the plant reserve system can be set up with the decision left to the states,
>
> (Folsom 1934)

Folsom's mention of the importance of the "plant reserve system" as a fallback position if the "inter-state industry funds" were not included is an important reminder that market considerations were a major issue for the corporate moderates. They could gain a cost advantage if they maintained their workforce at a steady size and therefore have lower unemployment insurance payments than smaller companies that were more likely to take on or drop workers with small swings in demand. That is, the need to maintain a company reserve might give the big companies a competitive advantage in the pricing of their products (Swenson 2002, pp. 226–231 for a detailed discussion of this issue).

Meanwhile, the CES already had agreed to reconsider the issue even before it received the report from the Advisory Council on Economic Security. This was in part because it had received a new report sent to Roosevelt by the BAC's Committee on Unemployment Insurance, which recommended the federal plan. As might be suspected by now, the BAC report was written by Stewart (Schlabach 1969, p. 140). The CES then decided on a federal system after all, but then changed back again after floating the federal option with key members of Congress. As Perkins later explained:

> After long discussion we agreed to recommend a federal system. We went back and informed colleagues in our own Departments. Within the day, I had telephone calls from members of the Committee saying that perhaps we had better meet again. There was grave doubt, our latest interviews with members of Congress had shown, that Congress would pass a law for a purely federal system. State jealousies and suspicions were involved. So we met again, and after three or four hours of debate we switched back to a federal–state system.
>
> (Perkins 1946, pp. 291–292, my italics)

In the end, it seems most likely that the corporate moderates and the IRC lost to members of Congress on the federal-level versus state-level issue, not to Roosevelt, the AALL, or those who wanted to protect the unemployment program that had been launched in Wisconsin. That is, it appears that the decision was a political one, not a constitutional one. But what were the "state jealousies and suspicions" to which Perkins alluded? Some social scientists and historians argue that supporters of the AALL and Wisconsin's state program were the key opponents (e.g., Finegold and Skocpol 1995; Kessler-Harris 2001; Orloff 1993) But back in the blatantly racist and Southern-dominated 1930s, it seems more likely that the strongest opponents of Stewart's plan were the Southern Democrats, a conclusion based on the objections that soon surfaced in Congress. IRC expert Murray Latimer, whose credentials on this issue include the fact that he was raised in Mississippi, wrote as follows in a frank personal letter to a professor at the University of Virginia early in 1935:

> Almost without exception, congressmen and Senators from the South indicated extreme skepticism of the wisdom of any legislation of a social character which would concentrate further power in Washington. Behind this feeling was obviously a fear that unsympathetic administrations in Washington would require southern states to pay Negroes a benefit which would be regarded locally as excessive.
>
> (Latimer 1935)

The Origins of the Social Security Act 273

Latimer's social background and his deep involvement in the Social Security Act give his observations considerable weight. As with so much else in American history, many crucial issues have been shaped by the intransigence of the former slaveholders and their progeny. The plantation owners were not as wealthy as their Northern counterparts after they lost the Civil War, but they had veto power through their dominance within the Democratic Party. When the AALL is matched up against the Southern Democrats on issues of power, it does not seem to be much of a contest. The Wisconsin supporters were a minor add-on.

Stewart's opponents were clear and visible when it came to the rejection of his proposal to have both employers and employees contribute to unemployment insurance. Both organized labor and reform-oriented social workers opposed contributions by workers. They still believed that unemployment was the fault of the corporations, which therefore should take full responsibility for compensating workers when they lost their jobs. In their eyes this "fact" made unemployment compensation different from old-age pensions, for which employee contributions were considered to be fair. Unfortunately for the reformers and average workers, this line of reasoning reduced unemployment benefits, made them easier to stigmatize, and put payment levels and the number of months of coverage at the mercy of Congress in later decades. The liberal-labor "victory" over the IRC on this issue therefore was a shortsighted one, which they insisted upon despite hearing many good arguments against it from friendly sources since they had first raised it the year before.

The failure to include employee contributions to the unemployment insurance fund in the legislation is also very telling in light of Roosevelt's statement at the outset of the process that he favored a contributory plan for both old-age pensions and unemployment compensation. Nevertheless, he quietly accepted the narrow demands by the nascent liberal-labor alliance on this issue. Perhaps future commentators on the New Deal should keep this point in mind when they praise Roosevelt for claiming that he insisted on contributions by workers "to give the contributors a legal, moral, and political right to collect their pensions and unemployment benefits" and thus ensure that "no damn politician can ever scrap my social security program" (Schlesinger 1958, pp. 308–309). But workers did not contribute to unemployment benefits, at least at the outset, which is striking because unemployment insurance seemed to be more important to Roosevelt. So it seems most likely that he simply decided not to challenge the liberal-labor alliance on an issue about which it felt very strongly. If that is the case, it is an example of how elected officials provide politically appealing rationales for policy outcomes which are based in power battles that the after-the-fact rationales later obscure.

Although this conflict and its resolution were an important step in the policy-making process, legislation still had to be enacted, which means there is another opportunity to see how the corporate moderate/IRC/

274 Social Insurance Created and Undermined

SSRC network did in its battle with the Southern Democrats. And beyond the legislative enactment, there is the fact that several important amendments were added to the Social Security Act just a few years later, which marks the point at which the corporate moderates won out almost entirely.

The Legislative Gauntlet

The CES's overall Social Security legislation for the range of social insurance programs mentioned at the outset of the chapter, not just for old-age pensions and unemployment insurance, was introduced into Congress in mid-January 1935. At the outset it had the apparent support of a wide cross-section of the corporate community, including a committee of the NAM (Brents 1984; Jenkins and Brents 1989). Then, too, a committee of the Chamber of Commerce endorsed the bill in March, while it was still being dissected by Congressional committees, and went one step further by favoring the nationally oriented federal plan for unemployment insurance that Teagle and Stewart advocated (Nelson 1969, p. 214). The plans embodied in the draft legislation also had the backing of reformers and labor leaders. It thus seemed for a moment that the plan might face clear sailing.

However, the support for the legislation by the ultraconservatives was soon reversed for political reasons that are often overlooked, and the Southern Democrats raised their own separate objections. The proposal therefore had to survive a seven-month legislative gauntlet that included highly critical testimony by the NAM and the leaders of its organizational affiliates in leading industrial states, followed by a complete redrafting in the House and near defeats in key Congressional committees (Altman 2005, for an insightful account of the legislative battles). There were also last-minute changes in the preamble due to a Supreme Court decision. Finally, the revised legislation almost failed due to a last-minute amendment to allow companies with their own pension plans to opt out of the government plan. In the end, though, all of the policy provisions survived, even though Southern Democrats insisted upon further restrictions on federal regulation of both the old-age and unemployment insurance provisions.

The IRC Memorandum to Clients, No. 5, provided a detailed eight-page overview of the original bill for its clients on January 25, eight days after it was introduced. It then criticized the unemployment insurance plan because it would lead to 48 sets of state records, causing many costly problems in transferring files in what was coming to be a nationwide labor market. The IRC also was disappointed by the small measure of control that the federal government would have over state plans. It predicted opposition to the unemployment provisions for several reasons, all of which reflected the IRC's ongoing preferences for a national plan. The IRC also still favored a tax on employees as well as employers for unemployment

The Origins of the Social Security Act 275

insurance as well as for old-age pensions, and uniform federal standards that must be adhered to by all states.

The memorandum was more positive toward the old-age insurance provisions, noting that the contributions to the program were low "as compared with the pension plans of progressive companies..." (Industrial Relations Counselors 1935a, p. 10). However, it did worry that the government might not be able to "assure the contractual character of this obligation so long as Congress has the power later to change the terms of the law." It also expressed concern that the bill gave "no recognition to industrial pension plans that have been adopted in several industries, and a number of which have become well established and have accumulated considerable reserves" (Industrial Relations Counselors 1935a, p. 10). Within a few days, however, they saw this lack of recognition for established industrial pension plans as a very real opportunity for the companies that had them.

Testimony Before Congress

As Roosevelt and Perkins had feared, most of the discussion in Congress focused on old-age social insurance. This part of the legislation was explained and defended at length and in detail by Witte, Brown, and Latimer. Latimer and others believe that Witte was by far the most creditable witness for the great majority of congressmen (Schlabach 1969, p. 14). However, Brown and Latimer's testimony is of greater theoretical interest because it stressed labor market concerns, which supports the claim that the program was created with industrial relations in mind, not social welfare (Graebner 1980, pp. 187–189). For example, Latimer's only concern was that higher benefits might be needed to induce the large number of retirements that he thought necessary to help improve the unemployment problem. (Armstrong's oral history suggests the same kind of emphasis, which is worth mentioning because she speaks from an independent perspective. She told her interviewer that the objective "was not only to protect the older worker, but it was also to get him out of the labor market" (Armstrong 1965, p. 255).)

Responding to the concerns of companies that already had their own pension plans, the IRC's Memorandum to Clients, No. 6, for February 1, 1935, explained for the first time that the government plan would be less costly for these companies. It also proposed that the current company plans could be seen as supplementary to the government program, making it possible to provide more attractive pensions for higher-income workers: "The combined cost to companies of the revised company plan and the national plan would presumably be less than the cost of their present plans, since the contribution rates levied by the Security Bill are set below actual cost on the assumption that the additional amounts needed later will be drawn from general tax funds" (Industrial Relations Counselors 1935b, p. 1). This memo is very important because it proves that the IRC realized there would be cost savings and the opportunities to provide better retirement benefits for executives much earlier than previous accounts state, which give no credit to the IRC (e.g., Hacker 2002; Klein 2003).

Memorandum No. 6 then explains why the employees themselves might prefer Social Security to company plans that claimed they would pay higher benefits. These reasons are also an admission of the weaknesses inherent in company pension plans discussed by Sass (1997). It first notes that there is an "absence of real guarantees" in company plans, which is a damning admission if there ever was one. Second, it notes that there had been "widespread cuts in the amounts paid to pensioners and reductions in the rate of pension which have occurred during the past four years," which is an admission that many company plans were not actuarially sound over the long run (Industrial Relations Counselors 1935b, p. 2).

Memorandum to Clients No. 6 is also important because it provides the first mention of "contracting out," which would "permit a company to operate a separate plan outside the federal scheme if it is in no way less favorable than that of the government and has its current credits fully financed." The memorandum concedes that such a provision would have "a decided appeal from the industrial relations viewpoint of the individual company," implying that privately controlled pension plans might help the company in retaining and restraining employees. But it then adds, "[W]e understand that the experts who drafted the bill believe such a provision would weaken the effectiveness of the measure for the great number of wage earners who are not under company plans" (Industrial Relations Counselors 1935b, p. 2). In other words, the IRC experts, as exemplified by Latimer and Stewart, had decided that contracting out was not a good idea for the corporate community. The memorandum then added that a separate plan would be burdensome besides: "Certainly the inclusion of the proposed provision would be accompanied by requirements for financial guarantees from the companies of a character that might prove burdensome and difficult to meet and to that extent would lessen its acceptability" (Industrial Relations Counselors 1935b, p. 2).

These comments are part of a process of disseminating a new perspective within the corporate community, starting with the Rockefeller-related oil companies and the large companies with membership in the Special Conference Committee. They are also the first of several pieces showing that some social scientists are incorrect when they conclude that most of the corporate moderates were in favor of contracting out because of their alleged continuing opposition to federal old-age insurance (e.g., Hacker 2002, p. 101; Orloff 1993, p. 293).

The depth of the IRC experts' concern over contracting out is revealed in a letter that Brown sent to Witte shortly thereafter, on February 13,

The Origins of the Social Security Act 277

reporting on what he had learned through his discussions of contracting out with corporate executives at the annual meetings of the American Management Association. Once again serving as the eyes and ears of the Rockefeller group, Brown reported that most of the executives understood that this provision was not to their advantage. He also had learned that the Philadelphia insurance agent who was lobbying for the idea, Walter Forster, had very little support among insurance agents or the large insurance companies, with the exception of Prudential and Metropolitan:

> The Prudential Company has been rather inept in the matter and I think that you will find that the dozen or more companies other than the Prudential and the Metropolitan are not particularly in sympathy with the tactics of those two companies. I heard in Pittsburgh, however, that the Metropolitan, at least on the surface, is saying the bill will be a boon to the insurance companies in expanding the demand for supplementary group annuity contracts. Both the Prudential and the Metropolitan are somewhat frightened by the threat of investigation of industrial insurance, and may not be as anxious to push the amendment on account of a backfire in this respect.
>
> (Brown 1935a)

Brown had further encouraging conversations that he reported on in a letter to Witte on February 23. The list of companies he provides that lacked interest in contracting out is long and impressive:

> I am continuing to receive word from industrial relations executives of their lack of interest in the contracting out amendment. Confidentially, the last word I had was from Art Young, Vice-President of the United States Steel Corporation. [Brown is referring to Arthur Young, the former head of IRC, who had moved to U.S. Steel in 1934 to help the company fight off unions.] I have been in touch also with the American Telephone and Telegraph Company, Socony-Vacuum, DuPont, United States Rubber, Union Carbide and Carbon, Western Electric, and a number of other companies. The men in question are the chief personnel officers, and since I have known most of them for six or eight years, I have confidence in what they tell me.
>
> (Brown 1935b)

While committees in the House and Senate were deciding whether to permit the report from the Committee for Economic Security to be voted upon by the full House and Senate memberships, Stewart and the SSRC hosted a conference in Atlantic City on March 22–23. It was the outcome of the funding request they had submitted in the spring of 1934, when they had anticipated that amendments to the final legislation would be necessary. This conference unanimously recommended funding for studies of the soon-to-be social security administrative board. Two SSRC committees, the Committee on Public Administration and the Committee on Social Security, would carry out the studies. The Rockefeller Foundation immediately gave approval to this request, which led to donations of $611,000 ($11.1 million in 2018 dollars) (Fisher 1993, p. 139).

Shortly after the SSRC conference, the IRC's next Memorandum to Clients included two attached statements from (unnamed) insurance companies stating their belief that the legislation will "result in renewed appreciation and greater stimulation of life insurance activities both individual and group rather than the reverse" (Industrial Relations Counselors 1935c, March 27, p. 8). This is further evidence that the IRC and at least some insurance companies understood the potential of the Social Security Act well before the date claimed by earlier researchers.

At the same time as the IRC and the insurance companies were realizing that contracting out was not a good idea, the administration's general legislative proposal was being totally rewritten in the House Ways and Means Committee for reasons that had nothing to do with IRC and the insurance companies. Minimum benefits and merit hiring of state-level administrators were eliminated at the insistence of Southern Democrats on the committee, which is of course further good evidence for an emphasis on their power during the New Deal (Witte 1963, pp. 125, 143–145).

The IRC's Memorandum to Clients, No. 10, dated April 10, provided a thorough summary and evaluation of the revised legislation that the Ways and Means Committee introduced into the House on April 4, starting with the fact that the title had been changed from the Economic Security Act to the Social Security Act. It noted that the unemployment section of the new bill "makes no provision" for any of the major concerns expressed in Memorandum to Clients, No. 5, leaving that portion of the legislation very unsatisfactory:

> Coverage is reduced and federal supervision of state personnel is struck out. In short, the principles of broad coverage and competitive equality insisted on at the outset have been violated while a door has been opened to permit political appointments and high administrative costs.
>
> (Industrial Relations Counselors 1935d, p. 2)

There were also changes in the plans for old-age insurance that did not meet the IRC's expectations. For example, benefits would now be higher for low-wage workers than they were in current company plans and lower than they would be for high-wage workers. Death benefits would now be higher than planned after short periods of employment and lower than planned after lengthy periods of employment. When the revised

The Origins of the Social Security Act   279

legislation reached the House floor on April 12, it first had to survive two brief challenges—one by the Communist Party, the other by the pressure group for the elderly called the Townsend Plan. Both received attention in the media at the time and subsequent attention by historians and social scientists, but in fact neither alternative had any chance of passage or any influence on the proceedings. The Communist bill, with a sweeping call for a guaranteed annual income adjusted for region of the country, received only 40 votes, and the Townsend Plan, which originally called for payments of $200 per month to every person over age 60, with the proviso that all of it be spent within the month, only received 56. Moreover, *over half* of the votes in both instances came from ultraconservatives who opposed any form of government social insurance (Witte 1963, p. 99). If the votes on the Communist and Townsend bills are any indication, there were no more than 15 to 20 representatives in the House who stood to the left of the New Deal.

However, some social scientists place great emphasis on pressure on Congress from the Townsend Plan, so more should be said about it.

The Townsend Plan

It is sometimes asserted that the Townsend Plan helped put old-age pensions on the agenda (Starr 2017, pp. 267–268, 278) or had a major impact on the passage of the Social Security Act (e.g., Hacker 2002; Hacker and Pierson 2002; Weir, Orloff, and Skocpol 1988). The plan had its origins in a series of letters-to-the editor in early 1934 to a local newspaper in Long Beach, California, by a 66-year-old physician and former real estate salesman, Francis Townsend. They began to appear shortly after he was eased out of a position in city government. The letters simply presented his own version of various plans that were being discussed in retirement communities in that city and nearby Los Angeles (Bernstein 1985, pp. 61–66, for a colorful and informative portrait of Townsend, who was a first-class self-promoter).

Townsend suggested that in order to revive the economy and at the same time help the elderly, the federal government should give $200 a month to every American citizen over age 60, on the condition that they would retire, thereby making room for younger employees, and spend all their pension money by the end of each month. The funds would come from a new 2 percent sales tax. (Later the plan called for a more general transaction tax, "with features essentially similar" to the value-added tax (VAT) that is now used in many European countries (Manza 1995, p. 347).)

Based on an enthusiastic local response to his letters, Townsend and one of his former real estate partners incorporated a rough outline of his plan as a nonprofit organization in the summer of 1934. They did so at the same time as the Committee on Economic Security's staff already was working on its plan. Shortly thereafter, the plan founders began to set up local groups in the Los Angeles area and established a newsletter that had a greater outreach.

The Townsend Plan first received major media attention in late November 1934, due to its barrage of letters to Congress and the White House opposing the possible removal of the old-age provisions from the Social Security Act, which Roosevelt had hinted might occur in the speech that had led Armstrong, Brown, Latimer, and others to fear that he might delay on old-age pensions. Since Roosevelt and Perkins quickly denied any such intent, it might seem that these letters may have had some impact. But according to detailed archival research work on the Townsend Plan by sociologist Edwin Amenta (2006, p. 76), the letters began to arrive well after Roosevelt and Perkins had given public assurances that those provisions would be included. (Amenta's exhaustive research may be especially credible because he doubts the role of corporate moderates in the passage of the Social Security Act.) Earlier, another sociologist who is not an advocate of theories claiming class or corporate dominance, came to a similar conclusion, as one part of a more general project on the role of experts during the New Deal (Manza 1995, pp. 31, 245).

Despite the fact that the Townsend Plan's total membership and ability to lobby were not as impressive even in early 1935 as they appeared to be in some media accounts, Townsend himself was able to draw national media attention during the Congressional debate over the Social Security Act. He was invited to testify before House and Senate committees in February, where his lack of specifics, or even a clear understanding of his own plan, proved to be an embarrassment (Amenta 2006, pp. 85, 87–88; Manza 1995, pp. 348–349; Witte 1963, pp. 85–86). Although the plan had suffered a resounding defeat a month after his testimony, as recounted in the previous subsection, one trio of sociologists and political scientists claim that the Townsend Plan did have an impact in Congress because it had membership groups in many congressional districts that might challenge those legislators that opposed the plan (Weir, Orloff, and Skocpol 1988). This claim is contradicted by another fact reported by Amenta (2006, p. 98): at that time the Townsend Plan "had little presence outside the far West and had not yet decided on targeting congressional districts."

Given all this evidence that the Townsend Plan was too late and too weak to matter, it is interesting that Witte (1963, p. 103) would mention it in mid-May 1935, well after it had been completely rejected in the House, when he was asked by members of the Senate Finance committee to present the best argument he could for the administration's old-age social-insurance proposal. In reply, he said that something like the Townsend Plan might be forced upon Congress if the administration's bill did not pass. This kind of statement sounds like a rhetorical assertion in the midst

The Origins of the Social Security Act   281

of delicate negotiations within a Senate committee. However, it is taken at face value in two accounts, which claim that the Social Security Act was a "strategic accommodation, driven by fear of less attractive alternatives," a fear that was generated by "well-organized populist challenges, such as the Townsend Movement for old-age pensions" (Hacker and Pierson 2002, p. 308; Hacker and Pierson 2004, p. 187). Contrary to those accounts, Amenta (2006, p. 96) concludes that the Townsend Plan had little or no impact on the creation or passage of the Social Security legislation:

> [I]t is difficult to identify anything the Townsend Plan did in Washington that buoyed old-age benefits. Almost all the beneficial effects of the Townsend Plan on old-age policy would doubtless have materialized regardless of whether its leaders had drafted the McGroarty [the sponsor of the Townsend Plan in the House] bill, come to Washington to testify and lobby for it, induced Townsendites to threaten legislators to pass it, to amend it, and to attack the security bill and support no alternatives, as they did.

This conclusion, along with a similar one reached in the mid-1990s by Manza (1995, pp. 31, 245), presents a major challenge to the various claims about the effects of the Townsend Plan. There is no evidence that the Townsendites' bill-drafting, testifying, lobbying, or threatening had any impact. Furthermore, it may be a stretch to use the phrase "the Townsend movement" to characterize these efforts (Hacker and Pierson 2002, p. 308). A social movement involves collective opposition to established rules and customs by people who have organized to make sustained challenges against elite opponents and authorities, and such challenges usually involve social disruption, whether violent or nonviolent (e.g., Piven 2006; Tarrow 1994). But the Townsend Plan did not involve its elderly members in rule-breaking, let alone marching and demonstrating. It was a traditional interest group—a narrow group that seeks to influence specific legislative issues of concern to it. To call the Townsend Plan a "movement" drains the concept of any real meaning beyond the idea of interest groups and pressure groups, which are long familiar and carefully studied in political science (e.g., Berry 1999, p. 142, for this general critique of the misuse of this concept).

The Senate and the Business Advisory Council Have Their Say

The Senate Finance Committee, which Witte feared as the biggest threat to the legislation because it contained many Southern conservatives, finished its hearings in February, but then postponed further action on the Social Security proposal until April. It did not approve a report until

282   Social Insurance Created and Undermined

May 17, after coming within a vote or two of stripping the bill of old-age insurance. During the final weeks of deliberation, a new element was added to the picture when corporate anger over the imminent passage of the National Labor Relations Act led to a harsh attack on the Social Security Act. It came in early May from the newly elected ultraconservative president of the Chamber of Commerce at the group's annual meeting in Washington, who had replaced a corporate moderate. The attack came as a surprise because the previous Chamber leadership had been quietly accepting of the Social Security Act.

In response to the new Chamber president's criticism, the BAC decided that it had to restate its support for Social Security by going to the White House the next day, despite its opposition to the National Labor Relations Act. "Business Leaders Uphold President," said the *New York Times* headline on page 1 on May 3. Among the 20 people appearing at the White House was, first and most symbolically, the outgoing Chamber president, who was also a Boston utility company executive. Next in symbolic importance might be the head of Chase National Bank, who was also John D. Rockefeller's brother-in-law. The top partners in two Wall Street investment banks, Brown Brothers Harriman and Goldman Sachs, were present, along with the presidents or chairs of Remington Rand, Kennecott Copper, United States Rubber, Cannon Towels, Procter and Gamble, Lambert Pharmaceutical Company, and the Mead Corporation (Domhoff 1970, pp. 214–215 for the full list of names and corporate affiliations).

In the aftermath, but not because of the BAC's visit to the White House, the Senate Finance Committee's bill ended up much improved over the version passed by the House, in spite of Witte's fears. According to the IRC's Memorandum to Clients, No. 12, for May 27, 1935e (p. 1), the Senate Finance Committee "restored to the bill several features that appeared in it originally but were omitted in the House draft." This may have been in good part because the Southern-dominated committee was extremely impressed by the testimony of their fellow Southerner, Folsom of Eastman Kodak, which led to changes in the details of the bill's unemployment provisions that were more in keeping with the corporate moderates' top preferences (Jacoby 1993; Jacoby 1997, pp. 211–212; Swenson 2002, p. 228–229).

The bill also had a new preamble due to a Supreme Court decision in early May declaring the Railroad Retirement Act unconstitutional. Because the reduction of unemployment and the efficiency and morale of the workforce could no longer be considered within the purview of the constitution, the emphasis in the revised preamble was on the country's general welfare. This change, which obscured the major role of industrial relations experts such as Latimer and Stewart in writing the act, was made because the constitution allows the government to support the general welfare through its taxing power:

> Now, to achieve the original purpose, the administration turned to the taxing power and the general welfare clause of the Constitution. In the process, the ideology of social security was given formal sanction. After May 1935, proponents of retirement legislation talked less about efficiency, economy and unemployment relief than about social security and the needs of older workers, which were now a central policy goal rather than ancillary to some larger purpose.
>
> (Graebner 1980, pp. 162–163)

Put another way, the Social Security Act was first and foremost concerned with labor relations, but that fact could not be stated directly due to the composition of the Supreme Court and the nature of its past decisions. It was therefore necessary to refer to the general welfare clause. With the role of industrial relations experts in creating the Social Security Act soon lost from view, the preamble and subsequent accounts of the Social Security Act by some historians opened the way for claims about the role of social workers that appear in a sociologist's full-length treatment of the Social Security Act, which is based on secondary sources (Orloff 1993).

Just as the bill was about to pass the Senate, it faced one final obstacle: an amendment to allow the "contracting out" for companies with established pension plans, which had been vigorously opposed by IRC and most of the corporate moderates interviewed by Brown a few months earlier. The amendment was formally offered by a conservative Democrat from Missouri, Bennett Champ Clark, so it came to be called the Clark Amendment. From the point of view of the corporate ultraconservatives and the Senators that opposed the whole social-insurance program, the amendment was a perfect way to undercut the Social Security Act without voting against it. Despite protests from Roosevelt and Perkins, along with actuarial arguments against the amendment by Witte and other experts, it passed by the wide margin of 51 to 35 on June 19, followed by passage of the act in general by a 77 to 6 vote the same day (Witte 1963, p. 106). The large vote for the Clark Amendment is revealing—and supportive of my general analysis—because it underscores the power of Southern Democrats and others sympathetic to corporate ultraconservatives in a seemingly liberal Senate.

Roosevelt then made it clear that he would not sign legislation that included the Clark Amendment because it would create major actuarial and administrative problems, especially when companies—or their pension plans—went bankrupt, or when employees left companies that had private pension funds before their retirement age. The standoff led to a

284   Social Insurance Created and Undermined

two-month delay while a Congressional conference committee argued about the issue and searched for a compromise. Congress finally agreed that the bill would be passed without the Clark Amendment, but with the provision that the Clark Amendment would be reconsidered in the next session of Congress after experts had a chance to see if contracting out could be made compatible with the overall system. Roosevelt signed the legislation on August 14, 1935.

The IRC sent out a brief summary of the act's provisions on August 16. The memorandum first repeated its disapproval of the Clark Amendment, concluding, "It seems clear that from the practical operating viewpoint such companies would have nothing to gain from the amendment" (Industrial Relations Counselors 1935f, p. 1). It then noted that members of the IRC staff were meeting with "the representatives of leading insurance companies and other interests concerned primarily with the sections on pensions." Finally, the memorandum announced that the organization already was working on supplemental plans:

> Industrial Relations Counselors is now engaged in the formulation of several types of private plans which will *supplement* the pension benefits provided under the federal scheme and more adequately cover employees in the higher salary brackets. Our recommendations on future procedure may vary as between companies installing a plan for the first time and companies that have operated a formal plan for some years.
>
> (Industrial Relations Counselors 1935f, p. 1, my italics)

This brief memorandum was followed on August 23 by a longer and more reflective one, No. 15, which nicely reveals the corporate moderates' viewpoint and presages their agenda for defeating the Clark Amendment. By and large, IRC experts were satisfied with the overall legislative outcome, calling it a program that "will increase mass purchasing power and act as a shock absorber for our economic system," which makes them sound like proto-Keynesians (Industrial Relations Counselors 1935g, p. 2). The memorandum also said that the old-age pension provisions "were much better drawn than the unemployment compensation phase," a conclusion that comes as no surprise because IRC experts—and their ally, Barbara Armstrong—wrote them (Industrial Relations Counselors 1935g, p. 3). In addition, the memorandum also contained some surprisingly moderate and even progressive comments that explained the empirical basis for their policy analyses. For example, the report said that IRC's cross-national studies of social-insurance systems convinced its authors "that a very considerable proportion of the costs must be borne by the public treasury," which put them in greater accord with the social workers than originally seemed to be the case (Industrial Relations Counselors 1935g, p. 3).

The summary also contained several criticisms of the Clark Amendment that past memorandums had refrained from mentioning because the IRC's leaders wanted "to avoid any comment which might have been misconstrued as being political argument..." (Industrial Relations Counselors 1935g, p. 6). First, contracting out would be more costly for corporations by as much as 33 to 100 percent. Second, the need to make back payments to the government for "each employee leaving a company before retirement age would subject a company fund to an unpredictable cash withdrawal, which would tend to force investments into a form suitable for commercial banks rather than proper insurance investments" (Industrial Relations Counselors 1935g, p. 7). Third, private plans would have "burdensome administrative and reporting problems" so that the government could oversee them properly. Finally, the existence of private plans "would tend to weaken the actuarial basis of the government old-age benefit plan" due to the fact that companies with the lowest costs were most likely to set up their own plans, leaving the government "to deal with the poorest risks" (Industrial Relations Counselors 1935g, pp. 6–7).

This list of objections to the Clark Amendment was the opening salvo in the effort to make sure that it was not adopted. In the end, no substitute for the Clark Amendment was ever offered, but the behind-the-scenes effort to deal with it will be discussed in the next chapter because it provides further evidence for the power of the corporate moderates in and around the Rockefeller/IRC/SSRC network.

In concluding this detailed account of the origins of the Social Security Act, it should be noted again that the process was long and drawn out, and that the corporate moderates lost on several specific issues. Along the way, restive workers made their presence felt through the grassroots activity of the Railways Employees National Pension Association. And the AFL demonstrated its power by inserting its non-systemic view of the economy into the provisions for unemployment insurance by rejecting contributions by workers, which proved to be extremely shortsighted.

As for liberals and social workers, they wanted something better and more generous than the corporate moderates' plans, but they ended up as lobbyists for the plan that emerged from the policy-planning network. Finally, the agitation and plans from the Communists and Townsend Plan advocates, while drawing headlines at the time, and many academic what-if and if-only analyses decades later, had little or no impact on the formulation or passage of the act. Overall, the final outcome fits well with the idea that corporate moderates created its most important principles. It also shows they did the state-building in this case because the federal government lacked both capacity and autonomy during the New Deal on legislation concerning social insurance. Based on the work by Amenta (2006), any future claims about the importance of this old-age pressure group in frightening the corporate moderates into action perhaps should be regarded as a failure to read the scholarly literature on the origins of the Social Security Act.

As for the Southern Democrats, they were the Disposers. They were the reason why agricultural and domestic workers were not covered by old-age insurance until 1950, even though an early study by the Committee on Economic Security's research staff said that such coverage was feasible (Alston and Ferrie 1999). And as noted earlier, the legislative battles in Congress strongly suggest that the Southern Democrats were the main reason why unemployment insurance was placed under the control of the states. Southern Democrats also eliminated the civil service requirements for the staff that administered the programs and any minimal federal standards for payment levels, which both the IRC experts and the AALL reformers favored. These changes allowed the representatives of the plantation owners to put their local cronies in charge of agencies and keep benefit payments low enough to maintain full control of their workforce (see Quadagno 1988, for detailed information on the powerful impact of the Southern Democrats on this legislation). In the end, then, it was a battle between corporate moderates and the fledgling liberal-labor alliance on the one side and ultraconservatives and plantation owners on the other. The corporate moderates and their hired experts shaped the general act, but the Southern Democrats carved out the exceptions the plantation owners wanted.

References

Ahmed, Amel. 2013. *Democracy and the politics of electoral system choice: Engineering electoral dominance.* New York: Cambridge University Press.

Alston, Lee J. and Joseph P. Ferrie. 1999. *Southern paternalism and the American welfare state.* New York: Cambridge University Press.

Altman, Nancy. 2005. *The battle for Social Security: From FDR's vision to Bush's gamble.* New York: John Wiley & Sons.

Altmeyer, Arthur. 1968. *The formative years of Social Security.* Madison: University of Wisconsin Press.

Amenta, Edwin. 2006. *When movements matter: The Townsend Plan and the rise of social security.* Princeton: Princeton University Press.

Anderson, Mary and Mary Winslow. 1951. *Women at work.* Minneapolis: University of Minnesota Press.

Armstrong, Barbara N. 1932. *Insuring the essentials: Minimum wage, plus social insurance—a living wage problem.* New York: Macmillan.

———. 1965. "Oral History." *Social Security Oral History Project.*

Baltzell, E. Digby. 1964. *The Protestant establishment: Aristocracy and caste in America.* New York: Random House.

Bernstein, Irving. 1960. *The lean years: A history of the American worker, 1920–1933.* Boston: Hougton Mifflin.

———. 1985. *A caring society: The New Deal, the worker, and the Great Depression.* Boston: Houghton Mifflin.

Berry, Jeffrey M. 1999. *The new liberalism: The rising power of citizen groups*. Washington: The Brookings Institution.

Brents, Barbara. 1984. "Capitalism, corporate liberalism and social policy: The origins of the Social Security Act of 1935." *Mid-American Review of Sociology* 9:23–40.

Brown, J. Douglas. 1935a. "Letter to Edwin Witte, February 13." In *Brown Papers, Box 15, 1935 File*. Princeton: Mudd Library, Princeton University.

———. 1935b. "Letter to Edwin Witte, February 23." In *Brown Papers, Box 15, 1935 File*. Princeton: Mudd Library, Princeton University.

———. 1965. "Oral History." In *Social Security Oral History Project*. New York: Columbia University Library.

———. 1972. *An American philosophy of social security: Evolution and issues*. Princeton: Princeton University Press.

Brown, Josephine. 1940. *Public relief, 1929–1939*. New York: Henry Holt & Company.

Burns, Eveline. 1966. "Oral history." In *Social Security oral history project*. New York: Columbia University Library.

Carter, Franklin. 1934. *The New Dealers*. New York: Simon and Schuster.

Castrovinci, J. 1976. "Prelude to welfare capitalism: The role of business in the enactment of workmen's compensation legislation in Illinois, 1905–1912." *Social Service Review* 50:80–102.

Chambers, Clarke. 1952. *A historical study of the Grange, The Farm Bureau, and the Associated Farmers, 1929–1941*. Berkeley: University of California Press.

Cohen, Adam. 2009. *Nothing to fear: FDR's inner circle and the hundred days that created modern America*. New York: Penguin.

Cowdrick, Edward. 1928. *Pensions: A problem of management*. New York: American Management Association, Annual Convention Series, No. 75.

Darknell, Frank. 1975. "The Carnegie Council for Policy Studies in Higher Education: A new policy group for the ruling class." *The Insurgent Sociologist* 5:106–114.

———. 1980. "The Carnegie philanthropy and private corporate influence on higher education." Pp. 385–411 in *Philanthropy and cultural imperialism: The foundations at home and abroad*, edited by R. F. Arnove. Boston: G. K. Hall.

Davies, Gareth. 1999. "The unsuspected radicalism of the Social Security Act." Pp. 56–71 in *The Roosevelt years: New perspectives on American history, 1933–1945*, edited by R. Garson and S. Kidd. Edinburgh, Scotland: Edinburgh University Press.

Domhoff, G. W. 1970. *The higher circles*. New York: Random House.

———. 1996. *State autonomy or class dominance? Case studies on policy making in America*. Hawthorne, NY: Aldine de Gruyter.

Downey, Kristin. 2009. *The woman behind the New Deal: The life of Frances Perkins, FDR's Secretary of Labor and his moral conscience*. New York: Doubleday.

Eakins, David. 1966. "The development of corporate liberal policy research in the United States, 1885–1965." Ph.D. dissertation Thesis, History, University of Wisconsin, Madison.

Eden, Elizabeth. 1936. "Letter to Thomas Devevoise, October 30." In *Rockefeller Family Archives, Record Group III 2H, Box 122, Folder 909*. Sleepy Hollow, NY: Rockefeller Archive Center.

288 Social Insurance Created and Undermined

Finegold, Kenneth and Theda Skocpol. 1995. *State and party in America's New Deal*. Madison: University of Wisconsin Press.

Fishback, Price and Shawn Kantor. 2000. *A prelude to the welfare state: The origins of workers' compensation* Chicago: University of Chicago Press.

Fisher, Donald. 1993. *Fundamental development of the social sciences: Rockefeller philanthropy and the United States Social Science Research Council*. Ann Arbor: University of Michigan Press.

Folsom, Marion. 1934. "Letter to Frank W. Lovejoy, December 12." In *Folsom Papers, Box 108, Folder 3*. Rochester: University of Rochester Library.

Fosdick, Raymond. 1933. "Letter to John D. Rockefeller, April 27." In *Rockefeller Family Archives, Record Group 2 (OMR), Economic Reform Interests, Box 16, Folder 127*. Sleepy Hollow, NY: Rockefeller Archive Center.

Fox, Daniel M. 2006 "The significance of the Milbank Memorial Fund for Policy: An assessment at its centennial." *The Milbank Quarterly* 84:5–36.

Garraty, John. 1960. "The United States Steel Corporation versus labor: The early years." *Labor History* 1:3–38.

Gordon, Colin. 1994a. *New Deals: Business, labor, and politics in America,1932–1935*. New York: Cambridge University Press.

———. 1994b. *Pitied but not entitled: Single mothers and the history of welfare, 1890–1935*. New York: Free Press.

Graebner, William. 1980. *A history of retirement*. New Haven: Yale University Press.

Hacker, Jacob. 2002. *The divided welfare state: The battle over public and private social benefits in the United States*. New York: Cambridge University Press.

Hacker, Jacob and Paul Pierson. 2002. "Business power and social policy: Employers and the formation of the American welfare state." *Politics & Society* 30:277–325.

———. 2004. "Varieties of capitalist interests and capitalist power: A response to Swenson." *Studies in American Political Development* 18:186–195.

Hansen, Alvin, Merrill Murray, Russell Stevenson, and Bryce Stewart. 1934. *A program for unemployment insurance and relief in the United States*. Minneapolis: the University of Minnesota Press.

Hayes, Erving. 1936. *Activities of the President's Emergency Committee for Unemployment*. Concord, NH: Rumford Press.

Hicks, Clarence. 1930. "Letter to John D. Rockefeller, Jr., October 2." In *Rockefeller Family Archives, Educational Interests, Box 80, Folder 573*. Sleepy Hollow, NY: Rockefeller Archive Center.

———. 1941. *My life in industrial relations*. New York: Harper & Brothers.

Huthmacher, J. Joseph. 1968. *Senator Robert F. Wagner and the rise of urban liberalism*. New York: Atheneum.

Industrial Relations Counselors, Inc. 1934a. "Memorandum to Clients No. 1." New York: IRC.

———. 1934b. "Memorandum to Clients, No. 4." New York: IRC.

———. 1935a. "Memorandum to Clients, No. 5." New York: IRC.

———. 1935b. "Memorandum to Clients, No. 6." New York: IRC.

———. 1935c. "Memorandum to Clients, No. 9." New York: IRC.

———. 1935d. "Memorandum to Clients, No. 10." New York: IRC.

———. 1935e. "Memorandum to Clients, No. 12." New York: IRC.

———. 1935f. "Memorandum to Clients, No. 14." New York: IRC.

The Origins of the Social Security Act 289

————. 1935g. "Memorandum to Clients, No. 15." New York: IRC.

Irons, Peter. 1982. *The New Deal lawyers*. Princeton: Princeton University Press.

Jacobs, Lawrence and Robert Shapiro. 2000. *Politicians Don't Pander*. Chicago: University of Chicago Press.

Jacoby, Sanford. 1993. "Employers and the welfare state: The role of Marion B. Folsom." *The Journal of American History* 47:525–556.

————. 1997. *Modern manors: Welfare capitalism since the New Deal*. Princeton: Princeton University Press.

Jenkins, J. Craig and Barbara Brents. 1989. "Social protest, hegemonic competition, and social reform." *American Sociological Review* 54:891–909.

Kelly, Laurence. 1987. *Industrial relations at Queen's: The first fifty years*. Kingston, Canada: Industrial Relations Centre, Queen's University.

Kessler-Harris, Alice. 2001. *In pursuit of equity: Women, men, and the quest for economic citizenship in 20th century America*. New York: Oxford University Press.

Klein, Jennifer. 2003. *For all these rights: Business, labor, and the shaping of America's public-private welfare state*. Princeton: Princeton University Press.

Lagemann, Ellen. 1989. *The politics of knowledge: The Carnegie Corporation, philanthropy, and public policy*. Middletown, CT: Wesleyan University Press.

Latham, Earl. 1959. *The politics of railroad coordination, 1933–1936*. Cambridge: Harvard University Press.

Latimer, Murray. 1932. *Industrial Pension Systems in the United States and Canada*. New York: Industrial Relations Counselors, Inc.

————. 1933. "Memorandum on work for federal government." In *Rockefeller Foundation Collection, Record Group 1.1, Series 200S, Box 348, Folder 4143*. Sleepy Hollow, NY: Rockefeller Archive Center.

————. 1934. "Correspondence with Industrial Relations Counselors, Inc., on salary and taxes." In *Latimer Papers, Box 9, Folder 12*. Washington: Special Collections, George Washington University Library.

————. 1935. "Letter to Robert Gooch, March 20." In *Latimer Papers, Box 1, Folder 2*. Washington: Special Collections, George Washington University Library.

Latimer, Murray and Stephen Hawkins. 1938. "Railroad retirement system in the United States." In *Latimer Papers*. Washington Special Collections, George Washington University Library.

Loetta, Louis. 1975. "Abraham Epstein and the movement for old age security." *Labor History* 16:359–377.

Loth, David. 1958. *Swope of G. E. The story of Gerard Swope and General Electric in American business*. New York: Simon and Schuster.

Mann, Michael. 1993. *The sources of social power: The rise of classes and nation-states, 1760–1914*, Vol. 2. New York: Cambridge University Press.

Manza, Jeff. 1995. "Policy experts and political change during the New Deal." Ph.D. dissertation Thesis, Sociology, University of California, Berkeley, Berkeley.

Mink, Gwendolyn. 1995. *The wages of motherhood*. Ithaca: Cornell University Press.

Moss, David. 1996. *Socializing security: Progressive Era economists and the origins of American social policy*. Cambridge: Harvard University Press.

Nelson, Daniel. 1969. *Unemployment insurance: The American experience, 1915–1935*. Madison: University of Wisconsin Press.

NICB. 1931. *Elements of industrial pension plans.* New York: National Industrial Conference Board.

Orloff, Ann. 1993. *The politics of pensions: A comparative analysis of Britain, Canada, and the United States, 1880–1940.* Madison: University of Wisconsin Press.

Orloff, Ann and Eric Parker. 1990. "Business and social policy in Canada and the United States, 1920–1940." *Comparative Social Research* 12:295–339.

Perkins, Frances. 1930. "Letter to Beardsley Ruml, November 5." In *Spelman Fund, Series 4, Box 9, Folder 275.* Sleepy Hollow, NY: Rockefeller Archive Center.

———. 1946. *The Roosevelt I knew.* New York: Harper & Row.

Pierce, Lloyd. 1953. "The activities of the American Association for Labor Legislation in behalf of social security and protective labor legislation." Ph.D. dissertation Thesis, Economics, University of Wisconsin, Madison.

Piven, Frances. 2006. *Challenging authority: How ordinary people change America.* Lanham, MD: Rowman & Littlefield.

Poole, Mary. 2006. *The segregated origins of Social Security: African Americans and the welfare state.* Chapel Hill: University of North Carolina Press.

Quadagno, Jill. 1988. *The transformation of old age security: Class and politics in the American welfare state.* Chicago: University of Chicago Press.

Quadagno, Jill and Deana Rohlinger. 2009. "Religious conservatives in U.S. welfare state politics." Pp. 236–266 in *Religion, class coalitions, and welfare states,* edited by K. Kersbergen and P. Manow. Cambridge: Cambridge University Press.

Roberts, Alasdair. 1994. "Demonstrating neutrality: The Rockefeller philanthropies and the evolution of public administration, 1927–1936." *Public Administration Review,* pp. 221–228.

Sass, Steven A. 1997. *The promise of private pensions: The first hundred years.* Cambridge: Harvard University Press.

Saunders, Charles B. 1966. *The Brookings Institution: A fifty-year history.* Washington: The Brookings Institution.

Schlabach, Theron F. 1969. *Edwin E. Witte: Cautious reformer.* Madison: State Historical Society of Wisconsin.

Schlesinger, Arthur 1957. *The decline of the old order.* Boston: Houghton Mifflin.

———. 1958. *The coming of the New Deal.* Boston: Houghton Mifflin.

Skocpol, Theda. 1992. *Protecting soldiers and mothers: The political origins of social policy in the United States.* Cambridge: Harvard University Press.

Skocpol, Theda and Edwin Amenta. 1985. "Did the capitalists shape Social Security?" *American Sociological Review* 50:572–575.

Skocpol, Theda and Kenneth Finegold. 1982. "State capacity and economic intervention in the early New Deal." *Political Science Quarterly* 97:255–278.

Skocpol, Theda and John Ikenberry. 1983. "The political formation of the American welfare state in historical and comparative perspective." In *Comparative social research,* edited by R. Tomasson. Greenwich, CT: JAI.

Slaughter, Sheila and Edward T. Silva. 1980. "Looking backwards: How foundations formulated ideology in the Progressive Period." Pp. 55–86 in *Philanthropy and cultural imperialism: The foundations at home and abroad,* edited by R. F. Arnove. Boston: G. K. Hal & Co.

Starr, Paul. 2007. *Freedom's power: The true force of liberalism.* New York: Basic Books.

———. 2017. *The social transformation of American medicine: The rise of a sovereign profession and the making of a vast industry.* New York Basic Books.

Stewart, Bryce. 1925. "An American experiment in unemployment insurance in industry." *International Labor Review* 11.

———. 1928. *Financial aspects of industrial pensions.* New York: American Management Association.

———. 1930. *Unemployment benefits in the United States: The plans and their setting.* New York: Industrial Relations Counselors, Inc.

———. 1933. "Memorandum: Government work of Bryce M. Stewart." In *Rockefeller Foundation Collection, Record Group 1.1, Series 200S, Folder 4143.* Sleepy Hollow, NY: Rockefeller Archive Center.

Stewart, Bryce and Meredith Givens. 1934a. "Planned protection against unemployment and dependency: Report on a tentative plan for a proposed investigation." In *Rockefeller Foundation Collection, Record Group 1.1, Series 200, Box 398, Folder 4723.* Sleepy Hollow, NY: Rockefeller Archive Center.

———. 1934b. "Project report: Exploratory study of unemployment reserves and relief (economic security)." In *Rockefeller Foundation Collection, Record Group 1.1, Series 200S, Box 408, Folder 4824.* Sleepy Hollow, NY: Rockefeller Archive Center.

Swenson, Peter. 2002. *Capitalists against markets: The making of labor markets and welfare states in the United States and Sweden.* New York: Oxford University Press.

Tarrow, Sidney. 1994. *Power in movement: Social movements, collective action and politics.* New York: Cambridge University Press.

TCF. 1935. *American foundations and their fields, 1934.* New York: Twentieth Century Fund.

Traynor, Roger, Adrian Kragen, Herma Kay, Stefan Riesenfeld, Sam Kagel, Richard Dinkelspiel, and Kathryn Gehrels. 1977. "Barbara Nachtrieb Armstrong in memoriam: The light-years of Barbara Armstrong, 1890–1976." *California Law Review* 65:920–936.

Weinstein, James. 1968. *The corporate ideal in the liberal state.* Boston: Beacon Press.

Weir, Margaret, Ann Orloff, and Theda Skocpol. 1988. "Understanding American social politics." Pp. 3–27 in *The politics of social policy in the United States,* edited by M. Weir, A. Orloff, and T. Skocpol. Princeton: Princeton University Press.

Weischadle, David T. 1980. "The Carnegie Corporation and the shaping of American educational policy." In *Philanthropy and cultural imperialism: The foundations at home and abroad,* edited by R. F. Arnove. Boston: G. K. Hall & Co.

Witte, Edwin E. 1963. *The development of the Social Security Act.* Madison: University of Wisconsin Press.

Young, Arthur. 1933. "Grant from Rockefeller Foundation to cover expense of cooperation with government agencies, December 22." In *Rockefeller Foundation Collection,* Record Group 1.1, Series 200S, Box 348, Folder 4143. Sleepy Hollow, NY: Rockefeller Archive Center.

Chapter 7

Revising and Augmenting Social Security, 1937–1973

No sooner did the Social Security Act pass than the corporate moderates and their experts began to plan for the several changes that would be necessary to make the legislation fully to their liking. The way in which those changes were worked out is highly revealing in terms of the role of the policy-planning network in implementing social policies that are favored by the corporate moderates. In this instance, two SSRC committees mentioned in the previous chapter, the Public Administration Committee and the Committee on Social Security, were the key links to government. It is also noteworthy that the Rockefeller Foundation was standing behind them with both advice and money (Fisher 1993).

The IRC is not mentioned in the previous paragraph because the Rockefeller Foundation and the SSRC committees gradually edged the IRC to the sidelines precisely because it was too closely identified with employers. However, this decision did cause hard feelings, which is revealed by two memos in the Rockefeller Foundation papers at the Rockefeller Archive Center. The first was sent by Stacy May, the coordinator for public administration programs for the Rockefeller Foundation, to Joseph P. Harris, the research director for the SSRC's Public Administration Committee. May told Harris that "it is entirely sound for you to attempt to straighten out on the feeling of strain between your committee and the Industrial Relations Counselors" (May 1936). May then stated the basis for the tension, namely, a decision to give the SSRC the visible role because it would have more legitimacy as a disinterested source: "It seems to me clear that your group is much more apt to be accepted than the Industrial Relations Counselors as an objective body the advice of which might be of service to the Social Security Board" (May 1936). So any corporate involvement would be one step removed, and that fact in part explains why some scholars do not allow for any role for any corporate leaders.

Nonetheless, the IRC would continue to be valuable, the letter continues, because it had compiled very useful information and might be helpful in reassuring reluctant companies that it made sense to support the Social Security Administration:

> On the other hand, the Industrial Relations Counselors has done an impressive amount of work in the field and, as I have reviewed their publications recently, it seems to me that they have collected a considerable amount of material even on the detailed administrative aspects of the problem such as forms, etc. Furthermore, the field is so huge that I am all in favor of having everyone who is equipped to make any contribution to it proceed to do so. Everyone, I suppose, accepts the fact that administrative procedure will not get very far unless it is able to win the support of industrial groups, and it is likewise agreed that those industrial groups have a considerable experience which may be drawn upon for guidance in the operation of their own pension schemes, etc., because of the fact that many of the largest firms have operated abroad and have had actual experience in working under social insurance schemes of a number of types. If, then, the Industrial Relations Counselors are interested in continuing their past work and have the resources to do so it would seem to me that they might be encouraged to make it their special task to see that the industrial side of the case is heard and that the industrial experience is available.
>
> (May 1936)

According to a memo on March 26 to top Rockefeller Foundation officials from one of their employees, who was associate director of the foundation's Division of Social Sciences, and its major contact with the SSRC's two committees, IRC's Bryce Stewart probably came to terms with the new arrangement:

> I lunched today with Bryce Stewart. The main purpose of the meeting was to discover to what extent he felt aggrieved by the Foundation's recent action in appropriating funds for the investigations of the Public Administration Committee notably in the field of unemployment insurance administration and employment office procedures. He appeared to have accepted our action as evidence that it would not be feasible for him to push ahead with his own project.
>
> (Van Sickle 1936)

This two-page memo, which is also of interest because it once again spotlights how the Rockefeller Foundation combined money and information to play a pivotal role in the implementation of the Social Security Act, then went on to summarize the work that the IRC was doing and discuss how that work might fit into the SSRC committees' larger plans.

294 Social Insurance Created and Undermined

A possible grant request to the foundation from Stewart is mentioned, along with the fact that the IRC would remain valuable in advising employers about meeting the requirements of the Social Security Act. In short, the IRC and Stewart would now have a more peripheral role than they did in the drafting of the act. These memos show beyond the shadow of a doubt that the Rockefeller Foundation was at the center of the network to amend the Social Security Act.

Although the SSRC's Public Administration Committee made many contributions to the development of the Social Security Board between 1935 and 1937, its Committee on Social Security took primary responsibility for Social Security in 1937, which made it possible for the Public Administration Committee to concentrate on other governmental issues. In 1937–1938 industrial relations expert Joseph Willits of the Wharton School, whose work with Rockefeller industrial relations experts and the SSRC reached back to the early 1920s, took over as chair of the Committee on Social Security. In addition, J. Douglas Brown joined the committee. He thereby provided another close link to the Rockefeller labor-relations network, and to the staff that wrote the Social Security Act as well. Then he became chair of the committee the next year.

The committee also included an AT&T executive, Chester I. Barnard, who was the president of New Jersey Bell Telephone; he had made somewhat of a scholarly name for himself with his lectures on enlightened management, which became a Harvard University Press book, entitled *The Functions of The Executive* (1938). The other member from the corporate community was Albert Linton, the president of a major insurance company in Philadelphia, Provident Mutual Life. In addition to Brown, there were three other university professors with expertise on unemployment or old-age benefits, along with the director of the Russell Sage Foundation, the head of the railway and steamship clerks union, and representatives of the American Public Welfare Association and the American Association of Social Workers.

There is evidence that the officers of the Rockefeller Foundation were "exerting direct control over appointments to the committee" (Fisher 1993, p. 148). For example, they vetoed the idea of including Leo Wolman, the professor of economics at Columbia, mentioned in Chapter 2, who served as an adviser to Hillman of the CIO and as a member of the original National Labor Board. Instead, the union leader for railway and steamship clerks was appointed. Then, too, the SSRC accepted a Rockefeller Foundation suggestion that a representative of the American Public Welfare Association be added to the committee.

The Clark Amendment Once Again

The first key issue facing the SSRC committees concerned the defeat of any attempt to revive the Clark Amendment. The task was assigned to the

Committee on Social Security, which hired a highly respected actuarial expert, Rainard B. Robbins, who had first worked on old-age pensions for the Carnegie Foundation for the Advancement of Teaching 15 years earlier. Robbins began by writing to the industrial relations officers at a wide range of companies, along with the relevant executives at six major insurance companies, to find out if they were favorable to the amendment. The way in which he operated can be seen in an exchange of letters he had with Marion Folsom of Eastman Kodak, who had served to the Committee on Economic Security's Advisory Council on Social Security.

Robbins' letter to Folsom on December 16, 1935, began by calling attention to the well-known people who served on the committee: "The Committee indicated by this letterhead has asked me to find for them, if possible, the views of a number of leading employers with reference to a provision for 'contracting-out' in the old age annuity sections of the Social Security law" (Robbins 1935). He then asked if Eastman Kodak had "reached a decision as to how it will modify its retirement plan, if at all," and invited Folsom to lunch if he happened to be coming to New York City in the next few weeks.

Folsom replied two days later saying he would be happy to discuss the issue, but first he noted that "I was quite interested in seeing the personnel of your committee; it is a high-grade committee and I am sure that this investigation will be very helpful" (Folsom 1935). In other words, the names on a letterhead do matter, which means that status matters in understanding power in America. He then went on to say he had originally supported the Clark Amendment, but that he had changed his mind because of the headaches of transferring funds to the government when an employee leaves before retirement and of dealing with government oversight. (These two issues were among the concerns mentioned in the IRC's Memorandum to Clients, No. 15.). After noting that Eastman Kodak already had supplemental plans to attract higher-wage workers to its factories in France, Belgium, and The Netherlands, where government pensions were low, Folsom said that the company would turn its current American pension plan into a supplemental plan.

According to the report written by Robbins (1936), there were many executives with views similar to those expressed by Folsom. Of the 17 who were acquainted with the details of the amendment, 13 were opposed to it, two were working to improve it, and two were undecided. When Robbins asked executives if they were aware of the various restrictions and standards built into the amendment, he learned that most of them replied, "I had not thought of that" (Robbins 1936, p. 9). Based on this line of questioning, perhaps we can infer that the questions asked by Robbins were also meant to educate executives about the amendment and to discourage them from supporting it.

In the case of insurance companies, Robbins found that five of the six had "no enthusiasm for the Clark Amendment" (Robbins 1936, p. 22). However, they did favor "the general idea of an employer being permitted to conduct his retirement plan independently of the government plan if a way can be found" (Robbins 1936, p. 9). At the same time, they did not see any practical way to improve upon the unsatisfactory Clark Amendment, so they were advising corporate employers to develop plans that supplemented the government plan (cf., Klein 2003, Chapter 3). Most corporate executives caught on fast, although a few ultraconservatives used the passage of the Social Security Act as an opportunity to shrink their plans (Quadagno 1988, p. 118).

Robbins' findings were made known to both friends and critics of the Clark Amendment. In addition, they were used by Latimer as one basis for a report he submitted to the Social Security Board on March 23, 1936. Latimer also drew upon his own personal discussions with executives and a letter to him from Brown, which reported that he had talked to "scores" of executives on a visit to several western states, but found "never even a wishful thought for the Clark Amendment." Brown then added, "I think Forster [the insurance agent who led the lobbying effort for the Clark Amendment] and Graham [an executive for one major insurance company] will have something to explain away" (Brown 1935). Latimer concluded his memorandum summarizing what he had learned from Brown's letter, the SSRC report, and his own inquiries by asserting that "With the possible exception of Standard Oil Company of New York, I know of no industrialists favoring the Clark Amendment, if such amendment has all or most of the following features" (Latimer 1936, p. 1).

The report then lists several basic features, such as being at least as favorable as the Social Security Act. When it came time for a joint Congressional committee to convene in the spring of 1936 to discuss the Clark Amendment, the meeting was cancelled. According to the recollections of one labor department lawyer assigned to help draft a new version of the Clark Amendment, the meeting was cancelled because Forster, and the insurance companies that had sided with him, no longer had any interest in it (Eliot 1992, p. 130–131). I therefore conclude yet again that the advantages of accepting and then building upon the government's social security program were understood by corporate moderates and their experts earlier than some historians and political scientists realize when they overlook the role of the IRC in creating the Social Security Act and of the SSRC in its implementation (e.g., Hacker and Pierson 2002; Klein 2003).

The SSRC Prepares New Amendments

Once the Clark Amendment was finally out of the way, SSRC committee members could turn their full attention to providing advice on Social

Security Board procedures and suggesting changes in the Social Security Act. The SSRC also arranged "for the employment of people when the government was unable to hire [them] because of the inflexibility of federal personnel recruitment or because of the restrictions against the employment of noncitizens" (Fisher 1993, p. 155). Even before the Social Security Board (later renamed the Social Security Administration) was established, the Committee on Social Security was providing technical assistance and helping with the selection of personnel:

> The committee assisted in the selection of personnel, brought together officials and nongovernmental experts, advised on research plans generally, and, on the details of specific studies, called attention to sources of pertinent data or accumulated experience, participated in innumerable technical conferences and discussions, and facilitated interagency coordination.
>
> (Fisher 1993, p. 150)

In addition to the massive informational, organizational, and staffing problems that faced such a major undertaking, the SSRC committees and the Social Security Board had to deal with the many criticisms that had been raised about the program by businesses, liberals, social workers, and supporters of the Townsend Plan and similar senior citizen pressure groups. (These pressure groups had gained strength, not lost it, after the passage of the Social Security Act, and often were able to directly influence state legislatures to improve their old-age assistance programs; this meant they were in a position where they could have an indirect influence on the Social Security Board and Congress to improve benefits (Amenta 2006, Chapter 7, especially p. 173).)

Corporate leaders were most exercised by the reserve fund that Roosevelt and his secretary of treasury had insisted upon at the last minute so that general tax revenues would not have to be used to finance the program decades later. They first of all worried that a large reserve fund would lead to pressures to raise benefits or be used to buy public enterprises, a concern that Teagle (1935) already had expressed to Swope three years earlier. They also feared that the money might be used to help pay for other government social-welfare projects, such as public housing. Their concern about what the government allegedly might do with the reserve fund is further evidence of their wariness about government and their determination to make sure it did not become any more independent than it already was.

On the other side of the fence, liberals, social workers, and advocates from old-age groups wanted to raise pension payments and extend them to more occupational groups than were originally covered, including the self-employed, agricultural workers, and domestic workers. Most

298 Social Insurance Created and Undermined

worrisome of all to the centrist social-insurance experts and leaders of the Social Security Board, many social workers and liberals wanted to merge the old-age insurance program with the old-age assistance plan for those who had not contributed enough money to the fund over the years to qualify for old-age insurance. The centrists rejected this option, also supported by the Townsend Plan and its imitators, as a form of welfare that could be easily stigmatized and cut back by ultraconservatives. Furthermore, the social workers still wanted to pay for this generous old-age benefit for everyone out of general tax funds.

The Corporate Community Lobbies for a New Advisory Council

In the face of the corporate community's criticisms of the reserve fund, which were soon voiced by Republicans in the Senate, the Social Security Board's chair, Arthur Altmeyer (the former John R. Commons student and Perkins' one-time assistant in the Department of Labor), reluctantly agreed to a temporary Advisory Council. It was charged with examining the program's problems closely and recommending any needed amendments to Congress. J. Douglas Brown, still serving on the SSRC's Committee on Social Security, became chair of the 25-member Advisory Council. One other member of the Committee on Social Security joined him on the Advisory Council, Linton of Provident Mutual Life. The council also included six other business leaders in addition to Linton (Swope of GE and Folsom of Eastman Kodak were among them, along with a high-level executive from U.S. Steel). Six union representatives were appointed, three from the AFL and three from the CIO. There were six other professors in addition to Brown, including Witte, by this time back to teaching economics at the University of Wisconsin, and economist Alvin Hansen, the former member of the Technical Board, who by this point was a professor at Harvard. The general secretary of the National Consumers' League was appointed, along with a recent president of the Association of Schools of Social Work.

Based on historian Edward Berkowitz's (1987, pp. 62–66) analysis of the Advisory Council's minutes, which read as if they are almost verbatim transcripts of the meetings, Witte, Linton, Folsom, and Brown took the lead in the arguments and compromises. The labor leaders once again seldom attended meetings and had very little impact, as had been the case in 1934–1935. It seems likely, then, that sociologist Donald Fisher (1993, p. 155), who studied the issue from the perspective of the Rockefeller Foundation's internal documents and its exchanges with the SSRC's Committee on Social Security, is correct when he concludes that research and reports by the Committee on Social Security "laid the basis for the 1939 amendments to the Social Security Act." For example, in a study similar to the earlier analysis of business leaders' attitudes toward the Clark Amendment, the Committee on Social Security surveyed organized labor, insurance companies, and other businesses on their attitudes toward various proposed modifications of the act. The results of the survey very likely provided Brown and Linton with a good sense of what amendments would be acceptable to all parties.

After months of negotiations, usually with Witte in one corner and Linton and Folsom in the other, Brown was able to fashion a compromise that satisfied just about everyone. To begin with, all parties agreed that the reserve fund should be whittled down to a "reasonable contingency" size by several means. They included raising benefits, providing higher benefits for married couples, extending benefits to widows at age 65 and to the dependent children of deceased recipients, and starting to pay out benefits in 1940 rather than waiting until 1942, as originally planned (Berkowitz 1987, p. 72). Furthermore, all concerned could agree to a payment schedule that gave a slight boost to low-income retirees while restraining benefits at the top. Liberals, social workers, organized labor, and Townsendites favored these changes because of their concern that low-income people might not otherwise have enough money to live on. The changes suited Keynesian economists such as Hansen because they put money into the hands of those most likely to spend it and avoided the drag on the economy that a reserve fund might create.

As part of this bargain, the insurance companies and other corporations were reassured that payroll taxes would be kept as low as possible. The corporate moderates also appreciated the fact that the reserve fund would decline, although the issue of its continuing existence was purposely left ambiguous. Additionally, insurance companies liked the compromise because it left plenty of room for their profitable private plans for employees with higher incomes, especially for the corporate executive plans that were their largest customer target. To hurry things along, Linton even helped finance some of the liberal reformers who lobbied the Congress for "adequacy" in old-age pensions (Sass 1997, p. 282, ftn 17).

Congress accepted most of these recommendations, but no new occupational categories were added, which reflected the continuing desire of the Southern Democrats and ultraconservatives to exclude low-wage workers, especially agricultural workers. Very significantly in terms of future arguments over the solidity of Social Security reserves, the 1939 amendments put tax collections earmarked for Social Security into an inviolate trust fund. Based on a strong unanimous statement from the advisory council, and its endorsement by Congress, the corporate moderates and their experts in the policy-planning network thought they had "to put to rest claims that the Treasury bonds in which the Social Security funds were invested were somehow not real and in some way represented a misuse of funds..." (Altman 2005, p. 132).

300 Social Insurance Created and Undermined

The ultraconservatives had made false claims about the alleged shakiness of the reserve funds from the moment the Social Security Act passed, so the transformation of the reserves into a trust fund, based on 1,000 years of Anglo-Saxon and American custom, precedents, and laws, did not deter them in the least from continuing their efforts. They were determined to undermine public confidence in a government program they heartily despised as contrary to their deeply held market fundamentalism and their claims about the need for individual autonomy and a limited role for government in caring for citizens. As shown in Chapter 8, libertarians revived and augmented these efforts in the 1970s as part of their deliberately "devious and deceptive" strategy to undermine Social Security (MacLean 2017, pp. 177–181 for the libertarian plan, and p. 178 for the quote).

The 1940–1947 Social Security Advisory Council

The conservative coalition made possible by the 1938 elections froze Social Security pensions during the eight-year period following the enactment of the 1939 amendments. It did so in an attempt to put an end to the expansionary plans for the Social Security Act being developed by the Wisconsin reformers that staffed what was by then called the Social Security Administration. As a result, means-tested old-age assistance became more important in terms of both number of recipients and the size of the benefits, putting guaranteed pensions in a precarious position by the late 1940s (Brown 1999, pp. 112–113). By 1947, however, all moderates and many ultraconservatives in the corporate community were in general agreement that expansionary changes could be made in old-age insurance, thanks in fair measure to the conservative way in which the system was administered. This change also involved ongoing educational efforts within the corporate community by Committee for Economic Development (CED) trustee Folsom of Eastman Kodak, who chaired the social-insurance committees of both the NAM and the Chamber of Commerce (Manza 1995, p. 370). At this point, Congress agreed to appoint yet another Advisory Council to reconsider Social Security.

The chair of U.S. Steel headed the new Advisory Council, which should not come as a shock by now, especially since he also served on the Advisory Council leading to the 1939 amendments. But it is a little surprising that he rarely attended meetings and left most decisions to the associate chair, Sumner Slichter, a Harvard economist. Slichter was well known in the corporate community as a key economic adviser to the CED. Slichter also was a consultant for several major corporations and had two brothers who were corporate executives.

As the de facto leader of the Advisory Council, Slichter worked closely with the member with the most experience on these matters, J. Douglas Brown, who had helped write the old-age provisions of the original act and then chaired the 1938 Advisory Council. The new council also included two business holdovers from the previous council, Folsom and Albert Linton, the insurance company executive. Along with a policy analyst from the AFL and another from the CIO, Slichter, Brown, Folsom, and Linton were part of a six-person steering committee (Altman 2005, pp. 152–153).

At Brown's suggestion, the steering committee hired a former Social Security administrator, Robert M. Ball. Brown had come to know Ball after Ball took a position at a new University-Government Center on Social Security, which provided training sessions for professors and federal employees about the Social Security program. Ball, whose previous work as a Social Security employee had given him the opportunity to develop an understanding of the business viewpoint, proved to be both knowledgeable and pragmatic, which made it possible for him to introduce new ideas and fashion compromises, a role he was to play for the next 36 years in relation to new developments in the Social Security system (Berkowitz 2003, pp. 55–73).

The representatives of organized labor, by this point eager and forceful participants in the process, wanted to raise the level of income that could be taxed for Social Security purposes to $4,800, with most corporate leaders insisting on a much lower level, $3,000. In the end, the advisory council compromised at $4,200 (Altman 2005, pp. 155, 165). Benefits were increased by 77 percent, but most of this increase simply overcame the 74 percent rise in prices since the first payments were made, and the increase was only two-thirds as large as the rise in wages since 1939, so retired workers were falling behind those who were employed in terms of their purchasing power. The Advisory Council also recommended the inclusion of self-employed, agricultural, and domestic workers, but most agricultural workers in the South would still be excluded because they worked part-time or seasonally (Quadagno 1988, p. 148). A majority of the Advisory Council also advocated the addition of disability insurance, but Folsom and Linton were opposed, as were the Chamber of Commerce and the American Medical Association.

Congress once again accepted most of the recommendations, but pared down the number of occupations to be included. Disability insurance was supported in the Senate, but it lost to the conservative coalition in the House. In general, Social Security became somewhat more inclusive, but not more generous. More importantly from the liberal-labor perspective, the changes seemed to guarantee that old-age pensions, not means-tested old-age assistance, would be the way in which most of the elderly would receive benefits in the future.

Small Gains During the Eisenhower Years

When Republicans won control of both the White House and Congress in 1952 for the first time since 1928, ultraconservatives in the corporate community and Congress made their usual pitch to limit old-age benefits to a single flat sum for anyone over age 65, whatever a person's work record or previous income levels. But at this point organized labor was poised to put up a major battle, and in any case President Dwight Eisenhower rejected the ultraconservative's proposal. He thereby sided with the corporate moderates, who favored the strengthening of Social Security through raising the cap on the amount of a person's income subject to the Social Security tax and slight increases in benefit levels. Moderates also wanted to enlarge the Social Security pool by expanding coverage to include public employees, self-employed professionals, farmer-owners, farm workers, and domestic workers, and to make payments slightly higher for some beneficiaries by only counting years in which the person could work enough months to contribute to the pension fund (Altman 2005, pp. 180–181). The ultraconservatives and the AMA opposed all of these improvements when they were presented to Congress, but the new amendments to the Social Security Act passed in August 1954, after self-employed professionals were removed due to AMA lobbying. It was a clear victory for the corporate moderates and the liberal-labor alliance.

A year later, the liberal-labor alliance won its first victory on its own on a Social Security initiative, due to concessions it made to the Southern Democrats, on an amendment to include disability benefits. Based on concerted Congressional lobbying and a compromise with insurance companies and Southern Democrats, the amendment covering all disabled workers passed in the House in spite of the fact that the Eisenhower Administration and the AMA opposed it. Then the conservative coalition in the Senate Finance Committee delayed the bill. The bill went to the floor for a vote by the full Senate after the finance committee ended up in a 6-6 deadlock as to whether it should be sent forward. At this point liberal and labor lobbyists made two key concessions that opened the way for partial success. They supported an amendment that would give states control of the program, which met the key demand by Southern Democrats. Then they agreed to exclude employees under age 50, which neutralized opposition from insurance companies. In exchange, a majority of Southern Democrats in the Senate voted for the compromise and the insurance industry did not lobby against the bill (Quadagno 2005, pp. 53–55).

In 1958 Congress extended the disability program to include benefits for the families of disabled workers, and in 1960 it was extended to include employees under age 50. It was at this point that conflict over Social Security more or less subsided for the time being. Social Security now seemed to be a fact of life, except for libertarians and other ultraconservatives. At about the same time, however, concerns about health insurance were rising for a confluence of reasons.

The Passage of Medicare and Medicaid

After the complete failure of health-insurance legislation during the Progressive Era and the New Deal, the passage of legislation establishing Medicare and Medicaid as amendments to the Social Security Act in July 1965, was in many ways a major triumph for the liberal-labor alliance over the American Medical Association and the ultraconservatives in the corporate community. However, the reasons for this success, and its considerable limitations, reveal a great deal about the power of corporate interests in the United States, which ultimately benefited from this legislation and were strengthened by it.

Although the economics and politics of the Medicare battle are detailed and complicated, the essence of the matter from a power perspective is that health services are a perfect example of "market failure" for many reasons and in all senses of the term: for example, you can't know when you will need health services, can't shop around while you are sick, don't have enough information to make a sensible choice even if you have the time to find the right surgeon beforehand, and usually can't afford the high-to-astronomical costs that go with major illnesses (Arrow 1963, for the classic argument in terms of irregular demand, product uncertainty, and other economic concepts; Haas-Wilson 2001; Kuttner 1997, Chapter 4, for a general analysis and summary). The most dramatic issue in relation to market failure is seen in the events that gradually led to health insurance for everyone in most industrial democracies, through employers or government, and to coverage for about 75–85 percent of Americans in the second half of the twentieth century.

The owners of retail stores can boot customers out if they don't have the money to pay for the products or services they desire. But hospitals, and most physicians, cannot easily refuse treatment to patients who come to emergency rooms without money or insurance, whether due to ethical qualms or potentially embarrassing negative publicity. Still, the practice was extensive enough that eventually, in 1986, the government passed the Emergency Medical Treatment and Active Labor Act, which prohibits the "dumping" of patients and assesses fines on hospitals that are found guilty of breaking the law. As a result, the practice declined considerably, but the costs of the unpaid treatment of indigent patients were 5.8 percent of hospital costs at the end of the twentieth century (Altman and Shactman 2011, p. 265; Meyer 2016). Nor can doctors and hospitals ignore the moral qualms of refusing to treat elderly patients who could benefit from the many new but expensive methods of prolonging lives.

Since refusal of services to those who can't afford to pay is illegal as well as unethical, hospitals and physicians often try to recover their costs by charging more for paying patients and/or private insurance companies ("cost-shifting"), which is one of the key reasons why government

304 Social Insurance Created and Undermined

support for healthcare eventually became necessary. That is, the financial needs of hospitals overcame their anti-government ideology. At the same time, the more general change toward government-supported healthcare in one form or another for as many citizens as possible occurred primarily because the liberal-labor alliance forced the issue. The alliance then made enough concessions to gain the cooperation of the American Medical Association and the votes of some members of the conservative coalition serving on key Congressional committees.

As explained in Chapter 6, the efforts to establish government health insurance in the United States stretched back to the failed attempts by the American Association for Labor Legislation in the Progressive Era and the Committee on Economic Security during the New Deal. The liberal-labor alliance and New Deal Democrats in Congress had revived the issue in the late 1930s, but once the conservative coalition came to power in Congress in 1939, there was little likelihood of any success; at the same time, Roosevelt turned his attention to the looming wars in Europe and the Pacific (Starr 2017, pp. 275–277). As a result, hospitals organized local hospital insurance programs to keep payments flowing in, while at the same time fending off both government and commercial insurers. These local programs led to a nationwide Blue Cross Association in 1938, with the hospitals lobbying state governments to exempt this nonprofit venture from laws that regulate commercial insurance regulation (Quadagno 2005, p. 23). Physicians followed suit and created insurance plans to cover their fees, which in 1943 eventuated in Blue Shield, "a national organization of medical care plans designed and controlled by doctors" (Quadagno 2005, p. 25).

Once World War II ended in 1945, Democratic President Harry S. Truman called for a national health-insurance plan. However, he did not put forward any legislation because he knew it would have no chance against the conservative coalition. Showing once again the pivotal role of Southern Democrats, the first federal government payments for medical services (outside of the Veterans Administration) did not materialize until the Southern Democrats agreed to subsidies in 1946 for the construction of hospitals, but on the condition that they could not be integrated in states with legalized segregation (Poen 1979, p. 87). This legislation was the result of a lobbying campaign by the American Hospital Association (AHA), which began as early as 1939, and had the strong support of the construction industry and the building-trades unions.

By the late 1940s, many nonprofit and public hospitals, which predominated in that era, signaled that they could no longer continue to care for indigent patients without government help. Similarly, the leaders of Blue Cross told government officials that they could not offer affordable medical insurance to working-age adults as long as they had to sell insurance to the elderly as well. They were especially handicapped in competing with the relatively few, but large, for-profit insurance companies, which developed formulas ("experience ratings") that tended to eliminate elderly patients and concentrate on healthy young adults ("cherry picking" for profits). In order to deal with its cost problems, Blue Cross also began to work with trade unions that had health plans, which laid the groundwork for a possible insurance industry/labor union alliance (Poen 1979, p. 137; Quadagno 2005, p. 24).

The AMA, the Chamber of Commerce, and the conservative coalition blocked a liberal-labor plan for government health insurance for everyone in 1950, but allowed Congress to pass "an obscure provision" that "provided matching funds to the states for payments to doctors and hospitals for medical services to welfare recipients," which bolstered a program that had been "growing quietly since the Depression" (Starr 2017, p. 286). This program, which provided what were called vendor payments for the purpose of reimbursing physicians and hospitals, became one of the prototypes for Medicaid in 1965. The acceptance of these vendor payments by the conservative coalition clearly reveals that Medicaid is a way to give government subsidies to physicians and hospitals to provide services to low-income Americans, but it is as a matter of course stigmatized by ultra-conservatives as a free handout to the undeserving poor.

In the wake of their defeat in 1950, liberals and labor leaders reconsidered an idea first proposed in the late 1930s and early 1940s, the creation of a hospital insurance plan that would be restricted to the Social Security Administration's elderly beneficiaries. However, the idea of limiting a new proposal to include only the elderly, with the thought that success might open the way for including younger adults at a later date, was initially rejected at the top levels of the Social Security Administration because of their commitment to health insurance for all. Moreover, organized labor's interest in government health insurance began to decline somewhat because of its increasing ability to achieve healthcare for its members and retired members through union contracts. In making this choice, union leaders fully understood that their stance left non-unionized workers holding the bag, but they also knew they could not win universal health insurance without first diluting the strength of the conservative coalition by defeating some of its members in elections, as already discussed in Chapter 3. The most liberal of the labor leaders hoped they could eventually bring about this change through creating black-white voting alliances in the South, but this possibility never materialized.

One sociological analysis claims that this situation led over the next 15–20 years to a "health policy trap" (Starr 2011, pp. 122–123). According to this analysis, the expensive and complicated combination of employment-based insurance and Medicare made it difficult, if not impossible, to fashion government programs to help the significant minority of Americans who cannot afford health insurance. After 1965, there were too many

306 Social Insurance Created and Undermined

people that did not want to risk major changes in a system that was by and large satisfactory for them (Starr 2011, pp. 122–123).The liberal-labor alliance is thus hamstrung, and the power of the corporate moderates on government insurance benefits is also limited to some extent, even if they happen to favor some health-care reforms, as they often did in the years after 1970.

From a corporate-dominance perspective, this policy trap was created by the same historical and structural factors that tilt all power struggles in favor of the corporate rich and the plantations owners. The existence of both a Southern agricultural economy based on slave or low-wage labor, and the electoral rules that lead inexorably to a two-party system, made the policy trap inevitable. As a result of these two factors, the conservative coalition could dominate on health-insurance issues, just as it did on other issues of concern to it. By the late 1940s and early 1950s, the liberal-labor alliance therefore had to settle for corporate-based health-care benefits, but attaining them was a major struggle in any case, even with the reasonably strong unions of the 1950s. However, victory was made possible, as mentioned in Chapter 3, by the precedents set by the National War Labor Board and the IRS during World War II, along with a Supreme Court ruling in 1949, which rejected U.S. Steel's refusal to grant benefits to its unionized workforce (Brown 1999, pp. 153–156 for the original account).

Although unions were able to win many forms of benefits for their members, there were limits to how much unions could gain on health-insurance issues by the late 1950s, which fairly quickly made government health insurance for the elderly a priority for the AFL-CIO. This change in direction occurred in 1957, shortly after the automobile companies insisted that the UAW should not "demand negotiations for those in retirement" in the next round of collective bargaining (Quadagno 2005, p. 57). Even without this ultimatum from the automobile executives, union officials were painfully aware that more benefits for retirees meant lower wage increases for their current workers, which was a very difficult trade-off. Union leaders also knew it was a propitious moment for a new campaign because hospitals were coming under even more financial pressure. In fact, the AHA had let it be known that it was rethinking its official opposition to government support for taking care of low-income patients of all ages (Altman 2005, p. 186).

As part of its new campaign for hospital insurance, the AFL-CIO provided the major financial support for a new senior citizen's council, which proved to be very effective in organizing Social Security recipients as a pressure group (Marmor 2000, p. 18). The campaign also had the support of professional associations for social workers and nurses. In addition, union health-insurance experts and legislative strategists worked closely with two experienced hands that knew the system best. Robert M. Ball, back at the Social Security Administration after his brief time out of government, provided advice from the inside. Wilbur Cohen, who had worked for the Social Security Administration from 1935 until 1956, when the Eisenhower Administration pushed him out, took time off from his position as a professor of social work at the University of Michigan and helped with strategy and lobbying (Berkowitz 2003, Chapters 2 and 3).

The new approach adopted by the liberal-labor alliance was not immediately successful. The conservative coalition, supported by substantial lobbying by the AMA, the newly formed Health Insurance Association of America, the Pharmaceutical Manufacturers Association, the Chamber of Commerce, and the Farm Bureau, rejected hospital insurance for the elderly. But the AMA and the private insurance companies, whether nonprofit or for-profit, also felt compelled to come up with alternative plans, most of which relied on federal subsidies to state governments or private insurance programs. At this point the AMA even asked its members to consider lowering their fees to elderly patients as a way to fend off government health insurance. This idea went nowhere, of course, but it reveals once again the degree to which the AMA disliked potential government regulation.

Liberal-labor hopes for health insurance were frustrated by the Democrats' loss of several dozen House seats in the 1960 elections. Their proposals therefore died in the Ways and Means Committee during the Kennedy years. The decisions to kill the proposals were made by the chair of Ways and Means, Wilbur Mills. A Southern Democrat from Arkansas. Mills knew that sentiment for hospital insurance for the elderly was about evenly distributed pro and con within his committee, and short of a majority in the overall House. He did not want to force his colleagues "to clarity their public record with anything so concrete as a yes or no vote when there was little to be gained by it" (Marmor 2000, pp. 40–41). At the same time, the Austin-Boston alliance, still managed by two of its leaders from the late 1930s, agreed to the Kennedy Administration's request to enlarge the Ways and Means Committee. They also agreed that no one would be appointed to the committee that might keep Medicare from going to the House floor if and when there were enough votes.

By 1962–1963, most Medicare opponents knew that they were fighting a losing battle. Rearguard legislation had passed in 1960 to give federal matching grants to states to support hospital care for low-income patients but it was helping a mere 1 percent of these patients. Only 32 states were willing to pay the state's share, and most of the meager federal subsidies were going to five large industrial states. Nationwide, the number of elderly Americans, most of whom were unable to pay for hospital care, grew from 12 to 17.5 million between 1950 and 1962. The American Hospital Association came to the conclusion that its member hospitals needed some form of major federal support as costs increased. Furthermore, the commercial insurance companies were doubtful that their new attempts to insure the elderly could be profitable. They began to think in terms of selling supplemental insurance to fill any gaps in a government plan (Quadagno 2005, p. 72). Still, neither the American Hospital Association nor the Health Insurance Association of America dropped its official opposition to Medicare. Both continued to resist the liberal-labor plan as much as possible, while at the same time trying to shape it to their liking.

Due to the Democrats' strategy of delay mixed with gradual change, and the realization by their opponents that private insurance was not sufficient, the Democratic landslide in 1964 meant that some form of health insurance for the elderly would be passed in the next Congressional session. The Democrats came forward with their proposal for hospital insurance, which the Republicans countered through a bill adapted from a plan written by experts at Aetna, the giant private insurer. The Republican plan called for supplementary private insurance, in part subsidized by the government, which would pay for physicians' services as well as hospitalization. At the same time, the AMA tried to stave off the Democrats' proposal by updating past Republican plans for federal subsidies for the purchase of private hospital care. Renamed Eldercare, the AMA plan also included provisions for payment for physicians' services, so it was obvious that the physicians wanted to make sure they would increase their incomes if the legislation did pass.

The AMA's clout had been augmented in 1964 through an arrangement with the powerful tobacco lobby, through which the AMA's Education and Research Foundation received $10 million from the tobacco interests for further study of what the Surgeon General had announced to be an established fact, that smoking is "causally related to lung cancer in men" (Proctor 2011, p. 235). One historian called this arrangement a "hush fund funded by cigarette manufacturers as part of a deal struck (in 1964) with the AMA to help stave off Medicare" (Proctor 2011, p. 189). The deal increased the reach of the AMA to Southern members of Congress, most of whom supported Big Tobacco, and usually voted with the conservative coalition (Kluger 1996, pp. 285–287).

The Ways and Means Committee then decided to include all three proposals in a single package: Medicare A, which provides hospital and nursing-home insurance; Medicare B, which pays the doctors' bills; and Medicaid, an expansion of the AMA's Eldercare proposal, to include hospital and physician payments for low-income patients of any age. The Republican's emphasis on private insurance, paid for at least in part by government subsidies, reappeared throughout the next 35 years, and became a feature of the Affordable Care Act in 2010. As to Medicaid, which actually had its origins in the 1950 legislation to reimburse states for some of their medical expenses related to welfare recipients, it left healthcare for African American citizens in the 17 segregationist states in the hands of the white Southern Democrats, who had opposed the civil rights and voting rights bills. More generally, this decision "relegated the poor to a variable, lower tier of protection, with sharply restricted eligibility in the South and Southwest" (Starr Forthcoming, p. 1).

Despite this major compromise, many Republicans and the AMA still resisted, as did the Chamber of Commerce, of course, with the opponents fearing any governmental expansion as well the loss of professional autonomy for physicians. Northern and Southern Democrats, at this point mostly united, were therefore forced to include private insurance companies as intermediaries for Part B, giving the insurers an opening into a market in which they previously had only minor involvement. In the process, insurance companies also won the right to administer Part A (hospital insurance) as well. As for the AMA, it continued to resist on its own. It was successful in its insistence that physicians that worked in hospital settings, such as radiologists and anesthesiologists, must be able to maintain their independence by submitting their bills directly to the insurance companies, rather than through the hospitals, as both the hospitals and Medicare advocates desired (Marmor 2000, p. 54).

As this brief overview demonstrates, Medicare and Medicaid never would have been created without the unflagging efforts of the liberal-labor alliance, which received most of its funding on this issue from the AFL-CIO. Ironically, though, the liberal-labor alliance ended up fashioning a compromise that perhaps saved the private insurance system. According to the AFL-CIO's chief strategist on government medical insurance, the liberal-labor alliance had no other choice than to save the private insurance system in order to obtain government insurance for the elderly. "What we were really doing," he explained, "was making voluntary insurance viable for almost all of the working population in the country" by having government pay for the elderly patients who made private insurance unprofitable. "Now without Medicare," he continued, "had this burden existed as a threat or had they attempted to meet it, their system would have broken down, which in either case would inevitably have brought on national health insurance" (Quadagno 2005, p. 75). The AFL-CIO strategist may have been wrong to think that the system could not be patched up, and overly optimistic in thinking that the conservative coalition would have accepted national health insurance, as future events showed. But the fact remains that the Republicans did force a compromise that greatly bolstered and benefited the burgeoning medical-industrial component of the corporate community, and at the same time unexpectedly eliminated any strong public backing for national health insurance for everyone.

To add insult to injury, the union officials that had done so much to bring about Medicare were not consulted on key details of the final legislation. The result was an agreement between President Johnson and his many congressional friends and allies in the conservative coalition, which gave insurance companies the large administrative role mentioned two

310 Social Insurance Created and Undermined

paragraphs ago. As union experts presciently feared, this bargain opened the way for rampant inflation, especially because any attempts at price controls were also eliminated out of fear that physicians might boycott the program. According to two of the union experts that helped formulate the AFL-CIO's policies and strategies related to health and medicine, the labor movement actually had very little direct access to the White House on this issue. They thought the consultations the administration held with labor leaders were mostly meant to keep "the labor boys happy without anything of real substance happening as a result." Labor had "fought like the dickens against letting the insurance companies into this program" out of cost concerns, so "[i]t was disappointing to be working on this for years and years in every detail, and then within a matter of an hour have the entire picture changed totally and be presented with this and not really have had a part in it" (Quadagno 2005, pp. 74–75, for the information and quotations in this paragraph).

In the eyes of another sociologist, the longtime Social Security advocate, Wilbur Cohen, was also culpable: "As the administration's representative in the negotiations, Cohen bears responsibility for the legislation's abject concessions to the healthcare industry" (Starr Forthcoming, p. 7). As Cohen later explained, the legislation paid hospitals on the basis of costs, which can quickly become inflated, because "that is what the hospitals wanted" (Starr Forthcoming, pp. 7–8). But the same source shows that Johnson was willing to give the providers of medical services what they wanted to avoid confrontations with the conservative coalition. When Johnson asked Cohen if a doctor could charge "what he wants," Cohen explained that decisions about physicians' fees would be made by insurance companies, such as Blue Shield, which would "have to do all the policing so that the government would have its long hand," at which point Johnson interrupted to say, "All right, that's good" (Starr Forthcoming, p. 8).

From a corporate-dominance perspective, there was no way Cohen could have done better, as shown by the fate that befell the ideas put forward by the union experts. If there was going to be Medicare and Medicaid, it would have to be on terms acceptable to the corporate community and plantation owners. This claim is also supported by the subsequent failures of liberal-labor efforts to enact their versions of government health insurance, as shown in Chapter 9. This point also reveals the limits on any institutional analysis of power in the United States that does not give enough weight to the institutions undergirding the power elite and the policy-planning network, or stress class conflict on economic issues.

Due to Johnson's rejection of various policy suggestions put forth by the union experts and the liberals in Congress, the costs of the program were soon twice what the administration originally estimated, led by physicians and corporate medical interests. The result was a wage-push inflation of the first order, at the very time that corporate CEOs, most of them Republicans, were blaming union demands for the rising inflation. In fact, "both hospital and physician charges more than doubled their past average rate of yearly increase" in 1966, the program's first year in operation (Marmor 2000, p. 51). In the process, the health-insurance companies became a powerful lobby in and of themselves as their profits grew rapidly. For-profit hospitals were able to enter the market in a significant way for the first time, and earn outsized profits. They often did so by buying, or buying out and closing, a large number of nonprofit and public hospitals.

More generally, medicine became an organized business sector that had strong incentives to overcharge patients and the government due to the fact that taxpayer monies were underwriting a big part of the bill. The new system thereby created a relentless inflationary pressure in relation to medical costs. Over the first five years after the passage of Medicare and Medicaid, hospital costs increased 14 percent, far more than most other costs were rising at the time (Marmor 2000, p. 98). Within a few years, health spending as a percentage of Gross Domestic Product was at least twice as high as in other industrialized democracies, such as Canada, France, and Germany, leading President Nixon to keep his wage-price freeze on healthcare as well as food, oil, and construction after he had ended it in general (Starr 2017, p. 399). Meanwhile, millions of people still had no insurance coverage of any kind because they did not work for a large corporation or a government agency, but were not poor enough to qualify for Medicaid (Krugman 2007, Chapter 11).

In 1968, in a vain attempt to remedy the defects in the government's health-insurance program, UAW chief Walter Reuther kicked off a new drive for national health insurance for everyone. He eventually enlisted the entire liberal-labor alliance and gained the backing of the most famous of the liberal senators, Ted Kennedy of Massachusetts. Reuther even thought that some corporate leaders might be supportive of his efforts now that they faced stronger foreign competition and were looking for ways to lower their wage-and-benefit costs (Quadagno 2005, p. 111).

Instead, the corporate moderates gradually developed their own plans to foster greater coverage of employees through private health-care plans. The most important and enduring codification of these plans was contained in a CED report, *Building a National Health-Care System* (1973). It officially appeared somewhat belatedly for several reasons, including the death of the chair of the subcommittee in late 1971. Its eclectic sources are made clear by footnotes in the report. They included studies of key issues by corporate executives in New York as leaders on Governor Nelson Rockefeller's Committee on Hospital Costs in 1965, and on his *Report On Health Services and Costs* in 1971, with one or more CED trustees and other corporate executives serving on these committees (CED 1973, pp. 47, 74). In general, corporate executives thought highly of the new prepaid plans for comprehensive medical care, which are generically called "managed care." In particular, the CED had "sung the virtues" of managed care through Health Maintenance Organizations (HMOs) ever since they were included in legislation introduced in 1971 by President Nixon, based on presentations by corporate-oriented policy experts (Starr 2017, p. 396).

Although the CED report had been delayed, it did appear at a moment when it seemed possible that a more complete health-insurance plan for working-age adults might be enacted. With all 50 members of its Research and Policy Committee approving the statement, as did all but the physician and pharmaceutical representatives on the subcommittee, its summary of recommendations called for the "enactment of a health-insurance program that would require that a basic level of protection be made available to all Americans regardless of their means, age, or other conditions" (CED 1973, p. 22).

The report began with a mandate that all large-scale employers had to offer prepaid health-insurance plans for their employees, which would be supported by contributions from both employers and employees. As part of this support for mandated corporate health insurance, the CED incorporated its argument for purchasing this healthcare from HMOs, which would compete among themselves on the basis of price and adequacy of services in providing the whole range of health services for business employees, Medicare patients, and Medicaid recipients. The liberal-labor alliance had successfully resisted Nixon's 1971 initiative that included a provision incorporating HMOs, but HMOs were given federal endorsement and financial support eight months after the CED report appeared. The Health Maintenance Organization and Resources Development Act of 1973 provided $375 million in grants and loans to encourage the kind of HMOs envisioned by the corporate moderates (Brown 1983). It included a strong push to make HMOs part of health coverage by requiring that companies with 25 or more employees and an established healthcare plan had to "provide an HMO option" if there was one within their geographical area (Quadagno 2005, p. 375).

Smaller employers, on the other hand, would receive some degree of help in their payments by being part of private insurance pools, thereby making any government funding of employee health insurance unnecessary. Once again, the CED wanted these health-insurance pools to make as much use as possible of HMOs. Finally, there would be federally sponsored community trusteeships with basic benefits for everyone else, including "the poor or near-poor," who would not have to pay premiums or co-payments (CED 1973, p. 25). The Medicaid program would have responsibility for overseeing the community trusteeships, but would gradually assume a more residual role (CED 1973, p. 25).

As for the issue later called the "individual mandate" which became a bugaboo for many ultraconservatives as the ultimate in governmental assumption of a Big Brother role, the CED made clear that the purchase of health insurance would have to be legally required for everyone above a specified income level (those below that level would be proportionately subsidized). The report crisply and firmly stated, quite contrary to what ultraconservatives claimed, that "disputes over whether the government has the right to do this have long been resolved" in terms of both public and private insurance (CED 1973, p. 65). It then listed as examples "the mandated coverage of occupational injury, old-age, survivors, disability, health for the aged, unemployment, automobile insurance, and temporary disability in a few jurisdictions" (CED 1973, p. 65). Most of all, mandates to buy health insurance were essential for insurance companies to be able to offer profitable insurance plans to everyone without excluding people with preexisting conditions.

Perhaps even more surprising, the CED suggested there might be a need for temporary "governmental controls over some or all health care charges and wages" at first because "market forces work imperfectly to supply care at reasonable costs;" controls therefore might be needed to avoid "runaway costs" during the "transition period" (CED 1973, pp. 25, 75, for this twice-stated point). Since ultraconservatives inside and outside the corporate community always have disputed the legality of individual mandates, as well as any need for price controls outside of wartime, this CED report provides further evidence that there are moderate conservatives within the corporate community.

Despite the willingness of some leaders in the corporate community to consider their own version of universal health insurance when Nixon introduced new legislation in 1974, union leaders and many liberals held out for universal government health insurance paid for by payroll taxes and managed by the Social Security Administration. They felt they had been burned in 1965 by Johnson's decisions, and that the 1974 elections would strengthen the liberal-labor alliance in Congress. At his point, Senator Kennedy urged unions to compromise, but they were adamant. In fact, they felt betrayed by Kennedy's decision to offer an alternative bill not to their liking; they wanted no part of any healthcare legislation that included private insurance companies, and they objected to high co-payments and deductibles (Altman and Shactman 2011, pp. 55–58). As a result, no legislation was passed because the liberal-labor alliance did not have the strength to prevail in Congress, and the ultraconservatives and the conservative coalition did not like several features of the corporate moderates' plan (Quadagno 2005, pp. 110–124).

As will be shown in Chapter 9, the Affordable Care Act of 2010 shares several commonalities with the 1973 CED proposal, which demonstrates that the corporate moderates held firm for 37 years as to what kind of universal health coverage they were willing to accept. Medicare would continue for those over age 65 in both plans, companies had to offer health insurance to their employees (those with one or more full-time employees in the CED plan, those with over 50 employees in the Obama plan), and individuals without coverage would be required to purchase health coverage (through community trusts in the CED plan, through state-level insurance exchanges in the Obama plan). Both plans provided government subsidies for insurance purchases by low-income people that were not employed and not eligible for either Medicare or Medicaid. The main difference is that the Obama proposal had to exempt millions of small businesses from offering insurance plans and give a bigger role to private insurance companies, which by then had vastly larger health-insurance programs than they did earlier (e.g., Potter 2010; Quadagno 2011; Quadagno 2014).

References

Altman, Nancy. 2005. *The battle for Social Security: From FDR's vision to Bush's gamble*. New York: John Wiley & Sons.

Altman, Stuart and David Shactman. 2011. *Power, politics, and universal health care: The inside story of a century-long battle*. Amherst, NY: Prometheus Books.

Amenta, Edwin. 2006. *When movements matter: The Townsend Plan and the rise of social security*. Princeton: Princeton University Press.

Arrow, Kenneth. 1963. "Uncertainty and the welfare economics of medical care." *American Economic Review* 53:941–973.

Barnard, Chester. 1938. *The functions of the executive*. Cambridge: Harvard University Press.

Berkowitz, Edward. 1987. "The first Advisory Council and the 1939 amendments." Pp. 55–78 in *Social Security after fifty: Success and failures*, edited by E. Berkowitz. New York: Greenwood Press.

———. 2003. *Robert Ball and the politics of Social Security*. Madison: University of Wisconsin Press.

Brown, J. Douglas. 1935. "Letter to Murray Latimer, August 12." In *Latimer Papers, Box 1, Folder 2*. Washington: Special Collections, George Washington University Library.

Brown, Lawrence. 1983. *Politics and health care organization: HMOs as federal policy*. Washington The Brookings Institution.

Brown, Michael K. 1999. *Race, money and the American welfare state*. Ithaca: Cornell University Press.

CED. 1973. *Building a national health-care system: A statement on national policy*. New York: Committee for Economic Development.

Eliot, Thomas. 1992. *Recollections of the New Deal: When the people mattered*. Boston: Northeastern University Press.

Fisher, Donald. 1993. *Fundamental development of the social sciences: Rockefeller philanthropy and the United States Social Science Research Council*. Ann Arbor: University of Michigan Press.

Folsom, Marion. 1935. "Letter to Rainard Robbins, December 18." In *Folsom Papers, Box 108, Folder 3*. Rochester: University of Rochester Library.

Haas-Wilson, Deborah. 2001. "Arrow and the information market failure in health care: The changing content and sources of health care information." *Journal of Health Politics, Policy and Law* 26:1031–1044.

Hacker, Jacob and Paul Pierson. 2002. "Business power and social policy: Employers and the formation of the American welfare state." *Politics & Society* 30:277–325.

Klein, Jennifer. 2003. *For all these rights: Business, labor, and the shaping of America's public-private welfare state.* Princeton: Princeton University Press.

Kluger, Richard. 1996. *Ashes to ashes: America's hundred year cigarette war, the public health, and the unabashed triumph of Philip Morris.* New York: Alfred A. Knopf.

Krugman, Paul. 2007. *The conscience of a liberal.* New York: W. W. Norton & Co.

Kuttner, Robert. 1997. *Everything for sale: The virtues and limits of markets.* New York: Knopf.

Latimer, Murray. 1936. "Memorandum to members of the Social Security Board." In *Altmeyer Papers, Box 2, Folder on the Clark Amendment.* Madison: Wisconsin Historical Society Archives.

MacLean, Nancy. 2017. *Democracy in chains: The deep history of the radical right's stealthy plan for America.* New York: Viking.

Manza, Jeff. 1995. "Policy experts and political change during the New Deal." Ph.D. dissertation Thesis, Sociology, University of California, Berkeley, Berkeley.

Marmor, Theodore. 2000. *The politics of Medicare.* Hawthorne, NY: Aldine de Gruyter.

May, Stacy. 1936. "Letter to Joseph P. Harris, February 1." In *Rockefeller Foundation Collection, Record Group 1.1, Series 200S, Box 397, Folder 4714.* Sleepy Hollow, NY: Rockefeller Archive Center.

Meyer, Harris 2016. "Why patients still need EMTALA." *Modern Healthcare,* March 26. https://www.modernhealthcare.com/article/20160326/MAGAZINE/303289881.

Poen, Monte. 1979. *Harry S. Truman versus the medical lobby: The genesis of Medicare.* Columbia, MO: University of Missouri Press.

Potter, Wendell. 2010. *Deadly spin: An insurance company insider speaks out on how corporate PR is killing health care and deceiving Americans.* New York: Bloomsbury Press.

Proctor, Robert. 2011. *Golden holocaust: Origins of the cigarette catastrophe and the case for abolition.* Berkeley: University of California Press.

Quadagno, Jill. 1988. *The transformation of old age security: Class and politics in the American welfare state.* Chicago: University of Chicago Press.

———. 2005. *One nation, uninsured: Why the U.S. has no national health insurance.* New York: Oxford University Press.

———. 2011. "Interest-group influence on the Patient Protection and Affordability Act of 2010: Winners and losers in the health care reform debate." *Journal of Health Politics, Policy and Law* 36:449–453.

———. 2014. "Right-wing conspiracy? Socialist plot? The origins of the Patient Protection and Affordable Care Act." *Journal of Health Politics, Policy and Law* 39:35–56.

Robbins, Rainard. 1935. "Letter to Marion Folsom, December 16." In *Folsom Papers, Box 108, Folder 3.* Rochester: University of Rochester Library.

316 Social Insurance Created and Undermined

———. 1936. "Preliminary report on the status of industrial pension plans as affected by old age benefits sections of the Social Security Act." In *Social Science Research Council Archives, Record Group 1.1., Box 261*. Sleepy Hollow, NY: Rockefeller Archive Center.

Sass, Steven A. 1997. *The promise of private pensions: The first hundred years*. Cambridge: Harvard University Press.

Starr, Paul. 2011. *Remedy and reaction: The peculiar American struggle over health care reform*. New Haven Yale University Press.

———. 2017. *The social transformation of American medicine: The rise of a sovereign profession and the making of a vast industry*. New York Basic Books.

———. Forthcoming. "The Health Care Legacy of the Great Society." In *Reshaping the federal government: The policy and management legacies of the Johnson years*, edited by N. J. Glickman, L. E. Lynn, and R. H. Wilson.

Teagle, Walter. 1935. "Letter to Gerard Swope, October 1." In *General Electric Archives, Downs Collection, 898.15.1, Series 5, Box A-19a*. Schenectady: Schenectady Museum Archive.

Van Sickle, John. 1936. "Memorandum on interview with Bryce Stewart, March 24." In *Rockefeller Foundation Collection, Record Group 1.1, Series 200S, Box 348, Folder 4146*. Sleepy Hollow, NY: Rockefeller Archive Center.

Chapter 8

Social Disruption, New Social Benefits, and then Cutbacks, 1967–1999

In the fall of 1967, after rioting and destruction in Detroit, Newark, and dozens of other cities, the moderate conservatives in the corporate community and the White House began to think about raising taxes and committing a significant amount of resources to dealing with African American exclusion and poverty. Based on the close ties Johnson had established with the corporate moderates, he made a major effort at restoring order through a corporate jobs program that would replace an unsuccessful government job-training program (Brown 1999, pp. 287–290). The new initiative developed quickly after he invited leading executives to the White House in late 1967 and asked for their help.

Calling themselves the National Alliance of Businessmen, the corporate leaders agreed to hire and train long-term unemployed youth for entry-level jobs in the private sector. This new initiative worked closely with the nonprofit National Urban Coalition, which had been created about the same time to encourage dialogue between leaders in black and white communities, along with advocating greater government attention to urban problems. A former Carnegie Corporation president, who recently had served as secretary of health, education and welfare, chaired the National Urban Coalition's board of directors; its board also included a cross-section of the corporate community, along with labor leaders, civil rights leaders, and local public officials.

Managed by executives who were on loan from corporations, the National Alliance of Businessmen and its publicists estimated that it hired approximately 430,000 people over the next two years and provided summer employment for another 300,000. The program was formally subsidized by the federal government, but only one-fourth of the corporate participants applied for payments because of the government's documentation and auditing procedures. The corporate community therefore saw its effort as a voluntary one, "a chance to show what the private sector could do" (Delton 2009, p. 229).

As conditions nonetheless went from bad to worse, the Committee for Economic Development (CED) took a step in a more moderate direction

318 Social Insurance Created and Undermined

with regard to government social spending, shortly after the formation of the National Alliance of Businessmen. It did so first of all through the publication in 1968 of a new set of policy recommendations in *The National Economy and the Vietnam War* (CED 1968). Kennedy's former secretary of treasury, a Wall Street financier recently elected to the CED board of trustees, joined with eight other members of the subcommittee in unanimously recommending a temporary tax increase, restraint in the growth of the money supply, and a reduction in the projected rate of increase in government expenditures. In terms of spending restraints, the subcommittee, rather surprisingly, both at the time and in retrospect, called for cuts in programs that in one way or another aided the corporate community: agribusiness subsidies, highway construction, improvements for rivers and dams, and the space program.

Rather notably, the policy statement abandoned CED's efforts in 1966 to reduce social spending as part of a focus on controlling inflation without tax increases. After stating that expenditures for new programs related to health, manpower training, welfare, education, housing, and community development had risen from $5.9 billion in 1960 to $7.5 billion in 1964, and an estimated $20.1 billion for 1969, the report pointed out that this was still only one-seventh of total federal spending (CED 1968, pp. 37–38). In making its recommendations, the subcommittee had the advice of two Democratic and two Republican economists. The Business Council changed to a somewhat similar perspective about the same time (McQuaid 1982, pp. 248–254).

Furthermore, the CED leaders said that most of the money that would become available when the war ended should be used to deal with problems of poverty and racial tension, rather than reducing taxes, so they perhaps perceived the domestic unrest as a serious matter by this point: "We, and we believe the country generally, are impressed by the need to do more than we have been doing to reduce extremes of poverty, improve the conditions of urban life, improve education, and to give positive support to equal opportunity to all without racial discrimination" (CED 1968, p. 45). Although the report was overly optimistic about how quickly the war would end, it proved to be the first of several CED reports that in effect expressed approval for the ongoing efforts by both Democratic and Republican administrations to strengthen the federal government's social-insurance and social-support capabilities. This support for most social-insurance programs lasted into the 1970s, well after the all-out offensive against unions began with the election of Richard Nixon to the presidency and the strengthening of the conservative coalition in Congress.

The efforts by the National Alliance of Businessmen and the CED, along with the government's increased spending in urban hot spots, seemed to be doing little good in terms of quelling unrest as the 1968 elections drew near. Since the summer of 1964, and in the aftermath of the assassination of Martin Luther King, Jr. in April 1968, there had been 329 major disturbances in 257 cities, resulting in 220 deaths, 8,371 injuries, and 52,629 arrests (Downes 1970). The primary impact of their efforts was to prompt corporations to seek out and promote well-educated African American executives. In the past, black executives had been relegated to minor positions, or else forced to find work in government agencies (Collins 1997). Diversification of the corporate community and the power elite, not the amelioration of poverty, became the corporate community's primary response to the pressures from the black community (Zweigenhaft and Domhoff 2003; Zweigenhaft and Domhoff 2018, Chapter 4).

CED Recommendations and the Nixon Administration

As a result of the 1968 elections, the problem of trying to decrease unrest through social spending fell to President Richard M. Nixon, who also wanted to strengthen his presidential majority in 1972 at the same time. As was the case during the Kennedy-Johnson years, Nixon's White House initiatives often drew upon, or paralleled, CED policy statements. Although some social scientists see this continued social spending as a puzzle or enigma (e.g., Block and Somers 2014, p. 194; Hacker and Pierson 2010; Pierson and Skocpol 2007), it is very comprehensible in the context of the concern with further potential upheaval that motivated the corporate moderates to a considerable degree until as late as 1974–1975.

Big Gains for Social Security in the Nixon Years

As part of an effort to solidify the elderly vote for Republicans, Nixon focused on spending increases for Social Security, which had received little attention during the battles over passing Medicare and Medicaid in 1965, and in the face of the upheavals generated by inner-city uprisings and turmoil, The relatively minor cost-of-living adjustments (COLAs) occasionally legislated by Congress barely kept up with inflation, if at all. Within the context of the corporate moderates' general support for social insurance, Nixon felt free to woo elderly voters by increasing Social Security benefits by 15 percent in 1969, 10 percent in 1971, and 20 percent in 1972, albeit in the face of growing inflation.

Then a major breakthrough occurred in the months before the 1972 presidential election. Nixon indicated his support for a seemingly small, but momentous advance in Social Security, which legislated automatic cost-of-living increases that would begin in 1975. In connection with the significant increases in benefits between 1969 and 1972, the automatic COLAs momentarily seemed to guarantee that most elderly Americans could live the remainder of their lives above the poverty line, a dramatic change from just a few years earlier. In addition, Congress put benefits for low-income, blind, disabled, and elderly people into a new federal program, Supplement Security Income, which was funded out of general revenues and administered by the Social Security Administration (Altman 2005, p. 211; Bernstein and Brodshaug 1988, p. 34). Liberals in Congress enthusiastically supported all of these changes, as did moderate Republicans, which created a winning coalition. More generally, the contrast between the corporate moderates' support for government insurance programs and the campaign they were carrying out against unions at the time, as discussed in Chapters 5 and 6, could not be more dramatic. This difference continued a pattern that began in 1935, as readers may recall.

New Forms of Social Benefits

In addition to the increases in benefits for those who were elderly, blind, or handicapped, Nixon and the corporate moderates made a concerted effort in the early 1970s to create a program that provided families with a minimum guaranteed level of income. Although that plan, entitled the Family Assistance Plan (FAP), ultimately failed, the legislative battle led to policy clarity in the corporate community. Future increases in governmental social support for low-income people would come through two programs that in no way discomfited the corporate community, agribusiness, and the Southern economy—and in fact benefited them in some ways.

Showing the depth of the corporate moderates' support for the kind of social spending Nixon was soon to propose, the CED issued a series of reports on improving welfare (1970a), job training (1970b), and urban education (1971), which built on several years of work on these issues by corporate moderates and their advisers. In terms of the first and most important of the three, the family assistance plan, the initial influence was a series of meetings by business leaders. They were called together in March 1967 by Governor Nelson Rockefeller of New York to answer the question: "If the problem of public welfare was given to you, what would you recommend as sound public policy in the next decade?" Led by the CEO of Xerox, the group came to the conclusion that it could support either of two alternatives.

The first alternative called for a "negative income tax." Both Keynesian and monetary economists advocated this idea, which boiled down to mandating the Internal Revenue Service to send checks to individuals if their incomes fell below a specified minimum. The second possibility called for "family allowances," in which government would send monthly payments to families with low incomes to provide them with help in raising their children. Governor Rockefeller's corporate committee said that it "leans in the direction of a negative income tax" as long as the system contains "strong incentives to work" (Moynihan 1973, pp. 56–57). A presidential commission appointed by Johnson in 1967, with a CED trustee—who also served as the CEO of Chicago and Northwestern Railways—as its chair, similarly recommended a negative income tax in a report that appeared in November 1969, but it did not include a work requirement.

The new CED family-support statement (1970a) appeared just after the House of Representatives passed Nixon's version of welfare reform and income maintenance, the Family Assistance Plan, which had been developed by a staff of Democrats and Republican experts. The Nixon and CED plans both built on the idea of family allowances, not a negative income tax, which meant that they would not cover single individuals or couples without children. The Nixon plan called for a minimum annual income benefit of $2,400 through a combination of government payments and food stamps for families with children. The new plan helped the working poor as much as, or more than, those on welfare, contained a workfare component for those on welfare, and was especially favorable for low-income African American families in the South. It was fashioned so that it would not cost more than $4 billion in the first year, which was considered the feasible economic and political limit by the Nixon Administration.

Ultraconservatives in the corporate community waged a spirited campaign to defeat the bill. Members of the conservative coalition serving on the Senate's most powerful committee, the 17-member Finance Committee, blocked it in the summer of 1970. This majority consisted of seven Republicans from small states with few welfare recipients or African Americans (Arizona, Delaware, Idaho, Iowa, Nebraska, Utah, and Wyoming), and three Southern Democrats. These members had been placed on the committee to guard against attempts to raise taxes, reduce agricultural subsidies, or lower the depletion allowances granted to the domestic oil industry. Their rejection of the plan was spearheaded by one of the staunchest anti-welfare Republicans in the Senate, the senior senator from Delaware, a rich state with very low welfare benefits. He was joined in his attack by the committee's chair, a Southern Democrat from Louisiana, who claimed to be for the legislation in principle. However, he sabotaged it in numerous ways, including misleading statements about its provisions and procedural delays that kept it from coming to the Senate floor in a timely fashion as a rider on other bills (Welsh 1973, p. 17).

Although a representative of the NAM testified that one of its own committees had found the plan's incentive structure workable, ultraconservative Senators insisted that they wanted more work incentives in the bill. As they well knew, their demands would raise the cost of the program well beyond what were considered reasonable limits. They also complained that the support for working adults was an expansion of welfare, which frustrated the proponents because they saw their program as a step toward shrinking the welfare rolls. On the liberal side of the table, an increase in work incentives raised the danger of forcing single mothers of pre-school children to work outside the home. This upset liberal Democrats and was anathema to a coalition of leftists and welfare recipients, who had created a National Welfare Rights Organization to bring pressure for higher welfare benefits (Piven and Cloward 1977, Chapter 5).

After the White House made numerous revisions in the program in a vain attempt to satisfy members of the conservative coalition on the Senate committee, the final vote of 10–6 against the plan included three negative votes from liberal Democrats. For the most part, though, wrote one of the expert advisers who helped shape the plan, the defeat was "a triumph of conservative strategy" (Moynihan 1973, p. 534). Ultraconservatives on the committee made the program too costly through work incentives for any Republican to vote for it, and too seemingly punitive for all but one of the four liberal Democrats to lend support.

Efforts were made to revive the plan in 1972, and a consensus between liberal Democrats and Nixon Republicans seemed to be close at one point. After once again passing the House, the new version lost in a 10–4 vote in the Senate Finance Committee, with liberals on one side and conservatives on the other. By that point there was less pressure to institute a new program. There had been no major urban riots since the summer of 1968, the upsurge in welfare recipients had leveled off, and there were fewer likely jobs for current welfare recipients at a time when the unemployment rate was increasing. In the final analysis, however, the program was blocked by the Southern Democrats' racial animus and their desire to maintain a low-wage workforce, in conjunction with the anti-government mentality of hard-core ultraconservative Republicans (Quadagno 1990; Quadagno 1994, Chapter 5).

More important in the long run, however, the debate over the various policy options for helping low-income families legitimated year-end support payments from the federal government for the working poor with a spouse or children. The payments came to be called the "Earned Income Tax Credit" (EITC), a far more positive name than "negative income tax." It is in effect a "transfer program that happens to be administered through the tax code" (Hoynes and Rothstein 2016, p. 3, whose new analysis also summarizes the large literature in economics on the EITC).

From the corporate point of view, the EITC program is a wage subsidy to business that is paid for out of general taxes and could be understood as an offset for the taxes low-income workers pay into Social Security through the payroll tax (Quadagno 1994, p. 122). Moreover, members of the conservative coalition, who always oppose both welfare payments and the creation of government jobs, could champion it as an incentive to work and a bonus. In the 1970s it had particular appeal to Southern Democrats, who had "repeatedly blocked or reduced social welfare benefits for the poor (including Aid to Dependent Children and its successor, Aid For Families With Dependent Children)," which inadvertently "paved the way for the EITC" (Howard 1997, pp. 67, 74, 143–144). Southern Democrats also made the EITC program more attractive to anti-government ultraconservatives by excluding public-sector workers, which made it possible to keep wages low for state and local government employees in the South. In 2018 dollars, the program provided up to $6,336 for a family with two or more children.

The general support the program attracted is revealed by the fact that liberals and conservatives in Congress agreed during the Ford Administration to double the level of income necessary before EITC payments were gradually phased out. Then the EITC benefits were increased slightly and made available to workers with somewhat higher incomes during the Carter Administration, as one part of a big push for large tax cuts in 1977 led by the Business Roundtable, and the program became permanent for the first time as well (Howard 1997, p. 144). The EITC program later received its largest expansion ever in 1993.

Government Cutbacks, Private Ameliorations

While the corporate community and agribusiness owners were slowly finding a way to provide some semblance of support for low-income people in the face of economic displacements and periodic social upheaval, it gradually became clear by 1972 or 1973 that the turmoil of the 1960s might be a thing of the past. The civil rights movement gradually grew smaller and less confrontational after it attained two of its most important goals, civil rights and voting rights in the South, even though African Americans still faced many caste-like obstacles. At this point a small percentage of African Americans, sometimes with the help of new scholarship programs, could enroll in previously all-white colleges and then obtain white-collar, professional, and high management positions (Collins 1997; Zweigenhaft and Domhoff 2003; Zweigenhaft and Domhoff 2018, Chapter 4).

With the military draft ended and American involvement in the land war in Vietnam winding down, young adult males could pursue their educational and career aspirations without fear of facing injury or death in Southeast Asia. There had been no student demonstrations of any moment since the massive spontaneous response to the Cambodian invasion in the spring of 1970. Feminists and environmental activists were being accepted into graduate schools or working through channels. In particular, the women who fought for expanded rights went to law school, medical school, and business school in far greater numbers than at any time in the past—and eventually would rise, albeit in small numbers, to high positions in business, politics, and federal agencies (Zweigenhaft and Domhoff 2018, Chapter 3).

Moreover, with no sign of inner-city upheavals since 1968, urban landowners and commercial real estate developers in the local and regional growth coalitions could focus on improving land values through plans for tax-subsidized people magnets, such as convention centers, music halls, museums, medical centers, university expansions, and sports arenas and stadiums (e.g., Sanders 1992; Sanders 2014). Due to ample federal funds for law and order, city leaders were also prepared by this point to deal with any future social disruptions with immediate and overwhelming force, by deploying the well-armed Special Weapons and Tactics (SWAT) teams that had been developed post-1968 in 200 cities across the country (Kraska and Kaeppler 1997, p. 6, Figure 1).

As routinization slowly returned, the Nixon Administration and subsequent Republican administrations gradually began a series of cuts or alterations in Johnson's Great Society programs: reducing funds for the Job Corps and closing most of its offices, giving governors a veto over Legal Services programs, reducing Office of Economic Opportunity funding by $292.1 million, limiting federal authority to reduce school desegregation, and defeating the Family Assistance Plan. What remained of Johnson's War on Poverty was divided up and tucked away within existing departments (Quadagno 1994, p. 175).

Most of all, there were cuts in subsidies for rent support and for building low-income housing. By 1968, 29 percent of new housing was due to federal subsidies, but that figure was down to 14 percent in 1972. In addition, low-income families had to pay 30 percent of their incomes toward housing, up from 25 percent (Quadagno 1994, p. 114). While these cuts were being made, a growing portion of the Department of Housing and Urban Development's budget was spent on nearly 1,000 urban renewal projects that had not been completed. The remaining urban grants from the Johnson Administration's Model Cities program were largely shifted from social service programs for the poor to "hardware" for the "most affluent communities," which were primarily white (Frieden and Kaplan 1975, pp. 259, 261, 264–265). Some of the money was spent on tennis court complexes in high-income neighborhoods and the extension of municipal golf courses.

As a result of these shifts, the drive to improve downtown land values through gentrification eliminated most of the remaining single-rooms and small apartments that were once available as rentals in or near downtown areas. Finally, the closing of state mental hospitals across the country, which were not replaced by the promised community-based facilities to nearly the extent they were needed, added to the homeless population (Rosenthal 1994, pp. 12–17, 152–166 for concise analyses of the processes through which ultraconservatives created homelessness in the United States).

By the late 1970s a small part of these cuts was being ameliorated by a network of nonprofit social-service providers that had slowly and haltingly developed around the Ford Foundation since the 1950s. These organizations were originally meant to aid and protect the burgeoning federal urban renewal programs of that era. They were strongly supported by the

Social Disruption and Benefits; Cutbacks   325

corporate moderates as one way to ensure adequate postwar demand, improve property values, and expand the postwar economy (e.g., Greer 1965; Rossi and Dentler 1961). Some of these programs had been incorporated into President Johnson's War on Poverty in slightly altered and expanded form, but by and large it was clear by 1965 that they had failed in terms of their main purposes.

At this point the Ford Foundation decided that inner-city issues would have to be approached from a new angle. The new programs would serve as "a proxy for local government, concentrating much more on economic development and on residential and commercial building and renewal, a distinction of considerable significance" compared to past poverty programs (Magat, 1979, p. 123). In theoretical terms, they were an attempt to create an organizational structure relatively independent of local government for improving conditions in the inner city (Domhoff 2005, for the detailed story and an assessment of its success; Liou and Stroh 1998). Most of these organizations took the form of Community Development Corporations (CDCs). They aimed to stimulate community development programs that would provide affordable housing and financial support for new small businesses, as well as providing some educational and social services. Although the CDCs grew in the early 1970s, they did not have nearly enough money to have a serious impact. The Ford Foundation tried to overcome this problem by creating a Local Initiatives Support Corporation in 1979 with an initial grant of $4.5 million, along with another $4.8 million from six corporate sponsors. Its purpose was to raise money for CDCs in many different cities, which would eventually establish offices around the country to service both urban and rural areas.

As part of the Reagan Administration's efforts to control social spending after massive tax cuts for wealthy individuals and corporations, there were further large cutbacks in social spending via an Omnibus Budget Reconciliation Act. The act reduced the *rate of growth* in spending on, among many social programs, housing subsidies, food stamps, unemployment insurance, school lunches, and welfare payments, so the impacts were gradual (Mayhew 2005, Table 4.1). Many of the cuts were gradual or small, but the declining budget did lead to closing down the Community Services Administration and other neighborhood-oriented agencies, which ultraconservatives considered outposts of the left. By 1985, federal funding for community development activities had diminished by $1 billion. But the cuts in subsidies for housing were even more drastic, dropping from $26.1 billion to $2.1 billion between 1981 and 1985. Once again, ultraconservatives created an even larger homeless population, which generated more tensions in cities throughout the country.

To partially offset the impacts of the Reagan cuts on housing and social services, the Ford Foundation donated just over $9 million between 1982 and 1991 to a new nonprofit housing investment company, the Enterprise

326 Social Insurance Created and Undermined

Foundation, which had been created recently by a real estate developer (Liou and Stroh 1998, p. 583; Peirce and Steinbach 1987). The Ford Foundation also developed a new Community Development Partnership Strategy in 1983, which called for the pooling of resources from the private sector, foundations, government agencies, and nonprofit institutions to support efforts to revitalize neighborhoods. As of 2002, the foundation had given $30 million to this partnership strategy.

While the Ford Foundation was advocating partnerships, the nonprofit Cleveland Housing Network, backed by the leadership of Standard Oil of Ohio, lobbied for a new federal tax break for wealthy individuals to induce them to invest in low-income housing. Called the Low Income Housing Tax Credit, it was built on an idea from an Indiana insurance company. It had strong support from both the Local Initiatives Support Corporation and the Enterprise Foundation (Guthrie and McQuarrie 2005; Tittle 1992, pp. 239–240; Yin 2001, p. 89).

The real breakthrough as far as building more low-income housing is concerned came when someone (it is not clear exactly where the idea came from) suggested that corporations as well as wealthy individuals should be offered this tax inducement. The legislation sailed through Congress (Guthrie and McQuarrie 2005). Although it took a few years for this new tax break to be used by the corporate rich in a widespread way, it grew by leaps and bounds after corporate executives established the nonprofit National Equity Fund to publicize the Low-Income Housing Tax Credit, which was reaffirmed and as a result further legitimated by Congress in 1990. Both the Local Initiatives Support Corporation and the Enterprise Foundation made extensive use of the new loophole to provide large sums of money for projects sponsored by CDCs. By the early 1990s, there were over 2,000 CDCs involved in a range of neighborhood improvement activities, based on support by the Local Initiatives Support Corporation, and the number had almost doubled by 2005. As of the early twenty-first century, roughly 90 percent of the low-cost housing built each year was financed by tax credits given to for-profit corporations (Guthrie and McQuarrie 2005).

The new Low Income Housing Tax Credit, in conjunction with the CDCs, the Local Initiatives Support Corporation, the Enterprise Fund, the National Equity Fund, and numerous other nonprofit agencies funded by corporations, gradually morphed into a new private network to deal with problems in inner-city neighborhoods in a way that was satisfactory to both factions within the power elite. The ultraconservatives were satisfied because tax breaks reduced the direct role of the federal government and encouraged initiatives by the private sector. Moderate conservatives liked it because it could deliver needed resources to the inner city and at the same time minimize a direct role by local government agencies. In effect, there was now the potential for a private government of nonprofit organizations controlled by the foundations and corporations, with CDCs at the center.

The social problems facing the urban poor were not even close to being solved by the corporate and foundation funding for the urban nonprofit networks. The Johnson-era government support programs, which were originally focused on downtown neighborhoods, were slashed, redirected toward the middle class, and/or dismantled altogether in the 1970s and 1980s. But the nonprofit CDCs and the constellation of organizations around them, when joined with the corporate-funded United Way, churches, and local charities, were able to provide just enough support for some semblance of order to persist in and near the downtown areas of cities (e.g., Domhoff 2005; Domhoff 2014, pp. 116–117).

The Right Turn on the Social Security Act

Shortly after Social Security benefits reached a level in the mid-1970s at which they were alleviating poverty among the elderly and making it possible for a widowed parent to raise children in at least modest circumstances, the program began to have financial problems. These problems soon led both corporate moderates and ultraconservatives to call for drastic immediate curtailments, which were eventually whittled down by the liberal-labor alliance to smaller and more gradual cuts. In the long run, though, these cutbacks added up to significant erosions from the high point that had just been reached.

The problems began with the large increase in inflation in and after 1973, generated for the most part by the sudden and unexpected increases in the price of foodstuffs, raw materials, and most of all oil, which caused prices to rise faster than wages. This totally unprecedented situation distorted benefit formulas in ways that involve technicalities that are not relevant to the story being told in this chapter (see Altman 2005, p. 216 on the lack of funds and her Chapter 12 for an explanation of why the trust fund had financial problems). The problems were compounded by the fact that the recent indexing of Social Security benefits made it impossible to cut monthly benefits through inflation, as had been the case in the past. In addition, more people than expected were leaving the workforce through successful claims for disability benefits (Kingson 1984, p. 134). This combination of events caused pensions and benefits to rise faster than payroll tax payments, resulting in a decline in the small cushion in the Social Security Trust Fund. As early as 1975, Social Security actuaries warned that the funds could be gone by 1979.

Despite the general thrust of the right turn that was taking place at the time, Congress dealt with the problem in 1977 in a bipartisan way by raising the maximum income that could be taxed for Social Security purposes and increasing payroll taxes equally on employers and employees.

Nevertheless, the outcome did involve slight long-term cutbacks in benefits. Actuaries then reassured the general public in the annual trustees' report that the amendments "restore the financial soundness of the cash benefit program throughout the remainder of this century and into the early years of the next one" (Bernstein and Brodshaug 1988, pp. 34–35).

However, the second round of oil shocks in 1979 unexpectedly proved them wrong. Instead of 28 percent inflation and 13 percent growth in real wages between 1978 and 1982, there was 60 percent inflation and a decline in real-wage growth by 7 percent (Pierson 1994, p. 65). The ensuing economic upheaval once again threw the projected relationship between payroll tax collections and cost-of-living increases out of balance. Further adjustments therefore were seen as necessary so the fund would not be exhausted during 1983 (Altman 2005, p. 222; Kingson 1984, pp. 136–138).

Although Congress had been able to fashion a reasonable compromise for dealing with this second wave of unanticipated inflation, ultraconservatives inside and outside the government realized they might have a new opportunity. Nixon and Ford's gradual cutbacks, along with Republican gains in the 1978 elections, might make it possible to define the new problem as a major crisis, not the temporary shortfall projected by centrist and liberal experts. Ultraconservatives now claimed that Social Security was another reason to worry about future government debt, even though it was funded by payroll taxes, not federal income and excise taxes.

It was in these altered circumstances that the new ultraconservative ("libertarian") think tank funded by Charles and David Koch, the multibillionaire owners of one of the largest privately owned corporations in the country, put the new anti-government economic ideas created by James B. Buchanan and other "public-choice" theorists into action (Estes 1983; Myles 1981). Called the Cato Institute because the Roman leader Cato The Elder had declared that "Carthage must be destroyed" (MacLean 2017, p. 140), the Cato Institute and other ultraconservative think tanks used the new actuarial assessments to claim that experts were either covering up the deep problems in the system or else did not know what they were talking about. Based on these distortions, they published several reports that readily gained dramatic coverage in the media, in part because any "crisis" attracts readers and viewers, in part because the media tries to report all sides of an issue.

The Cato Institute, joined by the equally anti-government Heritage Foundation, called what they were doing a "Leninist strategy," meaning that they were completely determined to revolutionize the system of social insurance no matter what actions were needed to win (Altman 2005, Chapter 14; MacLean 2017, pp. 138–140, 180). To this end, their reports talked of "bankruptcy," even though the worst-case scenario involved shortfalls of 4 percent to 10 percent without any increases in payroll taxes, and even though bankruptcy was impossible because payroll taxes always would continue to flow into the Social Security Trust Fund. The inviolate nature of the trust fund established by Congress in 1939 was now ignored or forgotten by the anti-government libertarians as part of their efforts to define the situation as a crisis (Estes 1983; Myles 1981).

Taking advantage of the ultraconservative media campaign based on Buchanan's general suggestions, Congressional conservatives made a further change in Social Security in 1980 by reducing disability benefits on the grounds that they were overly generous (Bernstein and Brodshaug 1988, pp. 34–35). Then came a right turn on Social Security by the corporate moderates, which became fully apparent during the Reagan Administration.

Corporate Moderates Join the Attack on Social Security

The Reagan Administration's original attempt to cut Social Security, which in part backfired, revealed that the corporate moderates, as exemplified by reports from the CED, were now ready to join with ultraconservatives in limiting the program severely. However, the liberal-labor alliance, even though it was on the defensive by then, was able to hold on to most of the basic features of the Social Security program because it made concessions and played its cards well. Moreover, it had some built-in advantages due to the structure of the program, such as its inclusiveness, the fact that higher earnings lead to higher payroll taxes and higher pensions, and the sheer number of people already receiving benefits due to its long history (Pierson 1994, Chapter 3).

As was the case just two years earlier, relatively easy adjustments could have been made, but this time the corporate rich and the power elite mounted an even larger scare campaign. Although national surveys soon reported that most people, and especially those under 35, believed that the system would be bankrupt by the time they were eligible to receive benefits, the respondents also made it clear they wanted to preserve the system through tax increases. Their fears were encouraging to the libertarian ultraconservatives who wanted to privatize Social Security, but the fact that most people wanted to preserve the current system was encouraging for the program's supporters (Bernstein and Brodshaug 1988, p. 42).

The CED contributed to the crisis atmosphere with a report entitled *Reforming Retirement Policies*, which claimed "a retirement disaster is on the way early in the twenty-first century." Using projections that assumed a declining birth rate and an increasing number of retired workers, the CED warned that the rate of growth in the labor force might decline and that older workers would become a "burden" on "future generations" (CED 1981, pp. 3–5). In addition, the presumed shrinkage in the growth of the workforce, which was in fact being countered by millions of immigrants

330 Social Insurance Created and Undermined

from Latin American and Asia in the 1970s, supposedly meant that older workers who remained productive might have to continue working for the sake of the economy. The CED report therefore concluded that the retirement age should be gradually raised two months a year until it reached age 68 in the year 2000. After all, people were living longer, although in fact it was only people in the upper half of the income distribution that were living longer among those who made it to age 65. If death rates by income class are taken into account, the payroll taxes paid into the system by shorter-lived blue-collar workers would be funding the retirement lives of the top 20–30 percent of the income ladder. The CED also called for changes in the formula used to determine cost-of-living increases, which were said to "overcompensate" for inflation (CED 1981, pp. 3–5).

As with other issues, the seemingly nonpartisan, nonpolitical CED did extensive non-lobbying lobbying in relation to this report. One retrospective CED historical document (N.D.), put together in the late 1980s by a longtime CED staff member, reported that trustees and staff discussed it with every member of the Senate Finance Committee as well as with every member of the House Ways and Means Committee (CED, N.D.). The CED's chief lobbyist of the previous few years, by then on the White House staff as a deputy assistant for the president for legislative affairs, encouraged the distribution of the CED report. On February 11, 1981, he wrote a note from the White House to a member of the CED's public relations staff, saying that "the report will come in handy," and in the process urged that if one of CED's employees "would only hurry with the retirement statement, we might be able to do something positive about Social Security (while assuring the integrity of the program, of course)" (Duberstein 1981).

At this point, Reagan, with the encouragement of his most zealous advisers, overplayed his hand. In doing so he drew on suggestions from a Social Security Task Force set up during the 1980 presidential campaign, which was chaired by an economist at the ultraconservative Hoover Institution. More generally, the task force consisted primarily of free-market economists at several universities. Building on this report, one of Reagan's libertarian advisers, who served as the director of the Office of Management and Budget, created a draconian plan in early May 1981. It would have produced twice as much savings as were actually needed through a variety of benefit cuts, with a special—and politically shortsighted—focus on solving the administration's looming general deficit problems with large immediate cuts in Social Security, even though the deficit problem had everything to do with the Reagan income tax cuts and nothing to do with Social Security funds (Altman 2005, p. 231; Kingson 1984, pp. 140–141).

The result of this series of audacious blunders was a barrage of criticism aimed at the White House, including from some Republicans, who

Social Disruption and Benefits; Cutbacks   331

feared that such drastic changes might put them in danger of losing their Congressional seats in 1982. The proposed policies also solidified and energized Save Our Security, a liberal-labor-elderly leadership group formed in 1979, which spoke for a coalition of nearly 100 liberal, labor, and senior citizens' organizations. The well-known liberal of that era, Wilbur Cohen, whose involvement in Social Security stretched back to a minor role in the creation of the original Social Security Act, and included his strategic role in the passage of Medicare, served as the Save Our Security chair.

The ambitious White House plan was withdrawn before it was formally presented to Congress. But the unfavorable publicity it received short-circuited the efforts to cut Social Security that were moving forward quietly in the House under the direction of a Southern Democrat from Texas, who chaired the Social Security Subcommittee of the Ways and Means Committee. His plan would have dealt with the short-term budgeting problems by means of a six-month delay in the next cost-of-living adjustment (COLA) and with the elimination of long-term shortfalls by increasing the retirement age to 68 between 1990 and 2000, both of which were consistent with the CED's recommendations. His plan also would have eliminated minimum benefits and payments to college children of deceased beneficiaries. Due to the outcry caused by the Reagan plan, the ultraconservatives had to settle in 1981 for a cutback in payments to the 775,000 children of deceased beneficiaries who were 22 years old or older and still in college. The average reductions of $259 a month for these students saved $700 million the first year (less than 1 percent of the Social Security payments in 1982). (It is through frequent small nicks such as this one, a form of budget guerilla warfare, that the ultraconservatives gradually created the new poverty discussed earlier in this chapter.)

Faced with a potential political backlash, the White House suggested to Thomas ("Tip") O'Neill (a Boston Democrat, a leader of the Austin-Boston Alliance, and the Speaker of the House) that the president and Congress should jointly appoint a bipartisan Commission on Social Security to examine the issues and make recommendations. The plan called for Reagan to select three Republicans and two Democrats. In addition, the Republican leader of the Senate would suggest three Republicans and (with the advice of the Senate Minority Leader) two Democrats. Finally, O'Neill would add three Democrats and (with the advice of the Republican Minority Leader) two Republicans. This formula led to an eight-to-seven majority for the Republicans, but the more important point is that conservatives outnumbered liberals by ten to five because two of the Democrats appointed by Reagan were ultraconservatives. The first of these nominal Democrats—a former oilman and chemical executive—was the president of the ultraconservative NAM. The second, a small-town banker from Louisiana, had been an informal leader among Southern Democrats in the House from 1961 until his retirement in 1979.

332 Social Insurance Created and Undermined

For the chair, Reagan selected the libertarian business economist, Alan Greenspan, who had been the chair of President Gerald Ford's Council of Economics Advisors. Greenspan in turn selected as his assistant a former tax lawyer, Nancy Altman, who had worked on private pension funds for the corporate firm Covington & Burling, and then served as a legislative assistant and adviser on Social Security to a Republican senator. Based on her up-close experience of the commission's work, she developed a keen understanding of Social Security and became a strong lifelong advocate for the program. In addition, she wrote two useful and revealing books on the program's history and present-day functioning (Altman 2005; Altman and Kingson 2015) and became a leader in the Pension Rights Center, Social Security Works, and Strengthen Social Security.

Reagan also appointed the president of Prudential Life, who was the chair of the Business Roundtable's task force on Social Security, a member of the CED's Research and Policy Committee, and a trustee of both the Conference Board and the Business Council. In a meeting with the president of the CED two years earlier, the Prudential president had told him of his interest in the CED's Social Security project and said he wanted "to keep the two projects [i.e., the CED and Business Roundtable projects] coordinated insofar as feasible." The CED president then asked him "to name a staff man that we could invite to all our retirement meetings," and he sent one of his Prudential employees, who worked on corporate pension plans (Holland 1979). Based on his high position at Prudential and his many connections to policy-discussion groups, it can be safely inferred that he represented the general corporate-moderate view on Social Security at that time. Reagan's final appointment was a business woman, who earned a B.A. from Cornell and an MBA from Harvard, took her first job at her family's automobile dealership, and then worked in middle-level roles for McKinsey and Co., Citibank, and Blyth Eastman Dillon before becoming the vice president for finance with the Shaklee Corporation in 1981. She had legitimacy on the Social Security issue as a member of a 1979 Advisory Council on Social Security. Her husband, also a business executive, was a White House aide who had been in charge of organizing business support during Reagan's presidential campaign.

The Republican congressional representatives included three moderates: Senator Robert Dole, chair of the Senate Finance Committee; John Heinz, chair of the Senate Special Committee on Aging; and Barber Conable, a member of the House Ways and Means Committee. There were also two Republican ultraconservatives, Colorado Senator William Armstrong, chair of the Senate Finance Committee's Subcommittee on Social Security, and William Archer of Texas, the ranking Republican member of the House Ways and Means Committee's Subcommittee on Social Security. Both Armstrong and Archer were outspoken opponents of the Social Security program.

The Democratic appointees started with two emblematic elected Democrats. Senator Patrick Moynihan, a one-time CED adviser who also helped draft Nixon's Family Assistance Plan, had been elected to the Senate from New York in 1976. Representative Claude Pepper, who first served in Congress as a liberal Senator from Florida from 1936 to 1951, had been a member of the House from a Miami district since 1963. The third and fourth Democrats were a former House member from Michigan, Martha Keyes, who had been the Assistant Secretary of Health and Human Services during the Carter Administration, and Lane Kirkland, the president of the AFL-CIO.

Perhaps most significant of all, the fifth Democratic appointee was Robert M. Ball, the executive director for the Advisory Committee on Social Security in 1947 and a key strategist in the fight for Medicare. Still highly respected for his patience and ability to forge compromises, he immediately became the de facto leader for the other four liberal Democrats, who knew that he spoke for Speaker O'Neill on Social Security issues. Ball was in almost daily touch with O'Neill. He also consulted regularly with the leaders of Save Our Security, the American Association of Retired Persons (AARP), the National Council of Senior Citizens, and dozens of individuals, so that there would be no surprises for any of them, thereby making it possible to alter the Democrats' bargaining stance rapidly as the process moved forward (Ball 2010, pp. 12–13; Bernstein and Brodshaug 1988, p. 39). (The NAM president and the Louisiana Southern Democrat turned banker, although nominal Democrats, did not attend the frequent meetings held by the other five Democrats to discuss strategy.)

Overall, the balance of forces represented a classic match-up between the corporate-conservative and liberal-labor alliances. The commission met seven times before the elections, heard testimony, and discussed numerous issues. For the most part, the commissioners did no serious bargaining during this period because the main unstated goal of the Republicans was to keep Social Security out of the forthcoming midterm elections. However, the commission did agree to set Medicare aside, which greatly simplified the problems, despite repeated objections by the president of Prudential Life, who wanted to deal with both issues at the same time so that major cuts could be made in benefits. It also ruled out a quasi-privatization plan put forward by a prominent young Stanford economist, who later went on to chair the Council of Economic Advisors under President George W. Bush (Ball 2010, pp. 20, 27). More generally, it agreed to leave the basic structure of the system as it was and then to work from the most pessimistic projections concerning the short run and more moderate projections about the long run. Within that context, it also agreed that it had to close a short-run deficit of between $150 and $200 billion and make up for a gap of about 1.8 percent over the 75-year period between 1983 and 2056. The Democrats doubted that any meaningful projections could be made over such a long time period, but they accepted them as part of their plan to restore confidence in the stability of the system (Bernstein and Brodshaug 1988. pp. 41–43).

Despite the Republicans' hope that the establishment of the commission would render the Social Security issue less visible until after the elections, the Democrats made the earlier Republican attempt to cut Social Security a major campaign issue in 1982. They did so by deploying Representative Pepper from Miami. Eighty-two years old and widely known to senior citizens as "Mr. Social Security," Pepper delivered fiery speeches in favor of Democratic candidates in a large number of House districts. Although the ongoing recession and the unemployment induced by the high interest rates were the Republicans' most serious electoral problem, some Republicans believed that the overreach on Social Security contributed to the near loss of the Senate majority and a decline of 26 seats in the House. These electoral defeats made it more likely that they would seek compromise on Social Security.

The commission met for three consecutive days shortly after the elections and made substantial progress toward a bargain. The five liberal Democrats then decided to offer a three-month delay in the COLA, but there was no further give on the Republican side. At this point a key Reagan aide of a moderate stripe held secret discussions with Ball that signaled that Reagan and at least some members of his staff wanted to make a deal. Then, just when it seemed unlikely that any agreements could be reached, Senator Dole wrote an op-ed column for *The New York Times* in early January 1983, stating in effect that the crisis was solvable "through a combination of relatively modest steps" (Altman 2005, pp. 245–246). This public signal led to a discussion between Moynihan and Dole on the Senate floor, and then a suggestion from Dole that a small group of commissioners (Dole, Conable, Greenspan, Monyihan, and Ball) begin a series of private meetings. The meetings soon involved Reagan's White House Chief of Staff, and then two of his assistants, along with the libertarian director of the Office of Management and Budget.

One of the White House assistants who regularly attended the private meetings, the former CED employee who had lobbied Congress for the organization, had an important go-between role in the compromise, but he is often overlooked because he said little at the meetings. However, as Ball told me in a telephone interview in 1990, he was important because he was a likable person who had good relations with both Democrats and Republicans in Congress, and was committed to bringing about an agreement. In particular, he had a close connection to the machine Democrat from Chicago who chaired the Ways and Means Committee. Ball later made similar assertions about the former CED employee's role in a posthumously published account of how the negotiations unfolded (Ball 1990; Ball 2010, p. 36).

Social Disruption and Benefits; Cutbacks   335

With Reagan's approval ratings lower than President Jimmy Carter's at a comparable point in his administration, the White House was faced with a deadline for reporting the likely large deficits that would occur in the unified budget, due to the large tax cuts that Congress passed in 1981. Reagan and his aides therefore became even more eager to find a compromise. The final bargain started with the six-month delay in the COLA. It added up to about a 2 percent cut in benefits in the long haul, which is not trivial, and savings in the short run that cut one-fourth of the gap. In return, the Republicans agreed to tax those retirees in higher income brackets on up to half of their Social Security benefits, a significant concession of the kind no Republican ever would agree to by the 1990s. However, in this case Republicans could spin the compromise as a cut in benefits rather than a tax increase, which made it symbolically acceptable. They also agreed to move forward a payroll tax increase to 1984, which originally had been scheduled for 1999. This change added up to a large increase in the taxes on middle-income individuals. In addition, they agreed to extend coverage to new federal employees and to the small percentage of employees in nonprofit organizations who were not yet covered, which would help to build up a substantial reserve in a short time. There were a few smaller changes as well, some quite technical, but most of the savings and new revenues came from the large changes just mentioned (Ball 2010, pp. 46–52; Bernstein and Brodshaug 1988, pp. 50–55).

By agreeing to the acceleration in payroll tax payments, the Republicans in effect agreed to something that had been anathema to them before, a large reserve fund that might ensure the full stability of Social Security for 50 to 75 years. This time, though, it was left unmentioned that such reserves could be used to fund ongoing government operations until the Treasury bonds purchased by the Social Security Trust Fund with the new taxes came due in future decades (Altman 2005, p. 135, for an excellent discussion of the firm legal status of these trust assets). According to an analysis by a former State Department official, who was also a retired vice chair of Goldman Sachs, the large reserve fund created by this deal provided the American government with "a surplus it could draw on to cover increases in the regular operating deficit" (Hormats 2007, p. 241). He then added: "And American leaders did not hesitate to raid those funds on a regular basis, relieving the pressures on the president and Congress to slash the deficit" (Hormats 2007, p. 241). More specifically, the payroll tax could be used to partially cover tax cuts for the wealthy and increases in the defense budget. This large gain for the corporate rich and the power elite should of course come as no surprise at this point in the book, but it was never spoken about in those terms, then or later, by any Republicans or their public relations employees.

In spite of the general agreement forged between the five Democrats and the Republican moderates on the major issues, there was nonetheless resistance to the overall deal by six conservative members of the commission. The fact that the three business representatives were part of this dissident group was of great concern to the White House staff. It arranged a personal meeting for Reagan with the president of Prudential, which led to his decision to join the majority. He then convinced two other business members to join the compromise, which left the retired Southern Democrat/banker, the Republican Senator Armstrong, and the Republican Representative Archer on the losing end of a 12–3 vote to accept the report (Altman 2005, p. 248, on Reagan's meeting with the Prudential president; Ball 2010, p. 50, for the Prudential president's influence on the other business representatives).

To complete the compromise, the commission left it up to Congress to fill the remaining one-third of the long-run gap through one of two options. The conservative members, including the two ultraconservative Democrats, suggested that the retirement age should be raised from 65 to 67 through monthly increments that would begin in 2000. The five liberal Democrats proposed that the gap should be filled through gradual tax increases that would begin in 2010 *if* they were needed.

With the 1982 elections safely over, the conservative coalition accepted the general compromise offered by the commission. Then it opted to increase the retirement age starting in 2000 rather than leave it to a future Congress to decide if taxes actually needed to be raised in 2010. This preemptive decision once again reveals the ultraconservatives' deep-seated desire to limit any government support for social benefits as much as possible. Since many non-college working people retire from strenuous and physically wearing jobs before age 65, it also in effect meant another benefit cut for lower-income people. Fewer of them were likely to be hardy enough to wait until age 67 in order to collect full benefits (Pierson 1994, p. 67).

Both Republicans and Democrats declared victory and breathed a sigh of relief. But the CED leaders stated publicly that they were disappointed in the results, which they had tried to influence through meetings with Greenspan, Dole, and other key participants, as well as with staff members of the relevant Senate and House committees. In the aftermath, they expressed their dissatisfaction in a 1984 report, *Social Security: From Crisis to Crisis* (1984), which repeated CED's 1981 recommendations. They complained that the cuts were too small and cautious, allegedly leaving too narrow a margin of safety. Ball called the new CED report "quite irresponsible" and predicted large surpluses by 1988, while claiming that the CED was "looking for any excuse to push their proposals for further benefit cuts" (AP 1984, p. 16). According to Ball in my interview with him, the corporate executives he knew were willing to support Social Security at a minimum level of payments, but they did not want to see any increases because of their general anti-government ideology and their

Social Disruption and Benefits; Cutbacks   337

resulting preference for private pension plans (Ball 1990). For corporate moderates, matters had come full circle since the early 1930s, when their private pension plans were in crisis amidst the turmoil of the Great Depression. By the 1980s, by contrast, they felt confident they could enact cutbacks in the government program their predecessors had helped to create, without risking any pushback or voter backlash.

Ball turned out to be more than correct in predicting large surpluses. According to testimony before Moynihan's Senate Subcommittee on Social Security and Family Policy in 1988, the trust fund was taking in $109.4 million per day by that year and had grown to almost $100 billion in just four years (Moynihan 1988). By 2010, the Social Security Trust Fund had $2.6 trillion in Treasury notes, enough to pay benefits until 2035. However, ultraconservatives continued to claim that Social Security was in crisis because the Social Security Administration did not have any actual money in the bank, only the "IOU's" from the Treasury. They thereby continued to ignore the fully protected legal standing of the trust funds. Or perhaps they hoped a Supreme Court dominated by ultraconservative corporate lawyers would take their side if the issue came to a court fight. In the eyes of liberal economists, the issue that really concerns the conservatives is that federal taxes might have to be raised somewhat, including income taxes on the well-to-do, when the time comes in the 2030s for the Social Security Trust Fund to collect on its Treasury bonds in the same way that wealthy investors and foreign countries expect to do (e.g., Baker 2001; Baker and Weisbrot 1999).

Still, the fact remains that the corporate community and the Reagan Administration did not win all that they had hoped to on Social Security in the early 1980s. True, benefits were trimmed significantly through delaying the COLAs and increasing the retirement age, and the money collected for the trust fund was used to pay for part of the large budget deficits over the next 30 years. But the liberal-labor alliance was able to restore public confidence in the system and give it legitimacy for the next 20–25 years in the face of a predominantly conservative Congress eager to make larger reductions or privatize the whole system. It was also able to make some changes that benefited women and brought all employees of the federal government and nonprofit organizations into the system. The overall result accurately reflects the power differential between the two rival power alliances in the early 1980s. The corporate-conservative alliance, with the full support of the richest of the corporate rich, consistently pushed national policy in a rightward direction, but in this instance the liberal-labor alliances had been able to fend off a worst-case scenario and even make a few improvements by way of inclusion, while at the same time accepting gradual declines in the purchasing power of individual payments.

338 Social Insurance Created and Undermined

The Attack on Social Security Continues, 1985–1999

The ongoing corporate attack on Social Security was renewed shortly after the 1984 compromise. Ultraconservatives took the lead in this process. But for all the distortions in the ultraconservative onslaught, the corporate moderates tolerated most of it because, at the least, they also wanted to limit the program severely, as evidenced by the broadside scare statement by the CED (1984) at about the same time. Then, too, one of CED's trustees, Peter Peterson, whose long career spanned the CEO position at Bell & Howell, two years as Secretary of Commerce in the Nixon Administration, and two decades as a Wall Street investment banker, where he amassed several billions of dollars in wealth, took up the cudgels for fiscal responsibility and deficit reduction. His solutions to these putative problems involved significant cuts in Social Security. He spent tens of millions of dollars to publicize his claims, and wrote three books with alarming titles (Peterson 1993; Peterson 1996; Peterson and Howe 2004).

By the late 1990s, a Democratic president, Bill Clinton, was ready to make a compromise in order to defuse the issue, which would have led to further cuts in Social Security. However, any possibilities for such a compromise were cast aside when the Republicans turned to the scorched-earth policy of trying to impeach Clinton due to his lack of truthfulness about past sexual escapades, which were asked about in the context of an investigation that began on the basis of an alleged real estate scam in which he had participated. But the Social Security issue was a "phony crisis" all along, as two economists explained in great detail (Baker and Weisbrot 1999, for the technical legerdemain concerning Social Security used by Peterson and those who agree with him). It was a scare tactic, and it might well have worked for a second time if not for the impeachment hearings.

References

Altman, Nancy. 2005. *The battle for Social Security: From FDR's vision to Bush's gamble*. New York: John Wiley & Sons.

Altman, Nancy and Eric Kingson. 2015. *Social Security works! Why Social Security isn't going broke and how expanding it will help us all*. New York: The New Press.

AP (Associated Press). 1984. "Business leaders urge cuts in Social Security." P. 16 in *San Francisco Chronicle*, February 19:16.

Baker, Dean. 2001. "Defaulting on the Social Security Trust Fund bonds: Winner and losers." Washington: Center for Economic and Political Research.

Baker, Dean and Mark Weisbrot. 1999. *Social Security: The phony crisis*. Chicago: University of Chicago Press.

Ball, Robert. 1990. "Telephone interview with G. William Domhoff, August 7."

———. 2010. *What really happened: The Greenspan Commission*. New York: The Century Foundation Press.

Social Disruption and Benefits; Cutbacks 339

Bernstein, Merton and Joan Brodshaug. 1988. *Social Security: The system that works.* New York: Basic Books.

Block, Fred and Margaret Somers. 2014. *The power of market fundamentalism: Karl Polanyi's critique.* Cambridge: Harvard University Press.

Brown, Michael K. 1999. *Race, money, and the American welfare state.* Ithaca: Cornell University Press.

CED. 1968. *The national economy and the Vietnam War.* New York: Committee for Economic Development.

———. 1970a. *Improving the welfare system.* New York: Committee for Economic Development.

———. 1970b. *Training and jobs for the urban poor.* New York: Committee for Economic Development.

———. 1971. *Education for the urban disadvantaged: From pre-school to employment.* New York: Committee for Economic Development.

———. 1981. *Reforming retirement policies.* New York: Committee for Economic Development.

———. 1984. *Social Security: From crisis to crisis?* New York: Committee for Economic Development.

———. N.D. "CED Impact: Reforming retirement policies and Social Security." in *Hurwitz Papers.* Washington: Committee for Economic Development.

Collins, Sharon M. 1997. *Black corporate executives: The making and breaking of a black middle class.* Philadelphia: Temple University Press.

Delton, Jennifer. 2009. *Racial integration in corporate America, 1940–1990.* New York: Cambridge University Press.

Domhoff, G. W. 2005. "The Ford Foundation in the inner city: Forging an alliance with neighborhood activists." WhoRulesAmerica.net. https://sociology.ucsc.edu/whorulesamerica/power/ford_foundation.html.

———. 2014. *Who rules America? The triumph of the corporate rich.* New York: McGraw-Hill.

Downes, Brian. 1970. "A critical re-examination of the social and political characteristics of riot cities." *Social Science Quarterly* 51:349–360.

Duberstein, Kenneth. 1981. "Memo to Sol Hurwitz, February 11." In *Committee for Economic Development Archives, President's Staff Files: Duberstein.* Washington: Committee for Economic Development.

Estes, Carroll. 1983. "Social Security: The social construction of a crisis." *Milbank Quarterly* 61:445–461.

Frieden, Bernard and Marshall Kaplan. 1975. *The politics of neglect: Urban aid from Model Cities to revenue sharing.* Cambridge: MIT Press.

Greer, Scott. 1965. *Urban renewal and American cities.* Indianapolis: Bobbs-Merrill.

Guthrie, Douglas and Michael McQuarrie. 2005. "Privatization and low-income housing in the United States since 1986." Pp. 15–51 in *Research in political sociology: Politics, class, and the corporation,* vol. 14, edited by H. Prechel. Oxford, UK: Elsevier.

Hacker, Jacob and Paul Pierson. 2010. *Winner-take-all politics: How Washington made the rich richer—and turned its back on the middle class.* New York: Simon & Schuster.

Holland, Robert. 1979. "Memo to CED Staff on Beck, October 22." In *Committee for Economic Development Archives, President's Trustee Files: Beck File.* Washington: Committee for Economic Development.

Hormats, Robert. 2007. *The price of liberty: Paying for America's wars.* New York: Times Books.

Howard, Christopher. 1997. *The hidden welfare state: Tax expenditures and social policy in the United States.* Princeton: Princeton University Press.

Hoynes, Hilary and Jesse Rothstein. 2016. *Tax policy toward low-income families.* https://www.nber.org/papers/w22080.pdf. Cambridge: National Bureau of Economic Research.

Kingson, Eric. 1984. "Financing Social Security: Agenda-setting and the enactment of the 1983 amendments to the Social Security Act." *Policy Studies Journal* 13:131–155.

Kraska, Peter and Victor Kaeppler. 1997. "Militarizing American police: The rise and normalization of paramilitary units." *Social Problems* 44:1–18.

Liou, Thomas Y. and Robert C. Stroh. 1998. "Community development intermediary systems in the United States: Origins, evolution, and functions." *Housing Policy Debate* 9:575–594.

MacLean, Nancy. 2017. *Democracy in chains: The deep history of the radical right's stealthy plan for America.* New York: Viking.

Magat, Richard. 1979. *The Ford Foundation at work: Philanthropic choices, methods, and styles.* New York: Plenum Press.

Mayhew, David. 2005. *Divided we govern: Party control, lawmaking, and investigations, 1946–2002.* New Haven: Yale University Press.

McQuaid, Kim. 1982. *Big business and presidential power from FDR to Reagan.* New York: Morrow.

Moynihan, Daniel. 1973. *The politics of a guaranteed income: The Nixon Administration and the Family Assistance Plan.* New York Random House.

———. 1988. "Conspirators, trillions, limos in the night." P. A15 in *The New York Times*, May 23.

Myles, John. 1981. "The trillion dollar misunderstanding." *Social Policy*, July-August:25–31.

Peirce, Neil R. and Carol F. Steinbach. 1987. *Corrective capitalism: The rise of American community development corporations.* New York: Ford Foundation.

Peterson, Peter. 1993. *Facing up: How to rescue the economy from crushing debt and restore the American dream.* New York: Simon & Schuster.

———. 1996. *Will America grow up before it grows old? How the coming Social Security crisis threatens you, your family and your country.* New York: Random House.

Peterson, Peter and Neil Howe. 2004. *On borrowed time: How the growth in entitlement spending threatens America's future.* New Brunswick: Transaction Publishers.

Pierson, Paul. 1994. *Dismantling the welfare state? Reagan, Thatcher, and the politics of retrenchment.* New York: Cambridge University Press.

Pierson, Paul and Theda Skocpol. 2007. *The transformation of American politics: Activist government and the rise of conservatism.* Princeton: Princeton University Press.

Piven, Frances and Richard Cloward. 1977. *Poor people's movements: Why they succeed, how they fail.* New York: Random House.

Quadagno, Jill. 1990. "Race, class, and gender in the U.S. welfare state: Nixon's failed Family Assistance Plan." *American Sociological Review* 55:11–28.

———. 1994. *The color of welfare: How racism undermined the War on Poverty.* New York: Oxford University Press.

Rosenthal, Rob. 1994. *Homeless in Paradise: A map of the terrain.* Philadelphia: Temple University Press.

Rossi, Peter and Robert Dentler. 1961. *The politics of urban renewal.* New York: Free Press.

Sanders, Heywood. 1992. "Building the convention city: Politics, finance, and public investment in urban America." *Journal of Urban Affairs* 14:135–160.

———. 2014. *Convention center follies: Politics, power, and public investment in American cities.* Philadelphia: University of Pennsylvania Press.

Tittle, Diana. 1992. *Rebuilding Cleveland: The Cleveland Foundation and its evolving urban strategy.* Columbus: Ohio State University Press.

Welsh, James. 1973. "Welfare Reform Born, Aug. 8, 1960, Died, Oct. 4, 1972: A sad case study of the American political process." Pp. 14–17, 21–23 in *The New York Times Sunday Magazine,* January 7.

Yin, Jordan. 2001. "The community development system: Urban politics and the practice of neighborhood redevelopment in two American cities from the 1960s to the 1990s." Ph.D. dissertation Thesis, Department of Planning, Cornell University, Ithaca.

Zweigenhaft, Richard L. and G. William Domhoff. 2003. *Blacks in the white elite: Will the progress continue?* Lanham, MD: Rowman & Littlefield.

———. 2018. *Diversity in the power elite: Ironies and unfulfilled promises.* Lanham, MD: Rowman & Littlefield.

Chapter 9

The Circuitous Path to the Affordable Care Act, 1974–2010

Although the major health-care reform proposed by Nixon and the corporate moderates in 1974 was not passed, there were several changes in laws and circumstances over the next 19 years that prepared the way for another effort at reform in 1993. After that attempt by President Bill Clinton failed, still further small changes in the ensuing 15 years set the stage for the eventual passage of the Affordable Care Act in 2010. During the same period, most liberals and labor leaders gradually adjusted their goals in the face of the repeated defeats they suffered on health insurance at the hands of the corporate community and the conservative coalition.

In the same year that the CED (1973) report *Building a National Health-Care System* appeared, the newly formed Business Roundtable took several steps to make the corporate community more effective in shaping national health policy. It first of all created its own temporary task force on health policy to keep an eye on new developments and perhaps offer new policy initiatives. To aid the task force in taking a more proactive role on health issues, the leaders of the Business Roundtable created a small, quasi-independent think tank, the Washington Business Group on Health (WBGH), whose "initial purpose was to defeat national health insurance," but it soon "became involved in other medical policy issues..." (Starr 2017, p. 444). More specifically, it was charged with developing a "market-based strategy for health care" that would provide policies to contain cost increases and reinforce "private control over medical care resources" (Bergthold 1990, p. 45). Several CEOs attended the WBGH's early meetings, but it was primarily engaged with middle-level corporate benefits executives via seminars, reports, and newsletters as its staff grew from one or two in the mid-1970s to 12 in 1984 and 26 in 1988 (Bergthold 1990, pp. 41–47 for the most complete discussion of the first ten years of the WBGH, based in good measure on her own interviews).

In keeping with the Construction Users Anti-Inflation Roundtable's strategy of creating local business groups to deal with the local building-trades unions, as discussed in Chapter 5, the Business Roundtable and the WBGH advocated local and regional health alliances, which brought together a range of health-care purchasers in an attempt to contain cost growth. The alliances grew in number from about 25 in 1982 to 178 in 1987 (Bergthold 1990, p. 51). Case studies and surveys suggest that they had an impact in California and Massachusetts, and were active in most of the other 48 states (Bergthold 1990, p. 51, Chapters 6–9).

At the same time as the Business Roundtable was building an institutional infrastructure for active corporate involvement in health-care policy at all governmental levels, it was also taking policy positions in reaction to initiatives by the liberal-labor alliance and the federal government. In 1977 the Business Roundtable and WBGH joined with the National Association of Manufacturers (NAM) and the Chamber of Commerce to successfully urge the conservative coalition to defeat a proposal by President Jimmy Carter to institute price controls on hospitals in the face of the continuing rise in hospital costs. The corporate community did not like the rising hospital costs, but it disliked government price controls even more (Quadagno 2005, pp. 125–128).

In terms of potential impact, the most important change encouraged by the WBGH gave Medicare more control over physicians and hospitals, which "proved to be a turning point in the relationship between government and health" (Starr 2017, p. 54). It occurred quietly during the Reagan Administration as one small part of the 1983 changes in the Social Security Act that were discussed at length in Chapter 8. The change occurred through "a little-noticed provision that was slipped into the Ways and Means Committee bill at the last minute by members of the Health Subcommittee"; although there was no debate in the House, it was in fact "a radical restricting of Medicare" because Medicare would no longer reimburse hospitals when they submitted a bill (Quadagno 2005, p. 135). Instead, "hospitals would receive a predetermined amount based on what treatment was provided," and they would have to make sure they lived within what was in effect their budget on that issue, or else lose money (Quadagno 2005, p. 135). On the other hand, they could keep the whole prepayment if they controlled their costs better than expected.

The WBGH worked hard to see that this provision appeared in the bill, even though it gave new power to government on pricing issues (Bergthold 1990, p. 45). The new government-control policy was then adopted in some states for use in containing Medicaid costs. In addition, the WBGH "helped some private companies adopt similar accounting procedures for their own health plans" (Quadagno 2005, p. 136), demonstrating once again that it was fully focused on reducing costs for corporations that purchased health-care plans. The American Hospital Association decided to accept the change gracefully, but many hospitals solved their cost problems by shortening hospital stays, which put an increasing number of patients into nursing-care facilities. Hospitals also found ways to shift costs to private insurance plans. This cost-shifting, in turn, led to rapid increases in

344 Social Insurance Created and Undermined

the costs of private insurance, and then to a renewed effort by corporations and insurance companies to create managed care plans, including Health Maintenance Organizations (HMOs) (Starr 2017, p. 455).

The large industrial corporations and the WBGH made their boldest move toward cost-cutting via government legislation by supporting an initiative in the late 1980s to create a catastrophic insurance benefit within Medicare. This resort to a government bailout might have cut corporate costs for retiree social benefits as much as 30 percent (Quadagno 2005, p. 156). Since 80 percent of retirees had purchased Medigap insurance through private companies, this was not a change sought by advocates for elderly organizations. Furthermore, at first glance it seemed to be opposed to the interests of insurance companies, but they stepped aside because selling Medigap had not been highly profitable (Quadagno 2005, p. 152). Once Reagan made clear that the insurance had to be financed with higher taxes on those elderly with comfortable incomes, which might amount to as much as $1,500 a year, most conservatives pronounced themselves willing to accept the new government insurance plan.

At the same time, the liberal-labor alliance and other advocates for the elderly were mounting a campaign to add a long-term nursing-care benefit to Medicare for the frail elderly. The highly visible and respected advocate for the elderly in the House, Carl Pepper, by then 87 years old, led the campaign. They also wanted federal regulation of the nursing-home industry as well, due to the lax regulation provided in most states. However, the insurance companies were adamantly opposed to both the new Medicare benefits and any attempt at federal regulation, and they had the support of the Chamber of Commerce and the NAM because the bill would entail an increase in the payroll tax (Quadagno 2005, p. 177). At that point Pepper, by then the chair of the House Rules Committee, threatened to keep the WBGH's catastrophic insurance amendment from a vote unless the nursing-home legislation also was voted upon. In late June 1988, the conservative coalition rounded up 243 votes (99 from Democrats, 144 from Republicans) to defeat the nursing-home insurance legislation, and then in early July the same coalition led the way to the passage of catastrophic insurance (Quadagno 2005, pp. 155, 177).

The defeat of the liberal-labor-elderly initiative and the apparent success of the corporate community's push for catastrophic insurance provide a graphic example of the power disparity between the rival camps at that time. However, the story did not end there. Advocacy groups sympathetic to the middle-class elderly, who would have to bear the new tax burden, brought about a repeal of the catastrophic insurance legislation in 1989 through a spirited campaign, including demonstrations. Republican legislators were not prepared to face the wrath of elderly centrist and conservative voters that could afford Medigap insurance, so the conservative coalition did not form to preserve the legislation. The Business

Roundtable and the WBGH were thwarted on this issue, but not by the liberal–labor alliance.

Emboldened by the Reagan Administration's ongoing attacks on unions and Social Security, the corporate community also initiated private efforts to lower health-care costs at the same time as its small policy victories in Washington on health issues were having little or no impact on corporate costs. These efforts included higher deductibles on private insurance, higher co-payments, reduced benefits, and moving as many jobs as possible out of the country. The corporations and the WBGH also redoubled their efforts to build private purchasing alliances at the state and local levels in an effort to reduce payments to insurance companies, hospitals, and physicians. They also increasingly turned to self-insuring, which was beneficial to them in terms of avoiding many federal requirements. This new angle was made possible by a 1974 federal pension law, which made the regulation of self-insured plans a state-level function. The change to self-insuring by many of the largest employers also added to the difficulties that were facing the smaller insurance companies, some of which dropped health-care insurance or went out of business entirely. At the same time, though, the largest insurance companies continued to prosper and the insurance industry became even more powerful on health-care policy issues (Quadagno 2005, pp. 169–170).

A Democratic President, a Failed Healthcare Plan

The rising costs of health care and the increase in underinsured and uninsured low-income citizens, along with the shortcomings in Medicare and Medicaid, generated a new round of thinking about general reforms in the early 1990s. The impetus in this direction was given an unexpected boost when a liberal Democratic candidate for the Senate achieved an unexpected victory in 1990, at least in part because there was strong voter support for his emphasis on improving government health insurance.

Some corporations joined with unions and other advocacy groups in the early 1990s to form a National Leadership Coalition for Health Care Reform as a venue to discuss possible solutions. Both for-profit and the remaining nonprofit hospitals, including the Catholic Hospital Association, were also willing to consider wider health-care coverage. By this point, the American Medical Association (AMA) wanted to see expanded health-care coverage, but it was only a shadow of its former self in terms of power due to "the continued search by government and employers for control over medical expenditures," which led to "the rise of corporate enterprises in health services" (Starr 2017, p. 421).

As a result of all this activity, Democrat Bill Clinton's presidential campaign in 1992 emphasized that he would have a plan, which during the campaign primarily meant that many policy experts in and around his campaign were discussing a range of ideas. Although a full plan did not emerge until the fall of 1993, well after Clinton was in office, the effort may have been doomed to failure by a decision he made at a meeting with his health-care advisers on January 11, 1993, nine days before the inauguration. In the face of projections that the costs for Medicare and Medicaid might rise as much as 13 percent a year, and drawing on his knowledge of health-care issues as a person interested in policy details, the president-elect decided he needed a plan that would provide universal coverage and at the same time contain mechanisms to contain costs. But most policy analysts thought that it would be difficult if not impossible to obtain both objectives at the same time. No business or individual was willing to give up what they had if they thought it was adequate, especially if they feared the new plan might be worse for them (e.g., Altman and Shactman 2011, pp. 94–96)

Those who doubted that costs could be controlled while expanding coverage included members of Clinton's transition team on health care. When they told him their cost estimates, he was furious with them. He and one of his most trusted advisers, a friend from his years as a Rhodes Scholar, who had become a business consultant, thought there were excessive costs that could be squeezed out of the system (Hacker 1996, pp. 119–121, for the arguments among advisers; Johnson and Broder 1996, pp. 103–108, for a portrait of the business consultant). The health advisers that made the higher cost estimates moved to the margins or left the health advisory group entirely (Altman and Shactman 2011, pp. 62–63, 74; Johnson and Broder 1996, pp. 108–111).

Although the president appointed a White House Task Force for Health Care Reform shortly after his inauguration to reach out to many groups and examine several options, with his wife Hillary Clinton in charge, it did not have a decision-making role. Its members wrote numerous position papers and gathered considerable testimony from a wide range of individuals and groups, but they had made no recommendations by the time the committee was disbanded in late May, after a little over four months of existence. Moreover, the main options and negotiations were already in the hands of a small group of White House advisers by March, with the president serving as their chair, and as the person who made the decisions (Starr 2011, pp. 81–82, who was a member of this advisory group and therefore writes as a participant-observer who kept notes and records at the time).

The plan the president decided upon as most likely to fulfill his objectives had its immediate origins in work by sociologist Paul Starr, who had continued to involve himself in health-care policy after writing his well-received history of medicine in the United States from its early years to 1982 (Starr 2017, for the updated edition that carries the story to 2016). In this plan, which built on a plan developed earlier for possible use at the state level, Medicare and the private prepaid insurance plans provided by large employers would remain intact. However, smaller companies would pay a tax to nonprofit "regional health alliances," which would also receive funds from a significant boost in cigarette taxes. The cooperatives would then offer individuals a range of insurance options, which would be put together by competing private insurance companies. In a book meant to explain the rationale of the Clinton plan to policy experts and interested members of the general public, Starr (1994. p. XL) called it "a public framework for insurance that allows Americans to choose among a variety of private health plans." Finally, there would be a "national health board to establish regional and national spending limits," and it would have "the authority to set limits on insurance premium hikes" (Quadagno 2005, p. 188).

Starr explained the rationale for the regional health alliances in the course of a telephone interview with future political scientist Jacob Hacker, at the time doing graduate research on the unfolding of the policy-making process. In Hacker's words, such a plan "represented a potential source of 'countervailing power' in medical care—an institutional means by which the diffuse interests of patients could be brought to bear against the concentrated interests of the medical profession" (Hacker 1996, p. 95; see Starr 1978, p. 97 for his first use of the term "countervailing power" in discussing what he was then calling "regional health system agencies"). The regional health alliances also would "sever the tie between employment and coverage" for a large number of people (Hacker 1996, p. 96). More specifically, in the final Clinton plan, over 99.5 percent of the nation's 3.9 million employers would be required to drop their insurance plans, if they had one, and pay a premium ("a payroll tax dressed up as a premium") to one or more of the regional health alliances (Hacker 1996, p. 124). However, large corporations, those with more than 5,000 employers, were not required to join a separate insurance purchasing plan, which exempted 933 corporations at the time.

The rising health costs were very annoying to moderate corporate leaders. Higher costs raised the prices of their products, perhaps thereby hurting their competitive position, and also contributed to a federal debt they heartily disliked. But it is important to keep in mind that they did not feel compelled to insist on reforms, or accept genuine compromises, because they had other options. They could continue to adopt their own self-insured plans, receive tax write-offs for their benefit payments, make gradual increases in co-payments, and outsource jobs to non-union employers inside and outside the United States. It therefore seems plausible that the corporate community's final stance on health-insurance reforms might have been based on other considerations, including its general attitude toward government and its concern with the control of labor markets to the greatest extent possible.

348　Social Insurance Created and Undermined

Just as important at that juncture, and contrary to the dire projections, it turned out the rising health costs were being brought under control while the reform process was unfolding. The various forms of prepaid medical insurance, and most especially HMOs, were finally coming into their own due to the very strong push for them by corporations in the 1980s. As sociologist Linda Bergthold, a member of the White House task force, recounted in a retrospective analysis, shortly after Clinton's plan failed, "reform of the marketplace was proceeding headlong before Clinton focused the national spotlight on health reform" (Bergthold 1995, p. 10). (In the three years before her appointment to the task force, Bergthold had recommended health plans for corporations as an employee of Mercer, Inc., a San Francisco-based consulting firm, and most recently had been on loan to the WBGH for two months, so she was very familiar with corporate views on health-care issues.) Other policy analysts came to the same conclusion (Swenson and Greer 2002, pp. 610–61, 623–626, for a very detailed account of supporting evidence), including Starr (2011, p. 118), when he noted that "health care inflation eased in 1993 and 1994, and some employers came to believe that managed care provided them with a long-term solution." Based on the unexpected good news on cost inflation, along with the scope of the Clinton plan, "the initial response from all groups was cautious support," with unity on what they opposed and disagreements on what they might support (Bergthold 1995, p. 6).

Nor was it simply business interests that decided to remain cautious about their support for health reform. Liberal supporters of expanded health insurance took the same stance, with varying degrees of skepticism. Strong liberals and leftists still wanted government health care for everyone through a single-payer system. They did so despite the fact that Senator Ted Kennedy and union leaders had abandoned hope for such a large-scale reform in 1979 because it encountered too much resistance from both the corporate community and the large percentage of employees that were satisfied with their present health insurance. On the other hand, conservative Democrats wanted a system in which employers either provided a range of health-insurance plans for employees to choose from, or else paid a payroll tax of 7–9 percent that would make it possible for large nonprofit organizations or a government agency to provide insurance plans. (Such plans were called "pay-or-play" by those who debated these issues.)

Once the broad outlines of Clinton's plan became clear, the various sectors of the corporate community, and virtually all Republicans in Congress, saw it as a threat or as government overreach. Since money for extending the insurance program to low-income people would come from the increase in cigarette taxes, Southern agribusiness interests and white Southern Democrats opposed that aspect of the plan. Moreover, and unknown at the time, the tobacco industry's trade association repeated the clandestine role it had played during the legislative battle over Medicare.

The Tobacco Institute, with most of its money coming from the two largest tobacco companies, secretly funneled large, unknown sums of money to both the liberal and leftist groups that supported a single-payer plan, as well as to ultraconservative groups that completely opposed the Clinton plan, as part of the tobacco industry's efforts to defeat the Clinton proposal (Tesler and Maloner 2010).

The most vocal and sustained opposition from the outset came from the Health Insurance Association of America, which at that point represented the smaller insurance companies because the five giants of the industry (Aetna, MetLife, Cigna, Prudential, and Travelers) had resigned from it. Moreover, the large insurers had formed their own Alliance for Managed Competition, which favored a reform involving competition among health-care providers. It would include government subsidies for low-income individuals and families, but there would be much less government regulation. The remaining members of the Health Insurance Association of America, which made their money by selling policies to healthy young adults, saw the Clinton plan as their death knell, and pulled no punches.

The ultraconservative front group called the National Federation of Independent Businesses (NFIB), which was still being treated by most social scientists as a legitimate business association, joined the small insurers in their early and outright opposition. However, the evidence available clearly shows that the NFIB was the same unrepresentative pseudo-association that it had been when it allegedly represented small business in the defeat of the Labor Law Reform Act in 1977, as discussed in Chapter 5 (Hamilton 1975, Chapters 2 and 7; Zeigler 1961, pp. 31–32). Located in Virginia since 1992, by that juncture the NFIB had 700 employees and annual revenues of over $58 million (Domhoff 1995, p. 6). Its opposition to any government intervention in the marketplace on this issue was not consistent with the opinions of many small-business owners (Kazee, Lipsky, and Martin 2008). It also was the lobbying group most closely intertwined with the Republicans in the 1990s, with a staff drawn in good part from a pool of people that had worked for the Republican Party or Republican elected officials (Shaiko and Wallace 1999).

In keeping with its narrow partisan role, and still not at all representative of small business, over 90 percent of the NFIB's campaign donations went to Republicans between 1989 and 2010, with many of those non-Republican donations very likely going to the remaining Democratic members of the conservative coalition (Mandelbaum 2009a). The chair of the NFIB board of directors during the Clinton years was prototypical of its leadership. He owned a snack-food business that employed 800 workers and grossed $50–75 million a year, and he gave $130,000 to Republican candidates between 1985 and 1993. Another board member at the time had a landscaping and nursery business that employed 100 people and took in $6 million a year. Still another was an executive for a sugar cane and land company, which employed 60 people and had sales of $1–3 million (Domhoff 1995, p. 10). These companies are obviously nowhere close to the *Fortune*-1000 level. But they also are not the small mom-and-pop stores with seven or fewer employees and sales under $300,000, which the NFIB claimed to represent.

The NFIB later received credit in some academic post-mortems for its alleged role in forcing the Chamber of Commerce to reconsider its initial stance of keeping an open mind on the issue. But leaders within the Chamber of Commerce immediately expressed their concerns about the new proposal once its general outlines were clear. They wanted the regional health alliances to be voluntary for any company with over 100 employees, which is a huge drop-off from exemptions only for companies with over 5,000 employees (Judis 1995, p. 67). More generally, corporate leaders, including leaders in the Business Roundtable, also were concerned that the regional health alliances might become involved in a form of regulatory oversight (Johnson and Broder 1996, pp. 319–320; Martin 1995).

In terms of costs and savings, there were in theory potential self-interested divisions between companies that might end up paying more and those that might save more, but most of the businesses that might have benefited through reduced costs ended up opposing an employer mandate. According to Bergthold (1995, p. 9), their anti-reform unity was based at least in part "on the grounds of ideological opposition to government mandates of any kind." However, there were more general power issues at stake as well. The corporate executives expressed "tensions between the economic self-interest of firms (e.g., wouldn't it be cheaper to simply pay for but not manage health benefits?) and the fear of loss of control over benefits to government" (Bergthold 1995, p. 12). From a corporate-dominance perspective, the corporate leaders once again were concerned with retaining as much power as they could in terms of controlling labor markets, while at the same time keeping government from becoming bigger and potentially more powerful.

Drawing in part on the account of the policy process that he wrote at the time (and later put on the Internet for one and all), Starr (2011, p. 122) concluded: "During the spring and summer of 1993, in what may really have been the crucial shift, the nation's elites abandoned health care reform entirely" because "[t]hey had become impatient with its complexity and nervous about its cost." This conclusion was shared by the mainstream leaders in the Senate as well as business interests. Another sociologist, Beth Mintz (1998, p. 217), came to a somewhat similar conclusion based on her independent research: "The defection of big business can be viewed as a unified action, based not on the ability of a narrow, self-interested segment to dominate the decision-making process, but on the uncertainty that the Clinton proposal generated for the big business community."

Circuitous Path to the Affordable Care Act 351

From a corporate-dominance perspective, the core of the corporate community, the *Fortune*-500 companies, and, more generally, the *Fortune*-1000, found themselves in a very uncomfortable situation. Viewed from one angle, they were being offered an exemption from dropping their insurance plans, many of which were loosely regulated because they were self-insured plans. But accepting that bargain might needlessly separate them from other businesses on a very visible issue. From a dollars and cents perspective, they would become small fish in a big insurance pond dominated by the regional health plans: "If a large business remained self-insured, but most of the small and mid-sized employers in the community joined a regional pool, the large business would quickly become a very small buyer facing an increasingly consolidated delivery system" (Bergthold 1995, p. 12). In addition, their worksite health-promotion and fitness centers might disappear, and "what control would a company have over its workforce if it could not use benefits to attract and retain employees?" (Bergthold 1995, p. 12).

Despite being wary about the plan well before it was even introduced into Congress by Clinton, leaders within the Business Roundtable continued to bargain with the White House throughout the summer of 1993. At the same time, the president's primary attention was focused into early August on passing the budget, an issue that had taken much longer than expected. Any remaining hope for an agreement on health-care legislation had all but ended by October when the negotiations became "strident" and the Roundtable decided that Clinton's proposal had to be defeated (Judis 1995, p. 70). By February 1994, the Business Roundtable had indicated that it thought a plan advocated by a member of the Conservative Democratic Forum in the House deserved consideration as well. Since this plan did not include the most objectionable features of the Clinton plan, many observers, correctly or not, perceived the Business Roundtable's statement as an indirect way to express its hostility to the Clinton initiative (Johnson and Broder 1996, pp. 319–320).

"Indeed," journalist John Judis of *The New Republic* concluded (1995, p. 71), based on his interviews at the time, "the Roundtable's vote was decisive in shifting overall business sentiment," and at the least "opened the door for other business groups to reject the Clinton Plan," which the NAM did "three days later" (Judis 1995, p. 71). Moreover, the White House "desperately attempted to keep the Roundtable in the fold," claimed it would compromise on several key issues, and arranged for the Business Roundtable's leaders to meet with the chair of the House Ways and Means Committee so they could learn first-hand from him how he intended to win a majority (Judis 1995, p. 71). But nothing came out of these efforts (Johnson and Broder 1996, pp. 318–325 for a similar account of White House and Business Roundtable interactions based on their own interviews).

Once it was clear that the corporate community would not be pressuring members of Congress to pass reform legislation, the more centrist Republicans felt free to reject the plan for political reasons. "After business backtracked from its earlier support for reform," Starr (2011, p. 118) concludes, "Senate Republicans reassessed their position" in March 1994. By that time, both ultraconservative Republicans and white Southern Democrats in the House were already approaching the issue with their eyes on the 1994 Congressional elections, and the ultraconservative Republicans of course claimed full credit for the eventual defeat of the health-care plan. In September 1994, the Democratic leaders in the Senate decided it would not be politically sensible to bring the plan up for a vote in the face of a sure defeat.

Although this analysis strongly suggests that the corporate community and the conservative coalition defeated the Clinton initiative, that conclusion is disputed by political sociologist Mark Mizruchi (2013; 2017). In his view, the previously well-knit and politically effective corporate moderates (which he calls "the corporate elite") were too fractured after 1990 to have any influence on health-care insurance: "By the early 1990s, the corporate elite was incapable of acting collectively to address the crisis over the cost of health care and this inability to act has persisted into the present" (Mizruchi 2017, p. 108).

In the case of Clinton's plan specifically, he claims that "the largest American companies were initially strongly supportive of the government playing a significant role in providing health care," an analysis that is based in part on his interview with a business leader: "According to a leading figure in American business with whom I spoke, who had attended a speech by Hillary Clinton to a group of major corporate executives, 'Hillary had them eating out of her hand'" (Mizruchi 2017, p. 110). However, this claim is contradicted by the analysts who conclude that the process began with cautious support, and with no agreement on solutions (Bergthold 1995, p. 6; Starr 2011, p. 80).

Mizruchi (2017, p. 110) also claims "there was evidence to suggest that a number of companies were cowed into opposition by Republican members of Congress, who threatened to punish the companies that supported the president." Based on this analysis, he concludes that: "In the 1990s, Congress was exercising its muscle on the corporate elite rather than vice versa" (Mizruchi 2017, p. 110). In an earlier and more detailed analysis of the same issue, he concluded that the Clinton plan lost for many reasons, including the all-out opposition of the NAM, the Chamber of Commerce, and small business, but the weakness of the corporate elite was crucial: "Ultimately, however, what prevented constructive reform from occurring was the ineffectuality of the corporate elite" (Mizruchi 2013, p. 252). To the contrary, Clinton's health-care plan lost because both the moderate conservatives and the ultraconservatives in the corporate community (that

Circuitous Path to the Affordable Care Act   353

is, the Business Roundtable, the Chamber of Commerce, and the NAM) decided they opposed it for a variety of reasons, especially in the context of the apparent control of costs through HMOs and other types of prepaid managed care. The defeat of the plan had nothing to do with any of the issues raised by Mizruchi (2013; 2017).

The Affordable Care Act

There were several small changes in government support for health care in the late 1990s and early 2000s that were acceptable to, or actively encouraged by, the corporate community and the Republican-dominated Congress. The most important in terms of low-income citizens was a new benefit for children whose parents made less than two times the poverty level. It aided several hundred thousand children at the outset, and eventually several million. More relevant from a corporate point of view, which favored as much privatization of health-care services as possible, the Medicare Modernization Act of 2003 offered major incentives to insurance companies to press harder for HMOs, with initial payment rates 25 percent higher for Medicare patients enrolled in HMOs than for those who preferred traditional fee-for-services physicians; it also included "tax incentives to encourage higher-income elderly to purchase private health-care as a substitute for Medicare" (Quadagno 2005, pp. 199).

In addition, the Medicare Modernization Act added coverage for Medicare patients' medication costs, which passed with ease once the drug companies were given the right to set the price. Medicare would pay for medications, with no possibility that Medicare could try to bargain (Quadagno 2005, pp. 199). More generally, the 2003 Medicare legislation was supported by a "mammoth coalition" that was opposed by an "equally heavy set of groups," but the supporting groups in this instance had been created by the health insurance and drug corporations, who created this benefit in the face of opposition from the entire liberal-labor coalition (Baumgartner, Berry, Hojnacki, Kimball, and Leech 2009, p. 231). (The generosity of the Republican Congress to the health services industry in 2003 was an important basis for the "cost savings" that were negotiated by the Democrats to make the Affordable Care Act affordable a few years later.)

The compromises contained in a new insurance package legislated in Massachusetts in the early spring of 2006 created a prototype for a similar package of health-care assistance that eventually became the Affordable Care Act in 2010 (hereafter usually the ACA). This unanticipated new opportunity originated in 2004 when the Bush Administration refused to renew special payments of $385 million per year to the state to support its expanded Medicaid program. This rejection came in the context of the budget deficits the Bush Administration had created for itself with its large

2001 and 2003 tax cuts, along with the impending expense for its new Medicare drug benefit. It was also looking to trim back Medicaid expansions in other states as well, not just in Massachusetts.

Faced with a potential budget crisis due to this refusal, the Republican governor, Mitt Romney, who already had a task force thinking about health-care issues, reached out to the state's powerful liberal voice in Congress, Senator Ted Kennedy. Romney sought Kennedy's help in convincing President Bush and his secretary of health and human services to grant another three-year extension (McDonough 2011, p. 39). Kennedy had friendly relationships with both the president and the health and human services secretary, and he lobbied them heavily. However, the fact that the governor was a Republican with potential national appeal very likely had a more important role in convincing the Bush Administration to provide the extension. This time, however, if Massachusetts did not develop its own self-financed program within a three-year window, it would have to reimburse the federal government for its extra annual federal supplement, which would add up to nearly $1.2 billion for those three years. This provision created a powerful incentive to compromise.

Even with a billion-dollar IOU looming in the background, the wrangling between the state's business community and the liberal-labor activists, along with the conflicts between Romney and the Democratic legislature, were not settled until shortly before the federal deadline. The cohesive state-level corporate coalition created for this issue feared a possible tax increase for business if the federal money disappeared and the debt had to be paid. Since the issue concerned expanding access to the uninsured, it was not directly threatening to businesses, but the plan the corporate coalition supported was a minimal one. It included an individual mandate to buy health insurance, but not an employer mandate to offer insurance to employees. The Massachusetts Business Roundtable, the Associated Industries of Massachusetts, the Greater Boston Chamber of Commerce, and the Massachusetts Taxpayers Foundation worked together to keep costs for business low, but it was moderate on this issue in that it could lean a little left of center if need be (McDonough 2018).

At the same time, the Affordable Care Today coalition, which called itself ACT!, in concert with its liberal allies in the Massachusetts House, and with strong support from the Service Employees International Union (SEIU), demanded an expansion of the current state Medicaid program and the coverage of more children from low-income families. To pay for the program, it wanted an employer mandate to complement the individual mandate. To develop support for its program, ACT! held numerous rallies and engaged in vigorous lobbying. It also circulated a petition to put its health-care plan on the ballot in November 2006, if the legislature did not act before the deadline (McDonough 2011, pp. 38, 40).

The liberal-labor alliance had a silent ally, the Blue Cross Blue Shield Foundation. In the late 1990s, Blue Cross Blue Shield of Massachusetts had an abundance of cash and was thinking about emulating the various Blue Shield Blue Cross companies in other states that began to convert to a for-profit status beginning in 1994. However, it decided to stay nonprofit and use some of its extra money to create a foundation, which had the explicit mission of working toward universal coverage in the state. The company's leadership also decided to hire a former liberal aide to a Democratic governor to head the foundation, who at the time worked for the Massachusetts Hospital Association. The foundation issued a series of reports on reform options, held forums, and served as a bridge that helped connect the business community, ACT!, and the legislature (McDonough 2011, p. 38).

After a long stalemate, and in the face of the federal deadline, ACT! accepted a much smaller employer mandate than it had advocated at the outset. The Democratic majorities in both houses of the state legislature, with liberal House members prodding the more mainstream Senate Democrats, substantially expanded the Romney plan. It now included deeper and broader financial subsidies, an expansive statewide set of benefits, and a $295 per employee penalty (brokered by the business leaders in negotiations with the governor and the legislature) for those businesses with 11 or more employees that did not provide health insurance (McDonough 2011, p. 40). Even then, Romney used his veto powers to eliminate the employer mandate when he signed the legislation in April 2006. The legislature then overrode this and several other Romney vetoes of specific provisions.

Because the plan in essence called for everyone to pay as much as they could, it was a societal effort to cover major health-care expenses for every citizen in Massachusetts that might need extra help some day. In that regard, it was a "collective" endeavor that is consistent with liberal values. However, Romney also could construe ("frame") the legislation in conservative terms as the ultimate in individual self-responsibility because everyone had to look out for themselves by having insurance. In doing so, Romney drew on the fact that the ultraconservative Heritage Foundation had reintroduced the Committee for Economic Development's endorsement of an individual mandate into the health-care argument in 1990, and had recommended that insurance exchanges should be set up to make it easier to individuals to shop for an insurance plan. To underscore these points, Romney had a Heritage representative as one of the speakers at the celebration of the enactment of the plan (McDonough 2011, pp. 37–38, 40).

In other words, both liberal and ultraconservative ideologies could be used to justify the same program to their very different constituencies. However, by that point, some 16 years after Heritage first spoke, most national-level ultraconservatives had decided to reject the idea of an individual mandate as an imposition on individual freedom. They also had concluded that their opposition to any form of government-sponsored health insurance would be a winning electoral strategy if they constantly invoked the threat to freedom that government social insurance allegedly posed. They therefore derided Romney's involvement in "Romneycare" when he made an unsuccessful bid for the Republican presidential nomination in 2008 (McDonough 2011, p. 43).

In the immediate aftermath of this legislative success, there was renewed corporate, liberal-labor, and Congressional interest in the possibility of national reform along similar lines. The program seemed to work and it had potential ideological appeal to both liberals and at least some Republicans. In February 2007, the Business Roundtable agreed to join a diverse coalition to discuss possible reforms, which also included the SEIU and AARP. It even included the NFIB for a short time due to the willingness of its new president, appointed in late 2006, to take part. (In terms of his business background, as might be expected from the NFIB by this point, the new president had made many millions of dollars when he sold the Virginia-based high-tech company he headed to a large British technology corporation for $300 million (McCarthy 2005).)

The new health-care coalition, called Divided We Fail, had the modest goal of determining if its members shared enough common ground to recommend or support a possible plan (McDonough 2011, p. 54). In May 2007, the CEO of Safeway organized a Coalition to Advance Health Care Reform, which included 36 other companies (McDonough 2011, pp. 53–54; Nizza 2007). The Business Roundtable (2007) endorsed the individual mandate a month later. In doing so, it borrowed a page out of Romney's playbook by saying that it is the *responsibility* of all Americans to obtain insurance, which is in effect an endorsement of the individual mandate in the name of personal responsibility.

By this point, a new, all-encompassing insurance trade association joined the parade as well. America's Health Insurance Plans (AHIP) had been created in 2003 to represent the large insurance companies as well as some large managed care companies that did much of their billing to insurance companies. The new association also included the smaller companies that had completely opposed Clinton's plan from the start in 1993 through their Health Insurance Association of America (Altman and Shactman 2011, pp. 260–261). The new AHIP, including the smaller insurance companies that had joined it, had started to rethink its position shortly after the passage of the Massachusetts health-care legislation, and began putting out plans to save money on health care in late 2006 and early 2007 (McDonough 2011, p. 55). It expressed support for an individual mandate in 2007.

In making this transition, AHIP's members may have had their eye on increasing their business opportunities in a context in which they were losing their biggest customers to self-insurance plans (Brill 2015, p. 51).

By 1999, according to research by the nonprofit Employee Benefit Research Institute, 66 percent of companies with 1,000 or more employees had at least one self-insured health plan, a figure that reached 84 percent by 2011; similarly, the percentage of all private-sector employees in self-insured company plans rose from 41 percent in 1999 to 59 percent by 2011 (Fronstin 2016, p. 3; Miller 2012). Whether members of AHIP worried about this trend or not, at the least they knew a new corporate-friendly government health-care program that incorporated many more millions of people could be a potentially lucrative market for them.

The legislation the corporate moderates were willing to support at this point would include both an employer mandate and an individual mandate, make maximum use of private-sector health insurance and HMOs, and retain Medicare. In fact, all of these features were already part of a proposal in 1993 by moderate Republicans in the Senate, which was offered as an alternative to the Clinton initiative. As Quadagno (2014, p. 35) concluded, "[t]he ACA's key provisions, the employer mandate and the individual mandate, were Republican policy ideas, and its fundamental principles were nearly identical to the Health Equity and Access Reform Today Act of 1993, a bill promoted by Republican senators to deflect support for President Bill Clinton's Health Security plan." These principles also parallel the assumptions underlying the proposal put forth by corporate moderates in the early 1970s, including the individual mandate, as best embodied in the report by the CED (1973).

The highly visible public statements in 2007 by many corporate leaders concerning their views on health insurance are consistent with the expectations theory of policy change, which hypothesizes that clear signals from leaders in the corporate community are one of the ways in which large corporations influence policy decisions (Swenson 2002, Chapters 9–10). Whether these signals were the reason or not, the early frontrunner for the Democrat presidential nomination in 2008, Hillary Clinton, made clear at a forum for Democratic presidential hopefuls, sponsored by the SEIU in late March 2007, that she had a plan that included these provisions. However, her most visible liberal opponent at that moment made a strong play for her liberal supporters. A former trial lawyer who had been the Democratic senator from North Carolina from 1999 to 2005, and the Democratic nominee for vice president in 2004, he in effect endorsed a plan advocated by many liberals and labor leaders through Health Care for America Now (HealthCAN). As a large umbrella organization, it had major financial backing of at least $26 million dollars from liberal philanthropies. HealthCAN eventually collected signatures from 140 members of Congress, who said they backed the general principles of the organization's overall plan (McDonough 2011, p. 57).

Called the "public option," this left-liberal idea called for a government-sponsored health-care plan that could be included within the array of private insurance plans that would be made available. The ostensible aim was to provide competition for the private insurers to force them to offer plans at reasonable prices, but the implicit hope of strong liberals, and leftists who liked the idea as well, was that it would be favored by the general public to a large extent, or be ready to fill the gap if the private insurance market became too expensive or failed. The specifics of the plan advocated by HealthCAN were developed by political scientist Jacob Hacker (Hacker 2007; McDonough 2011, pp. 56–57, 133–134), who earlier wrote the book on the failed Clinton Plan (*The Road To Nowhere*, 1996).

Many mainstream liberals, centrists, and health economists thought Hacker's plan was more problematic than strong liberals claimed. Whatever the merits of the plan according to different groups of liberals and centrists, it was anathema to the insurance companies because it might shrink their market to a size at which they could not agree to accept applicants with previously existing conditions. It was also unacceptable to hospitals and physicians because they feared it might eventually lead to price controls (Altman and Shactman 2011, pp. 296–302).

As for the third major Democratic candidate, future President Barack Obama, he expressed doubts that people should be forced to buy insurance. When he released his own plan in late May, which built on the existing system, he pledged that it would not contribute to the federal debt. The plan would bring in low-income individuals through tax credits and subsidies, and create Heritage-style state-run insurance exchanges that would include a public option. It called for a provision that would allow Medicare to negotiate prices with the drug companies, but did not include an individual mandate. Instead, there was only a mandate that parents had to purchase health care for their children.

The Obama plan hewed as close to the center of the political spectrum as possible. Three economists known to be concerned about cost control wrote most of its provisions. One of them, a professor of economics at Brandeis, had led the small government staff that created the Nixon plans for 1971 and 1974. He also had been among those marginalized or dismissed by president-elect Bill Clinton in January 1993, based on his doubts that it would be possible to control costs as effectively as Clinton and his trusted adviser believed to be possible (Altman and Shactman 2011, pp. 34, 53, 62–63, 245.) Obama's rivals for the nomination heavily criticized his plan's omission of the individual mandate because it was widely agreed that such a mandate was necessary. It was therefore inadequate from a policy point of view. However, there are indications that Obama soft-pedaled the individual mandate because he knew from polling that many voters did not like the idea, and in any case he wanted to appear more centrist than Clinton and her rivals to her left (Altman and Shactman 2011, p. 249; Brill 2015, pp. 36, 61; Starr 2011, pp. 186–187).

While Republican Senator John McCain and Democrat Obama campaigned for the presidency in the months before the election, the two Senate committees most crucial to health-care issues, the Finance Committee and the Committee on Health, Education, Labor and Pensions, hosted an all-day bipartisan meeting for approximately 250 elected officials and staff members at the Library of Congress. The purpose was to keep the health-care issue alive in Congress, with the hope there would be health-care reform whichever candidate won the presidency. Then, in October, with a month remaining before the elections, Senator Kennedy, the chair of the Committee on Health, Education, Labor and Pensions, instructed members of his staff to meet with approximately 20 officials from a wide range of organizations that represented various business groups, along with mainstream liberals, centrists, and even a few conservatives.

In arranging for this meeting, Kennedy wanted to learn if the members of this potentially broad coalition were still in favor of health-care reform. As everyone at the meeting was well aware, the Business Roundtable had released a four-part health plan a week or two before the meeting, which included the individual mandate despised by ultraconservatives, along with subsidies for low-income people (McDonough 2011, p. 53). It soon became clear as the discussion unfolded that no one in the room was for any of the more liberal plans that had been offered in recent months. Nor did any of them favor a slow, incremental approach that would start with federal support for state-level initiatives. When it came to an approach similar to Romneycare, there was large majority support. However, the representatives from five business groups, including those from the Business Roundtable and the Chamber of Commerce, conspicuously abstained. They soon met separately and decided they were on board under two conditions: (1) it would be a uniform national plan so businesses would not have to deal with 50 different state governments; and (2) there would be no tampering with the 1974 pension legislation that made it possible for corporations to self-insure at the state level (McDonough 2011, p. 37). There were no objections to these two provisos from the other participants in the fledgling coalition.

By this point the ultraconservative front group, the National Federation of Independent Business, which continued to mislabel itself as a business association, had returned to its usual all-out opposition (and the president who had joined the Divided We Fail coalition was no longer its president) (Mandelbaum 2009b; McDonough 2011, p. 54). Meanwhile, the NFIB continued to be treated as a legitimate representative of small business in the academic literature, despite all the evidence to the contrary. Consistent with that past evidence, a 2008 national survey of small-business owners with 100 or fewer employees showed that approximately one-third said they were Democrats and 29 percent said they had no party affiliation,

360 Social Insurance Created and Undermined

leaving only about one-third as self-declared Republicans; then too, most of the NFIB's campaign donations continued to go to Republicans, even while insisting it was a nonpartisan organization (Mandelbaum 2009a). In 2011–2012, shortly after the Affordable Care Act passed, the NFIB gave over 98 percent of its campaign contributions to Republicans, drawing in good part on large donations it obtained from a secretive Republican Political Action Committee (CMD 2012).

More generally, the Divided We Fail coalition failed because the Business Roundtable on the one side and AARP and the SEIU on the other could not agree. However, the Business Roundtable did not reject the possibility of new legislation. It therefore continued to work for the kind of reforms it wanted (McCanne 2009). Looking at the failure of the Divided We Fail coalition in terms of the likely calculations of AARP and the SEIU, and the liberal-labor alliance more generally, the reformers very possibly believed they could win more in the governmental arena than the Business Roundtable was willing to concede to them to be part of a broader center-liberal coalition.

Staying consistent with his campaign promises, and against the advice of some of his political advisers, Obama continued to state that he wanted to make health-care legislation his first order of business and a potential legacy. He further said he would leave the details of the legislation to the Congressional committees that had been setting the stage through their public and private meetings with key stakeholders. In that context, he carefully avoided any statement on the individual mandate. Veteran Democratic staff members from the two key Senate committees then wrote a detailed draft of the bill between June 17 and July 15, 2009, which included the individual mandate. At this point the president said he would accept it (McDonough 2011, p. 60).

Although President Obama did not involve himself in the details of the legislation, he and his White House aides did make a concerted effort to line up as much business support as they could, which in good part involved bargaining over the amount of cost savings each business sector was willing to provide. By late June the White House, with the considerable help of the Democratic chair of the Senate Finance Committee and his staff, could announce that the trade association for the drug companies had agreed to have its member companies provide $80 billion in discounts to Medicare patients over a ten-year period, partly in exchange for the greatly expanded market that would be created by the new legislation (McDonough 2011, p. 76). In addition, the pharmaceutical manufacturers were in effect foregoing some of the riches handed to them by the Medicare Modernization Act in 2003 by helping to cover a gap in that legislation. This gap had been necessitated by a constraint Congress had imposed on itself in terms of how much a new spending bill could contribute to an increase in the national debt. This show of proper budgetary caution had left some of the elderly paying a higher percentage of their prescription costs once they had spent more than a certain minimum and before they reached a high point at which the government paid most of the cost (McDonough 2011, p. 172–173). The drug companies further cemented the bargain by spending an estimated $150 million in lobbying and media coverage in support of the legislation (Kirkpatrick 2009; Mizruchi 2013, p. 257).

The Obama Administration then entered into negotiations with three major associations representing a wide range of hospitals. They were able to reach agreement by early July for $155 billion in savings over a ten-year period (McDonough 2011, p. 78). In exchange, the hospitals were exempted for a ten-year period from any general payment cut that might be made by a new Independent Payments Advisory Board, which would be mandated to make general payment cuts if certain overall spending levels were exceeded (Altman and Shactman 2011, p. 371). The large for-profit hospitals and hospital chains, represented by the Federation of American Hospitals, were fully accommodated on their main issues at that point, although they insisted it would not be a reasonable deal for them if less than 95 percent of the population was covered. The nonprofit Catholic Hospital Association, which strongly supported coverage for everyone for moral reasons, was able to reach an acceptable compromise with the Democrats for dealing with the highly charged issue of public funding for abortion. However, negotiations with the largest association of hospitals, the American Hospital Association, took much longer because it included a wide array of hospitals. Its member hospitals in rural regions felt they were being short-changed by a reimbursement formula that seemed to favor large urban hospitals, so lengthy negotiations within the association and with the government were necessary to resolve the issue to everyone's satisfaction (Altman and Shactman 2011, p. 266).

The AMA did not come out in favor of the plan until December after lengthy bargaining in which it gained little or nothing. The AMA was the only major organized body that was not asked for a cost saving, but it did not receive solid guarantees for any of the changes it had sought, although a few medical specialties gained some small breaks. The potential for yearly cuts in Medicare payments to physicians, which had been included in legislation in 2000, but usually suspended on a year-to-year basis, was not rescinded, although it was suspended for at least another year. A promised independent vote on the issue did not occur because the bill had to be finalized in a hurry when the Democrats unexpectedly lost a Senate seat in Massachusetts in a special election after the death of Senator Kennedy.

Nor could the AMA modify or remove the plan for an Independent Payment Advisory Board, which worried physicians because they felt they would be the first to be hit by any cutbacks the board recommended. The AMA also saw the public option as a threat for similar reasons (Altman and Shactman 2011, pp. 271–273; McDonough 2011, pp. 52, 173–176).

Similarly, negotiations with the trade association for medical devices also took longer than expected, despite a willingness to compromise by both sides, so the final details, and a cost saving of $20 billion, were not agreed upon until the same month, December, that agreement was reached with the AMA.

Despite the efforts to accommodate as many major sectors of the healthcare community as possible before introducing the legislation into Congress, the Democrats could not reach agreement on a range of issues with the insurance companies represented by AHIP. The most important of these issues involved the size of the cost givebacks expected of the industry through its individual companies. The Democrats, working through the chair of the Senate Finance Committee and his staff in this instance, asked for the same level of cost savings that the pharmaceutical companies had agreed to, $155 billion over a ten-year period. However, AHIP offered only $80 billion based on its own studies. An independent assessment by a Wall Street firm concluded that the insurance industry could afford to go higher, and the nonpartisan Congressional Budget Office said that none of AHIP's suggested efficiencies would save any money. But AHIP would not budge on this issue (Altman and Shactman 2011, pp. 262–264; McDonough 2011, pp. 78, 169).

At the same time, liberals successfully added what they considered to be necessary provisions that would limit insurance company profits. For example, the companies would be required to pay out 80 percent of what they received from companies with small plans and 85 percent of what they received from companies with large plans. Then, too, the AHIP negotiators were deeply angry about the exemption of hospitals from any payment cuts by the Independent Payment Advisory Board for a ten-year period. In those circumstances, the insurance industry claimed there could be considerable cost increases for them (Altman and Shactman 2011, p. 371). Nor did the insurance industry want the liberal plan for a public option included in the bill because of the uncertainties it would introduce into the actuarial analyses used in pricing decisions. In the face of this entangled bundle of differences, the negotiations ended in July 2009, and AHIP began lobbying against the plan, claiming it would increase insurance premiums dramatically. AHIP also quietly started to give what eventually added up to $86.2 million to the Chamber of Commerce to attack the plan in the name of small businesses (McDonough 2011, pp. 78–79, 169). (In 2011, AHIP gave $850,000 to the NFIB as part of an effort to convince Congress to repeal a provision in the ACA it did not like (Potter 2013).)

Once the details of the legislation were agreed upon by the White House and Democratic leaders in Congress, virtually all of the Republicans in Congress opposed the legislation for their usual reasons, including those advanced by AHIP, the NFIB, and the Chamber of Commerce. At that point, however, the Democrats had 60 votes in the Senate and a

Circuitous Path to the Affordable Care Act   363

258–177 majority in the House, so any disagreements that mattered were among Democrats. With the exception of the public option in the Senate, those disagreements did not include the issues that had been negotiated with representatives of the corporate community. Instead, they primarily involved social issues relating to religion, sexuality, and most of all, abortion, which led to prolonged and highly contentious battles.

Ignoring the reassurances and appeals of the Catholic Hospital Association, which had a strong representation of nuns in its leadership, the conservative male hierarchy of the Catholic Church, with the help of Protestant evangelicals, came close to defeating the legislation in the House on the basis of their shared opposition to abortion. However, enough liberals very reluctantly accepted a compromise on abortion for the bill to pass (Altman and Shactman 2011, pp. 288–291). In the end, only one Republican in the House, a Vietnamese American from New Orleans, supported the bill, to the great displeasure of his colleagues.

When the bill returned to the Senate for final consideration, the corporate community's opposition to the public option rose to the fore within the context of the effort to win the final few Democratic votes that were needed. As already noted, the public option was anathema to the insurance companies, including the large insurance companies in Hartford and New York, and they had a sympathetic friend in the centrist Democratic senator from Connecticut. The price of his vote, along with that of a conservative Democrat from Nebraska, was the removal of the public option (Altman and Shactman 2011, pp. 290–291, 296–302, for a detailed discussion of this contentious issue). The Senate majority leader also had to make specific deals with three Democratic senators to secure their votes. The Nebraska senator demanded that the federal government pay the full cost for any Medicaid expansion in his state. The senator from Louisiana received special Medicaid payments for her state, and the Senator from Arkansas won the elimination of any penalties for employers that did not provide health insurance for provisional employees (McDonough 2011, p. 91–92)

Following the passage of the Affordable Care Act, the health-care industry became even more concentrated due to a new wave of mergers, with hospitals more clearly at the center of the system (Starr 2017, pp. 274–275). At the same time, health care in the United States remained more expensive than in most countries, primarily because of higher administrative costs, higher drug costs, and higher salaries for physicians. Then, too, and not insignificant in terms of the importance of consumer demand, the higher cost of American health care also involved the wider use of potentially life-saving surgeries and other intensive medical applications; they had been strongly demanded by middle- and upper-middle-class Americans, many of whom voted Republican. Most physicians also had advocated intensive medical procedures as well. Nevertheless, the ACA did

364 Social Insurance Created and Undermined

cut projected health-care costs, as Obama's economists and the Congressional Budget Office had predicted it would (Altman and Shactman 2011, pp. 246, 251; Cutler and Sahni 2013).

This general analysis of the power struggle over the Affordable Care Act contrasts once again with that of the political sociologist who sees the "corporate elite" as fractured. Although he notes that some corporate leaders were "involved at all stages of the process" that led to the Affordable Care Act, he concludes that the corporate elite was "far less central than it had been during the debate of the Clinton plan, and had "essentially sat on the sidelines" (Mizruchi 2013, p. 258). Whatever the merits of this surprising claim about sitting on the sidelines may prove to be if new archival evidence appears, several conclusions seem to be firmly established based on detailed analyses of the origins and passage of the legislation that were not taken into consideration in making his assertion (Altman and Shactman 2011; McDonough 2011; Quadagno 2011). All of them provide information showing that the corporate moderates played a major role.

There are numerous indications of this central role: (1) the act was based on principles that were created and insisted upon by the moderate conservatives in the corporate community; (2) many corporate moderates joined health-insurance coalitions with non-business groups in 2007, and the Business Roundtable endorsed the individual mandate in 2007 and offered its own plan in 2008; (3) corporate moderates were involved in all stages of the legislative process (recall that the Business Roundtable was consulted as late at December 24, 2009); (4) the issues of concern to the pharmaceutical, hospital, and medical devices sectors of the corporate community were accommodated before the legislation went to Congress; (5) the corporate moderates did not try to block the bill; (6) the concerns of the insurance companies—and hospitals and physicians—were assuaged to some extent by the removal of the public option; and (7) the efforts to defeat the bill by AHIP, the Chamber of Commerce, and the NFIB failed.

The passage of the ACA, which corporate moderates favored, when juxtaposed with the failure of the Clinton health-care plan in 1994, which the corporate moderates opposed, provides strong evidence that they were a pivotal point in the ACA process. But it is also true that the legislation could not have passed if the liberal-labor alliance had not been willing to give ground on abortion funding. The act was therefore the product of a coalition of corporate moderates, the liberal-labor alliance, and the Democratic Party, a coalition that had rarely appeared after the 1960s.

For the most part, as already mentioned at the end of Chapter 7, the ACA was more similar to than different from the CED's report on *Building A National Health-Care System* (1973). As in the CED plan, corporate employees still had employer-provided health-insurance plans, and Medicare remained in place for the elderly. The CED had called for community trusts for the poor and near-poor, which would be overseen by Medicaid officials, whereas the ACA has state-level insurance exchanges that offer a range of federally subsidized private insurance plans. The CED projected that Medicaid would decline in its importance, and the ACA proponents similarly projected that Medicaid would be at least partially replaced by the state insurance exchanges.

Instead, Medicaid has continued to grow over the decades, so once again the corporate moderates were neither seers nor all-powerful. In 2017, perhaps as many as 19 percent of all those with any form of health insurance were covered by Medicaid. More generally, about one-third of those with health insurance were in one of three government insurance programs: Medicare, Medicaid, or the Veterans Administration (Pear 2017).

Conclusion

The Social Security Act of 1935, which was clearly based on principles that emerged from the experience of corporate moderates with their private insurance plans, and then honed into specific plans within the policy-planning network, was the first major government program to provide social insurance to a majority of Americans. Its provisions for old-age pensions, unemployment insurance, and assistance for single mothers with young children, along with old-age assistance for those who do not receive Social Security pensions, established the foundations for an expanded system of social benefits in the future. The Social Security Act was gradually supplemented by disability benefits, Medicare, Medicaid, the Earned Income Tax Credit, job-training programs, rent support, subsidies to developers for building low-income housing, and the expansion of supplemental nutritional assistance in times of major crisis. Finally, the Affordable Care Act, in conjunction with expansions in Medicaid, helped to reduce the percentage of Americans without health insurance from 16.0 percent in 2010 to 9.1 percent in 2015, and it would have been even lower if many Republican-dominated state legislatures had not refused to accept the expansion of Medicaid (Starr 2017, p. 472).

Taken together, these government programs made it possible for the elderly, low-income people, the unemployed, and single mothers with young children to squeeze by on a day-to-day basis, especially after Social Security pensions were indexed for inflation in the mid-1970s, and food stamps were made more readily available in times of economic crisis. In addition, as noted in Chapter 8, the urban poor and the homeless received some help, albeit very limited, from foundation-funded and tax-subsidized Community Development Corporations, corporate-sponsored low-income housing programs, United Way, churches, and local charities.

Nevertheless, the fact remains that the poverty rate, which fell from 22.4 percent in 1959 to 11.1 percent in 1973, due in part to the creation

366 Social Insurance Created and Undermined

of various crisis-generated social benefits that were later cut back, such as rental and low-income housing subsidies that benefit the poor, varied between 12 and 15 percent between the late 1970s and 2012 (Seefeldt, Abner, Bolinger, Xu, and Graham 2012). As a result, the United States had the most meager welfare state among the 35 industrialized democracies that are compared by means of information compiled by the Organisation for Economic Development and Cooperation.

All of these outcomes are further evidence for the power of the corporate rich and the power elite through their policy-planning network and the conservative coalition in Congress. New social-insurance programs were created in the 1930s and then again in the 1960s in the face of economic calamity or social unrest. They grew little or were reduced in size when a united corporate community opposed any further expansions. The lack of further growth in these programs indicates that the power elite were able to starve the federal government by limiting taxes on high incomes and capital gains, by holding wages to a minimum, and by supporting an opinion-shaping network that repeatedly blamed the victims of corporate power for their poverty and lack of education.

It is also notable that the one program that continued to grow, federally supported health insurance, was not close to universal until 2010, and it was based on the principles that the corporate moderates had first decided upon by 1973. Put another way, the health-care program did not reach its early twenty-first century form until the liberal-labor alliance abandoned its hopes for a single-payer ("Medicare-For-All") system and for a system of regional health alliances that would replace most employer-based insurance programs.

With the exception of their acceptance of health insurance for nearly everyone, the corporate rich and the power elite had increased poverty after the 1970s, while most similar countries were reducing it. In 1979, the average American could expect to live about 1.6 years longer than people in other well-to-do nations, but by 2015 they were likely to die nearly two years earlier than citizens in comparable countries (Ingraham 2017). At the same time, differences in life expectancies between higher-income and lower-income people in the United States grew as well (Chetty, Stepner, Abraham, Cutler, Lin, Scuderi, Turner, and Bergeron 2016).

References

Altman, Stuart and David Shactman. 2011. *Power, politics, and universal health care: The inside story of a century-long battle.* Amherst, NY: Prometheus Books.

Baumgartner, Frank, Jeffrey M. Berry, David Hojnacki, David Kimball, and Beth Leech. 2009. *Lobbying and policy change: Who wins, who loses, and why.* Chicago: University of Chicago Press.

Bergthold, Linda. 1990. *Purchasing power in health: Business, the state, and health care politics.* New Brunswick: Rutgers University Press.

————. 1995. "American business and health care reform: 'Do we have to move so fast?'." Paper presented to the American Sociological Association. Washington, DC.

Brill, Steven. 2015. *America's bitter pill: Money, politics, backroom deals, and the fight to fix our broken healthcare system*. New York: Random House.

Business Roundtable. 2007. "Business Roundtable unveils principles for health care reform." Washington. https://www.businessroundtable.org/archive/media/news-releases/business-roundtable-unveils-principles-for-health-care-reform.

CED. 1973. *Building a national health-care system: A statement on national policy*. New York: Committee for Economic Development.

Chetty, Raj, Michael Stepner, Sarah Abraham, David Cutler, Shelby Lin, Benjamin Scuderi, Nicholas Turner, and Augustin Bergeron. 2016. "The association between income and life expectancy in the United States, 2001–2014." *Journal of the American Medical Association* 315:1750–1766.

CMD. 2012. "The National Federation for Independent Business: A front group for big business." Madison: Center for Media and Democracy. www.sourcewatch.org.

Cutler, David and Nikhil Sahni. 2013. "If slow rate of health care spending growth persists, projections may be off by \$770 billion." *Health Affairs* 32:841–850.

Domhoff, G. W. 1995. "Who killed health care reform in Congress, small business or rich conservatives, and why did they do it?" Paper presented to the *American Sociological Association*. Washington, DC.

Fronstin, Paul. 2016. "Self-Insured Health Plans: Recent Trends by Firm Size, 1996–2015." *Employee Benefit Research Institute: Notes* 37:1–6.

Hacker, Jacob. 1996. *The road to nowhere: The genesis of President Clinton's plan for health security*. Princeton: Princeton University Press.

————. 2007. *Health care for America: A proposal for guaranteed affordable health care for all Americans building on Medicare and employment-based insurance*. Washington: Economic Policy Institute.

Hamilton, Richard. 1975. *Restraining myths: Critical studies of U.S. social structure and politics*. New York: Sage Publications.

Ingraham, Christopher. 2017. "Americans are dying younger than people in other rich nations." *The Washington Post*, December 27, https://www.washingtonpost.com/news/wonk/wp/2017/12/27/americans-are-dying-younger-than-people-in-other-rich-nations.

Johnson, Haynes and David Broder. 1996. *The system: The American way of politics at the breaking point*. Boston: Little, Brown & Company.

Judis, John. 1995. "Abandoned surgery: Business and the failure of health reform." *American Prospect*. https://prospect.org/article/abandoned-surgery-business-and-failure-health-reform.

Kazee, Nicole, Michael Lipsky, and Cathie Jo Martin. 2008. "Outside the big box: Who speaks for small business?" *Boston Review*, July/August. http://bostonreview.net/BR33.4/kazee.php.

Kirkpatrick, David. 2009. "Drug industry to run ads favoring White House plan." P. A13 in *The New York Times*.

Mandelbaum, Robb. 2009a. "Whom does the N.F.I.B. represent (besides its members)?" *The New York Times*, August 26, pp. https://boss.blogs.nytimes.com/2009/08/26/whom-does-the-nfib-represent-besides-its-members.

———. 2009b. "NFIB's trailblazing president hits the highway." *Inc.com*, January 16. https://www.inc.com/the-entrepreneurial-agenda/2009/01/nfibs_trailblazing_president_h.html.

Martin, Cathie. 1995. "Stuck in neutral: Big business and the politics of national health reform." *Journal of Health Politics, Policy and Law* 20:431–436.

McCanne, Don. 2009. "Comment." In "'Divided We Fail' is divided and failing." *Chicago Tribune*, February 16. Reproduced by Physicians for a National Health Program. http://pnhp.org/blog/2009/02/17/divided-we-fail-is-divided-and-failing.

McCarthy, Ellen. 2005. "Apogen sold to British tech firm." *The Washington Post*, August 3. http://www.washingtonpost.com/wp-dyn/content/article/2005/08/02/AR2005080201899.html.

McDonough, John. 2011. *Inside national health reform*. Berkeley: University of California Press.

———. 2018. "Background information on the passage of Romneycare." Personal email to G. W. Domhoff.

Miller, Stephen 2012. "More employees covered by self-insured health plans." Society for Human Resource Management. https://www.shrm.org/resources andtools/hr-topics/benefits/pages/self-insured-health-plans.aspx.

Mintz, Beth. 1998. "The failure of health care reform: The role of big business in policy formation." Pp. 210–224 in *Social Policy and the conservative agenda*, edited by C. Lo and M. Schwartz. Malden, MA: Blackwell.

Mizruchi, Mark. 2013. *The fracturing of the American corporate elite*. Cambridge: Harvard University Press.

———. 2017. "The Power Elite in historical context: A reevaluation of Mills's thesis, then and now." *Theory and Society* 46.

Nizza, Mike. 2007. "A C.E.O. pitches universal health care." in *The New York Times*, May 7.

Pear, Robert. 2017. "Moves to shrink health law add to federal role." *The New York Times*, December 27, p. A1.

Potter, Wendell. 2013. "NFIB and AHIP: Hidden influence-peddling in Washington." Center for Media and Democracy. https://www.prwatch.org/news/2013/05/12117/nfib-and-ahip-hidden-influence-peddling-washington.

Quadagno, Jill. 2005. *One nation, uninsured: Why the U.S. has no national health insurance*. New York: Oxford University Press.

———. 2011. "Interest-group influence on the Patient Protection and Affordability Act of 2010: Winners and losers in the health care reform debate." *Journal of Health Politics, Policy and Law* 36:449–453.

———. 2014. "Right-wing conspiracy? Socialist plot? The origins of the Patient Protection and Affordable Care Act." *Journal of Health Politics, Policy and Law* 39:35–56.

Seefeldt, Kristin, Gordon Abner, Joe Bolinger, Lanlan Xu, and John Graham. 2012. "At risk: America's poor during and after the Great Recession." School of Public and Environmental Affairs, Indiana University, Bloomington.

Shaiko, R. and M. Wallace. 1999. "From Wall Street to Main Street: The National Federation of Independent Business and the new Republican majority."

Pp. 18–35 in *After The Revolution: PACs, lobbies, and the Republican Congress*, edited by R. Biersack, P. Herrnson, and C. Wilcox. Boston: Allyn and Bacon.

Starr, Paul. 1978. "Controlling medical costs through countervailing power." *Working Papers for a New Society* 5:10–11, 97–98.

———. 1994. *The logic of health-care reform: Why and how the president's plan will work*. New York: Whittle Books in association with Penguin Books.

———. 2011. *Remedy and reaction: The peculiar American struggle over health care reform*. New Haven: Yale University Press.

———. 2017. *The social transformation of American medicine: The rise of a sovereign profession and the making of a vast industry*. New York Basic Books.

——— (Forthcoming). "The Health Care Legacy of the Great Society" in *Reshaping the Federal Government: The Policy and Management Legacies of the Johnson Years*, edited by N. J. Glickman, L. E. Lynn, & R. H. Wilson.

Swenson, Peter. 2002. *Capitalists against markets: The making of labor markets and welfare states in the United States and Sweden*. New York: Oxford University Press.

Swenson, Peter and Scott Greer. 2002. "Foul weather friends: Big business and health care reform in the 1990s in historical perspective." *Journal of Health Politics, Policy and Law* 22:605–638.

Tesler, Laura and Ruth Maloner. 2010. "'Our reach is wide by any corporate standard': How the tobacco industry helped defeat the Clinton Health Plan and why it matters now." *American Journal of Public Health* 100:1174–1188.

Zeigler, Harmon. 1961. *The politics of small business*. Washington: Public Affairs Press.

Part 3

The Rise of an International Economic System, 1939–2000

The five chapters in Part 3 focus on the readily traceable, gradual, step-by-step creation of a new international economic system during and after World War II. The early chapters reveal the key role of domestic economic considerations in explaining why the corporate moderates, in their role as internationalists, crafted an international economic framework. Their reasons included the fear of losing power to the liberal-labor alliance in a more domestically oriented economy, as well as a desire for even greater profits. By 1946 or 1947, their concern with defeating the Communist countries became an added motivation. (To make the chapters as reader-friendly as possible, the month and year of some important events are repeated so that it is not necessary to keep them in mind or leaf back in the chapter.)

The chapters first of all focus on the role of two major policy-discussion organizations in the postwar era, the Council on Foreign Relations and the Committee for Economic Development, the latter introduced in Chapter 3, and in later decades on the Business Roundtable, in formulating the policies necessary for an international economic system. These three organizations, with important assistance from foundations, think tanks, and a wide range of special committees they helped to create, brought these policies to the attention of the federal government through a variety of avenues. They then played a major role in creating the governmental structures for implementing them. They carried out their plans in the face of continuing setbacks at the hands of the ultraconservatives and the conservative coalition until the mid-1970s.

At about the same time as the ultraconservatives began to soften their stance on trade issues, the corporate moderates lost the support they had enjoyed earlier from the liberal-labor alliance, which by the early 1970s vehemently rejected the off-shoring of jobs that became one of the most visible features of later phases of the internationalization process. Despite these challenges, the corporate moderates' plans, which took far longer to realize than they originally imagined, finally were successful. They culminated, for all intents and purposes, with the passage of the North

American Free Trade Agreement (NAFTA) in 1993, Congressional approval of American participation of the World Trade Organization (WTO) in 1994, and the establishment of permanent normal trade relations with China in 2000.

Based on findings that unfold in these chapters, it also can be added that previous analyses of the international economic system tend to overlook the early years of the planning for it, underestimate the degree to which the corporate moderates had a coherent vision, and ignore the role of the policy-planning network. More specifically, most of these earlier analyses miss the fact that the important corporate and governmental figures they rightly focus upon were part of the policy-planning network, and drew most of their new ideas and advisory experts from it. Then, too, some earlier analyses either make the internationalization of the economy seem like a natural unfolding of the inner workings of an enterprise-and-market system, or suggest that its development was more ad hoc and piecemeal than it was, and usually in reaction to specific events and new opportunities.

Chapter 10

The Council on Foreign Relations and World Trade

This chapter explains how and why corporate moderates, Wall Street financiers, and experts in the policy-planning network created the general plans between 1939 and 1945 that shaped the economic framework for an increasingly internationalized postwar economy. As part of this analysis, the chapter sets the stage for demonstrating in the following chapter that this same planning process laid the groundwork for the creation of the International Monetary Fund (IMF) and the International Bank for Reconstruction, which is commonly known as the World Bank. Finally, the chapter also provides the context for understanding how postwar planning set the stage for the possibility of 30 years of anti-colonial warfare in Vietnam, first by the French, with large amounts of financial aid from the United States, and then by the Americans themselves, as detailed in a subsequent chapter.

The plans that are discussed in this and the next two chapters were developed within the Council on Foreign Relations and its war-peace study groups between 1939 and 1942, beginning days after World War II broke out in Europe. This claim builds on detailed archival studies by historian Laurence Shoup (1974; 1975; 1977), along with my historical research in several archives to verify and expand on Shoup's efforts, including the same archives he utilized. (To indicate my preference for Shoup's original research, I do not cite again below the book-length account he and a co-author later wrote (Shoup and Minter 1977).) The analysis in this chapter also makes use of research by other scholars as well.

In putting great emphasis on the Council on Foreign Relations (hereafter, usually called the CFR), I am not denying that other private organizations and the internationally oriented American mass media had a role in influencing government officials and the small percentage of people who pay attention to the specifics of foreign policy. As shown in detail decades ago, there were many such organizations supported by internationalists around the country (Divine 1967). Moreover, the magazines established by publisher Henry Luce, and in particular *Time* and *Fortune*, pushed very hard for postwar planning from 1940 to 1944, often chiding

374   Rise of an International Economic System

the White House and State Department for allegedly failing to keep up with a public opinion that they claimed to be increasingly in favor of American involvement in the war and in postwar planning, once France fell and Germany attacked the United Kingdom.

As early as January 1940, for example, a 19-member *Fortune* Roundtable discussion group, consisting of a cross-section of business leaders, lawyers, and association officials, called for United States participation in organizing the postwar peace discussions. In addition, there were turf wars between CFR leaders and other international organizations, along with competition among them for funding from foundations, which demonstrates once again a point that was made in the Introduction. Corporate leaders and experts suffer from the same personal ambition and competition for prestigious positions that lead to an egosystem, resentments, and tensions within any group (Schulzinger 1984, pp. 109–111, for evidence of this point in the case of the various foreign-policy organizations).

Nor was the Business Advisory Council silent on these issues. In June 1940, the longtime executive director of the Business Advisory Council (BAC) made clear in a speech to a trade association meeting that BAC members intended to be fully involved in the defense mobilization, and that they were concerned about a major war's impact on the economy. A year later a BAC committee sent a 13-page memorandum to the secretary of commerce outlining its concerns, and soon thereafter began a large-scale reorganization. This series of events eventually led to the BAC's involvement in postwar planning through the creation of the Committee for Economic Development in 1942 (Collins 1981; Whitham 2016, pp. 51–55). Two liberal, but corporate-oriented organizations, the National Planning Association (NPA) and Twentieth Century Fund (TCF), also made contributions to the overall effort through reports based on discussions that brought together a wide range of experts, including some of those working for the Council on Foreign Relations (Whitham 2016).

Despite all this other activity, and the personal and financial rivalries among leaders of the various groups, it is also the case that many of the leaders of these organizations were members of the CFR or its postwar planning groups. This generalization includes Luce of *Time* magazine. It also includes the organizer of Luce's roundtable discussion groups, who was also the president of the Foreign Policy Association, which had more of an outreach function in terms of the attentive public, and had many overlaps with the CFR in personnel and funding. In fact, the Luce empire's published reports were sometimes less technical versions of what academic experts were proposing to the State Department as part of their confidential work for the CFR. In short, the CFR was the sustained and well-financed core of the internationalist perspective, which projected a very large role for the United States in the postwar world. Its function was to create and organize the policy goals of the corporate moderates.

The CFR had its origins in the years after World War I, when many American leaders returned from the peace conference dissatisfied with both their preparation for the negotiations and the outcome of the conference. They also believed that the growing economic power of the United States should lead to greater involvement and leadership in world affairs than the nation previously had shown, but events were proving their hopes and predictions to be wrong. Even so, the CFR did not spring up overnight. Instead, there were at least two discussion groups originally, one made up primarily of Wall Street financiers, the other of former statesmen and academic experts interested in international affairs. The fact that the CFR was not formally founded until 1921 reflects the difficulties entailed in bringing the two groups together (Shoup 1974; Wala 1994, Chapter 1). The eventual merger was based on the fact that the financiers needed expertise they did not have and the academicians and statesmen needed financial support and the ties to people with influence that they lacked.

As Robert Divine (1967, p. 20) summarizes, the new organization was restricted to 650 members, 400 from New York and 250 from the rest of the country. Even though it had a significant number of expert members, its membership roster read like a *Who's Who* of American leaders, including financiers, corporate executives, and corporate lawyers. It also included a handful of syndicated columnists, clergymen, and State Department officials. This small membership constantly has to be kept in mind because the CFR from the 1920s to the late 1960s cannot be thought of in quite the same way as the much larger CFR that evolved and grew in the 1970s, with a gradual change in some of its roles within the larger corporate community. (In essence, it later developed its own in-house think tank and became a publisher as well, even while continuing to sponsor well-funded small discussion groups, which carried on the organization's traditional mode of operation and had a considerable impact on government.)

In any event, there is ample systematic evidence to support Divine's contention that the CFR originally was the province of internationally oriented bankers and corporate executives in New York and surrounding areas, as well as of academic experts and journalists. It also is well established that its funding for projects came from large foundations directed by business leaders, who were also members of the CFR in significant numbers (e.g., Beckmann 1964; Domhoff 1970, Chapter 5).

The CFR also went to great lengths to encourage and influence the scholarly study of international relations (Beckmann 1964, for the foundation funding of such programs). In April and May of 1946, for example, it organized six regional conferences in cities such as New York, Chicago, Denver, and Berkeley to discuss the educational and social objectives of teaching and studying international relations. These day-long roundtable discussions were attended by 126 faculty members from 76 universities,

376 Rise of an International Economic System

including professors in political science, international law, history, economics, and geography (Kirk 1947, p. v).

The most visible leaders of the early CFR were widely known in the power elite and Washington. They begin with its honorary chair, Elihu Root, who was a Wall Street lawyer before and after his years in the federal government as Secretary of War for President William McKinley and Secretary of State for President Theodore Roosevelt. Later he served as the chair of the three main Carnegie foundations—the Carnegie Corporation, the Carnegie Endowment for International Peace, and the Carnegie Institution of Washington. CFR director Henry L. Stimson, a New York corporation lawyer for most of his adult life, and widely considered to be Root's one-time protégé, was the Secretary of War for President William Howard Taft, then Secretary of State under President Herbert Hoover, and later the Secretary of War under President Franklin D. Roosevelt from June 1940 until the end of the war.

The role of the individual members of the war-peace study groups, some of whom also served as appointed officials or consultants in the state and treasury departments, are chronicled in other scholarly accounts of the planning for the postwar world. However, these accounts do not give much if any attention to the involvement of these individuals in the CFR. Instead, they in effect trace the role of a network of individuals, sometimes noting their former roles as financiers, executives, or professors. But they do not discuss the organizational network, that is, the policy-planning network, of which the individual networks are a part.

To take one example, a textbook on diplomatic history in the twentieth century notes that there was a private foreign-policy "establishment," whose members worked in law firms, banking houses, universities, foundations, and individual corporations, and alternated between "tours of government service" and private institutions (Schulzinger 2002, p. 8). It lists a large number of secretaries of state as examples, but does not note that after 1944 most of them were also leaders in the CFR (Schulzinger 2002, p. 6). However, in this case the book does point out that "theorizing about foreign affairs often originates in the minds of members of universities and organizations such as the Council on Foreign Relations, The Brookings Institution, and the American Enterprise Institute"; this role is attributed to the fact that "the daily business of conducting foreign affairs demands so much attention that officeholders rely on the ideas of outsiders with the leisure to create plans for the future" (Schulzinger 2002, p. 8). This is exactly the role played by the CFR and its several war-peace study groups between 1939 and 1945.

Both then and later, the Council on Foreign Relations attempted to realize its internationalist aims through discussion groups, research studies, booklength monographs on a wide variety of countries and issues, and articles in its journal, *Foreign Affairs*, which was widely respected and read in foreign-policy circles. In attempting to foster its perspective, the CFR saw its primary adversaries as isolationists in Congress and the nationally oriented and protectionist ultraconservatives in the corporate community. The ultraconservatives by and large did not want the United States to become entangled in world affairs outside America's own "backyard," meaning for the most part the southern half of the Western Hemisphere and some of the Asian countries on the shores of the Pacific Ocean.

Trade Policy in the Interwar Years

The years between 1917 and 1930 should have been good ones for CFR policies if the internationalization of the economy through new tariff and trade policies were inevitable due to American power. By all measures, the United States was the foremost economic, political, and military power in the world following World War I, and many European leaders thought it should take the lead because the United Kingdom could no longer do so. The United States had more direct foreign investments than any other country, and it was the largest trading power even though foreign trade was only a very small part of its huge economy (Frieden 1988, pp. 59–61; Frieden 2006). But "the pendulum swung back towards protectionism and little public U.S. government involvement in international monetary issues" (Frieden 1988, p. 61).

The international investment banks on Wall Street had major involvements in capital investments in many foreign countries, and the most internationally oriented corporations were very large and expanding rapidly overseas, but they failed again and again in their attempts to influence Congress, or even Republican presidents, because the ultraconservatives had greater political strength, especially in Congress. In the face of the Great Depression, however, the ultraconservatives were in retreat as their industrial base crumbled and the Democratic Party took control of Congress (Frieden 1988, p. 83).

Nor did the CFR have much if any impact in the early New Deal. Its leaders vigorously entered a national debate in the early 1930s in opposition to "selfsufficiency" and greater government control of the economy, and instead supported such steps toward internationalism as the Reciprocal Trade Act of 1934 (Gardner 1964; Shoup 1974; Woods 2003). However, the success of the Reciprocal Trade Agreements Act was largely due to the insistence of the Southern Democrats, who dominated the key Congressional committees. As exporters of agricultural products and importers of finished goods, the Southern rich were thoroughgoing "free traders" at the time (Haggard 1988). The Southern plantation owners therefore were crucial to whatever success the internationally oriented bankers and corporations enjoyed during the New Deal, as well as in their attempts to internationalize the economy in the first several years after World War II ended.

378   Rise of an International Economic System

It was only in the late 1930s that the general balance of forces between the internationalists and isolationists began to change, in part due to Roosevelt's desire to develop a better relationship with internationally oriented Wall Street bankers, whom he knew well personally through long-standing social connections, but had kept at arm's length for both policy and political reasons. Roosevelt also believed that the largest corporations would be essential to the industrial conversion to military production that would be necessary if another world war broke out. In this context the CFR had the necessary ingredients to become a major factor in the policy-making process. Its leaders had personal access to the government officials who would be making the key decisions, knew what kinds of arguments and information would be useful in making these decisions, and could learn when important decisions were likely to be discussed and made. Furthermore, CFR leaders had legitimacy in the eyes of decision-makers because respected scholars conducted their studies, and they were therefore regarded as highly informed about foreign affairs. Then too, government officials had often been members of CFR discussion groups, and many CFR members from the private sector had been appointed to government positions in the past.

Perhaps the best single example of this point about access and legitimacy for the crucial years under consideration in this chapter, 1939 to 1945, is banker Norman H. Davis, a founding director of the CFR and its president from 1936 until his death in 1944. His relationships with top decision-makers in the State Department and White House were longstanding and close, particularly with Roosevelt. The son of a successful businessman in Tennessee, Davis became a millionaire by means of financial dealings in Cuba between 1902 and 1917. Through his friendships with a partner in J. P. Morgan and the president of Hartford Fire Insurance, Davis became a financial adviser to the secretary of treasury on foreign loans during World War 1.

Davis also was a financial adviser to the American delegation to the Paris Peace Conference in 1919, where he worked with another Morgan partner, who became a founding member of the CFR. He then served briefly as an assistant secretary of treasury and undersecretary of state before turning to a banking career in New York in March 1921. At this point Davis involved himself in the affairs of the Democratic Party in New York, which was the party to which all self-respecting wealthy Southerners belonged at the time. It also gave him the opportunity to be a potential go-between for Northern Republicans on Wall Street. In that regard the New York Democratic Party was also a very important northern outpost for Southern Democrats, partly because of the plantation owners' involvement in exporting, but also as a source of campaign support for the party throughout the United States (Alexander 1992; Overacker 1932; Webber 2000).

As it turned out, Davis's most important new friendship through his party involvement was with a fellow Tennessean, Cordell Hull, the chair of the national party and a congressman, and later Roosevelt's secretary of state throughout his entire administration. From 1921 onward, Hull and Davis often were the spokespersons for the Democrat Party on foreign economic policy in the face of the Republican Party's strong isolationist/protectionist wing (e.g., Adams 1976, Chapters 1–2). It was during this time that Davis also became friends with Roosevelt. In 1928 Roosevelt had begun work as a private citizen on an international development trust to stimulate foreign trade, and Davis helped him with the project (Gardner 1964, p. 19, and see also the letter from Roosevelt to Davis dated October 8, 1928, in the Davis Collection in the Library of Congress). In addition, Davis was a delegate to international conferences under Republican presidents in 1927 and 1932, and Roosevelt made him an ambassador-at-large in 1933 and head of the American Red Cross in 1938.

Outside the political sphere, Davis was considered a "well-known friend of the Morgan Company," according to former Roosevelt adviser Raymond Moley (Shoup 1974, p. 27, quoting Moley 1939). (For Davis' own account of his relation to the Morgan interests, see his undated memorandum to Hull in the Davis Collection in the Library of Congress, which I found to be extremely detailed and informative, although it would be tedious to recount here). As early as 1912, Davis had become the Morgan partners' Cuban representative, negotiating a $10 million loan from Morgan for the Cuban government in 1914. By the time Davis was elected CFR president, he also was a director of the Bank of New York and Trust Company. Davis had direct and frequent access to Roosevelt and Hull in the years between 1940 and 1942, when postwar planning was in its crucial formative phase. For example, there were two telephones in Davis' office at the American Red Cross, one for normal calls, the other a direct line to the White House. As for Hull, his appointment calendar shows that Davis met with him in his office several times a week; he also played croquet with Davis most nights of the week (Shoup 1974, p. 30).

Similar relationships between CFR leaders and foreign-policy leaders will become apparent as the details of postwar planning are discussed. However, the more important question is whether this access shaped the thinking of foreign-policy officials, or whether they instead relied on the information and recommendations of people hired by the State Department to do government planning from the inside. This critical issue is addressed in the next subsection, which substantiates that the CFR's postwar planners did provide the bulk of the State Department's postwar planning from the outside in 1940 and 1941. They then became part of the State Department in 1942, when serious planning within the government finally was undertaken.

The CFR and the "Grand Area" Strategy

World War II began in Europe in early September 1939. By September 12, CFR leaders were meeting with Assistant Secretary of State George

Messersmith, a longtime member of the CFR, to offer their services on postwar planning. If a smoking gun exists as to the moment that marked the beginning of the planning for the internationalization of the world economy in the second half of the twentieth century, this is it. Messersmith spoke later in the day with Secretary of State Hull and Undersecretary of State Welles, both of whom expressed interest in the idea. Shortly thereafter CFR president Norman Davis talked with his friend Hull and received verbal approval of the plan (Shoup 1974, p. 64).

The State Department also conveyed its approval of the plan to the Rockefeller Foundation, which gave the CFR $44,500 on December 6 to begin its work. This foundation support continued for the life of what turned out to be a five-year project, and it amounted to about $10.8 million in 2018 dollars. This is the first clear-cut example of a foundation and a policy-discussion group working closely with a specific department in the executive branch on a foreign-policy issue. As will be shown, it led to state-building by the corporate rich, the power elite, and their policy-planning network, and a set of policies that went well beyond what Secretary of State Hull had long expounded on as "free trade."

Members of the State Department and the CFR met at Messersmith's home in mid-December to finalize the arrangements. According to the plan, the CFR would set up study groups to "engage in a continuous study of the course of the war, to ascertain how the hostilities affect the United States and to elaborate concrete proposals designed to safeguard American interests in the settlement which will be undertaken when hostilities cease" (Shoup 1974, pp. 64–66, quoting a CFR Memorandum). In short, the aim was to create blueprints for the postwar world.

"Studies of American Interests in the War and the Peace," as the project was officially named, began with five study groups: Economic, Financial, Security and Armaments, Territorial, and Future World Organization. The first two groups were soon merged into one Economic and Financial Group, and the Future World Organization Group became the Political Group. Later, in May 1941, a Peace Aims Group was created to ascertain the peace aims of other countries through private discussions in New York with their leaders and representatives. However, many of the plans emanating from several of these groups were very short-range, such as suggestions for what American "war aims" should be at one crucial moment, or suggestions on territorial concerns that were "overtaken by events," such as the Nazi invasion of the Soviet Union and the Japanese attack on Pearl Harbor (Schulzinger 1984, p. 77). The study groups involved with short-term issues had little or no impact in terms of postwar events, so they are not dealt with in this book. Instead, the focus is on the postwar planning that led to a framework and strategy for realizing and protecting the large geographical area that would be needed for the full functioning of the American economy in the postwar era without large-scale government

Council on Foreign Relations, World Trade **381**

intervention and direction. To this end, harmonious postwar economic relations with the United Kingdom and Japan were always a primary consideration of the deliberations.

Each group had a leader, or "rapporteur" in CFR language, along with a research secretary and 10 to 15 members. Three of the groups had co-rapporteurs. Almost 100 people participated in the groups between 1940 and 1945. They were a cross-section of top-level American leadership in finance, business, law, media, universities, and the military, and they included academic experts in economics, geography, and political science as well as White House advisers and other government advisers. "Through these individuals," Shoup (1974, p. 68) reports, "at least five cabinet-level departments and 14 government agencies, bureaus, and offices were interlocked with the war-peace studies at one time or another. They collectively attended three hundred and sixty-two meetings and prepared six hundred and eighty-two separate documents for the Department of State and President. Up to twenty-five copies of each recommendation were distributed to the appropriate desks of the Department and two for the President."

Isaiah Bowman, the president of Johns Hopkins University, a founding director of the CFR, and one of the nation's leading geographers, was the leader of the Territorial Group. His role within the CFR and in the government from the 1920s to 1950s has been chronicled in great detail in a biography of him (Smith 2003). Whitney H. Shepardson, another founding director of the CFR and a lawyer-businessman in New York, with economic and personal relationships with the J.P. Morgan banking interests, headed the Political Group. Shepardson had served as an assistant to President Woodrow Wilson's closest adviser at the Paris Peace Conference. In 1924 he went to London to help set up a parallel set of committees within the Royal Institute of International Affairs, which was the United Kingdom's counterpart to the CFR. International lawyer Allen W. Dulles, a director of the CFR since 1927, and later the head of the CIA in the Eisenhower Administration, was a co-leader of the Security and Armaments Group, along with *The New York Times*' military expert, Hanson W. Baldwin. Hamilton Fish Armstrong, a founding CFR director and the editor of *Foreign Affairs*, and a major coordinator in the overall war-peace studies as its vice chair, was the leader of the Peace Aims Group.

The key figures in the Economic and Financial Group, which played by far the most prominent role on the issues of concern in this chapter, were economists Jacob Viner and Alvin H. Hansen, both of whom were former presidents of the American Economic Association and had small roles in the development of the Social Security Act (as mentioned in Chapter 6). Viner was the most highly regarded international economist of his era. He began his career of advising government in the Department of the Treasury in the 1930s, as well as being an adviser to the CFR. Hansen moved

382 Rise of an International Economic System

to Harvard from the University of Minnesota in 1937 and became the most visible and renowned Keynesian economist in the country (Galbraith 1971, pp. 49–50). He had numerous advisory roles within the federal government, serving as a consultant to the State Department, Federal Reserve Board, and the National Resources Planning Board (a small liberal planning agency within the White House), during the time of his involvement with the CFR project.

On the basis of their social backgrounds, neither Viner nor Hansen could be considered a likely candidate for an important advisory position. Both were raised in modest financial circumstances, far from the centers of American wealth and power. Viner was born in Canada and did not become an American citizen until he was 22 years old; however, he did receive his Ph.D. at Harvard and rose quickly in the professorial ranks at the University of Chicago and later at Princeton. Hansen was born and raised in South Dakota, the son of immigrants from Scandinavia. He earned his B.A. at Yankton University in South Dakota and earned his Ph.D. at the University of Wisconsin. Both Viner and Hansen, then, are testimony to the social mobility that is possible through involvement in American academic circles and the policy-planning network.

Despite somewhat differing theoretical orientations, Viner and Hansen worked closely in the Economic and Financial Group. Other economists with a similar range of views, including such well-known figures of the time as Winfield Riefler, Eugene Staley, and Arthur Upgren, joined them (Helleiner 2014, pp. 124–127 for evidence on the important roles played by Hansen, Riefler, Staley, and Viner in early postwar planning). CFR employees William Diebold, Jr., who went on to write several books, served as research secretary (Diebold 1941; Diebold 1959; Diebold 1972); and Percy Bidwell, originally trained as an agricultural economist, served as the CFR's director of studies. The fact that experts of diverse orientations were hired by the CFR for its project yet again suggests a flexibility on the part of at least some corporate moderates, which is said to be lacking in the higher circles by the skeptics concerning the capacity of the corporate moderates to create new policy alternatives.

The Economic and Financial Group had two direct connections to the White House. The first was economist Lauchlin Currie, an early Keynesian who had worked at the Federal Reserve Board in the mid-1930s. He joined the White House in 1939 as Roosevelt's administrative assistant with special duties in the field of economics, a position he held until 1945. He was considered the White House liaison to the group (Roosevelt 1933–1945, Official File 3719, November 27, 1941). He joined the discussion group officially in February 1943. The group's other connection to the White House, Benjamin V. Cohen, a New York corporation lawyer, was famous for his partnership with another corporate lawyer in crafting important New Deal legislation, including the Securities and Exchange

Council on Foreign Relations, World Trade 383

Commission Act and the Public Utilities Holding Company Act. He was quiet, discrete, and loyal to Roosevelt to a fault; he joined the CFR group in September 1941, well after the general strategy was formulated.

The Economic and Financial Group later developed ties with the new policy-discussion group created by the BAC and the Department of Commerce in 1942, the Committee for Economic Development (CED). One of the CED's founders, business executive Ralph Flanders, joined the Economic and Financial Group in July 1942. Another important connection between the CFR and the CED was provided by one of the aforementioned economists, Arthur Upgren, who had a major role in organizing the CED through his work for the Commerce Department. In 1945, Viner, Upgren, and Currie advised the CED on its first report on *International Trade, Foreign Investment, and Domestic Employment* (CED 1945). More generally, five of the 11 original members of the CED's overall Research Committee, which was essentially the group's coordinating agency, were also members of the CFR.

At the same time as the CFR was organizing its war-peace study groups, the Department of State created its own internal structure for postwar planning. In mid-September 1939, after a series of meetings with CFR leaders, Hull appointed a special assistant, Leo Pasvolsky, to guide government postwar planning. Shortly thereafter, on December 12, Pasvolsky drafted a plan for a new departmental division to study the problems of peace and reconstruction (Shoup 1974, p. 70). Then, in late December, the department formed a policy committee, named The Advisory Committee on Problems of Foreign Relations, with Undersecretary Sumner Welles, a member of the CFR, as chair. All the members of the committee were employees of the State Department, except CFR president Norman Davis, and lawyer George Rublee, who was a founding member of the CFR and the director of the federal government's Inter-governmental Committee on Political Refugees.

It is important to look more closely at the State Department's new and understaffed planning structure in order to understand the central role the CFR had inside of it. The division of policy studies envisioned by Pasvolsky in his memorandum of December 12, 1939, did not come into being until early in 1941 due to the lack of personnel in the department. Indeed, his memorandum indicated that the division's own research would be minimal at first and stated that it "would stress assembly of materials and the attempt to influence the research activities of unofficial organizations" (Shoup 1974, p. 71, his paraphrase of the memorandum). Not to mince words, any early planning would come from the CFR under the general guidance of the State Department, which lacked any planning capacity at the time. Much of this guidance came from Pasvolsky himself, who regularly attended meetings of the Economic and Financial Group once it was formed. He had joined the CFR the year before,

384 Rise of an International Economic System

It is therefore useful to next examine Pasvolsky's career up to the point that he joined the State Department and then the CFR's Economic and Financial Group. From 1923 to 1935, he had been an employee of The Brookings Institution, the largest and most visible private think tank of the 1930s (and thereafter). He eventually received his Ph.D. in international economics from Brookings itself in 1936. After also working for the Bureau of Foreign and Domestic Commerce in 1934–35 and the Division of Trade Agreements within the Department of State in 1935–36, he became a special assistant to Hull from 1936 to 1938, and then again from 1939 to 1946, when he returned full time to The Brookings Institution until his death in 1953. This demonstrates that Pasvolsky was one of those many experts who moved back and forth between the policy-planning network and government service. His career path therefore suggests he was as close to private postwar economic planners as he was to the decision-makers on foreign policy in the State Department.

As for the State Department's policy-level Advisory Committee on Problems of Foreign Policy, it did little or nothing before it became defunct in the summer of 1940. The pressure of immediate events was too great for thinking about postwar problems in the understaffed department as the war in Europe escalated in 1940. It was not replaced until late December 1941, after the United States had entered the war, when it was enlarged and renamed the Advisory Committee on Postwar Foreign Policy (of which more later). It is in this context of meager State Department postwar planning, then, that the CFR carried out its own postwar planning efforts. It was an ideal situation in which an outside group could have great influence. That is, the department of the government concerned with foreign policy was both understaffed (and therefore "weak") and permeable, which meant that outsiders such as the members of the CFR might be able to influence it directly. When it comes to the State Department, this situation is almost completely the opposite of any theory that emphasizes the autonomy or relative autonomy of the government from societal influences.

As already noted, the earliest and most important CFR planning for the purposes of this chapter took place within the Economic and Financial Group. It began modestly with four reports dated March 9, 1940. They analyzed the effect of the war on United States trade, concluding that there had been no serious consequences up to that point. Similarly, five reports dated April 6 were primarily descriptive in nature, dealing with the possible impact on American trade of price-fixing and monetary exchange controls by the belligerents. Two reports dated May 1 provide an indication of the direction the CFR planning might take.

The first of these reports warned that a way would have to be found to increase American imports in order to bring about a necessary increase in exports. The second concluded, contrary to the traditional advocates of expanded trade, that high American tariffs had not had a big influence in restricting American imports. Although reducing tariffs would help to increase imports, boosting industrial activity and the incomes of American consumers would do even more to increase imports. In retrospect, this brief report can be seen as an early harbinger of what became one of the biggest problems the CFR's planning efforts faced between 1945 and 1947, increasing American consumption to increase foreign trade, as discussed in more detail in Chapter 13. The CFR planners did not even attempt to solve the problem in the early 1940s.

Given the almost exclusive emphasis Hull, other Southern Democrats, Wall Street bankers, and traditional economists put on reducing foreign and domestic tariffs to foster the international economy, the early reports from the Economic and Financial Group are the first pieces of evidence that the CFR was going to develop its own analysis, rather than reinforcing the State Department's usual conception of how to further the country's economic interest. Due to the fact that many international relations experts believe the State Department's economic policy was based on an amorphous "Wilsonianism" between 1940 and 1947 (e.g., Ikenberry, Knock, Slaughter, and Smith 2011; Krasner 1978), any divergences between Hull and the CFR perspective are evidence for CFR influence.

The Nazi invasion of France in May 1940, and the subsequent attack on the United Kingdom, turned the attention of both the State Department and the CFR to the problems of stabilizing the economies of Latin American countries that previously had depended upon their exports to continental Europe. This problem led step-by-step to the studies that culminated in a vision of the American economy in the postwar world, which I emphasize because it shows that the grand design for the postwar era did not spring out of abstract thought exercises or from poring over general statistical tables. There were numerous meetings and exchanges of information between the State Department and the CFR leaders from May to October in relation to this work. At a plenary meeting of all war-peace study groups on June 28, the project's official contact with the State Department urged that materials given to the department should be couched as practical recommendations (Shoup 1974, p. 91). Pasvolsky then outlined the close relationship that had developed with the war-peace studies, stating that:

> He had gone over many details with Mr. Hansen, had suggested some directions of work, and had pointed out to Mr. Hansen the great usefulness of the work already done. The relations between the groups and the State Department were such that, for economic matters, he might be asked at any time about the usefulness of a proposed investigation.
>
> (Shoup 1974, p. 91, quoting the "Memorandum of Discussions of First Plenary Session, Council on Foreign Relations," June 28, 1940)

386 Rise of an International Economic System

On June 10, 1940, State Department planners suggested it might be necessary to set up a single trading organization to market all surplus agriculture production in the Western Hemisphere. This would make it possible to bargain in the face of Germany's great economic power. However, it was soon realized that this kind of solution would be criticized by the corporate community and was not in keeping with American values. When Roosevelt asked on June 15 for a recommendation by June 20 on what to do about the economic problems of Latin America, it was decided as an interim measure that the government's Reconstruction Finance Corporation (a lending source created during World War I and used extensively during the New Deal) should supply the money to buy the surplus products. On September 26, Congress gave the Reconstruction Finance Corporation $500 million to carry out this policy.

Moreover, the Economic and Financial Group had concluded in a paper of June 7, three days before the first State Department memorandum, that a "Pan-American Trade Bloc" would not work because it would be weak in needed raw materials and unable to consume the agricultural surpluses of Canada and the southern half of Latin America. There were too many national economies in the hemisphere that were competitive with each other rather than complementary. Furthermore, economic isolation in the Western Hemisphere would cost the United States almost two-thirds of its foreign trade (Shoup 1974, p. 102). As if that were not enough, CFR planners shortly thereafter concluded that any Western Hemisphere cartel for selling to Germany was doomed to failure because the self-sufficiency of the German bloc was such that it could not be forced to trade with the Western Hemisphere (Shoup 1974, p. 106).

It was in analyzing this series of issues that the Economic and Financial Group of the war-peace studies began to think about the postwar international economy in terms of the minimum geographical area that would be necessary for the productive functioning of the American economy without drastic controls and major governmental intervention, both of which were completely out of the question for the entire corporate community. First, a report completed in June 1940, entitled "Geographical Distribution of United States Foreign Trade: A Study in National Interest," showed both the increasing importance of the country's manufacturing exports as compared to agricultural exports and the increasing importance of Asia and Oceania for both exports and imports. As Shoup (1974, pp. 107–108) summarizes, "They concluded that the Far East and Western Hemisphere probably bore the same relationship to the United States as America had to Europe in the past—a source of raw materials and a market for manufactures."

Equally important, and essential in understanding the leadership role undertaken by the United States after World War II, other studies soon concluded that the economies of the United Kingdom and Japan could not function adequately in harmony with the American economy without a large part of the world as markets and suppliers of raw materials. It was emphasized that Japan's trade needs could be accommodated as part of a larger solution to world economic problems, but that the United States' problems could not be solved if Japan excluded the American economy from Asia. This economic argument, as discussed again in Chapter 12, provides the starting point for the policies that later led to a Communist containment policy in Southeast Asia. While other strategic and ideological dimensions were also later added to the concerns about Southeast Asia, such as showing that the United States would protect its allies, the original economic issues in relation to the economies of the United Kingdom and Japan are often overlooked.

The CFR refined its analysis from July through September with a "detailed study of the location, production, and trade of key commodities and manufactures on a worldwide basis and within the framework of blocs [of nations]" (Shoup 1974, p. 109). The four blocs were (1) the Western Hemisphere; (2) continental Europe and Mediterranean Basin (excluding the Soviet Union); (3) the Pacific area and Far East; and (4) the United Kingdom and its colonies. Due in good part to the export competition between the southern countries of Latin America on the one hand and Australia, New Zealand, and India on the other, the United Kingdom itself was seen as an essential market for dealing with agricultural surpluses. Only with the United Kingdom and its colonies included was there a non-German area that was self-sufficient and harmonious, as a memorandum of September 6 concluded (Shoup 1974, p. 110).

These economic issues were embodied in a memorandum of October 19, 1940, which was the first full statement of the CFR's vision for the postwar international economy. It "set forth the political, military, territorial and economic requirements of the United States in its potential leadership of the non-German world area including the United Kingdom itself as well as the Western Hemisphere and the Far East" (Shoup 1974, p. 111, quoting Memorandum E–B19). After summarizing changes in the nature and direction of American trade, it stated that "the foremost requirement of the United States in a world in which it proposes to *hold unquestioned power* is the rapid fulfillment of a program of complete rearmament" (Shoup 1974, p. 113, quoting Memorandum E–B19; my italics). However, the "coordination and cooperation of the United States with other countries" was also necessary in order to "secure the limitation of any exercise of sovereignty by foreign nations that constitutes a threat to the minimum world area essential for the security and economic prosperity of the United States and

388 Rise of an International Economic System

the Western Hemisphere" (Shoup 1974, p. 113, quoting Memorandum E-B19). Finally, there would have to be new monetary, investment, and trade arrangements, which are discussed in the next chapter.

Members of all four war-peace study groups discussed this stunning memorandum, which is breathtaking in its scope, on October 19, 1940, the same date it was formally issued. (Pasvolsky of the State Department was present as well). The members of the Political Group present at the plenary session doubted that Germany would settle for a stalemate in the war, so Pasvolsky ventured that the Political Group might

> suggest blocs that it thought might result from the war, and then see what could be done in economic terms within each area. There would be two cores to start on; the first, Germany and the minimum territory she could be assumed to take in the war; the second the United States. Working outward from these cores, one could build up several possible blocs on a political basis, and then examine their economic potentialities
> (Shoup 1974, p. 11, quoting Discussion Memorandum E-A 10)

At about the same time, State Department planners at the staff level, inactive from July to October on postwar questions, resumed their meetings on October 15. They had been organized as the Interdepartmental Group to Consider Postwar Economic Problems and Policies because the group now included representatives from the Tariff Commission, the Federal Reserve Board, and the Agriculture, Treasury, and Commerce departments. Pasvolsky, as chair of the group, proposed a series of commodity studies that paralleled those already completed by the CFR; he also gave all members a set of the CFR studies (Shoup 1974, pp. 124–127). The interdepartmental group's work on commodity issues was more extensive than that of the CFR because of the greater resources the departments and agencies started to receive at that point, but "the Council's initial goal of giving direction to the work of the government had clearly been achieved" (Shoup 1974, p. 128).

As the State Department resumed its planning studies, the Political Group at the CFR refined its remaining questions about several of the basic assumptions in an October 19 report for the Economic and Financial Group. It reaffirmed its belief that Germany would not cease its efforts against the United Kingdom under any circumstances, meaning that the prolonged coexistence of a German bloc and an American-led bloc was politically unlikely even if it were economically feasible. The Political Group also questioned the political viability of one non-German bloc dominated by the United States; such a large area might bring charges of imperialism and perhaps alienate some Latin American countries. The Political Group therefore raised the possibility of two democratic blocs in the non-German world, one led by the United Kingdom, one led by the United States, with close coordination between the two (Shoup 1974, pp. 132–134). In other words, there were differences in perspective between the Political Group and the Economic and Financial Group that needed to be discussed further before a conclusion could be reached.

Members from all war-peace planning groups attended a general meeting to discuss these issues on December 14, 1940. While some disagreements remained after the meeting, a general consensus was reached on three key issues. First, most participants thought there was a need to plan as if there would be a Germanized Western Europe for the immediate future; however, everyone agreed they preferred the defeat of Germany and the integration of Western Europe into the Western Hemisphere/United Kingdom/Asia bloc, which by then was formally called the "Grand Area." Second, there was general agreement that the Grand Area could not be broken into two democratic blocs because of the danger that the United Kingdom might try to maintain its empire and exclude the United States from free trade and investment within it. This concern proved to be well-grounded, and the basis for numerous conflicts between the two countries on monetary issues and loans. Third, it was agreed that important American economic and strategic interests in Asia were being threatened by Japanese expansionism.

By mid-1941, CFR leaders and planners began to take positions within the government, a process that was to be intensified a year later. For example, when an Economic Defense Board headed by Vice President Henry Wallace was established on July 30, 1941, to consider postwar economic issues, Wallace appointed economist Riefler of the Economic and Financial Group as his chief adviser. About the same time, Upgren, an economist in the same planning group as noted above, became head of the newly created National Economics Unit within the Department of Commerce. It was from this position that he performed staff functions in the creation of the Committee for Economic Development. Finally, Hansen was appointed as the United States chair of the Joint Economic Committee of the United States and Canada (Shoup 1974, p. 160). It is likely that these positions provided CFR economists with new outposts for arguing the CFR perspective. At the least, they were listening posts from which more could be learned in terms of any independent government thinking related to postwar planning.

Council on Foreign Relations planners also emphasized their criticisms of the State Department's free-trade approach in published statements. For example, the research secretary for the Economic and Financial Group, William Diebold (1941, p. 111), in his book *New Directions in Our Trade Policy*, stated the larger and more power-oriented view held by CFR planners as follows: "The war has made it crystal clear that trade policy is an instrument of foreign policy which must be made to serve the national interest

390 Rise of an International Economic System

as a whole rather than the limited ends implied in the slogan 'to promote foreign trade.'" What the CFR leaders had in mind for the postwar world, then, as already has been emphasized, was far more than "Wilsonianism" based in "Lockean liberalism" (Ikenberry, Knock, Slaughter, and Smith 2011; Krasner 1978). Instead, CFR spokespersons saw the United States as a nation that should use its political and military power to create international economic and political institutions necessary for the larger world economy they believed essential for the proper functioning of the American, British, and Japanese economies.

Once the United States entered the war after the attack on Pearl Harbor in December 1941, CFR leaders worked closely with appointed officials to intensify planning efforts inside the government, and to assure that these efforts were controlled within the State Department, not by some other agency or department. On December 28, 1941, President Roosevelt decreed "all recommendations on postwar problems of international relations from all departments and agencies of the government should be submitted to the president through the Secretary of State" (Shoup 1974, p. 200). This decision put the Department of the Treasury and Vice President Wallace's Economic Defense Board, now renamed the Board of Economic Warfare, in subordinate roles.

On December 28, three weeks after the United States entered the war, the president also approved a new 14-member Advisory Committee on Postwar Foreign Policy. CFR president Norman H. Davis had a large hand in its formation. The members of the Advisory Committee came primarily from the State Department and the CFR, which provides further evidence that the CFR and the government were tightly linked on postwar planning. Nine were government officials and five were private citizens chosen "because of their high personal qualifications for policy consideration and because of their capacity to represent informed public opinion and interests" (Notter 1949, pp. 72–73). Four of the five private citizens (Armstrong, Bowman, Davis, and former United States Steel chair Myron Taylor) were members of the Council on Foreign Relations. The fifth, *New York Times* journalist Anne O'Hare McCormick, could not be a CFR member because it was a male-only organization until the 1970s. Of the government officials, four were also members of the CFR or its war-peace studies, including White House adviser Cohen and planner Pasvolsky. (Later, in early 1943, after the Advisory Committee faded in importance, six of the members (Hull, Welles, Davis, Taylor, Bowman, and Pasvolsky) took the main responsibility for political issues and became known as the Informal Political Agenda Group. Roosevelt called them "my postwar advisers" (Shoup 1974, p. 203). All but Hull were members of the CFR, and two, Davis and Bowman, were highly involved in the war-peace studies.)

During 1 and 1942, the Advisory Committee worked primarily through a series of subcommittees. Once again, the details on the members of these

Council on Foreign Relations, World Trade 391

subcommittees are important in providing evidence of the close ties between the CFR and government planning at this point. Bowman, rapporteur of the CFR's Territorial Group, also chaired the government's Territorial Subcommittee. Davis chaired both the Security Subcommittee and the Coordination Subcommittee, whose function was to provide "contact with private organizations actively discussing postwar problems," a vague-sounding mandate that certainly included the CFR, and thereby legitimated its role as a governmental link to the private sector (Notter 1949, p. 80). Welles chaired the Political Subcommittee. When a Special Subcommittee on European Organization was created in May 1943 to consider boundary questions and region-wide organizations, Armstrong chaired it. Of the eight members of this special subcommittee drawn from other subcommittees, five were members of the CFR or its war-peace groups. As for the two members of the special subcommittee from outside the already established subcommittees, they were Percy W. Bidwell and Jacob Viner, revealing once again the importance of experts from the CFR's Economic and Financial Group to the government.

Although the Advisory Committee and the subcommittee appointees provided a close liaison between the CFR and the State Department at the policy level, CFR leaders nonetheless sought similar coordination at the research level as well. The issue was discussed at a meeting between CFR leaders and department officials on February 21, 1942.

> Early in this meeting Armstrong proposed that a decision about liaison and coordination between the Council on Foreign Relations and the Advisory Committee should be made. Welles then asked if the Advisory Committee could take over the research staff of the Council without disrupting its endeavors. Armstrong replied that the Council's labors might be seriously impaired and proposed instead that the research secretaries of the Council should work in the Department two or three days each week, attending the subcommittee meetings. The Council would thus be in "close relation to the actual functioning of the Advisory Committee." Welles agreed, stating that he "wished to have the most effective liaison that could be devised."
>
> (Shoup 1974, p. 208, with the two internal quotes drawn from the minutes of the meeting)

Due to this rather extraordinary degree of coordination, the CFR's policy-planning groups held their meetings early in the week in New York, freeing the research secretaries to meet with the departmental subcommittees in Washington later in the week. This gave the government employees the opportunity to communicate the department's research needs to the CFR groups. The CFR planners were given the title of "consultants," and received travel expenses and a per diem allowance from the government.

392 Rise of an International Economic System

This combination of appointments at both the policy and research levels of the State Department's postwar planning structure is further evidence that the CFR played a major role in shaping government decisions on the postwar international economy.

Moreover, additional evidence for the importance of these appointments arises from the fact that some regular staff members believed that the consultants were dominating the State Department's research work through prior consultation with each other and CFR leaders. In particular, Harley Notter, who later wrote the official departmental history of postwar planning, complained bitterly about what he perceived as a CFR takeover in several memos to Pasvolsky in early 1942 (Shoup 1974, pp. 247–249). Finally, in September, Notter drafted a letter of resignation stating his situation was no longer tenable for two reasons. The first was that he was receiving one set of instructions from Welles and another from Pasvolsky, which reflected a departmental power struggle that included both personal conflicts and complex issues concerning the structure of the projected United Nations (which need not concern us for the purposes of this chapter). The second involved the power of the CFR within the department's Division of Research:

> I have consistently opposed every move tending to give it increasing control of the research of this Division, and, though you have also consistently stated that such a policy was far from your objectives, the actual facts already visibly show that Departmental control is fast losing ground. Control by the Council has developed, in my judgment, to the point where, through Mr. Bowman's close cooperation with you, and his other methods and those of Mr. Armstrong on the Committee, which proceed unchanged in their main theme, the outcome is clear. The moves have been so piecemeal that no one of them offered decisive objection; that is still so, but now I take my stand on the cumulative trend.
>
> (Shoup 1974, p. 250, quoting a letter in the
> Notter File in the National Archives)

Notter apparently changed his mind about resigning. The letter was never sent even though nothing changed in the relationship between the CFR and the department. In his official history of postwar economic planning by the State Department, Notter (1949) gives no real sense of how large the CFR's role was nor of his dissatisfaction with it. Since his superficial account of postwar planning is one source for several histories of postwar planning, it may contribute to any scholarly notions that the State Department was more independent of outside influences at that time than it in fact was.

The CFR's vision of the postwar economic system had been accepted within the government by the end of 1942 at the latest. The state-building on this crucial issue, including the placement of personnel inside the government, was complete. The only new postwar policy issue of major import that faced CFR planners and government decision-makers between 1943 and 1946 was the incorporation of the German economy and Western Europe into the Grand Area. The CFR planners had decided by 1945 that a reconstituted and demilitarized Germany could be an essential engine to a fast and strong recovery for the European economy as a whole. They were also determined that the mistake of burdening Germany with large reparation payments, as was the case after World War I, should not be repeated (Gramer 1995; Gramer 1997, Chapter 5).

While CFR planners expected there might be some resistance to their plans for Germany, they were caught by surprise by a plan put forth at the last minute in 1945 by Secretary of Treasury Henry Morgenthau at a meeting between Roosevelt and Churchill. It called for a de-industrialized Germany, which would have a predominantly agricultural economy. CFR leaders worked very diligently to defeat this new initiative, and they met with no disagreement when it came to a decision point early in the presidency of Harry S. Truman.

Taking nothing for granted, the CFR created a new study group on "The Problem of Germany" in late 1946, which included several of its most prominent members, including a corporate lawyer who became the U.S. High Commissioner of Germany in September 1949. Viner from the Economic and Financial Group was also a member (Gramer 1997, Chapter 5; Wala 1994, Chapter 4). The issue became even more salient when the Cold War reached a critical point due to the Soviet blockade of Berlin that began in June 1948, just two months after Congress approved of a massive rebuilding plan for Europe, discussed in Chapter 13, which centered around the restoration of West German industry.

The Committee for Economic Development Enters the Picture

As important as the CFR's war-peace studies were in creating a new framework for American postwar foreign policy, there were limits to its usefulness because it did not include the many corporations that would not be involved in foreign trade in the first several years after the war, if ever. Nor did the CFR's planning in close coordination with the department of state do anything to publicly counter the highly visible postwar planning that was being carried out by experts in the liberal-labor alliance. Liberal planners and economists, working in and around the small planning agency within the White House, the National Resources Planning Board, were issuing widely distributed Keynesian economic prescriptions that called for continued government spending and new government planning agencies. These liberal-labor plans would perforce limit the power of corporations and make foreign markets less important in avoiding a return of

394 Rise of an International Economic System

the depression-level economic conditions that did not abate until World War II spending began.

At the same time, the corporate moderates were convinced that the ultraconservatives' economic plans for a return to the same old free-market verities would slow the economy, and thereby risk falling profits, depression, and renewed social disruption. It was in this context that the CED trustees hired four of the most experienced economists advising the CFR's Economic and Financial Group to consult for the CED as well. Complementing the CFR's international planning, the CED's committee on international trade policy made important additions to the corporate moderates' understanding of how to create a strong international economic system, as discussed in Chapter 13.

The Absence of Concerns about the Soviet Union

In concluding this chapter, it is striking in the light of postwar events that the war-peace discussion groups and the CED devoted little or no time to discussing the Soviet Union or communism, and offered no recommendations on these topics. In the case of the CFR, it is clear that none of the members of its war-peace group had any use for Communist economic policies or the Soviet dictatorship, except as a military ally that was essential to the defeat of Germany. In that context, any issues relating to the Soviet Union were discussed primarily in connection with Eastern Europe. Recognizing the weak and underdeveloped nature of the fragmented economies in the small countries of that region, some CFR planners suggested the creation of an Eastern European customs union. Such a customs union might lead to a regional economy that could serve as a market for Western Europe and as a buffer against the Soviet Union (Shoup 1974, p. 241).

However, CFR leaders and government decision-makers were divided as to the possibility of such an outcome. When Armstrong argued at a State Department subcommittee meeting in March 1942, that steps should be taken to keep those countries from becoming Communist, Assistant Secretary of State A. A. Berle, Jr. "immediately reminded Armstrong that Soviet help was indispensable for a United Nations victory and that the department should be cautious about moves to put hostile states on that country's borders" (Shoup 1974, p. 241, paraphrasing State Department minutes). When Armstrong pressed the same point at a meeting of the department's Territorial Subcommittee on October 9, 1942, Bowman thought there was no choice but to accept a Soviet takeover of those countries (Shoup 1974, p. 242). Historian John Gaddis (1972, p. 137) also uses comments by Bowman to suggest that by 1943 American decision-makers were prepared to acquiesce in Soviet dominance in Eastern Europe.

In short, there was neither strong emphasis nor great unity on the question of Eastern Europe, the area in which there was the greatest threat of

Soviet domination. Instead, Germany and Japan were the immediate and overwhelming dangers to the Grand Area with regard to developing the necessary living space for the American economy. Moreover, and very importantly, neither the Soviet Union nor Eastern Europe was a part of the Grand Area that now was seen as ample enough to accommodate a post-Nazi Germany as well as the United States, the United Kingdom, and Japan in a harmonious fashion.

References

Adams, Frederick. 1976. *Economic diplomacy: The export-import bank and American foreign policy 1934–1939.* Columbia University of Missouri Press.

Alexander, Herbert E. 1992. *Financing politics: Money, elections, and political reform.* Washington: CQ Press.

Beckmann, George. 1964. "The role of the foundations." *The Annals of the American Academy of Political and Social Science* 356:12–22.

CED. 1945. *International trade, foreign investment, and domestic employment.* New York: Committee for Economic Development.

Collins, Robert M. 1981. *The business response to Keynes, 1929–1964.* New York: Columbia University Press.

Diebold, William. 1941. *New directions in our trade policy.* New York: Council on Foreign Relations.

———. 1959. *The Schuman Plan: A study in economic cooperation, 1950–1959.* New York: Praeger.

———. 1972. *The United States and the industrial world: American foreign economic policy in the 1970s.* New York: Praeger.

Divine, Robert. 1967. *Second chance: The triumph of internationalism in America during World War II.* New York: Atheneum.

Domhoff, G. W. 1970. *The higher circles.* New York: Random House.

Frieden, Jeffry A. 1988. "Sectoral conflict and U.S. foreign economic policy." Pp. 59–90 in *The State and American foreign economic policy,* edited by G. J. Ikenberry, D. Lake, and M. Mastanduno. Ithaca: Cornell University Press.

———. 2006. *Global capitalism: Its fall and rise in the twentieth century.* New York W. W. Norton.

Gaddis, John. 1972. *The United States and the origins of the cold war, 1941–1947.* New York: Columbia University Press.

Galbraith, John. 1971. *Economics, peace and laughter.* New York: Penguin Books.

Gardner, Lloyd. 1964. *Economic aspects of New Deal diplomacy.* Madison: University of Wisconsin Press.

Gramer, Regina. 1995. "The German question from recovery to rearmament: The Council on Foreign Relations and its voices of dissent, 1942–1950." The Society for Historians of American Foreign Relations, June 21–24. Annapolis.

———. 1997. "Reconstructing Germany, 1938–1949: United States foreign policy and the cartel question." Ph.D. dissertation Thesis, Department of History, Rutgers University, New Brunswick.

Haggard. 1988. "The institutional foundations of hegemony: Explaining the Reciprocal Trade Agreements Act of 1934." Pp. 91–120 in *The state and American foreign economic policy*, edited by G. J. Ikenberry, D. Lake, and M. Mastanduno. Ithaca: Cornell University Press.

Helleiner, Eric. 2014. *Forgotten foundations of Bretton Woods: International development and the making of the postwar order.* Ithaca Cornell University Press.

Ikenberry, G. John, Thomas J. Knock, Anne-Marie Slaughter, and Tony Smith. 2011. *The crisis of American foreign policy: Wilsonianism in the twenty-first century.* Princeton: Princeton University Press.

Kirk, Grayson. 1947. *The study of international relations in American colleges and universities.* New York: Council on Foreign Relations.

Krasner, Stephen. 1978. *Defending the National Interest.* Princeton: Princeton University Press.

Moley, Raymond. 1939. *After seven years.* New York: Harper & Brothers.

Notter, Harley. 1949. *Postwar foreign policy preparation, 1939–1945.* Washington: U.S Government Printing Office.

Overacker, Louise. 1932. *Money in elections.* New York: Macmillan.

Roosevelt, Franklin D. 1933–1945. "Papers as President," Official File. Franklin D. Roosevelt Presidential Library & Museum. Hyde Park, NY.

Schulzinger, Robert. 1984. *The wise men of foreign affairs: The history of the Council on Foreign Relations.* New York Columbia University Press.

———. 2002. *U.S. diplomacy since 1900.* New York Oxford University Press.

Shoup, Laurence. 1974. "Shaping the national interest: The Council on Foreign Relations, the Department of State, and the origins of the postwar world." Ph.D. dissertation Thesis, History, Northwestern University, Evanston.

———. 1975. "Shaping the postwar world: The Council on Foreign Relations and United States war aims." *Insurgent Sociologist* 5:9–52.

———. 1977. "The Council on Foreign Relations and American policy in Southeast Asia, 1940–1973." *Insurgent Sociologist* 7:19–30.

Shoup, Laurence and William Minter. 1977. *Imperial brain trust.* New York: Monthly Review Press.

Smith, Neil. 2003. *American empire: Roosevelt's geographer and the prelude to globalization.* Berkeley: University of California Press.

Wala, Michael. 1994. *The Council on Foreign Relations and American foreign policy in the early Cold War.* Providence: Berghahn Books.

Webber, Michael J. 2000. *New Deal fat cats: Business, labor, and campaign finance in the 1936 presidential election.* New York: Fordham University Press.

Whitham, Charlie. 2016. *Post-War business planners in the United States, 1939–1948.* New York: Bloomsbury Publishing.

Woods, Tim. 2003. "Capitalist class relations, the state, and New Deal foreign trade policy." *Critical Sociology* 29:393–418.

Chapter 11

The Grand Area and the Origins of the International Monetary Fund

The policy discussions in the Council on Foreign Relations (CFR)'s war-peace study groups in 1940 and 1941 provide the starting point for understanding American postwar monetary policy and the origins of the IMF. Based on leads in historian Laurence Shoup's dissertation (1974), the case for this claim builds on my archival research in the war-peace documents and the CFR's "Digests of Discussions", and in the papers of three key participants, as supplemented and contextualized by the work of numerous historians and policy analysts. The documents and discussions are highly detailed and not easily summarized, and perhaps would not even be believed if not presented at somewhat greater length than usual. Many documents are therefore quoted at length. *Caveat lector.*

Economists Jacob Viner and Alvin Hansen are once again the critical connections between the war-peace studies and the government on a very important issue, and in this case essential links to the United Kingdom and their key postwar monetary and trade representatives as well. To recall and extend an earlier point, Viner was active in the CFR during the 1930s and at the same time an adviser to Secretary of Treasury Henry Morgenthau until the mid-1940s. In 1934 he helped create and manage the exchange stabilization fund within the Treasury, which was a precursor of the IMF, and in 1935 and 1936 he helped Morgenthau in negotiating a pact with the United Kingdom and France through which national exchange stabilization funds were used to stabilize currency values (Blum 1959, Chapter 4).

This Tripartite Pact grew to include several smaller democratic countries as well. At that point it was only a step or two in principle from an international monetary stabilization fund, which was the original and main purpose of the IMF. Not insignificantly, and indeed crucially in terms of one of the key differences of this account from earlier ones, Viner also was the person who first brought economist Harry Dexter White, who is usually credited as the American who contributed the most to the creation of the IMF, into the treasury department. He hired White in the summer of 1934 to write a summary report on American monetary and banking legislation "with a view to planning a long term legislative program for the

Administration" (Rees 1973, p. 40, quoting Viner's letter to White; Steil 2013, pp. 22–23). White then joined the Department of the Treasury on a temporary basis in late 1935, resigning his professorship at little Lawrence College in Wisconsin, with about 1,000 students. White had accepted a professorial position there after a series of one-year appointments at Harvard without any likelihood of tenure, where his work was considered "superficial" (Skidelsky 2000, p. 240) and "academically unexceptional" (Steil 2013, p. 21). Put frankly, he was seen as a second-rate economist by professors of economics at the most prestigious universities.

White's stature in the eyes of the university community of that era is a more important issue than it may seem. As is still the case today, it was widely believed at the time that the allegedly best and the brightest preferred to be employed at high-status universities, wherein they received higher salaries and had greater freedom than if they worked as mere civil servants and appointees in a government department. In addition, CFR leaders, and by inference corporate leaders, who knew the top academicians through policy-planning groups, and often served as university trustees, were well aware of the status rankings among professors and universities. For example, in a summary of a discussion with British planners at a war-peace studies meeting in January 1942, it was agreed that the people in government service with the time to plan ahead were the "washouts." To have a plan with the stature to be taken seriously by "operational" appointees, it would have to be developed by experts outside of government that commanded the respect of those in key positions (Council on Foreign Relations 1942, pp. 10–11).

In other words, Viner and Hansen had far more status than White did, including in the eyes of the Secretary of the Treasury, Henry Morgenthau, as shown later in this chapter. In fact, Morgenthau never made a decision in regard to international monetary policy and the creation of the IMF unless he knew that Viner had examined and approved of the relevant documents. He had great respect for Viner's views, which meant that the changes Viner suggested were usually made.

Hansen, as the leader of the liberal Keynesians, was best known for his emphasis on public spending for domestic projects, but he was knowledgeable about monetary issues as well. As will be shown shortly, he had a role in coordinating international monetary policy with John Maynard Keynes and the other economists who worked for the United Kingdom's Treasury Department at the time. Other economists from the Economic and Financial Group, especially Winfield Riefler and Arthur Upgren, also were active on the IMF project, so the expert links between the war-peace studies and the drafting of the IMF proposal were numerous.

There is another intriguing dimension to White's involvement in the origins of the IMF. Although it was unknown to most people at the time except for a few Soviet spies, and therefore had no impact on

The Grand Area and the Origins of the IMF   399

how he was regarded, he did provide classified government information to Soviet spies inside and outside the American government from 1935 to 1939, and then again from 1941 to 1945 (e.g., Craig 2004; Haynes and Klehr 1999, pp. 138–145; Steil 2013, pp. 35–39, 293–298). It is important to note that White was not a Communist and did not consider himself to be a spy, but he did write down the gist of classified information to give to close friends in the State Department, whom he knew to be Communists, and he very likely provided at least some classified documents (Olmsted 2002, pp. 48–51, 100–103). He felt justified and guiltless because the information he provided to his Communist friends furthered the possibility of positive Soviet-American relations, which he thought very important as a non-Communist liberal internationalist. He did not think the information he passed along harmed the interests of the American government (Craig 2004, who provides new information and the most detailed analysis, especially pp. 148–155, 261–262 and Chapter 12; Steil 2013, pp. 6, 35–39, 44–46, for a gripping account, with new information on White's pro-Soviet activities in the late 1930s).

Although White's relationship to the Soviet Union through American spies and his private discussions with Soviet officials at Bretton Woods were not an issue at the time, they became a serious matter in late January 1946, shortly after he was appointed as the American director of the IMF. An American woman who ran a major Soviet spy ring in Washington went to the FBI unbidden in November 1945, and described in great detail her extensive role in spying over the space of many years. In the process she stated that White had provided Communist spies with information (Craig 2004; Olmsted 2002; Steil 2013, pp. 36, 44, 294–296). He was forced to resign quietly in March 1947 (Casey 2001, p. 188). In 1948 he was brought before the House Un-American Activities Committee, where he denied any wrongdoing (Rees 1973; Steil 2013, pp. 318–320).

However skeptics may regard the evidence as to whether White gave classified government information to those who were not supposed to have it, and that he knew to be Communists, the important point at this juncture is that Stalin and his main advisers had inside information about postwar American monetary plans. This information showed that the monetary plans were not designed to undermine them. In addition, Soviet representatives were active participants at the founding IMF conference. Many of Stalin's advisers thought the Soviet Union should join the new IMF, so it is unlikely that the IMF was seen as a provocation by the Soviets.

The starting point for the deliberations that led to the IMF appear in a document from the CFR's Economic and Financial Group on international monetary questions, report E-B34, dated July 24, 1941, just over four months before the United States declared war on both Germany and Japan after the Japanese attacked Pearl Harbor early in December 1941. The new CFR document was meant primarily as a general framework for

400   Rise of an International Economic System

studies of the international monetary, investment, and trade organizations that would be needed to integrate the Grand Area. Entitled "Methods of Economic Collaboration: The Role of the Grand Area in American Economic Policy," it includes a review of the Grand Area concept that is useful for its conciseness and directness. It is quoted in detail not only to support the claim that the CFR's war-peace studies were foundational to postwar monetary policy, but to tell readers that this and other documents usually are not discussed in studies of the origins of the IMF (e.g., Block 1977; Eckes 1975; Oliver 1975; Steil 2013; van Dormael 1978). It begins as follows:

> The purpose of this memorandum is to summarize the concept of the Grand Area in terms of its meaning for American policy, its function in the present war, and its possible role in the postwar period. The memorandum is the introduction to a series concerned with the methods of integrating the Grand Area economically.

It continues with a section on "The Grand Area and American Defense," which begins with an excellent overview of the American economy and its needs:

> The economy of the United States is geared to the export of certain manufactured and agricultural products, and the import of numerous raw materials and foodstuffs. The success of German arms from the invasion of Poland onward brought most of Europe under Nazi domination and threatened the rest of the world. Faced with these facts, the Economic and Financial Group sought to determine the area (excluding continental Europe, which for the present was lost) that, from the economic point of view, was best suited to the defense of the United States. Such an area would have to: (1) contain the basic raw materials necessary to the full functioning of American industry, and (2) have the fewest possible stresses making for its own disintegration, such as unwieldy export surpluses or severe shortages of consumers' goods.

The memorandum then states the empirical basis for the claims that are made in it:

> With this end in view, a series of studies was made to ascertain the "degree of complementarism" in trade of several blocs: the Western Hemisphere, the British Empire (except Canada), the Far East. From the point of view of the United States, the Western Hemisphere is an inadequate area because it lacks important raw materials, which we get from southeastern Asia, and it is burdened with surpluses normally exported to Europe, especially the United Kingdom. An extension

The Grand Area and the Origins of the IMF   401

of the area in opposite directions to take in these two economically important regions thus becomes necessary. The extension brings new problems, but it was found that the United States can best defend itself—from an economic point of view—in an area comprising most of the non-German world. This has been called the "Grand Area." It includes the Western Hemisphere, the United Kingdom, the remainder of the British Commonwealth and Empire, the Dutch East Indies, China, and Japan.

(Council on Foreign Relations 1941a, p. 1)

After a discussion of the German-controlled bloc and the relative unimportance of the Soviet Union to the American economy, the memorandum stresses the role of the Grand Area in military preparedness and in avoiding adjustments in the American economy:

The Grand Area, then, is the amount of the world the United States can defend most economically, that is, with the least readjustment of the American economy. To maintain a maximum defense effort, the United States must avoid economic readjustment caused by constriction of the trading area if the military cost of defending the area is not too great. What such constriction might mean in weakening the defense economy can best be seen by imagining the strain on American supplies of labor, materials, and industrial capacity of the attempt to manufacture substitutes for or to do without rubber, tin, jute, and numerous vegetable oils, instead of importing these products from southeastern Asia. Similarly, to the extent that the United States and other countries can continue to export their surpluses, some dangerous stresses in the domestic economy are prevented from developing.

The above paragraphs might seem more than enough as a blunt call for an international economy built around American needs, but there is more that is said by way of frank geopolitics concerning the military costs and risks that might be involved in securing this area, which might lead to American wars in Asia:

It is important for the United States to defend the Grand Area and to prevent the capture of any of its parts by the Germans. Similarly, the Grand Area must be defended from defection from within, (1) by making it economically possible for all member countries to live in the area, and (2) by preventing any country—particularly Japan— from destroying the area for its own political reasons. Some studies of the economic aspects of these problems have been made, others are projected. It is not the role of the Economic and Financial Group to determine how the area is to be defended nor to assess whether

402 Rise of an International Economic System

such a defense is feasible, though broad military considerations have of course played some part in determining the area, and it has been assumed that keeping the area intact is not patently impossible from a military viewpoint. Similarly, the methods of political collaboration needed to integrate the area, and the diplomacy required for keeping it intact, do not fall into the Group's sphere, except insofar as economic weapons and enticements are part of that diplomacy and the institutional structure for solving economic problems is called political.

(Council on Foreign Relations 1941a, pp. 2–3)

Two pages later, the document turns to the importance of collaboration with the United Kingdom in integrating the Grand Area, emphasizing that this economic collaboration must begin during the war, not afterwards:

Anglo-American collaboration is the key to the integration of the Grand Area, both as a wartime measure and in forging an enduring peace on the lines desired by the two countries. Many of the problems facing the peacemakers will be determined by wartime policies and the developments of war economics. It is likely to be easier to continue economic collaboration begun in wartime than to start anew at the peace settlement. It seems important, then, that the United States and Empire countries work together within the framework of the Grand Area economy in wartime, and plan their policies—so far as is compatible with the immediate war effort—to provide the best possible basis for coping with problems of the peace.

(Council on Foreign Relations 1941a, pp. 4–5)

The document goes on to say that there would be problems in integrating the Grand Area. There would be a need for a "conscious program" to insure that it did not come apart:

The statistical neatness of the Grand Area will not cause it to function automatically simply because Germany controls most of Europe although the blockade and its consequences stimulate this development. The condition of "buying first from one another," on which it is based, would itself require a considerable degree of trade readjustment and raise certain problems of transportation. The Grand Area was defined on the basis of peacetime trade; the conditions of war change demand patterns and create hazards, such as the destruction of shipping and production capacity. Japan's expansionist policy continues to threaten the integration of the Grand Area. These problems may not be ignored; some have already been the subjects of study. Above all, it appears certain that the integration of the Grand Area requires a conscious program of broadly conceived measures for (1) knitting the parts of the area closer together economically and (2) securing the full use of the economic resources of the whole area.

(Council on Foreign Relations 1941a, p. 5)

In fact, as also mentioned in the previous chapter, the American planners sensed that there might be problems with the United Kingdom in particular, whose government very likely would resist opening up their empire to American corporations, so the CFR experts thought it would be critical to force the issue under the pressure of war:

> The integration of the Grand Area is based on American-British collaboration. At the same time, America and British interests are neither identical nor entirely parallel. Not only will there be disagreements as to what policy is best, but also real clashes of interest which can be resolved only to the hurt of certain groups within one or the other country. In wartime the tendency is for such clashes of interest to be submerged and subordinated to the single goal of winning the war. At the peace and after it, they tend to re-emerge, sometimes more sharply than ever. With outside pressure of a common enemy removed, such conflicts of interest can easily destroy the whole program of continued international cooperation. One of the most important tasks of the Grand Area studies will be to detect present and prospective clashes of interest, define them so far as possible, and seek means of eliminating, alleviating, or compromising them.
>
> (Council on Foreign Relations 1941a, p. 5)

Finally, there is an outline of proposed studies relating to the economic integration of the Grand Area. Those concerning "Financial Collaboration" and "Monetary and Exchange Problems" directly relate to the origins of the IMF. They show that at least some corporate moderates with access to the White House, state, and treasury departments were proposing a way to facilitate the dramatic extension of the American economy into much of the world. The outline included financial collaboration, international financial institutions, stabilization of exchange rates, international anti-depression measures, trade arrangements, and development programs (Council on Foreign Relations 1941a, p. 6). In fact, CFR planners thought that generating a plan for an international exchange stabilization fund was, as Viner (1942, p. 174) pointed out, a "comparatively easy" task.

Nevertheless, and as the CFR planners feared, there were major problems in creating a plan that suited the United Kingdom. The subsequent negotiations proved to be highly complex and seemingly endless over a three-year period. In order to understand the interactions between British and American planners, it is first of all, necessary to understand the British perspective on the key issues as well as the American view outlined above.

The United Kingdom's economic and financial position had not only been greatly weakened by its war with the Nazis, which is obvious, but by its financial dealings with the United States as well. Due to the neutrality laws passed by Congress in 1935 at the insistence of isolationists, the United Kingdom's purchases of war-related materials from the United States between 1939 and 1941 had to be on a cash-and-carry basis. This arrangement rather quickly drained their reserves of American dollars. As the pressure on their finances increased, the American Treasury insisted that the United Kingdom sell their assets in the United States to make their payments. While these asset sales made further immediate payments possible, they also meant that the United Kingdom would be less able to earn American dollars in the future.

American officials in the Treasury Department kept a sharp eye on the United Kingdom's gold supply as well. They wanted to be sure that the country was not hoarding gold before they tried to convince Congress to make changes in the neutrality laws it had enacted just a few years earlier. For example, when Morgenthau learned in December 1940 that the United Kingdom had $42 million in new gold waiting in Cape Town, he immediately recommended that Roosevelt ask for it, and it was picked up a few weeks later with much fanfare. The British were deeply insulted by what they saw as a crass maneuver by a nation already in possession of most of the world's gold supply. From their point of view, the Americans seemed to be out to weaken the British Empire (Dobson, 1986, pp. 25–28). Then, in March 1941, with the United Kingdom nearing bankruptcy in terms of dollars and gold, Roosevelt pushed a "Lend-Lease" bill through Congress, which made it possible to provide unrestricted aid to the United Kingdom in exchange for future repayments or *considerations*. The word "considerations" is in italics because some decision-makers thought the vague and undetermined nature of those considerations might prove to be a major bargaining chip in dealing with a near-bankrupt nation. This is especially the case because the Lend-Lease bill gave the president the discretion to decide what the repayments or considerations would be. This freedom was to become very important in negotiations concerning the nature and scope of the IMF.

However, Lend-Lease did not solve all of the United Kingdom's immediate problems. The American Treasury quickly insisted on restrictions on British commercial exports that were in competition with American exports. Ostensibly, these restrictions were demanded in order to maintain American public support for the Lend-Lease program; rightly or wrongly, there was considerable suspicion in the United Kingdom that these restrictions also were meant to further diminish its declining economic power (Dobson 1986; Gardner 1980, pp. 173–175). Whatever the intent, the restriction on its exports did keep the United Kingdom on a short financial tether.

The United Kingdom's leaders also were very wary of American pronouncements in favor of free trade because they had long been a staple of the State Department under Secretary of State Cordell Hull. There were two reasons for this wariness. First, they were not at all sure that the Americans would accept free trade in practice. (When the United Kingdom dominated world trade during most of the late nineteenth and early twentieth centuries, it had pushed for free trade for others, but found ways to practice protectionism (often in indirect ways), so its well-schooled diplomats knew whereof they worried (Lachmann 2015, p. 469).) Second, free trade by itself was seen as a very antiquated and dangerous doctrine by a British government influenced at that time by the experience of the Great Depression and Keynesian doctrines. Simply put, the British firmly believed that free trade without firm commitments to anti-depression fiscal, monetary, and social policies in the United States would drag the world economy into any future American depressions that were allowed to run their course. They believed American policy failures had contributed to the abandonment of relatively free trade in the early 1930s, and they did not want to see those failures repeated at their expense.

Although British officials realized that many leaders in the State Department, treasury department, and CFR understood this point, they were not at all confident that the reactionaries, nationalists, and isolationists so prevalent among ultraconservatives in the corporate community and Congress would accept the New Deal and Keynesian policies necessary to safeguard an open world economy. Indeed, American ultraconservatives, who clung to classical laissez faire (market-fundamentalist) thinking, in the face of considerable evidence showing it was not realistic to do so, already openly hated Keynesianism. Keynes was even despised by conventional New Dealers such as Secretary of Treasury Morgenthau, who had little or no understanding of economics. In addition, as noted in earlier chapters, numerous studies of Congressional voting patterns show that the conservative coalition controlled Congress when it came to taxes, business regulation, and labor relations from 1939 onward (e.g., Katznelson, Geiger, and Kryder 1993; Shelley 1983). Still further, the ultraconservatives were in the process of dismantling numerous New Deal agencies between 1943 and 1945 as they gradually won even greater control of Congress in the 1942 and 1944 elections. More generally, they were the major influence in forcing a fast and unregulated transition from wartime controls to almost complete deregulation very soon after the war ended (Domhoff 2013, pp. 41–48; Whitham 2016, Chapter 4).

Given the antipathy Morgenthau and many members of Congress had toward Keynesian economics, it is ironic that Keynes himself was one of the chief British advisers and negotiators in relation to Lend-Lease repayments and a future international monetary stabilization fund. I say ironic because Keynes not only saw the larger economic issues better than most

406   Rise of an International Economic System

officials, making him a brilliant adversary for the American negotiators, but he instinctively generated strongly negative personal reactions in many American leaders due to his polished, arrogant, and non-macho style.

In terms of Keynes' involvement in the issues of concern in this chapter, he first arrived in the United States in May 1941, to negotiate the details of the Lend-Lease agreement that had been passed by Congress two months before. It was right at a time when CFR leaders and officials in the State Department were thinking about how to gain British acceptance of the Grand Area plan. Anticipating that there would be British resistance to these ideas because they implied the United Kingdom's subordination to the United States, the American negotiators hit upon the idea of linking the Lend-Lease agreements with their plans for the postwar world. That is, the *consideration* they sought from the United Kingdom in exchange for vast amounts of war materiel and other supplies was acceptance of the American plan. The United States would forego financial repayments in exchange for power, which meant the United Kingdom's acquiescence to American leadership in the international economy, including within its still-large colonial empire. Instances such as this seem to provide strong evidence that power, not profits or balanced government budgets, are the primary concern of the corporate rich and the power elite.

The Lend-Lease negotiations were therefore focused on the issue of lowering tariffs and removing other trade barriers, which meant in practice that the United Kingdom's colonies, protected by "imperial preferences," would be opened up to American trade and investment. But Keynes kept pointing out that the United Kingdom would have a balance of payments problem after the war, and that the Americans therefore would have to accept more imports and give loans to the United Kingdom if they expected to increase trade with the British Empire. Furthermore, the acceptance of more imports might necessitate Keynesian policies in the United States in order to increase the level of activity in its domestic economy, just as CFR planners also had stated in one of their brief early reports. To repeat, any plan for international economic cooperation would have to include more than simple "free-trade" agreements. Keynes also was aware of the fact that there were important conservatives in London, in both the treasury department and the central bank, that would oppose American postwar plans because they might undermine the empire and hasten the United Kingdom's decline as a world power. Eckes (1975, p. 39) provides a graphic summary of the issues involved in the negotiations:

> John Maynard Keynes, England's leading financial negotiator, realized that, without parallel arrangements to assure an expansionary world economy, to reconstruct war-debilitated nations, and to erase currency imbalances, Britain could not adjust to the cold shower of American competition. Thus, on one visit to Washington in 1941, Keynes bluntly

The Grand Area and the Origins of the IMF   407

dismissed the "lunatic proposals of Mr. Hull," and warned that without American financial assistance Britain might be compelled to select an autarkic course in the postwar period. Of course, more than economic considerations shaped the British position. Advocates of imperial preference argued vigorously that nondiscrimination spelled the death of Britain's historic empire and England's decline as a world power.

Not surprisingly, then, there was very little meeting of the minds during the spring and summer of 1941. The British knew the Americans would not cut off aid in the midst of the war. They also hoped that the United States eventually would come into the war on their side, and that the terms of Lend-Lease could be made less onerous for the United Kingdom in that event. As for the Americans, they did not try to become more specific than acceptance of the general principles of the Grand Area strategy. This was partly because officials of the executive branch did not wish to make promises until they were sure Congressional opinion had become more sympathetic to internationalism. However, it also involved a point I emphasized in the previous chapter. The State Department had very little planning capability at the time, to which it now can be added that the Treasury had not officially begun to develop any plans for monetary policy. Then, too, recall from the previous chapter that Roosevelt did not decide whether state, treasury, or Vice President Henry Wallace's Economic Defense Board would take the lead in coordinating postwar planning until two weeks after the United States entered the war.

It is in this context that planning for what came to be called the International Monetary Fund (Keynes acerbically pointed out that the "fund" was really a "bank") officially began in the fall of 1941. Most commentators on the origins of the IMF believe that the planning began independently in the United States and the United Kingdom, with White taking the lead for the Americans and Keynes for the British (e.g., Gardner 1980, p. 71; van Dormael 1978, Chapter 4). However, evidence in the Viner Papers, Hansen Papers, and the Morgenthau Diaries verifies that the situation was more coordinated than some accounts suggest, with Hansen and Viner playing a mediating role between experts from the two countries and with the American federal government. For example, the Economic and Financial Group initiated a series of four off-the-record meetings with British economists on September 20, 1941, to discuss general issues of collaboration. The secretary of the Royal Institute of International Affairs, which was mentioned in the previous chapter as the United Kingdom's counterpart to the CFR, was also present. According to the summary of the discussion, a wide range of economic topics was covered in a general way (Council on Foreign Relations 1941a).

Shortly thereafter, Hansen traveled to London, where Keynes was drafting a plan to implement American proposals in a way that would be

408 Rise of an International Economic System

satisfactory to the United Kingdom. Despite anti-internationalist assertions by Keynes while in the United States a few months earlier, he realized that it would be very hard to resist the economic and political power of the Americans. He also knew that the United Kingdom's recovery would be slow and painful without American trade and loans. He therefore suggested methods for international currency stabilization that could lead to the liberalized expansion of international trade that the Americans sought. The essence of his plan was the establishment of a very large international currency exchange and credit-granting institution that could be drawn upon with relative ease by any country that was temporarily short of any given foreign currency due to trade imbalances (Skidelsky, 2000, Chapter 6).

Functioning on the principle of a friendly and trusting bank, the "international clearing union," as Keynes called the projected institution, would make it possible for countries to "overdraft" their accounts for a period of time so that expansionary trade could be continued. In effect, it was a bank that made temporary loans of foreign currencies from a fund that was based on no more than the promise of the member countries to provide the needed currencies when called for. Each country would provide the clearing union with a line of credit, but would not have to deliver the currency until it actually was needed. As will be seen shortly, the Americans were very nervous about this plan. They were afraid that some countries would not immediately provide the currency when it was asked for. Even more, they feared there would be an unlimited call for American currency, but with no assurance that the countries needing the loans were living within their means.

It was during this time that Hansen arrived on the scene in London to confer personally with Keynes and other British economists (Helleiner 2014, p. 125). Keynes' first major biographer, economist Roy F. Harrod (1951, pp. 527–528), explained the visit as follows, noting that Hansen's "mandate" from the government was "obscure":

> At this period there occurred a useful visit by Professor Alvin Hansen, the well-known economist, and Mr. [Luther] Gulick, a consultant of the National [Resources] Planning Board and expert on the TVA. [Gulick was the head of the Institute of Public Administration, an organization in the urban policy-planning network.] Although sponsored by the State Department, the nature of their mandate was obscure. They advocated Anglo-American cooperation to prevent world depression, and proposed the establishment of an International Economic Board to advise collaborating governments with respect to internal policy designed to promote full employment, economic stability, and world trade. . . They also advocated an International Resources Survey and an International Development Corporation, with a view to promoting wise development overseas.

The Grand Area and the Origins of the IMF   409

The British were somewhat surprised by these progressive proposals according to Harrod (1951, p. 528), who also recalled that the proposals were on a higher level of political sophistication than the simple Wilsonian trade doctrines of Hull: "These proposals were cordially welcomed; the doctrine seemed to belong to a different world of thought from that which took the elimination of discrimination in foreign trade to be the panacea for the world's ills."

In keeping with this cordial welcome, Hansen wrote an enthusiastic two-page letter to Viner upon his return to the United States about his "numerous conferences" with British economists "now in government service" and with "a number of high officials in the Treasury and other branches of government, including some members of the Cabinet..." (Viner Papers: Hansen to Viner, Box 13, Folder 9, October 20, 1941). Hansen continued his account by stating the discussions were "encouraging" and that there was interest in an international Reconstruction Finance Corporation "along the lines of the discussion at our own Council on Foreign Relations." He already had discussed the new proposals with Hull and Wallace, and would be talking with Morgenthau the next day. He closed with the hope that they could have a discussion of these matters at "a meeting of the Council on Foreign Relations November 1" (Viner Papers: Hansen to Viner, Box 13, Folder 9, October 20, 1941).

Viner replied with equal enthusiasm in a letter of October 24, saying that he found Hansen's letter "interesting and encouraging," and thought they were on the "right path." He also suggested that Hansen be in touch with Riefler, who had been in the Economic and Financial Group from the outset and was now working with Vice President Wallace at the Economic Defense Board. He made this suggestion because Riefler "is working intensively along the same lines and has a very interesting draft of a specific Anglo-American post-war financing organization" (Viner Papers: Viner to Hansen, Box 13, Folder 9, October 24, 1941). Hansen replied on October 28 with news that he had a revised draft of his plan based on "numerous conversations." He reported that he had been unable to contact Riefler as yet. He then suggested that the next meeting of their CFR planning group might be the place for further discussions:

> I see no reason why our Council on Foreign Relations, in view of its confidential relations with the State Department, might not have a full discussion of this draft, as well as of Riefler's proposals. Possibly you, Riefler, and I might have a special discussion of it at lunchtime on Saturday.
>
> (Viner Papers: Hansen to Viner,
> Box 13, Folder 9, October 28, 1941)

It is noteworthy that there is no suggestion that White should be part of the discussion, and in fact he did not come into the picture for another

410 Rise of an International Economic System

month or two. (Helleiner 2014, pp. 124–125 makes many of these same points based on his own archival research, and adds on p. 127, note 144, that White was not a member of the CFR.)

In a reply to Hansen in early November, Viner "stressed the importance of including small countries in the *management* of international lending institutions in order to avoid the appearance of what he called an Anglo-American 'financial monopoly'" (Helleiner 2014, p. 125, my italics). Putting the issue in a phrase from Viner's letter to Hansen, political scientist Eric Helleiner (2014, 125) quotes him as saying, "to be successful the proposed body must avoid the odium of two-power imperialism." Once the IMF was in place, however, the American bankers who had oversight over it ignored that concern, as documented in work by historian Kevin Casey (2001, Chapter 7) and as discussed in Chapter 13.

Unfortunately, this particular paper trail ends at this point, a problem that will recur at other crucial junctures in the archival record because none of the key American economists was a compulsive record keeper. In this instance, however, the line of thought can be picked up to some degree in other documents. On November 28, 1941, for example, the Economic and Financial Group summarized the proposals by Hansen and Riefler in a memorandum entitled "International Collaboration to Secure the Coordination of Stabilization Policies and to Stimulate Investment" (E–B44). The emphasis was once again placed on the need for expansionary domestic policies in order to make possible open or "multilateral" international trade, so White's later eagerness to include spending promises in his draft would hardly have come as a surprise to members of the CFR's Economic and Financial Group, or to Keynes.

A few days later, Hansen was able to make this general point again through another avenue, the governmental-sponsored Canadian-American Committee that he co-chaired. On December 5, the committee sent the White House and State Department a proposal for an International Stabilization and Development Board that would make suggestions about how the United States, the United Kingdom, and Canada could coordinate their economies. However, none of the documents or resolutions discussed in this paragraph deals with the specific problem of monetary policy. As will be shown, Viner was carrying this issue forward within the treasury department in conjunction with White, and very likely supervising White's drafting. (In making this claim, I am not suggesting that Viner was "behind the scenes" or secretive; I am instead suggesting that previous researchers on this issue did not find all the archival evidence that is available.)

It was at this point in the monetary and currency discussions that the Japanese attack on Pearl Harbor brought the United States into the war. Although American involvement in the war focused official attention even more on day-to-day issues, it also led to decisions on postwar

The Grand Area and the Origins of the IMF   411

planning that had been delayed for over a year. Morgenthau consolidated Treasury responsibility for foreign economic planning in White's hands early in December. A week later, on Sunday morning, December 14, Morgenthau called White to ask him to begin work on a monetary stabilization fund. White summarized this call the next day in a memo for the files (Morgenthau Diaries: Treasury Department Order No. 43—see list of Archival Sources at the end of the book). Then, in late December, Roosevelt gave the order putting the State in charge of postwar planning and assigning a secondary role to Treasury and the Economic Defense Board, as already noted in the previous chapter.

I was unable to determine why Morgenthau decided to call White about monetary policy on that particular Sunday in mid-December. There are no hints in his detailed records for the two previous weeks, or in White's papers. On the basis of retrospective accounts by White's associates (Eckes 1975, p. 46), there is some reason to believe that White actually had been working on monetary plans throughout the fall, and that Morgenthau's call only made official what had been going on unofficially. Such a possibility would not be surprising because White's longstanding involvement with monetary policy began with his work for Morgenthau and Viner on exchange stabilization in the mid-1930s, as noted earlier in the chapter (Blum 1959, Chapter 4). Whatever the exact origins of Morgenthau's order, the more general issue for theoretical purposes is the possible influence of CFR planners on White's plan. As the Treasury Department's liaison with the State Department on postwar planning issues in the previous two years, White was well aware of the internationalist proposals being sent to the State Department by the CFR's war-peace studies (Notter 1949). We also know from Harrod (1951, p. 539) that White had direct conversations about foreign economic issues with Hansen, and from the Morgenthau Diaries we know that White "continually supported the fiscal proposals of Alvin Hansen" (Blum 1970, p. 430).

However, Viner was by far the most important CFR intermediary to White, and Morgenthau. The Morgenthau Diaries reveal that he was present for general meetings at the Treasury on December 1, 2, 11, 12, 22, and 23. Moreover, there is documentary evidence in his reappointment letter of January 1, 1942, and subsequent memos by White and another department official, that Viner aided in the crafting of the original proposal for an International Monetary Fund. Given Viner's earlier relationship with White and his deep involvement in the CFR's postwar planning, the documentary evidence concerning Viner's work with White at Treasury exemplifies the influence of highly regarded private experts on the American government. True enough, there are state "structures," and there is a general ideological "atmosphere," but in addition there is also direct input from an outside expert deeply involved in a corporate-sponsored policy-planning network on a specific decision in a situation

412 Rise of an International Economic System

of potential conflict and great uncertainty. Given the volatility of the economic system and uncertainty as to how the executive and legislative branches might respond to one or another crisis, it is essential for the corporate community to have direct access to all parts of the government to be sure its interests will be protected (DiTomaso 1980, for an excellent statement of the importance to organizations that they reduce uncertainty in their environments, as emphasized in organizational theory).

The first evidence of Viner's direct involvement in the creation of the IMF drafted by White is his letter of appointment for 1942, which states that he would be paid from the "Exchange Stabilization Fund":

> January 1, 1942: Sir: You are hereby appointed Special Assistant and Consulting Expert in the Office of the Secretary, with compensation at the rate of nine thousand dollars per annum, payable from the appropriation "Exchange Stabilization Fund." In addition to your salary, you will be allowed five dollars per diem; in lieu of subsistence while on duty in Washington, D.C. Signed, Henry M. Morgenthau.
>
> (Morgenthau Diaries, Book 483, p. 180)

In 2018 dollars, Viner was receiving $138,500 per year for his services, along with $76 a day in expense money for the days he was in Washington.

In the first week of January, when the first plan seems to have been finalized, Viner was at the Treasury Department on the fifth, sixth, and seventh. On January 6 White asked Undersecretary of State Sumner Welles if he would be interested in introducing a resolution in favor of an "interallied" stabilization fund at the conference of American ministers in Rio de Janeiro later in the month (Helleiner 2014, pp. 107–108, 116 also discusses this conference). When Welles responded positively, White sent a memo to Morgenthau on January 8. It included the plan and reported that White had asked Viner to approve it, which is further evidence that Viner was overseeing White's work for Morgenthau:

> In the event Mr. Welles decides at Rio to propose a resolution on the establishment of a Stabilization Fund, I have in mind submitting the appended draft for his consideration. This draft was prepared in this Division, and is a much shorter draft than the one I showed you before. I have asked Mr. Southard [a department employee] to go over it with the Legal Division and Mr. Viner, and after they have approved, to submit it to you for your tentative approval.
>
> (Morgenthau Diaries, Book 483, p. 222)

One week later, on January 15, Southard sent a copy of the proposal to Undersecretary of Treasury Daniel Bell [this is not the sociologist named

The Grand Area and the Origins of the IMF 413

Daniel Bell] with the following preface, which mentions the role of Viner in creating the plan:

> Mr. White discussed the proposal for such a Fund with the Secretary early in January and received the Secretary's approval of the idea in principle. The draft prepared by Mr. White grew out of several discussions within the Treasury which included Mr. Bernard Bernstein [a department employee] and Jacob Viner.
>
> (Morgenthau Diaries, Book 486, p. 1)

On the same day as the Southard memo, White contacted Morgenthau from Rio, where White was assisting Welles at the Inter-American Conference. White asked permission for Welles to submit the proposal to the meeting. Before making a decision, Morgenthau called in Bernstein to brief him on the issue. Bernstein wrote the following memo to the file after the briefing. It is quoted here because it once again shows the major role played by Viner as an outside adviser to the Treasury Department:

> I told him that there was one point which Jacob Viner thought should be cleared with him [Morgenthau] and that was whether the subject of this resolution should be cleared first with the British before it is presented down there, and if presented, whether it should be done by the British and Treasury representatives in Washington or by the President to Churchill.
>
> (Morgenthau Diaries, Book 486, p. 4)

Morgenthau thought about the question and then decided to wait on introducing any resolution rather than bothering the president. Two days later, however, Welles himself wired Morgenthau asking him to reconsider. Welles argued that he did not think it was necessary to check with the British. He also enclosed a simplified statement of the possible resolution. On January 19, Morgenthau telephoned White, asked him if Welles felt strongly about the issue, and then gave the go-ahead when White replied in the affirmative (Morgenthau Diaries, Book 486, pp. 179, 208).

There are other reasons to believe that Morgenthau relied heavily on and fully trusted Viner. On January 21, for example, Morgenthau asked Viner and Lauchlin Currie, the White House economist who kept track of the war-peace studies for the President, to suggest ways to raise money for the war in all 12 Federal Reserve Districts. Even more intriguing is the following departmental conversation about Viner, which appears in the Morgenthau Diaries for February 1. (My reading in the so-called Morgenthau "diaries" for late 1941 and early 1942 convinced me that they are for the most part, if not completely, a stringing together of the

414 Rise of an International Economic System

transcriptions of his secret telephone tap and his office tape recorder, along with telegrams he received.) In this instance the tape recorder captured a freewheeling discussion that involved (1) a possible new employee, and (2) a loan to China. Just when it comes to the point at which we might learn something about White's personal feelings toward Viner, the tape recorder fails. However, I believe enough is said to suggest Viner's role was very large by way of oversight and that White had personal reasons to play down Viner's role in the department:

MORGENTHAU: Harry [i.e., White], get Viner to help you.

WHITE: Mr. Secretary, anything at all that is even in Mr. Viner's field, I always ask him to help me. I am always glad of his help.

MORGENTHAU: Well, that hasn't always been so.

WHITE: That has always been true except where we have questions where I know we are opposed on domestic policy and in which I didn't think it would be a help but a hindrance, as far as I was concerned, but on foreign policy.

MORGENTHAU: Well...

WHITE: Or monetary matters.

BELL: It is always better to have Jake in after something is prepared, because he will argue for two hours before he gets started.

WHITE: He is helpful and I am always glad to have him.

BELL: It is very helpful to get his criticism on documents that have been prepared.

WHITE: But again, thinking of somebody for Haas' division, you know, Viner is in a little different position than he would be if Haas had somebody in his division. There are men who might come in the same capacity as Viner, but who might or might not come in a...

MORGENTHAU: Well, the man I had in mind would be in the same relation to the rest of us as Viner is. Now, if you ask me who Viner is responsible to, I don't know. He has never raised the question. He is here to help all of us.

BERNSTEIN: Well, he is responsible to you, but we all use him.

MORGENTHAU: Including Harry.

WHITE: Very definitely, and I am very glad to.

BERNSTEIN: He really sits in on most of our conferences.

FOLEY [another department official]: He has been in on all this China thing.

WHITE: Whenever he is in the Treasury he is always in.

FOLEY: He was in Harry's office on all of this (the loan to China).

MORGENTHAU: I believe Harry. I don't know why Harry is suddenly sensitive on that one.

WHITE: Because three times in the last week you have reminded me to get him in. I always do. I don't know whether that was an indication that you think I don't.

MORGENTHAU: Well, sometime when we are alone I will tell you why.

WHITE: O.K. I will try to give you some names of those [possible employees] I hear about and I will ask other men about Hardy. Maybe I got a peculiar notion about him (Hardy).

MORGENTHAU: Well, you men needn't wait. I will just tell Harry now and get it off my chest, that is all.

(Morgenthau Diaries, Book 491, p. 72)

And there the dialogue abruptly ends. But later sources note that Morgenthau felt that White was "overly zealous," among other defects, and others who knew White noted several negative qualities (Steil 2013, pp. 34–35).

The 12-page plan drawn up by White and Viner in either late December 1941 or early January 1942 can be compared with the Keynes plan at this point as background for assessing Hansen and Viner's later role. Briefly, the plan called for a fund of $5 billion, considerably less than what Keynes envisioned. The fund would be "subscribed," unlike Keynes' plan, meaning that each country would put in a certain amount of its currency and gold beforehand so that the fund would have currencies to lend and exchange. The size of the subscription would depend on the size, power, and trade volume of the country. The voting arrangements on policy issues were structured in such a way that the United States would have 60 percent of the votes as long as its friendly Latin American neighbors voted with it (Eckes 1975, p. 49).

Generally speaking, the differences between the American and British plans reflected the economic situations of the two countries. The United Kingdom, as a debtor nation, wanted an institution that could make currency loans without putting heavy restrictions on the borrowing countries. As a country without much gold, it did not want gold to have the large role proposed for it by the Americans. The British government also wanted to be sure that creditor nations such as the United States would be forced to loan out their currency rather than holding on to it in times of economic downturn or trade imbalance. The United States, as a creditor nation with a huge gold supply, wanted the fund to be able to insure that borrowing countries were not headed for financial disaster or using the currency loans as disguised investment loans. It wanted a role for its gold as a restraint on overall borrowing and as an assurance to conservative bankers and members of Congress. In that sense, the United States wanted a financial policeman (Skidelsky 2000, p. 467).

The negotiations over the two plans proved to be long and difficult, but the British ultimately had to concede to the Americans on almost every basic point (Skidelsky 2000, Chapters 9 and 10). The United Kingdom's acquiescence became easier when the Americans agreed to a mechanism by which other countries would be assured that the Americans could not limit the supply of their currency without suffering some penalty. Despite the American dominance, Keynes was not totally disappointed by

416 Rise of an International Economic System

the outcome because he thought the American plan was far better than nothing at all, and far more than he had expected from the American government. In a confidential letter to fellow British negotiators of April 19, 1943, before the most intense debates had taken place, Keynes concluded that the White plan "represents a big advance," but added that "it is a long time too soon to even breathe a suggestion of compromise" (van Dormael 1978, p. 27).

The draft IMF plan of early 1942 was finalized in late April. A clean draft was typed for presentation to Morgenthau on May 8, but was backdated to March for some unknown reason (van Dormael, 1978, p. 45). Morgenthau quickly accepted the final draft, and then strategized with White about the next step to take. Both hoped to move quickly, and White wanted to avoid the State Department by sending the plan directly to the White House. Morgenthau compromised on that suggestion by sending the plan to the president and the State Department at the same time, but Roosevelt put a stop to any unilateral moves by sending his copy to Hull and telling him to work on the project with the Department of the Treasury. At the same time, Roosevelt lodged responsibility for carrying through the project with the treasury department. In actuality, Roosevelt's decision reflected arrangements for interdepartmental cooperation on monetary issues that went back to early 1940, which respected the treasury department's large role on foreign economic issues since the 1930s (Blum 1970; Notter 1949 Chapter 2).

At this point an interdepartmental committee was created to discuss White's proposal and make alterations if necessary, with White as chair. The main conflicts within the committee were between the state and treasury departments, but they were not over substantive matters. Rather, the main issues were the timetable and format for international discussions (Eckes 1975, pp. 60–62). The State Department wanted to move slowly until other international economic issues with the United Kingdom were resolved and public opinion and Congress were sure to be favorable. The State Department also wanted to honor the British government's insistence that it have agreement with the United States before other nations were consulted. Treasury, on the other hand, wanted to move more rapidly and consult widely with other nations. It was not nearly as concerned with British sensibilities as was the State Department, a fact understood by the British (Dobson 1986).

Morgenthau had a tendency to interpret the State Department's concerns as a dislike for the plan, but it seems more likely that Hull, and then Roosevelt, decided on a more cautious course for political reasons: "Hull seemed genuinely convinced that the administration must prepare the public for the United States' global responsibilities, and he was certain that premature disclosure would only polarize the public, damage the Democratic Party, and shatter the prospects for international cooperation"

(Eckes 1975, p. 63). Although Hull resisted high-level and visible negotiations on monetary stabilization issues, he finally agreed in July 1942 to preliminary talks if they were confined to experts from a few major nations. He did so because the two officials in his own department involved in monetary planning, former corporate lawyers Dean Acheson and A. A. Berle, Jr., argued that further delay might weaken British supporters of international economic cooperation and increase the possibility that other countries would turn to unilateral decisions to solve their economic problems (Eckes 1975, p. 63).

In addition to preliminary discussions with a few countries, the Americans continued to argue among themselves about the relative merits of what came to be called the White Plan and the Keynes Plan. But for all the disagreements over the two plans, they were in fact more similar than they were different. This point became clear in a lengthy discussion of them in the CFR's Economic and Financial Group on March 6, 1943. The discussion also is of interest because it reveals differences between Viner and Hansen, with Viner favoring the fund approach and Hansen favoring Keynes' overdraft proposal. However, Viner carried the day by pointing out that many countries do not recognize a line of credit as a real obligation. He therefore argued that it was better to have the money (and gold) beforehand:

> Mr. Viner thought that the memorandum [by Hansen] overemphasized the case in favor of the overdraft method of stabilization as opposed to the fund arrangement. Both require the same basic commitment to be made in the first instance, that a country will provide a certain amount of money—whether as a direct contribution to the Fund or as a line of credit for the Clearing Union—for use in connection with exchange stabilization. Under the Fund plan, the money is made available from the start and there is never any question that the Fund has access to it; under the overdraft plan, however, subsequent legal action may be necessary actually to make available money that has been nominally put aside for this purpose. If a Central Bank claimed it had no free assets when the Clearing Union wished to draw on the line of credit, no money might be forthcoming unless a priority had been legally arranged for. A country wishing to avoid its obligations might find it easier to cancel a line of credit than to seize a deposit of the International Fund.
>
> (Council on Foreign Relations 1943, p. 4)

By the end of the discussion, Hansen said "the difference between the two stabilization plans was less than he had believed" (E-A24, 1943, p. 5). He therefore made changes in the memorandum on the two plans that he was preparing for circulation in the White House and State Department,

418 Rise of an International Economic System

and from that point on he worked to improve the fund concept and to convince the British government to accept it. Viner clearly had the final say on this issue in CFR discussions, and probably at the Treasury as well. More generally, this discussion is an excellent example of the kind of differences that are analyzed in depth and ironed out within the settings provided by the major policy-discussion groups.

Hansen and Viner continued to mediate between Keynes and White in the spring and summer of 1943, and Keynes and Viner corresponded (Gardner 1980, p. 86; Skidelsky 2000, pp. 303–305, 312–313; Viner, Keynes Correspondence, Box 16, Folder 21). After his discussions with Viner, Hansen sent Keynes an advance copy of a revised memorandum via the auspices of a British economist, Redvers Opie, who served as his country's liaison with the United States Department of the Treasury, and especially with White. Opie replied with a lengthy letter marked "personal and private" to Hansen on May 19 regarding Keynes' reactions. It shows that Hansen was trying to shape the American proposal to deal with Keynes' concerns, and that he was being kept abreast of Keynes' latest thoughts. It also reveals that parts of the negotiations were considered "difficult points" that Opie could not "deal with in writing." This resort to personal conversations makes it harder to reconstruct the decisional process, but the thrust of the negotiations is nonetheless quite clear, as this revealing letter from Opie to Hansen shows:

> Just before I left for the Food Conference I received a letter from Keynes thanking me and you for sending him an advance copy of your memorandum on "International Adjustment of Exchange Rates." As you expected Keynes was very glad that you stressed the need for getting creditor countries to share responsibility for making adjustments to restore international equilibrium. There are one or two points arising out of Keynes' letter to me that I should like to take up with you orally on the first opportunity but, since that is unlikely to be until after June 3, perhaps I had better raise one or two points now. The first is interesting in the light of your revised figure of $12 billion for the resources of the Fund. Keynes suggested that it would be easier to reach acceptable quotas if the total were raised to $15 billion leaving the United States at $4 billion, on the assumption that the whole world has to be covered.

Opie continued:

> The second point refers to the limitation on the obligation of creditor countries. Keynes surmises that a maximum obligation will have to be accepted and he believes that $4 billion for the United States should be reasonably adequate. The real problem which then arises is the same

in the Stabilisation Fund as in the Clearing Union, namely what to do when a currency becomes scarce. We have the same difficulty in understanding what the processes would be in the Stabilisation Fund solution. I should like very much to discuss this with you off the record when I return. Thirdly, Keynes agrees that the source of funds for long-term foreign investment should be a different institution and also that for the Commodity Control the case for separation for the reasons which you give is not equally clear. I should be most grateful if you could treat this letter as a personal exchange between you and me and I look forward to discussing one or two more difficult points which I cannot deal with in writing

> (Hansen Papers, Opie to Hansen, May 19, 1943,
> HUGFP 3.16, Box 1, Correspondence 1943)

A technical committee formed in May 1943 honed the final American plan. Among the 24 experts from five different departments and agencies were two members of the CFR's Economic and Financial Group, Benjamin V. Cohen, representing the White House, and Hansen, as one of the representatives from the Federal Reserve Board. As might be expected by now, it was Hansen and the Federal Reserve delegation that raised the most serious questions. Hansen continued to push to make the plan more acceptable to Keynes, and the other Federal Reserve participants raised concerns relating to the amount of gold each country had to contribute and the way it would be utilized. The thrust of these recommendations can be found in several letters and outlines, but the main points and their political implications are best stated in a personal letter from Hansen to White on June 11:

> Since we had our conference with you, the staff at the Federal Reserve has again gone over the whole matter and Goldenweiser is sending you a summary statement of the main points. I am sending you this personal note since I can't come Monday so that you will know my own point of view. It seems to me that our suggestions can quite easily be incorporated into your plan. You have frequently stressed the importance of having a plan that could get the approval of Congress. In my judgment, the modifications which we have suggested would help very much to get this approval, for the following reasons:
>
> 1. The American contribution would not be increased beyond the $2 billion you have suggested.
> 2. The contribution of other countries would be very greatly increased to $13 billion.
> 3. The Fund would be stronger in its gold holdings under our proposal. This, I think, would be pleasing to Congress.

420 Rise of an International Economic System

4. The American voting power while small (rightly so with our relatively small contribution) would rapidly grow if we purchased large amounts of gold from the Fund.
5. The plan looks toward future limitation by the Fund of new gold production. This meets one type of opposition to gold purchases.

Our proposal suggests that decisions can be made by majority vote. While this may not be pleasing to many Congressmen, I think they can be sold on our suggestion since if in fact we buy a large amount of gold, our voting power would rapidly rise. Thus, the ultimate control by the United States would become very great if in fact we were called upon to supply a large amount of the credit. It seems to me that these suggestions would really greatly strengthen your plan and I hope that you will give them, as I am sure you will, earnest consideration. I regret that I cannot be at your meeting on Monday.

> (Hansen Papers: Hansen to White, June 11, 1943,
> HUGFP 3.16, Box 1, Correspondence 1943)

The general similarity in outlook between Hansen and White did not mean that White gracefully accepted Hansen's suggestions. In fact, White became annoyed with Hansen and the Federal Reserve experts when they raised their fears about the consequences of unlimited American gold purchases during a three-day conference later in June with monetary specialists from 19 countries. Eckes (1975, p. 95) tells the story:

When Alvin Hansen openly questioned the wisdom of an American commitment to accept all gold mined in the world, White lost his patience. Such theoretical ideas sound good at an economic conference, he retorted, but that group does not determine government policy. To allay fears that Washington might do as Hansen proposed—restrict its gold purchases—White vigorously reaffirmed the Treasury's long-standing promise to buy and sell gold at $35 per ounce. From White's standpoint this commitment to interconvertibility was imperative if others were to have confidence in the postwar system.

Still, White made several of the changes suggested by Hansen, the Federal Reserve, and experts from other nations. For example the size of the fund was increased to $8 billion, the amount of gold in each country's quota was increased to 50 percent, and countries were given more flexibility in adjusting their exchange rates during the first three years of the fund's operation (Eckes 1975, pp. 95–96; van Dormael 1978, p. 86). The new draft became the basis for formal technical discussions between the United States and the United Kingdom in September 1943. With both countries now eager for agreement for their separate political reasons, the discussions

The Grand Area and the Origins of the IMF 421

moved along very easily compared to the past. Keynes even abandoned his plan for a clearing union based on an overdraft principle, asking in return for a fund of $10 billion, not $8 billion, and agreement that countries would not be deprived of their flexibility in altering their exchange rates. Although White and Keynes continued to argue and compromise for three weeks over technical issues, it was understood once the clearing-union concept was dropped by the British that there were no differences that could not be resolved (Eckes 1975, pp. 97–98).

The stage was now set for a meeting of 44 nations in Bretton Woods, New Hampshire, which took place during the first three weeks of July in 1944. In terms of the international harmony and cooperation the meeting symbolized, the Bretton Woods Conference was the historic occasion it is usually said to be. It also provided the opportunity to bring congressional leaders of both parties as well as interest-group leaders into the process. All such people who were present at the conference became enthusiastic supporters of the outcome, including Republican Senator Charles Tobey of New Hampshire, who had been feared as a potential isolationist opponent. Another positive outcome of the meeting was the enormous media coverage for the idea of international monetary agreements, which was seen as the opening round in shaping elite public opinion in favor of the agreement.

In terms of substance, however, very little was changed in the draft proposal for the IMF that had been agreed to by the American and British negotiators (Gardner 1980, p. 110). Most of the arguments among nations concerned the relative size of their contributions to the fund, with countries lobbying for larger contributions than their rivals and neighbors for two reasons. First, they wanted to look like greater powers in the eyes of their own citizens and other countries than they in fact were. Second, the larger a nation's contribution, the more it could draw upon the fund for the currencies of other countries.

In keeping with White's widely shared hope for a positive relationship between the United States and the Soviet Union in the postwar era, he kept the Soviet representatives (who included one of their spymasters) fully apprised of the American perspective in official meetings in which other American representatives were present. He also went out on a "diplomatic limb" by meeting privately with some of them both during and after the conference, and "provided them with information on the American negotiating strategy" on several occasions (Craig 2004, p. 149). In the end, though, the State Department wanted to delay on loan promises to the Soviets that the treasury officials thought would be wise to offer. But this desire for delay did not matter. Stalin already had decided to decline the invitation for fear that joining the IMF would be interpreted by other nations as "a sign of weakness" and "a forced step taken under the pressure of the USA" (Craig 2004, p. 153).

In addition to ratifying the plan for the IMF, the Bretton Woods Conference also agreed to plans for the International Bank for Reconstruction and Development (World Bank). Plans for the bank had been discussed in both the Economic and Financial Group and the treasury department from 1941 onward. However, they had been put to the side during the disputes over the exchange stabilization fund because the World Bank was relatively noncontroversial in the eyes of government officials and American bankers. Originally, there were aspects of White's suggestions for it that were highly liberal and controversial. But these aspects were removed in informal discussions within the American government at a fairly early stage, as explained in a very detailed history of the bank (Oliver 1975, pp. 110–125, 138–144). Keynes and other European experts wrote their own plan for the bank on the cruise to the United States for the conference, which turned out to be very similar to a moderate plan drafted by White and sent to Keynes. It was little more than a fund for guaranteeing foreign investments, and there was no opposition to it in Congress, even from those who vigorously opposed the IMF (Eckes 1975, p. 132).

The final hurdle facing the Bretton Woods agreements was approval by a majority in the House and Senate. The State Department fully supported the plan and worked closely with the treasury to win its acceptance (Eckes 1975; Gardner 1980; Oliver 1975; van Dormael 1978). Taking no chances, officials in the state and treasury departments made an all-out effort to spread their message through speeches, endorsements, and favorable newspaper and magazine articles. Most of those in the general public who knew anything about the plan were positive, but only 23 percent of the respondents in one poll "could even relate Bretton Woods to world affairs" (Eckes 1975, p. 196). As is so often the case, the battle would be fought out among highly interested partisans in the attentive public and Congress.

There was widespread business and agricultural support for the IMF and World Bank. The ultraconservative Farm Bureau testified in favor of it, and a Business and Industry Committee for Bretton Woods was formed that included officers from such major corporations as General Mills, American President Lines, Bristol-Myers, and Hilton Hotels (Paterson 1973, p. 151, footnote 15). Significantly, the support committee included two prominent leaders of the ultraconservative NAM.

Despite the support from ultraconservatives in the corporate community, outspoken ultraconservatives in Congress continued to oppose it. By far the most visible and prominent of these critics, Senator Robert Taft of Ohio, the son of President William Howard Taft, said that American wealth was a "weapon, and I hope it will be used as a weapon;" as far as the IMF was concerned, it would be like "pouring money down a sewer" because the United States would provide all the money and other people would decide what would be done with it (Casey 2001, p. 42). However, by far the most effective opposition came from the banking industry, especially from big banks in New York. It needs to be stressed that their opposition was not anti-internationalist. Instead, it was based first of all on a desire to maintain the large influence on monetary policy that traditionally had been enjoyed by large New York banks, and second on a fear that overly liberal currency policies might lead to postwar inflation (Eckes 1975, p. 176). That is, bankers are as power- and profit-oriented as other corporate leaders, and not eager to compromise for the common good of the corporate community if they can avoid it.

Working through the American Bankers Association and the Federal Reserve Bank of New York, the bankers' alternative was an approach based on British-American collaboration in currency stabilization. Called the "key currency" approach, which in effect meant that currency stabilization would be a joint matter for Wall Street and its London counterpart, the plan would first stabilize monetary relations between the United States and the United Kingdom. It would do so in part through a large loan to the British, and then build out to other nations. An international organization would come later if at all (Eckes 1975, pp. 88–89). The Canadian and the British governments opposed the plan, which reinforced the opposition to it on the part of American officials and their advisers (Eckes 1975, pp. 176–177; Williams 1944, p. 234). The author of this alternative plan was economist John H. Williams, vice president of the New York Federal Reserve Bank and dean of the Harvard Graduate School of Public Administration. He also had been a member of the Economic and Financial Group from February through November of 1940. Like Hansen, he recognized that the success of any monetary plan was dependent on avoiding depression in major countries. His ideas were discussed within the Economic and Financial Group of the war-peace studies and published in *Foreign Affairs* (Williams 1943; Williams 1944). Clearly, then, there were differences over the IMF among members of the CFR, with Williams and major commercial bankers fighting a proposal that had been shaped and supported by the war-peace studies.

The board of the Federal Reserve Bank of New York, which was a Wall Street outpost, urged the key currency plan on the board of governors of the Federal Reserve in Washington. But the Washington board rejected its pleas in favor of the White Plan. Revealing once again the degree to which this battle was within the in-group, Hansen played a major role as an adviser to the board of governors in defeating Williams' plan:

> Consultant Alvin Hansen, who was instrumental in shaping the Federal Reserve position on this issue, asserted that, if Bretton Woods failed, there was little hope for supplementary economic agreements on investments, commodities, and commercial policy. And, without a network of international ties, parallel political agreements designed to assure future peace would surely fail. "Having become internationalists

424 Rise of an International Economic System

on political lines," Hansen claimed, "there is the gravest danger that the United States will remain isolationist on economic lines." Unless the United States provided the leadership and demonstrated its commitment to permanent international arrangements, "nationalistic policies tending toward economic isolation are almost certain to prevail. Economic nationalism and isolationism, rival economic blocks, and international friction will likely be intensified."

(Eckes 1975, p. 119)

Moreover, Williams and the New York bankers did not speak for all American bankers. For example, Edward Brown, president of the First National Bank of Chicago, described by Keynes as "the star performer amongst the American delegation," with "a complete intellectual understanding," joined the aforementioned Business and Industry for Bretton Woods Committee (Paterson, 1973, pp. 150–151; Skidelsky 2000, p. 356). In addition, Brown claimed that many other bankers throughout the country agreed with him (van Dormael, 1978, p. 254). Earle Cocke, an Atlanta banker, wrote of his approval of the agreements because the IMF would increase export sales of the South's cotton, tobacco, and peanut crops (Eckes, 1975, p. 170). Since Southern Democrats were great believers in free trade until the mid-1950s, they needed little prompting from Cocke.

Although the New York bankers were relatively isolated within the corporate community in their opposition to the Bretton Woods agreements, and were seen as engaging in a special-interest kind of pleading by other corporate leaders, they nonetheless were an important factor in the legislative battle because they gave great moral support to the isolationist Republicans on the House Banking and Currency Committee. In particular, they had a close relationship with Congressman Charles Dewey of Illinois, the main isolationist spokesperson. Until two weeks before the final vote, it looked as if Dewey had organized a majority on the committee to block the plan (Eckes, 1975, pp. 192–194). This temporary coalition between internationalist New York bankers and isolationist House Republicans was held together in good measure by the claim that the IMF would be wrongly used by needy countries to provide themselves with short-term reconstruction and transition loans under the excuse of monetary adjustments.

The answer to this argument came in a "Hegelian compromise intended to satisfy both the government and the bankers" (Eckes, 1975, p. 191). Its sponsor was the CED, the then-new organization of corporate moderates. As also noted briefly in the previous chapter, the CED's goal was to plan for the transition to a postwar economy in a cooperative way in conjunction with the government and other groups, but its unstated goal was to minimize government involvement in the economy (Eakins, 1966). In 1943, it had hired John H. Williams as well as Viner and Upgren to help with a major study of international policy, the conclusion of which was the need to develop mechanisms to avoid depressions and advance free trade (Whitham 2016, Chapter 5). With regard to dealing with Wall Street bankers, the CED suggested that any possibility of the fund being used wrongly for short-term loans could be dealt with by authorizing the proposed World Bank to make short-term stabilization loans as well as long-term loans for reconstruction and development:

> With the bank taking a more active role in the abnormal postwar period, the fund, designed primarily to cushion short-term fluctuations in an orderly world where international transactions tended to balance, would not have to assume the burden of financing unstable conditions. According to the CED analysis, if the bank engaged in stabilization lending, the fund would not misuse its resources and become frozen with unwanted currencies, as the bankers feared.
>
> (Eckes 1975, p. 191)

Some observers argued at the time that the Hegelian compromise was largely symbolic, but the CED proposal, however anodyne, did give the bankers a way to save face and accept the inevitable, at least until the IMF proposal reached a venue within the federal government in which they had clout (Eckes 1975, p. 192). This seeming capitulation by the bankers, along with the ascendancy of Harry S. Truman to the presidency after Roosevelt's death in April 1945, led to a "remarkable turnaround" on the House Banking and Currency Committee; the majority that had opposed the bill was now reduced to three isolationist "irreconcilables" from the Midwest (Eckes 1975, p. 197). The bill authorizing the president to accept membership in the IMF and the World Bank sailed through both the House and Senate by wide margins. It reflected the Americans' "desire for an updated gold standard as a means of liberalizing trade" and "to concentrate financial power in Washington" (Skidelsky 2000, p. 357).

Still, for all this apparent success, the bankers were in fact empowered by an amendment to the final legislation that in effect was demanded by the New York banking community. Winthrop Aldrich, the chair of Chase National Bank, still claimed, in a widely reported speech, that the IMF agreement provided "automatic borrowing privileges," which would use American dollars and ignore a country's ability to repay its loans, leading to currency depreciation in the process (Casey 2001, p. 45). The bankers' main spokesperson, who was an employee of the Federal Reserve of New Bank, and also a representative of the American Bankers Association, told Morgenthau that he and other bankers were "distrustful of any program for giving away American gold" and of "all spending programs, especially when sponsored by Lord Keynes" (Casey 2001, p. 42).

Based on worst-case arguments and the access and high status they enjoyed, the New York bankers had enough influence with the House Banking and Currency Committee to force the treasury department to offer a

426 Rise of an International Economic System

compromise. It established a high-level government advisory committee to coordinate postwar foreign economy policy, the National Advisory Council on International Monetary and Financial Problems. It consisted of the secretaries of treasury, state, and commerce, and the chairs of the Federal Reserve Board and the Export-Import Bank. When President Truman replaced Morgenthau as Secretary of Treasury with a close friend he trusted from their days in the House in the 1930s, and later with a banker from St. Louis, the New York bankers felt assured that their voices would be heard. As shown in Chapter 13, their assurance was justified shortly thereafter through their influence on postwar government loan polices and on the World Bank.

Once the IMF, the World Bank, and the National Advisory Council on International Monetary and Financial Problems were legislated, there was one more battle to be fought by the corporate community. It was against the British at a conference of all member nations at Savannah, Georgia, during March 1946. By this point the lead negotiator on the American side was William L. Clayton, the Assistant Secretary of State for Economic Affairs since late 1944. Clayton was a formidable figure in his own right as a co-owner of Anderson, Clayton, and Company, the largest cotton trading company in the country, and a founding trustee of the CED. In addition, he was a member of a new CFR study group set up in November 1945, four months before the Savannah Conference, to collaborate with the State Department on studies of American foreign economic policy (Viner Papers: Winfield Riefler to Jacob Viner, November 2, 1945, Box 22, Folder 12). With Clayton leading the way as a firm believer in the CFR view that a hard bargain had to be driven with the United Kingdom to open up its colonies to American corporations, Keynes and his colleagues lost on the location of the two institutions and on the degree to which political overseers would hedge in experts. By the end of the conference the fund and the bank were clearly dominated by the American government. Keynes left the conference disappointed by the Americans' high-handedness (Skidelsky 2000, pp. 464–468). However, he did later say that the National Advisory Council on International Monetary and Financial Problems was a "step forward" because it was "relatively independent of Congress" (Casey 2001, p. 63).

And yet, as the liberal CFR adviser Hansen later wrote, in the face of the disappointments concerning moderate plans that were blocked by the ultraconservatives, "[n]o one familiar with the political realities of the time is likely to argue that a more ambitious scheme could have been realized" (Eckes 1975, p. 79; Hansen 1965, p, 177). In that sense, the final outcome illustrates the great power of bankers and of ultraconservative leaders in Congress through the conservative coalition. But the very existence of international monetary and redevelopment organizations that would play the role planned for them by the CFR confirms the even greater power of the corporate moderates in shaping the larger picture. At both levels, the

The Grand Area and the Origins of the IMF **427**

general and the specific, it was corporate leaders that had the real power, not the experts the corporate moderates employed through the policy-planning network or the moderate and liberal members of Congress.

Despite all the detailed planning and the bitter arguments, the IMF could not come into its own until the late 1940s due to the fact that it was not designed to handle the transition to peacetime. It was well understood by the corporate moderates during the Bretton Woods negotiations that the United States would have to make a large loan to the United Kingdom after the war ended. Even with this understanding, the planners underestimated the devastation to the British and European economies, as well as the long stretch of time that would be needed to reconstruct them. In addition, the Americans linked the granting of the loan to the United Kingdom's ratification of its participation in the IMF (Gardner 1980, pp. 191, 196–197, and Chapter 11; van Dormael 1978, pp. 274–275).

However, the corporate moderates suddenly faced unexpected postwar problems in their efforts to realize the plans they had forged through the war-peace studies and the Bretton Woods agreement. Those problems are dealt with in Chapter 13. But first it is useful to show how the potential for an American war in Vietnam was created by the strong emphasis the CFR put on the need for a Grand Area within which the American corporate economy could expand and coexist with the United Kingdom and Japan.

References

Block, Fred. 1977. *The origins of international economic disorder: A study of United States international monetary policy from World War II to the present.* Berkeley: University of California Press.

Blum, John. 1959. *From the Morgenthau diaries.* Boston: Houghton Mifflin.

———. 1970. *Roosevelt and Morgenthau.* Boston: Houghton Mifflin.

Casey, Kevin. 2001. *Saving international capitalism during the early Truman presidency: The National Advisory Council on International Monetary and Financial Problems.* New York: Routledge.

Council on Foreign Relations. 1941a. "Methods of Economic Collaboration: The Role of the Grand Area in American Economic Policy." Economic and Financial Group. *Studies of American Interests in the War and the Peace.* Report E-B34, July 24. New York.

———. 1941b. "Digests of Discussions." E-A20, September 20. New York: CFR.

———. 1942. "Digests of Discussions." E-A25, Part II, January 24. New York: CFR.

———. 1943. "Digests of Discussions." E-A24, March 6. New York: CFR.

Craig, R. Bruce 2004. *Treasonable doubt: The Harry Dexter White spy case.* Lawrence: University Press of Kansas.

DiTomaso, Nancy. 1980. "Organizational analysis and power structure research." Pp. 255–268 in *Power structure research,* edited by G. W. Domhoff. Beverly Hills: Sage.

Dobson, Alan. 1986. *U.S. wartime aid to Britain, 1940–1946.* London: Croom Helm.

Domhoff, G. W. 2013. *The myth of liberal ascendancy: Corporate dominance from the Great Depression to the Great Recession.* Boulder: Paradigm Publishers.

428 Rise of an International Economic System

Eakins, D. (1966). "The development of corporate liberal policy research in the United States, 1885–1965." Unpublished Ph.D., University of Wisconsin, Madison.

Eckes, Alfred. 1975. *A search for solvency: Bretton Woods and the international monetary system, 1941–1971.* Austin: University of Texas Press.

Gardner, Richard. 1980. *Sterling-dollar diplomacy in current perspective: The origins and the prospects of our international economic order.* New York: Columbia University Press.

Hansen, Alvin. 1965. *The dollar and the international monetary system.* New York: McGraw-Hill.

Harrod, Roy. 1951. *The life of John Maynard Keynes.* New York: Harcourt Brace.

Haynes, John and Harvey Klehr. 1999. *Venona: Decoding Soviet espionage in America.* New Haven: Yale University Press.

Helleiner, Eric. 2014. *Forgotten foundations of Bretton Woods: International development and the making of the postwar order.* Ithaca Cornell University Press.

Katznelson, Ira, Kim Geiger, and Daniel Kryder. 1993. "Limiting liberalism: The Southern veto in Congress 1933–1950." *Political Science Quarterly* 108:283–306.

Lachmann, Richard. 2015. "Neoliberalism, the origins of the global crisis, and the future of states." Pp. 463–484 in *The sociology of development handbook*, edited by G. Hooks, S. Makaryan, and P. Almeida. Berkeley: University of California Press.

Notter, Harley. 1949. *Postwar foreign policy preparation, 1939–1945.* Washington: U.S Government Printing Office.

Oliver, Robert. 1975. *International economic co-operation and the World Bank.* London: Macmillan.

Olmsted, Kathryn. 2002. *Red spy queen: A biography of Elizabeth Bentley.* Chapel Hill: University of North Carolina Press.

Paterson, Thomas. 1973. *Soviet-American confrontation: Postwar reconstruction and the origins of the Cold War.* Baltimore Johns Hopkins University Press.

Rees, David. 1973. *Harry Dexter White: A study in paradox.* New York: Coward, McCann & Geoghegan.

Shelley, Mack. 1983. *The permanent majority: The conservative coalition in the United States Congress.* Tuscaloosa: University of Alabama Press.

Shoup, Laurence. 1974. "Shaping the national interest: The Council on Foreign Relations, the Department of State, and the origins of the postwar world." Ph.D. dissertation Thesis, History, Northwestern University, Evanston.

Skidelsky, Robert. 2000. *John Maynard Keynes: Fighting for Britain*, Vol. 3. New York: Macmillan.

Steil, Benn. 2013. *The battle of Bretton Woods: John Maynard Keynes, Harry Dexter White, and the making of a new world order.* Princeton: Princeton University Press.

van Dormael, Armand 1978. *Bretton Woods: Birth of a monetary system.* New York: Holmes & Meier.

Viner, Jacob. 1942. "Public Policy Papers." in *Jacob Viner Papers, 1909–1979.* Princeton: Department of Rare Books and Special Collections, Princeton University Library.

Whitham, Charlie. 2016. *Post-War business planners in the United States, 1939–1948.* New York: Bloomsbury Publishing.

Williams, John. 1943. "Currency stabilization: The Keynes and White plans." *Foreign Affairs* 21:645–658.

———. 1944. "Currency stabilization: American and British attitudes." *Foreign Affairs* 22:233–247.

Chapter 12

The Grand Area Strategy and the Vietnam War

The plans developed between 1940 and 1944 to create a postwar Grand Area and an international monetary regime within which the United States economy could reach its full potential also provided the framework that eventually made the contemplation of a war in Vietnam plausible in the late 1940s and 1950s. This chapter explains how the requirements of the corporate moderates' international economic plans, and in particular their desire to find ways for the American, British, and Japanese economies to work together peacefully, were the original driving factors in setting the stage for war. In addition, the Americans' inability to convince France to free its colonies compounded the problem.

This account of the original foundations for this ill-fated war is important because it helps explain why the corporate rich and the power elite would later accept the risks of disruption they knew might arise within the United States if they prosecuted the war during the domestic turmoil in the 1960s. However, war was never a foregone conclusion and could have been avoided because the economic rationales for it discussed in this chapter no longer made much sense by the early 1960s, and even less sense by the late 1960s.

Recalling from Chapter 10 that the plan for the Grand Area was being developed in 1940, the analysis begins with the first steps that put the United States on a path that might lead to war. They occurred at the general meeting of members from all the Council on Foreign Relations (CFR) war-peace studies groups on December 14, 1940, which was a full year before American entry into World War II. Among several important issues, the agenda for this meeting included a discussion of Southeast Asia. The conclusions that arose from this discussion on Southeast Asia were considered so pressing in terms of American interests in Asia that they were embodied in a memorandum under the title "American Far Eastern Policy," which was dated January 15, 1941.

Using one quote from this policy report, Shoup (1974, p. 137) summarizes the new perspective on the American-led postwar interest in Asia as follows, and in the process demonstrates the strategic factors that

430 Rise of an International Economic System

combined with economic issues in shaping early postwar policies toward Southeast Asia:

> The main interests of the United States in Southeast Asia were dual in nature. The first was purely economic. The memorandum stated that the "Philippine Islands, the Dutch East Indies [now Indonesia], and British Malaya are prime sources of raw materials very important to the United States in war and peace; control of these lands by a potentially hostile power would greatly limit our freedom of action."

The second CFR concern was a strategic one that had political, economic, and psychological aspects. A Japanese takeover of Southeast Asia would impair the British war effort against Hitler, threatening sources of supply and weakening the whole British position in Asia. Moreover, it was feared that many people might view a Japanese takeover in that region as the beginning of the disintegration of the British Empire. In addition, there was concern that Australia and New Zealand might decide to focus on home defense (Shoup 1974, p. 137).

If we keep in mind, then, that Southeast Asia was considered essential to the Grand Area by late 1940, then we can begin to appreciate the considerable continuity that is found on the importance of Vietnam in the postwar era in reports and books from the CFR. It is also seen in the official position papers of the National Security Council (NSC), an agency established in the White House in 1947 through the efforts of corporate moderates, with the goal of coordinating military and foreign policy (Huntington 1961). But it is also true, as all sources stress, that the Cold War and the resulting containment policy, along with a fear of appearing soft on communism in the eyes of other nations and American voters, eventually came to have weight in the thinking of postwar government officials. Still, in terms of needing Southeast Asia as part of the Grand Area, only the specific enemies to that necessity had changed, not the policy. The Germans and Japanese were the enemies during World War II, and the Soviet Union and Communist China were the potential threats in the 1950s. The primary concerns remained, first, healthy Japanese and British economies that could function in harmony with the American economy and, second, the ability to limit the power of nations that threatened this corporate-based conception of American foreign economic interests. The concern with establishing and defending the Grand Area therefore preceded the advent of the Soviet and Chinese threats. The importance attached to Vietnam in the early 1940s therefore cannot be attributed to a Lockean dislike of communism or a fear of a Sino-Soviet bloc, which are sometimes set forth as explanatory factors in discussions of the Vietnam War because there allegedly were no economic or strategic interests at stake for the United States (Krasner 1978, pp. 320–326).

All this said, it is once again necessary to state, in order to avoid any misinterpretations of this chapter, that the step-by-step process that led to the Vietnam War was not inevitable and foreordained by events in the 1940s, or even in the early 1960s. As demonstrated in the work of the preeminent historian of the Vietnam War, Fredrik Logevall (2012, p. 710), the American leaders always "had real choices about which way to go," and those choices were "evident not only in retrospect but also at the time," even though "the policy always moved in the direction of deeper U.S. involvement." Furthermore, the world economy and power relations among nations kept changing throughout the decades, as did the American power wielders' conception of their interests.

Based on the Economic and Financial Group's call for the inclusion of Southeast Asia in the Grand Area in 1940, the first step toward a possible war in Vietnam began in the deliberations of the war-peace studies' Territorial Group, which first discussed postwar political arrangements for Southeast Asia on March 18, May 20, and July 6, 1942. There were three main CFR members who figured prominently in these discussions and had later involvement in government planning through lobbying or formal appointments of one kind or another. As stated in Chapter 10, Isaiah Bowman, the geographer and president of Johns Hopkins University, was the leader of the Territorial Group. Hamilton Fish Armstrong, mentioned earlier as one of the leaders of the war-peace studies and as the editor of *Foreign Affairs*, was a member of the Territorial Group and the chair of the Peace Aims Group. Finally, Rupert Emerson, a Harvard political scientist, who was an expert on Southeast Asia with a special focus on the rise of nationalism in the area, was a member of the Territorial Group.

As the "Digests of Discussions" for the meetings of the Territorial Group make clear, the question of freedom for the native peoples of Southeast Asia was constantly balanced with the need to secure American interests. In the context of anticipating what pre-Communist China might want in Indochina, Bowman drew some conclusions about power that seem to reflect the bottom line for later American strategizing about the area:

> The course of the discussion led Mr. Bowman to observe that a general idealized scheme, as, for example, of complete Asiatic freedom, sometimes runs counter to proposals which were more practical. He was not opposed to the aspirations of the Chinese, but he did not think we could proceed from victory to the ideal, but must go from victory to that security which is a prime condition for the realization of the ideal. Security must take first precedence. It is, in the first instance, a matter of power—power exercised from critical points. The problem is *how to make the exercise of that power international in character to such an extent that it will avoid conventional forms of imperialism.* The eventual

432 Rise of an International Economic System

question will be how to provide for a later period of genuine international collaboration on a wider basis.

(Council on Foreign Relations 1942, p. 9, my italics)

Bowman's suggestions reveal the mindset of the American foreign-policy establishment at that time. The issue was power, and the United States had preponderant power, as historian Melvyn Leffler (1992) convincingly argues in his account of the rise of the United States in the 1940s. It is within that context that the problem was to "avoid conventional forms of imperialism." As part of that process, Bowman thought it would be helpful to use President Roosevelt's adoption of a good-neighbor policy toward Latin America as evidence that the United States would not abuse its new imperial power.

In terms of state-building and the CFR's role within the government itself, Bowman, Armstrong, and Emerson also played central roles in official governmental postwar planning for Southeast Asia, a story that was pieced together by historian Gary Hess (1987). Recalling from Chapter 10 that Bowman chaired the State Department's Subcommittee on Territorial Problems, and that Armstrong served on that committee with him, here it can be added that Bowman and Armstrong were also members of the State Department's Subcommittee on Political Problems. It was within that subcommittee that "the most extensive discussion and significant recommendations" concerning Southeast Asia took place in 1943, well after the original discussions by the Territorial Group that was part of the war-peace studies (Hess 1987, p. 62).

At the outset, both departmental subcommittees, whose members overlapped almost entirely, hoped to push the European colonial powers into a worldwide anti-colonial policy. As the idea crystallized in the Subcommittee on Political Problems in August 1942, there would be a trusteeship arrangement whereby the major powers would oversee a gradual movement to independence by former colonies. However, the overbearing and counterproductive way in which France dealt with its colony in Indochina might require a special arrangement there according to Sumner Welles, the CFR member who was also a State Department official:

> Welles drew an important distinction between the French colony and those of Britain and the Netherlands. While the French record necessitated international administration of Indochina, the British and Dutch could be restored to authority in their colonies provided they agreed to general supervision of, and to report to, the regional international trusteeship council. Hence the Southeast Asian trusteeship council, as envisioned in August, 1942, would have an overall responsibility for assuring the development of self government, but would exercise direct control only in Indochina.

(Hess 1987, p. 66)

The Grand Area Strategy and the Vietnam War 433

But this solution, which was consistent with Roosevelt's views on French policy in Indochina, was not acceptable to anyone. Hull and others in the State Department did not like the plan because the department had pledged that it would treat all colonies the same, and in addition they did not want to weaken France in Europe (Kattenburg 1980, pp. 13–14). The British did not like it because it forced them to give up some sovereignty over their colonies, and divided them from their French allies. The French did not like it because it took away their colony. In the face of these disagreements, Bowman wrote a document for the State Department a little over a year later, dated October 29, 1943, which led to the eventual early postwar American position on Vietnam. Its substance parallels his earlier thinking and that of CFR planners in both the Territorial Group and the Economic-Financial Group. In doing so, he was drawing in part on a September 1943 memorandum for the CFR's Territorial Group, "Regionalism in Southeast Asia," in which Emerson floated the idea of a regional council "to establish non–discriminatory trade policies;" this regional council would place "political and economic control in hands likely to be friendly to the United States" (T-B67 1943, p. 6).

Bowman's official report listed four alternatives for dealing with Vietnam, which ranged from independence to complete French control without supervision. Independence was ruled out because of a fear of instability in the region. Complete French control was considered unacceptable due to France's terrible record in Indochina, which was heavily criticized by CFR planners and Roosevelt. Furthermore, a trusteeship such as Roosevelt favored was ruled out because, as Hess (1987, p. 74) summarizes, such a plan "depended upon all colonial powers accepting similar international control of their possessions," which was out of the question as far as the British were concerned. Thus, Bowman argued that the area had to be returned to French control through British-American power, but with "an international system providing for review and inspection of colonial areas" (Hess 1987, p. 74). Bowman's conclusions were reinforced by a report for the State Department subcommittee by Emerson dated November 16, 1943. He too held that French control should be restored, but subject to international review and with the presumption it would lead to self-government for the country in the long run. In other words, the combination of Bowman and Emerson meant that a view similar to that of the CFR planners was adopted within the government.

When the United Kingdom and France would not agree to any oversight, the State Department and the White House concluded they had no choice but to support France because of their distaste for an independent Indochina that most likely would be dominated by Communist-nationalists. Then, just two years later, with the rise of a Communist-led nationalist movement fighting for independence in what was by then called Vietnam, not Indochina, and with the movement's temporary takeover of many of the country's provinces, American leaders were faced with a decision

434 Rise of an International Economic System

about supporting the French once again. They decided they could not risk granting independence to Vietnam because the nationalist movement had Communist leadership, which suddenly loomed much larger because the first signs of the Cold War were beginning to emerge. The American leaders made their decision in spite of the close ties that had been developed between the Vietnamese nationalist movement and a handful of American government officials in Vietnam, who were part of the intelligence gathering activities of the Office of Strategic Services (OSS) (Logevall 2012, pp. 82–86, 98–105; Spector 1983, pp. 36–42). Some of the OSS members, and perhaps a few officials in the State Department back in Washington, thought it would make sense to support the Communist leader of the movement, Ho Chi Minh, who was known personally by several of them. However, it soon became clear that top decision-makers in Washington, who tended to be more conservative and concerned about Europe, would support nationalists against a minor nation such as the Netherlands, as demonstrated in Indonesia in 1947–1948, but not the likes of Ho Chi Minh, with his close ties to Soviet and Chinese Communist leaders (Kattenburg 1980, pp. 5–8; Lawrence 2005, Chapters 5–6).

In deciding to oppose the Communist-led nationalists, American leaders knew from the start that they were likely to lose, based on reports from the field about the strength of Vietnamese nationalism. As one OSS officer wrote in 1945, shortly before he was killed by the nationalists later that day: "Cochincina is burning, the French and British are finished here, and [the United States] ought to clear out of Southeast Asia" (Logevall 2012, p. 117). Their policy goal became the simple one of denying the area to communism for as long as possible. Given that minimal goal, their policy was successful until 1975, as Leslie Gelb and Richard Betts (1996) argue. Members of the policy-planning network and the CFR did not deceive themselves about Vietnam, but they did not make their pessimistic views known to the general public. The policy advice they received from their experts on the ground in Vietnam was accurate about the great strength of the Communist-led nationalists, so the decision to fight for a stalemate was made with their eyes wide open.

For that reason Gelb and Betts (1996) title their book *The Irony of Vietnam: The System Worked*; it is their reaffirmation of the rationality of CFR leaders, American experts, and the U.S. government from the 1940s through the late 1960s, when leaders within the CFR convinced President Johnson to de-escalate the war and seek an eventual settlement. The corporate moderates and the Vietnam specialists in the CFR changed their views at this point because the world was now different, the American armed forces were losing, and the anti-war movement was contributing to the domestic upheaval in the United States. (Gelb was the director of the secret 1960s Department of Defense project that compiled a detailed account of American involvement in the Vietnam War, which was later

The Grand Area Strategy and the Vietnam War 435

stolen and published as *The Pentagon Papers*. In the late 1970s he was an assistant secretary of state in the Carter Administration, and from 1993 to 2002 he was the president of the CFR.)

Eventual defeat or not, once the decision was made to support France in Vietnam, the Truman Administration had little choice but to follow French policy and at the same time provide indirect financial support for the fighting through economic grants in the 1940s, as well as large amounts of direct military support from 1950 to 1954 (Friedberg 2000; Logevall 2012). The Americans could suggest, cajole, and even threaten, but the French now had the ultimate weapon: the threat to leave.

If any American leaders ever were inclined for a minute to deal with the Vietnamese Communist leadership in the immediate postwar era, based on the assessment that these leaders were first and foremost nationalists, that temptation disappeared when the Communists won in China in 1949, followed shortly thereafter by the Korean War. From that point forward, according to historian Robert M. Blum (1982, p. 214) in his study of postwar policy in Southeast Asia, "The American containment policy in Southeast Asia arose from the ashes of its failed policy in China." Similarly, historian Brian VanDeMark (1991, pp. 4–5) says that the United States aided France because of a need for French cooperation in Europe, and later out of fears of Communist expansion in Asia. Still another historian, Andrew Rotter (1987, p. 84) provides a detailed account of policy-making within the Truman Administration to demonstrate that Burma, Malaya (which faced a small but tenacious Communist insurgency at the time), Thailand, and Indonesia (which had a significant Communist opposition throughout this era) were factored into the administration's thinking, along with Indochina and Japan:

> As the problems in China, Japan, and Western Europe intensified during 1949, drawing attention to Southeast Asia, U.S. policymakers came to regard Indochina, and especially Vietnam, as the key to the resolution of regional and international crises. Officials saw stability and prosperity in Indochina as necessary for the achievement of similar results in Burma, Thailand, Malaya, and Indonesia, and, more and more, as a prerequisite to the political and economic successes of the developed, non-Communist world.

Even though it is true that Southeast Asia in general became a more critical issue for the United States due to the revolution in China, there is still somewhat of a mystery in terms of including Vietnam within the area to be defended militarily unless the economic considerations set forth in the war-peace studies are entered into the equation. As historian John Gaddis (1987, pp. 74, 89) points out, the inclusion of Indochina within the American "defensive perimeter" in Asia in the late 1940s actually was an

436 Rise of an International Economic System

"anomaly" from a military standpoint. Earlier, the military had suggested a defense rooted primarily in islands stretching from the Aleutians, Midway, and Okinawa to British and Dutch islands in the southwest Pacific. Thus, any explanation of the increasing Americanization of the Vietnam War is incomplete if it overlooks the larger American agenda that is embodied in the CFR's war-peace studies and the delineation of a Grand Area.

Put another way, despite the military's recommendation concerning the specific details of where the defense perimeter should be located, which did not include Vietnam, a study by the State Department's policy-planning staff in March 1949, and a review by the NSC in December of the same year, concluded that Southeast Asia as a whole, not just Vietnam, was more vital than either Taiwan or Korea. Gaddis (1987, p. 90) then lists the several reasons why American officials came to this conclusion, one of which, the importance of the area as a source of food and raw materials, is consistent with the early concerns of the CFR planners in relation to the Grand Area:

> American officials appear to have made an exception to their general rule of not regarding mainland areas as vital, in the case of Indochina, for several reasons: (1) the conviction that Ho Chi Minh was a more reliable instrument of the Kremlin than Mao Zedong; (2) the belief that the Soviet Union had designated Southeast Asia as a special target of opportunity; (3) concern over the importance of Southeast Asia as a source of food and raw materials; and (4) in an early version of what would come to be known as the "domino theory," fear of the strategic and psychological consequences for the rest of non-communist Asia if Indochina should fall to communism.

Drawing on research on the American occupation of Japan by historian Michael Schaller (1985), Gaddis stresses that the concern with food and raw materials involved support for the Japanese economy as well as keeping needed supplies from the Chinese Communists. Then too, the importance of Southeast Asia at the time as a source of raw materials and markets for Europe as well as Japan is stressed in an account of an aid mission to Southeast Asia in 1950 written by its deputy chief (Hayes 1971). In short, there are several sources that acknowledge the role of economic concerns in making decisions about Southeast Asia.

The CFR itself devoted little direct attention to Southeast Asia in the postwar years until March 1950, when it formed a study group to reconsider the region. During the next year it created a joint study group with the Royal Institute of International Affairs to discuss the same area. The views of CFR leaders resulting from these two discussion groups are best revealed in the book that came out of the joint study group. Shoup

(1977, p. 20) summarizes the book as follows, with the internal quotes coming from the book:

> The book produced by the joint study group in January 1953 defined the American national interest in Southeast Asia almost exactly as had the War and Peace Studies Project—in economic and strategic terms. The book argued that "Southeast Asia contributes some of the most critical raw materials needed by Western Europe and the United States. It also makes an essential contribution to the food supply of India." Strategically, the "loss of any further portion" of the Far East in general "could well have decisive effects on the balance of world power in the years ahead."

W. Averell Harriman, a director of the CFR and President Truman's Director of Mutual Security, wrote the first official statement of the American national interest in Southeast Asia in January 1952. Shoup (1977, p. 23) concludes that Harriman's document was "identical" with the CFR view on why the area was of importance. Six months later, the NSC, as part of its charge to centralize military decision-making in the White House, approved a statement of policy concerning Southeast Asia that had the usual emphasis on raw materials and the strategic role of the region. It added that "the loss of any single country would probably lead to a relatively swift submission to or an alignment with communism by the remaining countries in this group" (Shoup 1977, p. 24, quoting NSC memorandum 124/1). In addition, and in keeping with the Grand Area conception of the American national interest, the statement concluded "the loss of Southeast Asia, especially of Malaya and Indonesia, could result in such economic and political pressures in Japan as to make it extremely difficult to prevent Japan's eventual accommodation to Communism" (Shoup 1977, p. 24, quoting NSC memorandum 124/1).

In October 1953, the CFR organized a 40-person discussion group on Southeast Asia. Its research director wrote a pamphlet for the closely related Foreign Policy Association in March 1955, based on his work for the group. It called Southeast Asia an "economic and strategic prize" that was "worth fighting for" (Shoup 1977, p. 20). A 1954–55 CFR study group on the same region resulted in a book by the group's research director, a professor at the University of Virginia, which claimed the area was "of global strategic importance roughly comparable to Panama and Suez" (Shoup 1977, p. 21). Raw materials and the importance of the area to Japan also were part of his argument.

The Eisenhower Administration maintained an equally strong, if not stronger, overlap between the CFR and key foreign-policy decisions. Wall Street lawyer John Foster Dulles, a CFR member who had been highly

438 Rise of an International Economic System

involved in various study groups since the 1930s, served as Secretary of State. As mentioned earlier, his brother Allen, a member of the war-peace studies, and the CFR president in the late 1940s, served as the director of the CIA. Then, too, Eisenhower had chaired a CFR study group on aid to Europe in 1949–1950, with Armstrong, Baldwin, and Viner from the war-peace studies among its 14 members; three of the staff members to his aid-to-Europe study group had been staff members for the war-peace studies (Wala 1994, pp. 126–135, 254). At its final meeting, several months after the Chinese Communist Army came to the rescue of their North Korean allies, and just before the news broke that Eisenhower had been appointed as the Supreme Allied Commander in Europe, he and other members of the group, with the help of National Security Director Harriman, wrote an urgent letter to President Truman. It called for an immediate military build-up in Europe (Wala 1994, pp. 136–139).

With Eisenhower and the Dulles brothers playing the major roles on foreign policy during the Eisenhower Administration, there was even more emphasis placed on the strategic importance of Vietnam. Eisenhower was ready to escalate support for French troops and land American troops as long as he had hopes that such actions might work (Logevall 2012, Chapters 16–21). When French leaders and the growing anti-war movement in France asked why the Americans felt they could settle for a truce in Korea, but not in Vietnam, the Eisenhower Administration replied with arguments about strategic and economic issues similar to those discussed in the war-peace studies, with frequent mentions of the implications of Vietnam for the economic health of Japan. In March 1954, for example, Secretary of State Dulles told a large audience at the Overseas Press Club in New York City that

> Southeast Asia is the so-called "rice bowl" which helps to feed the densely populated region that extends from India to Japan. It is rich in many raw materials, such as tin, rubber, and iron ore. It offers industrial Japan potentially important markets and sources of raw material. The area has great strategic value.
>
> (Logevall 2012, p. 462)

In keeping with arguments put forth during the Truman years, it was asserted that the loss of Vietnam and its nearby neighbors might lead to the possible fall of Burma, Malaya, and Indonesia. When military actions appeared to be futile, the Eisenhower Administration refused to join France and the United Kingdom in negotiating a graceful exit, leaving the door open for future unilateral American involvement (Logevall 2012, Chapter 24). At the same time, the National Security Council statements of 1954, 1956, 1958, and 1960 continued to define the national interest in Southeast Asia in terms of concepts similar to those invoked by the CFR's

The Grand Area Strategy and the Vietnam War   439

war-peace studies and the Truman Administration. The statements usually began with the immediate situation and then spelled out the possible military options for dealing with the latest Communist successes. They always explained the need for drastic actions in terms of the same concerns expressed by the Economic and Financial Group within the war-peace groups. Moreover, the last paragraph in the Eisenhower Administration statements were almost identical in language to the last paragraph of the policy statement under Truman: "The loss of Southeast Asia, especially of Malaya and Indonesia, could result in such economic and political pressure on Japan as to make it extremely difficult to prevent Japan's eventual accommodation to communism" (Shoup 1977, p. 24, quoting NSC memorandum 5405).

In 1959, the CFR established yet another study group on Southeast Asia to determine whether or not the Truman-Eisenhower stance toward Vietnam should be altered. Among the 43 members were several people that had been in the earlier studies of the subject, along with a former research secretary in the war-peace studies, who became a State Department adviser on Southeast Asia after the war. The main expert adviser to this new committee summarized the group's outlook in his *Southeast Asia in United States Politics* (Fifield 1963). He repeated the same themes found in the work of CFR leaders and research scholars since the early 1940s. He also called for military involvement and supported the interdependency theory that had come to be known as the "falling dominoes" principle: "Military defense against direct and indirect aggression must be a fundamental United States objective in Southeast Asia, for without security all other goals collapse like a row of dominoes when the first is pushed over" (Fifield, 1963, p. 407).

With this CFR definition of America's strategic interest firmly established over nearly a 20-year period, the Kennedy Administration seemingly had little discussion of basic assumptions as it gradually involved itself in Vietnam. Many commentators at the time had the impression that United States involvement in the war was unthinking and almost accidental, with no real understanding of the risks and costs. For example, Gelb and Betts (1996, p. 73) conclude that during the Kennedy years, "Vietnam policy debates from the beginning of the administration centered on how to save Vietnam, not whether to save it." But it was only after the revelations in the Pentagon Papers (e.g., Gravel 1971) that most people came to understand that the president, cabinet leaders, and their advisers from the policy-planning network knew from the start that they could not win the war. Even so, the Kennedy Administration's escalation was not quite that simple or unthinking.

The president and his many appointees with longstanding involvement in the CFR believed they could do better than the French because they were not defending a colonial empire. In addition, they proudly thought

440   Rise of an International Economic System

of themselves as being sympathetic to an independent non-Communist Vietnam, and they thought they had a hugely superior air force to that of France besides. Overlooking the major differences between the Communist insurgencies in Malaya and Vietnam, they drew hope from the fact that the British believed they finally had triumphed in Malaya by 1960 (Logevall 2012, pp. 707–708). (Malaya was the main constituent country in newly formed Malaysia in 1963.) The number of American troops in Vietnam soon jumped from 900 in 1960 to 8,000 in mid-1962, to almost 16,300 at the time that President John F. Kennedy was assassinated in November 1963, and to 23,300 in 1964 (Logevall 2012, pp. 705–706).

As already mentioned in Chapter 4, former Vice President Johnson won the presidency in his own right in 1964, with 61.1 percent of the vote, in part by implying he was for peace in Vietnam, unlike his openly hawkish Republican challenger. Moreover, the overwhelming opposition to the escalation of the war in newspaper editorials and opinion polls, along with the large Democratic majorities in both Houses of Congress, suggested it would be politically possible for Johnson to draw back from a situation that had only become worse during the Kennedy Administration (Logevall 1999). In addition, the relative handful of foreign-policy officials involved in the decision-making process now understood the depth of the Sino-Soviet split and knew that neither the Soviet Union nor China had any interest in pressing for an expansion of the war. As for the Communists in Hanoi, they had made it clear they would accept a coalitional government in South Vietnam. They also were willing to "negotiate an agreement that would have allowed the United States a face-saving means of disengagement," which might minimize any super-patriotic voter disapproval based on right-wing claims about unnecessarily losing a war (Logevall 2004, p. 104).

However, once the full record of discussions and negotiations involving the major powers of the time became available, which included archival information from Australia, Canada, and the United Kingdom as well as from the Soviet Union, China, France, and the United States, it became even more certain than it was in the mid-1960s that the American leaders had no intention of negotiating despite the many new circumstances and a likely defeat. Instead, they were planning to escalate the war as needed, and President Johnson made several secret decisions during and after the election campaign that prepared the military for that possibility (Logevall 2001).

At the same time, it is also obvious that their decisions were not based on the need to defend a "Grand Area," a term that had faded from usage many years earlier, or on insuring that a now-thriving Japanese economy had access to the former Indochina region. They expressed little concern about China's possible territorial aims. Moreover, many of them doubted that North Vietnam and South Vietnam would become a puppet of China if they became one country under Communist rule. In particular, and this

The Grand Area Strategy and the Vietnam War   441

is a damning admission in terms of risking lives for nothing, two longtime CFR foreign-policy experts, who served as the top war planners for the secretary of state and the secretary of defense during the Kennedy and Johnson administrations, wrote as follows to their bosses and the president concerning the likely outcome if the American government did not escalate: "the most likely result would be a Vietnamese-negotiated deal, under which an eventually unified Communist Vietnam would reassert its traditional hostility to Communist China and limit its own ambitions to Laos and Cambodia" (Logevall 2001, p. 75).

In other words, the fears expressed by CFR experts from the late 1940s through the 1950s, along with the plans they suggested for Southeast Asia, were no longer necessary by the early 1960s at the latest. By late 1964, and contrary to what is often believed, the key decision-makers who had the option of escalating the war or negotiating a graceful exit were no more worried about the Communist threat than the CFR planners had been in the early 1940s. This time, though, they talked in terms of American "credibility" and the country's "standing" in the world. That is, they now seemed to be concerned with maintaining the country's status as the dominant world power with the ability to protect and police the system created over the previous two decades by CFR planners and government officials. As for the Democratic leaders in Congress and at party headquarters, some of them said they were worried about a hawkish backlash, even though a majority of the public opposed the war.

Whatever the political worries of some Democrats, it is certain that the most visible members of the corporate community, including those who were leaders in the CFR and the CED, believed that the war should be escalated. This included the CFR members who were serving in key positions in the Johnson Administration (e.g., Shoup 1977). To show their backing for a larger war, CFR and CED leaders therefore organized a 48-person public relations committee, called the "Committee for an Effective and Durable Peace in Asia," to bolster public support for the war effort. The country's chief negotiator at the talks that ended the fighting in Korea, a Wall Street lawyer, chaired the committee. Most of the 48 members were bankers, corporate lawyers, and college presidents from all parts of the country, but there were several corporate CEOs as well. Several of them served on the "Citizens Committee for Peace and Freedom in Vietnam" and other pro-war committees that attempted to shape public opinion (Brinkley 1992, pp. 248–250). The new faux committee ran an ad in *The New York Times* and 13 other newspapers across the country in early September 1965, which expressed its agreement with Johnson's war aims in a ten-point statement of principles. It stressed that he "acted rightly and in the national interest" in sending American troops into Vietnam.

By 1967, however, after a rapid troop escalation to 586,100 in 1968 and two years of intense fighting, combined with growing anti-war protests on the home front, many CFR leaders began to express private doubts

442 Rise of an International Economic System

about further escalation in the face of continuing military failure (Logevall 2012, pp. 705–706). These doubts led to a new study group on "A Re-examination of American Foreign Policy." Then, in late March 1968, shortly after a surprise attack on South Vietnam's capital city, Johnson called together his senior advisory group on Vietnam for consultation because of divided opinion among his government advisers about what steps to take.

Officially named the President's Consultants on Foreign Policy, and informally called the "wise men," the advisory group had been constituted in September 1964 and duly announced in *The New York Times*. Most of the 16 original members were members of the CFR as well as being former top State Department appointees in the Truman, Eisenhower, and Kennedy administrations, or else leaders on Wall Street. They had supported Johnson's decisions to escalate the war, including the dispatch of combat troops in July 1965, and had reassured him again in early November 1967 that he was on the right path (Gibbons 1989, pp. 347–350; Gibbons 1995, pp. 874–878; Isaacson and Thomas 1986, Chapter 23).)

At the March 1968 meeting, though, the great majority of those in attendance thought that de-escalation, negotiation, and eventual withdrawal were the only sensible steps. Fully 12 of the 14 men present at this crucial turning point were members of the CFR (Shoup 1977, p. 26). Shortly thereafter, Cyrus Vance, a Wall Street lawyer, as well as the Deputy Secretary of Defense in the Kennedy Administration and a CFR director, explained the group's thinking to a former State Department official, who was writing a book on the dramatic change in Vietnam policy: "We were weighing not only what was happening in Vietnam," said Vance, "but the social and political effects in the United States, the impact on the U.S. economy, the attitudes of other nations; the divisiveness in the country was growing with such acuteness that it was threatening to tear the United States apart" (Hoopes 1969, pp. 215–216).

At this point all of the CFR leaders and advisers, not just those working in government, had been well aware of the tensions between China and the Soviet Union for several years, which made any lingering fear of a coordinated Communist effort against American, European, and Japanese corporate involvement in the Third World even less likely. They also knew that in 1965, Indonesian leaders, with behind-the-scenes encouragement from American CIA and military personnel, had decimated the Indonesian Communist Party, which eliminated the third-largest Communist Party in the world and ended communism as a threat on that large and resource-rich island empire. Within this changed geopolitical context, and knowing there was no chance of victory, they thought it was time to grapple with the increasing economic and political disruption on the home front (i.e., rising inflation, urban unrest, and an anti-war movement). When Richard M. Nixon was elected president in 1968, it fell to a longtime CFR adviser, Harvard-based strategist Henry Kissinger, to negotiate a gradual withdrawal from Vietnam as a special assistant to the president for national security affairs. In attempting to do so, Kissinger worked closely with members of a newly formed CFR study group on "the Vietnam Settlement." The study group was created in late 1968 to discuss the terms of a political settlement and suggest negotiating positions in talks with the Vietnamese Communists (Shoup 1977, p. 27).

Chaired by CFR director and former Undersecretary of the Treasury Robert V. Roosa, its official purpose was to "explore possible paths toward a settlement." One of the wise men, Vance, was a member, along with CFR director and MIT professor, Lucian Pye, a well-known foreign affairs expert of the day, along with former government officials and two CFR staff members. The chair and the CFR staffers crafted a proposal that was supported by a majority of the participants. It "envisioned a standstill cease-fire and a division of power based on a recognition of territory controlled by the Saigon Government and the Vietcong, a formula the framers conceded was 'rigged' to favor the government" (Shoup 1977, p. 27). In May of 1969, the group met with Undersecretary of State Elliot Richardson and Kissinger. When Nixon announced his own five-point peace plan in October 1970, it had many parallels with the CFR's plan, including a standstill cease-fire and a political settlement based on the existing relationship of political forces in South Vietnam. Vance later said that he thought the CFR's Vietnam study group "had some influence" on the eventual peace treaty (Shoup 1977, p. 27).

Although the war dragged on for another five years as the United States continued bombing while at the same time withdrawing troops, it was not again a major policy issue. American troops were officially withdrawn in 1973. The remaining American officials, and the Vietnamese leaders and advisers they worked with, had to leave in a hurry in late April 1975, when North Vietnamese troops captured Saigon from what remained of the South Vietnamese army and government. Recriminations, regrets, and lingering questions persisted for many of the veterans and their families, but the 30-year military operation in Vietnam, first through the financing of French troops, then through the commitment of American military forces, had been a successful one for the power elite in terms of keeping Vietnam out of the Soviet and Chinese orbits for 30 years.

For all intents and purposes, the wise men, the CFR leaders, and the rest of the power elite had moved on to other issues after 1968, including the successful opening to China. Southeast Asia and Japan were secure, and the battle over containment had moved elsewhere. However, the domestic damage that been part of the wise men's concerns in 1968 continued to generate problems. Moreover, as difficult as the inflation was for the domestic economy, it caused even greater problems for the corporate moderates' plans for the international economy, as explained in Chapter 14.

444 Rise of an International Economic System

Before turning to that issue, though, it is necessary to discuss whether or not the leaders in the CFR and CED were successful in implementing their immediate postwar plans as World War II wound down in 1944 and 1945.

References

Blum, Robert. 1982. *Drawing the line*. New York: Norton.

Brinkley, Douglas. 1992. *Dean Acheson: The Cold War years, 1953–1971*. New Haven: Yale University Press.

Council on Foreign Relations. 1942. "Digests of Discussions." E-A25, Part II, January 24. New York: CFR.

Fifield, Russell. 1963. *Southeast Asia in United States policy*. New York: Praeger.

Friedberg, Aaron. 2000. *In the shadow of the garrison state: America's anti-statism and its Cold War grand strategy*. Princeton: Princeton University Press.

Gaddis, John. 1987. *The long peace*. New York: Oxford.

Gelb, Leslie and Richard Betts. 1996. *The irony of Vietnam: The system worked*. Washington: The Brookings Institution.

Gibbons, William. 1989. *The U.S. government and the Vietnam War: Executive and legislative roles and relationships. Part III: January-July, 1965*. Princeton: Princeton University Press.

———. 1995. *The U.S. government and the Vietnam War: Executive and legislative roles and relationships. Part IV: July 1965–January 1968*. Princeton: Princeton University Press.

Gravel, Mike. 1971. "The Pentagon Papers." Boston: Beacon Press.

Hayes, Samuel. 1971. *The beginnings of American aid to Southeast Asia*. Lexington, MA: Heath.

Hess, Gary. 1987 *The United States' emergence as a Southeast Asian power*. New York: Columbia University Press.

Hoopes, Townsend. 1969. *The limits of intervention: An inside account of how the Johnson policy of escalation in Vietnam was reversed*. New York: D. McKay Company.

Huntington, Samuel. 1961. *The common defense*. New York: Columbia University Press.

Isaacson, Walter and Evan Thomas. 1986. *The wise men: Six friends and the world they made*. New York: Simon and Schuster.

Kattenburg, Paul. 1980. *The Vietnam trauma in American foreign policy, 1945–75*. New Brunswick, NJ: Transaction Books.

Krasner, Stephen. 1978. *Defending the National Interest*. Princeton: Princeton University Press.

Lawrence, Mark. 2005. *Assuming the burden: Europe and the American commitment to war in Vietnam*. Berkeley: University of California Press.

Leffler, Melvyn. 1992. *A preponderance of power*. Stanford: Stanford University Press.

Logevall, Fredrik. 1999. *Choosing war: The lost chance for peace and the escalation of war in Vietnam*. Berkeley: University of California Press.

———. 2001. *The origins of the Vietnam War*. New York: Longman.

———. 2004. "Lyndon Johnson and Vietnam." *Presidential Studies Quarterly* 34:100–113.

———. 2012. *Embers of war: The fall of an empire and the making of America's Vietnam*. New York: Random House.

Rotter, Andrew. 1987. *The path to Vietnam: Origins of the American commitment to Southeast Asia*. Ithaca: Cornell University Press.

Schaller, Michael. 1985. *The American occupation of Japan: The origins of the Cold War in Asia*. New York: Oxford University Press.

Shoup, Laurence. 1974. "Shaping the national interest: The Council on Foreign Relations, the Department of State, and the origins of the postwar world." Ph.D. dissertation Thesis, History, Northwestern University, Evanston.

———. 1977. "The Council on Foreign Relations and American policy in Southeast Asia, 1940–1973." *Insurgent Sociologist* 7:19–30.

Spector, Ronald. 1983. *Advice and support: The early years, 1941–1960*. Washington: Center of Military History, U.S. Army, U.S. Government Printing Office.

VanDeMark, Brian. 1991. *Into the quagmire: Lyndon Johnson and the escalation of the Vietnam War*. New York: Oxford University Press.

Wala, M. 1994. *The Council on Foreign Relations and American foreign policy in the early Cold War*. Providence: Berghahn Books.

Chapter 13

Rebuilding Europe in the Face of Ultraconservative Resistance, 1945–1967

Introduction

Although Vietnam loomed large in the United States in the 1960s, it was not a major foreign-policy issue as the postwar transition began in 1945. By far the largest problem for the corporate moderates in terms of realizing the ambitious expansionary economic plans put forth by the Council on Foreign Relations and the Committee for Economic Development was a smooth transition to a peacetime economy, which included the rebuilding of the European economies that fell within the Grand Area as quickly as possible.

However, those involved in managing the transition underestimated the depth of the rebuilding problem because Europe seemed to be recovering faster during the first postwar year than it had after World War I. In addition, they were thwarted at every turn by the ultraconservatives in the corporate community and the conservative coalition in Congress, which had gained still more seats in the 1944 elections, even in the face of Roosevelt's successful campaign for a fourth term. Moreover, the Republicans took control of both the House and the Senate in the 1946 midterm elections in the context of the large postwar strike wave, which meant that passing the kind of trade and aid legislation the corporate moderates sought would be all the more difficult.

As a result of these several factors, the corporate moderates made little or no progress between the end of the war in August 1945, and the spring of 1947, when the key European economies began to fail and Communist parties grew stronger. Even with their successes over the next two or three years, they were then stymied by the ultraconservatives during the Eisenhower years. They did not achieve their most immediate goals on tariff reduction until 1967, just as a whole round of new international monetary and trade problems began due to the economic consequences of the Vietnam War.

The Sudden Transition in 1945

When the war with Japan ended sooner than expected in mid-August 1945, the decontrol and reconversion processes were far faster than the corporate moderates advocated. Controls on raw materials, wages, vehicle purchases, gasoline, and processed foods were gone within a few weeks, 165 wartime government agencies were dismantled within the year, and government spending was cut by $102 billion (Whitham 2016, p. 151). The excess profits tax was repealed as of January 1, 1946, which was a key factor in union leaders' decision to strike for large wage increases very quickly, especially in light of their concern over the loss of overtime pay. Inflation, major strikes, and consumer anger over rising prices became the defining features of 1946. At the same time, the National Advisory Council on Financial Issues, created as part of the ultraconservatives' price for accepting the IMF and World Bank legislation, also took a conservative approach. It threatened to cut off lend-lease aid to the United Kingdom within weeks of the end of the war, but relented when Undersecretary of State Will Clayton, the cotton exporter and Committee for Economic Development (CED) trustee, argued at length that this would be a great mistake (Casey 2001, pp. 75–76).

In addition, the National Advisory Council on Financial Issues was slow to launch the World Bank, even though it pushed for the bank to be the primary source of loans for projects in other countries. When private funds to provide the bank with loan capital did not materialize from the expected Wall Street sources, Truman appointed a Presidential Committee for Financing Foreign Trade in late June 1946, to make recommendations on how to increase private loans to the bank. The committee was chaired by Winthrop Aldrich, the chair of Chase Manhattan Bank, and consisted primarily of other bankers. One of the two exceptions was the chair of International Harvester, who was a brother-in-law to Aldrich. The other non-banker was Paul Hoffman, the head of Studebaker, a trustee of the CED, and a member of the Business Advisory Council (BAC). The committee's suggestions had no impact because bankers had ample investment opportunities in America and wanted strong government guarantees to protect any money they invested in the World Bank (Casey 2001, pp. 165–170).

In February 1947, the National Advisory Council on Financial Issues appointed a Wall Street lawyer, whose most important client was Chase Manhattan Bank, as the World Bank's new president. He in turn appointed a Chase Manhattan vice president to be the executive director, and in the process "consolidated Wall Street's influence over the World Bank," which was now managed as a "conservative, business-oriented bank that private investors could trust" (Casey 2001, pp. 144–145). Moreover, the World Bank placed its initial focus on Europe, for which its leaders had grave concerns. But that meant several less developed countries, including Brazil and Chile, which were originally supposed to be the primary focus of the bank, were unsuccessful in obtaining loans (Casey 2001, Chapter 6).

448 Rise of an International Economic System

In the case of the IMF, the National Advisory Council on Financial Issues slowed its launching and made its procedures more cumbersome. It first of all focused on strengthening its own control of the IMF though the appointment of several executive directors that had to scrutinize requests for currency loans. The process thereby became far less routine than Keynes and the Council on Foreign Relations (CFR) planners had advocated. When the British asked for a currency loan, the price the executive directors demanded was that the United Kingdom would make its currency convertible to other currencies sooner than seemed prudent to the British government and the CFR planners. The new plan did not work and by late 1946 the country faced a financial crisis (Casey 2001, p. 197).

In addition to hampering the corporate moderates, the ultraconservatives and the conservative coalition also defeated the liberal-labor alliance by eliminating the main provisions from its first major initiative of the early postwar era. The Employment Act of 1946 was originally meant to make the federal government responsible for full employment. It would provide loans and development contracts for private companies and projects if the economy began to falter, and then start new government building projects if necessary. These ideas were of course anathema to the entire corporate community. However, the corporate moderates were concerned with maintaining high employment in order to sustain domestic consumer demand, and at the same time reassure its potential international trading partners that the federal government would not let another Great Depression happen, and thereby drag down Europe in the process.

The CED therefore worked with ultraconservatives in Congress to salvage some parts of the legislation that were useful for its own purposes. By the time the president signed the Employment Act in early 1946, the government was given the responsibility of paying more attention to the economy through a yearly report by a new Council of Economic Advisors (CEA) located in the White House. A new Joint Committee of Congress would then study the report as a basis for suggesting possible legislation (Domhoff 1990, Chapter 7; Whitham 2016, pp. 172–175, 177–178).

The bill also had major implications in terms of the relationship between the corporate community and the federal government. It included a specific mandate for the CEA and the Joint Committee on the Economic Report to utilize the work of "private research agencies" (Bailey 1950, p. 232). Thus, the policy-discussion groups and think tanks within the policy-planning network were being given a more formal standing. Due to the fact that the conservative coalition had abolished the small White House planning agency in 1943, and stipulated that no other government agency could take over its functions, the modified Employment Act helped to ensure that much of the small amount of planning there might be in postwar America would take place outside the government, within organizations closely related to the corporate community in terms of their financing and high-level governance. The Employment Act thereby blurred the line between the federal government and the private sector, which helped to reinforce corporate dominance by increasing government reliance on the policy-planning network for new policy alternatives. In that sense, the corporate rich and the power elite had engaged in the active dismantling of state capacity for their own benefit.

The corporate community's success in making use of the CEA as a direct link between the policy-planning network and government is demonstrated most clearly by the fact that 24 of the 41 people appointed to it between 1945 and 1983 served as consultants for either the CED or the Commission on Money and Credit (a special one-time policy commission sponsored by the CED in the late 1950s). Many of the appointees also had consulted for other think tanks or policy-discussion groups. Most striking, 11 of the 13 chairs of the CEA in that time period previously had been employed by or consulted for the CED or a major think tank. There were very few career differences between the seven Republican and six Democratic appointees to the chair position, except in the case of two liberal chairs appointed by Democratic presidents (Domhoff 1987, for a detailed accounting of the careers of postwar CEA appointees before and after their CEA service). However, it also needs to be emphasized that almost half of the appointees were young economists, who were often without any strong political views, or even with views that were very different from the administration they were temporarily serving. Their primary contacts were within the academic community, and they usually returned to academe after their appointments ended.

By late 1946, it was not just the United Kingdom that was facing serious economic problems. The other European economies were not recovering either. In addition, several European governments faced potential domestic unrest, and some people were near starvation in Germany in the winter of 1946–1947. Then, too, the communist party in Greece had started a civil war in early 1946, the Italian communists seemed poised to win the 1948 elections (the CIA sent millions of dollars to influence that election), and the Communist Party in France was the country's largest political party, with support from about 25 percent of the electorate. By March 1947, the United Kingdom was no longer able to continue to provide foreign aid to Turkey—which faced direct Soviet pressure— or Greece, as its army fought the communist insurgency. At that point, Congress quickly voted to provide military and economic aid that would not require repayment. It did so in support of the "Truman Doctrine," promulgated three months earlier, which stated that the United States would resist Soviet expansion. Soon after the aid to Turkey and Greece was provided, it was clearly understood by all but the most isolationist ultraconservatives that all of Western Europe needed economic aid in large amounts.

450 Rise of an International Economic System

There was debate and uncertainty on how to provide this aid, but the corporate moderates won the day in the new international economic and political context. Surprisingly, and in a testament to their flexibility under pressure, they did so by assimilating ideas that originally came from the two most liberal organizations in the policy-planning network, the National Planning Association (NPA), and the Twentieth Century Fund (TCF) (Whitham 2016, Chapter 5). The leaders and experts in these organizations, which shared two or three overlapping business leaders with the CED, and several economists as well, realized sooner and more fully than other policy experts that the country's large-scale wartime industrial expansion had made the rapid expansion of market demand in both the United States and Europe even more acute than it had been in the 1930s.

The basic starting point for the new line of thinking appeared in a November 1944, NPA report, which directly confronted the problem of how to increase American imports so other countries could pay for American exports. This issue, first briefly mentioned in one of the early reports by the CFR's Economic and Financial Group in 1940, turned out to be an even bigger problem than the CFR economists had anticipated. (One of the economists working on this NPA report, Winfred Riefler, had been part of the Economic and Financial Group since its inception.) The NPA report, *America's New Opportunities in World Trade* (1944), said that the "wartime industrial expansion" had compounded the problem to the point that the productive capabilities of the United States alone "could meet both foreign and domestic demand" (Eakins 1969, p. 156). As a result, the country would not only have to increase demand at home to greatly enhance the domestic market, but it had to figure out ways to increase demand in other countries so that the United States could export *twice* as much as it had in the best peacetime years, 1929 and 1941.

To deal with this very large problem, the report urged the export of capital by private enterprise, but claimed that "the government would have to help by providing some investment funds and by exercising 'general supervision' over both private and public American investment abroad" (Eakins 1969, p. 157, citing the 1944 NPA report). It also recommended a major expansion of the role played by the IMF, World Bank, Export-Import Bank, and Reconstruction Finance Corporation in supporting foreign investments by American corporations.

But the export of capital was not seen as a sufficient answer to the problem. There would have to be a large increase in imports as well, which would be in the national interest in terms of dealing with the country's own postwar problems. A small part of the problem could be solved by lowering American tariffs, which had not been done to the extent needed. In the end, though, other countries would have to be able to export products to the United States for Americans to buy. These imports would come "at the expense of American industries 'whose functions can be performed more efficiently abroad'" (Whitham 2016, p. 140, citing the 1944 NPA report). In other words, labor-intensive industries with minimum start-up costs, such as the textile and furniture industries, would lose out. Here, then, was the basis for the protectionist coalition that would lobby its elected representatives in Congress very vigorously over the next 50 years, with the increasingly Southern-based textile industry in the forefront.

The report received widespread attention, including a front-page story in *The New York Times*, and drew praise from the State Department's Assistant Secretary for Economic Affairs, Dean Acheson, a corporate lawyer and CFR member, who later served as Secretary of State from 1949 to 1952. However, the report did not explain how foreign countries could eventually pay back their loans without delaying their full recoveries, and its call for a new government agency overseeing foreign investment would very likely be rejected by most corporate leaders and the conservative coalition (Eakins 1969, p. 159; Whitham 2016, p. 141).

In any event, it soon became apparent that important corporate leaders fully understood the need for imports that is stressed in the NPA's report. In October 1943, the Texas cotton exporter and CED trustee, Will Clayton, at the time serving as the Assistant Secretary of Commerce, already had told a large audience at the meetings of the National Foreign Trade Council that the world was experiencing "the greatest economic expansion of all times," so there would be a need for "great new markets abroad," and for the United States to "import more and invest heavily abroad" (Whitham 2016, p. 135).

Following the NPA report, the TCF took the next step when it decided to carry out an ambitious study of the issue in the summer of 1945. It hired a University of California, Berkeley, economist to work with economists at the Institute for Advanced Study at Princeton to produce a very detailed economic analysis. By the end of the year, four chapters had been drafted, along with a brief summary. At that point the TCF leaders realized they would have to move faster if they were going to influence the ongoing debate. They therefore assembled a research committee to "oversee the project and to write a report with recommendations for action" (Whitham 2016, p. 147). It included representatives from business and labor, along with three economists that had been involved in two or more of the projects within the policy-planning network that were concerned with the rebuilding of the postwar economy.

Paul Hoffman, by now very familiar to readers as the president of Studebaker, a CED trustee, and a member of the BAC, was the most prominent business representative on the committee. He was joined by a longtime vice president at Chase Manhattan Bank, Joseph Rovensky. Rovensky had been an assistant to Nelson Rockefeller, one of John D. Rockefeller's five sons, from 1941–1943, at a time when Nelson Rockefeller served as the federal government's Coordinator of Inter-American Affairs. The director

452 Rise of an International Economic System

of education and research for the CIO and the international representative for the AFL were also active members of the committee.

The three economists touched all the bases with regard to postwar planning and involvement with government. Percy Bidwell, the director of studies at the CFR, directed the new TCF committee. Winifred Riefler, an original member of the CFR's Economic and Financial Group within the war-peace studies, also had worked on the 1944 NPA study as well, and had just joined the CED Research Advisory Board. The CED also was represented by another one of its economic advisers, Theodore Schultz, an expert on agricultural economics, and a professor at the University of Chicago. Schultz had also helped with the 1944 NPA report. More generally, five economists were at the center of the policy planning for the postwar era in terms on serving on two or more of the main reports— Bidwell of the CFR, Riefler, Schultz, Arthur Upgren, and Jacob Viner. The most central economist was Riefler, who received his Ph.D. at The Brookings Institution, served as a minister of warfare in London, and was affiliated with the Institute for Advanced Study at Princeton from 1935 to 1949 (NYT 1974). He was involved in reports for the CFR, CED, NPA, and TCF. The other four were involved in at least two of the groups. Four of the five were involved in the CFR's War-Peace Studies, and three were involved in the TCF report. Thus, it seems very likely that the TCF report represented the culmination of what they had learned during the war years, and conveyed to Hoffman and others in the CED, CFR, and BAC.

The TCF group discussed back and forth with each other and the economists who wrote the background chapters for several months. Their *Report of the Committee on Foreign Economic Relations* (TCF 1946) appeared in June 1946, and contained the arguments and recommendations that were ultimately discussed in Congress several months later. The fact that the union representatives were in full agreement with the thrust of the report made it likely that there would be a coalition of corporate moderates, plantation owners, and the liberal-labor alliance on this critical issue.

Although the term Grand Area had been abandoned, the report and the pamphlet stated that the Western European and British economies, in conjunction with the former British colonies, Japan, and Southeast Asia had to be reconstituted immediately (TCF 1946, p. 9). Furthermore, simply lending the United Kingdom and Western European countries the money needed to rehabilitate the core of the Grand Area would not work, no matter how low the interest rates or how long the term of the loans. The problem of repayment still would remain, and it would be a continuing drag on the necessary consumer spending. In that regard, the authors of the report concluded it had been a "mistake" by the National Advisory Committee on Financial Issues to give the World Bank the authority for rehabilitation loans, and then went so far as to say that the committee "deplores this use" of the new bank for this purpose (TCF 1946, pp. 11–12).

The only solution was to find a politically acceptable way to give the European countries vast sums of money, an outright gift (Eakins 1969, p. 160; Whitham 2016, pp. 145–148, 154–164 for in-depth accounts). But where would the money come from? In effect, it would come from a "new domestic tax that was needed to finance American exports as the means to full employment" (Eakins 1969, p 160). For the corporate moderates, this solution had the added virtue that it would not require any government intervention into the American economy, as had happened during the worst stages of the Great Depression, and as had been recommended in the 1944 NPA report. Based on this new approach, the corporate moderates could begin to focus exclusively on the long-term international expansion of a rejuvenated corporate community that was capable of producing more than the American market could consume.

Due to the growing tensions between the Soviet Union and the United States, and the threat to Western Europe represented by the communist parties in Greece, Italy, and France, the argument for financial gifts became more palatable to the ultraconservative Republicans in control of Congress. In other words, without the Cold War, it is not certain that the corporate moderates' plans for an international economy, even with the Southern plantation owners and the liberal-labor alliance as their allies on this issue, could have overcome the ultraconservatives in the corporate community and the Republican isolationists and protectionists in Congress.

The pivotal role of the Cold War in furthering the corporate moderate's internationalization plans is the big grain of truth that anchors most scholarly accounts of the postwar era. But the fact remains that these accounts downplay or ignore the work done in the policy-planning network between 1939 and 1945, treating it as a side issue at best, or a historical relic worthy of only a passing footnote. These accounts therefore lack a full picture and thereby overlook the role of the corporate moderates and the policy-planning network. In particular, no matter what various scholars' theoretical perspectives might be, it is almost as if the Council on Foreign Relations and the war-peace study groups never existed. Due to that oversight, the expansionary goals of the corporate moderates, along with their desire to minimize government control of the American economy, is lost from view. The explanatory power of most extant theories is therefore limited by a failure to include this larger historical context.

Enter the Marshall Plan

Building on the TCF report, corporate moderates and several of the organizations in the policy-planning network lobbied for what came to be known as the Marshall Plan, because its broad outlines were introduced in a speech by Secretary of State George Marshall, a leading World

454   Rise of an International Economic System

War II general. President Truman then accepted a suggestion by Senator Arthur Vandenberg of Michigan, the chair of the Senate Foreign Relations Committee, and a one-time isolationist, to appoint a blue-ribbon presidential commission to develop Marshall's proposal. The chair, a railroad heir and investment banker, W. Averell Harriman, first introduced in Chapter 12 as President Truman's national security director in 1952, was a former chair of the BAC and a member of the CFR. Five of the nine corporate appointees, including Hoffman, were trustees of the CED. Several of the others were members of the CFR. Three of the six academic representatives were members of the CED's Research and Policy Committee. The commission's report called for a four-year program of financial aid to 16 Europe countries, which would provide $113.2 billion in 2018 dollars. (Even in these dire circumstances, the first 20 percent of the aid was originally supposed to be in the form of loans.) (Eakins 1969; Hogan 1987; Whitham 2016, pp. 178–182).

Hoffman and the other CED trustees on the commission added a compromise that dealt with a major sticking point. Ultraconservatives did not want to give money to seemingly "socialist" economic systems. (They were actually welfare states governed by social-democratic parties with views fairly similar to those of the liberal-labor alliance in the United States). In order to accomplish the two main corporate goals in backing the plan (guarding against Soviet-backed Communist takeovers and creating new customers for American corporations), the corporate moderates successfully argued that the report should say that each country would be free to choose its own economic system: "While this committee firmly believes that the best method of obtaining high productivity is the American system of free enterprise, it does not believe that any foreign aid program should be used as a means of requiring other countries to adopt it" (Schriftgiesser 1967, p. 119).

Since this point continued to raise concerns among ultraconservatives, the CED soon thereafter published its own statement in support of the Marshall Plan, *An American Program of European Economic Cooperation* (CED 1947). It stated that the trustees firmly believed the American free enterprise system was the best way to create a productive economy, but that they also thought it was fair and just that "each country must be left free to decide on its own methods of organizing production" (CED 1947, p. 15; Schriftgiesser 1967, pp. 118–119). In addition, the CED report (1947, p. 22) suggested that the program should be carried out by a new agency directed by people chosen from "the large number of able men who served our country during the war years and gained fruitful experience in dealing with questions similar to those presented by the program of cooperation" (Schriftgiesser 1967, p. 119). The report provided the basis upon which the Republicans in the Senate could justify their insistence that the program be taken out of the State Department and placed in a new independent government agency, which would be headed by a corporate executive (Whitham 2016, p. 180).

The CFR and CED also made major efforts to sell the Marshall Plan to the general public, a majority of whom did not like the idea that the United States was giving taxpayer money to foreigners, without any strings attached, any more than ultraconservatives did (Wala 1994, for a highly revealing case study of this massive opinion-shaping effort). The private Committee for the Marshall Plan therefore stressed again and again in its pamphlets and media advertising that the grants would not only revive European economies, and thereby make communism less attractive. They also would help the American economy because most of the money had to be used to buy American machinery and consumer goods. They emphasized that the Marshall Plan money should be seen as a form of domestic economic pump priming by the American government (Eakins 1969, pp. 166–167). The key unions in the liberal-labor alliance endorsed these promotional efforts because their leaders had been calling for increased government spending since the late 1930s. Although the union leaders preferred domestic spending, they understood that the foreign aid would have the same effect because most of it was being spent in the United States.

Once the Marshall Plan legislation finally passed in April of 1948, Truman appointed Hoffman as head of the European Economic Cooperation Administration at the insistence of Senator Vandenberg. Hoffman in turn included several CED trustees among the numerous corporate executives who staffed his agency in the United States and in the 16 European countries receiving aid, and Harriman was appointed as a special ambassador to coordinate the program in Western Europe (Schriftgiesser 1967, p. 119; Whitham 2016, p. 178).

In the aftermath of the Marshall Plan, the corporate moderates were able to realize another goal first set forth in the war-peace studies. They lobbied for an international trade organization to set up basic ground rules that countries had to adhere to in order to make the system more beneficial for all concerned. It would also be involved in settling disputes among importers and exporters in the various countries. However, the corporate moderates had to make do with a second-best option. Although the Americans and the British already had agreed they would begin work on such an organization after the Bretton Woods conference was completed, they were delayed by British hesitation when Republican protectionists took control of Congress in 1946. As the 1946 TCF report had warned, many foreign countries doubted that American leaders could ensure that the ultraconservatives inside and outside Congress would do what was necessary to end a major depression in the United States before it dragged down other economies (TCF 1946, p. 14). These countries also frankly doubted the Americans would reduce tariffs enough for foreign countries

456   Rise of an International Economic System

to earn the money they would need to pay for American exports. In this regard, the TCF report presented a telling contrast with the international economy that had been led by the United Kingdom: "The British market stood ready to absorb imports in quantity without important official barrier or hindrance, and in this way helped foreign debtors to repay their loans" (TCF 1946, p. 15).

As a result of the hesitations concerning the capacity of American leaders to create a stable international economy, a 23-nation conference in late 1947 led to demands by the British and other foreign leaders for opt-out clauses and other protections and guarantees. These demands, which were agreed to somewhat reluctantly by American negotiators, went too far for many corporate moderates as well as all ultraconservatives and the conservative coalition in Congress (Whitham 2016, pp. 170, 182). Despite this legislative failure, the Americans and other participating nations were able to put together a new agreement that they all could accept, and that did not involve approval by Congress. Called the General Agreement on Trade and Tariffs (GATT), it was a "grand version" of the Reciprocal Trade Act of 1934, which had been strengthened by Congress in 1945 (Whitham 2016, p. 182). It was based on a series of reciprocal agreements among the several nations, which provided the necessary rules to regulate trade. The agreement also included clauses that made it possible to settle disputes through negotiation and arbitration. GATT then played the same role as an official international trade organization for the next 47 years, when Congress approved American involvement in a new World Trade Organization in 1994.

As the European Cooperation Administration took charge of recovery in Europe, the role of the National Advisory Council on Financial Issues narrowed considerably, but it still oversaw the World Bank, IMF, and Export-Import Bank. The World Bank slowly turned to the role it was intended for, helping less developed countries with development loans, but still under the control of American private bankers. It was not until mid-July 1947, that private bankers made their first modest contribution to the postwar efforts by buying $250 million in World Bank securities to use as a basis for loans to less developed countries (Casey 2001, p. 167). As for the IMF, the National Advisory Council on Financial Issues implemented a policy of "requiring more stringent financial and monetary conditions to members' use" of its quota of IMF funds, and more generally sought to save "the majority of the IMF's resources for use after Western European recovery was complete..." (Casey 2001, p. 223).

Although the success of the Marshall Plan depended on the arguments provided by the NPA and the TCF, both of these organizations became marginal in their importance once the CED and other corporate moderates had assimilated their main ideas and arguments. Their future studies primarily concerned the economies of various European countries, or

Europe as a whole. In the case of the NPA, it also lost out because it favored more government oversight than most corporate moderates were willing to accept, and also because it included labor leaders and representatives of liberal farm organizations. Corporate moderates were on occasion willing to listen to ideas suggested by more liberal groups, or to take part in their forums and serve on their committees. But most of them were not prepared to be part of permanent organizations with unions, due to their many disagreements with them on most issues. As far as farm issues were concerned, the corporate community was more in tune with the Farm Bureau and its surrounding network of foundations and think tanks (McConnell 1953; McCune 1956).

Defense Spending and the Korean War

At the same time as aid began to flow into Europe, American foreign-policy leaders became even more convinced that Soviet intentions were antithetical to American interests. A new secretary of state, the aforementioned Dean Acheson, with the help of his advisers in the State Department, began thinking in terms of a substantial military build-up in Western Europe. Nevertheless, Truman disappointed the internationalists by asking the Defense Department to cut its spending by $2 billion in July 1949. Although the more conservative members of the Truman Administration, along with conservative leaders in Congress, perceived the Soviet Union as a menace, they insisted that the need to control deficits should constrain any increases in military spending (Friedberg 2000; Schriftgiesser 1960, p. 167).

However, Truman did agree to a major reevaluation of the country's foreign and military policies. The resulting national security policy statement, "United States Objectives and Programs for National Security," which came to be known as "NSC-68," recommended a 300 percent increase in military spending over the next few years to rearm Western Europe and station 100,000 American troops there as well. Despite NSC-68's urgent tone, it still seemed unlikely that the military spending proposal would go anywhere because Truman and most Republicans in Congress opposed it. Then the sudden and unexpected North Korean invasion of South Korea in June 1950 changed the economic and military equations as American troops were sent into action to repel the attack. Shortly thereafter, the 1950 midterm elections brought an increased number of ultraconservatives back into the House, which in effect spelled the end for the European Cooperation Administration.

Even with a war against communists being fought by American troops in South Korea, it was not a foregone conclusion that ultraconservative Republicans would support spending for troops and rearmament in Western Europe. In anticipation of this problem, the corporate moderates created a new lobbying and opinion-shaping organization, the Committee on the Present Danger, in December 1950, five months after the Korean War began. The 54-member group included Paul Hoffman, four other CED trustees, and an economist on the CED's Research Advisory Board, as well as numerous leaders and members in the CFR. In a campaign reminiscent of the effort to sell the Marshall Plan three years earlier, along with even more direct lobbying of Congress, the Committee on the Present Danger pulled out all the stops in an effort to convince the general public and Congress of the importance of taking NSC-68 seriously. After several months, Congress eventually agreed to troops in Western Europe and funding for European rearmament (Friedberg 2000; Sanders 1983). A new Mutual Security Administration then succeeded the European Cooperation Administration as the American coordinating agency in European countries.

The increase in defense spending, along with military assistance to European countries, most of which was used to buy American weaponry, replaced the $3.7 and $4.1 billion spent on the Marshall Plan in 1949–1950 and 1950–1951, and provided a major economic stimulus to the American economy. In combination with the spending for the Korean War, military spending on Europe brought unemployment down from 5.4 percent in June 1950, to below 4.0 percent for most of 1951 and 1952. It then fell below 3.0 percent until the last three months of 1953, with low points of 2.5 percent in May and June of that year, a postwar record that the economy would never again come close to attaining.

Just as was the case with Marshall Plan money, defense spending had the side benefit that it did not require government-based direction of the domestic economy, nor competition with any sector of the corporate community. It consisted primarily of large contracts for a relative handful of major corporations—and the subcontractors they hired. By early 1951, the Korean War had been fought to a stalemate at the original dividing line between North and South Korea. Peace talks began at that point, but it took another two years before a truce was signed in late July 1953, and there were several fierce battles while the talks were being concluded.

The Battle Over Tariff Policies

With the Korean War finally at an end, the corporate moderates faced a new set of uncertainties in their efforts to realize their international objectives. In 1953, the Republicans controlled the presidency and both houses of Congress—the first time this had happened since 1929—thanks to a sweep of the 1952 elections. As a result, the many ultraconservative protectionists would be in powerful positions from which they could block trade expansion. The question was whether the Republicans would move in a more internationalist direction or revert to protectionism. In terms of providing a wide-lens view of what unfolded, the CED and the National Association of Manufacturers (NAM) provide the best vantage points.

The ensuing argument between the moderate conservatives and ultra-conservatives in the corporate community was complicated by the fact that the corporate moderates were strong backers of General Dwight D. Eisenhower for the Republican presidential nomination in 1952. In the process of helping him win the nomination, they aided in the defeat of the ultraconservatives' favorite candidate, Senator Robert Taft of Ohio, the staunch isolationist who had opposed joining the IMF. This conflict reignited the ultraconservatives' simmering resistance to the internationalist, supposedly "Eastern" elites, leading some ultraconservatives to accuse the corporate moderates of conspiracy and pro-communist leanings for the next several decades.

Nor were the corporate moderates mere background supporters of Eisenhower's campaign. They served in both his primary and presidential campaigns in many different roles, and were determined to have an influence on his policies once he was elected. To steal a march on their opponents, eight CED trustees met with the president-elect in New York six days before he was to leave for the White House. They urged the general CED program on him, including a liberalization of such aspects of trade policy as tariffs, shipping restrictions, and "buy American" legislation (Schriftgiesser 1960, p. 162–164).

Shortly thereafter, CED came out with a policy statement on foreign economic policy entitled *Britain's Economic Problem and its Meaning for America* (CED 1953). As the title implies, the report focused on the need to strengthen the British economy by making it possible for the United Kingdom to sell more products in the United States. Moreover, a strong British Commonwealth (created in 1949 and consisting of the United Kingdom and its former colonies, the largest of which are Canada and Australia) was seen as important to the United States for both economic and geopolitical reasons, just as it had been in the early 1940s by CFR planners. That is, a strong economy in the British Commonwealth would make it possible for the United States to export more goods and services, but it also would insure that the British Commonwealth would remain a strong political ally. Moreover, the report is also of general significance because it called for lower tariffs and the removal of other trade restrictions for all American allies.

But the majority of Republicans in Congress blocked the corporate moderates' legislative initiatives. The Eisenhower Administration had to settle for a one-year extension of the Reciprocal Trade Act and a special investigatory commission, the Commission on Foreign Economic Policy, which was supposed to come up with trade recommendations for the next legislative session. In terms of the series of delays and defeats on international issues that the corporate moderates would in fact suffer throughout

460 Rise of an International Economic System

Eisenhower's presidency, they would have been better off with a Democratic presidency and Congress. However, as explained in the chapters in Part 1, support for the Democrats was out of the question for most corporate moderates due to their overriding desire to eliminate unions.

The newly created Commission on Foreign Economic Policy is a case study in how the corporate moderates and the ultraconservatives sparred throughout the Eisenhower years, with the ultraconservatives winning most of the rounds. The commission included ten Congressional members and seven private citizens. There were three Republicans and two Democrats from each house of Congress, five corporate executives, one economist, and one labor leader. Several of the Republicans were arch-protectionists. All four Democrats were from the South and had been advocates of low tariffs and expanded trade in the past. The chair was the former head of Inland Steel and a strong advocate of increased trade, as were most of the other corporate executives on the commission. However, one of them, a leader in the NAM, was staunchly protectionist. The lone labor leader on the commission, the president of the United Steel Workers, also favored further increases in foreign trade because that would very likely mean more jobs for steelworkers.

Once again fully realizing the magnitude of the problems they faced, the CED leaders formed their own study group on the issue at the same time as the commission was appointed. It included top officers from General Electric, Standard Oil of New Jersey, Bankers Trust, the Bank of America, and H. J. Heinz Company, among many major banks and corporations. One of its three technical advisers was economist Jacob Viner, who is familiar to readers as a leader in the CFR's war-peace studies and as a key adviser to the Department of the Treasury concerning the IMF.

Most interesting of all with regard to events in the early 1960s, the CED committee was chaired by Howard C. Petersen, the chair of Fidelity Philadelphia Trust Bank. Petersen's first job had been as a corporate lawyer with a major Wall Street firm in New York in the 1930s. During World War II he served as an assistant to the undersecretary of war. As head of the subcommittee, Petersen spent a considerable amount of time talking with leading spokespersons for protectionists industries (Schriftgiesser 1960, p. 182). One of them, the president of the Manufacturing Chemists Association, was on the subcommittee. In other words, Petersen was becoming a generalist on trade policies, and also learning more about the concerns of the protectionists in the corporate community.

The report by Petersen's subcommittee, entitled *United States Tariff Policy* (CED 1954), made the case for expanding both imports and exports in a familiar fashion. It claimed that economic specialization by countries tends to raise the standard of living in all countries through more efficient use of resources. It argued that the United States had to encourage more imports if other countries were to have the money to buy American

Resistance to Rebuilding Europe 461

exports. Finally, in a noneconomic argument, it insisted that low tariffs were necessary to help American allies, and especially the United Kingdom, which relied far more on trade than the United States. That is, geopolitical concerns entered into the argument once again.

Still another corporate committee appeared about the same time as the presidential commission and the CED subcommittee were formed. This one was an advocacy committee to urge public support for an expansive trade policy through publicity and lobbying. Called the Committee for a National Trade Policy, all but six of its numerous officers and directors were either trustees of the CED or members of the CFR. One of the lawyers working with the committee, George W. Ball, whose credentials as an internationalist went back to government service on foreign economic policies in the war years, figures almost as prominently as Peterson later in this chapter (Bauer, de Sola Pool, and Dexter 1963, p. 380).

Despite their efforts, the corporate moderates lost ground in the 1955 legislative session. They won permission to lower tariffs by only 15 percent over the next three years, and they had their hands tied slightly by a number of protectionist amendments, which there is no need to outline here (Pastor 1980, p. 103). These setbacks were somewhat unexpected in that Democrats had taken control of both the House and Senate after the 1954 elections. The key committees were headed by traditionally low-tariff Southern Democrats, not Republican protectionists, and in the past their efforts had been essential in holding the losses to the protectionists to a minimum.

But something else had changed between 1953 and 1955. The textile industry, now largely located in the South, began to clamor for protection for the first time. After dominating the American market in the years when American allies were still rebuilding from the war, the textile manufacturers were now feeling a slight pinch from foreign imports. Less than 10 percent of the market had been captured by lower-cost imports, but the trend was such as to make the Southern textile owners fearful for the future. Working through their longstanding trade association, the American Textile Manufacturers Institute, industry leaders put on a vigorous campaign throughout the South. They held scores of meetings with other business owners and executives, encouraging them to contact their Congressional representatives. They enlisted the support of textile workers. They sponsored letter-writing campaigns. And they lobbied in Washington.

An interview-based study by a pioneer power structure researcher, Floyd Hunter (1959, Chapter 10), provides insights into how the corporate moderates operated on the textile issue. What he found is consistent with the NPA report from ten years earlier, *America's New Opportunities in World Trade* (1944), which warned that low-end industries would have to be sacrificed in the process of strengthening the economies of Europe and Japan. His study included 33 returned questionnaires on the issue from top

462 Rise of an International Economic System

national leaders, interviews in Tokyo with Japanese textile and government leaders, and interviews with textile leaders in North Carolina and South Carolina, as well as interviews with leading corporate moderates.

The study documents the constant communication between textile officials and general leaders in the corporate community, including those who favored lower tariffs and expanded trade. Moreover, several of the corporate moderates reported that they had supported a recent compromise whereby Japan "voluntarily" limited its exports of textiles into the United States. Voluntary restraint preserved the general policy stance of increasing foreign trade while at the same time responding to the textile industry: "The nontextile men who had called upon the administration and Congress, particularly a number of national nongovernment leaders who were identified as communicators on the question, were satisfied with the compromise. They had spoken forthrightly in favor of keeping trade channels open, and had stressed the need to keep Japan in the Western allied policy orbit" (Hunter 1959, p. 241).

The textile owners' efforts apparently had an impact on Southern Democrats. They changed from free traders to cautious protectionists (Bauer, de Sola Pool, and Dexter 1963, pp. 35–360). More generally, the conversion of the Southern Democrats to a more protectionist stance on textiles meant that the Southern rich were now aligned on some trade issues with Northern ultraconservatives in the same way they were on labor and social-insurance issues. With the conservative coalition now forming on some trade and tariff issues, it was strictly no contest when that coalition decided to take on the internationalists. The corporate moderates had won some victories in the 1940s that advanced their policy goals, but they were in trouble in Congress on foreign trade when they could not count on the Southern Democrats.

Not surprisingly, then, the legislation for renewal of the Reciprocal Trade Act in 1958 was not a victory for the Eisenhower Administration. While renewal was granted for four years, the protectionists hemmed in the executive branch by granting Congress the right, by a two-thirds concurrent vote, to "force the President to implement a recommendation of the Tariff Commission" (Pastor 1980, p. 103). The ultraconservatives also rewrote a national security escape clause "so that virtually any domestic industry could obtain protection from foreign competition if it were determined that such competition were weakening the internal economy and thereby impairing national security" (Pastor 1980, pp. 103–104).

Despite this stalemate, the efforts of the CED and other internationally oriented corporate-moderate organizations continued unabated during the late 1950s. The CED published several reports that continued to call for liberalized trade policies, chaired by the corporate executives from major corporations of the day. By far the most important and prescient of three reports concerned the new European Economic Community, now more commonly known as the European Common Market (CED 1959). The report called the European Common Market "one of the most important undertakings of the twentieth century," sounded warnings about possible U.S. exclusion from European markets, and anticipated many of the issues that would be discussed in the Kennedy Administration in regard to the Trade Expansion Act of 1962 (Schriftgiesser 1967, pp. 123–124).

The European Common Market And Its Meaning To The United States (1959) was also a first for the CED because it was based on discussions with one of its European counterparts, the Committee for Progress Economic and Social, which consisted of French, German, and Italian corporate executives. The CED also had similar interchanges with policy-discussion organizations in the United Kingdom and Sweden. Moreover, the CED report included within it a report by the Committee for Progress Economic and Social on the problems the European Economic Community confronted (CED 1959, pp. 63–91). It also included an appendix that summarized the lengthy and detailed treaty that established the European Economic Community, so the CED was clearly attempting to make it possible for members of the corporate community, lawmakers, and journalists to digest the full import and potential of this new development in the most palatable way possible (CED 1959, pp. 92–113).

The Trade Expansion Act of 1962

It was a new day for the corporate moderates with regard to their plans for the international economy when Democrat John F. Kennedy won the presidency and the Democratic Party held on to its majority in both houses of Congress, which it had regained in the 1954 elections. Their first victory concerned the passage of the Trade Expansion Act of 1962, which went significantly beyond previous trade legislation in allowing the executive branch to negotiate lower tariffs.

The internationalist intentions of the Kennedy Administration in the trade area were clearly signaled by the appointment of George W. Ball, the lawyer who had worked for the opinion-shaping Committee for a National Trade Policy in the mid-1950s, to chair a pre-inauguration task force that would recommend new initiatives in foreign policy. Ball then went on to serve as the assistant secretary of state for economic affairs. The potential for success for the corporate moderates on this issue was also indicated by the appointment of banker and CED trustee Petersen as the president's special trade adviser. He was put in charge of drafting new trade legislation with the help of a staff of ten people (Pastor 1980, p. 106; Preeg 1970, pp. 44–45).

Just as Peterson had done in his work with the CED, he also served as a negotiator with the protectionist industries: "The campaign by the administration on the chemical industry was carried as far as a private meeting between Peterson and industry leaders in February at a session of the Manufacturing Chemists Association in New York" (Bauer, de Sola Pool, and Dexter 1963, p. 351, who provide this information in the context of a generally flawed account that ignores the role of the policy-planning network). In the case of the even more politically crucial textile industry, a Democratic lawyer who had been an aide to Kennedy since his Senate days carried out the negotiations. After the Kennedy Administration agreed to impose import quotas on foreign textiles and increase subsidies for Southern cotton growers, the ultraconservative protectionists in Congress no longer opposed the legislation: "It was the indirect effect of the administration's approach to and conversion of the textile lobby and to numerous other businessmen that indirectly affected Congress" (Bauer, de Sola Pool, and Dexter 1963, pp. 78, 362, 422).

The CED tried to move things along by publishing a new report, *A New Trade Policy for the United States* (CED 1962), just as the legislative process began. It argued that a more expansionary trade policy would stimulate the economy and help deal with unemployment, unused productive capacity, and the balance of payments problem. It warned yet again that the United States could be shut out of the European Common Market if it did not open its own markets, and added that Third World countries might "turn to the Soviet bloc" if "they cannot find markets in the Free World..." (CED 1962, pp. 5–6). It provided 11 specific recommendations in regard to the nature of the policy negotiations with foreign countries, along with a discussion of the size and distribution of tariff reductions by the United States.

The legislation as agreed to by the White House and Congress also included a provision for "adjustment assistance" (financial compensation) to workers who were directly harmed by import competition, a provision that was vigorously opposed by the CED. It was a concession that Kennedy insisted upon to win support from organized labor. In fact, the head of the steelworkers union had suggested this provision during the Eisenhower years when he served on the presidential Commission on Foreign Economic Policy, but the majority of commissioners had rejected it. Its inclusion in the Trade Expansion Act of 1962 is a reminder of why corporate moderates remain wary of Democratic presidents even when they help them achieve most of what they desire on an issue such as trade.

Even with that legislative concession to organized labor, the bill was a complete victory for the corporate moderates because the pro-labor amendment was rarely used, and "not a single case of adjustment was authorized" for the 15 petitions that were filed between 1962 and 1968 (Chorev 2007, p. 90). This unbroken string of rejected petitions was a clear indication that the general growth in the economy made possible by trade expansion would not be shared with workers. There would be no large severance pay packages that lasted for two or three years, or any of the other ways of helping everyday workers, for which there were precedents in past legislation. In particular, the GI bill for veterans of World War II included provisions for educational support for those who went to college or trade schools, government-backed lower interest rates on mortgages, and slight preferences (a forerunner of "affirmative action") for lower-level government positions.

The legislation also included an important institutional change that proved to be a powerful Trojan horse within the executive branch for the corporate moderates, and therefore another example of state-building by the corporate rich, the power elite, and their policy-planning network. It set up an Office of the Special Trade Representative that was insulated from the State Department, which made it less likely that other foreign-policy issues would compromise trade negotiations. Once the bill was signed, a CED trustee from a multimillionaire San Francisco shipping family, William M. Roth, was named the President's new Special Representative for Trade. (This title was changed slightly to "Special Trade Representative" and backed by a permanent staff via legislation in 1974, which will be discussed in Chapter 14.) At the same time as Roth was beginning his work, the CED organized a major study that searched for a common North American-European trade policy in relation to Japan and Southeast Asia. It did so with the help of a grant from the Ford Foundation and through the involvement of the parallel committees of corporate leaders that the CED had established in Japan as well as the several countries in Western Europe (Schriftgiesser 1967, Chapter 17).

Petersen, who had by then resigned from his role in the White House on trade policy and returned fulltime to his position at Fidelity Philadelphia Trust Company, headed the new CED Subcommittee on East-West Trade. The subcommittee included the presidents or chairs of American Electric Power, Bank of America, Crown Zellerbach, Gillette, MGM, Pitney-Bowes, Sperry and Hutchinson, and Standard Oil of California, and the editor-in-chief of Cowles Magazines and Broadcasting. The advisers to the committee included an economist from the University of California, Berkeley, and the director of the European Institute at Columbia University (CED 1965).

Once again the CED counterparts, consisting of the French, German, and Italian corporate leaders in the Committee for Progress Economic and Social, and this time joined by the Japanese Committee for Economic Development as well, contributed input to the CED subcommittee's deliberations. They did so through position papers and the inclusion of some of their own expert employees at subcommittee meetings. Members of both the European and Japanese delegations to the CED discussions also wrote supporting or dissenting comments that were published as part of the final report. This involvement of European and Japanese representatives indicates that the parallel committees in Europe and Japan were part of

466   Rise of an International Economic System

the infrastructure within the American-based policy-planning network, which was in the process of creating a more fully international economy.

The CED's 1965 annual report noted: "There was a very large area of agreement on trade and credit policy toward the East by these groups of businessmen and scholars in the five leading industrial countries, policy toward Red China being the biggest exception." It then added: "The agreement between these five groups probably exceeded that achieved by their governments," which may be a commentary on the growing solidarity within an enlarged international corporate community, and also on the problems the corporate communities in the United States, Europe, and Japan faced in dealing with separate governments (CED 1966, p. 6). It is also an example of coordinated, close-in work by corporate leaders in stitching together an international economy. This infrastructural work is sometimes overlooked or not fully appreciated by the many social scientists with a narrow focus on government officials as the main power actors in the United States, and as the only power actors that can create new government structures.

Roth and his several assistants, guided in part by suggestions in the CED report, along with the suggestions in many other reports as well, then led the lengthy negotiations that culminated in a pact among 50 nations. Finalized in 1967, the agreement decreased tariffs on industrial products by one-third (Schriftgiesser 1967, p. 136). These negotiations were a very crucial step in the internationalization of the economy that corporate moderates had been advocating for a little over 20 years, often without much progress. But at the same time as these successes were finally being realized, the international economy was in turmoil due to the impact of the Vietnam War and the resulting inflation in the United States, and soon thereafter, in the rest of the world as well. As a result, protectionist concerns were heightened in Congress, and there was talk of new trade wars, with the AFL-CIO now increasingly opposed to trade expansion as inimical to its interests.

In a quick reaction to this new turn of events, and acting in part on the basis of warnings by the special trade representative and a Republican senator, 21 top corporate executives created a new Emergency Committee on Foreign Trade, led by David Rockefeller, the president of Chase Manhattan Bank and a director of CFR, and Arthur K. Watson, the vice chair of IBM as well as being the president of the International Chamber of Commerce and a member of the CFR (Martin 1994, p. 60). (Martin underestimates the importance of corporate power, and does not include the information on Rockefeller and Watson's roles in the policy-planning network; she also makes the false claim that a new business activism began in the 1960s, when in fact this activism had existed for decades.) And, contrary to interviews with "experienced Washington veterans," the Emergency Committee on Foreign Trade was not created at the suggestion of high-level officials in

Resistance to Rebuilding Europe **467**

the executive branch (Destler and Odel 1987, p. 119). The corporate leaders already were carefully monitoring the situation, and then the warning bell was rung for them by CED trustee and Special Trade Representative Roth at a meeting of the private National Foreign Trade Council, and seconded by a former corporate lawyer, Jacob Javits, who was by then the senator from New York (Dreiling and Darves 2016, pp. 129–130).

The new organization's 21 founding members included nine members of the Business Council. Six were members of the CFR and six were trustees of the CED, with three in both the Business Council and the CED (and three members were in none of the three groups). ECAT, as the Emergency Committee on Foreign Trade came to be known, became a main focal point for the efforts by corporate leaders within the policy-planning network to block and at the same time accommodate protectionists in Congress for the next 40 years. It soon played a role in stopping a protectionist coalition, led in good part by the AFL-CIO, from succeeding on legislative efforts in the early 1970s (Chorev 2007; Dreiling 2001; Dreiling and Darves 2016). At the same time, organized labor's objections to increased foreign trade grew even stronger over the next 35 years as Mexico, Southeast Asia, and ultimately China replaced the Southern states as the corporate community's safe haven from unions, but the setbacks in the early 1970s proved to be the first in an unending series of defeats for the liberal-labor alliance on trade issues.

References

Bailey, Stephen K. 1950. *Congress makes a law: The story behind the Employment Act of 1946.* New York: Columbia University Press.

Bauer, Raymond, Ithiel de Sola Pool, and Lewis Dexter. 1963. *American business and public policy: The politics of foreign trade.* New York: Atherton Press.

Casey, Kevin. 2001. *Saving international capitalism during the early Truman presidency: The National Advisory Council on International Monetary and Financial Problems.* New York: Routledge.

CED. 1947. *An American program of European economic cooperation.* New York: Committee for Economic Development.

———. 1953. *Britain's economic problem and its meaning for America.* New York: Committee for Economic Development.

———. 1954. *United States tariff policy.* New York: Committee for Economic Development.

———. 1959. *The European Common Market and its meaning to the United States.* New York: Committee for Economic Development.

———. 1962. *A new trade policy for the United States.* New York: Committee for Economic Development.

———. 1965. *East-West trade: A common policy for the West.* New York: Committee for Economic Development.

———. 1966. *CED in 1965: A report of activities.* New York: Committee for Economic Development.

468 Rise of an International Economic System

Chorev, Nitsan. 2007. *Remaking U.S. trade policy: From protectionism to globalization.* Ithaca: Cornell University Press.

Destler, I. M. and John Odel. 1987 *Anti-protection: Changing forces in United States trade politics.* Washington: Institute for International Economics.

Domhoff, G. W. 1987. "Where do government experts come from? The CEA and the policy-planning network." Pp. 189–200 in *Power elites and organizations,* edited by G. W. Domhoff and T. Dye. Beverly Hills: Sage.

———. 1990. *The power elite and the state: How policy is made in America.* Hawthorne, NY: Aldine de Gruyter.

Dreiling, Michael. 2001. *Solidarity and contention: The politics of class and sustainability in the NAFTA conflict.* New York: Garland Press.

Dreiling, Michael and Derek Darves. 2016. *Agents of neoliberal globalization: Corporate networks, state structures and trade policy.* New York: Cambridge University Press.

Eakins, David. 1969. "Business planners and America's postwar expansion." Pp. 143–171 in *Corporations and the Cold War,* edited by D. Horowitz. New York: Monthly Review Press.

Friedberg, Aaron. 2000. *In the shadow of the garrison state: America's anti-statism and its Cold War grand strategy.* Princeton: Princeton University Press.

Hogan, Michael. 1987. *The Marshall Plan: America, Britain, and the reconstruction of Western Europe, 1947–1952.* New York: Cambridge University Press.

Hunter, Floyd. 1959. *Top leadership, U.S.A.* Chapel Hill: University of North Carolina Press.

Martin, Cathie. 1994. "Business and the New Economic Activism: The Growth of Corporate Lobbies in the Sixties." *Polity* 27.

McConnell, Grant. 1953. *The decline of agrarian democracy.* Berkeley: University of California Press.

McCune, Wesley. 1956. *Who's behind our farm policy?* New York: Praeger.

NPA. 1944. *America's new opportunities in world trade.* Washington: National Planning Association.

NYT. 1974. "Winfield Riefler, Monetary Expert." *The New York Times,* April 10. https://www.nytimes.com/1974/04/10/archives/winfield-riefler-monetary-expert-exaide-to-federal-reserve-chief-is.html.

Pastor, Robert. 1980. *Congress and the politics of U.S. foreign economic policy, 1929–1976.* Berkeley: University of California Press.

Preeg, Ernest. 1970. *Traders and diplomats: An analysis of the Kennedy round of negotiations under the General Agreement on Tariffs and Trade.* Washington: The Brookings Institution.

Sanders, Jerry. 1983. *Peddlers of crisis: The Committee on the Present Danger and the politics of containment.* Boston: South End Press.

Schriftgiesser, Karl. 1960. *Business comes of age.* New York: Harper & Row.

———. 1967. *Business and public policy.* Englewood Cliffs, NJ: Prentice Hall.

TCF. 1946. *Report of the Committee on Foreign Economic Relations* New York: Twentieth Century Fund.

Wala, Michael. 1994. *The Council on Foreign Relations and American foreign policy in the early Cold War.* Providence: Berghahn Books.

Whitham, Charlie. 2016. *Post-War business planners in the United States, 1939–1948.* New York: Bloomsbury Publishing.

Chapter 14

From Turmoil to the World Trade Organization, 1968–2000

The mobilization for the Vietnam War without government controls on the economy, as there had been during World War I, World War II, and the Korean War, led to an increase in inflation from a mere 1.0 percent in January 1965, to 4.7 percent in December 1968. This accelerating inflation greatly complicated the corporate community's project to internationalize the economy. By failing to control inflation, the American government also exported inflation to its trading partners by insisting that those countries hold on to the dollars they were earning through their exports, rather than requesting the American gold reserves they were entitled to under the terms of the Bretton Woods agreement.

The rapid increase in "Eurodollars" (American dollars held by people, banks, corporations, and government entities outside the United States) fed into the growing Eurodollar market, which the London financial district and the Bank of England had slowly constructed in the late 1950s and early 1960s. Perhaps somewhat ironically, Eurodollars helped to restore the large role that British banks had enjoyed in the decades before World War II. Nevertheless, American bankers were glad there might be a new American-Anglo financial dominance, which would reprise the Anglo-American dominance of the first several decades of the century. Furthermore, as one of the American bankers' first benefits from this restored alliance, they began to borrow British Eurodollars to circumvent the restraints on their lending that the Federal Reserve Board (Fed), and the federal government more generally, were trying to impose (Burn 2006, pp. 9, 72, 129–130, and Chapter 6; Fourcade-Gourinchas and Babb 2002, pp. 549–556; Mann 2013, pp. 141–142). As part of the process, British banks were making a considerable portion of their rising profits after 1968 by lending Eurodollars to foreign banks, and especially the large American banks on Wall Street.

Wall Street bankers were of course staunch internationalists, but they also wanted to maintain their own prominence and profits, just as they did during the process that created the International Monetary Fund. Due to their relationship with the British banks, they were able to make the

470 Rise of an International Economic System

large loans that American industrial corporations were eagerly seeking so they could respond to a booming American market and the even bigger opportunities that now existed overseas. In other words, the financiers' profit-making decisions, based on the inevitable logic of expand or lose out, at least partially undermined the impact of the Fed's high interest rates on inflation. The only acceptable way to control inflation was, once again, to force workers to absorb its costs through declining wages and higher consumer prices, not limitations on profit-making opportunities or higher taxes on wealthy individuals. But that remedy was not immediately available in the face of tight labor markets and strong unions in the manufacturing and construction sectors of the economy.

In June 1969, six months after Nixon took office, the bankers in charge of his Treasury Department began to work on this issue as the leaders of an intra-governmental committee that included representatives from the state and commerce departments, as well as the Federal Reserve Board, the Export-Import Bank, and the Council of Economic Advisors. Their subsequent report concluded that the administration should do nothing for the time being to deal with its burgeoning balance-of-payments problem. That is, it should honor the government's agreement to exchange dollars for gold for as long as it could, rather than devaluing the dollar. But if and when the problems became unmanageable, it should stop providing gold for dollars. In the parlance of the day, it should "close the gold window," immediately and without negotiations, when it became necessary to do so for domestic economic and political reasons: "Keep the gold window open for now, the report advised, but be prepared to close it if necessary," (Matusow 1998, p. 128).

This harsh policy alternative had become possible to contemplate because the United Kingdom, Western Europe, and Japan had fully recovered from the devastation of World War II, and there was no danger of Communist takeovers anywhere in Europe. Put another way, and contrary to those critics that claim Europe and Japan had taken advantage of the United States in previous years, the hardline policies advocated by these critics (usually in retrospective accounts) would have been unthinkable for corporate moderates in the first 15 to 20 years after World War II ended. Moreover, large financial companies and corporations benefited far more from American policies than may be contemplated by those who look primarily at trade imbalances and factory job losses in making their assessments.

Several of the economists that recommended this proposed policy came from the policy-planning network. Paul Volcker, the Under Secretary of Treasury for International Monetary Affairs, and a member of the Council on Foreign Relations (CFR), was the central figure in the interagency governmental group that suggested policy alternatives on international monetary issues (the group was informally known as the "Volcker

From Turmoil to World Trade Organization 471

Group") (Gowa 1983, pp. 60, 62–63). (Volcker's career moving back and forth from Chase Manhattan Bank to the government from the late 1950s until his appointment to the Nixon Administration was briefly mentioned in Chapter 5). As part of the effort to deal with the continuing gold drain in the early Nixon years, Volcker worked closely with an economist from Washington University in St. Louis, who was a former adviser to the CED, and the assistant secretary of treasury at the time. Volcker also interacted with two members of Nixon's Council of Economic Advisors, one of whom had been a consultant to the CED since the late 1950s, and the other a staff economist for the CED for 23 years before he left to become a fellow at The Brookings Institution.

Closing the gold window would come as no surprise or disappointment to the new generation of bankers and corporate executives that came to power in the 1960s. One of the co-founders of the Emergency Committee on Foreign Trade (ECAT), David Rockefeller, criticized the gold standard as constraining international trade expansion in remarks to a Congressional committee in 1961, a year after he became president of his family's Chase Manhattan Bank. It was a position from which he would be in the forefront of virtually every major American international initiative until his retirement in 1981. (As noted earlier, he was also a director of the CFR.) Rockefeller suggested steps to Congress to "remove the requirement that gold be held against the note and deposit liabilities of the Federal Reserve Banks," which would allow banks to enlarge their role as a "major part of the financing of our exports and imports of goods and services" and thereby "exercise a role of leadership in international financial matters" and in "the defense and development of the free world" (Dreiling and Darves 2016, p. 128). Similarly, in regard to the gold standard, the other ECAT co-founder, Arthur K. Watson, who was in charge of IBM's World Trade Corporation, commented in 1967: "It matters little to free world industry whether the monetary system is ultimately based on gold, paper or sea shells;" instead, what mattered is "a system that will allow fairly wide swings in debt and credit" because "trade is expanding and it must have an international monetary system that expands with it" (Dreiling and Darves 2016, p. 127).

As the American wage-price spiral continued to roil the international economy, foreign countries increased their demand for gold in exchange for dollars in order to deal with the inflation in their own countries, or to limit American power, as in the case of France. In August 1971, about a year after Nixon received the policy recommendation from Treasury, he decided to take action at the same time as he instituted the wage-price freeze already discussed in Chapter 5. In effect, the government "declared economic warfare against its astonished allies" in Europe and Japan, with the strong backing of the corporate community (Matusow 1998, p. 162). It did so through two changes in international economic policy designed to stimulate the American economy and reduce unemployment, while at the same time helping American corporations sell more goods overseas. Capitalizing on the fact that the American dollar was also the international medium of exchange, the first change put an end to the postwar international monetary system by announcing that the government would no longer give American gold to foreign countries in exchange for American dollars (Gowa 1983, who tells the story without any mention of any organization in the policy-planning network, or any discussion of the careers of the policy-makers).

In closing the gold window, Nixon was making the best of his options in terms of dealing with domestic economic problems and corporate concerns. In effect, the federal government's previous efforts to maintain the Bretton Woods system as long as possible had kept the dollar at a high value that made American exports too expensive, rendering them less competitive in European and Japanese markets. At the same time, allowing imports to be less expensive made them more attractive to American buyers. In the process, both corporate profits and some American jobs were being lost.

In this context, the most attractive alternative for Nixon was simply to assert American power by refusing to convert dollars into gold, "thus reneging on dollar liabilities and expanding domestically without regard to international repercussions" (Dahlberg 1984, p. 586). The chair of the Federal Reserve Board, and leaders at the New York Federal Reserve Bank, which traditionally managed the country's international monetary affairs, expressed concerns that closing the gold window might trigger retaliation or more inflation. But Nixon did it anyhow. As historian Allen Matusow (1998, p. 148) wryly notes, he closed the gold window simply "because he wanted to. It was his opening move in a historic offensive to correct the overvalued dollar and reorder the trading world to serve his political purposes." That is, to put the historic change within a power context, at this point the corporate rich and the power elite believed they could make American economic expansion their one and only international goal now that the European and Japanese economics were fully recovered from World War II.

To make clear just how much power Nixon intended to exert, his confrontation with American allies also included three other policy changes. He first of all doubled the effective tariff on all imports into the United States to 10 percent, thereby forcing other countries to negotiate new terms of trade with the American government or lose imports into the world's largest market. Moreover, the president announced a 10 percent reduction in foreign aid and provided new tax subsidies for American exports (Matusow 1998, p. 167).

Importantly, the new international economic policies removed any conflict between the corporate community's domestic goals—low inflation and high employment—and an integrated world economy in which large corporations could prosper. Closing the gold window also dealt with several of the negative consequences of the American failure to control inflation between 1967 and 1971. It gave the Nixon Administration the freedom to follow expansive domestic policies and continue to spend money abroad, while at the same time trying to control the wage-price spiral through the freeze.

Although the issues involved in the wage-price freeze and closing the gold window were talked about in terms of wage-push inflation, balance of payments problems, trade barriers, exchange rates, and the convertibility of dollars to gold, the underlying issues were clearly concerned with power. Would American unions continue to have the power to win wage increases under conditions of labor scarcity and inflation? Which countries might have to suffer inflation or unemployment, or both? Whose corporations would have the best opportunities to sell their products in other countries? For Nixon, the goal was to "keep the United States number one and help rally a new majority for '72" (Matusow 1998, p. 148). For all the confusion and consternation the package generated at home and abroad, it in fact furthered the interests of both the White House and the corporate community.

As for the corporate moderates, the pressures they exerted in favor of dramatic government actions showed they were now willing to do battle with both the unions at home and their trading partners overseas, just as they had done with the unions at home and the Soviet Union overseas from the 1940s through the 1960s. Rather than being evidence of American decline, as some social critics claimed at the time, the new directions were an indication that the power elite intended to compete even more vigorously for profits in the international arena.

Shortly after the new economic policies were announced on August 15, Nixon appointed William Eberle, the president of American Standard, a manufacturer of plumbing and heating equipment, and the chair of a two-year CED project on trade and currency issues in relation to Europe, as his special trade representative (STR). The new CED statement on trade policy and inflation led by Eberle, *The United States and the European Community* (1971), was based on discussions over a two-year period, which included international economists from major universities that had served as advisers or appointees in the federal government. Perhaps the most important expert participant was a Harvard-trained economist who served as the head of the Federal Reserve Board's Division of International Finance, and was a "well-regarded" member of the Volcker Group at the same time he was meeting with the CED policy committee (Gowa 1983, pp. 114–115 for information on Robert Solomon's participation in the Volcker Group). His presence on a private-sector corporate committee while serving in government is another instance of the way in which the line between the

474 Rise of an International Economic System

policy-planning network and government is blurred in the United States. In any event, the report turned out to be a source of information, possible guidelines, and expert contacts for Eberle's future efforts. The position took Eberle to dozens of meetings in capital cities across the world over the next three years.

The first several months of negotiations led to a temporary monetary arrangement in December 1971, in which the Europeans resisted a devaluation of the dollar by more than 12 percent. This was less than the 15–20 percent desired by the United States, and the new arrangement collapsed within a year. Henceforth the money markets would determine the value of each currency, which also meant a more advantageous devaluation of the American dollar. The country's trading partners were left with unpleasant choices. For example, they could continue to accept the flood of dollars let loose by the Fed's easy money policies—$10 billion in 1970, $30 billion in 1971—despite the negative consequences for their own economies. Or they could revalue their currencies upward, which would reduce any trade advantages their corporations had in relation to American companies. They might even restrict American capital inflow, but that would invite American retaliation. In the end, their only reasonable choice was to allow the international market to determine the value of each currency.

As might be expected, CED trustees reacted positively to Nixon's policy changes. They expressed their strong approval through a new programmatic statement, *U.S. Foreign Economic Policy and The Domestic Economy* (CED 1972b), which was assembled by one of its standing leadership committees without bringing in outside expert consultants. The group included the CED's longstanding trustee leader on trade expansion, Howard C. Peterson of the Fidelity Bank in Philadelphia, and representatives from Standard Oil of New Jersey and Caterpillar Tractor. It is noteworthy that the group included Kennedy and Johnson's STR, William M. Roth, as well as the current trade representative, Eberle. The CED's annual report on activities during 1971 claimed some credit for the role of its international reports in shaping recent events and expressed pleasure with Eberle's appointment as STR (CED 1972a).

The CED's Research and Policy Committee continued to focus on international monetary and trade issues throughout Eberle's tenure. In 1973 it issued a report on *Strengthening The World Monetary System* (CED 1973). Reflecting its concerns with the growing tensions between protectionist industries and Japan, the next year it issued two reports concerning American trade relations, the first of which provided a joint American-Japanese perspective on how to improve the international economic system (CED 1974a). The second report was based on a dialogue on how the two countries viewed each other (CED 1974b). These efforts not only provided specific proposals and an exchange of perspectives, but also brought together corporate executives and international economists from both countries, who might later provide advice to their respective countries, or work together as government appointees in the future. When Eberle resigned as the STR in December 1974, he was replaced by another CED trustee, the president of his family-owned Mayfair Mills in Spartanburg, South Carolina, who then held the position until the end of the Nixon-Ford Administration. Since textiles were the main bone of contention between the two countries, it is likely that the new STR found the 1974 CED reports and his CED contacts helpful over the next two years.

Due to the changes in monetary policy and the continuing threat from protectionists, corporate moderates also turned their attention to new governmental institutions for expanding trade and limiting the impact of Congressional supporters of protectionism. With Eberle playing an active role (Chorev 2007, pp. 89–91), the Trade Act of 1974 became the latest instance of state-building on international economic policy by the corporate rich, the power elite, and their policy-planning network. The corporate moderates also could count on direct interventions with President Nixon by the CEO of Pepsi, who recently had been appointed chair of ECAT (Chorev 2007, p. 89). The Pepsi CEO had been Nixon's friend and supporter since the 1950s, and had hired Nixon as a business ambassador for Pepsi between 1963 and 1967, while he was ostensibly out of politics (Hoffman 1973, p. 106). More generally, and as a result of ECAT's standing and connections, it "actively participated in the drafting deliberations, and its recommendations received equal attention as those provided by state agencies" (Chorev 2007, p. 89). Then too, a "well-place source" told two international trade economists that President Nixon would not have sent the proposed legislation to Congress "had he not been assured of that group's strong support" (Destler and Odel 1987, p. 118).

The new trade act first of all created what came to be called "fast-track" authority, which gave the executive branch the primary authority to formulate and initiate trade legislation. Under this new arrangement, Congress could only vote for or against the new package within a 90-day period, with no possibility for amendments, and a majority was sufficient for passage, with no filibusters possible. Trade legislation thereby became the only issue on which there could be timely and simple majority rule in the United States, with no chance for even a large minority of elected officials to block it. This arrangement reflected not only the power of the corporate rich and the power elite to shape international economic policy, but an admission by Congress, based on painful past experience, that its members were too susceptible to overwhelming local and regional interests, and therefore too divided among themselves, to come to agreement on general trade expansion.

However, because there are limits on the degree to which Congress can cede its authority to the executive branch, fast-track authority had to be renewed for each new initiative. In each case of renewal approved in the remainder of the twentieth century (in 1979, 1988, and 1991), there was conflict, and temporary concessions were made to protectionist industries. Moreover, and showing the limits of this Congressional grant of authority, attempts at renewal were rejected in 1994 because the corporate community did not agree with President Bill Clinton's efforts to include more provisions related to demands by unions and environmentalists, and in 1997 because liberals and labor did not think Clinton's provisions went far enough (Destler 2005, pp. 219–220, 262–269, for accounts of both of these failures).

In addition to making it possible for the executive branch to take the initiative on specific trade issues, the Trade Act of 1974 also created a set of advisory committees, which in effect made the trade committees within trade associations and some parts of the policy-planning network part of the official process. There were 30 or more advisory committees that were incorporated into the decision-making process. At the next level, there was a more general Advisory Committee on Trade Policy and Negotiations (known by the acronym ACTPN). It was appointed by the president to advise both an enlarged Office of the U.S. Trade Representative and the president. Although the appointments were made to individuals, in practice those who were appointed came overwhelmingly from the Business Roundtable, the Chamber, the NAM, and other organizations in the policy-planning network.

The legislation also included a wide range of possible policy options, including import quotas and escape clauses, which could be used by aggrieved industries in an effort to convince the Office of the U.S. Trade Representative and the president that companies in other countries were selling products in the United States for less than their production costs. The law also provided provisions offering redress if industries could show that foreign companies were violating various unfair trade laws. In those cases, the law made adjustment assistance available for companies that might lose out to importers, and for employees that lost jobs due to increasing imports. This array of available options made the legislation more politically plausible for members of Congress, and in any case gave the Office of the U.S. Trade Representative and the president the power to decide which options they wanted to use. Thus, future disagreements between those who wanted to expand and those who wanted to limit trade would be carried out within the advisory committees and the Office of the U.S. Trade Representative, with the president making the final decisions.

The legislation faced opposition from the large contingent of Democrats that was sympathetic to the concerns of the liberal-labor alliance, and from the few protectionist industries that remained completely dissatisfied. The opponents may have been partially hampered in their efforts to derail the legislation by the fact that "protectionist industries did not cooperate with organized labor" (Chorev 2007, p. 89). The act passed by

From Turmoil to World Trade Organization   477

the wide margin of 278-143 with the support of 163 Republicans and 115 Democrats, mostly from the South. With a majority of non-Southern Democrats opposed, it was a victory for the conservative coalition.

Once the law was in place, the protectionist industries lost for the next 20 years in their various attempts at the restriction of imports, starting with their failure to gain presidential support for import quotas. As for the escape clause, it was made "obsolete" by the Ford and Carter administrations because they did not want to set any precedents for protectionism (Chorev 2007, p. 116). Nor could protectionists convince either Republican or Democratic presidents to make use of the unfair trade provisions (Chorev 2007, pp. 143–146). Recalling that adjustment assistance was rejected in 15 different instances in the Kennedy-Johnson years, it may come as no surprise that it was seldom granted to workers in the face of opposition from most business sectors, which claimed that additional costs might cause them to lose export opportunities (Chorev 2007, pp. 92–93). Nevertheless, protectionist industries and unions continued to file claims and make demands at a high rate, even though they rarely succeeded (Chorev 2007, p. 139).

Although the corporate moderates worked against the measures preferred by protectionists, the new, more insulated institutional arrangements for trade led them to respond positively to remedies that did not conflict with trade expansion, such as initiatives that made it more feasible for domestically oriented businesses to compete in the world market. To this end the corporate moderates vigorously pursued efforts to force foreign governments to reduce the subsidies and preferential purchasing they used to further or protect some of their home industries. In this way, the internationalists' strategy both defeated and accommodated the protectionist industries.

The Trilateral Commission and the Carter Administration

President Jimmy Carter's views and policies relating to trade were largely informed by his export-oriented Southern heritage (he was a multimillionaire peanut farmer) and his involvement in the Trilateral Commission, a joint project created in 1973 by the Council on Foreign Relations and its counterparts in Europe and Japan. Carter was recommended for membership by the members of the Atlanta Committee of the Council on Foreign Relations, many of whom were among his financial backers (Shoup 1980, p. 45). He had spent considerable time as governor of Georgia from 1971 to 1975 flying around the world singing the praises of Atlanta as a corporate headquarters, and of the Atlanta-based Coca Cola Company, which provided him with a corporate jet and paid a large part of the expenses for his travel (Biven 2002, p. 16; Shoup 1980, p. 29). A few years

478 Rise of an International Economic System

earlier, Carter had already met with David Rockefeller, who orchestrated the founding of the Trilateral Commission, and was in the small group that made the final decision on membership (Shoup 1980, p. 43).

In regard to the Trilateral Commission itself, Carter later told one of his White House aides that its meetings "for me were like classes in foreign policy—reading papers produced on every conceivable subject, hearing experienced leaders debate international issues and problems..." (Biven 2002, p. 18). Carter came to know his choice for vice president, liberal Minnesota Senator Walter Mondale, through their shared involvement in the Trilateral Commission, and also his Secretary of State, Cyrus Vance, one of the CFR members who advised Johnson to deescalate the Vietnam War in 1968. So, too, for his secretary of defense, secretary of treasury, national security adviser, and special trade representative, the latter a corporate lawyer for international businesses and a longtime Texas Democrat and party fundraiser (Dryden 1995, Chapter 6, for an account of the STR's efforts during the Carter years). Overall, the early Carter Administration included 20 appointees who were members of the Trilateral Commission; four were trustees of CED and five were either trustees or employees of The Brookings Institution, one of the two or three most internationally oriented think tanks in the policy-planning network (Shoup 1980, pp. 51, 104).

Within this internationally oriented, Trilateral Commission environment, there was little chance that the protectionist industries, or the liberal-labor alliance, would have any impact on trade policy (Chorev 2007, pp. 116, 119–121 for Carter's actions on several specific issues), although the Carter Administration did use a marketing agreement to slow imports in the labor-intensive shoe industry (Biven 2002, pp. 228–230). The Carter Administration's policies to lower inflation and increase trade were based on projected improvements in the international economy that were supposed to follow from joint expansionary efforts led by Germany and Japan, a recommendation from the Trilateral Commission known as the "locomotive strategy." In July 1978, Carter agreed to deregulate the price of domestically produced oil by the middle of 1979 because America's artificially low prices were exporting inflationary pressures to Europe. In exchange, Germany and Japan agreed to support new stimulus measures that would presumably help the American economy, too (Biven 2002, p. 153).

At that point, large price increases by OPEC at the beginning of 1979 upset all the administration's plans, both international and domestic. The price hikes doubled the previous price of oil, which had an even larger impact on the American economy than the quadrupling in 1973–1974 because the United States was by then much more reliant on imported oil. The OPEC price jump, along with the partial deregulation of oil prices that Carter had agreed to, led to a 32 percent rise in oil prices in the first four months of 1979. The American economy, along with most others, then suffered from renewed high inflation, which increased political turmoil just about everywhere and caused many governments to topple (Fourcade-Gourinchas and Babb 2002; Mann 2013). Faced with double-digit inflation, the president decided to pressure the Fed for higher interest rates.

After moving his moderate, handpicked chair of the Fed to the recently vacated position of secretary of treasury, in came Paul Volcker, by this point a member of the Trilateral Commission as well as the CFR, and the president of the Federal Reserve Bank of New York, in addition to his past roles mentioned earlier in this chapter and in Chapter 5. And, as also noted in Chapter 5, he immediately started raising interest rates indirectly through targeting the money supply. At the same time the CED, the Business Roundtable, and other business groups urged him not to relent.

In 1979, the Carter Administration did make a change in the way in which trade issues would be handled. It moved the authority over the Office of the U.S. Trade Representative from the Department of the Treasury to the Department of Commerce, which was the longstanding home for many of the agencies that were supportive of all sectors of American business. It also meant that the secretary of commerce might be more sympathetic to the general and specific concerns of a wider range of businesses than the Wall Street-oriented Department of the Treasury.

New Reagan Administration, Same Trade Polices

Although Ronald Reagan appointed many ultraconservatives to positions concerning taxes, labor, welfare, and other domestic issues, the key positions relating to international issues were held by corporate moderates from internationally oriented organizations within the policy-planning network. Despite protests from ultraconservatives, Reagan had already shown his hand on international issues by choosing a strong internationalist as his vice presidential running mate, George H. W. Bush, which led to open criticism by some ultraconservatives and protectionists. Bush was a member of the CFR and the Trilateral Commission, and spent much of his time on international issues during the eight years he was vice president.

President Reagan's first secretary of state was a former army general, a recently appointed CEO of a major internationally oriented corporation, United Technologies, and a member of the CFR. The person who succeeded him several months later was the CEO of an international construction company, the Bechtel Corporation, a member of the CFR, and a trustee of the CED. The secretary of treasury, the recent chair of Merrill Lynch, was a member of the policy committee of the Business Roundtable, as well as being a member of the CFR and a CED trustee. The secretary of defense, a corporate lawyer who came to the government from a position as vice president and general counsel of the Bechtel Corporation, was a member of the Trilateral Commission. In all, 31 Reagan appointees

480 Rise of an International Economic System

were members of the CFR, including the director of the CIA, the secretary of commerce, and eight high-level appointments at the State Department (Jenkins and Eckert 2000; Sklar and Lawrence 1981).

By this time corporate moderates in the Business Roundtable and ECAT had organized a multilateral trade negotiations coalition, whose members were found to be "highly active in the President's Advisory Committee on Trade Policy and Negotiations (ACTPN) during the 1980s" (Dreiling and Darves 2016, p. 147). However, the Reagan Administration's primary focus on cutting taxes, eliminating domestic programs, and defeating labor unions resulted in a lack of forward motion in terms of trade expansion during Reagan's first term. Nor was any relief from competition granted to petitioning industries, which led to several Congressional bills that had to be defeated or significantly watered down (Chorev 2007, pp. 133–136). There was talk in Washington that protectionist sentiments were becoming more ascendant (Destler and Odel 1987, Chapter 6).

Moreover, Volcker's attempt to wring inflation out of the economy through increasingly high interest rates overwhelmed any possibilities for trade expansion by making some domestically manufactured products too expensive to compete against imports from Western Europe and Japan. In addition, the high-interest policies encouraged large industrial firms to move some of their production overseas and then import the finished products back into the United States. Still, Volcker's efforts continued, with the full backing of President Reagan and the corporate community, until the early months of 1982. By that point the Mexican government began to teeter on the brink of financial disaster because it could not service its loans from American banks. It is also seemed possible that any further delays in lowering interest rates might force Citibank into bankruptcy because of its risky loans throughout Latin America. With the inflation rate tumbling from 13.5 percent in 1981 to 3.2 percent in 1983, Citibank was able to stretch out the loans ("extend and pretend," "delay and pray," as these negotiations were called), with the hope that the cash-strapped countries would be able to resume their payments.

After Reagan's reelection in 1984, his new Secretary of Treasury, corporate lawyer James F. Baker of Houston, a close friend of vice president Bush as well as being the White House chief of staff during Reagan's first term, took the lead on trade issues. To make American exports competitive once again, he met with American allies and developed a process that would lead to a decline in the high value of the American dollar. He also initiated investigations of potentially unfair trading practices in other counties, rather than waiting for industries to go to the time and expense of bringing their cases to government. At the same time, he continued to resist any protectionist measures (Chorev 2007, pp. 133–135, 139).

Working with Bush and the new STR, who had been the Deputy STR for two years in the Carter Administration, Baker took the initiative on

From Turmoil to World Trade Organization 481

two major issues that later came to fruition in the 1990s. He first focused on a new round of GATT negotiations that would strengthen legal mandates and sanctions, but with the understanding that the negotiations also might lead to an agreement for a World Trade Organization (WTO), backed by government sanctions. Second, he engaged the United States in bilateral negotiations with Canada, which came to fruition in a free-trade agreement in 1987. Three years later, after Bush had been elected president in 1988, and with Baker serving as his Secretary of State, the trade pact with Canada unexpectedly led to the tripartite negotiations among the United States, Mexico, and Canada that eventually created the North American Free Trade Agreement (NAFTA).

The Bush Administration Negotiates NAFTA

The informal negotiations leading to NAFTA began in early 1990, after a Harvard-trained Mexican economist, Carlos Salinas, won the presidency of Mexico and began to think about an ambitious plan for the development of the Mexican economy. To do so he assembled a team of American-trained Mexican economists, and after some hesitations, indicated his intentions to American officials. He met in Houston with Bush and Baker shortly thereafter, and developed close relations with them (Mayer 1981, pp. 38, 42). He also reached out to the American corporate community through the CEOs of two corporations, American Express and Eastman Kodak, which had a strong economic presence in Mexico; they were also the co-leaders of the Business Roundtable's task force on trade expansion (Mayer 1998, pp. 39, 42). In addition, Salinas contacted Senator Bill Bradley (D-NJ), who had taken an interest in Mexican economic development since 1985, after serving on a Senate committee that helped resolve the Mexican debt crisis (Mayer 1981, p. 37).

Based on post-NAFTA interviews with participants from all three countries, two Canadian political scientists pieced together the highly complex negotiation process that then unfolded (Cameron and Tomlin 2000). The researchers were able to conduct frank and in-depth interviews that made it possible to construct a sophisticated, multi-level analysis of the negotiations. It was possible to develop this analysis because they started with a deep understanding of the secretive negotiations due to the background information they obtained from an extremely well-informed confidential informant within the Canadian government. The interviewees often expressed surprise at what the interviewers already knew, and were usually very forthcoming (Cameron and Tomlin 2000, pp. 12–13, for the interview strategy, and Chapter 4 for the motivations and goals of the leaders in each country; Mayer 1998, Chapter 3, for an independent parallel analysis).

The informal negotiations that later would lead to the formal negotiations, along with the major role the Business Roundtable would play,

482 Rise of an International Economic System

first came into notice within the formal political arena in late September 1990. At that point President Bush notified the relevant Congressional committees that he would seek an extension of his fast-track authority for both NAFTA and possible American entry into a World Trade Organization if the negotiations ended satisfactorily (Cameron and Tomlin 2000, p. 70). Liberals, union leaders, and grassroots environmental activists immediately made their all-out opposition to both NAFTA and the WTO abundantly clear for a variety of reasons relating to job loss, union decline and possible environmental degradation (Dreiling 2001, Chapter 4; Mayer 1998, pp. 69–77). By January 1991, they had joined forces to create a coalition to defeat the Bush proposal.

With Democrats holding solid majorities of 55-45 in the Senate and 265-165 in the House, the two most important Democrats on the fast-track issue, Lloyd Bentsen, a Texas rancher and insurance magnate, who was chair of the Senate Finance Committee, and Dan Rostenkowski, a Chicago machine Democrat, who was chair of the House Ways and Means Committee, wrote to the president. They stressed the need for any fast-track agreement to address the rights, health, and safety of workers as well as environmental protections. At the same time, Rostenkowski contacted the Business Roundtable leaders active on trade issues, warning them that it was "time to get your asses in gear if *you* want to win this thing" (Cameron and Tomlin 2000, pp. 74–75, my italics). They responded by expanding their Coalition for Multilateral Trade Negotiations into the Committee for Trade Expansion, which included the NAM, the Chamber of Commerce, and ECAT, as well as numerous individual corporations. They then began lobbying for fast-track authority, primarily through the Washington representatives of the member corporations, along with several law, lobbying, and public relations firms. Three months later, fast-track won 233-194 in the House with strong Republican support and mixed Democratic support. Reflecting the initial opposition of textiles and other protectionist industries in the South, a majority of the Southern Democrats opposed the measure, 43-41 (Destler 2005, p. 206).

The formal negotiations among the official representatives from the three countries were based in the American case on the deliberations within "more than 30 advisory committees on such broad topics as investment, intellectual property, agriculture and labor as well as more narrowly focused topics such as chemicals, paper products, textiles, and dairy and livestock products" (Mayer 1998, p. 114). These committees met regularly with the relevant U.S. negotiators. Overall coordination for the negotiations was provided by ACTPN, most of whose members were corporate executives, although there were two labor representatives and an environmental representative as well. The co-chairs of ACTPN were the same CEOs from American Express and Eastman Kodak that had been part of the process since its informal beginnings, and they were still the co-chairs of the Business Roundtable's trade task force (Mayer 1998, p. 114). The STR, corporate lawyer Carla Hills, who was a CED trustee, orchestrated the overall process. The details of the deliberations were secret, and the participants had security clearance.

The negotiations were completed in mid-August 1992. President Bush, the Mexican president, and the Canadian prime minister formally signed the agreement on December 17, 1992. Leaders within the Business Roundtable then met with other business leaders, the president of Mexico, and the Mexican counterpart to the NAM to discuss strategy (Mayer 1998, p. 234). The Americans also used the occasion to greatly expand their Committee on Trade Expansion into USA*NAFTA, which soon claimed to have 2,300 corporate members, along with 46 trade associations and a number of law firms (Dreiling 2001, p. 95).

An Eastman Kodak executive that advised the company's CEO on international trade was placed in charge of managing the day-to-day operations of USA*NAFTA (Mayer 1998, p. 234). The Washington representatives for large corporations once again did most of the legwork, aided by lawyers, Republican and Democratic lobbying firms, and public relations and advertising agencies (Mayer 1981, p. 235). Following the past precedents set by the Business Roundtable in dealing with construction unions in the 1970s and local healthcare systems in the 1980s, USA*NAFTA appointed "state captains" in all 50 states, most of whom came from highly visible local and regional corporations, to work with the lobbying and public relations specialists in arranging visits with the Senators and members of the House from their states (Dreiling 2001, p. 95). In 20 of these states, the state captain appointed regional and local committees to bring the efforts even closer to local business communities and to elected officials in the House that were sitting on the fence on the issue.

The most detailed policy and political account of the NAFTA process, written by a political scientist serving as an aide to Senator Bill Bradley, concludes that the Business Roundtable was the "effective parent" of USA*NAFTA (Mayer 1998, p. 252). Subsequent quantitative work on a network of 228 pro-NAFTA corporations, along with several major policy-discussion groups, supports his conclusion. It demonstrates that the Business Roundtable was near the center of the network, along with ECAT and NAM. The president's Advisory Committee on Trade Policy Negotiations and numerous trade advisory committees were in the network as well, through their direct corporate links (Dreiling 2001, pp. 95, 99, 129).

In a follow-up study with a similar database for 1997 and 2003, sociologists Michael Dreiling and Derek Darves (2016, Chapter 6) found that being part of a policy-discussion group significantly increased the chances that one or more of a corporation's executives would serve on a trade advisory committee, belong to one of the temporary pro-trade alliances, or testify before a Congressional committee on a trade issue. In particular,

484 Rise of an International Economic System

involvement in the Business Roundtable increased the chances that at least one of a corporation's executives would serve on a trade advisory committee by 152 percent, be a member of one of the temporary pro-trade alliances by 234 percent, or testify before a Congressional committee on trade policy by 346 percent (Dreiling and Darves 2016, pp. 215–216, 218). Thus, there can be little doubt, based on a combination of case-study and network-analysis findings, that the policy-planning network, and especially affiliation with the Business Roundtable, had a major impact in the realm of international trade issues.

As the approval process began in January 1993, there was one large new factor in the equation. A little over a month before President Bush signed the agreement with Canada and Mexico, he had lost the presidency to Democrat Bill Clinton in a three-way race. A single-issue, anti-trade candidate, billionaire H. Ross Perot, one of the 25 richest Americans at the time, received 18.9 percent of the votes while spending $72 million of his own money. The new president, who had most recently been the governor of Arkansas and the chair of the Democratic Leadership Council, a centrist party organization with a strong contingent of Southern Democrats, would therefore assume the task of shepherding the NAFTA package through Congress.

The Clinton Administration and NAFTA

The first Democratic president since Jimmy Carter continued in the bipartisan tradition of appointing corporate moderates from the policy-planning network to top positions in his administration. President Clinton's first secretary of state practiced corporate law in Los Angeles and served on the board of directors for Lockheed Martin, Southern California Edison, and First Interstate Bancorp, and was also a vice chair of the CFR. There were also another 31 members of the CFR in Clinton's administration, most of them in the State Department, including the president of the CFR as the undersecretary of state for political affairs by 1995. The director of the CIA, the American representative to the United Nations, the chair of the Council of Economic Advisors, and the director of the Office of Management and Budget also were members (Domhoff 1998, pp. 251, 254–255). The STR, born and raised in Nashville, was a Los Angles corporate lawyer and fundraiser for the Democratic Party (Dryden 1995, pp. 384–390).

As pro-trade as the administration was, there were still delays and problems before NAFTA was finally signed in December 1993, just as fast-track authority for NAFTA was about to expire. The problems arose because Clinton had campaigned on the promise of supporting NAFTA, but also said that adding side provisions would provide stronger guarantees for environmentalists and trade unions than the Bush Administration had included. As useful as this added wrinkle was in gaining support from both liberals and centrists in the electorate, the new side agreements proved to be difficult for the Clinton Administration to agree upon, and difficult to negotiate with Mexico and Canada. Moreover, Clinton's early focus as president was on passing a budget and implementing his health-care plan, which took much longer than he expected. It was not until mid-August 1993, that he gave NAFTA any time at all, right about the time the final round of negotiations was completed. With the vote already scheduled for November 17, it was not until the few weeks before that date that Clinton gave NAFTA his full attention.

These delays meant that there was little that USA★NAFTA could do while it waited, and in any case many of the Business Roundtable leaders and other corporate policy groups were focused on the budget and health care as well. Further complicating the problems for the corporate executives and groups that were charged with making sure that NAFTA passed, they were concerned that the NAFTA process would stall out, or that the side agreements would go too far for them. They therefore withheld their full support until they were certain as to what they would be supporting, or opposing, as the case might be. In fact, within a month after discussions of the side agreements began, lawyers employed by the Business Roundtable were warning its leaders that the results might not be to their liking. The Business Roundtable, ECAT, NAM, and the Chamber of Commerce then sent a joint letter of concern to the new STR (Mayer 1998, pp. 181–182).

Once the new side agreements were announced in mid-August, they were enthusiastically endorsed by the seven large, national-level environmental groups, which had been part of the process of creating the environmental regulations (Destler 2005, p. 202; Mayer 1998, p. 291). These groups, which included the National Wildlife Confederation, the National Resources Defense Council, the Environmental Defense Fund, and Nature Conservancy, were part of the policy-planning network through their corporate and foundation financing as well as their shared corporate directors, as also evidenced by the fact that they been instrumental in creating the Environmental Policy Administration and the White House Council on Environmental Quality during the Nixon Administration (Domhoff 2014, pp. 84–85; Gonzalez 2001; Mitchell 1991; Robinson 1993).

Unlike the corporate moderates' relationship with mainstream environmentalists, there was little or no chance from the start that the corporate moderates could accommodate union leaders, who could see no sensible way in which they could safely be anything but opposed (Mayer 1998, p. 178). They were therefore entirely dissatisfied with the labor side agreements and remained in complete opposition. They were joined in their opposition by the liberal grassroots environmental activists that had been opposed to the granting of fast-track in 1991 (e.g., Friends of the Earth, Greenpeace, and the Sierra Club) (Destler 2005, p. 202). Working together through the Citizens Trade Committee, which also included

486 Rise of an International Economic System

consumer and religious groups, they recognized that they could not sway Congress via lobbying. They therefore focused their efforts on creating strong grassroots pressure that might convince Clinton and other Democrats that there would be serious electoral costs if they did not find a way to delay or defeat NAFTA (Dreiling 2001, Chapter 4; Mayer 1998, p. 185). If there would have been any added strength in a united opposition, it was lost to the fact that union leaders and most liberals would have nothing to do with Perot, who continued his anti-trade crusade through speeches at big gatherings and through television time that he purchased.

With the Congressional side deals finally in place, and the Citizens Trade Committee already staging grassroots rallies and spending whatever it could on media advertising, the White House turned to the selling of NAFTA to Congress. This process in good part involved trying to provide fence-sitting Democrats with the political cover they felt they needed before they exposed themselves to potential electoral defeat by supporting NAFTA (Mayer 1998, pp. 277, 279). Clinton appointed a corporate lawyer from Chicago, William M. Daley, to coordinate the lobbying and public relations campaign. He was the son of a legendary Chicago mayor, who had served for 21 years in tumultuous times (1955–1976), and the brother of the person who had been serving as Chicago's mayor since 1989, so he was well known in both the Democratic Party and the corporate community. To provide reassurances and outreach to Republicans in Congress, he was joined by a recently retired Republican member of the House from Minnesota, who was at the time a guest scholar at The Brookings Institution.

Daly then hired two lobbying firms, one that worked primarily with Democrats, the other primarily with Republicans, to put together grassroots campaigns in 50 districts represented by Democrats and about 30 Republican districts (Mayer 1998, p. 288). In conjunction with the US-A★NAFTA state and local captains, their goal was to locate people that might prove influential in supporting NAFTA in talks with other local residents. As indicated by the political scientist who had been an aide to Senator Bill Bradley, Daley spent much of his time coordinating the efforts of the White House and USA★NAFTA (Mayer 1998, pp. 275, 279–280, 286, 289). By that point USA★NAFTA had its own office in the Capitol building, so it had ready access to members of Congress (Dreiling 2001, p. 95).

However, the corporate leaders were not fully convinced that Clinton would provide strong backing for NAFTA and stay the course. They therefore sought face-to-face reassurances in a White House meeting with the president and his White House NAFTA team. The two sides met under the auspices of a joint invitation from David Rockefeller, by then the 78-year-old patriarch of Wall Street, the corporate community, and the CFR. Although the corporate leaders were skeptical and suspicious, all of the White House participants except for the president were part of the corporate community, starting with Daley. Clinton's national economic adviser was the former chair of Goldman Sachs and a member of the CFR; the secretary of treasury was the multimillionaire founder of a large insurance company in Texas before being a senator; the secretary of commerce was a corporate lawyer in Washington; the White House chief of staff was the former president of a large natural gas company in Little Rock; and the STR was a corporate lawyer from Los Angeles (Domhoff 1998, p. 252).

Following this meeting, the leadership of USA*NAFTA passed from the CEO of Eastman Kodak to the CEO of Allied Signal, who in turn brought in one of his top corporate assistants to run the day-to-day operations. Reacting to concerns expressed by the public relations firms hired by USA*NAFTA in regard to the impact the opponents seemed to be having on public opinion, the Business Roundtable then contributed $5 million for advertising as the corporate campaign began in earnest in September (Mayer 1998, p. 248). At this point corporate CEOs were asked to make telephone calls and personal visits to the representatives from House districts in which their companies had headquarters or large corporate facilities (Mayer 1998, pp. 280, 285–286). The corporate grassroots and media campaigns began in earnest at this time as well (Mayer 1998, pp. 282–292 for an overview). The full extent of these efforts is spelled out in an interview-based case study by the multimillionaire publisher-editor of *Harper's Magazine*, who entitled his book *The Selling of "Free Trade": NAFTA, Washington, and the Subversion of American Democracy*, to highlight the extreme lengths to which he thought the corporate leaders went to pass the legislation (MacArthur 2000).

The opponents in Congress, led by the House majority whip, a senior Democrat from Michigan, thought they had the necessary votes to defeat the measure. However, the pro-NAFTA forces won by a large margin in the House, 234-200, where the vote was expected to be very close. Most of the surprise came from a 53-32 vote in favor by 85 Democrats from the South, who finally had been satisfied by the provisions concerning textiles and citrus fruits on which they had demanded concessions.

The passage of NAFTA proved to be the last major piece of legislation on which white Southern Democrats and the conservative coalition would have a significant role in providing a winning margin. Most of these white Southern Democrats were swept out of office a year later by either black Southern Democrats or white Republicans due to the gerrymandering bargain between the black Democrats and the Republicans. Black Democrats won 12 new seats and Republicans picked up 32 seats in the space of the three Congressional elections between 1992 and 1996 (McKee 2010, p. 72; Zweigenhaft and Domhoff 2018, pp. 122–123, 214). Then, too, recall that five white Southern Democrats in the House and one in the Senate switched to the Republican side after the 1994 elections.

488 Rise of an International Economic System

From GATT to WTO

As mentioned earlier, the GATT negotiations that began in 1986 included the possibility that a new World Trade Organization (WTO) might eventually emerge from them. This possibility became a reality in April 1994, when 123 nations signed on to the new plan, with the United States one of the last to do so. The eventual Congressional approval of American entry into the WTO culminated the efforts by the corporate moderates that began in the mid-1940s, when they had to settle for the GATT organizational structure in 1947, due primarily to opposition from the ultra-conservatives in the corporate community and the conservative coalition.

The new agreement first of all mandated a dispute settlement process that included legal sanctions. It also strengthened legal protections for intellectual property rights, such as drug and software patents, movie and television show rights, and publisher royalties. It created greater investment opportunities in foreign countries for financial companies and it limited government subsidies for specific companies or industries, even while supporting government grants for research. Finally, it included agricultural products within a multilateral trade agreement for the first time, although most of the initial goals and specific guidelines concerning agriculture were very modest (Chorev 2007, pp. 161–169, on key provisions).

The possibility of joining the WTO generated relatively little controversy in the United States at the time, at least compared to the conflict over NAFTA, in part because organized labor largely sat on the sidelines. However, with the White House and the corporate community still arguing about Clinton's health-care plan, and with the Office of the U.S. Trade Representative once again struggling to resolve internal policy disagreements, there was another long hiatus between the end of the negotiations and the legislative approval process. The vacuum was filled by various pressure groups that claimed the United States might lose some of its sovereignty if it joined the WTO. For consumer advocate Ralph Nader and his many supporters, who were generally on the liberal-labor side of the political divide, the danger was said to be in the possible overriding of American laws protecting the environment and ensuring product safely. For the hard right, led by the ultraconservative nativist Republican provocateur of the day, Patrick Buchanan, the WTO raised the threat of "world government" (Destler 2005, p. 221). For the anti-trade advocate Perot, the danger was once again the loss of jobs, which would sap American economic power. In this context, the textile industry took the opportunity to lobby successfully for further short-term concessions that kept Southern Democrats in support of the legislation.

As a result of the delays, party politics entered into the equation and the vote was postponed until after the fateful 1994 Congressional elections. At this point the corporate moderates stepped into the process with

From Turmoil to World Trade Organization 489

a lobbying campaign in October and November (the Alliance for GATT Now), asking Congressional members to withhold any decisions or announcements on their votes until after the elections (Chorev 2007, p. 159). This campaign seemed especially important in the case of the Senate, where the vote was expected to be close (Destler 2005, pp. 226–227). After an easy 293-123 victory for the WTO in the House, the price the Republicans in the Senate exacted was agreement to a "WTO Dispute Settlement Review Commission." It would provide important symbolic assurances to those everyday citizens who worried about the possibility that joining the WTO might threaten the nation's sovereignty. The commission's five members, all Federal appellate court judges, appointed by the president in consultation with Congressional leaders, would review all dispute settlements that went against the United States position. If it found three decisions in any five-year period that were demonstrably unfair, Congress would have to vote on whether or not to stay in the WTO. With that agreement in place, both parties in both houses supported the legislation by at least a two-to-one margin in December 1994 (Destler 2005, pp. 227–228).

Normalizing Trade With China

A small amount of trade with China began in a halting fashion shortly after President Nixon decided the time was right in the early 1970s to move toward an accommodation with the Chinese Communist leadership that had come to power in 1949. However, the authorization for trade with Communist countries, under a clause in the Trade Act of 1974, necessitated a year-by-year Congressional approval of trade relations. During the 1980s the volume of trade began to grow significantly after China adopted a market economy, albeit one in which the dictatorship exercised unquestioned control over it. Moreover, China became eager for membership in the WTO soon after it was established in 1995. Its representative on trade issues offered the United States a long list of concessions in 1999 in exchange for permanent normal trade relations with the United States and American support for China's admission to the WTO.

Eliminating the need for yearly renewal of trade relations with China would mean an end to any constraints on China's internal and external policies that were created by the need for yearly renewal. However, Clinton already had removed any considerations of human rights issues from the annual renewal process in 1994, due to dust-ups with the corporate rich and the power elite. His secretary of state had been "publicly rebuffed" while he was in China for asserting the need for such a linkage; a day after his return to Washington he was publicly criticized once again, this time by his former colleagues at the Council on Foreign Relations. They did so through their sponsorship of an "unprecedented public forum

490 Rise of an International Economic System

in which three former secretaries of state and numerous other notables attacked the linkage policy" (Destler 2005, p. 212). Clinton himself had earlier received sharp corporate criticism as well. In May 1993, the Business Coalition for U.S.-China Trade, consisting of 37 trade associations and 298 companies, including such international giants as Boeing and General Electric, sent Clinton a letter opposing such conditions on trade with China (Destler 2005, p. 211).

On the other hand, normal trade relations and Chinese membership in the WTO might provide further safeguards for foreign investment in China and further legal protection for intellectual property rights. (However, the Chinese government's respect for intellectual property rights remained minimal.) More certainly, normal trade relations would remove any corporate hesitation in off-shoring American corporate production to China, which was seen as a seemingly endless source of disciplined low-wage labor. Clinton's trade and foreign-policy advisers were for the change, but the president and his political advisers worried that it might not be the right time to approach Congress. His hesitations were reinforced by his main economic adviser, the former chair of Goldman Sachs, who by this point had been elevated to secretary of treasury. Clinton decided to wait, and even thought a better deal might be possible.

The corporate moderates were deeply disappointed by this possible delay because Europe had entered into normal trade relations with China several years before, and they did not want to lose out to their counterparts in Europe and Asia in the growing Chinese investment, labor, and consumer markets. Nor did they think the United States could gain anything by way of further concessions by waiting. They made their unhappiness known directly to Clinton, who soon found a way to resume the process after one or two face-saving maneuvers (Destler 2005, p. 275).

By the time Clinton introduced the necessary legislation in late November 1999, the liberal-labor alliance had gained the full support of leftist activists on union and environmental issues. These activists had picked up momentum after playing a part in thwarting further progress at the third annual meeting of the recently formed WTO, which was held in Seattle. Their marches and nonviolent blockades at entrances had blocked access to the meeting hall for many of the assembled national trade ministers, and the subsequent unexpected breaking of windows and setting fires in trash bins by anarchist activists had brought out the National Guard. To the degree that discussions could be held, a coalition of leaders from less developed countries made their displeasure known concerning labor and environmental regulations, which they felt might slow their own growth and possibly give marketing advantages to foreign multinationals in their own countries. In that regard, their concerns were more nearly the opposite of those expressed by the union and environmental activists at the heart of the street protests (Destler 2005, pp. 271–273; Yuen, Burton-Rose, and Katsiaficas 2001).

Still, the anti-globalization coalition's seeming success was significant for what it might portend in the future, so the new corporate coalition for trade normalization, USA★Engage, was taking nothing for granted. In fact, the chief lobbyist for the Chamber of Commerce told a newspaper reporter, shortly after the WTO fiasco, "Seattle happened with plenty of time for us to get that wake-up call" (Dreiling and Darves 2016, p. 225). USA★Engage hired two highly visible firms to carry out many of the needed lobbying tasks. One was a lobbying firm directed by the son of the renowned Speaker of House in the 1980s, Tip O'Neill, who was a key power actor in blocking the most draconian changes in the Social Security Act sought by the Reagan Administration, as recounted in Chapter 8. O'Neill's son also had once been an aide to Lloyd Bentsen, the multimillionaire former senator from Texas and the secretary of treasury in the first Clinton Administration, so he was a well-known and highly visible figure in his own right. The other lobbying firm hired by USA★Engage was the Chicago-Washington corporate law firm in which William M. Daley, the former White House director of the lobbying effort for NAFTA, and by this point the Secretary of Commerce, had been a partner. Based on a December 1999 report released by the Business Roundtable, USA★Engage focused its grassroots advertising and lobbying efforts on 71 House districts in which the representatives had not stated their support for permanent trade relations with China (Woodall, Wallach, Roach, and Burnham 2000, p. iii).

The full extent of these targeted pressures is chronicled in a detailed report by a public-interest watchdog group, Public Citizen (Woodall, Wallach, Roach, and Burnham 2000). The undecided representatives received visits by the USA★Engage state campaigns, which were aided once again by lobbying, public relations, and media specialists hired by the members of the Business Roundtable. They also received timely deliveries of PAC campaign donations, which at the least served as reminders that businesses are an important source of their financial support, and perhaps served as warnings that such donations could go to an opponent in the next election. For example, individual members of the Business Roundtable alone gave "$68.2 million in PAC, soft money and individual donations to Members of Congress and the Democratic and Republican parties between January 1999 and May 2000," the month in which the Congressional vote was held (Woodall, Wallach, Roach, and Burnham 2000, p. iii). Then too, some representatives claimed that they had been threatened in the business press with reprisals by named and unnamed sources (Dreiling and Darves 2016, pp. 292–293).

Although opinion polls showed that the general public opposed anything that might transfer jobs to China, the corporate moderates had a

492 Rise of an International Economic System

very strong factor working in their favor inside Congress, which mattered well beyond CEO visits and PAC donations in its importance. Those who voted against the measure would be risking the loss of established economic relationships if they did anything that would disrupt American involvement in China. In short, "there were clear and serious costs to rejection," and the members of Congress "were very much aware of this—and aware they would be blamed for any damage" (Destler 2005, p. 276). Liberals in Congress therefore looked for ways to vote for the measure by adding provisions that were consistent with their general political views.

Since the bill still seemed to be lacking majority support in early May, shortly before it would be officially introduced, the conservative Republicans in charge of key committees allowed Democrats to add a provision that would limit the size of any sudden surges in Chinese imports that might impact a specific business sector, and to establish a commission that would oversee and report on bilateral relations concerning human rights in a wide range of countries, with no specific mention of China (Destler 2005, p. 276). When the crucial vote was taken in the House in late May 2000, 73 Democrats joined 164 Republicans to provide a winning margin of 237-197.

Summary and Conclusions

Although there had been a very large international trading system in the several decades before 1914, little survived from it after World War I and the 1920s, except for some cautionary lessons. In addition, most nations were too destitute and/or inwardly turned to do much trading during the 1930s. Starting on September 12, 1939, however, the Council on Foreign Relations tried to make sure the setbacks experienced by internationally oriented businesses during the previous 25 years would not be repeated. Its members also wanted to ensure that this time around the United States would play the role expected of it by top leaders in the United Kingdom and Western Europe. In the long run, the corporate moderates fulfilled their goals, but it was a very long run due to the many successful rearguard actions by the ultraconservatives in the corporate community and the conservative coalition in Congress, which forced changes in plans and caused delays until the mid-1970s. But their success in the 1990s on NAFTA, the WTO, and permanent trade relations with China brought their plans to something very close to full fruition.

In the process of achieving their goals, the corporate moderates lost the support of the liberal-labor alliance because of the way they used the international economy to help them undercut unions, even while refusing to share much if any of the bountiful rewards of an international trading system with workers in general. Once again, that is, it is not only the massive size of the American multinationals, along with the counterparts they helped create in other countries, or the very large profits they make, that measures their enormous success. The low and stagnant wages for 85–90 percent of Americans, and the desolation in the cities that corporations abandoned throughout the country, starting in the late 1970s, also can be used as measures of their power (Autor, Dorn, and Hanson 2016; Autor, Katz, and Kearney 2008, for evidence of the havoc trade normalization with China created in numerous American cities). Their international trade victories also contributed to the growing wealth and income gaps. Put another way, the power of the corporate rich not only can be measured by how much they won. It also can be measured by who suffered the most from their decisions, namely, the 85–90 percent of Americans who are not owners, business executives, corporate lobbyists, famous entertainers, or professionals with advanced college degrees.

Focusing more specifically on the findings on the role of the Business Roundtable in the events that led to NAFTA, the WTO, and normal trade relations with China, they stand as a refutation of any claim that the "corporate elite" in general, or the Business Roundtable in particular, were too fractured and divided by the 1990s to be effective (Mizruchi 2013, pp, 252–255; Mizruchi 2017). The tight relationships among corporations, the policy-planning network, trade advisory committees, ACTPN, and the Office of the U.S. Trade Representative, as shown by both quantitative network studies and case studies, demonstrate that the Business Roundtable, the corporate community, and the power elite were far from fractured on trade issues in the 1990s, any more than they were fractured on union issues or government social benefits at that time.

References

Autor, David, David Dorn, and Gordon Hanson. 2016. "The China shock: Learning from labor-market adjustment to large changes in trade." *Annual Review of Economics* 8:205–240.

Autor, David, Lawrence Katz, and Melissa Kearney. 2008. "Trends in U.S. wage inequality: Revising the revisionists." *Review of Economics and Statistics* 90:300–323.

Biven, W. Carl. 2002. *Jimmy Carter's economy: Policy in an age of limits.* Chapel Hill: University of North Carolina Press.

Burn, Gary. 2006. *The re-emergence of global finance.* London: Palgrave Macmillan.

Cameron, Maxwell A. and Brian W. Tomlin. 2000. *The making of NAFTA: How the deal was done.* Ithaca: Cornell University Press.

CED. 1971. *The United States and the European Community: Policies for a changing world economy.* New York: Committee for Economic Development.

———. 1972a. *Report of activities in 1971.* New York: Committee for Economic Development.

———. 1972b. *U.S. foreign economic policy and the domestic economy.* New York: Committee for Economic Development.

494 Rise of an International Economic System

————. 1973. *Strengthening the world monetary system.* New York: Committee for Economic Development.

————. 1974a. *Toward a new international economic system: A joint Japanese-American view.* New York: Committee for Economic Development.

————. 1974b. *How the United States and Japan see each other's economy: An exchange of views between the American and Japanese committees for economic development.* Edited by I. Frank and R. Hirono. New York: Committee for Economic Development.

Chorev, Nitsan. 2007. *Remaking U.S. trade policy: From protectionism to globalization.* Ithaca: Cornell University Press.

Dahlberg, Robert. 1984. "Review of 'Closing the gold window: Domestic politics and the end of Bretton Woods'." *Political Science Quarterly* 99: 585–586.

Destler, I. M. 2005. *American trade politics.* New York: Columbia University Press.

Destler, I. M. and John Odel. 1987 *Anti-protection: Changing forces in United States trade politics.* Washington: Institute for International Economics.

Domhoff, G. W. 1998. *Who rules America? Power and politics in the year 2000.* Mountain View, CA: Mayfield Publishing Company.

————. 2014. *Who rules America? The triumph of the corporate rich.* New York: McGraw-Hill.

Dreiling, Michael. 2001. *Solidarity and contention: The politics of class and sustainability in the NAFTA conflict.* New York: Garland Press.

Dreiling, Michael and Derek Darves. 2016. *Agents of neoliberal globalization: Corporate networks, state structures and trade policy.* New York: Cambridge University Press.

Dryden. 1995. *The Trade Warriors: USTR and the American Crusade for free trade.*

Fourcade-Gourinchas, Marion and Sarah Babb. 2002. "The rebirth of the liberal creed: Paths to neoliberalism in four countries." *American Journal of Sociology* 108:533–579.

Gonzalez, George. 2001. *Corporate power and the environment: The political economy of U.S. environmental policy.* Lanham, MD: Rowman & Littlefield.

Gowa, Joanne. 1983. *Closing the gold window: Domestic politics and the end of Bretton Woods.* Ithaca: Cornell University Press.

Hoffman, Paul. 1973. *Lions in the street.* New York: Saturday Review Press.

Jenkins, Craig and Craig Eckert. 2000. "The right turn in economic policy: Business elites and the new conservative economics." *Sociological Forum* 15:307–338.

MacArthur, John R. 2000. *The selling of "free trade": NAFTA, Washington, and the subversion of American democracy.* New York: Hill and Wang.

Mann, Michael. 2013. *The sources of social power: Globalizations, 1945–2011,* Vol. 4. New York: Cambridge University Press.

Matusow, Allen. 1998. *Nixon's economy.* Lawrence: University Press of Kansas.

Mayer, Arno. 1981. *The persistence of the Old Regime.* New York: Pantheon.

Mayer, Frederick. 1998. *Interpreting NAFTA: The science and art of political analysis.* New York Columbia University Press.

McKee, Seth C. 2010. *Republican ascendency in Southern U.S. House elections.* Boulder: Westview Press.

Mitchell, Robert. 1991. "From conservation to environmental movement: The development of the modern environmental lobbies." Pp. 81–113 in *Governmental and environmental politics*, edited by M. Lacey. Baltimore: Johns Hopkins University Press.

Mizruchi, Mark. 2013. *The fracturing of the American corporate elite.* Cambridge: Harvard University Press.

———. 2017. "The Power Elite in historical context: A reevaluation of Mills's thesis, then and now." *Theory and Society* 46.

Robinson, Marshall. 1993. "The Ford Foundation: Sowing the seeds of a revolution." *Environment* 35:10–20.

Shoup, Laurence. 1980. *The Carter presidency, and beyond: Power and politics in the 1980s.* Palo Alto, CA: Ramparts Press.

Sklar, Holly and Robert Lawrence. 1981. *Who's who in the Reagan Administration.* Boston: South End.

Woodall, Patrick, Lori Wallach, Jessica Roach, and Katie Burnham. 2000. *Purchasing power: The corporate–White House alliance to pass the China trade bill over the will of the American people.* Washington: Public Citizen.

Yuen, Eddie, Daniel Burton-Rose, and George Katsiaficas. 2001. *The battle for Seattle.* New York: Soft Skull Press.

Zweigenhaft, Richard L. and G. William Domhoff. 2018. *Diversity in the power elite: Ironies and unfulfilled promises.* Lanham, MD: Rowman & Littlefield.

Part 4

Conclusions

The chapter in this final section brings together the findings and conclusions from the previous chapters to assess the accuracy and adequacy of the three theoretical perspectives favored by a strong majority of social scientists and historians in the first two decades of the twenty-first century—interest-group pluralism, organizational state theory, and historical institutionalism. As part of these assessments, the chapter also draws upon new findings and insights from outside the purview of the battle over unions, the creation of government social benefits, and the expansion of foreign trade.

In the case of interest-group pluralism, the chapter presents new information on the role of the policy-planning network in proposing new legislation, and governmental structures in relation to the environment, which are said by interest-group theorists to be the results of liberal efforts. It also shows that the same corporate-moderate foundations that funded think tanks and policy-discussion groups continued to provide significant financial backing for advocacy organizations that worked for the inclusion of previously excluded African Americans and recent immigrants. Contrary to the claims by the most visible interest-group theorist discussed in this chapter, this ongoing support included the advocacy groups these foundations helped create.

In regard to organizational state theory, the chapter points to the ways in which several of its findings support the claims in this book about the special-interest process, including the emphasis on class conflict. At the same time, however, the theory's advocates ignore the information that would have led them to the policy-planning network. They also inaccurately characterize the concept of a power elite as including labor leaders, which leads them to refute a straw man in claiming that the power elite was not involved in the issue-areas they studied.

Finally, the critique of historical institutionalism draws together several general findings that call its emphasis on the relative independence of the government into question. First presented are findings from a comparative analysis of changes in the electoral systems in several European countries and the United States in the late nineteenth and early twentieth centuries, based on a detailed reading of parliamentary and congressional debates. This study revealed that the somewhat different electoral systems in these countries were the product of class conflicts in which the balance of power between organized business and the newly forming working class varied considerably from country to country. Similarly, there were major changes in both the structure of government and the nature of the electoral systems at the local level in the United States in the same time period, due to the unrelenting and nationally coordinated efforts of locally oriented businesses, which were reacting to challenges by the rapidly growing urban labor force.

In addition, the critique of historical institutionalism also presents several new examples of how the power elite and the policy-planning network created new governmental structures at the national level throughout the twentieth century, over and beyond those already documented for the policy conflicts related to labor unions, social benefits, and trade expansion, including the Agricultural Adjustment Administration during the early New Deal, and the Office of Management and Budget during the Nixon Administration. The analysis of historical institutionalism then concludes by outlining the several mistakes its main advocates make in explaining the more conservative policy stances adopted by corporate moderates beginning in the late 1960s, which they wrongly date to the mid-1970s. Until 2016, they also mistakenly underestimated the role of increasing white resistance to the civil rights movement in making it possible for Republicans to win the presidency and implement the corporate moderates' new agenda.

The chapter closes with a synthesis of the conditions under which the liberal–labor alliance was able to win in the legislative arena despite the structural and historical obstacles it faced, and then draws together the reasons for its failures in situations in which it might have been more successful.

Chapter 15

The Shortcomings of Alternative Theories

Introduction

The detailed findings on the role of the corporate rich and the power elite in shaping three major government policies, and in many cases creating new government agencies and committees to carry out those policies, speak for themselves in terms of corporate domination throughout the twentieth century. In addition, the theory, methods, and findings in this book can provide a starting point for anyone wishing to examine corporate involvement in other policy matters that impacted the lives of large numbers of citizens during that century.

Then, too, the new or seldom-considered archival findings that provide the main basis for this book also can be used by those who are theoretically oriented to decide for themselves whether or not three theories of policy-making that had gained ascendancy in the social sciences by the end of the last century should be altered or abandoned. Those theories—interest-group pluralism, organizational state theory, and historical institutionalism—have differing origins and use different methods of inquiry, but they have come to be more similar than different. They also share the same vulnerabilities in relation to the archival findings presented in this book. Since many readers are very likely to be familiar with these three theories, they will be highlighted only briefly as a context for suggesting how the findings in this book raise numerous problems for each of them, and may add up to a refutation of all three.

Interest-Group Pluralism

There are several versions of pluralism, but they all conceive of power in the United States as divided and to varying degrees fluid, whether based on temporary coalitions that form anew on different issues, a wide range of voluntary associations, or competing interest groups rooted in stable shared concerns (such as business groups, unions, environmental groups, social-justice groups, and single-issue nonprofit advocacy groups).

Additionally, all versions of pluralism agree that there are constraints on corporate power due to the right to vote, along with the checks and balances built into the governmental structure at the nation's founding, which make it difficult for any one group or class to dominate. They also point to the lack of a large unifying business association to bring together the many different types of businesses, and the successes of non-business interest groups, such as labor unions from the 1930s to the 1980s, the consumer movement in the early 1970s, and environmentalists in the 1970s and thereafter (e.g., Berry 1997; Vogel 1989)

Most interest-group studies of policy-making only partially discuss one or more of the three issue-areas that are analyzed in this book, and usually have a shorter time frame. It is therefore more instructive to look at a study by political scientist Jeffrey Berry (1999, p. 9), which employs a standard interest-group approach based on 205 legislative cases that were salient in 1963, 1979, or 1991, because they had been discussed in a Congressional hearing and received "at least minimal coverage in the press." The study includes information on the role of corporations, foundations, and think tanks as well as labor unions and citizen groups, the latter of which are defined as groups that are not primarily concerned with the business or professional interests of their members (Berry 1999, p. 2). The main finding concerns the increasing importance of citizen groups during this time period, which include environmental, consumer, civil rights, and social-justice organizations along with a decline in union power. The emphasis is therefore on the rise of a "new liberalism" since the 1970s, with liberal citizen groups having considerable success in defeating conservative citizen groups on cultural issues involving the religious right.

Although the study does not link corporations, foundations, and think tanks in any conceptual way, corporations and "corporate-based foundations" (that is, foundations directly managed by corporation employees) are mentioned together at one point. The corporations have tried to "buy credibility" through their "generous donations" to prominent mainstream think tanks, which are characterized as being modeled after universities, albeit without any students, and as "centrist" and "nonideological" (Berry 1999, pp. 137, 140). Moreover, several prominent family foundations, led by the Ford Foundation, had a major role in funding some of the new citizen groups focused on environmental or social-justice issues at their outset.

In addition to overlooking the more basic and long-term reasons for the links among corporations, foundations, and think tanks, the study goes astray in claiming that foundation funding for citizen groups declined in importance as these organizations established their own funding sources through fund-raising drives and membership dues. In fact, most of these liberal citizen groups, including advocacy groups for low-income communities of color, were very dependent on mainstream foundation money

The Shortcomings of Alternative Theories 501

from the 1960s to the end of the century, as determined by consulting widely available annual volumes, the *Foundation Grants Directory*, compiled by the foundation-financed Foundation Center (https://foundationcenter. org). In 1994–1995, for example, the Ford Foundation gave $3.2 million to the National Council of La Raza and $695,000 to the Mexican-American Legal Defense and Education Fund (MALDEF); in that same two-year period, the Ford Foundation gave $600,000 to the National Resources Defense Council, which also received grants from 52 other foundations as well (Domhoff 1998, p. 132, Table 4.2, and p. 133). There are numerous other examples of continuing mainstream foundation funding for citizen groups that could be provided, all of which can be explained in terms of a moderate conservatism that prefers accommodation and gradual change to confrontation and repression (e.g., Domhoff 2009).

The consumer movement that developed out of the activism of the civil rights and anti-war movements of the 1960s is held out in this and other interest-group studies as evidence for the success of citizen groups, based on the several consumer protection laws enacted between 1967 and 1974 (e.g., Berry 1999, pp. 43–44, 72; Vogel 1989, Chapters 3–5). However, the relevant business groups either agreed with the legislation or forced modifications to make it acceptable (Domhoff 1990, pp. 272–273). The most important exception is the automobile industry's objections to the National Traffic and Motor Vehicle Safety Act, an effort to force car manufacturers to make safer automobiles (Luger 2000).

In addition, the weaknesses of the consumer movement were exposed by 1978 when it could not win enactment for its cautious plan for an Agency for Consumer Advocacy, due to the efforts of the Business Roundtable and its allies, who worked with the conservative coalition to stop the legislation (Akard 1992; Schwartz 1979). The consumer movement also failed in its legislative efforts to increase corporate responsibility. Congress refused to consider the idea of federal charters for corporations, which allowed them to continue to incorporate in states with very weak laws governing corporations. Plans to increase shareholder rights and strengthen the laws on corporate crime were rejected. Several new initiatives at the Federal Trade Commission led to a strong reaction by Congress when it received complaints from the car dealers, funeral directors, and other business groups that would be regulated. The ultraconservatives tried to abolish the Federal Trade Commission entirely, but it was saved with the help of corporate moderates, who believed it still had some uses (Pertschuk 1982).

All environmental groups are counted as part of the new liberalism, but the key groups with regard to the formulation of environmental policy, some of them founded well before the 1960s by corporate moderates as part of the longstanding conservation movement, were funded by large foundations and are part of the policy-planning network (Domhoff 1998, pp. 132–133, 264–265; Gonzalez 2001; Mitchell 1991; Robinson 1993).

As noted in Chapter 14, these groups were integral during the Nixon Administration in creating and staffing the Council on Environmental Quality in the White House and the Environmental Protection Agency as a government agency (Mitchell 1991; Robinson 1993), and their ideas were incorporated into the successful effort to pass NAFTA by the Clinton Administration, as also discussed in Chapter 14 (Destler 2005, p. 202; Mayer 1998, p. 291). Environmental groups that were more liberal than the mainstream environmental groups had great success in sensitizing public opinion on environmental issues, creating watchdog groups whose reports received attention in the mass media, and developing new ideas and technologies for controlling some forms of pollution, which were grudgingly accepted by the corporate community in some instances. But after 1975 they were not able to pass any legislation opposed by the Business Roundtable.

Berry's *The New Liberalism* (1999) claims the reasons for labor's decline are varied. Most purportedly have to do with societal changes, such as the rise in affluence and the transition to a service economy. Some of the problem allegedly lies with workers themselves. Service workers are said to have a "greater reluctance" to join unions than workers in the manufacturing sector, and "many workers just do not believe that what unions will gain for them will outweigh dues that must be paid" (Berry 1999, p. 157). "Finally," the analysis concludes, "more aggressive antiunion efforts by business have also contributed to this trend" (Berry 1999, p. 157).

As the chapters in Part 1 demonstrate, it is far more likely that the unrelenting successful efforts by the corporate rich and the Southern plantation owners to chip away at union expansion and power were far and away the major reason for unions' decline. This historical analysis is supported by comparisons with Western Europe, where service workers joined unions, and with Canada, where the labor laws were stronger and more likely to be enforced (Freeman and Medoff 1984; Warner 2013). The claims about Canada are further supported by the fact that there was a gradual, but relatively small decline in unionization in Canada between 1977 and 2000, after six provinces mandated certification elections in several different years to replace the card-check method. This change gave Canadian employers the opportunity to deploy the same delaying tactics used in the United States (Riddell 2004; Riddell 2001; Warner 2013, pp. 117–119 for a summary). In the early 1990s, an increasing percentage of American workers expressed an interest in joining a union, which refutes any claims that workers had lost interest in unions (Freeman 2007).

Generally speaking, the bulk of the evidence presented in studies focused on the late twentieth century shows that business-based interest groups usually won in Congress on issues of concern to them, as had been the case in earlier studies ranging from obtaining family and corporate tax breaks to lobbying Congress on many issues, and thwarting or capturing regulatory agencies (Domhoff 1979, Chapter 2, for an overview of interest-group findings through the mid-1970s; Page and Gilens 2018, Chapter 5 for the early 1980s to early 2000s). These findings are consistent with a corporate-dominance theory at the level of the special-interest process. On the other hand, interest-group theories are not able to explain the major policy issues such as those discussed in this book, and seldom try to do so. In this regard, the discussion of the decline of organized labor in *The New Liberalism* (Berry, 1999, p 157) is highly indicative.

However, analyses of the victories for liberal citizen groups in the last 35 years of the twentieth century did affirm that the liberal and left activists that came of age in the 1960s were able to help expand opportunities and gain individual freedoms for many previously excluded individuals on non-business issues, and to enjoy some small specific successes on consumer, environmental, and health issues. They were also able to defend most of these gains through the rest of the century despite the efforts of ultraconservative foundations, think tanks, and advocacy groups, none of which had more than one or two links to the moderate conservatives through corporations or the policy-planning network.

Organizational State Views on Policy-Making

Organizational state theorists claim that organized private groups have a major impact on government by hiring professional lobbyists who are knowledgeable about the specific issues of concern to them. Their view is "pluralistic" in its emphasis on separate policy domains and competing groups that are able to influence government, but it stresses that there are usually powerful organizations behind these separate efforts, such as corporations, farm organizations, unions, and organized medicine (Heinz, Laumann, Nelson, and Salisbury 1993; Laumann and Knoke 1987). Their study of the main power actors and their success in the "policy domains" of agricultural, energy, health, and labor policy in the early 1980s was based on a three-step process. They first developed a sample of highly active business, trade association, union, and nonprofit organizations, whose spokespersons were then asked to identify the representatives and lobbyists they employed. In turn, the representatives and lobbyists were asked to name the five government officials or staff members they most frequently contacted. Both the organizational representatives and the government employees were interviewed and also asked to fill out various questionnaires inquiring about their actions, and their perceived degree of success on the issues in which they were involved (Heinz, Laumann, Nelson, and Salisbury 1993, pp. 17–21).

Conservatives claimed to be successful more often than liberals did, although liberals felt they were successful on some issues as well (Heinz, Laumann, Nelson, and Salisbury 1993, pp. 345, 409–410). However, self-reported

504 Conclusions

success on the five issues of the most concern to them is a very questionable measure of actual power outcomes. Furthermore, for the 94 success ratings (out of 442) on which they had ratings from two representatives, "the assessments of success differ substantially" (Heinz, Laumann, Nelson, and Salisbury 1993, p. 352). This weak indicator of power is clearly not very reliable. The serious weaknesses of their power indicator to one side, their research led to two findings that are very likely accurate.

First, representatives of trade associations were in one camp, and the representatives and employees of liberal and/or labor organizations tended to be in another on all four issues. Second, they report there is no distinct boundary between those employed by interest groups and government officials in terms of their career backgrounds. Forty-six percent of the representatives and lobbyists for interest groups had worked for the federal government at one point or another in their careers, and another 9 percent had worked in government at the state or local levels, which is consistent with earlier studies (Heinz, Laumann, Nelson, and Salisbury 1993, pp. 116–118).

As for the top-level government officials with whom the interest-group representatives interacted most frequently, they were mostly "in and outers" in terms of having careers both inside and outside of government (Heinz, Laumann, Nelson, and Salisbury 1993, p. 221). Even in the case of the "mid-level" officials, who constituted half of the government officials interviewed and surveyed, only one-third were "career officials with civil service status and substantial tenure in the federal government" (Heinz, Laumann, Nelson, and Salisbury 1993, p. 221). In the conclusion to the chapter on government officials, the researchers stress the similarity of government officials' careers to those of the interest-group representatives: "A substantial number in each set have served at one time or another on the other side of the relationship, and it is therefore not surprising that they have many things in common" (Heinz, Laumann, Nelson, and Salisbury 1993, p. 243). For this and other reasons, the authors conclude that any claims of government independence are not tenable for the United States because "both the power of private interests and the authority of the government agencies appeared to be relatively dispersed overall, and the outcome would probably be more accurately characterized as pluralist" (Heinz, Laumann, Nelson, and Salisbury 1993, pp. 395–396).

Based on their findings, they also reject the Millsian conception of the power elite because "we ought to find some of our notables functioning as go-betweens or brokers," but instead there is an empty space at the center of their networks (Heinz, Laumann, Nelson, and Salisbury 1993, p. 299). They therefore entitled their book *The Hollow Core* to emphasize their alleged refutation of the concept of a power elite (Heinz, Laumann, Nelson, and Salisbury 1993, pp. xvi, 299). In doing so, however, they wrongly think that Mills portrayed corporate lawyers and investment bankers as

The Shortcomings of Alternative Theories   505

playing an integrative role between corporations and labor organizations. Mills (1956, p. 289) actually said that corporate lawyers and investment bankers were "almost professional go-betweens of economic, political, and military affairs, and who thus act to unify the power elite," which does not include union leaders.

Organizational state theorists also reject any implication of general corporate domination, quoting with approval from an earlier, now-classic book concluding that many "largely autonomous elites" had gained control of the aspects of government of concern to them, but did not "rule" in the sense of "commanding the entire nation" (McConnell 1966, p. 339). Organizational state theorists agree with this claim because (1) no one set of closely knit organizations seems to control all of the specific policy domains, and (2) some of the most important policy issues, such as the functioning of the national economy and decision-making on national defense, are outside the purview of any of the specific policy domains (Heinz, Laumann, Nelson, and Salisbury 1993, pp. 304–305; McConnell 1966, pp. 339–340).

However, these claims are called into question by the fact that the organizational state theorists did not study the networks among the corporate rich themselves, but only the links created by the trade association leaders and lobbyists employed by the corporate rich. If they had harkened back to the interview study in the 1950s that is similar to theirs, by sociologist Floyd Hunter (1959), they would have seen that the leaders of large corporations knew each other well and often interacted in subsets on policy issues, such as in the case of lowering tariffs during the 1950s, as discussed in Chapter 13, and were often involved in organizations such as the Committee for Economic Development.

Moreover, if the organizational state theorists had examined the relevant network analyses available at the time they wrote, they would have found evidence for the close relationships among the corporate rich, corporations, and the network of foundations, think tanks, and policy-discussion groups that comprise the policy-planning network (Bonacich and Domhoff 1981; Burris 1992; Domhoff 1975; Eitzen, Jung, and Purdy 1982; Salzman and Domhoff 1983). If they had built on these analyses and traced the government connections of those who created links between corporations and the organizations in the policy-planning network, it would have led them to the Congressional testimony, federal advisory committees, presidential commissions, and cabinet appointments through which members of the policy-planning network impact government on the general issues that organizational state theorists wrongly think are the exclusive purview of government officials.

Subsequent network analyses of the links among corporations, the leaders of policy-discussion groups, and government committees and agencies relating to trade expansion, as discussed in Chapter 14, are in effect a refutation of the claims by the organizational state theorists concerning both the power elite and corporate domination (Dreiling 2001, pp. 95. 99, 129; Dreiling and Darves 2016, Chapter 6). In particular, this work not only replicated the close relationship between major corporations and the Business Roundtable found in other studies, but it demonstrated for the first time that corporations affiliated with the Business Roundtable were far more likely to serve on trade advisory committees than would be expected by chance. More generally, this network analysis, combined with case-study information, demonstrates that the corporate rich and the power elite, working primarily through the Business Roundtable and the wide-ranging advocacy groups it sponsored on each trade-expansion issue, were completely successful in reaching their major policy objectives on trade expansion in the 1990s.

Organizational state theory is useful in demonstrating once again that the boundaries between private interests and government are not very distinct or strong in the United States. It provides a good demonstration of the role of the special-interest network that is one part of the corporate-domination theory presented in this book. It also reveals there is conflict on a wide range of special-interest issues between the corporate community and the liberal-labor alliance, which is consistent with the class-conflict perspective that is one aspect of the theory presented in this book.

Historical Institutionalism

The third theory, historical institutionalism, stresses the persistence of the routine, institutionalized ways that are established to carry out one or another general task. Routinization soon leads to established sets of organizations in large-scale societies, which have specific goals and take each other's actions and likely reactions into account when they contemplate any changes in their own strategies for stability or expansion. Historical institutionalists also claim that the institutional structure of a government—for example, whether it is parliamentary or presidential, centralized or decentralized—has an important role in shaping party systems. They stress that the political strategies used by non-state institutions are an attempt to adapt to governmental structures, which is necessary if they are going to be successful in realizing their goals (e.g., Campbell and Pedersen 2001; Pierson and Skocpol 2007; Skocpol 1980; Skocpol 1985).

Based on comparative studies of the several industrialized democracies in Western Europe and the two in North America, the most distinctive feature of historical institutionalism at its outset was the degree of independence it accorded to governments, including the American government (e.g., Skocpol 1980). However, the most visible version of the theory was altered to some extent in the 1990s on the basis of studies of key issues during the Progressive Era. The success of organized activist women in shaping meaningful legislation, even though they did not have the right to vote, seemed especially relevant (Skocpol 1992). The new findings led to a "polity-centered approach," which stresses that the lack of strong government bureaucracies and an established church in the United States provided an opening for social movements, voluntary coalitions, pressure groups, and political parties to have an impact (Skocpol 1992, pp. x, 529). The theory's emphasis then turned to the need to create "broad, trans-partisan coalitions of groups—and ultimately legislators" that have to be "assembled for each particular issue" (Skocpol 1992, p. 368). This polity-centered approach has much in common with pluralism, although it puts more emphasis on the seeming independence of political institutions and the structured nature of the political process.

Even with the change to a policy-centered approach, historical institutionalists still overstate both the independence and the state-building capacity of the American government for two reasons. To begin with, they have underestimated the degree to which the electoral systems in both Western Europe and the United States were shaped by business leaders and landlords in their successful attempts to contain the potential political power of the working class in the second half of the nineteenth century. This point is demonstrated in a detailed comparative study of the records of legislative debates in Belgium, the United Kingdom, Norway, Sweden, and the United States (Ahmed 2013a; Ahmed 2013b). For example, this rapidly escalating conflict caused the business owners and the landlords in Belgium, Norway, and Sweden to adopt a system of proportional representation to insure that they retained at least some participation in the government. In the case of the United Kingdom, the Conservative and Liberal parties thought they could constrain parties emanating from the labor movement in the 1880s by relying on a system based on specific geographical districts using a plurality vote. Their judgment proved to be correct from 1884 to the 1920s, but then the surging Labour Party gained more adherents and reduced the Liberal Party to a minor third party.

These comparative results may seem at first glance to have nothing to do with the United States, which had a territorially based, single-member-district plurality system for the House of Representatives and the Senate from its founding. But, during the 1830s, ten of the 26 states—mostly smaller states in both the North and South—were using statewide elections to fill all their House seats in an attempt to gain more legislative power for their business or plantation leaders, a strategy that was made possible by the fact that the Constitution left it to the states to decide how they would elect members to the House. These problems were compounded by the formation of workingmen's parties between 1828 and the early 1830s. Although they were all focused on the local level, they quickly split into factions, and were short-lived (Ahmed 2013a, pp. 92–94; Laurie 1989,

508 Conclusions

pp. 80–83). Claiming in part that they feared increasing worker involvement in politics, conservative members of both the Whigs and the Democrats narrowly passed Congressional legislation in 1842 that reaffirmed the need to elect just one representative from a specific district for each House seat allotted to a state.

This issue, and sustained union agitation beyond the local level, declined in the 1840s and 1850s in the face of the rising divisions over slavery. But the possibility of electoral changes was raised again in the late 1870s due to the growth of the Greenback-Labor Party, an anti-corporate farmer-labor alliance, which won 13 of the 293 seats in the House in 1878. A small group of worried congressional conservatives thought that proportional representation might be necessary, but the collapse of the Greenback-Labor Party soon thereafter, due to mutual suspicions between its farmer and labor wings, ended any discussion of changing the electoral rules (Ahmed 2013a, p. 100). At that point the leaders of the two established parties decided they could contain any potential threats that might develop from a coalition of African Americans and low-income white farmers in the South, or a unified effort by the fast-growing working class in the North, with two simple but effective exclusionary strategies: manipulating the boundaries of House districts ("gerrymandering") and by engaging in various types of voter suppression, including literacy tests in the South (Kousser 1974) and poll taxes in both the North and South (Ahmed 2013a, pp. 102–104; Keyssar 2009, Chapter 5).

The idea that business leaders in the North were as concerned with exclusionary electoral structures as their counterparts in Europe is further and even more convincingly demonstrated by their successful attempts to make changes in both the electoral and legislative systems at the local level in the face of challenges that began in the 1870s and 1880s with rapid urbanization and an increasing number of immigrant workers. In the early twentieth century, a further threat to local growth coalitions arose from the newly formed Socialist Party, which elected 1,200 members in 340 cities across the country in 1912, including 79 mayors in 24 different states (Weinstein 1967, pp. 93–118).

The late-nineteenth century challenges at the local level led to the formation of an urban policy-planning group, the National Municipal League, at a meeting in 1894, which included 150 city developers, lawyers, political scientists, and urban planners from 21 cities in 13 states (Stewart 1950). It gradually developed a number of potential changes in electoral rules, each of which lowered voter turnout and made it more difficult for Democrats and Socialists to win elections (Alford and Lee 1968). These changes included off-year elections, allegedly needed because city issues were different; nonpartisan elections, which were said to be necessary because the citizens of a community have common interests that should not be overshadowed by partisan politics; and citywide elections, supposedly necessary because the problems facing members of a city council involve the city as a whole and not separate neighborhoods. They also advocated for smaller city councils and a new form of local government in which mayors would have less power and the city agencies would be managed by city managers (Domhoff 1978, pp. 162–163, for a more detailed overview).

Successes came slowly at first, but by 1919 one or more of these changes had been implemented in 130 cities, and local business leaders continued to make gains in the next several decades (e.g., Schiesl 1977). By 1991, 75 percent of American cities had nonpartisan elections and 59 percent used citywide elections. The successful efforts to reject the package of changes came from large cities with strong Democratic Party organizations (Renner and DeSantis 1994). These findings provide good evidence that the electoral and legislative structures in any given country, including the United States, cannot be taken as unproblematic evidence for the power of government officials. The electoral systems of the twentieth century have to be understood as "strategies of containment" devised by the land-owners and business owners of the nineteenth century, including in the United States at the local level, which appear to be nearly the opposite of what historical institutionalism might expect (Ahmed 2013b, Chapter 2).

Second, the historical institutionalists' emphasis on the way in which the American government is structured as an independent factor in the power equation completely overlooks the extent to which new additions to the government throughout the twentieth century were due to the state-building efforts by the corporate rich and the power elite. In addition to the many instances that are discussed at length in this book in relation to unions, social-insurance programs, and trade expansion, here it can be recalled that the National Civic Federation played a large role in the creation of the Federal Trade Commission (Weinstein 1968, Chapter 3), and add the fact that the Bureau of the Budget, established shortly after World War I, was in good part the work of organizations in the nascent policy-planning network (Kahn 1997). So, too, the Bureau of the Budget was expanded into an Office of Management and Budget in the late 1960s, with the help of a report by the CED, a presidential task force, and a presidential commission, all dominated by corporate executives. Both of these presidential advisory groups were chaired by members of the CED, the first during the Johnson Administration, the second during the Nixon Administration (Berman 1979, pp. 74, 85–90 and Chapter 5; CED 1966; Tomkin 1998, pp. 44–52).

The evidence that the corporate rich contributed to state-building through the efforts of the policy-planning network also includes one of the major new government agencies established very early in the New Deal, the Agricultural Adjustment Administration. This instance, which was one consequence of the Act mentioned in passing in Chapter 1, is of special interest because historical institutionalists claimed that it was primarily the result of work by agricultural economists within the Department of Agriculture, who were working from a "public interest" perspective (Finegold and Skocpol 1995, p. 61). (The main role of the agency was to provide subsidy payments to cotton, tobacco, and rice planters in the South, and wheat and corn-hog farmers in the Midwest, in exchange for limiting their planted acreage in order to reduce oversupply and thereby raise prices.)

Contrary to the historical institutionalists' account, based on limited sources, the archival record makes clear that the original idea for the domestic allotment program came from the president of the Laura Spelman Rockefeller Memorial Fund, who asked the Agricultural Committee of the Social Science Research Council (SSRC) to examine it more closely. This request in turn led to a detailed statement of the allotment plan by a Harvard agricultural economist who was a member of the committee (e.g., Black 1928; Black 1929a; Black 1929b; Domhoff and Webber 2011, Chapter 2, for a very detailed account). From there the plan was passed along to the president of the Chamber of Commerce for examination by one of its committees, where it met with approval. After further improvement by an agricultural economist who had worked in the policy-planning network as well as government, the Memorial Fund president put the plan in the hands of an agricultural economist who was an adviser to future President Franklin D. Roosevelt during the election campaign. Thus, the fact that an agricultural economist employed by the government's small Bureau of Agricultural Economics suggested something similar about the same time as the president of the Memorial Fund was advocating his plan is beside the point because his efforts did not lead to a proposal that made it to the policy agenda. Furthermore, the agricultural economist from Harvard hired by the Memorial Fund to flesh out the plan later incorporated the government employee's ideas into the new plan, and then asked him to provide comments on the overall plan (Domhoff and Webber 2011, pp. 94–96).

Once the plan was accepted by the Southern plantation owners, and the leaders of the American Farm Bureau Federation more generally, albeit after they made major revisions to make it even more beneficial to themselves, it moved through the Congress very quickly (Saloutos 1982, pp. 254, 259, 281). Although historical institutionalists stress the importance of experts already employed by the Department of Agriculture in implementing the plan, six of the top nine leaders of the Agricultural Adjustment Administration were employees of farm organizations, and only one of the three academic experts in a top position had been with the government for any length of time (Saloutos 1982, Chapter 5).

Similarly, historical institutionalists claimed that the National Labor Relations Board was created by government bureaucrats working for the original National Labor Board, in conjunction with liberal legislators. Although they ignore the role of Business Advisory Council members in

The Shortcomings of Alternative Theories   511

suggesting and serving on the original National Labor Board, as discovered by historian Kim McQuaid (1979) years before they wrote their account, the authors were partially on the right track in emphasizing the importance of "the urban liberals within the Democratic majority in 1935" in the passage of the act. At the same time, they completely ignore the veto power of the Southern Democrats and do not mention the importance of the exclusion of agricultural workers from the purview of the act until a later chapter (Finegold and Skocpol 1995, p. 138).

In terms of their claim of a temporary ascendancy for liberals as leading to the passage of the act, they later add a slight qualification: "Even during the liberal 'Second' New Deal (1935–1938), southern cotton planters were able to get their workers excluded from the Wagner Act, the Social Security Act, and the Wages and Hours Act" (Finegold and Skocpol 1995, p. 194). But there was no liberal ascendancy, however temporary, because of the continuing control the Southern Democrats had over general leadership positions and many key government committees in the 1935–1936 Congressional session. They therefore had far more general power in their dealings with President Roosevelt than the historical institutionalists' conventional "majority rules" viewpoint implies. Their emphasis on a non–Southern Democratic, urban-liberal majority within Congress, while at the same time ignoring the important support from Progressive Republicans, undercuts the accuracy and usefulness of their otherwise insightful account. The Progressive Republicans from the Midwest and West might have sided with the Southern Democrats in filibustering labor legislation if it had included agricultural labor within its purview.

Historical institutionalists also make empirical mistakes in claiming that the Social Security Act was created by government officials, independent experts, liberal political leaders, and pressures from social movements (e.g., Amenta 1998; Hacker and Pierson 2002; Orloff 1993; Skocpol and Ikenberry 1983; Weir, Orloff, and Skocpol 1988). They claim that the act was the product of a long historical experience with government pensions, and most importantly with pensions for the veterans who fought in the Civil War. However, as Chapter 6 of this volume mentions, most of those veterans and their widows had passed away by 1920 at the latest (Domhoff 1996, pp. 234–236 for a more detailed critique on this issue). Instead, as shown in Chapter 6, it was insurance companies, the Carnegie Institute for the Advancement of Teaching, and several large corporations that took the steps leading to the act, as later expanded and refined by experts working for Industrial Relations Counselors at the beginning of the New Deal.

The historical institutionalists conclude that the few corporate leaders who supported the act were marginal within the corporate community and not always central to the policy-formation process in regard to Social Security (e.g., Orloff 1993, pp. 288–289; Skocpol 1987). But that assertion is refuted by archival records demonstrating that the president of Standard Oil of New Jersey and other top corporate leaders had major roles, and were kept well informed by one of the top experts on social insurance employed by Industrial Relations Counselors, Inc. (IRC), and by reports from the Special Conference Committee and periodic IRC Memorandums. Similarly, it was an IRC Memorandum dated February 1, 1935, that explained to the president of Standard Oil of New Jersey and many other corporate executives why it would make sense to view their private pension plans as a supplement (primarily for executives, of course) to a government old-age insurance program. Based on this IRC Memorandum, it is evident that the ideas for the country's "divided welfare state" appeared much earlier and from a very different source than is asserted by historical institutionalists (e.g., Hacker 2002).

More generally, the historical institutionalists claim that the experts involved in the creation of the Social Security Act, including those employed by the IRC, were independent. One pair of historical institutionalists wrote that "by the early 1930s, IRC was a self-supporting industrial relations consulting firm," independent of the Rockefeller orbit (Orloff and Parker 1990, p. 306). Another said that the drafters of the Social Security Act were "social workers, scholars, private economists, actuaries, and the like," who were "not reliable allies of capital"; J. Douglas Brown, who wrote reports for the IRC, is characterized only as a professor at Princeton, and Murray Latimer, an employee of the IRC even while in government service, is identified as an employee of the government's Railroad Retirement Board (Amenta 1998, pp. 97, 117, 304)).

Several of the historical institutionalists who have written about the New Deal regard the Clark Amendment as evidence that business opposed the Social Security Act, and lost (e.g., Amenta 1998, pp. 118–119; Hacker 2002, p. 101; Orloff 1993, p. 293). Their best evidence consists of a list of 145 corporations that the insurance agent who was the strongest advocate for the amendment put together for lobbying purposes. (It was later obtained by the SSRC's Committee on Social Security for possible use as part of its effort to defeat the Clark Amendment (Hacker and Pierson 2002, pp. 302, 321 ftn. 80).) This evidence does not have the weight of the survey findings by the SSRC that few corporations or insurance companies supported the substance of the amendment as it was passed by Congress. Moreover, the evidence that the IRC experts opposed the Clark Amendment is far more formidable than a lobbyist's list that could have been used as a self-serving selling point in talking with members of Congress.

Finally, several historical institutionalists wrongly insist that any corporate support for the Social Security Act was due to a fear of the Townsend Plan as a far more undesirable option that might pass (e.g., Hacker and Pierson 2002; Weir, Orloff, and Skocpol 1988). The unlikely nature of the

The Shortcomings of Alternative Theories   513

Townsend Plan and the strong vote against it by Congress in the spring of 1935, as reported in many past accounts of the Social Security Act, always made this conclusion extremely unlikely, but in any case it was completely refuted in every detail on the basis of careful archival work by sociologist Edwin Amenta (2006), which was discussed in Chapter 6.

Overall, the extensive state-building by the corporate rich, the power elite, and the policy-planning network throughout the twentieth century, from the Federal Trade Commission to the Agricultural Adjustment Administration to the Office of the Special Trade Representative, seems once again to be very different from what historical institutionalism would expect due to its emphasis on government officials as the state-builders.

The Turn to More Conservative Policies on Labor and Social Insurance

Historical institutionalists also have an inadequate analysis of the ultraconservative turn in government policy, which they incorrectly locate in the second half of the 1970s (Hacker and Pierson 2010, pp. 58–58, 127–130). In their view, the right turn began with a new corporate mobilization, epitomized by the founding of the Business Roundtable in 1972, which they describe as the equivalent of a "domestic version of Shock and Awe" in terms of its impact (Hacker and Pierson 2010, p. 118). Tired of being defeated and shoved around, this account continues, the corporate leaders then created a more united, active, and sophisticated lobbying effort with which they could "flood Washington with letters and phone calls" (Hacker and Pierson 2010, p. 121). The result was a level of pressure on Congress that allegedly had not been applied before, although they present no comparative evidence in relation to the battles over the National Labor Relations Act in 1935, the Marshall Plan in 1947, or the Taft-Hartley Act in 1948. As further evidence for their assertion of corporate weakness in the 1960s and early 1970s, they focus on the increases in government spending between 1964 and 1977, which corporate leaders allegedly opposed (Hacker and Pierson 2010, p. 96).

In making their analysis, historical institutionalists overlook or ignore the evidence that the corporate community was already well organized in the 1950s and 1960s by the overlapping members of the Business Council, the Committee for Economic Development, and the Construction Users Anti-Inflation Roundtable. Their account of the origins of the Business Roundtable reveals that they do not understand that its primary concern was the strong collective-bargaining position organized labor had gained during the turmoil in the 1960s, as shown in Chapter 2 through the use of original archival work by Gross (1995, pp. 234–239) and Linder (1999, Chapter 7), not due to a concern with regulatory agencies or enlarged budgets in the early 1970s.

Nor do historical institutionalists recognize that corporate moderates were by then supportive of increased domestic spending in the face of the civil rights movement, rising tensions in the inner cities, and the turmoil generated by the anti-war movement, as seen most clearly in the policy statements and lobbying coalitions put together by the Committee for Economic Development at the time, and as documented in Chapter 8. These efforts by corporate moderates, carried out at the same time that they were working very hard to limit union power, demonstrate that increased government budgets cannot be assumed to be evidence for the power of liberals or the government, as many historical institutionalists do, without understanding the constellation of forces that were for and against those budgets. It is also evident that by the mid-1970s the corporate moderates had switched their emphasis to the earned income tax credit and the expansion of food stamps, neither of which interfered with labor markets or was very costly to them.

Also contrary to the historical institutionalists' conclusions about the right turn beginning in the second half of the 1970s, the liberal-labor alliance did in fact began to splinter over racial integration and how to deal with disruption in large Northern cities between 1961 and 1968. From 1968 on, facing an enlarged conservative coalition and a revived ultra-conservative grassroots movement, organized labor went downhill as a legislative and lobbying force, even though many large unions in construction and heavy industry continued to win wage gains during the 1970s. The historical institutionalists therefore overlook the central role of white resistance to the civil rights movement's push for the integration of neighborhoods, schools, and jobs, which brought the Republicans to power in 1968 and made possible the right turn that the corporate moderates wanted to take at that point for their own separate reasons (which, recall, concerned rising foreign competition, accelerating inflation, and the increasing bargaining power of unions in the context of a very tight labor market) (Hacker and Pierson 2010).

Six years later, the two historical institutionalists cited at the end of the previous paragraph, Jacob Hacker and Paul Pierson (2016), had altered their views to some extent. By then they agreed that the Committee for Economic Development had a major role in the postwar era as an "unusual hybrid" of "establishment figures, heavily weighted toward prominent members of the business community," as well as a "proto-think tank with a major role for academics"; however, they then went overboard by incorrectly asserting that the CED "accepted the role of unions..." (Hacker and Pierson 2016, pp. 141–142). Based on "several recent sophisticated studies," and "careful analyses by political scientists," they now agree with the general consensus, based on many past studies, that "race is a major ingredient in the GOP's antigovernment cocktail" (Hacker and Pierson 2016, pp. 250–251). In the final chapter they make a cheerful political argument for the revival of a "positive-sum society," which is neither here nor there as far as a power analysis is concerned. Nevertheless, their earlier chapters can be usefully read as evidence that historical institutionalists are catching up with the past by citing more recent studies that support earlier analyses they overlooked.

Conclusion

As this chapter demonstrates, theorizing in terms of the corporate community, the power elite, and the policy-planning network explains far more about policy-making in the United States in the twentieth century than pluralism, organizational state theory, or historical institutionalism. When the policy-planning capabilities available to the corporate community and the power elite are combined with the significant independent power possessed by the Southern rich, who could modify or block corporate moderates' state-building proposals by backing the conservative coalition, then the theory presented in this book can explain much of what needs to be explained in terms of how and why some legislation was passed, how and why some new government agencies and committees were created, and how and why most liberal-labor legislation opposed by the power elite was defeated in the twentieth century.

The theory also explains when the liberal-labor alliance could be successful, despite being constrained from its outset by the impossibility of creating a non-divisive third party in the American electoral context. To win on any issue, it usually had to have at least the tacit support of the controlling faction within the Democratic Party, namely, the Southern rich, often through liberal-labor support for the spending coalition in Congress, which invariably generated special benefits for the South as well. The theory also can explain why the liberal-labor alliance gradually lost the power it gained through the passage of the National Labor Relations Act and the need for government support of workers and their unions during World War II and the Korean War. Although this decline was halting and modest in the late 1950s and early 1960s, the eventual fate of private-sector unions was in good part sealed once the entire corporate community and the Southern rich became united as early as 1938–1939 by their determination to destroy unions, although that fact could not have been known until the full sweep of the archival and union-density record became available many decades later.

Even then, the corporate rich and the Southern rich might not have succeeded so soon and so completely in expanding their strong anti-union base in 11 of the 17 former slave-and-caste states, five Great Plains states, four Rocky Mountain states, and one state in the Southwest (Arizona) if they had not received a significant electoral boost due to the resistance of many middle-income white workers, blue collar and white collar, union

516 Conclusions

and non-union, to the overt nationwide push for integration by the civil rights movement in the 1960s.

Put another way, the United States remained a nation with a stratification system characterized by a caste-like system based on race, as well as by a class system based on wealth, income, and education, throughout the last 30 years of the twentieth century. This structural fact, which was readily apparent in neighborhood segregation, school segregation, job discrimination, and the low rates of intermarriage well into the 1990s, persisted much longer than had been expected by many social scientists, including this author. This persistence proved to be yet another factor that made it possible for the few tenths of one percent that comprise the corporate rich to dominate the federal government.

As the twenty-first century began, the corporate community and the power elite were more united than they had been at any time in the past 100 years. They had succeeded by 2000 in reducing union density in the private sector to 9.0 percent from its high points of 34.2 percent in 1945 and 33.5 percent in 1953. They had tamed Social Security and turned its trust funds into a piggy bank that covered deficits created by tax cuts for high-income earners, while at the same time putting stringent limits on welfare for those with low-income jobs or no jobs at all. They had created a framework within which American corporations could sell their goods and services, or contract for low-wage labor, just about anywhere in the world, including most former Communist countries, while at the same time making American markets available to trading partners in other countries.

The year 2000 therefore marked nothing less than the apparent triumph of the corporate rich, with unemployment as low as it had been since the late 1960s, thanks in part to a high-tech stock market bubble, and with a new Republican president about to take office after the Supreme Court's 5-4 decision to end the recount in Florida. The country's main geopolitical rival for nearly 45 years, the Soviet Union, was dead and gone, replaced by a smaller and economically declining Russia. From a corporate point of view, it may have looked like the best of all possible worlds. But of course no one could predict what the future might bring, as a series of completely unexpected and seemingly unlikely events would soon reveal.

References

Ahmed, Amel. 2013a. *Democracy and the politics of electoral system choice: Engineering electoral dominance.* New York: Cambridge University Press.

———. 2013b. "The existential threat: Varieties of socialism and the origins of electoral systems in early democracies." *Studies in Comparative International Development* 48:141–171.

Akard, Patrick. 1992. "Corporate mobilization and political power: The transformation of U.S. economic policy in the 1970s." *American Sociological Review* 57:597–615.

Alford, Robert and Eugene Lee. 1968. "Voting turnout in American cities." *American Political Science Review* 62:796–813.

Amenta, Edwin. 1998. *Bold relief: Institutional politics and the origins of modern American social policy*. Princeton: Princeton University Press.

———. 2006. *When movements matter: The Townsend Plan and the rise of social security*. Princeton: Princeton University Press.

Berman, Larry. 1979. *The Office of Management and Budget and the Presidency, 1921–1979*. Princeton: Princeton University Press.

Berry, Jeffrey M. 1997. *The interest group society*. New York: Longman.

———. 1999. *The new liberalism: The rising power of citizen groups*. Washington: The Brookings Institution.

Black, John D. 1928. "Letter to Beardsley Ruml, November 28." In *Black Papers, Chronological Correspondence File*. Madison: Wisconsin State Historical Society Archives.

———. 1929a. *Agricultural reform in the United States*. New York: McGraw-Hill.

———. 1929b. "Letter to Henry Taylor, March 19." In *Black Papers, Chronological Correspondence File*. Madison: Wisconsin State Historical Society Archive.

Bonacich, Phillip and G. William Domhoff. 1981. "Latent classes and group membership." *Social Networks* 3:175–196.

Burris, Val. 1992. "Elite policy-planning networks in the United States." *Research in Politics and Society* 4:111–134.

Campbell, John L. and Ove Pedersen. 2001. *The rise of neoliberalism and institutional analysis*. Princeton: Princeton University Press.

CED. 1966. *Budgeting for national objectives*. New York: Committee for Economic Development.

Destler, I. M. 2005. *American trade politics*. New York: Columbia University Press.

Domhoff, G. W. 1975. "Social clubs, policy-planning groups, and corporations: A network study of ruling-class cohesiveness." *The Insurgent Sociologist* 5:173–184.

———. 1978. *Who really rules? New Haven and community power re-examined*. New Brunswick: Transaction Books.

———. 1979. *The powers that be: Processes of ruling class domination in America*. New York: Random House.

———. 1990. *The power elite and the state: How policy is made in America*. Hawthorne, NY: Aldine de Gruyter.

———. 1996. *State autonomy or class dominance? Case studies on policy making in America*. Hawthorne, NY: Aldine de Gruyter.

———. 1998. *Who rules America? Power and politics in the year 2000*. Mountain View, CA: Mayfield Publishing Company.

———. 2009. "The power elite and their challengers: The role of nonprofits in American social conflict." *American Behavioral Scientist* 52:955–973.

Domhoff, G. W. and M. Webber. 2011. *Class and power in the New Deal: Corporate moderates, Southern Democrats, and the liberal-labor coalition*. Palo Alto: Stanford University Press.

Dreiling, Michael. 2001. *Solidarity and contention: The politics of class and sustainability in the NAFTA conflict*. New York: Garland Press.

Dreiling, Michael and Derek Darves. 2016. *Agents of neoliberal globalization: Corporate networks, state structures and trade policy*. New York: Cambridge University Press.

518   Conclusions

Eitzen, D. Stanley, Maureen A. Jung, and Dean A. Purdy. 1982. "Organizational linkages among the inner group of the capitalist class." *Sociological Focus* 15:179–189.

Finegold, Kenneth and Theda Skocpol. 1995. *State and party in America's New Deal.* Madison: University of Wisconsin Press.

Freeman, Richard B. 2007. *Do workers still want unions? More than ever.* EPI Briefing Paper. http://www.sharedprosperity.org/bp182/bp182.pdf. Washington: Economic Policy Institute.

Freeman, Richard B. and James L. Medoff. 1984. *What do unions do?* New York: Basic Books.

Gonzalez, George. 2001. *Corporate power and the environment: The political economy of U.S. environmental policy.* Lanham, MD: Rowman & Littlefield.

Gross, James A. 1995. *Broken promise: The subversion of U.S. labor relations policy.* Philadelphia: Temple University Press.

Hacker, Jacob. 2002. *The divided welfare state: The battle over public and private social benefits in the United States.* New York: Cambridge University Press.

Hacker, Jacob and Paul Pierson. 2002. "Business power and social policy: Employers and the formation of the American welfare state." *Politics & Society* 30:277–325.

———. 2010. *Winner-take-all politics: How Washington made the rich richer—and turned its back on the middle class.* New York: Simon & Schuster.

———. 2016. *American amnesia: How the war on government led us to forget what made America prosper.* New York: Simon and Schuster.

Heinz, John P., Edward O. Laumann, Robert L. Nelson, and Robert H. Salisbury. 1993. *The hollow core: Private interests in national policy making.* Cambridge: Harvard University Press.

Hunter, Floyd. 1959. *Top leadership, U.S.A.* Chapel Hill: University of North Carolina Press.

Kahn, Jonathan. 1997. *Budgeting democracy: State building and citizenship in America, 1890–1928.* Ithaca: Cornell University Press.

Keyssar, Alexander. 2009. *The right to vote: The contested history of democracy in the United States.* New York: Basic Books.

Kousser, J. Morgan. 1974. *The shaping of Southern politics: Suffrage restriction and the establishment of the one-party South, 1880–1910.* New Haven: Yale University Press.

Laumann, Edward and David Knoke. 1987. *The organizational state: Social choice in national policy domains.* Madison: University of Wisconsin Press.

Laurie, Bruce. 1989. *Artisans into workers: Labor in nineteenth-century America.* New York: Hill and Wang.

Linder, Marc. 1999. *Wars of attrition: Vietnam, the Business Roundtable, and the decline of construction unions.* Iowa City: Fanpihua Press.

Luger, Stan. 2000. *Corporate power, American democracy, and the automobile industry.* New York: Cambridge University Press.

Mayer, Frederick. 1998. *Interpreting NAFTA:Tthe science and art of political analysis.* New York: Columbia University Press.

McConnell, Grant. 1966. *Private power and American democracy.* New York: Knopf.

McQuaid, Kim. 1979. "The frustration of corporate revival in the early New Deal." *Historian* 41:682–704.

Mills, C. Wright. 1956. *The power elite.* New York: Oxford University Press.

The Shortcomings of Alternative Theories   519

Mitchell, Robert. 1991. "From conservation to environmental movement: The development of the modern environmental lobbies." Pp. 81–113 in *Governmental and environmental politics*, edited by M. Lacey. Baltimore: Johns Hopkins University Press.

Orloff, Ann. 1993. *The politics of pensions: A comparative analysis of Britain, Canada, and the United States, 1880–1940*. Madison: University of Wisconsin Press.

Orloff, Ann and Eric Parker. 1990. "Business and social policy in Canada and the United States, 1920–1940." *Comparative Social Research* 12:295–339.

Page, Benjamin and Martin Gilens. 2018. *Democracy in America?* Chicago: University of Chicago Press.

Pertschuk, Michael. 1982. *Revolt against regulation: The rise and pause of the consumer movement*. Berkeley: University of California Press.

Pierson, Paul and Theda Skocpol. 2007. *The transformation of American politics: Activist government and the rise of conservatism*. Princeton: Princeton University Press.

Renner, Tari and Victor DeSantis. 1994. "Contemporary patterns and trends in municipal government structures." In *The Municipal Yearbook 1993*. Washington: International City Managers Association.

Riddell, Chris 2001. "Union suppression and certification success." *Canadian Journal of Economics* 34:396–410.

———. 2004. "Union certification success under voting versus card-check procedures: Evidence from British Columbia, 1978–1998." *Industrial and Labor Relations Review* 57:493–517.

Robinson, Marshall. 1993. "The Ford Foundation: Sowing the seeds of a revolution." *Environment* 35:10–20.

Saloutos, Theodore. 1982. *The American farmer and the New Deal*. Ames: Iowa State University Press.

Salzman, Harold and G. William Domhoff. 1983. "Nonprofit organizations and the corporate community." *Social Science History* 7:205–216.

Schiesl, Martin J. 1977. *The politics of efficiency: Municipal administration and reform in America, 1800–1920*. Berkeley: University of California Press.

Schwartz, George. 1979. "The successful fight against a federal consumer protection agency." *MSU Business Topics* 27:45–56.

Skocpol, Theda. 1980. "Political responses to capitalist crisis: Neo-Marxist theories of the state and the case of the New Deal." *Politics & Society* 10:155–202.

———. 1985. "Introduction." In *Bringing the state back in*, edited by P. Evans, D. Rueschemeyer, and T. Skocpol. New York: Cambridge University Press.

———. 1987. "A brief reply." *Politics & Society* 15:331–332.

———. 1992. *Protecting soldiers and mothers: The political origins of social policy in the United States*. Cambridge: Harvard University Press.

Skocpol, Theda and John Ikenberry. 1983. "The political formation of the American welfare state in historical and comparative perspective." In *Comparative social research*, edited by R. Tomasson. Greenwich, CT: JAI.

Stewart, Frank. 1950. *A half century of municipal reform: The history of the National Municipal League*. Berkeley: University of California Press.

Tomkin, Shelley. 1998. *Inside OMB: Politics and process in the president's budget office*. Armonk, NY: M.E. Sharpe.

Vogel, David. 1989. *Fluctuating fortunes: The political power of business in America*. New York: Basic Books.

520 Conclusions

Warner, Kris. 2013. "The decline of unionization in the United States: Some lessons from Canada." *Labor Studies Journal* 38:110–138.

Weinstein, James. 1967. *The decline of socialism in America, 1912–1925.* New York: Monthly Review Press.

———. 1968. *The corporate ideal in the liberal state.* Boston: Beacon Press.

Weir, Margaret, Ann Orloff, and Theda Skocpol. 1988. "Understanding American social politics." Pp. 3–27 in *The politics of social policy in the United States,* edited by M. Weir, A. Orloff, and T. Skocpol. Princeton: Princeton University Press.

Archival Sources Consulted

Arthur Altmeyer Papers. Wisconsin Historical Society Archives. Madison, WI

William F. Benton Papers. Regenstein Library, University of Chicago. Chicago, IL

John B. Black Papers. Wisconsin Historical Society Archives. Madison, WI

J. Douglas Brown Papers. Mudd Library, Princeton University. Princeton, NJ

Committee for Economic Development Archives. General Files, President's Staff Files, and President's Trustee Files Washington, DC

Council on Foreign Relations. Studies of American Interests in the War and the Peace. New York, NY

Norman Davis Papers. Library of Congress. Washington, DC

John G. Feild Personal Papers. John F. Kennedy Presidential Library and Museum. Boston, MA

Marion Folsom Papers. University of Rochester Library. Rochester, NY

Ford Foundation Archives. Ford Foundation. New York, NY

Alvin H. Hansen Papers. Harvard University Archives, Harvard University. Cambridge, MA

Industrial Relations Counselors, Inc. Memorandums to Clients. IRC Library. New York, NY

Leon Keyserling Papers. Georgetown University Library. Washington, DC

Philip M. Klutznick Papers. Regenstein Library. Chicago: University of Chicago.

Murray Latimer Papers. Georgetown University Library. Washington, DC

Henry Morgenthau, Jr. Morgenthau Diaries. Franklin D. Roosevelt Presidential Library. Hyde Park, NY

Rockefeller Family Archives. Rockefeller Archive Center. Sleepy Hollow, NY

Rockefeller Foundation Collection. Rockefeller Archive Center. Sleepy Hollow, NY

Laura Spelman Rockefeller Memorial Archives. Rockefeller Archive Center. Sleepy Hollow, NY

Franklin D. Roosevelt, Roosevelt Papers, Franklin D. Roosevelt Library, Hyde Park, NY

Social Science Research Council Archives. Rockefeller Archive Center. Sleepy Hollow, NY

522 Archival Sources Consulted

Social Security Oral History Project. Columbia University Library. New York, NY

Gerard Swope Letters. Downs Collection. General Electric Archives. Schenectady Museum. Schenectady, NY

Jacob Viner Papers. Department of Rare Books and Special Collections. Mudd Manuscript Library. Princeton University. Princeton, NJ

Robert F. Wagner Papers. Georgetown University Library. Washington, DC

Harry Dexter White Papers. Department of Rare Books and Special Collections. Mudd Manuscript Library. Princeton University. Princeton, NJ

Index

Abbott, Edith 253, 255
abortion 361
ACA *see* Affordable Care Act 2010
accident insurance 47, 231, 233–4, 236
Acheson, Dean 417, 451, 457
ACT! (Affordable Care Today) 354–5
ACTPN (Advisory Committee on Trade Policy and Negotiations) 476, 480, 482–3, 493
ACW (Amalgamated Clothing Workers) 67–9, 100, 113, 140, 238, 240
adjustment assistance 464, 476–7
Advisory Committee on Employment Problems 242
Advisory Committee on Labor-Management Policy 178
Advisory Committee on Postwar Foreign Policy 383–4, 390–1
Advisory Committee on Unemployment Statistics 246
Advisory Council on Economic Security 259, 262, 266, 268, 270–2
advocacy organizations: and social security 259; ultraconservative use of 65; *see also* citizen groups
Aetna 308, 349
affirmative action 171–2, 190, 465
Affordable Care Act 2010 228; and 1974 CED proposal 313–14, 364–5; cost savings in 353; drafting of 360–2; employer and individual mandate in 357; passage of 363–4; private insurance in 308
AFL (American Federation of Labor): in automobile industry 112; and CIO 132, 138–9, 144–5, 150 (*see also* AFL-CIO); collaboration with corporate

moderates 57, 60, 62, 65, 113, 144–6, 151; divisions over industrial unions 119; exclusion of African Americans 122; and labor legislation 83–5, 92, 94–5, 104, 121, 127, 130, 138; in labor struggles 52–5, 116; membership of 68; and NRA 101; and NWLB 146; origins of 50–2; pension funds of 248; and post-war trade 452; in presidential elections 140, 154; relations with state 66, 68; and Social Security 233–5, 259, 271, 285, 298, 301; and spending coalition 19
AFL-CIO: and Fibreboard 167; and health insurance 306, 309–10; and international trade 466–7; lobbying Congress 158–9; Meany's leadership of 184–5; merger of 160; and public sector 169; and Social Security 333; and wage-price controls 180–1
African Americans: and Congressional Democrats 19; corporate inclusion of 193, 497; discrimination against 4–5, 150, 170–2; electoral power of 508; exclusion and poverty 317, 319, 323; in labor movement 45, 69, 122, 130, 138, 144, 161; and liberalism 31; and Medicaid 308; and social spending 321; and Southern Republicans 16; in UAW 186
agribusiness 2, 13, 16, 21, 129, 320
Agricultural Adjustment Administration 95, 97, 498, 509–10, 513
agriculture: business associations for 11; in New Deal legislation 95, 112, 120, 129, 511; and social security 262, 297, 301

524 Index

AHA (American Hospital Association) 304, 306–8, 343, 361

AHIP (America's Health Insurance Plans) 356–7, 362, 364

alcoholic beverages industry 140

Aldrich, Winthrop 425, 447

Alliance for Labor Action 185

Alliance for Managed Competition 349

Altmeyer, Arthur 253–4, 257, 260–1, 265, 269–70, 298

AMA (American Medical Association) 228; and government health plans 234, 262–3, 305, 307–9, 345, 361–2; and Medicare and Medicaid 303–4; and Social Security amendments 301–2

Amalgamated Association of Iron, Steel and Tin Workers 54, 116

Amenta, Edwin 280–1, 513

American Association for Old Age Security see American Association for Social Security

American Association for Social Security 238, 256, 259

American Association of Social Workers 253, 294

American Automobile Manufacturers Association 63

American Banking Association 127, 423, 425

American dollar: devaluation of 474; high value of 217; IMF use of 425; suspension of gold convertibility 197, 472; UK reserves of 404; see also Eurodollars

American Economic Association 117, 381

American Electric Power 168, 171, 465

American Enterprise Institute 376

American Express 231, 481–2

American Farm Bureau Federation see Farm Bureau

American Federation of Teachers 168

American Labor Legislation Review 232

American Liberty League 106, 137, 139–40

American Management Association 124, 242, 266, 277

American Public Welfare Association 254, 294

American Rolling Mill 240

American Textile Manufacturers Institute 461

anarchists 49–51

Anderson, Mary 254, 260

anti-colonial policy 432–3

anti-globalization movement 490–1

anti-lynching bill 127, 129

antitrust legislation 2, 91–2

anti-war movement 184, 187, 434, 442, 501, 514

apprenticeship programs 171–2, 195, 204

arbitration, voluntary labor 61

Armstrong, Barbara Nachtrieb 263–6, 269–71, 275, 280, 284

Armstrong, Hamilton Fish 381, 390–2, 394, 431–2, 438

Armstrong, William 332, 336

Associated General Contractors of America 193

Association of Railway Executives 82

AT&T 77, 98, 126, 175, 192, 277, 294

attentive public 8–9

Austin-Boston Alliance 18, 32, 307, 331

automobile industry: craft and industrial unions in 119; retirement benefits in 306; and safety legislation 501; separate labor board for 111–12, 114–15; and wage-price controls 180

BAC (Business Advisory Council) 97–8, 105; and CFR 383; Committee on Unemployment Insurance 268, 270, 272; consultation with union leaders 101; Industrial Relations Committee 98; and NLB 510–11; and postwar planning 374, 447, 452, 454; and social security 257, 282; in World War II 147–8; see also Business Council

Bacon, Robert 194

Baker, James F. 480–1

balanced budget 143, 148

balance-of-payments problems 470; see also international trade

Baldwin, Hanson W. 381, 438

Ball, George W. 461, 463

Ball, Robert M. 301, 306–7, 333–4, 336–7

Baltimore and Ohio Railroad strike 45–6

Bank of America 460, 465

bankers: in corporate community 55; Northern 7; opposition to IMF 423–5; relations with Europe 469–70; Southern 11; *see also* investment banks

Belmont, August 55

Bentsen, Lloyd 482, 491

Bergthold, Linda 348

Berkowitz, Edward 298

Berle, A. A., Jr. 394, 417

Bernstein, Bernard 413

Bernstein, Irving 78

Berry, Jeffrey 500, 502

Bethlehem Steel 77, 213

Betts, Richard 434, 439

Biddle, Francis 114–15, 117–20, 124

Bidwell, Percy 382, 391, 452

Birmingham, Alabama 172

Blough, Roger 178–9, 192–4

Blue Cross and Blue Shield 304–5, 310, 355

Blue Ribbon Committee 176, 207

Blum, Robert M. 435

Board of Control and Labor Standards for Army Clothing 68

boards of directors, overlapping 6

Borden's Milk 262–3

Bowman, Isaiah 381, 390–2, 394, 431–3

boycotts 51, 94; injunctions against 69; secondary 152–3, 158–9, 168, 211–12; and Taft-Hartley Act 157

Boyle, Kevin 184, 186, 221

Bradley, Bill 481, 483, 486

Brains Trust 91

Brandeis, Elizabeth 255

Brandeis, Louis 117, 233, 236, 255–6

Bretton Woods 421, 427; Harry D. White at 399; opposition to 422–4; *see also* IMF; World Bank

Brewery Workers Union 60

Britain *see* United Kingdom

British Commonwealth 401, 459

British Empire 400, 404, 406–7, 426, 430, 432–3

Brookings Institution 198; creation of 237; and foreign affairs 376; and Hoover administration 245; Pasvolsky at 384; and public sector unions 170; and Wagner committee 92, 94

Brown, J. Douglas: before Congress 275; historical institutionalists on 512; and old-age insurance 263–4, 266–7, 277, 280; and railroad pensions 250–1; Rockefeller funding of 25; on Social Security advisory councils 298–301; and SSRC 245, 254, 294; and unemployment insurance 269

Brown, Michael K. 156

Brown v Board of Education of Topeka 14, 65

Buchanan, James 65

Budd Manufacturing 104

building-trades unions *see* construction unions

Bureau of Labor Statistics 218

burial insurance 50

Burns, Arthur 193–4, 196

Bush, George H. W. 218, 479–83

Bush, George W. 218, 333, 353–4

Business Advisory Council; *see also* BAC

Business and Industry Committee for Bretton Woods 422, 424

Business Council: Blough in 179; and construction industry 195–6; and CUAIR 192; and Emergency Committee on Foreign Trade 467; and taxation 182

business principles, in social security 231, 233, 235–6

Business Roundtable 97; and ACTPN 476; aims of 203–4; and citizens groups 501–2; Construction Committee 203, 211; formation of 179, 192–3, 202–3, 206, 513; and healthcare 342–3, 345, 350–1, 353, 356, 359–60, 364; and inflation 479; and international trade 371, 480–5, 487, 491, 493, 506; and labor legislation 211, 213–15; Public Information Committee 203; and Social Security 332; and tax cuts 323

Cabinet Committee on Construction 194

Cambodia 441

Canada 28; agricultural surplus of 386; health spending in 311; and IMF 410; labor movement in 209, 502; trade negotiations with 481; *see also* Joint Economic Committee; King, Mackenzie; NAFTA

candidate-selection process 5, 7–8

526 Index

capital, export of 450
capitalism, challenges to 28–9, 60
Carnegie, Andrew 54, 237
Carnegie Corporation 237, 376;
  and public sector unions 170; and
  research on unemployment 246
Carnegie Endowment for International
  Peace 376
Carnegie Foundation for the
  Advancement of Teaching 237,
  295, 511
Carnegie Institution of Washington 376
Carter, Jimmy: and healthcare
  343; inflation under 200–1; and
  international trade 477–9; and labor
  legislation 212–13, 215
Casey, Kevin 410
caste, caste-like 4, 150, 161, 185–6,
  323, 516
catastrophic insurance 344
Catholic Hospital Association 345,
  361, 363
Catholics: and Democratic Party 141;
  immigrant 53
Cato Institute 328
CDCs (Community Development
  Corporations) 325–7, 365
CEA (Council of Economic Advisors)
  448–9, 471; chair of 193–4, 198, 333,
  484; and wage-price controls 178,
  180–1
CED (Committee for Economic
  Development): against unions
  168, 191; Blough in 179; and
  Business Roundtable 205; and
  Carter administration 478–9; and
  CFR 383, 394; Clayton in 426;
  and construction industry 195;
  and Employment Act 1946 448;
  and foreign policy 458; formation
  of 148–9, 374; and government
  social spending 317–21; and health
  insurance 311–14, 342, 355, 357,
  364–5; and inflation 182–3, 198–9,
  201–2; and international economic
  system 371, 424–5, 446; and
  international trade 459, 462–5, 467,
  483; and Marshall Plan 452, 454–6;
  and monetary policy 471, 473–4;
  and organizational state theory
  505; and policy-planning network
  449; political power of 513–14; and
  presidential advisory groups 509; and

Social Security 329–30, 332, 336,
  338; Subcommittee on East-West
  Trade 465–6; and Taft-Hartley Act
  153; and Vietnam War 441
Central Statistics Board 249, 253
CES (Committee on Economic
  Security): and drafting of Social
  Security Act 258–62, 265, 267–70,
  272; establishment of 257–8; and
  health insurance 304; report to
  Congress 274, 277, 286
CFR (Council on Foreign Relations)
  371; and Advisory Committee on
  Postwar Foreign Policy 390–1; and
  Carter administration 477; Clayton in
  426; and Clinton administration 484,
  487, 489; global vision of 389–90,
  392–3, 427, 446; and IMF 411, 448;
  influence on State Department
  383–4, 391–2; and international trade
  466–7, 492; Memorandum E-B19
  387–8; origins of 375–6; Peace
  Aims Group 380–1, 431; Political
  Group 380–1, 388–9; and postwar
  aid to Europe 452–5; and Reagan
  administration 479–80; relationships
  with foreign policy leaders 378–9;
  and Southeast Asia 429–30, 432,
  434–9, 441–3; study groups of 373–4,
  376–7, 379–81, 397; Territorial
  Group 381, 391, 431–3; and UK
  405–6; and universities 398; Volcker
  on 470, 479
CFR Economic and Financial Group
  380, 419; and CED 394; on Grand
  Area 399–403, 431; and IMF 402,
  407, 409–10, 417, 419, 423; members
  of 381–3; Pasvolsky at 383; and
  post-war economy 384–6, 450; and
  Roosevelt government 391; and
  World Bank 422
Chamber of Commerce: and ACTPN
  476; and healthcare 305, 307, 309,
  343–4, 350, 352–3, 359, 362, 364;
  and labor legislation 91, 96, 112, 124,
  158–9, 213; and LLRG 176; and
  New Deal agencies 510; and NFIB
  214; and NLRB 166; policy stances
  of 21; Powell memo to 205–6; public
  opinion of 151; and public sector
  unions 169–70; and Social Security
  Act 227, 274, 282, 300–1; and trade
  policy 482, 485, 491

Index 527

charities 73, 327, 365
Chase Manhattan Bank: Aldrich at 425, 447; and Rockefeller family 71–2, 282, 451, 466, 471; Volcker at 199, 471
Chase National Bank *see* Chase Manhattan Bank
cherry picking 305
Chicago Construction Users 193
child labor 68, 116, 127
China: People's Republic of 167, 430, 441, 466; split with Soviet Union 440, 442; trade relations with 372, 489–93; US investment in 467
CIA (Central Intelligence Agency) 381, 438, 449, 480, 484
Cigna 349
CIO (Congress of Industrial Organizations): in 1940s 146, 150; Communists in 142, 144, 152, 154; formation of 138; and NLRB 144; organizing victories of 141–3; and post-war trade 452; size of 145; and Social Security advisory councils 298, 301; in the South 128, 132
citizen groups 500–1, 503
Citizens Trade Committee 485–6
Civil Rights Act 1964 4, 21–2, 170, 186
civil rights movement 170–3; and construction industry 19; corporate reactions to 514; decline of 323; and liberal-labor alliance 2, 22, 184; white resistance to 183, 186, 498, 514–16
Civil Service Commission 169
Civil War, veterans of 230; *see also* veterans' pensions
Civilian Works Administration 250
Clark, Bennett Champ 283
Clark Amendment 283–5, 294–6, 299, 512
class conflict 29; during World War II 150; and electoral system 498; and government budget 149; and government offices 61; in IEMP theory 25; and intra-class conflicts 65, 144; and labor legislation 221, 235; and NLRB rulings 166; in organizational state theory 497; Rockefeller's attempts at managing 76
Clausen, Aage 17
Clayton, William L. 426, 447, 451
Cleveland Housing Network 326

Clinton, Bill 218; and healthcare 342, 345–53, 356–8, 364; and Social Security 338; and trade policy 476, 484–7, 489–90, 502; welfare reform 230
Clinton, Hillary 346, 352, 357–8
coal mining: corporatization of 55–7; eight-hour day in 49; in interlock networks 2; owned by steel companies 113; union-management collaboration in 94
Coalition for a Democratic Workplace 219
Coalition to Advance Health Care Reform 356
Cohen, Benjamin V. 382, 419
Cohen, Wilbur 307, 310, 331
COLAs (cost-of-living adjustments) 319, 330–1, 334–5, 337
Cold War 393; and postwar economic policy 453; and Southeast Asia 430, 434
collective bargaining 25; AFL promotion of 50, 66, 95–6; corporate moderate support for 98–9, 102–3, 114–15; legislative support for 93–4, 100, 107–8, 125, 130; multi-employer 56–7; NFC and 59–60, 63, 80–1; in public sector 169–70; relative power in 61; size of unit 121, 123, 130, 144; for social benefits 156; state support for 67–9, 81, 166; and Taft-Hartley Act 151–3; under NRA 97
collective power 22–3, 27, 187
Colorado Fuel & Iron 72, 75–6, 79, 99
Commission on Foreign Economic Policy 459–60, 464
Commission on Industrial Relations 66–7, 75, 102
Commission on Money and Credit 449
Committee for a National Trade Policy 461, 463
Committee for Progress Economic and Social 463, 465
Committee for the Marshall Plan 455
Committee for Trade Expansion 482–3; *see also* USA★NAFTA
Committee on the Present Danger 458
Commons, John R. 58–9, 83, 114, 232–3, 253, 260
communism: in Asia 387, 430, 433–7, 439–40; extension of 167; in Western Europe 449, 453, 470

528 Index

Communist countries 371, 489
Communist Party USA: AFL on 144;
as labor organizers 115–16, 139, 142,
152; and Social Security Act 279; and
Wallace campaign 154
Community Services
Administration 325
company unions 76; in legislation
96, 111; *see also* employee
representation plans
Compromise of 1877 45
Conable, Barber 332
Congress: agricultural committees in
130; approval of IMF and World
Bank 422; authority over trade
policy 475–6, 489; electoral system
of 507–8; seniority system 18, 21,
95, 210; trade policy committees
484; voting coalitions in 12–13;
see also House of Representatives;
Senate
Congressional Budget Office 362, 364
conservative coalition: in 1930s
132, 145, 405; in 1940s 150–1;
in 1950s 159; in 1970s 210, 212,
216; in Congress 12–16, 18–22;
and consumer legislation 501;
and economic planning 448; and
electoral districts 174; and filibuster
211; and healthcare 306–7, 313, 343;
and international economic system
371, 426, 446, 462, 477, 487; and
minimum wage 128; and monetary
policy 200; and Social Security 300–
1, 336; and spending coalition 17
Conservative Democratic Forum 351
Consolidation Coal 72, 79
Construction Industry Collective
Bargaining Commission 194, 196
Construction Industry Stabilization
Committee 196
construction unions: and CUAIR 342;
decline of 204, 217; and growth
coalitions 19, 53–4; growth of
144–5; and health insurance 304;
and labor legislation 160; and racial
discrimination 161, 172–3, 193;
state and corporate confrontation of
194–5
construction workers, response to
inflation 191
consulting firms, anti-union 160,
209, 217

consumer movement 500–1
containment, strategies of 509
contracting out 276–8, 283
contributory plans 237, 248, 273
Cornell University, Industrial and Labor
Relations Library 175
corporate community: beginnings of
1–3; and Clinton healthcare plan 351;
conflict among leaders of 8; domestic
and international goals of 472–3;
early years of 55–6; factions within
3, 21, 30, 64–6; healthcare initiatives
by 345; influence on policy-making
357, 412; international trade
argument within 459–60; Johnson
administration and 182; medical-
industrial component 309; and the
military 47; networks of dominance
5–7; and NLRB 166–7, 173; and
NRA 93, 97, 99; in Obama era
219; opposition to social insurance
366; and power elite 10–11; and
public image 127; relationship
with federal government 448–9;
response to civil rights movement
170–2; results of interactions within
10; social manifestation of 24–5;
and state capacity 251; triumph of
516; and Vietnam War 441; *see also*
corporate moderates; corporate
ultraconservatives
corporate lawyers: and NLB/NLRB
114–15, 117–18, 130–1, 207; and
NWLB 147; as opponents of labor
137, 158, 175–6; in organizational
state theory 504–5
corporate moderates 3; and Clinton
administration 484; and employment
448; and environmental movement
501; on federal budget 181–2;
flexibility of 30; and foreign
policy 430, 457–8; and healthcare
306, 311–12, 342, 347, 352, 357,
364–5; and international economic
institutions 371–4, 426–7, 429,
455; and international trade 178,
446, 458–64, 475–7, 488–92; and
Keynesian economics 149; and labor
law 91, 96, 111, 113–15, 127–8,
131, 175; and labor movement 50,
55–6, 59, 70, 100–2, 158, 183; and
liberal advocacy groups 497; and
monetary policy 473; and NLRB

118; and non-profit social service providers 324–5; and postwar aid to Europe 450, 452–4, 456–7; and postwar planning 394; right turn of 195, 199, 205–6; Rockefeller as leader of 80; social insurance plans by 227–8, 231–2, 237, 240–2; and social spending 317–20, 514; and spending coalition 14, 20–1; and Vietnam War 434; and workers' compensation 235; in World War II 148

corporate power, limits on 114, 118, 122, 131, 500

corporate rich 1–2 defined; 5 party of; and plantation owners 11; and policy-discussion groups 6; and policy-planning network 5, 74, 366, 505–6; and power elite 10, 59; and state-building 8, 59, 98, 102, 249, 253, 285 380, 392, 432, 449, 465, 475, 499, 509, 513, 515

corporate ultraconservatives 3; and Bretton Woods institutions 422, 426; and consumer legislation 501; creating poverty 331; dismantling New Deal 405; and health insurance 263, 313, 352; and international trade 371, 377, 405, 446, 455–6, 459–60, 462, 464; and labor legislation 96; and liberal-labor alliance 20; and Marshall Plan 453–5, 457; nationalism and nativism 65; and neoliberalism 30, 64–5; and non-profit social service providers 326; organizations of 63; in Senate 183; and Social Security 229–30, 257, 260, 274, 279, 283, 286, 328–9, 338; and Social Security reserve fund 299–300; and social spending 321–3; and spending coalition 13–14, 21–2; and Supreme Court 174; and Taft-Hartley Act 152–3; and workers' compensation 235

corporate-conservative alliance 12, 337

corporations: common bonds between 2; federal supervision of 59; legal privileges of 2

corporatization process 55–6

corruption, social psychology of 23

cost-shifting 303, 343–4

Council of Social Action 165

Council on a Union-Free Environment 213

countervailing power 347

Cowdrick, Edward S. 77–8, 98, 112, 123, 242, 266

Cox, Eugene 14

craft guilds 43, 50

craft unions: in 19th century 45; and civil rights movements 172; and industrial unions 119, 138–9; and national standards 84; railroad 82; and representation elections 111, 113, 121–2; and unskilled workers 67, 104; see also AFL

craft workers: collective bargaining by 114; and Democratic Party 130

cross-class coalitions 58, 61–2, 65

CUAIR (Construction Users Anti-Inflation Roundtable) 192–4, 196, 202–5, 342, 513

Cuba 379

currency stabilization 408, 423

Currie, Lauchlin 382, 413

cutthroat competition 57, 59, 92

Daily Worker 139

Daley, William M. 486–7, 491

Dark, Taylor 216

Dartmouth College 79

Davis, James 194

Davis, Norman H. 378–80, 383, 390–1

Davis-Bacon Act 194–6, 204, 218

death benefits 231, 278

decertification of unions 157, 160–1, 209

Deering Milliken 174

Democratic Leadership Council 484

Democratic Party: in 1948 elections 154–5; in 1970s 209–10; challengers to power elite in 11; and conservative coalition 14–16; control of Congress 21; and corporate moderates 55, 464; and du Pont family 105–6; and electoral system 508–9; and foreign policy 378–9; and international trade 482; and labor movement 29, 51, 53, 83, 130, 140, 143, 159; and liberal-labor alliance 515; professional voters for 221; and spending coalition 13, 17–20; and Vietnam War 441; white Southerners in 4–5, 7; white worker support for 186–7; see also liberal Democrats; machine Democrats; Southern Democrats; urban Democrats

Democratic Study Group 210

530 Index

Department of Labor, Advisory Committee 249
Detroit: riots in 317; Walk for Freedom in 173
Dewey, Charles 424
Dickinson, John 254
Diebold, William, Jr 382, 389
directors, interlocking 2–3, 55, 237
disability insurance 20, 230, 239, 301–2, 327, 329, 365
distributive power 22–3, 27
Divided We Fail 356, 359–60
Divine, Robert 375
Dole, Robert 332, 334
domestic labor 112, 120, 129, 286, 297, 301–2
domination, use of term 1
domino theory 436, 439
Dreiling, Michael 483
du Pont, Pierre S. 105–8
du Pont family: in 1936 election 139–40; and National Labor Relations Act 108, 111, 114
Dulles, Allen 381, 438
Dulles, John Foster 437–8
DuPont 77, 105, 126, 277

Eastman Kodak 243, 295, 481–3, 487
Eberle, William 473–5
ECAT 466–7, 471, 475, 480, 482–3, 485
economic classes 24–7
Economic Defense Board 389–90, 407, 409, 411
economic organizations 24; and political organizations 26–7
economic weapons 157, 402
EEC (European Economic Community) 462–4
efficiency wages 64
eight-hour day 48–9, 67, 81
Eisenhower, Dwight 157; and international trade 459–60, 462; and Social Security 302; and Southeast Asia 437–8; and steel industry 179
EITC (Earned Income Tax Credit) 322–3, 365, 514
Eldercare 308
elderly patients 303, 305, 307–9; see also Medicare
electoral systems 11–12, 145, 497–8, 507–9

Emergency Committee on Foreign Trade see ECAT
Emergency Medical Treatment and Active Labor Act 1986 303
Emerson, Rupert 431–3
Employee Free Choice Act 219
employee representation plans: CIO use of 142; corporate moderate support for 96, 98–9, 111, 137; legal restrictions on 104–5, 109, 111, 113, 121, 125–6; NLB on 106; and NLRB 119; Rockefeller promotion of 76–7, 79–81, 122–3, 143; unskilled workers forced into 82; see also representation elections
employers' associations 49, 61–3; see also NAM
Employment Act 1946 448–9
Employment Advisory Council 250
Enterprise Foundation 326
environmental groups 501
environmental policy 485, 488, 497
Environmental Protection Agency 485, 502
Equitable Life 236
Era of Good Feelings 55, 62–3
Eurodollars 469
Europe: in CFR analyses 387; colonial empires of 432; French role in 433, 435; labor movement in 41, 156, 502; labor-left coalitions in 234; postwar aid for 154, 393, 438, 446, 449–50, 452–3, 470 (see also Marshall Plan); social insurance in 230, 235, 247, 264; US economic warfare against 471; US military forces in 457–8; VAT in 279; wage-price policies in 180; and World Bank 447; World War I in 67; World War II in 373, 379, 384–5, 400, 402
European Common Market see EEC
European Cooperation Administration 456–8
excess profits tax 447
exchange stabilization fund 397, 403, 412, 422
expectations theory of policy change 257, 357
experience ratings 305
experts: independent 64, 240, 252, 263–4, 511; multiple affiliations of 241, 264
Export-Import Bank 426, 450, 456, 470

Fair Employment Practices Commission 150
Fair Labor Standards Act 1938 49, 127–8
family allowances 320–1
Fanning, John 165
FAP (Family Assistance Plan) 320–2, 324, 333
Farm Bureau 74, 307, 422, 457, 510
farm organizations, liberal 457
Federal Emergency Relief Administration 253, 257
Federal Mediation and Conciliation Service 153
Federal Reserve, proposed reforms to 127
Federal Reserve Bank of New York 199, 423, 425, 472, 479
Federal Reserve Board: chair of 199, 426; Division of International Finance 473; Hansen and 382; and IMF 419–20; and monetary policy 149, 469–70, 472–4; and Roosevelt Recession 145
Federal Trade Commission 59, 120, 130, 501, 509, 513
Federated Department Stores 171
Federation of American Hospitals 361
Federation of Organized Trades and Labor Unions 48
Feldstein, Martin 201–2
Fibreboard 167–8, 174–5, 208
Fidelity Philadelphia Trust Bank 460, 465, 474
Filene family 76, 102
filibuster: 1970s changes to 211; ending 15, 215; Southern Democrat use of 95, 129
Flanders, Ralph 383
Flint, Michigan, automobile strikes in 141–2
Folsom, Marion 243; and CES 259, 266; on contracting-out 295; and Social Security Act 271, 282, 300; on Social Security advisory councils 298–9, 301
food stamps: expansion of 20, 365, 514; strikers using 204
Ford, Gerald 210–12, 328
Ford Foundation: and CED 465; and citizen groups 500–1; and non-profit

social service providers 324–6; and public sector unions 170
foreign trade *see* international trade
Forster, Walter 277, 296
Fortune magazine 373
Fosdick, Raymond 78–80, 109, 247–9
Foundation Center 501
France: colonial empire of 429, 432–3, 435; health spending in 311; organized labor in 49, 295; raising capital in 55; in Tripartite Pact 397; in World War II 374, 385
Frankfurter, Felix 83, 116–17, 255, 264
Fraternal Order of Eagles 238, 259, 271
fraternal organizations 238
free trade 380, 424–5; US/UK differences on 389, 405–6; *see also* international trade

Gaddis, John 435–6
Garrison, Lloyd K. 117–19, 124, 147
GATT (General Agreement on Trade and Tariffs) 456, 481, 488–9
Gelb, Leslie 434–5, 439
General Education Board 79
General Education Fund 72
General Electric: and Business Roundtable 203; and CED 460; and CUAIR 192; employee representation plans 108; Hawthorne Studies at 80; and international trade 460, 490; and No-Name Committee 175; and PCEEO 171; and Social Security Act 227; in Special Conference Committee 77; union recognition at 142; *see also* Swope, Gerard
General Motors: board of 79; and CUAIR 192; and du Pont family 105; and NLRB 208; in Special Conference Committee 77; strikes at 141–2; use of violence against workers 137; and wage-price controls 180
gentrification 324
geopolitics 401, 461
Germany: health spending in 311; post-war 393; raising capital in 55; in World War II 374, 386, 388–9, 395, 401–2
gerrymandering 487
GI Bill 465

532 Index

Gitelman, Howard M. 75
Givens, Meredith 253, 255, 257–8, 261
globalization 29, 209
gold 197, 404, 415, 417, 419–20, 425, 469–73
Goldberg, Arthur 169, 173, 178
Goldman Sachs 282, 335, 487, 490
Goldwater, Barry 186
Gompers, Samuel 51; and capital-labor collaboration 58, 62; and health insurance 234–5
Goodyear 77, 137, 146
government contracts 171, 173, 213
government independence 504, 506
government officials 8; corporate influence on 1, 46, 148; pensions for 237; regulation of labor unions 159, 195; and social security 230, 232, 234, 253
Gramley, Lyle 199–200
Grand Area 389; abandonment of term 452; CFR memoranda on 400–1; integrating Europe into 393, 446; perceived threats to 395; UK acceptance of 406–7; and Vietnam War 427, 430–1, 436–7, 440
Great Depression: corporate reaction to 6, 131, 246; Democratic Party and 29, 377; and private pension funds 248; and social security 231, 239, 267
Greece 449, 453
Green, William 94, 101–2, 124
Greenback-Labor Party 508
Greenpeace 485
Greenspan, Alan 332, 334, 336
Griffin, Robert 158
Gross, James A. x, 120, 175
group insurance plans 237–8, 251
group-think 9
growth coalitions 7, 13, 16–17, 19
Gulick, Luther 408

Hacker, Jacob 347, 358, 514
Hanna, Mark 58
Hansen, Alvin: and CFR 381–2, 385, 397–8; defense of Bretton Woods 423–4, 426; on Joint Economic Committee 389; and origins of IMF 398, 407–10, 415, 417–20; and Social Security 246–7, 253, 269–70, 298–9
Harriman, Mrs. Borden 66
Harriman, W. Averell 437, 454

Harrod, Roy F. 408
Harvard Business School 80, 240, 243
Harvard Graduate School of Public Administration 423
Harvard Law School 116, 233, 255–6
Hatfield, Henry D. 250
Haymarket Square bombing 49
health alliances, local and regional 342–3, 347, 350, 366
health insurance: AALL plan for 234–5; attempts to legislate on 303–5, 308, 311, 313 (see also Affordable Care Act 2010; Medicare; Medicaid); Business Roundtable on 205; CED on 311–14; Clinton's proposal for 230; government-supported 228, 366; individual mandate for 312–13, 355–9, 364; and NFIB 214; private 344–5, 347–8, 356–7, 364–5; public option for 357–8, 361–4; and Social Security Act 228, 262
Health Insurance Association of America 307–8, 349, 356
health policy trap 305
HealthCAN (Health Care for America Now) 357–8
Helleiner, Eric 410
Heritage Foundation 328, 355, 358
Hess, Gary 432–3
Hicks, Clarence J. 77, 79–80, 99, 104–5, 108, 110, 239, 241–2, 247
Hill and Knowlton 176
Hillman, Sidney 294; as ACW leader 67–8; and ACW social insurance 240; and industrial organizing 138–9; and labor legislation 100–2, 113–15, 124, 131; political affiliations of 140
Hills, Carla 483
Himmelberg, Robert 96–7
hiring halls, union-controlled 194–5
historical institutionalism 497–8, 506–15
HMOs (Health Maintenance Organizations) 312, 344, 348, 353, 357
Ho Chi Minh 434, 436
Hoffman, Paul 447, 451–2, 454–5, 458
Holmes, Oliver Wendell 255
Homestead, Pennsylvania 54, 237
Hoover, Herbert 71, 79, 140, 244–6, 376
Hoover Institution 330

Index 533

Hopkins, Harry 253–4, 257–8, 262
hospital insurance 306–9; *see also* Medicare
hospitals: and ACA 361–4; for-profit 311; government subsidization of 228; price controls on 343, 358
House of Representatives: Agricultural Committee 210; Armed Services Committee 210; Banking and Currency Committee 210, 424–5; conservative coalition in 15–16; Un-American Activities Committee 399; Ways and Means Committee 182, 278, 307–8, 330–2, 334, 343, 351, 482
housing, federal subsidies for 324–5
Hull, Cordell 378–80, 383–5, 390, 405–7, 409, 416–17, 433

ideology organizations 24
IEMP model of social power 24–7
IMF (International Monetary Fund): Congressional approval of 422–6; expansion of role 450; Hansen at 246; launch of 427, 448; plans for 373, 397–8, 403, 407–21; and Soviet Union 399, 421; US oversight of 456; Viner and 269
immigrant labor 44, 52–3, 67, 130, 138, 329–30
imperial preferences 406–7; *see also* British Empire
imperialism, conventional forms of 431–2
income tax, negative 320–2
Independent Payment Advisory Board 361–2
indigent patients 303–4
Indochina *see* Southeast Asia; Vietnam
Indonesia 430, 434–5, 437–9, 442
industrial accidents 234
Industrial Advisory Board 97
Industrial Relations Counselors, Inc. *see* IRC
industrial relations departments, corporate 171
industrial unions: AFL divisions over 119; defeat of 218; in heavy industry 130; inclusion of African Americans 122, 132; and Landrum-Griffin Act 160; and representation elections 121; *see also* CIO

industrial workers: and AFL 104, 113 (*see also* industrial unions); and Democratic Party 130; migrant 53; militancy of 114–15; and National Labor Relations Act 112–13; response to inflation 191; Southern 128
inflation: after World War II 150, 447; corporate community response to 191–3, 195, 198, 201–5, 443; government action against 177–8, 181–3, 194–7 (*see also* wage-price guidelines); in healthcare costs 310–11, 347–8; and Keynesian economics 148–9; and Nixon's monetary policy 470, 473; and Social Security 327–8; under Carter 478–9; under Reagan 217–18, 480; and Vietnam War 442–3, 469; Volcker's response to 199–201
inflationary spiral 178, 183, 191, 194, 198, 200–1, 471, 473
informal leaders 23, 331
Informal Political Agenda Group 390
Institute of Government Relations 237
Institute of Government Research 73
Institute of Public Administration 79, 253, 408
insurance companies: and ACA 362, 364; and Clark Amendment 296; and health insurance 228, 305, 307–9, 313–14; and New Deal 511; and old-age insurance 244, 254; and social security 236–8; and workers' compensation 234–5
insurance exchanges 314, 355, 358, 365
Inter-American Conference 412–13
Interdepartmental Group to Consider Postwar Economic Problems and Policies 388
interest rates, high 183, 191–2, 196, 199–202, 217, 470, 479–80
interest-group pluralism 497–503
interlocks, nationwide 2–3
Internal Revenue Service 156, 320
International Association of Machinists 60, 62
International Bank for Reconstruction *see* World Bank
International Brotherhood of Railway Clerks 146
international economic system 371

534 Index

International Firefighters Association 168
International Harvester 47, 77, 79, 99, 447
International Ladies' Garment Workers Union 69, 100, 140
International Longshoremen's Association 158
international relations, scholarly study of 375
international trade: CFR on 385; and human rights 489; increasing 6, 181, 379, 385, 390, 408–9; multilateral negotiations on 480; post-war expansion of 450–1; Roosevelt on 379; under Kennedy 178; US share of 377; *see also* free trade; tariffs
international trade organization 455; *see also* WTO
international trading system 1, 492
internationalization of US economy 205, 209, 372, 377, 450–1, 466, 469
interorganizational alliances 27
intra-class differences 65
investment banks: and corporate lawyers 176; and corporations 1, 55; and Marshall Plan 454; and oil shocks 198; in organizational state theory 504–5; and Social Security 282; and trade policy 377
IRC (Industrial Relations Counselors, Inc.) 99, 113; and civil service requirements 286; and employee representation plans 123, 125–6, 137; Fosdick on 109–10; foundation of 78–9; and labor conflicts 143; and NLRB 118–19; and NWLB 146; sidelining of 292–4; and social insurance 227, 239–44, 248, 250–3, 257; and Social Security Act 258, 260–2, 265, 267–71, 274–6, 278, 282, 284–5, 295, 512; and unemployment 244–7, 273
Iron and Steel Institute 59, 63
Irving Trust 77
isolationists 377–8, 404–5, 424–5, 453–4, 459
Italy 449

Jacksonian Democrats 44
janitors 208
Japan: in postwar planning 381, 387, 390; trade with 217, 461–2, 474; US

economic warfare against 471; and US Southeast Asia policy 436–9; in World War II 380, 389, 395, 402, 410, 430
Job Corps 324
Johnson, Lyndon B.: and federal budget 181–3; and Keynesian economics 149; and labor relations 173; and Medicare 309–10, 313; and social spending 317, 321, 324–5, 327; and Vietnam 434, 440–2; and wage-price controls 180; white voters for 186
Joint (Canadian-American) Economic Committee 179, 389, 410
JPMorgan Chase 62, 71
Judis, John 351

Kennedy, John F.: and international trade 463–4; and Keynesian economics 149; and public-sector workers 169; and Taft-Hartley Act 159; and Vietnam 439–40; and wage-price controls 178–80
Kennedy, Ralph 207
Kennedy, Robert F. 177
Kennedy, Ted 311, 313, 348, 354, 359, 361
key currency approach 423
Keynes, John Maynard 398, 405–8, 410, 415–19, 421–2, 424, 426, 448
Keynesian economics: business or commercial version of 148–9, 191; Hansen converted to 246; and international trade 405; moderate 198, 201; and post-war planning 393; return to 31
Keyserling, Leon 120, 129–30
King, MacKenzie 75–6, 78, 143
King, Martin Luther, Jr. 173, 177, 319
Kirstein, Louis 102, 104, 108–10, 112
Kissinger, Henry 443
Knights of Labor 45, 47–51, 53, 60
Koch brothers 140, 328
Korean War: and defense spending 457–8; and labor movement 41–2, 132, 157, 160; and Vietnam War 435, 438

labor councils, citywide 44
labor injunctions 69, 83, 168; *see also* Norris-LaGuardia Act
Labor Law Reform Act 1977 212–16, 221, 349

Labor Law Reform Committee *see* LLRG 207

Labor Law Study Group 191, 202

labor legislation: conservative opposition to 127–8; corporate involvement in 108, 118; Cowdrick and 78; Rockefeller involvement in 70, 81, 97; *see also* Fair Labor Standards Act; National Industrial Recovery Act; National Labor Relations Act

labor markets: control over 53, 347; and Social Security 227, 275; in the South 131–2

labor movement *see* labor unions

Labor Policy Association 176

labor practices, unfair 122, 126, 146, 152, 168

Labor Relations Associates 160

labor shortages 68, 194–5

labor standards, national-level 84

labor theory of value 28

labor unions: in 19th century 41, 43–6, 48–9; collaboration with corporate moderates 57–8; conditions for success of 54, 60–1; congressional hearings on 158–60; decline of 183–4, 502–3, 513–14; employer measures against 157–8; health plans 305; impact of outsourcing and offshoring on 208–9; in interest-group pluralism 500; and international trade 485, 492; legislation on 13, 211–13, 215–16, 219; lobbying efforts of 504; membership of *see* union density; in NRA era 100–1; in presidential elections 139–41; private-sector 41, 185, 191, 206, 218–19, 515; Progressive Republican attitude to 82–3; providing social insurance 238, 248; public opinion of 143, 151; public-sector 42, 168–70, 191, 204, 216–18; racial integration of 128, 143, 161, 170, 220; recognition of *see* union recognition; rise and fall of 220–2; Roosevelt administration and 94–6, 130–1; single-company *see* employee representation plans; Southern Democrat opposition to 20; and wage-price controls 177, 180–1; *see also* craft unions; industrial unions

Labor-Management Reporting and Disclosure Act *see* Landrum-Griffin Act

labor-relations experts 114–15, 120, 124, 131, 138

LaGuardia, Fiorello 84

Landrum-Griffin Act 158–60, 175–6

Laos 441

Latimer, Murray: before Congress 275; on Clark Amendment 296; on Employment Advisory Council 250–1; at IRC 240–1, 252, 258; and old-age insurance 266–7, 276, 280; on private pensions 248–9; on Technical Board 263; and unemployment insurance 271–3

Latin America 330, 385–8, 415, 432, 480

Laura Spelman Rockefeller Memorial Fund 72–4, 79, 242, 510

Leeds, Morris 245, 254, 259

Leffler, Melvyn 432

Leiserson, William 138, 245, 269

Lend-Lease program 404, 406–7, 447

Lewis, John L.: and labor legislation 92–3, 100–2, 113–15, 131; as labor organizer 138–9, 142; in World War II 150

liberal Democrats, and spending coalition 20

liberalism: and neoliberalism 30–1; new 500–3

liberal-labor alliance 2; in 1970s 212, 215–16; breakup of 514; and civil rights 172, 187–8; in Congress 13, 20, 22, 49, 96, 498; and conservative coalition 15–16; and corporate internationalism 371; corporate opposition to 220; date of formation 234; and Fair Labor Standards Act 128; formation of 84–5; and healthcare 228, 304–7, 309, 312, 354–5, 360, 364, 366; and Henry Wallace campaign 154; and international trade 467, 476, 478, 490, 492; legislative defeats 151, 155, 166; and Marshall Plan 452–5; and Medicare 344; and National Labor Relations Act 108, 111, 115, 129, 131; and political parties 11–12; and postwar planning 393–4; Roosevelt as leader of 131; and Social Security 227, 229, 273, 286, 302, 329, 333, 337; successes of 515; and unions 147; version of Keynesian economics 148

liberal-labor power 42, 515

536 Index

libertarianism 65, 140, 300, 302, 328
life expectancies 366
Linton, Albert 294, 298–9, 301
LLRG (Labor Law Reform Group)
    175–7, 192, 205, 207
lobbyists 6, 215, 285, 503–5
local government 49, 141, 168, 325, 509
Local Initiatives Support Corporation
    325–6
Lockheed 171
lockouts 69, 168, 175
locomotive strategy 478
Logevall, Fredrik 431
longshoremen's unions 45
Los Angeles Times, dynamite attack on
    66, 84
Low Income Housing Tax Credit 326
Lubin, Isador 254
Luce, Henry 373–4
Ludlow Massacre 72, 75

machine Democrats 17–19, 334, 482
Magruder, Calvert 120
majority rule, in union representation
    elections 111, 113–14, 117, 120–3
Malaya 435, 437–40
Malaysia 440
MALDEF (Mexican-American Legal
    Defense and Education Fund) 501
managed care 311–12, 344, 348,
    353, 356
Mann, Michael 24
Manufacturing Chemists Association
    460, 464
market failure 303
Marshall, George 453–4
Marshall Plan 154, 453–6, 458, 513
Marxism 10, 28–30, 39, 51, 60, 115; *see
    also* communism
Maryland, voting patterns in 185, 187
mass media 141, 373, 502
Massachusetts, predecessor of ACA in
    353–6, 359
Matusow, Allen 196–7
May, Stacy 292
McCain, John 359
McCammon, Holly 221
McCormick, Anne O'Hare 390
McCormick, Cyrus 77, 79
McCulloch, Frank 165
McKinley, William 58, 376
McQuaid, Kim 511
Meany, George 184–5

Medicaid 308; and ACA 365; and
    HMOs 312; prototypes of 305;
    qualification for 311; state expansions
    353–4, 363, 365
Medicare: 1980s changes to 343–4;
    and ACA 357, 364; and Clinton
    healthcare plan 347; and drug
    companies 358, 360; establishment
    of 303, 307–8; final legislation on
    309–10; as health policy trap 305–6;
    Parts A and B 308–9
Medicare and Medicaid: and CED
    proposals 313–14; passage of 22, 228,
    303, 309–11, 319, 331
Medicare Modernization Act 2003
    353–4, 360
medication costs 353, 361
Medigap insurance 344
Messersmith, George 379–80
Metropolitan Life Insurance 72, 236,
    238–9, 248, 277, 349
Mexico 480–1, 483
Milbank Memorial Fund 262–3
military clothing 68
military organizations 24, 26
militias, and labor struggles 46–7
Miller, Berkeley 170
Mills, C. Wright 10–11, 31, 504–05
minimum wage: in coal mining 57;
    legislated 20, 84, 127–8; unions
    enforcing 114
Mink, Gwendolyn 53
Minneapolis teamster's strike 115
Mitchell, John 58, 64
Mizruchi, Mark 352–53
Model Cities program 324
Moley, Raymond 379
Mondale, Walter 478
monetary policy: CED on 149;
    international 397–8, 427–8,
    471–2, 474
monetary stabilization fund,
    international 397, 405, 411
money supply 149, 199–201, 318, 479
Morgan, J. P. 62
Morgenthau, Henry 393, 397–8, 404–5,
    409, 411–16, 425–6
Mortgage Bankers Association of
    America 17
mothers, unmarried 229–30, 322, 365
Moynihan, Patrick 333, 337
multinational corporations, power of
    492–3

Murray, Merrill 246, 253, 267–9, 271
Mutual Security Administration 458

NAACP 122, 161, 171
NAFTA (North American Free Trade
Agreement) 371–2, 481–8, 491–3, 502
NAM (National Association of
Manufacturers) 63–4; and ACTPN
476;, and Bretton Woods institutions
422; and civil rights 171–2;
confronting labor movement 69–70,
81; du Pont family in 106; and
healthcare 343–4, 351–3; and labor
legislation 82, 91–3, 96, 108, 112,
144, 151, 153, 159, 176, 213, 219; and
NLB 103–5; and NLRB 145, 166;
and public sector unions 169–70; and
Social Security 227, 274, 300, 331,
333; and social spending 321; and
trade policy 459–60, 482, 485; and
workers' compensation 235
NASA (National Aeronautics and Space
Administration) 169
National Action Committee for Labor
Law Reform 213, 215
National Action Committee on
Secondary Boycotts 212
National Advisory Council on
Financial Issues 447–8, 452, 456
National Advisory Council on
International Monetary and Financial
Problems 426
National Alliance of Businessmen 202,
317–18
National Association of Building
Owners and Managers 17
National Association of Real Estate
Boards 17
National Bureau of Economic
Research 74, 193; board of 79; and
Hoover administration 245; and
social security 253, 258; and Wagner
committee 92
National Civic Federation see NCF
National Constructors Association 193
National Consumers' League 232–3,
298
National Council of Senior Citizens
333
National Economics Unit 389
National Equity Fund 326
National Federation of Federal
Employers 168

National Foreign Trade Council
451, 467
National Grange 259
National Industrial Conference Board
92, 94, 243
National Industrial Recovery Act 1933
92–3, 95–7, 100, 129; Roosevelt's
defense of 116; unexpected outcomes
of 102
National Labor Relations Act, Supreme
Court on 143
National Labor Relations Act 1935:
amendments to 144, 147, 176–7;
and class conflict 29; corporate
resistance to 102, 124–7, 132, 137–8;
introduction of 107–9; lobbying
around 109–13; and National
Industrial Recovery Act 93; reasons
for success of 128–31; revised draft
of 119–24; Rockefeller influence
on 81; rolling back gains of 221;
and Social Security Act 282; and
Southern Democrats 21, 220, 511;
and Special Conference Committee
78; and temporary NLRB 117; union
support for 155
National Leadership Coalition for
Health Care Reform 345
National Metal Trades Association 62
National Municipal League 508
National Public Employers
Association 170
National Resources Defense Council
485, 501
National Resources Planning Board
382, 393, 408
National Traffic and Motor Vehicle
Safety Act 501
National Urban Coalition 317
National Welfare Rights
Organization 322
Native Americans 46
NCF (National Civic Federation) 57–9,
61, 63–4; and AALL 232, 234–5; and
Commission on Industrial Relations
66; and Federal Trade Commission
509; and New Deal 93, 102; and
Rockefeller group 80–1; Roosevelt
at 114
Nelson, Daniel 76
neoliberalism 29–31; origins of 197,
206; precursors of 65
Netherlands, colonial empire of 432

538 Index

network analyses 505–6

New Deal: agencies dismantled during WW2 405; and CFR 377, 382–3; and civil rights movement 19; conservative coalition opposition to 21; corporate opposition to 124, 141; corporate support for 98; du Pont attacks on 106; global application of 405; and liberal-labor alliance 2, 11; and policy-planning network 509–10; Rockefeller influence on 70, 72, 75, 81; role of unions in 120; and social insurance 236, 243; and Southern Democrats 278; and Special Conference Committee 78; and state capacity 251, 285

New Deal coalition 94, 260

New Deal Democrats 141–2, 304

New York Democratic Party 378

New York State Employment Service 247

NFIB (National Federation of Independent Businesses) 213–14; and healthcare 349–50, 356, 359–60, 362, 364

Nixon, Richard M. 173; in 1968 election 177, 185–7; and China 489; environmental institutions under 485, 502; and healthcare 311–13, 342; and inflation 194–7, 199; and Keynesian economics 149; monetary policy of 470–4; resignation 210; and social spending 318–22, 324, 328; trade policy of 475; and Vietnam 442–3

NL Industries 215

NLB (National Labor Board) 81, 102, 294; corporate opposition to 103–4; corporate support for 115, 510–11; Roosevelt weakening 111–12; split in 105–7; strengthening of 107–8; *see also* NLRB

NLRB (National Labor Relations Board): 1970s union-killing decisions of 207–9, 221; corporate compliance with 173; creation of 81, 102, 109; Eisenhower's appointments to 157–8; expansion of 213; Kennedy's appointments to 165–8; legislative establishment of 120–3; opponents of 143–5; policy-planning network role in 510–11; and racial exclusion 161; Reagan's appointments to 218;

and social benefits 156; Supreme Court overturning rulings 174–5; temporary version of 116–19, 124; in World War II 146

No-Name Committee *see* LLRG

Norris-LaGuardia Act 83–4, 93, 95, 103, 118, 120, 131

Northern Democrats 95, 131, 150, 212, 220

Northern Republicans 11, 13, 139, 378

no-strike pledge 67–8, 147, 150

Notter, Harley 392

NPA (National Planning Association) 374, 450–3, 456–7, 461

NRA (National Recovery Administration) 92, 96, 116; declared unconstitutional 124–5; Industrial Advisory Board 99, 101–2; Labor Advisory Board 101; management of 97–9

NSC (National Security Council) 430, 436–9, 457

NSC-68 457–8

nursing-care benefits 344

NWLB (National War Labor Board): and employee benefits 156; peacetime equivalents of 93, 101; World War I 68; World War II 146–7, 150, 306

Obama, Barack 219, 314, 358–61, 364

O'Brien, Ruth 120–21

Office of Economic Opportunity 324

Office of Management and Budget 484, 498, 509

off-shoring 209, 371, 490

Oklahoma 4

old-age assistance 229, 298, 300, 365

old-age insurance: 19th century precedents for 230; AFL unions on 84; corporate moderate thinking on 118, 242–4, 254–5; corporate ultraconservative attacks on 301–2; employee contributions to 273; liberal-labor victories over 20; private schemes 47, 231, 237–8, 248, 254, 275–6, 337, 512 (*see also* contracting out); and Social Security Act 227, 229, 263–7, 270, 275, 278–82

old-age pensions *see* old-age insurance

O'Neill, Thomas 331, 333, 491

Open Market Committee 127, 149

Opie, Redvers 418–19
opinion-shaping networks 5–6, 8–10, 366
organizational state theory 497, 503–6
organizations: divisions of labor within 22–3, 51; and social power 24
organized labor *see* labor unions
OSS (Office of Strategic Services) 434
Otis Elevator 239
outsourcing 167–8, 170, 175, 208–9, 223
overseas investment 182

Paris Peace Conference 1919 378, 381
Pasvolsky, Leo 383–5, 388, 390, 392
PATCO 216–17
payroll taxes: and healthcare 344, 347; and social security 265, 299, 322, 327–30, 335
PCEEO (President's Committee on Equal Employment Opportunity) 171
Pennsylvania: coal industry in 58; elections in 139, 141; garment industry in 103; steel industry in 54, 142
Pennsylvania Railroad 117, 231
pension plans *see* old-age insurance
Pepper, Claude 333–4, 344
Pepsi 475
Perkins, Frances: and Armstrong 264–5; and CES 258–60, 262; and IRC 242–3, 247, 249; and labor legislation 91, 94, 108, 130; and social security legislation 256–7, 266, 280; and unemployment insurance 270–2
Perot, H. Ross 484, 486, 488
Peschek, Joseph 206
Petersen, Howard C. 460–1, 463–5, 474
Petroleum War Service Board 71
Pharmaceutical Manufacturers Association 307
picketing 152, 157, 159, 166; common-situs 155, 211–12, 221
Pierson, Paul 514
Pinkerton Detective Agency 47, 54
Piven, Frances Fox 100
Plans for Progress 171–2
plant closings 221
plant reserve system 271
plantation owners 4; and corporate rich 11, 220; and health insurance 306;

and National Industrial Recovery Act 95; and National Labor Relations Act 129, 131; and New Deal agricultural agencies 510; and postwar economy 452; and social security staff 286; state aid for 16, 20; and state capacity 251; and unemployment insurance 268, 273
pluralism, biased 7; *see also* interest-group pluralism
policy domains 3, 29, 149, 210, 503, 505
policy-discussion groups 6; BAC as 97; functions and roles of 8–9; and power elite 10, 74; and trade advisory committees 483–4; and Wagner Act 92; in World War II 148
policy-planning network 6–10; and ACTPN 476; BAC in 97–8; Blough in 179; Business Roundtable in 204; and collective bargaining 115; environmental groups in 501; formal relationship with federal government 448–9, 509; and Hoover administration 245; impact on consensus 247; and international system 372–3, 376, 453; moderates in 206; and monetary policy 470–1; and New Deal 94, 102; and power elite 10–11; Rockefeller family in 73–5, 79; and social security 232, 236, 250–1, 253, 258, 261, 265, 285, 292, 365–6; theoretical perspectives ignoring 497–8; and trade policy 485, 493; urban dimension of 17–18
political machines 13, 17–19, 53–4
political organizations 25–7
postwar planning: CFR influence on 379–80; organizations pushing for 373–4; State Department structure for 383
poverty 264, 317–19, 324–5, 327, 331, 365–6
Powell, Lewis 205–7
power: four networks of 24–8; social psychology of 23
power elite: against National Labor Relations Act 220; broadening of 74; challengers and supporters 11–12; conservative turn after 1968 66; defined 10–11; diversification of 319; increasing poverty 366; influence over Congress 12–13; institutions

540 Index

undergirding 310; and non-profit social service providers 326; in organizational state theory 504–6; and social security 329; state-building by 59, 172, 249, 253, 465, 475, 498, 509; and tax cuts 335; triumph of 516

Presidential Committee for Financing Foreign Trade 447

President's Consultants on Foreign Policy 442

President's Emergency Committee on Employment 245–6

price boards 197

Princeton University: Industrial Relations Section 126, 241–2; Institute for Advanced Study 451–2; Rockefeller influence at 79–80

Progressive Era: Rockefeller family and 74; Socialist Party and 53; women's influence in 506–7

Progressive Party (1948) 154

Progressive Republicans 82–4, 92–4, 117–19, 121, 129, 511

prohibition, repeal of 105–6

property rights: intellectual 488, 490; in jobs 172, 187; and liberalism 30–1; libertarian appeal to 65; state protection of 46, 142

proportional representation: in national elections 507–8; in union recognition elections 106, 111, 113, 117

protectionism 377; and Cold War 453; UK version of 405

protectionists, in post-war US 455, 460–3, 467, 474–8, 480, 482

Protestants, white 7, 53

Provident Mutual Life 294, 298

Prudential Life Insurance 277, 332–3, 336, 349

Public Administration Clearing House 74, 253, 259

Public Citizen 491

public opinion, and corporate opinion-shaping 6–7

public-sector workers 168, 221, 302, 323

Pye, Lucian 443

racial intermarriage 4–5, 516

Railroad Labor Board 81, 130

Railroad Retirement Act 251, 282

Railroad Retirement Board 251, 263, 512

railroads: corporatization of 55; interlocking directorships of 2; old-age pensions on 231, 249–52; sabotage on 52

Railway Labor Act 1926 81–4, 93, 96, 108, 111, 117–18

Railways Employees National Pension Association 249–50, 267, 285

Raushenbush, Paul 255

Reading Formula 103–4

Reagan, Ronald: and health insurance 344–5; and labor unions 216–17; and Social Security 329–32, 334–7; and social spending 325; trade policies of 479

real estate interests 7, 13, 17, 21, 54, 323–4, 326, 365

recession of 1981–82 217

Reciprocal Trade Act 1934 377, 456, 459, 462

Reconstruction Finance Corporation 386, 450

reform clubs 17

reformers: liberal 235, 252, 299; middle-class 2, 56

replacement costs: and industrial unionism 113; for organized labor 52–4, 60, 69, 81, 103, 220

replacement workers: African Americans as 69; scarcity of 53, 61; Supreme Court on 217; thwarting introduction of 100; violence against 52; *see also* replacement costs

representation elections 103–4, 106–7, 111, 113–14, 117, 120–1, 146

Republican Party: in 1930s elections 139–40, 145; in 1940s 151; in 1960s elections 183, 186–7; allies of 12; and Chamber of Commerce 206; in conservative coalition 20–1; and healthcare legislation 308–9, 352–3; and immigrant labor 53; isolationists and protectionists in 379, 458–9; and NFIB 360; Northern rich in 7; on pensions in 19th century 230–1; white Southerners joining 5

resource dependency theory 3

retirement age 248, 283, 285, 330–1, 336–7

Reuther, Walter 173, 180, 184–5, 311

Index   541

Revolutionary War, middling classes in 43–4
Richardson, Elliot 443
Richter, Otto 263
Riefler, Winfield 382, 389, 398, 409–10, 450, 452
right to manage 167, 174, 184
right-to-work laws 152–3, 168, 213, 215, 220–1
Robber Barons 48
Robbins, Rainard B. 295–6
Rockefeller, David 72, 466, 471, 478, 486
Rockefeller, John D., Jr. 71–3, 75–8; and Arthur Young 99; and employee representation plans 126, 143; and IRC 110, 241, 258, 261, 268; and Milbank family 262
Rockefeller, John D., Sr. 70–1
Rockefeller, John D. III 241–2, 247
Rockefeller, Nelson 311, 320, 451
Rockefeller family, wealth of 70–2
Rockefeller Foundation 72–4; and CFR 380; Division of Social Sciences 80, 242; Economic Stabilization Program 246–7; and the Great Depression 244–5; and private pension funds 248–9; and social security 252–3, 257, 278, 292–4; trustees of 79
Rockefeller group 72–4, 79, 81, 243–4, 277
Rockefeller Institute for Medical Research 79
Rockefeller labor-relations network 75–81, 96–9, 115, 285, 294
Romney, Mitt 354–6
Romneycare see Massachusetts, predecessor of ACA in
Roosa, Robert V. 443
Roosevelt, Eleanor 260
Roosevelt, Franklin D.: and automobile industry 111–12, 114–15; CFR connections to 382–3; Congressional rebukes to 127; corporate support for 140–1; and du Ponts 106; and Felix Frankfurter 83; fourth term 446; as Governor of New York 242; and health insurance 304; and IMF 416; international policy of 378–9, 386, 432–3; and labor legislation 49, 91–5, 109, 124, 130–1; and labor unrest

115–16; and liberal-labor alliance 84–5; and NLB 102; and Rockefeller family 74; and Social Security Act 250, 256–9, 261–2, 265–6, 270–3, 280, 283–4; and Social Security reserve fund 297; and temporary NLRB 116–17, 119; in World War II 150, 390, 393, 404, 407, 411
Roosevelt, Theodore 376
Roosevelt Recession 143, 145
Root, Elihu 376
Rostenkowski, Dan 482
Rovensky, Joseph 451
Rublee, George 383
ruling class 25
Russell Sage Foundation 73, 294

sabotage, in labor struggles 50, 52, 64, 82
San Francisco, strike action in 115
Sass, Steven 248
Save Our Security 331
scabs see replacement workers
Schaller, Michael 436
Schiff, Frank 201–2, 205
Schlesinger, Arthur S., Jr. 94
Schultz, George 194–5
Schultz, Theodore 452
Schultze, Charles 198–200
Sears, Roebuck 160, 175
security guards 208
segregation 4–5; Southern Democrat support for 20, 144; and spending coalition 19; states institutionalizing 14; Supreme Court rulings against 174
SEIU (Service Employees International Union) 354, 356–7, 360
self-employed workers 297, 301–2
Senate: Committee on Education and Labor 112, 120, 123; Committee on Health, Education, Labor and Pensions 359; conservative coalition in 15–16; Finance Committee 281–2, 302, 321–2, 330, 332, 359–60, 362, 482; Foreign Relations Committee 454; Human Resources Committee 215–16; Judiciary Committee 177; Labor Committee 159, 207; Special Committee on Aging 332; see also filibuster
service workers 502

542 Index

sexual orientation 187–8
Shafer, Byron 17
Sherman Anti-Trust Act 1890 56
skilled workers: and early labor unions
  43–5; increasing supply of 193–4; in
  labor struggles 52–3
slave-and-caste states 4, 14–15, 187, 515
Slichter, Sumner 300–1
Smith, Howard 14, 145–6
social benefits: employer-provided 47,
  63, 122, 126, 147, 156; government
  programs 227
social insurance: American philosophy
  of 266; corporate plans for 238–9,
  249, 253–4, 256; private sector as
  model for 251–2; at state level 238;
  voluntary organizations and 259
social power, general theory of 22–8
Social Security: Commission on
  (1980s) 331–6; expansions under
  Eisenhower 301–2; expansions under
  Nixon 319–20; privatizing 186,
  329; Reagan-era attacks on 330–1,
  335–8, 343; recipients as pressure
  group 306; use of term 260; worker
  contributions to 322
Social Security Act 1935 227–8, 365;
  1930s amendments to 295–8, 300;
  before Congress 274–84; Carter-era
  attacks on 327–9; corporate role in
  creating 511–13; disability insurance
  in 20; drafting process 258–63; and
  IRC 79, 118, 240–1, 243, 250–1,
  258; and John Commons 59; old-age
  pensions in 263–74; precursors of
  231, 233–4, 236, 238; provisions of
  229–30; unemployment insurance
  in 246
Social Security Administration 293,
  297, 300, 305–7, 313, 320, 337
Social Security Advisory Council
  (1940–47) 300–1, 333
Social Security Board 292, 294, 296–8;
  Advisory Council 298–9; *see also*
  Social Security Administration
Social Security reserve fund 265,
  297–300, 335
Social Security Task Force 330
Social Security Trust Fund 327, 329,
  335, 337, 516
social spending 20, 182, 207,
  318–20, 325

social workers: in New Deal coalition
  260; and Social Security Act 271,
  273, 285, 297–9; and SSRC proposals
  252, 255, 258
Socialist Party 53, 68, 129, 139–40, 142,
  235–6, 508
socialists: in ACW 67; John Mitchell
  and 64; in labor unions 51–2, 60
socialization, informal 9
Solomon, Robert 473
Southeast Asia, US policy towards 387,
  429–38
Southern Democrats: and Clinton
  administration 484; as committee
  chairs 182, 210; in congressional
  voting coalitions 13–14, 16–21; and
  foreign trade 377, 385, 424, 461–2,
  482, 487–8; and health insurance 304,
  307–9, 348, 352; and labor legislation
  112, 124, 127–9, 143, 145, 151, 155,
  159, 176, 220, 511; and liberal-labor
  alliance 12, 131; and NRA 95, 97,
  112; and Republicans 13; and social
  insurance 236, 262, 268, 272; and
  Social Security Act 274, 278, 283,
  286, 299, 302; and social spending
  321–3
Southern Republicans 16
Southern rich 7, 11, 41, 210, 220, 377,
  462, 515
Southern states 15, 18–19, 132, 185,
  272, 467; *see also* slave-and-caste states
Soviet Union: absence of concern with
  394–5, 401; H. D. White's contacts
  with 398–9, 421; sale of agricultural
  reserves to 198; seen as threat 167,
  430, 457; and Southeast Asia 436,
  440; and Western Europe 449; in
  World War II 380
Special Conference Committee: and
  BAC 98; and IRC 118, 261–2; and
  labor legislation 104, 112, 123–4, 126;
  launch of 77–8; and Social Security
  Act 276, 512; use of violence against
  workers 137
Spelman Fund 74, 242–3, 245–6
spending coalition 12–13, 16–21, 515
SSRC (Social Science Research
  Council) 73–4, 80, 244; Agricultural
  Committee 510; and amendments
  to Social Security Act 294–7, 512;
  and Armstrong 264; and CES

Index 543

262; Committee on Development 244–5; Committee on Governmental Statistics and Information Services 249; Committee on Industry and Trade 245, 253; Committee on Public Administration 260, 278, 292–4; Committee on Social Security 278, 292, 294–5, 297–9, 512; Committee on Unemployment Insurance 253, 269; conferences on social security 252–5, 257–8, 261, 271, 277–8; and Hoover administration 245–6

stabilizing budget policy 148

Stalin, Josef 399, 421

Standard Oil of California 465

Standard Oil of New Jersey: and CED 460, 474; and CUAIR 192; employee representation plan at 110, 122, 126; Hicks at 80, 99; and IRC 268; labor unrest at 76–7, 84; Rockefeller family and 70–2; social benefits offered by 239–40; and Social Security Act 227, 512

Standard Oil of New York 146, 296

Standard Oil of Ohio 326

Starr, Paul 346, 348, 350, 352

state-building 8, 59, 98, 102, 249, 252–3, 285, 380, 392, 432, 465, 475, 507, 509, 513, 515

State Department: economic policy of 385–6, 405, 407; and IMF 416; and Marshall Plan 454; postwar planning structure of 379–80, 383–4, 388–92, 411; on Southeast Asia 436; Soviet agents in 399; Subcommittees on Territorial and Political Problems 432

steel industry: CIO organizing of 142–3; in era of inflation 181, 192; social benefits in 156

steel prices 179–80

steel workers 50, 62, 113, 464

Stevenson, Russell 246–7

Stewart, Bryce: Armstrong on 264–5; at IRC 240–1, 243, 252, 293–4; on labor advisory committees 249; and railroad pension plans 250–1; and Social Security Act 261–2, 267–73, 276; and SSRC 245–6, 253–4, 257–8

Stewart, Potter 174, 208

Stewart, Walter 249

Stimson, Henry L. 376

stock market crash of 1929 84

STR (Special Trade Representative) 397, 465–6, 473, 473–6, 478–80, 483–5, 487–8, 493, 513

strikebreakers 47, 52, 54

strikes 25; in 19th century 43–8; after World War II 447; in coal industry 58, 64, 68; general 48, 50, 62; led by Marxists 115; post-war 151; railroad 45–6, 48, 54; settled by NLB 103; sit-down 141–3, 145, 155, 220; spontaneous 52, 137–8, 231; in steel industry 69, 84, 116, 179; wildcat 152

Supplement Security Income 320

Supreme Court: attempted packing of 127, 144; *Bush v. Gore* 516; civil rights cases 4, 14, 65; and labor law 82–3, 116–18, 120–2, 130, 137, 143, 173–5, 208; and labor struggles 69, 137, 145, 155–6, 208, 211, 217, 221, 306; restraints on New Deal 93, 124–5; and social security 274, 282–3

SWAT (Special Weapons and Tactics) 201, 217, 324

Swenson, Peter 257

Swope, Gerard: in BAC 98, 101; on CES Advisory Council 259, 264, 266, 270–1; at General Electric 142; and National Labor Relations Act 108–11, 122; on NLB 102–4, 106–7; and social insurance 256–7; and Social Security reserve fund 297; on SS Board Advisory Council 298

Taft, Robert 151, 422, 459

Taft, William Howard 66, 68, 376

Taft-Hartley Act 145–6, 513; impact on labor movement 155–7, 159–60; labor opposition to 153–5; lawyers working on 175; provisions of 151–3

tariffs 377, 384, 450, 455, 458–63, 466, 472

tax breaks 13, 16–17, 326

taxation: of alcohol 105; class conflict over 149; corporate 182; corporate opposition to 5–6; Keynesian approach to 148, 181–2; power elite limiting 366

Taylor, Myron 390

544 Index

TCF (Twentieth Century Fund) 102; and postwar aid to Europe 450–3, 455–6; and postwar planning 374

Teachers Insurance and Annuity Association 237

Teagle, Walter C.: in BAC 98–9, 101; on CES Advisory Council 259, 266, 268, 270–1; and National Labor Relations Act 108–11, 122; on NLB 102–4, 106–7, 112; on NWLB 146; in Rockefeller network 77, 79; and Social Security reserve fund 297; at Standard Oil 71, 91

Teamsters, International Brotherhood of 69, 158, 160, 180, 185

Technical Board 259, 262–3, 265, 267–71, 298

ten-hour day 45

textile industry: corporatization of 55; and international trade 451, 461–2, 464, 482, 488; in the South 113, 128, 143, 168

think tanks 6; involvement in government 92, 206; and policy-planning network 8; and power elite 10, 74; Rockefeller supporting 73, 79

third parties 12, 154, 508

Time magazine 373–4

tobacco lobby 308, 348–9

Tobey, Charles 421

the Townsend movement *see* Townsend Plan

Townsend Plan 241, 279–81, 285, 297–8, 512–13

Trade Act 1974 475–6, 489

trade associations, lobbying efforts of 503–4

Trade Expansion Act 1962 178, 463–7

trade imbalances 408, 415, 470; *see also* international trade

Transportation Act 1920 81

Trilateral Commission 477–9

Tripartite Pact 397

Trotsky, Leon 115

Truman, Harry S.: and Bretton Woods institutions 425–6; and health insurance 304; and labor movement 151, 153, 155, 179; military policy of 435, 438, 457; and post-war Europe 393, 447, 454–5

Truman Doctrine 449

Tugwell, Rexford 259

Turkey 449

U.S. Building & Loan League 17

U.S. Mediation Board 82–4, 108, 120

U.S. Rubber 77, 105, 277, 282

U.S. Steel: Arthur Young at 99, 113; and CED 168; challenging New Deal legislation 106; coal mines owned by 100; labor disputes at 62–3, 69, 142; on No-Name Committee 175; social benefits at 231, 306; in Special Conference Committee 77; and wage-price controls 178–9

U.S. Trade Representative *see* STR

UAW (United Auto Workers) x, 142, 161, 173, 180, 183–6, 221, 306

UMW (United Mine Workers): benefits fund 152; collaboration with corporate moderates 58; at Colorado Fuel & Iron 76; congressional hearings on 158; and Democratic Party 140; formation of 57; and John Mitchell 64; membership of 69; and NWLB 146; organizing successes 100; and steel companies 113; and Wagner committee 92

unemployment: Depression-era responses to 244–7; high 74, 194, 200–1, 217–18; post-World War II 458

unemployment benefits *see* unemployment insurance

unemployment insurance: AFL unions on 84; company-provided 231, 236, 238, 243; corporate proposals for 261; early discussions of 230; IRC on 118, 227, 247; as liberal-labor victory 20; Reagan-era cuts to 325; Roosevelt on 94; and Social Security Act 227, 229, 267, 274–5, 285–6; SSRC on 73, 246, 254–5; in Wagner's legislation 256

Union Carbide 192, 277

union density 42; in 19th century 48–9; in 21st century 218–19, 222, 516; in 1930s 103; in 1940s 146, 157; in 1970s 204, 216; after World War I 69; decline of 151; in World War I 68

Union Programs for Fair Practices 172

union recognition: AFL lobbying for 83; corporate moderates and 63; delaying votes on 213; in Roosevelt era 142–3; strikes for 67; under NLB 106–8; in World War I 68

unionism *see* labor unions

Index

United Kingdom: colonies of *see* British Empire; electoral system of 507; and free trade 456; as global power 377, 387; and Grand Area 402–3, 406; and IMF 407–9, 415–17, 420–1, 423, 426–7, 448; labor struggles in 49; liberal-labor alliance in 234; neoliberalism in 197; postwar aid to 452, 459, 461; raising capital in 55; Royal Institute of International Affairs 381, 407, 436; in Tripartite Pact 397; unemployment insurance in 247; in World War II 374, 385, 388–9, 404–5

United Nations, projected structure of 392

United Rubber Workers 138

United States Employment Service 249, 252

United Steel Workers 156, 169, 178, 196, 460

United Way 327, 365

University of Chicago, and Rockefeller philanthropies 74

University of Minnesota, Economic Stabilization Research Institute 246–7

University of Wisconsin: and Brandeis/Frankfurter network 255–6; Commons at 59, 83, 232, 253, 260; Garrison at 117

unskilled workers: exclusion by NCF unionism 61; in labor movement 44, 48–9; railroad 82; use as replacement labor 53

Upgren, Arthur 382–3, 398, 424, 452

urban Democrats 17–19

Urban League 122

urban riots 161, 317–19, 322

USA★Engage 491

USA★NAFTA 483, 485–7

utility companies, regulation of 127

Vance, Cyrus 442–3, 478

Vandenberg, Arthur 454–5

VAT (value-added tax) 182, 279

vendor payments 305

Veterans Administration 304, 365

veterans' pensions 230–1, 237, 511

Vietnam, early US position on 433–5, 438–9

Vietnam War: Americanization of 436, 439–41; de-escalation of 434–5,

442–3; economic consequences of 178, 181–2, 446, 469; electoral impact of 187; end of 323, 443; origins of 427, 429–31; union support for 184, 207

vigilantes, anti-union 137

Viner, Jacob: at CED 424; at CFR 381–2, 397–8; and international trade 460; and origins of IMF 407, 409–15, 417–18; and postwar aid planning 438, 452; and postwar foreign policy 391; and unemployment insurance 269–70

violence: and civil rights movement 173; corporate community using 78, 137; in labor struggles 45–7, 50–2, 63, 66, 72, 75–6, 115–16; by state agencies 49

Volcker, Paul 199–201, 470–1, 479–80

Volcker Group 470–1, 473

Voss, Kim 48–9, 54

Voting Rights Act 1965 4, 19, 22

wage-price freeze 196–7, 311, 471, 473

wage-price guidelines 177–81

wage-price spiral *see* inflationary spiral

wages: stagnant 493; *see also* minimum wage

Wagner, Robert F.: and National Industrial Recovery Act 92–3, 95–6; and National Labor Relations Act 104–5, 107–9, 111–12, 115–25, 129; on NLB 101; and social security 250, 255–6; study group on unemployment 243

Wagner Act *see* National Labor Relations Act 1935

Wagner-Hatfield bill 250

Wallace, George 185–7, 221

War Labor Disputes Act 150, 152

WBGH (Washington Business Group on Health) 342–5, 348

wealth defense industry 6

Weber, Max 121

Weinstein, James 56

Weirton Steel 104

welfare, as stigmatizing label 229

welfare capitalism 76, 87, 156

welfare payments 20, 254, 322, 325

Welles, Sumner 383, 390–2, 412–13, 432

546 Index

West Coast Industrial Relations Associates 209
West Virginia 4
Westinghouse 77
Wharton School of Business 80, 204, 241, 244, 294
Whig Party 44, 508
White, Harry Dexter 397–8; and IMF 409–18, 420–1; passing information to Soviet Union 399; and World Bank 422
White House Council on Environmental Quality 485
White House Task Force for Health Care Reform 346, 348
white resistance 41, 183, 187–88, 206, 498, 514
white workers: exclusion of African Americans 150, 161; voting patterns of 183–8, 206–7, 220–1
Wilentz, Sean 31
Williams, John H. 423–4
Willits, Joseph 80, 244–6, 249, 258, 294
Wilson, Woodrow 59, 66–9, 72, 79, 381
Wilsonianism 385, 390, 409
Wisconsin Industrial Commission 246–7, 253, 260
Witte, Edwin 262; and Armstrong 264–5; before Congress 275; and contracting out 283; diary of 260–1; and old-age insurance 263, 266, 277, 280; and Social Security

Board Advisory Council 298; and unemployment insurance 270–1
Wolman, Leo 102, 294
Women's Trade Union League 67, 232
Woods, Arthur 79, 244–7, 249
work incentives 321–2
working class: militancy of 29; political division of 53; racial division of 150, 161, 173, 184, 216
workmen's compensation 234–6
Workplace Fairness Institute 219
World Bank: creation of 373, 422, 425–6; expansion of role 450; launch of 447, 456; and rehabilitation loans 452
World War I: business–government partnership in 92–3; class collaboration in 113; economic impact of 67; and union density 42
World War II: CFR in 379–80, 385–8, 390; corporate community in 147–8; end of 446–7; and union strength 146–7
WTO (World Trade Organization) 372, 456, 481–2, 492–3; China joining 489–90; Seattle protests against 490–1; US joining 488–9

Young, Arthur H. 99, 113, 116, 124–5, 243, 252, 258, 277
Young, Owen D. 79, 142